Plymouth Memories of an Octogenarian

PLYMOUTH MEMORIES OF AN OCTOGENARIAN

CHAPTER I.

Introductory.

In writing these memories I have in mind both the old and the young. With the old I may perhaps clear away some of the cobwebs which obscure their backward glance and reopen to their vision vistas of the past. With the young I may perhaps show how their fathers and grandfathers lived, and how through the results of their careers, the comforts and luxuries of the present generation have been evolved from the simple habits and ways of living of those who have gone before. An important lesson may be learned by the young, that, in this process of evolution, the achievements of today are only the culmination of the continuous labors of earlier generations; that all we are, and all we know, came to us from our fathers; and that the wonderful inventions and discoveries of which we boast, as if they were ours alone, would have been impossible without the lessons taught by the inventors and discoverers who blazed the way for our feet to tread.

Let me premise, without intending to enter the domain of history, by answering three questions, which, perhaps oftener than any others, are asked by visitors, and by young Plymoutheans who are beginning to study the career of their native town. The first question is—how and from whom did Plymouth receive its name? This question has been somewhat confused by the intimation of some writers that the name owes its origin, at least in part, to the Pilgrims. The facts show conclusively that such is not the case. In 1614 John Smith arrived on the coast of New England in command of an expedition fitted out under the patronage of Sir Ferdinando Gorges, the Governor of the castle in old Plymouth. Anchoring his ships near the mouth of the present Penosbcot river he embarked in a shallop to explore the coast, with the hope of making such discoveries of mines of gold and copper, and of finding such opportunities of obtaining a cargo of fish and furs, as would at least defray the expenses of his expedition.   While on his exploring trip he "drew a map from point to point, isle to isle, and harbor to harbor, with the soundings, sands, rocks and landmarks," and gave the country the name of New England instead of Virginia, the name by which it had been previously known.   Making a chart of the coast from the Penobscot to Cape Cod, he placed it on his return in the hands of Gorges, who submitted it to the inspection of Prince Charles, afterwards Charles the first, who affixed to it the names of three localities, which have adhered to them up to the present time.   These were, Plymouth, probably named in honor of Gorges, the governor of the Plymouth castle, and the patron of Smith's expedition; Charles River, named after himself, and Cape Ann named after his mother, Ann of Denmark.   Other names affixed by the Prince were Stuard's Bay for Cape Cod Bay, Cape James for Cape Cod, Oxford and London for two localities between Plymouth and what is now Boston, Cheviot Hills for the Blue Hills, and Bristol, Southampton, Hull, Ipswich, Dartmouth, Sandwich, Cambridge and Leith.

Nathaniel Morton, in his New England's Memorial, published in 1669, suggested that the Pilgrims adopted the name for the above reason, and also because "Plymouth in old England was the last town they left in their native country, and because they received many kindnesses from some Christians there." It seems to me that Morton was unfortunate in the use of language.   If he had said that the name given by Prince Charles was agreeable to the Pilgrims on account of its associations with their last port of departure, he would have undoubtedly spoken the truth, but it should not be stated that a name, already conferred on the landing place of the Pilgrims, was originated five years after its well known place on Smith's map. That the Pilgrims knew of the name there can be no doubt. Capt. Thomas Dermer was at Plymouth in the summer of 1620, and wrote a letter to Gorges, dated, Plymouth, in July of that year, advising any colony of fifty or more to settle there. That letter must have reached Gorges before the May-flower sailed from old Plymouth on the 6th of September, and of its contents the Pilgrims must have been made acquainted by Gorges, who was their adviser and friend. Besides, Ed-ward Winslow wrote a letter to England from "Plymouth in New England," dated December 11th, 1620, the very day of the Landing, a date too early for any formal action to have been taken by the Colony concerning a name for the locality; and further, Winslow uses the term, "New England," a title which Smith alone had given to the Northern part of Virginia, and which probably appeared nowhere else than on his map.

The second question is—when was Plymouth incorporated. The direct answer to this question, that Plymouth was never incorporated, would be very unsatisfactory without some ex-planation of the relations existing between the Colony and the town of Plymouth. It is all very well to speak of the settle-ment of the town instead of its incorporation, and fix the date at 1620, but the precise time, when the line was drawn between the colony and town, and when the town was clothed by of-ficial authority with the functions of a municipality, it is impos-sible to fix. In the records of 1626 Plymouth is called a plan-tation; in a deed dated, 1631, from John to Edward Winslow, the town of Plymouth is referred to; in accordance with the law passed by the General Court requiring towns to choose constables, one was chosen in Plymouth in 1633; and in 1638 at a meeting held for the purpose of considering the disposi-tion of the gift of stock by James Sherley of London for the benefit of the poor of the town, it was decided "that the town should be considered as extending from the lands of Wm. Pontus and John Dunham (now the lands of Thomas O. Jackson) on the south, to the outside of New street (now North street) on the north. Finally in the year 1637 the first entry in the town records was made, and on the second day of November, 1640, it was ordered at a meeting of the Court of Assistants that "whereas by the Act of the General Court held the third of March in the sixteenth year of his Majesties now reign, the Governor and Assistants were authorized to set the bounds of the several townships, it is enacted and concluded by the Court that the bounds of Plymouth township shall

extend southwards to the bounds of Sandwich township, and northward to the little brook falling into Black
Water from the commons left to Duxbury, and the neighborhood thereabouts, and westward eight miles up into the lands
from any part of the bay or sea; always provided that the
bounds shall extend so far up into the woodlands as to include
the South Meadows toward Agawam, lately discovered, and
the convenient uplands thereabouts." But notwithstanding
all these references, it is enough to say that Plymouth was
settled in 1620, but never formally incorporated.

The third question is: What was the disease which carried
off one-half of the Plymouth Colony during the first four
months after the landing. In answer to this question only
plausible conjectures can be made. Various theories have
been suggested by medical men and others, but unfortunately
insufficient data as to the symptoms and general characteristics
of the epidemic have been handed down to us to enable any
definite diagnosis to be made. Some have suggested smallpox, and some yellow fever, some cholera and some quick consumption. Some also have raised the question whether the
germs of the disease, which swept off the Indians living in
Plymouth four or five years before, still lurking in the soil or
in vegetation, might not have retained sufficient vitality to develop in the human system. This last suggestion would afford little satisfaction, for the question would remain unsolved
as to the nature of the disease. After much thought given
to the matter, I have come to what I think is the most natural
conclusion, that the disease was what was well known in the
days of Irish immigration, before ocean steam navigation was
available, as ship fever. Many readers will remember that
packet ships and transient vessels were constantly arriving at
New York and Boston, crowded with immigrants—after long
passages from England, and that long confinement below deck
resulted frequently in the breaking out of ship fever and caused
serious mortality. The voyage of the Mayflower from Southampton to Cape Cod harbor was more than ninety days in
length, and during that time imperfect ventilation and inadequate nourishment in a vessel of only one hundred and eighty
tons, carrying within her walls one hundred and twenty crew

and passengers, must have furnished all the conditions necessary for the presence of that terrible infection, which in our own day was so fatal to the immigrants from Ireland.

Let me further premise, in closing this introductory chapter, by saying that, of events occurring during a period of seventy-five years, of the changes in the external character of Plymouth, and of the manners and customs and ways of living of its people, I have a distinct recollection. Some of these, at a still earlier period, I can imperfectly recall. For instance in 1825, when I was a few months more than three years of age, my mother carried me on a visit to her father in Shelburne, Nova Scotia, and while I recall nothing of the voyage made in a fishing schooner on her way to the Grand Banks, the accuracy of my memory concerning many localities in Shelburne, was confirmed on a visit to that place twenty-six years later in 1851. My grandfather, Gideon White, a native of Plymouth, and a descendant from Peregrine White, was a loyalist during the revolution, and, holding a Captain's commission in the British army, served with his regiment in Jamaica during the war. With other loyalists he settled in Shelburne, where, receiving the appointment of Provincial Judge, he afterwards lived, making occasional visits to England, but none to the United States, until his death in 1833. He married Deborah Whitworth, the daughter of Miles Whitworth, a British Army surgeon, and four of his children married in Boston and Plymouth and Cambridge, while a son graduated at Harvard in 1812.

I remember, too, that at the age of four, in 1826, I was carried to my first school. It was kept by Mrs. Martha Weston, who was known as Mrs. Patty, or more generally Ma'am Weston, the widow of Coomer Weston, and grandmother of our townsman, Myles S. Weston, in the house on North street, the third below that of Miss Dr. Pierce, not long since occupied by Wm. W. Brewster. I remember well the school room, its sanded floor and the cricket on which I sat. From that dear old lady, with a pleasant smile and kindly voice, I first tasted the "sweet food of kindly uttered knowledge." She died July 27, 1841, and but few of her scholars can now be left to join with me in blessing her memory.

CHAPTER II.

Before proceeding to a general consideration of the streets and ways of Plymouth, and their changes, this is a fitting place to refer to an important alteration, in one of its chief highways, which, though occurring during my life time, is a little beyond the scope of my memory. In ancient times the route from Plymouth to Sandwich was through the district of "half way ponds," which thus received its name. When a stage line between the two towns was established the route ran through Chiltonville, leaving Bramhall's corner on the right, and passing over Eel River bridge, turned to the right and by a diagonal course reached a point on the present road near the estate of Mr. Jordan. At that time the road through Clark's valley by the cotton factory extended no farther south than the cross roads leading to the Russell Mills on the west, and by the old Edes & Wood factory on the east.

In 1825 this road was extended, making a junction with the old road, and thus establishing the present Plymouth and Sandwich highway.

In 1830 there were in Plymouth, north of Bramhall's corner in Chiltonville, seventeen streets so called, thirteen lanes, three squares, nine places and ways, and four alleys, concerning all of which something will be said in their order. The streets were Court, Howland, Main, North, Water, Middle, Leyden, School, Market, Spring, High, Summer, Pleasant, Sandwich, Commercial, Green and South streets. Court street, which took its present name by a vote of the town in 1823, owes its origin to no formal laying out. It practically followed the old Massachusetts path, and was a way of necessity gradually evolved from a footway, and bridle path, and cart way to its present condition. There is a tradition, which needs confirmation, that opposite the head of the present Murray street, it once made a detour to the west through the valley in the rear of the houses of Mr. Charles G. Hathaway and others, and came out into the present road at some point beyond Cold

Spring. There seems to have been no necessity for such a detour, and no available route for it to pursue, and I am inclined to the belief that the tradition is unfounded. There is another tradition, which may also be distrusted, that Tinker's Rock Spring, now known as Cold Spring, was removed by an earthquake in 1755 from the east to the west side of the street, where it now flows. There can be no doubt that it once flowed on the east side, but I was told by Mr. John Kempton Cobb, who always lived in the neighborhood of the spring, and would be now, if he were living, one hundred and nineteen years of age, that it was moved by owners of a pasture on the west side to supply water for their cattle. Within my own knowledge for many years the water after it left the pipe, turned into and out of the pasture referred to, before it crossed the street and passed through the Nelson field on its way to the harbor. When the trench was opened in 1904 for the purpose of laying a sewer, I noticed that the water from the site of the old spring on the east side was conveyed to the present outlet, through a pipe laid across the street, for which the story of the earthquake would fail to account. The boundaries of Court street, notwithstanding widenings and straightenings in various places, have remained practically as they were in 1830, except in two places. Until 1851, at what is now the head of Murray street, there was a watering place on the east side, through which teams were driven to water their horses. In the above year the easterly line of the street was straightened, and the old watering place thrown into the adjoining lots. The brook at this place was called "second brook" by the Pilgrims, the "first brook" being that which in my boyhood was called "Shaw's brook," and which flows, or recently did flow, between the houses of Mrs. Helen F. Hedge and Mr. Ripley, through pipes under the brick block to the harbor. The above mentioned "second brook" flows from a spring just within the lot on the west side of the street, and the bridge over it was long ago the terminus of the evening walks of loving couples who, as they turned for home formally rechristened the bridge in the most natural way as "Kissing bridge." The other place where the street underwent an important change was at the corner of North street, which in

1892 was cut off to meet the necessities of travel then increased by the recent construction of the street railway.

The greatest change which Court street has passed through in my day, has been brought about by the rows of elm trees along its sidewalks, all of which have been set out since 1830, and most of them as far as Cold Spring by the late Andrew L. Russell, to whose public spirit the town is chiefly indebted for one of its crowning glories.   In the above year the only shade trees within the bounds of Main and Court streets, between Town Square and Cold Spring, were two ash trees in front of the house on the southerly corner of North street. North of the trees set out by Mr. Russell were the old mile tree, which stood in front of the estate of the late Joab Thomas, and the trees beyond the estate of Mrs. Knapp, for which the town is indebted to the late Leavitt T. Robbins, father of our late townsman of the same name.   The mile tree was struck by lightning in 1829, and not long after was blown down and replaced by that now standing.   The beauty which these trees have added to the town, even lending grace and ornament to the many houses of ordinary styles of architecture along Court street, suggests a remark made many years ago by John Quincy Adams, while walking with a friend one bleak cloudy day in March, in reply to his companion who had expressed a wonder that the Pilgrims settled here.   "Oh," Mr. Adams answered, "you must remember that there were no houses here then." Mr. Adams must have been another Jonathan who

"Said he could not see the town
There were so many houses."

Howland street was laid out August 6, 1728, by Thomas Howland, through his land, and by deed of that date, under the name of Howland street, was dedicated to public use. For more than a hundred years it extended only as far as the present westerly line of the Gas works land, though originally laid out to the shore, but on the tenth of September, 1859, it was formally laid out in accordance with the original intent of Mr. Howland.

Main street, once called Hanover street, like Court street, was one of the original ways, not formally laid out, but from time to time changed along its lines.   The first important change was effected May 26, 1851, by straightening the westerly line from the corner of the land now owned by Wm. P. Stoddard, to the Plymouth Bank Building. Up to that time the Thomas house, now the Plymouth tavern, had a front yard perhaps twenty feet deep, and the law office of Wm. Thomas was on the southeast corner of the lot. Next south of the Thomas house and land, was an old house built out to the Thomas line, and both estates were cut off at the above date, thus establishing the present line of the street. Another important change was made August 3, 1886, by running a new line on the westerly side from the bank to Town Square, moving all the buildings back to the line, and giving the street at the narrowest point between Middle and Leyden streets, a width of fifty-eight feet seven inches. Its present name of Main street was adopted by the town in 1823. Middle street was laid out August 6, 1725, by Jonathan Bryant, Consider Howland, Isaac Little and Mayhew Little, owners of the land "for and in consideration of the public good, and for the more regular and uniform situation of the town of Plymouth, and to be forever hereafter called King street." At the time of the revolution it informally received its present name, which was finally adopted by the town in 1823, and on the 6th of March, 1899, it was widened to its present width. The way from the foot of the street to Water street, which for the purposes of this narrative, may be considered a part of the street, was laid out September 21, 1768, and May 13, 1807.

Two remarkable coincidences have occurred in connection with Middle street. In the early part of the 18th century one of the Bryant family kept a tavern on the corner of Main and Middle streets, which is called on the records Bryant's tavern, and in 1834 Danville Bryant kept a tavern on the same site. The other coincidence relates to the third Parish, which was established in Middle street, and built a meeting house in 1744, where the house occupied by Mr. Frink now stands. Rev. Thomas Frink of Rutland, Vt., was settled as its pastor, and more than a hundred years later our present townsman, bearing the same name, came to Plymouth, and now lives on the same site. These coincidences are constantly occurring as if men were mere puppets following unconsciously certain predestin-

ed lines.   When the Plymouth Woolen Mill went into operation about 1865, a Scotchman by the name of Fernside was
employed as a wool sorter.   After the manufacture of flan-
nels was abandoned he bought and settled on land in Duxbury,
which a man of the same name occupied more than two hundred years before.   A story of what perhaps may be called a
coincidence, was told me by our townsman Wm. Burns.   He
came from Scotland, and on his arrival between 1850 and 1860,
was employed in the Cordage Company's store at Seaside.
One day a man drove up to the store, and as he alighted, Mr.
Burns said to him, "Good morning, Mr. Glass,—when did
you come over?"   "What do you mean by coming
over?" replied the man.   "Why, from Scotland," said
Mr. Burns.   "I never was in Scotland, my ancestors have
lived in Duxbury since about 1640."   "Is not your name
Glass?" continued Mr. Burns.   "Yes," said the man.
"Why, I thought you were Mr. Glass, a neighbor of
mine in Scotland," said Mr. Burns.   This may, however, not
have been a coincidence, but a remarkable perpetuation of a
family type.   I have had in my own experience more than
one illustration of the descent of family types, through many
generations, one of which recently occurred. A stranger met me
in the street and asked me if I was Mr. Davis.   I said, "Yes,
and your name is Howland."   "How do you know that?" he
asked, "I have never seen you before."   I said, "I know by
your hand with its web fingers," instances of which I have
known in five generations of the family of Henry Howland,
one of the early members of the Plymouth Colony.   It is true
that he might have descended from a female Howland, and
thus borne another name, but I was right in calling him by
that name.

North street was laid out in 1633, and at various times was
called New street, Queen street, Howland street and North
street, which last name was adopted by the town in 1823. The
upper half of the street, on its northerly side, has been changed
since 1830 by the erection of the following houses; that of Dr.
Brown, built in 1833 by Jacob Covington, on the site of the old
Marcy house; the next house built in 1830 by Rev. Frederick
Freeman, the pastor of the Trinitarian Congregational church;
the easterly addition of the house of the late Edward L. Barnes

on the site of the house of Capt. William Rogers, and the house now occupied by Isaac M. Jackson, built about 1850, by Thomas T. Jackson, on the site of a house, which within my memory, was occupied by William Morton Jackson, and Richard Bagnall and others.

On the upper half of the street on the southerly side the following houses have been built since 1830; that built in 1838 by Ebenezer G. Parker, the cashier of the Old Colony Bank, and now occupied by the Misses Russell; that built in 1832 by Mrs. Betsey H. Hodge, recently occupied by Mrs. Thomas B. Drew; that occupied by Benjamin A. Hathaway, and built by Abraham Jackson on the site of one previously occupied by him, which was built about 1745 by Colonel George Watson; and finally the public library building built by the heirs of William G. Russell and Mary Ellen, his wife, on a part of the old Jackson land.

On the lower half of the street there have been several changes in its boundaries. From the way leading to the oil works, as Winslow street was called, at a point in front of the Willoughby house, there was for many years a way with steps running easterly and reaching the street below at an acute angle, thus breaking the continuity of the stone wall bounding the street. About 1858, while I was chairman of the selectmen, the board discontinued this way, and rebuilt the wall on a continuous line.

On the other side of the street there was another way with steps at its upper and lower ends opening opposite the northerly door of the Plymouth Rock House, and reaching the street below immediately above the house which stood on the corner of Water street. This way has also been discontinued by the selectmen. Through my youth a row of balm of Gilead trees stood below the wall extending from the elm tree in front of the house of Mrs. Ruth H. Baker to the way above mentioned. The Linden tree standing on the corner of Cole's Hill, has an interesting romance associated with it. The tree was planted by a youthful couple as a memorial of their engagement, and when not long afterwards, in 1809, the engagement was discontinued, and the memorial was no longer prized by the lady in whose garden it had been planted, she one day pulled it up, and threw it into the street.   My father, who happened to pass at the time, picked it up and planted it where it now stands.   He lived in the house now known as the Plymouth Rock House, where he died in 1824, and under his careful nursing it survived its treatment, and has grown into the beautiful tree, now blessing so many with its grateful shade. In that house I was born in 1822, and lived until I was more than twenty years of age, and hundreds of times I have climbed the branches of the Linden, often with book in hand, seeking shelter from the summer sun.

North street received a new laying out February 11, 1716, and still another on the 7th of October, 1765, and after the estates on Water street below Cole's Hill had been bought by the Pilgrim Society in 1856, and other dates, land was thrown out by the society, and the corner rounded.

So far as the houses on the lower half of North street are concerned, several changes have occurred since 1830. In my boyhood the double house now partly occupied by Miss Catherine Kendall, was a single house, occupied by the widow of Edward Taylor, who was then the wife of John Blaney Bates, whom she married in 1807.   After the death of Mrs. Bates and her husband, whom I well remember, Jacob and Abner Sylvester Taylor, sons of Mrs. Bates, remodelled the house and divided it into two tenements.   John Blaney Bates, the second husband of Mrs. Taylor, was one of the most skilful masons and master builders in southeastern Massachusetts, and was largely engaged in enterprises in other towns.   He built the Plymouth Court House in 1820, the Barnstable Court House, and as many as eight or ten brick or stone dwelling houses on Summer street and Winthrop Place in Boston.   A contract to build a house of hammered stone for George Bond in Winthrop Place, proved a disastrous one, and terminated his business career.   After the failure of Whitwell and Bond, the house referred to was sold to Henry Cabot, the grandfather of Henry Cabot Lodge, and occupied by him until Winthrop Place was extended to Franklin street, and made a part of the present Devonshire street.   Mr. Bates, as I remember him, was in his later days an inveterate sportsman, and would often spend hours behind an ice hummock, when the harbor was partially frozen, waiting for a possible shot at ducks in a sheet of open water near by. He died in 1831.

His stepsons, the Taylor brothers, who learned their mason's trade with him, also became skilful workmen and contractors in Plymouth and neighboring towns. In 1824 they built Pilgrim Hall for the Pilgrim Society, and Mr. Taylor told me that when they signed the contract in July, the stone was lying undisturbed in a virgin rock on the easterly side of Queen Ann's turnpike in Weymouth, and the timber stood uncut in the forests of Maine. So expeditiously, however, was the work performed that the hall was occupied by the Society at the anniversary celebration in the following December.

The house next east of the Taylor house was built in 1829 by the Messrs. Taylor on land of the Taylor estate. The Taylors had completed in that year their contract to build Long wharf and, having considerable material left, they put it into this house. I remember hearing it said that the partitions, and perhaps the walls, were constructed of some of the plank used in covering the wharf, and were consequently unusually solid and firm. The story was told that when Deacon Wm. P. Ripley, who bought the house, went to inspect it, he was told by one of the brothers that the partitions were so impervious to sound that conversation could not be heard from room to room. To confirm his statement he invited the Deacon to test it. After the doors were closed, the Deacon in one room and Mr. Taylor in another, the former called out loudly—"Do you hear?" and the answer. "No," came promptly back. The Deacon evidently was willing to take Mr. Taylor's word, thus confirmed, and bought the house. Deacon Ripley, son of Nathaniel and Elizabeth (Bartlett) Ripley, was born in Plymouth in 1775, and after his first marriage in 1805, owned and occupied the house on Summer street, which after 1845 was owned and occupied by Benjamin Hathaway. He kept a dry goods store in that house many years, and after the sale of the house in 1833 to the heirs of Robert Dunham, the store was occupied by the millinery establishment of Mrs. Thomas Long, one of the heirs. After giving up the store, Deacon Ripley entered into a partnership with his son-in-law, Andrew S. March, in Boston, under the firm name of Ripley & March, 21 Central street, but finally returned to Plymouth and took the store afterwards occupied by Southworth Barnes, on the site of the present Sherman block. He died November 10, 1842, and in the next year the house on North street was sold to Phineas Wells, to whom reference will be hereafter made.

Within my recollection no persons have been universally called Deacons, irrespective of their church connections, besides Deacon Ripley and Deacon John Hall. The latter was many years Deacon of the Baptist church, and was a farmer living at the corner of Court and Hall streets, where he raised a family of sons, well known by the last generations as industrious, useful and worthy citizens.

In his church he was the supervisor of every act. I remember that on one occasion the minister announced from the pulpit that on the next Thursday evening "the Lord willing, there will be a prayer meeting in this house, the weather permitting, if Deacon Hall has no objections, and on Friday evening, whether or no."

In middle life the Deacon bought a sloop and employed her in fishing, and in taking fishing parties into the bay. He scorned the fishing ledges generally resorted to, such as the Offer ledge, the House ledge, Faunce's ledge and the Thrum Caps, and fished on ledges of his own, the bearings of which he kept to himself. I was with him once, one of a party of ten, and before ten o'clock, the party caught one hundred and sixty cod and one hundred and forty haddock. In those days haddock were thought an inferior fish, and were difficult to dispose of in the Plymouth market at one cent a pound. In fact, they were not even dignified by the name of "fish," and I remember hearing a servant ordered to get a fish at the fish market, and if he could not get a fish, to get a haddock.

But some critical person found worms between the flakes of a codfish, and then another discovered that a haddock made a superior fry, and still another that in a chowder the flesh of a haddock was firmer than that of a codfish, and finally both came to be held in equal estimation. In my early days no lover of salt cod would eat anything but dunfish, and Deacon Hall was the only person in Plymouth, who cured them, Swampscott being generally looked to for a supply. They received their name from their dun color, which was of a reddish brown. They were caught in the spring, slack salted, and when partially dry, piled in a dark room covered with seaweed. After several weeks they were repiled, and after several weeks more, they were ready to be eaten.

In my mother's day short, thick fish were selected for the table, and every Saturday three were served with a napkin above and below, the upper one being removed to the kitchen, and the middle one eaten, while the other two supplied minced fish for Sunday's breakfast, and the Monday washing day dinner. A slice of dunfish cut up with potatoes, beets, carrots and onions, well covered with pork scraps and sweet oil, judiciously peppered, makes a dinner, which, with the white salt fish of today, it is impossible to prepare. Fish balls were not in vogue in my early days, but gradually took the place of mince fish, especially Sunday morning. Baked beans, now improperly called distinctively a New England dish, were according to my recollection, unknown in Plymouth, and were associated exclusively with Beverly, whose people were called Beverly beaners. A story was told of a vessel at sea running down to a schooner in distress, and finding that she was from Beverly, and out of beans. The first dish of baked beans I ever saw, was on a club dining table in Cambridge, after I entered college in 1838.

Deacon Hall understood the art of making a chowder as well as that of curing dunfish, or if his fishing party preferred a muddle, that is, a chowder with no potatoes and less liquor, he was equally skilful. Real lovers of fish and seafaring men I have generally found liked the muddle, as perhaps the following incident will attest. Capt. Ignatius Pierce, a man of dry humor, spent a number of years in California, never intimating in his letters any intention of an immediate return home. His wife, about nine o'clock one morning, received a telegram from him in Boston, merely saying, "have a muddle for dinner."

The good Deacon would have been amused at the following description of the ingredients of a genuine New England chowder by a professor of modern languages in the University of Virginia, in a work published by him in 1872, "A many sided dish of pork and fish, potatoes and bread, onions and turnips all mixed up with fresh chequits and seabass, black fish and long clams, pumpkinseed, and an accidental eel, well peppered and salted, piled up in layers, and stewed together." If such a dish as that had been placed before the Deacon he would in a changed form have followed the directions for cooking a coot—to wit, shoot your coot, pick it, parboil it, stuff it, roast it, baste it, and then throw it away.

CHAPTER III.

During my early life a house stood in North street between the house of Mrs. Ruth H. Baker and the present Plymouth Rock House, concerning the occupants of which I must say a word. It was a double house, the westerly end of which was occupied by Ebenezer Drew, his wife Deborah, or Aunt Debby, as she was called, and his brother Malachi. Ebenezer had no children and Malachi was a bachelor. They were the salt of the earth and the salt had not lost its savor. Without the three it would have been difficult for some of the neighbors, including my mother, to keep house. Malachi repaired the leaks in the roof, eased the doors, mended the chairs and kept the house generally in running order. Uncle Eben did the chores, fed and scratched the pig, sawed, split and piled the wood and wheeled our corn to the mill, taking care that Sylvanus Maxim, the miller, did not take out too much toll. In those days, every family bought or raised its own corn and sent it to the mill to be ground. When the steamboat arrived, if one happened to be running, Eben was always on the wharf with his handcart ready to take the luggage of passengers to their homes. I can see the old man now scraping with his jack-knife the apples I occasionally gave him, which, with his loss of teeth, he could neither bite nor chew. He died January 6, 1851, at the age of 77 years.

But chief of "the blessed three" was Aunt Debby. She assisted in making soap and candles, would nurse the sick, diagnose the various diseases of children, such as measles, by their smell, administer picra and "yarb" tea; staunch the blood of a cut finger with cobwebs and with the buds of the balsam poplar, or balm of Gilead, heal the wound. She was the forerunner, too, of those who with no more accuracy than she exhibited, foretell the number of a winter's snow storms. In my college vacation my first visit was always to her, and at Thanksgiving time it was often my privilege to bear a turkey and a couple of pies to her scanty board. She died April 15, 1844, at the age of 72. Peace to her ashes.

The easterly part of the house was occupied by William Collingwood, a worthy and intelligent Englishman, the father of our respected townsmen, George and James Bartlett Collingwood. He had been a manufacturer of pottery in Sunderland, in the shire of Durham, but owing to reverses he was induced to come to America, and took passage in 1819 with Capt. Plasket of Nantucket, bringing with him his wife Eleanor (Harrow) Collingwood and two sons, George and William, one year old. He settled in Nantucket, the home of Capt. Plasket, where he remained until 1825, when James Bartlett, who, with others, owned two ships in the whale fishery, induced him to come to Plymouth and take charge of the oil and candle works then recently established, which were situated between the house of the late Jesse R. Atwood and the shore. As long as the works remained in operation he was at their head, and afterwards for a time kept a restaurant at the corner of North and Water streets. He died in Plymouth in 1866, at the age of 76, and his wife died in 1884, at the age of 90. Three of Mr. Collingwood's sons died in the civil war. Joseph W., born in Nantucket January 5, 1822, was captain in Company H, 18th Massachusetts regiment, and died in a field hospital December 24, 1862, of wounds received at the battle of Fredericksburg on the 13th of that month. John B., born December 30, 1825, was adjutant of the 29th Massachusetts regiment and died in St. John's Hospital in Cincinnati, August 21, 1863. Thomas, born November 10, 1831, was a corporal in Company E, 29th Massachusetts regiment, and died at Camp Banks, Crab Orchard, Ky., August 31, 1863.

In 1843 Mrs. Collingwood was summoned to England to secure by identification an inheritance of property. She had then reached middle life, but, nevertheless, without a companion or attendant, she sailed on the 1st of July in the above year in the Cunard steamer Columbia, from Boston for Halifax and Liverpool. The Columbia, like all the earliest boats of the Cunard line, was a paddle wheel boat of about 1,200 tons. I know very well what those boats were, for I made a passage in the Hibernia of the same line in March, 1847, and I often wonder that in such small crafts, with one wheel buried in every roll of the sea, passengers were willing to expose themselves to the hazards of a winter passage. On Sunday, the second day out, when 240 miles from Boston, while still in charge of the pilot who, in accordance with the custom prevailing while the steamers called at Halifax, remained on board, the Columbia, in a thick fog, having been carried out of her course by an unusual Bay of Fundy current, struck a sloping rock on Black Ledge about a mile and a quarter from Seal Island, and 25 miles from Barrington, Nova Scotia, the nearest port on the mainland. Fortunately the sea was smooth and when the fog lifted a fishing schooner nearby came to the ship and with the boats of the steamer transferred to the island the passengers, 95 in number, including those in the steerage, and 73 officers and men, with luggage and the mails. The cargo was eventually saved, but the ship was a total loss. While on the island a sort of colonial government was established with Mr. Abbot Lawrence of Boston, one of the passengers at its head, to prevent excsses and possible disturbance, and a passing vessel was sent to Halifax with news of the wreck. In due time the steamer Margaret took them to that port, most of the passengers and crew continuing their passage in her to Liverpool. For the kindness and attention shown to Mrs. Collingwood by Mr. Lawrence she was always grateful. The valet of Mr. Lawrence was James Burr, a colored boy from Plymouth, who often with pride recounted to me the story of his adventure.

It is a little singular that our townsman, Robert Swinburn, recently deceased at an advanced age, came to Plymouth when a young man from Sunderland, the town in which Mr. Collingwood lived, and where he also was engaged in the employment of a potter, and should twenty years later than the voyage of Mrs. Collingwood have been also summoned to England for the purpose of obtaining an inheritance. A circumstance connected with the loss of the Columbia, which reminds us of the changes which have occurred in the facilities of communication, is the fact that the news of the wreck, which occurred on Sunday, the 2d of July, did not reach Boston until Sunday, the 9th.

I have given the loss of the Columbia a prominence in these memories because it was the only loss which the Cunard com-

pany has suffered during its career of 64 years, except that of
the Oregon, a steamer sold to the company by another line
after a collision and a transfer of her passengers to another
vessel, which foundered near Fire Island. Two other ocean
steamers had been previously lost, the President, with all on
board, in 1841, and the West India packet steamer Solway,
off Corunna, in April, 1843, with her captain and fifty lives.

Returning from this digression to North street, from which
I have wandered long and far, I wish to correct a statement,
based on misinformation, made by me in "Ancient Landmarks
of Plymouth," that the Willoughby house, built by Edward
Winslow in 1755, was confiscated. Mr. Winslow held the
office of collector of the port of Plymouth, registrar of wills
and clerk of the superior court of common pleas, and the
salaries from these offices, though he was not a rich man,
enabled him to live in luxury and ease. He was generous to
the poor and lavish in his entertainment of families in the aristocratic circles. He was a loyalist of the most pronounced
type, and consequently lost his offices at the breaking out of
the revolution. As nearly as I can learn from family records
he remained in Plymouth several years, evidently assisted by
friends, some of whom in a quiet way shared his loyalty to the
king. In December, 1781, he reached the British garrison in
New York with a part of his family, the remainder joining
him at a later period. Sir Henry Clinton allowed him a pension of £200 per annum, with rations and fuel. On the 30th
of August, 1783, he embarked with his wife, two daughters
and three colored servants from New York and arrived at
Halifax on the 14th of September. He died in Halifax the
next year, 70 years of age. The house in question was taken
on execution by his creditors, consisting of the town of Plymouth, Thomas Davis, William Thomas, Oakes Angier and
John Rowe, and in 1782, 1789, 1790 and 1791 it was sold by
the above parties to Thomas Jackson. In 1813 it passed under
an execution from Thomas Jackson to his cousin, Charles
Jackson, the father of the late Dr. Charles T. Jackson and Mrs.
Ralph Waldo Emerson.

Edward Winslow, son of the above, graduated in Harvard
in 1765, and at the time of the revolution was naval officer of

the port of Plymouth and held the offices of clerk of the court and register of probate jointly with his father. He joined the British army in Boston and went with Lord Percy on his disastrous expedition to Lexington and Concord, and was later appointed by Gen. Gage collector of Boston and register of probate for Suffolk county. At the evacuation of Boston, March 17, 1776, he went with the army to Halifax, where he was made by Sir William Howe secretary of the board of general officers, of which Lord Percy was president, for the distribution of donations to the troops. He afterwards went to New York and was appointed muster master general of the forces, and acted in that capacity during the war. In 1779 he was chosen by refugees in Rhode Island to command them, and served during two campaigns. After the war he was military secretary until the death of his father, and in 1785 went to New Brunswick, where he held the positions of king's counsellor and paymaster of contingencies, and died in 1815.

In the Winslow house above referred to Ralph Waldo Emerson married, August 22, 1835, Lydia Jackson, daughter of Charles and Lucy (Cotton) Jackson. I have a distinct recollection of the first time I ever saw Mr. Emerson, and I have no doubt that it was the first time he ever visited Plymouth. It was, I feel sure, in 1833, soon after he left the pulpit of the Second Unitarian church in Boston and after he had begun his career as a lecturer. It is said that his first lecture was delivered before the Boston Mechanics Institute on the very practical subject of "Water." At the time referred to he lectured in Pilgrim Hall on Socrates, and was the guest of Nathaniel Russell, whose daughter, Mary Howland Russell, born in 1803, was an intimate friend of Lydia Jackson, born in 1802. I believe that I am justified in assuming that on that visit he first saw his future wife. I remember well his appearance and manners on the lecture platform, and as a boy of eleven years I thought him oracular and dull. In the same year the wandering piper with his kilt and bagpipe appeared also in Pilgrim Hall, and Potter, the ventriloquist, entertained audiences by swallowing swords, and I am almost afraid to say that the exhibitions gave me more pleasure than the lecture. But my eyes had not at that early age been opened.

Dr. Holmes once asked an English gentleman to whom he had just been introduced, how he liked America, and on receiving the reply that he had been in the contry only nine days, told him that a pup required only nine days to open its eyes. But the doctor never hesitated to sacrifice courtesy for the sake of a joke, as the following story will further show: Hearing one evening at a party the name of a gentleman present, whom he had never seen before, he asked him if he were a relative of an apothecary of that name, and on receiving the answer that he was his son, he told him that he thought he recognized in his face the 'liniments" of his father. But to return to Mr. Emerson, my eyes have been opened.

In concluding the changes which have occurred in North street within my recollection, it only remains to be said that the Manter building on the corner of Water street was removed in 1859 from Pilgrim wharf, and stands on land formerly occupied by a tenement house, and by a small one-story building occupied by Thomas Maglathlen.

Water street, including its extension, was laid out by various acts of the town, as follows: On the 16th of February, 1715, in 1762, on the 4th of April, 1881, the 9th of December, 1893, and the 22d of June, 1895. The changes on the extension of the street, caused by the erection of the woolen mill of Mr. Mabbett, the utilization of the old Jackson lumber yard by Mr. Craig and the erection of the Brockton and Plymouth trolley electric plant, have been so recent that no reference to them is necessary. With the exception of the foundry, which was built to take the place of the foundry burned in 1856, and the electric light building on the corner of Leyden street, no new structure has changed in my day the general character of the street.

In my youth, and later, there were eight buildings on the westerly side of the street between North street and the steps at the foot of Middle street. In the rear of these houses there were two terraces supported by stone walls, and some of the houses were entered by flights of steps leading down from the top of the hill. In 1856, and in the years immediately succeeding, the Pilgrim Society bought all these estates, and after the removal of the houses graded the slope as it is seen today. The granite steps from the surface of the hill to the canopy over the Rock was built by private subscription. The graded bank is the property of the Pilgrim Society, and the surface of the hill, which belongs to the town, was placed by a vote of the town under the superintendence and care of the society.

Until recently there were also eight buildings between the way leading to the Middle street steps and the grass bank on Leyden street. By the will of J. Henry Stickney of Baltimore, who died May 3, 1893, the sum of $21,000 was given to a board of trustees for the purpose of buying and removing these houses and grading the bank. The board of trustees consists of the chairman of the selectmen, the presidents of the two national banks, the president and secretary of the Pilgrim Society, the president of the Plymouth Savings Bank, and the judge of probate and treasurer of Plymouth county, and their successors in said offices. All the estates have been bought except that owned by Winslow Brewster Standish, and the grading as far as practicable has been done.

The only remaining change in the street to be referred to is that associated with Pilgrim wharf and the Rock. Until 1859 the wharf was devoted to commercial uses. In that year the upper part of the wharf came into the possession of the Pilgrim Society, and the building which had stood on the northerly corner of the wharf was moved to the corner of Water and North streets, and eventually came into the possession of Mr. Manter, its present occupant.

Two buildings on the south side, between the wharf and the store of Mr. Atwood, were also bought by the society and removed. That on the corner had for many years been occupied in its lower story by a cooper shop and in its upper story by the sail loft of Daniel Goddard, and the other had been occupied as a store successively by Richard Holmes, Holmes & Scudder, Holmes & Brewster and John Churchill.

In 1883 the Pilgrim Society bought the entire wharf, and after removing the store houses standing on it fitted it for a steamboat landing exclusively. The corner stone of the canopy over the Rock was laid on the 2d of August, 1859, and the structure was completed in 1867. It was designed by Hammatt Billings, but follows very closely the plan of the Arch of Trajan built on one of the moles of the harbor of

Ancona on the shores of the Adriatic.   The use of scallop
shells on its top was suggested by the fact that this shell was
the emblem worn by the Pilgrims on their way to the Holy
Land.   The word Pilgrim, as applied to the Plymouth colonists, was never used, as far as I can learn, for more than a
hundred and seventy years after the landing.   They were
called "first-comers" and "forefathers" until 1794, when Judge
John Davis, in his ode written for the anniversary celebration
in that year first used the word "Pilgrim" in the following
verse :

> "Columbia, child of heaven,
> The best of blessings given,
>   Be thine to greet;
> Hailing this votive day,
> Looking with fond survey,
> Upon the weary way,
>   Of Pilgrim feet."

The next use of the word was made by Samuel Davis in a
hymn written by him for the celebration in 1799, the first
verse of which is as follows :

> "Hail Pilgrim fathers of our race!
> With grateful hearts your toils we trace.
> Again this votive day returns
> And finds us bending o'er your urns."

The word was undoubtedly suggested to Judge Davis by
a casual remark of Governor Bradford in his history of
Plymouth Plantation expressing the regret of the colonists at
leaving Leyden, as follows: "But they knew they were Pilgrims, and looked not much on those things but lifted up their
eyes to the heavens, their dearest country, and so quieted their
spirits."   The first use of the scallop shell associated with
the Plymouth Pilgrims was at the anniversary celebration in
1820, when at the ball in the evening some young ladies hung
a shell suitably decorated on the breast of Mr. Webster, the
orator of the day.   It simply expresses the sentiment that
man is a wayfarer travelling toward another and a better world.
I have seen it somewhere stated that it was worn by the Pilgrims returning from the Holy Land, and if such is the case as
the scallop is abundant on the shores of the Mediterranean, it
may have been adopted to attest their pilgrimage.   In the
chamber of the canopy are deposited four skeletons of Pilgrims

buried in the winter of 1620-1 on Cole's Hill, which were discovered in 1854 by workmen digging a trench for laying water pipes in Carver street, a little south of the foot of Middle street.

Before concluding what I have to say concerning Water street with its business, its stores and their occupants, I wish to refer more particularly to Plymouth Rock and its history, to supply necessary links in the chain of my narrative. Its first public recognition as the landing place of the Pilgrims occurred in 1742, after a grant had been made to individuals by the town of a strip of land extending from the top of Cole's Hill to low water mark, for the purpose of building a wharf. Thomas Faunce, the third elder of the Plymouth church, born in 1647, was ten years old when Governor Bradford died in 1657, twenty-six years old when John Howland died in 1673, thirty-three years old when George Soule died in 1680, and forty years old when John Alden died in 1687, all of whom were Mayflower's passengers. Hearing of the proposed wharf, and believing that the Rock would be buried from sight, he gathered on the spot his children and grandchildren and told them the story of the landing, which he had received from the Pilgrims themselves. Dr. James Thacher was told of this incident by witnesses of the scene, and through the channel of his history of Plymouth, the authenticity of the Rock has become a matter of historic record.

The second recognition of the Rock as the place of the landing, occurred in 1774, when the inhabitants of Plymouth under the lead of Col. Theopilus Cotton assembled about it with about twenty yoke of oxen, with the view of removing it to Liberty Pole square, as they called Town square, and consecrating it to the shrine of liberty. In attempting to raise it it separated into two parts, one of which was permitted to remain and the other was carried to its destination. There it remained until 1834, resting against the lower elm tree on the southerly side of the square. In that year the fourth of July was celebrated by its removal to the front yard of Pilgrim hall. A procession, of which Capt. Samuel Doten was marshal, preceded by the school children of the town, escorted a decorated truck bearing the Rock, then weighing 6,997 pounds, which was followed by a model of the Mayflower mounted on a car and drawn by six boys, of whom I was one. The Plymouth Band and the Standish Guards performed escort duty, and on reaching Pilgrim hall an address was delivered by Dr. Chas. Cotton, and a prayer was made by Rev. Dr. James Kendall. The ceremonies of the day closed with a dinner served in the basement of the hall by Danville Bryant, proprietor of the Pilgrim House, at which Hon. Nathaniel M. Davis presided, assisted by Hon. Isaac L. Hedge, Abraham Jackson, John Bartlett 3d, Nathaniel Wood and Eliab Ward as vice presidents. In June of the next year the Rock, in its new place, was inclosed by an iron fence designed by George W. Brimmer of Boston, the designer of the Gothic meeting house of the Unitarian parish, and so remained until 1880, when it was removed without display and placed within the canopy on that part of the Rock from which it was separated one hundred and six years before. The iron fence has since that time served to inclose a granite memorial in front of Pilgrim Hall bearing on its face the text of the Pilgrim compact.

As far back as I can recall, in 1832, Water street retained much of the business aspect, which had characterized it for about seventy-five years. The whaling and fishing industries were active and prosperous and Boston had not yet drawn away from Plymouth any considerable portion of its foreign trade. Molasses and sugar from the West India Islands, salt from Turks Island and Cadiz, and iron from Gothenberg, continued to come in, the last free of that burdensome duty, which has destroyed the iron industries of the old colony. I can hear today the rattling of the bars which Stephen Thomas and others carted through our streets to the various manufactories established in Plymouth, Carver, Wareham, Plympton and Kingston. I can count within my memory twenty-six establishments engaged in the manufacture of iron in Plymouth county, while with only two or three exceptions the few now at work are in a languishing condition. I have letters in my possession written in Plymouth, opposing the imposition of high duties, and predicting as a result of their operation the very conditions which now exist.

CHAPTER IV.

Living as I did on Cole's Hill through my youth, I have a distinct recollection of Water street and its business as far back as 1832. During the summer I spent much of my time out of school hours sculling a boat, or climbing vessels' rigging. At those times my special playmate was Winslow Whiting, who during the last years of his seafaring life commanded the bark Volant, and when the brig Hannah was in her berth on the north side of Hedge's wharf we laughed at the boys crawling through the lubber hole, while we proudly mounted the futtock shrouds.

At that time there were on Water street fourteen stores, three counting rooms, two blacksmith shops, two pump and blockmakers' shops, two painters' shops, one sail loft, one rigging loft, perhaps six cooper shops, one carpenter's shop, a wood carver's loft, and on the eight wharves leading from the street, sixteen storehouses. The stores were occupied by James Spooner, I. L. and T. Hedge, Richard Holmes, George Cooper, Elkanah Bartlett, William Nye, Josiah Robbins, Atwood L. Drew, Charles Bramhall, Phineas Wells, Levi Barnes, Scudder and Churchill, Leander Lovell and Henry Tillson.

James Spooner was the son of Deacon Ephraim Spooner, and lived all his life in the house on North street, now occupied by the widow of his grandson, James Walter Spooner. He occupied a store in the building still standing at the head of what is called Long Wharf. He owned several schooners engaged in the Grand Bank fishery, among which were the Swallow, Seneca and Leo. In the last named I was, though a boy, permitted to launch, and she was commanded for a time by the late Peter W. Smith. The Swallow had been a fisherman ever since 1803, but, nevertheless, continued in active busines until 1873, when she was lost. Mr. Spooner died, March 5, 1838. He was succeeded in the store by William Churchill, a native of Duxbury, and the son of Peleg Churchill, whose daughter, Eliza, married Joseph Chandler, the father of the late Peleg Churchill Chandler of Plymouth, who was named after his grandfather. Mr. Churchill built and occupied for several years the house on Middle street, now occupied by Charles H. Frink. While in Plymouth he carried on the mackerel fishery, employing as packers and coopers, his brother, Otis Churchill, and Winslow Cole. He removed in 1838 to Boston, where on Long Wharf he continued the same business.

The store of I. L. and T. Hedge, occupied the easterly half of the building which stood on the northerly corner of Hedge's wharf. With James Bartlett they were largely engaged in the whale fishery, having their counting room upstairs, and their store room below. Mr. Isaac L. Hedge moved in that year, 1832, into the house built by him, now owned and occupied by Father Buckley, where he died, April 19, 1867; Mr. Thomas Hedge was living in the house now owned by his daughter, Mrs. Lothrop, which he had bought of Thomas Jackson in 1830, and where he died, July 11, 1865.

John Thomas, who as a lawyer, occupied an office connected with the Hayward house on Main street, where the engine house now stands, was admitted to the firm in 1832, but in 1837 he removed to New York, where he engaged successfully in the wholesale iron business, and accumulated a handsome property. When retiring from business he bought an estate at Irvington on the North river, and built a house which he occupied until his death. He was killed by lightning in the hay field in July, 1855. He was the father of the late Wm. A. Thomas of Kingston.

Richard Holmes occupied a store standing immediately north of the present market of Anthony Atwood. He was a member of one of the oldest Plymouth families, and lived until 1835 in the house on Cole's Hill, now occupied by Anthony Atwood. In that year he bought a lot of land immediately north of the house of Mrs. Lothrop, extending from Court street to the shore, and built a house with fish houses and fish flakes in its rear, where he lived until his death. In 1833, his son-in-law, Alonzo D. Scudder, became his partner in business, and, after his death, July 4, 1841, continued with his son, Richard W. Holmes. After the death of Mr. Scudder, April 5, 1853, Isaac Brewster became the partner of Richard W. Holmes, after whose death, February 15, 1862, the store was occupied by John Churchill. Holmes & Scudder and Holmes & Brewster were many years engaged in the Grand Bank fishery, and general navigation, and their skippers, among whom were Oliver C. Vaughn, Benjamin Jenkins and William Atwood, regardless of equinoctial storms remained on the Banks until they had wet their salt. They owned at various times the schooners Volant, Flash, Abeona, Medium, Seadrift, Swallow, Challenge, Flora, Anna Hincks and Palestine, all of which, except the last two, were engaged in the Grand Bank fishery.

The next building at the head of Davis wharf contained for many years prior to 1826 the counting room of my grandfather, William Davis, who died, January 5, in that year. After a short occupation by William Spooner, it was in 1832 occupied as a store by George Cooper. For several years before that date, and many years after 1833, Mr. Cooper was employed as a clerk, and as far as I know, was never concerned in navigation. His occupation of the store was short, and he was succeeded by Elisha Whiting and Bartlett Holmes, Jr., and William Davis Simmons and others, until it came into the possession of Jesse R. Atwood, whose son, Anthony Atwood, now occupies it for a fish market. Mr. Cooper died April 29, 1864.

Elkanah Bartlett kept a store at the northerly corner of Carver's, now Craig's wharf, until his death. John Darling Churchill was connected as clerk, and in other ways with Mr. Bartlett, for many years, and succeeded him in business. Mr. Churchill, like Mr. Bartlett, was engaged in the Grand Bank fishery, and with Nathaniel E. Harlow, owned the schooners Conanchet, Engineer, Oronoco and Wampatuck.

William Nye had a store a little back from the street between Carver's wharf and Barnes' wharf, where he bought and sold old iron and junk. My associations with his store are among the pleasantest of my youth, for there by the sale of old iron, which I most assiduously picked up for two or three weeks before that holiday which was so delightful to all boys, the old election day, I found the wherewithal for the holiday feast, which was held in the barn or carriage house of some one of our families, and consisted of election cake and lobster and lemonade in the morning, followed by a stomach ache in the afternoon. The town baker always made up a good batch of election cake or buns, for the occasion, and these articles formed as important a part in the diet of the day as succotash on Forefathers' day. Mr. Nye would gather for his business at election time, a bag of bright new cents, and would tempt the æsthetic taste of the boys by asking them if they would take one bright cent or two dull ones. No day, not even Thanksgiving day, has such a firm seat in my memory as the old election day. It was the day of the meeting of the General Court, which until 1832, occurred on the third Wednesday in May. Mr. Nye lived in a house at the southerly end of Water street, which stood on the site of the house built and occupied by the late Rufus Churchill, who married one of his daughters. Mr. Nye came to Plymouth from Sandwich, and died February 25, 1849, and after his death, his house was moved across the street, where it now stands.

Alonzo D. Scudder, who came to Plymouth from Barnstable, began business in Water street with Lemuel B. Churchill for the sale of grain and flour, but precisely where their store was I cannot say. The partnership continued only a short time, and in 1833 Mr. Scudder became a partner with his father-in-law, Richard Holmes. He died as already stated, April 5, 1853, and Mr. Churchill died December 30, 1833.

Atwood L. Drew, I think, occupied a store, in 1832, in the basement of his father's house, near the corner of Leyden street, and was quite extensively engaged at various times in the whale and Grand Bank fisheries, and in general navigation. In 1839 he was associated as a partner with Leander Lovell, and built the store now standing at the northerly corner of Barnes' wharf. In later life he was associated in some capacity with his brother, William Rider Drew, an enterprising and prosperous manufacturer, who is still living, and whose extensive establishment for the manufacture of tacks and rivets is situated on Smelt Brook at Rocky Nook. Mr. Drew died November 25, 1877.

The store kept by Levi Barnes as early as 1830 was one of two in the building which stood on the southerly corner of the way leading to Middle street. In the latter part of his life he occupied the store which had been occupied by Phineas Wells. He died May 14, 1853, in the house on North street which he had owned and occupied since 1835.

Chas. Bramhall, who occupied the northerly store in the building above mentioned, was the son of Benjamin Bramhall, and one of a family of enterprising sons, five of whom I knew.   His brother William was a prosperous merchant in Boston, and for many years President of the Shawmut Bank, a position now occupied by our summer townsman, Jas. P. Stearns, his son-in-law.   Mr. Bramhall was actively engaged in the Grand Bank fishery, and died May 29, 1859, in the house where he had lived many years, recently occupied by B. O. Strong.

Henry Tillson was a son of Hamblin Tillson, and kept a shoe store on Water street, as early as 1828, and in 1832 removed to Market street, and died December 27, 1834.

Leander Lovell's store on Water street I cannot locate, but he was there as early as 1827, and on the tenth of November in that year his store was entered by burglars. In 1839 he was associated in business with Atwood L. Drew, and in the later years of his life was a partner with J. H. Harlow in the dry goods business in the store on Main street, now occupied by H. H. Cole. He was Town Clerk from 1852 to 1878, and as chairman of the Board of Selectmen and Moderator for many years, I am glad to put on record my appreciation of his courtesy and fidelity in the performance of his municipal duties. He came to Plymouth from Barnstable and married a daughter of Capt. James Bartlett, and died October 1, 1879.

Phineas Wells came to Plymouth from Maine, and married in 1828 Mercy, daughter of George Ellis. He opened in 1827 a grocery store which occupied the whole front of the building opposite the head of Hedge's wharf. He was a master of his business, prudent, methodical and industrious, and so far as salesroom and storeroom were concerned, his store has never been surpassed in Plymouth.   In or about 1850 he moved across the street and fitted up a store on the northerly corner of Hedge's wharf, where he remained until 1859, when he again moved to the store at the junction of Water and Leyden streets, where he remained until his death, December 8, 1869.

Josiah Robbins occupied a store at the head of Robbins' wharf. In looking over the files of the OLD COLONY MEMORIAL to verify my recollection of Water street, I find that he was there as early as 1827, and in that year advertised the sale of old currant wine. The temperance movement began in the above year, and I think in the sale of wines the lines must have been drawn at the product of currants, as the following officers of the Temperance Society organized in 1827 were chosen: Nathaniel Russell, President; Zabdiel Sampson, Vice-President; Wm. Thomas, Secretary; and Ichabod Morton, Nathan Hayward, Jacob Covington, Josiah Robbins, Thomas Atwood, John Russell, Thomas Russell and Isaac L. Hedge, Executive Committee. It is probable that up to that time every grocery store contained ardent spirits in its stock, and on the 8th of September, 1827, I. & E. Morton, whose senior partner was one of the above executive committee, advertised concerning their store at Wellingsley that "that prolific mother of miseries, that giant foe to human happiness, shall no longer have a dwelling place under our roof." The movement was followed up by temperance lectures delivered in the church at Training Green by Mr. Daniel Frost, and total abstinence pledges were signed by nearly one quarter of the entire population of the town. Though the grocers as a body abandoned the sale of spirits, obedience to popular sentiment was by no means universal. Family use and individual consumption were largely diminished, and with the erection in 1835 of the frame of the double house on the corner of Howland street, the practice of using liquor at "raisings" ceased. In the ship yards, however, for some years after that date, work was regularly knocked off every day at eleven and four o'clock for the distribution among the men of New England rum. Public opinion, however, without its re-inforcement by law, finally prevailed, and I should say that from 1835 to 1840 it would have been impossible to buy either ardent spirits or wines, except at the hotels, and that there were less than a dozen houses in which they could be found. I am inclined to think that even under the operation of stringent laws there has been a reaction, and that they are now more generally, though not excessively used than they were sixty-five years ago. It cannot, however, be denied, that if total abstinence less widely prevails, intemperance is less common, and more severely condemned. May it not be true that public opinion is more potent than law?

I have said that in 1832 there were three counting houses

on Water street, meaning such as were engaged in the business of foreign navigation. These were D. & A. Jackson, Nelson & Harlow, and Nathaniel Carver. The oldest and most important was that of D. & A. Jackson, which derived both its business and character from the old firm of Daniel and Charles Jackson, father and uncle of the members of the house. It did not immediately follow in chronological order the old house of Daniel and Charles Jackson, as for a time after the death of Charles Jackson in 1818 Daniel, the surviving partner, formed a partnership with his son Jacob, under the firm name of Daniel Jackson and son, which was dissolved in 1828. In this last year the firm of D. & A. Jackson had its origin. Though as far as the public knew only Daniel and Abraham were members of the firm, that at a later date their younger brother, Isaac Carver Jackson, became associated with them, there can be no doubt. It is within my recollection that the ship Iconium, the last ship built by the firm, was built in 1848 or thereabouts on the Sheepscott river, under Mr. Isaac C. Jackson's exclusive supervision.

The Jackson brothers were a remarkable set of men, six in number, all about six feet in height, gentlemen in bearing and dress, and with their blue coats and brass buttons, and in summer, white beaver hats, white trousers, low shoes and white stockings, their appearance in our streets gave character and expression to the town. They were all confident, self-centered men, who knew what they wanted and how to accomplish it, meddling in no man's business and permitting no man to meddle in theirs; neither asking for nor offering advice. They had means sufficient to carry out their enterprises and never sought outside of their family and their commanders, the contribution of a timber head to their ships.

The first vessels built by D. & A. Jackson were the Echo and Arno fishing vessels, which were sold. The Arno was probably the vessel of that name, which was many years one of the Plymouth fishing fleet. They next built a topsail schooner named the Janus, which made one voyage under command of Capt. Daniel Jackson to Russia, and was sold. In 1829 they built the brig Janus, commanded by Capt. William Holmes, who died in Valparaiso, May 10, 1831, while in command. They next built the brig Rhine of which Capt. Frederick Robbins was master a number of years, and which was finally lost on Fire Island. The brigs Maze and Autumn followed, engaged in general freighting business, and the brig Ganges commanded by Capt. Phineas Leach, and also the brig Cyclops. All of these vessels, including others up to perhaps 1835, were built in what was afterwards known as Battles' lumber yard. The brig Eurotas, one of the Jackson fleet, was bought in Duxbury and placed in command of Capt. Eleazer Stevens Turner, which he commanded until he took command of the ship Thracian, when he was succeeded in the Eurotas by Capt. Ira Potter.

How well I remember those bright waisted brigs, graceful and weatherly, and especially the Cyclops with her figurehead representing the mythological giant with a single eye in the middle of his forehead.

This head was doubtless the work of Samuel W. Gleason, who came to Plymouth from Middleboro and exhibited much talent as a wood carver. Two of his sons continued in business in Plymouth as long as ship building was active in Plymouth and Duxbury and Kingston, when they removed to Boston, and achieved some very commendable work on the clipper ships of the California and Australian period.

The Jackson firm were not long content with the building of brigs. While such vessels were well enough adapted to the iron trade, they were unsuited to the carrying of sugar from the West Indies to the North of Europe, and still more unsuited to the transportation of cotton. It was not an uncommon thing for vessels in the sugar trade bound from Havana to Cronstadt, to put into Plymouth to take out a clean bill of health. I remember well the ship Harvest, Capt. Lawton with George Warren supercargo, belonging to Barnabas Hedge, anchoring in Saquish cove, and proceeding with a new bill of health. The complete abandonment of the brig was effected when, at a later period, coal transportation became extensive on the Delaware and other rivers. The last full rigged brig in Plymouth was the old brig Hannah, which was owned by Barnabas Hedge, and commanded many years by Capt. Isaac Bartlett in the West India trade. Her last service was on a fishing trip to the straits, commanded by Capt. Ignatius Pierce, the father of the late Capts. Ignatius and Ebenezer Pierce.

The last American brig ever seen by me was in Salem harbor about thirty years ago, engaged in the African trade.

The ships Thracian and Persian were built in a yard about where the foot of Brewster street now is, by James Collins, master carpenter, who had already built the ships Brenda and Dromo for Arthur French of Boston, a brother-in-law of Abraham Jackson. The Jackson fleet of ships was completed by the purchase in Maine of the Tyrian and the building of the Iconium. Of each of these ships I have something to say. Many a trenail turned out by me in a trenail machine on a Saturday afternoon was put into the bottoms of the Thracian and Persian, and many a cracker and slice of cheese have I eaten in the ship house at their launchings. Capt. Frederick Robbins was transferred from the brig Rhine to the Persian, Capt. Eleazer Stevens Turner from the brig Eurotas to the Thracian, and Capt. Daniel Lothrop Jackson, son of the senior partner of the house, was given the command of the Tyrian.

Capt. Turner was eventually transferred to the Iconium, on which ship he was finally succeeded by Capt. William Davie. These ships were first class ships in every particular, and for one or each of them the schooner Capitol was bought in Maine and placed in command of Capt. Richard Rogers, who was sent to Virginia with wood choppers, teams and provisions and a gang of carpenters under Benjamin Bagnall, to get out frames on a tract of timber land, which the Jacksons had bought or leased for the purpose.

In December, 1846, I was in Marseilles waiting for a steamer to take me to Genoa and Naples. Having been in Paris away from the sea six months or more, I have never before or since experienced the pleasure which a sight of the Mediterranean gave me. My first excursion from the hotel, after my arrival, was as it would have been at home—down among the shipping. The new harbor had not then been opened, and the ships were made fast with their sterns to the mole. Seeing an American flag at one mast head, I soon read on the stern of the ship, "Persian of Plymouth." Inquiring of the ship keeper if Capt. Robbins, whom I knew was the captain, was on board, and learning that he was not, I walked along the mole, looking into the various stores, and soon saw him astride a chair, club house fashion, with his arms folded on the back, looking at

me as I entered. During the three days I was obliged to wait
for my steamer, I spent a half hour each day with him on
board his ship. He was soon to sail for New Orleans, and
as I afterwards learned he died while on the passage, or soon
after his arrival. He was succeeded by Capt. Thomas Ap-
pling, who had commanded the Cyclops, who died at sea of
yellow fever, and was succeeded by Capt. Lewis Robbins.
After leaving Capt. Robbins I walked farther down the mole
and read on the stern of a bark flying the stars and stripes,
the familiar name, "Griffin of Boston." I knew Capt. Charles
Blake, her owner and commander, who lived directly opposite
my grandmother's house in Winthrop place His vessel was
half yacht, half trader, and sometimes with guests, and sometimes without. He was a skimmer of the seas, taking comfort and pleasure, for which his freight list might pay in
whole or in part. While I was at Naples he came over and
anchored his bark directly in front of the hotel where I was
stopping.

But my story of Yankee vessels is not all told. On my way
down the coast of the Mediterranean a fellow passenger on
the steamer, an Englishman named James Buchanan, was
constantly boasting of the superiority of English vessels over
all others. Of course I defended my own, nor was it difficult,
in those days at least, to find fault with the squat sails, short
top gallant masts, clumsy blocks, poorly set up spars, and if at
anchor with sails furled, the untidy bunts which often looked
like bundles of rags on the yards of the Englishmen. As we
came to an anchor one morning in the harbor of Genoa, I
pointed out to Mr. Buchanan a very trig looking bark, anchored near by, which had a familiar look. "She's a tidy craft,"
said he, " and she'll be English, of course." I knew better,
and calling a boatman, directed him to row to the vessel. As
we rowed round her stern I was not very much surprised to
read, "Truman of Kingston," in hospitable letters. I had
often seen the Truman, Capt. Doane, as well as her sister ship,
the Cecilian, Capt. Dawes, belonging to Joseph Holmes, and
I spent a pleasant hour with the captain in his cabin before
going ashore for a day's stroll before leaving for Naples in
the evening. It was singular that the only three American
vessels visited by me in nearly a year's absence from home,

should have hailed from Plymouth, Kingston and Boston, and that all should have been commanded by men whom I knew. Another American vessel not actually visited by me during my trip to Europe in 1846, but seen under interesting circumstances, emphasized the environment enveloping me associated with home. On the second of May in the above year, Capt. John Eldridge of Yarmouth, Mass., master of the New York and Liverpool packet ship Liverpool, on which I was a passenger, sighted a dismasted vessel. She lay ahead of us directly on our course, and in answer to our hail as we rounded her stern, we found her to be the bark Espindola of and for New York from Liverpool, with four hundred steerage passengers, and commanded by Capt. Barstow of Hanover, Mass., fourteen miles distant from my house. Capt. Barstow reported that while he was in his cabin at eight o'clock on the morning before, the ship under full sail with a light northerly wind, without warning, was struck by a whirlwind, and completely dismasted. She wanted spars and provisions. The subsequent scenes were full of interest.

Luffing up into the wind and running close hauled about three miles, while spare spars were got out and lashed outside, and provisions were got in readiness, we ran back and layed to to the windward of the wreck. With a picked crew, under the command of the mate, the life boat was sent off in a rough sea, the mate holding in his hand a coil of lanyard attached to a Manila line that would float, fastened to the spars. When all was ready the lashings of the spars were cut, and when the boat was near enough the coil was thrown on board the wreck, and the spars pulled alongside. The mate backing up to the bark jumped into the chains, when she rolled to windward, and soon had the supply of meats and other provisions put on board. Capt. Barstow learning that a Plymouth man was on board the Liverpool, sent his compliments to me, and after about three hours' detention, we were again on our course. I afterwards saw that the Espindola obtained more spars from the packet ships, Ashburton and Hollinguer, and reached New York after a passage of forty days.

The Tyrian, commanded by Capt. Daniel Lothrop Jackson, met an untimely fate. During the Irish famine she loaded with corn for Glasgow, and after her departure from New

York no tidings of her were ever received. Of the Iconium I have a story to tell, as I received it from Capt. Turner's own lips on his way from Boston to Plymouth, the day after his marvelous escape from shipwreck in Boston Bay. It must have been in the month of March in the early 1850s that he came round the Cape with a load of cotton for Boston, and with a strong northeast wind, without rain or snow, he expected to find his way without trouble into lighthouse channel. But as the day wore on the wind increased to a gale, while the weather became so thick that to haul off shore, if possible, was the only safe course to pursue. With a light cotton ship, the sagging to leeward made it necessary, as night approached, to come to an anchor. With both anchors down and a long scope of cable, Capt. Turner hoped to ride out the gale. As near as he could judge he lay a mile and a half northeast and by north of the outer Minot's Rocks. The wind veered a little to the southeast, but as it veered it increased in intensity until about midnight one chain parted. He then cut away his spars, hoping that with an eased ship the other cable would stand by. But at daybreak the gale still increasing, the last cable parted, and the ship drifted, stern foremost, toward Strawberry Hill. The wind had veered at this time still more to the south, so that if the bow could be twisted to the northward and westward, and steerage way be got on the ship, it might be still possible to enter the harbor. Capt. Turner managed to set a piece of canvas on the foremast stump, but it did no good, and the ship continued to drift stern foremost. At this time the air had cleared, but the gale had not abated, and as a last resort he carried his kedge anchor aft, and dropped it over the stern, thinking it barely possible that it might catch long enough to turn the ship on her heel and give her steerage way. It worked as he hoped, and with the wind still veering, and hundreds on the shore awaiting a final disaster, he crawled along between Hardings and the breakers and rounded Point Allerton without a fathom to spare. A station pilot boat lying at anchor in the roads put a pilot on board, and Capt. Turner, as he told me, went into his cabin and crying like a child, thanked God for his deliverance. Not long after this he retired temporarily from the sea to recruit his enfeebled health, and was succeeded in the

Iconium by Capt. William Davie, but in 1861 was commissioned Sailing Master in the Navy, and while in command of the
storeship Relief, bound to the East Indies, he died at Rio
Janeiro, August 5, 1864. In just appreciation of his seamanship and skill, the Boston Underwriters made him a present
of five hundred dollars.

Daniel Jackson, the senior member of the Jackson house,
died July 1, 1852, Abraham Jackson died February 6, 1859,
and Isaac Carver Jackson May 23, 1875.

CHAPTER V.

Finding it difficult to define the ownership of vessels engaged in commerce, with which other counting houses on Water street were at various times within my memory associated, I shall subjoin a list as accurate as I have been able to make it, of all vessels except those engaged in the cod fishery hailing from Plymouth since about the year 1828.   Those vessels in the list engaged in whaling will be referred to more particularly in a narrative of the whaling industry, while it was carried on in Plymouth.   Those vessels engaged in the cod fishery, which only occasionally engaged in commercial pursuits, are not included in the list, but will be spoken of in a separate chapter.   Packets and coasters and smacks are included in the list, but the packets will be further considered under their own head.

SHIPS.

Arbella	Massasoit
Granada	Mayflower
Hampden	Persian
Harvest	Sydney
Iconium	Thracian
Isaac Allerton	Tyrian
Levant	

BARKS.

Abagun	Laura
Brontes	Liberia
Charles Bartlett	Mary and Martha
Chilton	Osprey
Condor	Plymouth
Crusoe	Triton
Edward Cohen	Victor
Fortune	Volant

BRIGS.

Attila	Cybelle
Aurora	Cyclops
Autumn	Daniel Webster
Chase	Eurotas
Cobden	Ganges

Garnet
Hannah
Isabella
James Monroe
Janus
Jennie Cushman
John Fehrman
Junius
Levant
Lucy
Maria
Massasoit
Maze
Miles Standish
Minerva
Oceanus

Old Colony
Plymouth
Plymouth Rock
Reindeer
Rhine
Rollins
Santiago
Sarah Abigail
Waverly
William
William Davis
Violet
Yeoman
Young America
Washington

SCHOONERS.

Anna D. Price
Atalanta
Capitol
Eliza Jane
Emma T: Story
Emma Winsor
Exchange
Fearless
Glide
Grace Russell
Independence
Janus
J. H. Racey
John Eliot
J. R. Atwood
John Randolph
Leader
Louisa Sears

M. R. Shepard
Maracaibo
Mary
Mary Allerton
Mary Eliza
Mary Holbrook
Martha May
Mercury
New York
Rainbow
Sarah Burton
Sarah E. Hyde
Sarah Elizabeth
Shave
Speedwell
Vesper
Wm. G. Eadie
Wm. Wilson

PINKIES.

Charles Augusta
George

Industry
Independence

SLOOPS.

Actress
Argo
Belus
Betsey
Comet
Coral
Eagle

Emerald
Falcon
Harriet
Hector
J. W. Crawford
Pennsylvania
Planet

Polly	Splendid
Russell	Susan
Sally Curtis	Thetis
Spartan	Wave

The four following ships, Granada, Hampden, Massasoit and Sydney in the above list were managed by Capt. John Russell, who bought or built them with the aid of contributions from Sydney Bartlett, William Perkins, William Thomas, Thomas Davis of Boston, and Thomas Russell of Plymouth.   I think the Massasoit was the only one of the four built in Plymouth, and she was lost on Point Allerton on her return from a Calcutta voyage in February, 1843.   A Mr. Holbrook of Dorchester, either passenger or supercargo, was lost.   The negro cook calling himself Professor Steamburg, some years afterwards opened a barber's shop in the Danforth building at the corner of North street, having been attracted here by the name of the town to which the ship belonged on which he was wrecked.

Exclusive of the packets and smacks, some of which were also built in Plymouth, a large majority of the vessels in the above list were launched in Plymouth yards.   There were building yards in Plymouth as early as the beginning of the eighteenth century, one of which was at the foot of Middle street, and another on the site of the electric plant at the foot of Leyden street.   The last must have been a well known and much used yard, and was situated on the northerly shore of the Mill pond, which was then an arm or cove of the harbor, with a broad entrance which was later traversed by the causeway and bridge existing today.   At the beginning of the Revolution John Peck, a naval constructor, was sent to Plymouth to design and build two vessels of war, which were named Belisarius and Mercury, the latter being put in the command of the noted Capt. Simeon Sampson.   It is probable that in early days, when only vessels of light draft of water were required, building yards were located on shores in close proximity to the woods, from which with short hauls building materials could be obtained.   Thus the ship building industries of the south shore of Massachusetts Bay were established and continued active until the exigencies of commerce demanded larger vessels, and the construction of railroads and the transport by water rendered it easy to supply with timber the yards of East Boston and Medford and Newburyport. I have no conclusive record to guide me, but I am inclined to think that up to the time of the civil war as many vessels were built in Plymouth and Kingston and Duxbury, and on the North River as in all the remainder of New England.

Some indication of the extent of the building of vessels in Duxbury may be seen in the following record of the industry in that town from 1826 to 1831, inclusive. In 1826 thirteen square rigged vessels, and three schooners were built; in 1827, seven square rigged and one schooner; in 1828, two ships, three brigs and five schooners; in 1829, two ships, six brigs and two schooners; in 1830, one ship, two brigs and eight schooners, and in 1831, four ships, three brigs and eight schooners.

In 1834 Ezra Weston of Duxbury, or King Cæsar, as he was called, who was reckoned the largest ship owner in the United States next to Wm. Gray of Salem, built the ship Hope of 800 tons, which I remember seeing anchored in the Cow Yard waiting to be towed to Boston to be rigged. She was the largest merchantman ever seen in Boston. In my vacation visits to my grandmother in Boston, where I was in the habit of rambling about the wharves, I remember the largest ships of that time, the Asia, the St. Petersburg and the Akbar, owned by Daniel C. Bacon and others, and none were larger than 400 tons. After the death of Mr. Weston, which occurred August 15, 1842, ship building in Duxbury practically ceased.

So far as the North River is concerned the building of vessels was begun as early as 1678, and the first one there built was launched on the Hanover side of the river, a little above the present bridge on the Plymouth and Boston road. Up to 1889, according to the record of Dr. L. V. Briggs, ten hundred and twenty-five vessels had been built, many of which before the Revolution were owned in England. The largest vessel was a ship of six hundred and fifty tons, and the classes numbered one hundred and one sloops, four hundred and eight schooners, sixty-six brigantines, one hundred and thirty-three brigs, fifty-three barks and two hundred and eight ships. The North River industry gradually declined as the demand for larger vessels than could float in the waters of the river, increased. The records of the ship building industry of the

Merrimac river, and those of Medford and East Boston, show where the industry went. The industry on the Merrimac river began at a very early period, it having the advantage of floating its timber from the northern woods directly to the ship yards. Before the Revolution, what were called Jew's Rafts, were built on the Merrimac for a London Jew named Levi, bolted and fastened with the equipment of a ship, and sent across the ocean. In an English newspaper of 1770 it was announced "that the Newbury," Capt. Rose, had arrived in the Thames, a raft of timber in the form of a ship, in twenty-six days from Newbury, New England.

No record of vessels built before the Revolution exists, but after the Revolution, up to 1883, about five hundred vessels were built on the Merrimac, and registered in the Custom House at Newburyport. The career of John Currier, Jr., of that city, was a remarkable one. Between 1831 and 1883, he built ninety-two ships, four barks and one schooner, of which the largest measured nineteen hundred and forty-five tons, and the average tonnage of the whole number was nine hundred and fifty-six.

Unfortunately there is no available record of the East Boston and Medford ships, but though the career of Donald McKay was shorter than that of Mr. Currier, it was more remarkable. Knowing something of Mr. McKay's origin and early life, I may be pardoned for making a special reference to him. He belonged to a family living in Shelburne, Nova Scotia, my mother's native town, and was engaged there in his trade as ship carpenter. My uncle, Cornelius White, a merchant, and the American Consul in that town, knowing his ability, advised him to go to Boston, and provided him with letters to such persons as he thought would advance his interests. Through these letters to my uncle, Isaac P. Davis, and William Sturgis, he at once secured work in the Charlestown Navy Yard. An entering wedge was enough for a man of genius like him, and the clipper ships which came one after another from his hands, soon placed him at the head of his profession in the country. A few years ago I had an interview in New York with his youngest brother, Nathaniel White McKay, named after another of my uncles, with regard to a steamboat for the Boston and Plymouth line, and I think the steamer Shrewsbury, which ran one season, was chartered through him.

The greatest triumph of Mr. McKay was the ship Great Republic, built at East Boston, three hundred and twenty-five feet long, fifty-three feet wide, and thirty-seven feet deep, with a capacity of four thousand tons.   She had four masts, the after one called the spanker mast of a single spar fore and aft rigged.   Her main yard was one hundred and twenty feet long, and her suit of sails contained 15,653 yards of canvas. She was partially burned at her dock in New York, and razeed to three decks and three masts.

In 1803 the foreign trade of Plymouth was at the height of its prosperity.   In that year it was carried on by seventeen ships, sixteen brigs and forty schooners, and the duties paid into the Plymouth Custom House amounted to nearly one hundred thousand dollars.   The above list of vessels shows how much the trade was reduced during the first quarter of the last century.   This was due to the embargo act passed Dec. 22, 1807, on the recommendation of President Jefferson, and later to the war of 1812.   The embargo act prohibited the departure from United States ports of all but foreign armed vessels with public commissions, or foreign merchant ships in ballast, or with such cargo only as they might have on board when notified of the law.   All American vessels engaged in the coasting trade were obliged to give bonds to land their cargo in the United States.   This embargo was repealed by a law taking effect March 15, 1809, except so far as it related to France and Great Britain, and their dependencies, and in regard to them also after the next session of Congress.   Of course such a law struck a severe blow at the trade on which Plymouth most depended for the support of its people, and at a town meeting held in August, 1808, a petition to the President for a suspension of the embargo, was adopted in which it was stated that "prohibitory laws that subject the citizens to grevious privations and sufferings, the policy of which is at least questionable, and the temptations to the violations of which from the nature of man are almost irresistible, will gradually undermine the morals of society, and introduce a laxity of principle and contempt of the laws more to be deplored than even the useless waste of property."

The President replied that "he would with great willingness have executed the wish of the inhabitants of Plymouth had the Berlin and Milan decrees, and the British orders in Council, which endangered the safety of neutral ships been repealed, but while the edicts remain, Congress alone can suspend the embargo."

During the fifteen months of the continuance of the embargo, many of the business men of Plymouth were seriously, crippled, and to some who survived its effects, the war which followed it, brought absolute ruin. During the war the wharves were crowded with vessels with their topmasts housed, and canvas bags, which received the name of Madison night caps, covered the hounds of their rigging. It is not to be supposed that yankee shrewdness entirely failed to evade the watchfulness of government officers, whose duty it was to prevent departures from port. Some of the vessels were already loaded with cargoes of fish for the West Indies when the war embargo began, and those which succeeded in the darkness of some stormy night in quietly setting up their rigging. and bending their sails, and getting to sea, found ready markets for their fish at from fifteen to twenty dollars per quintal.

I will close this chapter with a list of the captains of all vessels excepting those engaged in the cod fishery, who have served within my recollection.

Benjamin Nye Adams	Truman Bartlett
George N. Adams	Truman Bartlett, Jr.
Thomas Appling	Wm. Bartlett
Anthony Atwood	Wm. Bartlett
Edward B. Atwood	John Battles
Thomas Atwood	Edward W. Bradford
Thomas Atwood	Lemuel Bradford
Otis Baker	Samuel Briggs
Wm. W. Baker	Chandler Burgess
Bradford Barnes	John Burgess
James Barnes	Lewis Burgess
Zacheus Barnes	Wm. W. Burgess
Amasa Bartlett	Winslow Burgess
Andrew Bartlett	Horatio G. Cameron
Cornelius Bartlett	John Carlton
Flavel Bartlett	Nath'l Carver
Frederick Bartlett	Wm. Carver
Isaac Bartlett	Daniel D. Churchill
James Bartlett	Sylvanus Churchill
Josiah Bartlett	James M. Clark
Thomas Bartlett	Nath. Clark

Wm. Clark
Wm. Clark
George Collingwood
Joseph Cooper
James Cornish
Thomas E. Cornish
Nathaniel Covington
Robert Cowen
Dexter H. Craig
Ichabod Davie
Solomon Davie
Wm. Davie
Francis B. Davis
Samuel Doten
Samuel H. Doten
Simeon Dike
John Faunce
Elkanah Finney
Henry Gibbs
John Gooding
Albert G. Goodwin
Ezra S. Goodwin
Nath'l Goodwin
Ezra Harlow
Wm. O. Harris
Nathan Haskins
Gideon Holbrook
Albert Holmes
John F. Holmes
Kendall Holmes
Michael Holmes
Peter Holmes
Samuel D. Holmes
Truman C. Holmes
Wm. Holmes
Winslow Holmes
James Howard
Robert Hutchinson
Daniel Jackson
Daniel L. Jackson
Robert King
Thomas King
Clark Johnson
Wm. Langford
Phineas Leach
Augustus H. Lucas
Wm. Morton
Wm. Mullins
Thomas Nicolson
Wm. Nightingale
Grant C. Parsons

John Parsons
Ephraim Paty
John Paty
Gideon Perkins
Ebenezer Pierce
Ignatius Pierce
Ignatius Pierce, Jr.
Gideon V. Pool
Richard Pope
Calvin Ripley
Luther Ripley
Frederick Robbins
Isaac M. Robbins
Lewis Robbins
Nathan B. Robbins
Samuel Robbins
Richard Rogers
Samuel Rogers
Wm. Rogers ·
John Ross
Wm. Ross
John Russell
Merrick Rider
Marston Sampson
Amasa C. Sears
Benj. W. Sears
Hiram B. Sears
Thomas B. Sears
George Simmons
George Simmons, Jr.
Wm. D. Simmons
Nath'l Spooner
Nath'l Spooner
Wm. Swift
John Sylvester
Wm. Sylvester
Gamaliel Thomas
Thomas Torrey
Thomas Tribble
Eleazer S. Turner
Lothrop Turner
Wm. Wall
Charles H. Weston
Francis H. Weston
Harvey Weston
Gideon C. White
Henry Whiting
Henry Whiting, Jr.
Winslow Whiting
George Wood
George Weston

CHAPTER VI.

To the remaining features of Water street about the year 1830, it is not worth while to devote much space or time. The two blacksmith shops were conducted by Henry Jackson, with whom his son, Henry Foster Jackson, was associated, opposite the head of Davis's wharf, and by Southworth Shaw and his son Ichabod at the foot of Leyden street. A twelve-foot way from Leyden street, in direct continuation to Water street, separated the Shaw shop on the north from the building, which David Turner occupied as a pump and blockmaker's shop on the south. Thus the blacksmith building, the northerly part of which was converted into a grocery store, was surrounded by Water street, Leyden street and the way above mentioned. There is a photograph in Pilgrim Hall of the above buildings as they were before the changes were made which resulted in the present condition of that neighborhood.

These blacksmith shops as I remember them were confined to vessel and general work, and did not include horse shoeing in their business. Joshua Standish came to Plymouth from Middleboro in 1828, and established a blacksmith shop opposite the jail on what is now South Russell street, and went into the shoeing business; and there were shops of Lewis Perry near Bradford street, of Ezekiel Rider at Hobbs Hole, of Caleb Battles at Bramhall's corner, and of Isaac and Henry Morton at Chiltonville. The shop now on Summer street, and one carried on by Newell Raymond and Job Churchill at the head of North wharf, were started at a later period

Henry Jackson lived in the house at the corner of Middle street and Cole's Hill, and died there, September 29, 1835. His son, Henry Foster Jackson, who succeeded him in business, died in the same house, March 10, 1868. While I remember the personality of the father, I recall nothing of his character, but the fact that he was fourteen years a member of the board of Selectmen shows him to have been a respected and trusted citizen. The son, never taking special interest in town matters, was closely observant of public affairs, and was reliable authority on all questions relating to the nautical history of the town.

Southworth Shaw lived in the house now standing at the southerly corner of Court and Vernon streets, which had been occupied by his ancestors since 1701, when the southerly part of the house was built, and it is now owned and partially occupied by his granddaughter, Lucia Shaw, having been in the family more than two hundred years. He had seven children, Southworth, late of Boston, Ichabod, Betsey, who married the late Wm. Bramhall of Boston, Maria, Samuel of Plymouth, and the late George Atwood and James R. of Boston. He died January 18, 1847. His son, Ichabod, who continued the business, died March 20, 1873.

The two painters on Water street were Isaac and John Tribble. Isaac Tribble's shop was on his own premises a little north of the blacksmith's shop of Henry Jackson. He lived in the house to which his shop was attached, until 1834, when he bought the house recently standing next east of the house of John Russell on North street, where he died, Feb. 16, 1865. John Tribble's shop stood north of the shop now occupied by Winslow B. Standish, and he lived at the corner of High street and Ring Lane, where he died, June 2, 1862.

The pump and blockmakers on Water street were John Sampson Paine and David Turner. Mr. Paine lived for some years in a building set back from Water street, and facing the way leading from that street to the Middle street steps, and his shop was in the brick basement of the house, and facing Water street. Many years before his death, which occurred September 29, 1878, he bought and occupied the Samuel Robbins' estate on the north side of Middle street, including the hall, which for a long time was called Paine's hall.

David Turner occupied a shop at the foot of Leyden street already described in connection with the Shaw blacksmith shop. Over his shop was a hall, long known as Turner's hall, which was somewhat historic in its career. In that hall a public female school was first established in Plymouth in 1827, under the direction of the committee of the Central District. In 1827, Miss Laura Dewey from Sheffield, Mass., who married in 1832 Andrew Leach Russell of Plymouth, opened a private school for girls there, and in 1829 Horace H. Rolfe

opened a private school.   In 1832 Wm. H. Simmons, son of
Judge Wm. Simmons of Boston, opened a private school for
girls, and one of David Turner's sisters, and Miss Louisa S.
Jackson taught school there for a time.   For many years it
was a favorite hall for singing schools kept by Webster Seymour and Wm. Atwood and others.   I have always looked on
that hall as sacred to the memory of a lost musical genius, for
on my second day's attendance at Mr. Seymour's school I was
dismissed because I could not raise the octave.   When I have
heard some of my fellow pupils sing, who succeeded where I
failed, I have regretted that the dismissals were not more general.   If I am not mistaken, in that hall the Know Nothings
held their meetings during their period of incubation before the
demonstration of their strength in Town meeting in 1854.
There also the Mayflower Lodge, I. O. O. F., was instituted
Dec. 3, 1844.   The hall was only about thirty-five feet long
by about twenty wide, having an access to it by a flight of outside steps on the westerly end with a closed porch at the top.
So deficient was the town in halls before Pilgrim Hall was
built in 1824, and before the hall in the hotel on the corner of
Middle street, built in 1825 was available, that dancing parties
were often held in this hall, and I have heard my mother say
that she once attended an anniversary ball there, use being
made of the shop beneath for a supper room, to which access
was had by means of a trap door in the floor, and a stairway
built for the occasion.   Mr. Turner lived in a house a little
west of his shop on Leyden street, and died May 14, 1869.

The two sailmakers were Daniel Goddard, with a loft at
the southerly corner of Hedge's wharf and Water street, and
David Drew at a later period, with a loft in the Bramhall
building south of the way leading to the Middle street steps.
Mr. Goddard lived next to my mother's house on Cole's Hill,
and I had occasion many times as a boy to thank him for his
kindness.   If I wanted a ball of twine for my kite he gave it
to me, and if I picked out a pumpkin from the products of his
farm for a jack lantern, he made me a present of it.   He was
farmer as well as sailmaker, and employed on his farm as well
as in his loft, Alpheus Richmond, his brother-in-law, and his
brother Nathan and John A. Richmond, the son of Alpheus.
Associated with him in the loft was Lemuel Simmons, brother

of his wife, who a few years after the death of Mr. Goddard, which occurred October 30, 1844, retired from business.   Mr. Goddard married Beulah Simmons, and I have the liveliest recollections of her house and neat kitchen and cool dairy, where I, or some other member of our family, had our milk pail filled with morning and evening milk.   Those were not the days of milk carts, for a large portion of the families in town kept cows, and those who did not, sent daily to some neighbor who did.   The building up of the town has so far reduced available pasturage near its centre that reliance for a supply of milk now rests entirely on the remote districts of Plymouth and on the adjoining towns.   Not long ago I saw an old assessor's book for the year 1748, when with a population of about eighteen hundred, there were kept in town four hundred and thirty-eight cows, one for about every four of all the men, women and children.   In the last year, 1904, with a population of about eleven thousand, there were three hundred and forty-seven cows, or one for every thirty-two inhabitants.

In 1831 there were three or four besides Mr. Goddard, who kept small herds of cows, and among them was Lemuel Stephens, who near his residence at the foot of Fremont street, then known as Stephen's lane, had an abundance of pasturage. In the above year Mr. Stephens had a milk cart, supplying customers, and I remember his son Lemuel calling at our house on the morning of the 21st of November of that year, and telling us that the new Unitarian church had that morning been struck by lightning.   The son, Lemuel, must have been either merely assisting the driver of the cart, or driving it temporarily during Thanksgiving vacation, as in that year he entered Harvard College at the age of seventeen, and graduated in 1835.   The mention of his name recalls an incident in his life as Professor in later years in Girard College.   With many people the memory of Stephen Girard, the founder of the college was held sacred, and one of the articles on exhibition was a suit of clothes which had been worn by him.   Professor Stephens told me that during the absence from home one Saturday afternoon of himself and wife, he found on his return that quite a party had visited his house.   "What did they want," asked the Professor of the servant.   "Oh, sir, and for

sure, they wanted to see Brother Stephens' old clothes."
"Well Bridget, what did you do?" "Oh, and for certain, I
showed them some old clothes of your own hanging on a line
in the attic, and sir you ought to have seen what a time they
had over them, stroking and kissing them, and almost crying
over them." "Well, Bridget," said the Professor, "if they
call again, you may tell them they may have the lot for five
dollars."

As I am getting somewhat garrulous and running away
from the main thread of my narrative, I may be excused if I
tell another story, which the mention of Girard College suggests. It is well known that Mr. Girard provided in his will
that no clergyman should ever be admitted to the grounds and
buildings of the college. Some years ago a convention was
held in Philadelphia of the Masonic order, of which Dr. Winslow Lewis of Boston, a distinguished physician and surgeon,
was a member. One of the entertainments provided for the
convention was a visit to Girard College. Dr. Lewis, whom I
I remember well, always wore a high white clerical cravat, and
as the procession marched into the grounds, an official at the
gate said to him—"excuse me sir, but you cannot be admitted." "The hell I can't" said the Doctor. "Walk in
sir," said the official. It is an interesting commentary on the
will of Mr. Girard that profanity could serve as a ticket of
admission where the insignia of religion failed.

Returning from this digression, as I have spoken of Mrs.
Goddard, I cannot refrain from saying a word about her
brother, Capt. George Simmons, the father of the late George
Simmons. He sailed for my father and grandfather many
years in command of the brig Pilgrim in foreign trade, and
was one of their most efficient and trustworthy captains. My
father was in Boston in 1824, fitting the brig for a voyage,
when he was taken sick, and Captain Simmons brought him
home in a chaise, to die two days later. He named his second
son Wm. Davis Simmons, born in 1811, the master of the ill-
fated packet Russell, after my grandfather, and a daughter,
Joanna White, born in 1826, after my mother. It always
gave me pleasure to meet and talk with him when in later years,
enfeebled by lameness, he was employed as weigher of coal at
the pockets on the wharves. He died, July 26, 1863, at the

age of eighty-one years. I know no family with more marked physical traits than the family of which he and Mrs. Goddard and Lemuel Simmons were conspicuous members. I have noticed these traits in other families in Plymouth, not always the same, sometimes in figure, sometimes in walk, and again in voice, in mould of features, and in ways of doing things. They are such that neither time nor marriage can extinguish, and any close observer may have seen them in the Jackson, Kendall, Warren, Russell, Spooner and Simmons families, and in the Perkins family of Newfields street.

Not many years ago I was in the Town Clerk's office, and seeing a man dismounting from a wagon in the Square, I said to the clerk, "I never saw that man before but I feel sure that his name is Simmons, or he has Simmons blood in his veins." When I went out and addressed him as Mr. Simmons, I asked him if I was right in so calling him, and he said, "yes, that is my name." "Where do you live?" I asked him. "In West Duxbury," he replied. "Are you connected with the Plymouth Simmons family?" and he said he supposed he was distantly, but he was not acquainted with any of them. It has always been interesting to me to observe and study these family traits.

David Drew, the other sail maker, learned his trade of Mr. Goddard, and began business about 1840. He lived many years on Pleasant street, opposite Training Green, and died within a year or two, more than ninety years of age.

The old fashioned coopers who in the first half of the 19th century were numerous on Water street, have entirely disappeared. Mr. John C. Barnes now buys shooks and puts together twenty thousand barrels for cranberries annually. The coopers whom I recall were David and Heman Churchill, Otis Churchill, Winslow Cole, David Dickson, Ansel H. and Abner H. Harlow, Perez Pool and Gideon Holbrook.

Among the riggers who had their lofts on the wharves, may be mentioned, Lewis and Thomas Goodwin, John Chase, Merrick Ryder, Coleman Bartlett, Isaac J. Lucas and Peter W. Smith; and among the caulkers and gravers, Wm. Pearsons, Abbet and Atwood Drew, Clement Bates and Eliab Wood.

The master shipwrights, who ought to be mentioned were James Collins, Wm. R. Cox, Benjamin Bagnall, Richard W.

Bagnall, Wm. Drew and Joseph Holmes; and among the ship carpenters were, Gamaliel Collins, Samuel Lanman, Elias Cox, Richard and Samuel West Bagnall, Abijah Drew, David Thrasher and Isaac Lanman.

The house carpenter mentioned on Water street was Benjamin Weston, who, associated with his brother Lewis, had a shop south of the bridge opposite the foundry.   He lived for many years in the house inherited from his father, Lewis Weston, on North street, immediately west of the house of the late Edward L. Barnes, and died July 25, 1858.

Before closing this chapter it will be pertinent, in connection with those engaged in the equipment of vessels, to speak of the patent windlass invented by a native of Plymouth.   Samuel Nicolson was the son of Thomas and Hannah (Otis) Nicolson, and was born in the house which formerly stood on the north side of Court square, Dec. 22, 1791.   His father was a shipmaster, and in the revolution commanded the privateer sloop America, owned by Wm. Watson and Ephraim Spooner and others, carrying six swivels and seventy men, with Corban Barnes first lieutenant, and Nathaniel Ripley, second lieutenant, commissioned September 6, 1776.   Mr. Nicolson invented in 1830 what is known as the Nicolson windlass, and was the patentee of other inventions, among which was the Nicolson pavement.   He had two sisters, Hannah Otis, who married William Spooner, and Caroline, the wife of Edw. Miller, and the mother of the wife of Chief Justice George T. Bigelow. He died in Boston, January 6, 1866, and is buried on Burial Hill.

CHAPTER VII.

In speaking of the part Plymouth took in the whale fishery, it may be well to refer to the general history of that industry. In the year, 1640, Thomas Macy came from Chilmark, England, and settled in Salisbury, Mass. In 1659 he embarked from Salisbury in an open boat with his family and Edward Starbuck, and landed at Nantucket, where they were the first white settlers. Not long after their arrival, additions were made to the settlement, and to the appearance of a whale in their harbor, which they succeeded in capturing, seems to be due the origin of that great industry, for which Nantucket was for many years distinguished. Whales were abundant in the waters of the island, and for some years they were taken by boats, which brought the dead carcasses to the shore, where their blubber was peeled off and carried to the try pots of the fishermen.

In order to facilitate their work, the fishermen erected masts on the land with crow's nests at their tops, in which in suitable weather, observers were stationed, and when a spout was seen the boats were launched. This method was pursued for thirty or forty years, when small sloops were employed, making shorter or longer cruises during the summer months, and bringing in the blubber to be tried out on the island. Gradually larger vessels were employed, furnished with try pots, which made cruises to Davis straits as early as 1746, to Baffin's Bay in 1751, to the African coast in 1763, to the Brazil ground in 1774, and round Cape Horn to the Pacific in 1791. I have heard it said that Gamaliel Collins of Plymouth was one of the crew of the first American whaler to round the Horn.

It is a little singular that until 1821 no persistent effort was made in Plymouth to engage in the whale fishery. Whales were always at certain seasons abundant in the bay, but as far as I can learn only occasional attempts were made to take them. It is recorded that while the Mayflower was at anchor in Cape Harbor, "large whales of the best kind for oil and bone came daily alongside, and played about the ship." On the second of February, 1673, the town ordered that whatsoever whale, or part of a whale, or other great fish that will make oil, shall by the Providence of God be cast up, or come on shore, within the bounds of this township, that every such whale or part of a whale, or other such fish as will make oil; two parts of three thereof are to belong and appertain to the town, viz: the proprietors aforesaid, and the other third part to such of the town as shall find and cut them up and try the oil."

The following entry is made in the town records: "The marks of a whale left on record by Benjamin Drew of Plymouth, Dec. 17, 1737; the said whale was struck by Joseph Sachemus Indian at Manomet Ponds, the 25th of November, 1737, there were several irons put into her, one was a backward iron on her left side, and two irons on her right side pretty backward, and one lance on her right side, the iron on the left side was broke about six inches from the socket. She carried away one short warp with a drug to it, and a long warp with a drug without a buoy, one of the drug staves was made with a white birch, one of the irons was marked with an I on the head as the Indians think, with a blind S on the other side of the head, the rest of the irons we cannot give an account of the marks."

Thus it will be seen that though whales made their appearance in Massachusetts Bay, and the means for taking them were possessed in Plymouth, yet no serious movement was made to engage in the business of their capture. In 1821 a company was formed to prosecute the fishery, consisting of James Bartlett, Jr., Isaac Barnes, Isaac L. and Thomas Hedge, Benjamin Barnes, Henry Jackson, Ichabod Shaw, Southworth Shaw, Atwood Drew, Thomas Jackson, Jr., Daniel Jackson, Jacob Jackson, Josiah Robbins, John Harlow, Jr., Samuel Doten, Nathaniel Ripley, Nathaniel Ripley, Jr., William P. Ripley, Richard Holmes, Jr., Benjamin Bramhall, Wm. Davis, Jr., and John B. Bates of Plymouth, John Wheeler and Luther Gay of Cambridge and Stephen Griggs of Boston. Though at a later period Isaac L. and Thomas Hedge were active in the management of one or more whalers, they were young men at the time of the formation of the company, the former twenty-three, and the latter, twenty-one, and James Bartlett, Jr., was the projector of the enterprise, and the leader in its

management. The company contracted with Nehemiah New-
hall of Berkley to build the ship Mayflower of 345 59-95 tons,
and she sailed for the Pacific in September of that year under
the command of George Harris. The fitting of this ship with
the hopes, which the advent of a new industry inspired, seemed to arouse the dormant energies of the town, which the war,
so recently closed, had done much to paralyze. Coopers and
bakers and dealers in general supplies, as well as mechanics,
felt the quickening impulse, and the people of the town generally were ready to contribute their capital in enlarging and extending the new business. The Mayflower was absent nearly
three years, and landed between two and three thousand barrels of oil. How much of her cargo was sperm oil, and how
much whalebone she brought, I have no record to show. Before her arrival an oil and candle factory was established between what is now Winslow street and the shore, about where
the house stands recently occupied by George H. Jackson.

The Mayflower made two more voyages to the Pacific of
about three years each, under the command of Capt. Harris,
landing about five thousand barrels, and in 1830 she was sold
to Gideon Randall of New Bedford, an interest in her being retained in Plymouth by Jas. Bartlett, Jr., Abner S. Taylor and
the heirs of Atwood Drew. While the Mayflower was on her
first voyage, after the establishment of the oil and candle factory, Mr. Bartlett, while in Nantucket on business, induced
Mr. Wm. Collingwood, then living there, to come to Plymouth
and superintend the refining of oil, and the manufacture of
spermaciti candles.

In 1822 another company was formed consisting of James
Bartlett, Jr., Josiah Robbins, Isaac L. and Thomas Hedge, John
B. Bates, Thomas Jackson, Jr., John Thomas, Henry Jackson,
Jacob Covington, Daniel Jackson, Jacob Jackson, Allen Dan-
forth, Isaac Sampson, John Harlow, Jr., Richard Holmes, Jr.,
Ichabod Shaw, Isaac Barnes, Lemuel Bradford, George Bacon,
Rufus Robbins and Ephraim Harlow. They contracted with
Richard Currier of Amesbury to build the bark Fortune of
278 47-95 tons for the same service. She sailed for the Pacific
in September, 1822, under the command of Peter C. Myrick,
and returned in 1825 with two thousand barrels of oil. The
names of the members of both this and the other company show

the interest taken in the new industry by men of all occupations and professions, merchants, lawyers, traders, blacksmiths, owners of cod fishermen, silversmiths and masons, and a determination to make it a success. Among them appears the name of Allen Danforth, who became in that year a permanent resident of Plymouth as the editor of the OLD COLONY MEMORIAL.

The Fortune made a second voyage of three years in 1825, and a third in 1829, under the command of Charles P. Swain, and a fourth in 1833, under the command of David Upham. In 1837 she sailed under the command of Albert G. Goodwin of Plymouth, and in 1840 she made her last voyage from Plymouth under the command of Wm. Almy. I remember the Fortune well on her return in 1832, from her third voyage, and her sailing on her fourth in 1833. Owing to shoal water at the wharves, she made her fitting as did the other ships and barks in the Cow Yard, and the whale boats as they came and went loaded with supplies were especially attractive to the boys. One of my schoolmates, Nathaniel Lothrop Hedge, went with her. Being called out by Mr. Stoddard, the teacher of the high school, to receive a flogging for some offense, which must have been trivial, for he was never guilty of any other, he quietly took his cap from the nail above his head, and walked out of school to ship the next day for a three years' voyage. Two other Plymouth men, I think, shipped in the Fortune, John Barrett, who became the captain of a ship from New Bedford, and his brother, William, who became one of the best boat steerers of his day. On her voyage begun in 1837, George Collingwood of Plymouth was one of the crew, and Ozen Bates of Plymouth shipped on that or another voyage of the same ship. The Fortune was sunk to aid in blocking Charleston harbor in 1861.

In 1830 James Bartlett, Jr., Isaac L. and Thomas Hedge and Jacob Covington bought the ship Arbella of 404 26-95 tons, built in Bath, and in August of that year sent her to the Pacific under the command of George Harris, the first Captain of the Mayflower. She sailed again in 1834, and 1836 under the command of Ellis E. Eldridge, but what became of her after her return I have no means of knowing. I remember well the Arbella hove down near the end of the new Long wharf, with a raft under her bottom, being either caulked or sheathed or both. My impression is that most of the whalers made their voyages with either a bare or sheathed bottom. The process of heaving down was resorted to where docks were not available, and was safe in shoal water. The process of heeling for the purpose of making repairs below the water line is sometimes dangerous in deep water.   The British man of war, George, heeled at Spithead in 1782, was caught by a slight squall with her ports open, and sunk with the loss of six hundred lives.

In 1831 Isaac L. and Thomas Hedge, Jacob Covington, John Thomas and James Bartlett, Jr., bought the ship Levant of 332 34-95 tons, built at Newbury, and in July of that year, under the command of Thomas Russell of Nantucket, she sailed for the Pacific. She returned with 2,700 barrels of oil, and was sold February 14, 1835, for $15,600. This vessel was under the management of the Hedge firm.

In 1833 Jacob Covington, James Bartlett, Jr., Josiah Robbins, Jacob H. Loud and John B. Thomas, bought the bark Triton of 314 49-95 tons, built in Durham, N. H., and in November she sailed for the Pacific under the command of Mason Taber. She made two other voyages, one in 1835, under the command of Thomas Russell, and one in 1838 under the command of Chandler Burgess, Jr., of Plymouth. On her first voyage William Collingwood of Plymouth was one of the crew.

In 1838 James Bartlett, Jr., Daniel Jackson, Abraham Jackson, John B. Thomas, Jacob H. Loud, Nathaniel Russell, Nathaniel Russell, Jr., Allen Danforth, Thomas Russell and the heirs of Jacob Covington of Plymouth, and Thomas Russell of Nantucket, bought the bark Mary and Martha of 316 56-95 tons, built in Westbrook, Me., and in December she sailed for the Pacific on her only voyage from Plymouth, under the command of Thomas Russell. Wm. Collingwood of Plymouth was one of her crew.

The brig Yeoman, afterwards changed to a bark, was built in Plymouth in 1833, by James Spooner, Southworth Shaw, Ichabod Shaw, Ichabod Shaw, Jr., Benjamin Bagnall, Nathaniel C. Lanman, Wm. M. Jackson and Stephen Turner, and made several voyages to the South Atlantic, under the command of John Gooding and James M. Clark, and on several of her voyages George Collingwood was one of her crew.

The brig James Monroe, of 114 91-95 tons, built in Sandwich, was owned by Isaac L. Hedge, George Churchill, Nathaniel C. Lanman, Benjamin Hathaway, Southworth Barnes, John B. Thomas, Ichabod Shaw, Comfort Bates, Joseph W. Hodgkins, Nathaniel Russell, Albert G. Goodwin, Isaac Barnes, Thomas Hedge and Nathaniel M. Davis, and was engaged in the Atlantic fishery, under the command of Simeon Dike of Plymouth, and probably made a second voyage.

The schooner Exchange, of 99 91-95 tons, owned by Alonzo D. Scudder, Henry F. Jackson, James Collins, Wm. Nelson, and Rufus B. Bradford, was under the command of James King of Plymouth, and Rufus Hopkins of Provincetown. She made four voyages, in three of which George Collingwood was sailor, and in one, mate, and William Collingwood was a seaman when she was wrecked in the West India waters.

The schooner Maracaibo, 93 53-95 tons, built in Plymouth, and owned by Atwood L. Drew, Josiah Drew, Ephraim Harlow, James Doten, Ellis B. Bramhall, James Morton, Bartlett Ellis, Andrew L. Russell, Benjamin Barnes, 2d, David Turner, Lemuel Simmons, John Harlow, 3d, Robert Hatch, Nathaniel Holmes and David Holmes, engaged also in the Atlantic fishery, under the command of Capt. Pope and George Collingwood. She was lost September 19, 1846, off Bermuda.

The only other vessels engaged in the whale fishery were the schooner Mercury, of 74 34-95 tons, built in Middleboro and owned by Isaac Barnes, Southworth Barnes, Ivory L. Harlow, and Charles Goodwin, and commanded by Capt. Nickerson, and the schooner Vesper, of 95 52-95 tons, built in Essex, and owned by Bradford Barnes, Jr., William Atwood, Samuel Robbins, Jr., Benjamin Barnes, Bradford Barnes, Ellis Barnes, Nathaniel C. Barnes, Nathaniel E. Harlow, Bartlett Ellis, Joseph White, Robert Hatch, Heman Cobb, Jr., Corban Barnes, Jeremiah Farris, Samuel N. Diman, David Turner, Charles Goodwin, Southworth Barnes, Joab Thomas, Jr., Nathan H. Holmes, David Holmes, Ellis Drew, Ebenezer Ellis, Jr., and Edwin A. Perry. The Vesper afterwards entered the fishing and merchant service.

James Bartlett, the projector of the enterprise, which seemed to promise new life, and an aroused activity in Plymouth, stood in the front rank among the business men of his native town. He was the son of Capt. James Bartlett, a successful shipmaster in days when it was necessary that a captain engaged in foreign trade should be something more than a navigator and seaman. He had, to be sure, his sailing orders from his owners, seemingly controlling his actions, but sailing orders, in the many which I have read, written by my grandfather, really left the fortunes of a voyage to the discretion of the master. Capt. Bartlett died December 22, 1840, at the age of 81. There were others whom I might mention, some still living in Plymouth, who also represented the best class of merchant captains.

Mr. Bartlett, when quite a young man, was appointed supercargo on board a ship belonging to Barnabas Hedge, engaged in foreign trade. Such a position, with the responsibilities it imposed, was the best popular training school for a commercial life, and consequently when he projected the whaling industry in 1821, he possessed all the qualifications for its successful management. He occupied for some years the easterly part of the Winslow House on North street, but in 1832 he bought the LeBaron estate on Leyden street, at the corner of LeBaron's Alley, and built the house now occupied by his grandson, Wm. W. Brewster, where he died July 29, 1845, fifty-nine years of age.

With regard to the packet service of Plymouth there were four packets within my lifetime, which are not within my memory, the Belus, Capt. Thomas Atwood; the Falcon, Capt. Samuel Briggs; the Sally Curtis, Capt. Samuel Robbins, and the Betsey, Capt. Isaac Robbins. There was a fifth, the Argo, Capt. Sylvanus Churchill, which I have a hazy recollection of seeing at her berth at the end of Davis' wharf. Of the eight succeeding packets I have very definite pictures in my mind. These, in the order of their probable ages, were the Polly, Eagle, Splendid, Hector, Harriet, Atalanta, Thetis and Russell. The Polly was a black sloop, a dull sailer, unattractive in appearance, and poorly equipped for passengers. Her captain was Joseph Cooper, who lived in High street at the upper corner of Cooper's alley, leading to Town Square. At the northerly end of his garden on Church street, then known as Back street, there was a store house which, when he retired from the packet service in 1835, he altered into a grocery store, which he kept until his death, which occurred November 25, 1851, in the 83d year of his age. He was one of the last grocers in town to keep spirituous liquors for sale, and his stock in these was confined to Cicily Madeira wine. In 1835, or thereabouts, one of my mother's brothers, living in Nova Scotia, arrived unexpectedly one evening on the stage, and finding that she was out of wine to dispense the hospitalities of the occasion, she sent me with one of those square bottles made to fit partitions in the closet of the sideboard, up to Capt. Cooper's for two quarts of the above mentioned wine. I had nearly performed my errand in safety, when slipping on the icy sidewalk I fell near the doorstep and broke the bottle. Enough wine, however, was saved for immediate purposes, but it was the last wine my mother ever bought.

I remember that one afternoon in 1831, when two or three of the packets had been wind bound during a long spell of easterly weather, Capt. Cooper came down to the wharf in a hurried manner, evidently about to make a move. One of the other captains said: "What is the matter, old man, what are you going to do?" "I am going to cast off and hoist my jib," the Captain replied. "Parson Kendall's vane pints sou'west." "Hm," said the other Captain, "I'd stay here a month before I'd go to sea by Parson Kendall's rooster." This was before April, 1831, because in that month the old meeting house was taken down, rooster and all.

Sectarianism was active in those days, but Dr. Kendall was so little of a controversialist, and so much respected, that he occasionally exchanged pulpits with the evangelical ministers in Plymouth and adjoining towns. On one occasion he exchanged with Rev. Benjamin Whittemore of Eel River, and after church a conversation between two parishioners was heard—something to this effect: "Well, Captain, how did you like the parson?" The Captain replied, "I don't take much to this one God doctrine." "I guess," said the other, "one God is enough for Eel River, they only claim three in Boston."

In this connection it may not be improper to refer to an incident creditable to all concerned, which may interest my readers. The editors of the *Congregationalist*, the leading New England Trinitarian Congregational journal, inserted in its issue of March 4, 1851, the following notice:

"A premium of $30 is offered for a dissertation containing the most full and perfect and the best narrative of historical and other facts bearing upon the following question, viz: 'So far as Christian salvation is a change effected in individuals, and may be known to them and be by them described to others, does the saving power of Christ eminently attend upon a knowledge of his life, as it is revealed in his manifestations from his birth to his ascension; and is it reasonable to expect that the redeeming effect of this saving power will be proportioned to the faithfulness with which his life is studied, and the perfectness with which it becomes known, and is contemplated?' "

After the decision on the merits of the dissertations had been reached, it was found on opening the envelopes containing the names of the authors, that the premium had been awarded to Rev. Geo. Ware Briggs, pastor of the First Church in Plymouth, Unitarian.

The sloop Eagle had her berth at Hedge's wharf. She was a snub nosed, broad beamed craft, without a figure head, and painted a dull green, unattractive to the public and not a much better sailer than the Polly. She was commanded for a time by John Battles, Jr., but through most of the years of my boyhood, by Richard Pope. Captain Pope was a genial man, kind to his crew, and accommodating to his passengers, and by his popular ways secured his full share of both freight and passengers. After giving up the packet service, perhaps about 1840, he engaged in other pursuits, one of which will be mentioned in connection with the steamboats running on the line between Plymouth and Boston. In 1849 he went to California in the ship Samuel Appleton, sailing from New York, and on his return he was for a time sexton of the Unitarian church, and then was appointed keeper of the lighthouse at the Gurnet. Later he was a town watchman for some years, and died July 29, 1881, at 83 years of age.

The sloop Splendid was a handsome craft, well modelled, tall masted, had a figure head, was painted bright green, and was a fast sailer. To my youthful eyes she was the queen of the line. For a short time she was commanded by Richard Pope and Sylvanus Churchill, but through most of my boyhood, after 1832, by George Simmons. Capt. Simmons was an energetic man, taking advantage of every opportunity, running perhaps at times some risk, and making a trip to Boston and back, while the vessels of his prudent rivals lay in their berths. I remember seeing him leave the wharf one afternoon at sunset with a full load of hollow ware from the Federal furnace, and finding her the next morning but one, when I looked out of my window at Cole's Hill, lying in her berth with a full load of hemp for the Plymouth Cordage Company. Capt. Simmons, after he left the packet service, engaged for some years in the coal business, and as wharfinger of Hedge's wharf, and afterwards until his death, as the manager of trucking teams. He died June 4, 1886, eighty years of age. Capt. Sylvanus Churchill died March 2, 1878.

The sloops Harriet and Hector, both probably built in Plymouth, I speak of together, because they were of about the same age, and looked very much alike. Both were painted a bright green, and were good sailers. The Harriet had a berth at Barnes' wharf, and was commanded as long as I knew her by Samuel Doten Holmes. Captain Holmes bought in 1829 the house with a brick end, opposite the Universalist church, which he occupied until 1834, when he built and occupied until his death the house next above it. He died October 22, 1861.

The Hector had her berth at Carver's wharf, and was commanded by Bradford Barnes for a short time, but chiefly by Edward Winslow Bradford, who after the opening of the Old Colony Railroad established with Samuel Gardner, who had been a driver on the Boston stage line, the Bradford and Gardner express. After some years he sold his interest in the express to Isaac B. Rich, but again later he established Bradford's express, which he conducted until his death, which occurred December 27, 1874. Bradford Barnes, who for a time commanded the Hector, lived many years in the house on the southerly corner of Lincoln street, in the house which stood where Davis building stands, and in the house next north of the Universalist church. He died January 22, 1883.

The sloop Atalanta was built in Plymouth as early as 1830, and was commanded at first by Truman C. Holmes. She was afterwards rigged as a schooner, and as early as 1837 was commanded by Samuel H. Doten. I think she had her berth for a time at Carver's wharf, but I remember seeing her loading at Hedge's wharf on the 12th of June, 1837, the day after the Broad street riot in Boston, about which the crew talked as they took in their cargo. Of Capt. Holmes I shall have something to say in connection with the steamboat General Lafayette, and of Capt. Doten in connection with the Civil War.

The sloop Thetis was commanded by Isaac Robbins, and had her berth at Hedge's wharf. She was changed to a schooner in 1843, and I saw her last about 1865, at anchor off Marblehead Neck, loading with gravel.

The last packet equipped with any view to passenger service was the schooner Russell, owned by N. Russell & Co., Phineas Wells, and her commander William Davis Simmons, which had her berth at Davis wharf. Having the business of her owners she survived the advent of the railroad, and continued in service until her wreck. Her fate was a sad one. She left Boston on the afternoon of Friday, March 17, 1854, with a crew, besides her captain, consisting of Erastus Torrence, Alpheus Richmond and Ichabod Rogers, and with five passengers, Harvey H. Raymond, and his son, Benjamin B. Raymond, Elkanah Barnes, Edmund Griffin, son of Grenville W. Griffin, and Henry H. Weston, son of Henry Weston. The next day in a northwest gale, she went ashore near Billingsgate light on Cape Cod, and with the schooner a total wreck, all on board were lost. All the bodies came ashore at Wellfleet and Truro, and as I was requested to act as administrator of Capt. Simmons' estate, it became my duty to visit the tombs in those towns, where they were deposited, and after their identification to arrange for their removal to Plymouth.

The cause of the disaster can only be conjectured. The gale was from the west northwest, and as Billingsgate is about east southeast from the Gurnet, where the Russell was seen early Saturday morning, it is certain that she was driven helpless before it. And as the bodies came ashore in the immediate vicinity of the wreck, it is equally certain that those on board did not leave the vessel before she struck. I see no reason why if the rudder was under control, the schooner

could not, even with the partial loss of her sails, have been
sheered a little southerly to a lee under Manomet, or a little
easterly to a lee under Wood End. I am therefore inclined
to think that her rudder was disabled, either by striking a rock
at the Gurnet in getting away from her anchorage, or by
striking the tail of Brown's Island in missing stays, and that
in that condition she became the prey of the gale.

Since the loss of the Russell the following freighters have
run at different periods between Plymouth and Boston, though
not in the order stated:

The Glide, commanded by Thomas Bartlett and Capt. Joy.

The Wm. G. Eadie, commanded by Thomas Bartlett and
Kendall Holmes.

The M. R. Shepard and Eliza Jane, commanded by Thomas
Bartlett.

The Shave and Mary Eliza, commanded by Kendall
Holmes.

The Emma T. Story and Anna B. Price, commanded by
Wm. Nightingale.

The Martha May, commanded by Wm. Swift, and the Sarah
Elizabeth, commanded by Daniel O. Churchill.

Besides the above there were two sloops, the Comet, Capt.
Ephraim Paty, and the Coral, Capt. John Battles, Jr., which
were quasi packets, running on no special lines, but sailing
for any near port to or from which they could find freight.
Before railroads were built from Boston to the sea ports of
Massachusetts, all kinds of freight to and from those ports
were carried necessarily by water. Thus packets were running from Boston to every town of importance on the New
England coast. Those to the nearer places were sloops as to
Salem, Newburyport, Portsmouth, Barnstable, Plymouth and
Provincetown; those to places a little more distant topsail
schooners; those to Hartford, New York, Philadelphia, Baltimore, Richmond, Savannah and Charleston, brigs, and those
to Mobile and New Orleans, ships. Plymouth had a very considerable amount of freight to distribute, cotton cloth, nails,
anchors, hollow ware, cordage, fish and imported iron, sugar
and molasses. When these were sent in small amounts they
were sent to Boston by the regular packets, and transhipped
to the packets in Boston running on other lines. But if any

considerable amount of freight, a gang of rigging for instance
for Nantucket, a dozen or two anchors for New Bedford, or
twenty hogsheads of molasses for Hartford, or some other
port, were wanting transportation, then the Comet and Coral
found their opportunity, trusting to chance for more or less
of a return cargo for Plymouth or Boston. If they were needed to go to Maine ports they were reasonably sure of a lumber freight home. Indeed, as I remember, these vessels did
practically the entire lumber business of the town. Capt. Paty
died in California July 24, 1849, and Capt. Battles died in
Plymouth March 1, 1872.

There were other packets besides those of Plymouth seen
in our waters. There was the Juventa, a Kingston packet,
and there were the Duxbury packets Union and Glide, commanded by Capt. Martin Winsor, the Spy, the Jack Downing,
Capt. Holmes, the Traveller, Capt. John Alden, and the Reform, so that with the fifteen running to and from the three
towns there was rarely a day in suitable weather when more
than one did not pass the old square pier. In addition to all
the above, the Barnstable packet sloop Henry Clay not only
passed within sight, but frequently sought an anchorage in
the Cow Yard, or came to the wharves. The distance by stage
of Barnstable from Boston induced a large passenger traffic,
and she was fitted with a handsome cabin extending to the
main hatch, lighted by skylights, and containing ample and
luxurious accommodations.

There was one other vessel to whose memory I wish to pay
a tribute on account of the pleasant fishing parties on board of
her, in which I have participated. Her name was the Rainbow, but whence she came, what her regular business was,
and whither she went, I never knew. She was a queer craft,
sailing well on the starboard tack, but as dull as a log on the
port tack. She would loaf along up Saquish channel with the
wind southwest, but after rounding the pier she would come
up Beach channel like a race horse. She reminded me of the
story of a traveller, who said he saw in South America a race
of goats made with two long legs on one side and two short
ones on the other, so that they could walk easily round the
mountain side. A sailor in the group cried out: "Belay
there, Captain, how did them air goats sail on t'other tack?"

CHAPTER VIII.

It is singular that the spirit of invention and enterprise, which New England has displayed in the advance of civilization, should have been apparently indifferent in the development of steam navigation. It is true that her activities have been fully exerted in other directions, and that, as necessity is the mother of invention, the requirements of her manufacturing industries have demanded to the fullest extent the display of her genius. The Hudson River and New York bay seem to have been the theatre in which those early experiments were made, which laid the foundation in this country of successful navigation by steam. In these experiments, as early as 1803, Robert Fulton, assisted by Chancellor R. Livingston, seems to have led the way. In 1804 Col. John Stevens made a trial of a propelling power, consisting of a small engine and a screw. He later attached two screws to the engine, and the identical machine which he used is now owned by the Stevens Institute of Technology in Hoboken, New Jersey. It was placed on a new hull in 1844, and made on the Hudson eight miles an hour. In 1806 Robert Fulton built a sidewheel boat one hundred and thirty feet long, propelled by steam, with paddles 15 feet in diameter, and floats with two feet dip, and went to Albany at the rate of five miles an hour. This boat was called the Clermont, the name of the seat on the Hudson of Chancellor Livingston, and in 1808 made regular trips from New York to Albany.

While these operations were going on, causing a complete revolution in the commercial life of the country, New England never saw the smoke of a steamboat. The first boat to enter Massachusetts Bay was the Massachusetts, built in Philadelphia, and designed by its owners, Joseph and John H. Andrews, Wm. Fettyplace, Stephen White, Andrew Watkins and Andrew Bell, to run between Boston and Salem. After a few unsuccessful trips she was sent to Charleston, S. C., and was lost on the passage.

The next steamboat to enter the waters of Massachusetts was the Eagle, which was built in New York and had been for a time in Chesapeake Bay, under command of Capt. Moses Rogers, who was later commander of the steamboat Savannah, the first steam vessel to cross the Atlantic. She came to Plymouth in 1818, commanded by Lemuel Clark. Capt. Clark was either a Plymouth man, or the son of a Plymouth man, and had married in 1817 Lydia Bartlett, daughter of the late Ezra Finney, who lived, as many of my readers will remember, on the westerly corner of Summer and Spring streets. He had a son, William, one of my school and playmates, the father of William Clark, now living on Cushman street, who at one time was the master of the bark Evangeline of Boston. It is probable that Capt. Lemuel Clark was induced by his connection with Plymouth to bring his vessel here, where she must have been an object of great interest to the people of Plymouth and the adjoining towns. She remained here a number of days, having her berth at Carver's wharf and taking daily excursion parties into the bay. She was eight hours on her passage from Boston, making about five and one-half statute miles per hour. On her return to Boston she ran for a time on the Hingham line, but I have no record of her later history. A picture of her in oil hangs on the walls of Pilgrim Hall, taken from a contemporaneous drawing, and presented, through the good offices of Mr. George P. Cushing, the manager of the Nantasket Steamboat Company, by the artist to the Pilgrim Society, and occupies a frame given by the grandchildren of Capt. Lemuel Clark.

There is no record of the visit of any other steamboat to Plymouth until the advent of the General Lafayette, in 1828. She was built in New York in 1824, and bought in Boston by James Bartlett, Jr., James Spooner and Jacob Covington, with the view of establishing a steamboat line between Plymouth and Boston. According to her enrolment in the Plymouth Custom House, issued September 16, 1828, her name was General Lafayette, with one deck, two masts, 82 feet, 7 inches long, 6 feet, 1 inch deep, and measured 92 54-95 tons. For her better accommodation the owners of the boat bought Jackson's wharf at the foot of North street, and contracted with Jacob and Abner S. Taylor to build at the end of the wharf an extension nine hundred feet long and twenty-eight feet wide with a T at the end projecting northwesterly one hundred feet square. The extension built of piles and timber and plank was not completed until the autumn of 1828. In the meantime the Lafayette ran through the summer of that year from Hedge's wharf, leaving Plymouth at hours when the tide served, and leaving Boston at hours which on her arrival would enable her to reach her dock. Of course her fuel was wood, and she made the passage in five hours, making about eight and one-half statute miles per hour. The point reached by the wharf was that point on what was called the Town Guzzle, where at mean low tide there were four or five feet of water. With that depth of water a small steamboat like the General Lafayette could reach the extreme end of the wharf at all times of tide. The Town Guzzle was a circuitous one. It left Broad channel at its extreme southwesterly end, and running southwesterly five or six hundred feet, it made an easy curve; thence running northwesterly about eight hundred feet, and thence with another easy curve running southwesterly about four hundred feet to a point reached by the wharf. It was perhaps forty feet wide, and with sufficient water beyond that width for the dip of paddle wheels, at any time except within an hour of low water, there was rarely any detention. Steamboats of moderate length found little difficulty in rounding the curves, but those of greater length found it anything but easy work. I remember once the steamboat Connecticut left the wharf at near low tide, with a spring line from her bow to the wharf to twitch her round the curve, and as the line tautened, it snapped, the hither end coming back like a whip lash and tripping up, without serious injury, about a dozen persons standing near the cap log. I learned the lesson then and there to always stand at a distance from a spring line.

In the angle where the T joined the main wharf, there was a flight of substantial steps, where boats at all times could land, drawing not over two feet of water. This was a great convenience, enabling Sam Burgess, with his fish for the market, lobster boats from the Gurnet, and the Island and Saquish boats, to land without regard to the stage of the tide. Many a householder with his mouth made up for a fish dinner has sat by the hour together at the head of those steps, waiting for Sam. In those days, too, the only purveyor of lobsters was Joseph Burgess, the keeper of the light, and as regular as the day he would appear with his lobsters and wearing his red thrum cap, would wheel his barrow full about the town. There was no talk then of short lobsters, nor of extravagant prices, for nine pence, or twelve and a half cents in the currency of the time, would buy a three or four pound lobster. The scarcity and small size of this delicious shell fish in our day have not been satisfactorily explained. I am inclined to think that the cause is not to be found in the excessive amount of their catch, but in the appearance on our shores, and the increasing numbers, of the tautog, which not only exhausts the food, which the lobster feeds upon, but also feeds on the lobster itself. In my early boyhood, if I am not mistaken, the tautog was an unknown fish north of Cape Cod. The sandy shores of Barnstable county formed an effectual barrier to its northern migration. I think that about 1830 Capt. Josiah Sturgis, commander of the Revenue Cutter Hamilton, brought some live tautog round the Cape and dropped them in Plymouth Bay. A very few years afterwards the first tautog was caught off Manomet, and one or two years later several were caught off the Gurnet, while now they are found all along the shores of Massachusetts and Maine. To this new fish, in my judgment, may fairly be attributed the gradual disappearance of a food fish which was once abundant and cheap.

Returning now to the Lafayette, it can only be said that her career was a short one. Under the command of Capt. Truman C. Holmes, with Seth Morton as steward, she ran through the seasons of 1828 and 1829, the latter year making her berth at Long wharf, or steamboat wharf, as for many years it was called, and then was laid up in Tribble's Dock, or building yard, as it was called, north of the wharf to die. Her upperworks were removed, and her engine taken out, and my only recollection of the vessel is of a dismantled hulk with her planking stripped off, and her timbers fastened to the keel, standing otherwise unsupported, just visible at high tide above the surface of the water. The only incident of her service, which I remember, was an attempt with a party of excursionists, of which my mother was one, to go to Boston and return the same day. Night came without her return, and about midnight my mother reached home, having ridden from Scituate, where the steamboat had put in out of wood. Capt. Holmes, her commander, took command in 1830 of the new packet sloop Atalanta, and served with her several years until she was altered to a schooner, and placed under command first of Sylvanus Churchill, and then of Samuel H. Doten. He died March 14, 1880, eighty-five years of age.

In 1830, the year after the Lafayette ceased to run, the steamboat Rushlight, Capt. Currie, came to Plymouth and advertised to carry passengers to Boston for a dollar and a quarter, the fare by stage being two dollars, but how long this arrangement continued I do not know.

I know of no other steamboat in Plymouth until 1839, when the Suffolk ran on excursions to Boston and elsewhere during July and August. In 1840 a small steamboat, the Hope, Capt. Van Pelt, with a light draft, made regular trips to and from Boston during a part of the season. I recall an incident suggested by the mention of her name. On the 11th of September in that year I was called to Plymouth, being then in college, on account of the death of my brother-in-law, Ebenezer G. Parker, and left an order at the stage office in the City Hotel on Brattle street, to be called for by the stage at my grandmother's in Winthrop Place, leading out of Summer street. The Hope left Boston at two o'clock, reaching Plymouth at six. The leaving hour of the stage was the same, and as the passengers on that day were few in number, it was exactly two when I took my seat by the side of Samuel Gardner, the driver. As we started, Mr. Gardner said to me. "Mr. Davis, I am going to beat the boat today." The air was clear and exhilarating, the four horses were in good trim, and the road was in its best condition. Mr. Gardner did not leave the box during the trip, the horses were ready at the three places where changes were made, and as I dismounted at my mother's house at Cole's Hill, the boat passengers were coming up the wharf. I doubt very much whether any regular stage line in this country has ever travelled as our stage did that day, thirty-six miles in four hours.

Shortly after 1840 the steamboat Connecticut came to Plymouth and took excursion parties into the bay, but I do not remember that she made any regular trips to Boston. In 1844, if I am correct in the dates, the steamboat Express, Capt. Sanford, ran between Boston and Barnstable, stopping at Plymouth to leave and take passengers. She was a good boat, and made the passage to Plymouth in three and a half hours. Her managers had built a flat bottomed barge with scow ends, which, under the charge of Capt. Richard Pope, at low water met her at the upper end of Broad Channel, and exchanged passengers and freight. The return of the barge, by the way of the Guzzle, especially with wind and tide against her, was sometimes tedious, frequently consuming an hour. In 1844 the steamer Yacht ran a part of the season.

After 1845 I know of no steamboats coming to Plymouth, except occasionally on excursions from Boston for the day, until 1880. In the meantime the wharf began to suffer from storms and decay. Of course it was convenient for vessels to make fast to, until they could reach their regular berths, and in northeast storms it served as a barrier to protect the vessels at the short wharves from the wind and waves. At one time a bathing house was constructed beneath its flooring. Two bathing pools were built in two bays of the wharf, with plank floors and walls, and steps leading up into two dressing rooms above the wharf, to which subscribers, or those buying tickets, were admitted. These bathing rooms served their purpose for a time, but soon, like the wharf, needed repairs and were abandoned.

In 1880 the steamboat Hackensack, owned, I think, by the Seaver fish guano factory of Duxbury, made regular daily trips to or from Boston, or both, during the summer, except while she was repairing damages occasioned by a fire at Comey's wharf in Boston, where she lay. At that time the whole wharf, except about three hundred feet, which had been kept in repair, had by the action of storms and ice been practically destroyed, leaving only about a hundred piles within sight above the water. These were pulled up in 1880 by the tug Screamer, some of them requiring a force of thirty-three tons to start them from their beds.

In 1876 an appropriation made by Congress was expended in dredging a channel fifty feet wide, and six feet deep from Broad channel to the wharf, and in later years the width has been increased to one hundred and fifty feet, and the depth

to nine feet, at mean low water.   A basin connecting with
the channel has been dredged in front of the short wharves so
that not only can steamboats of sufficient size reach the docks,
but barges drawing sixteen feet of water find no difficulty in
berthing at the pockets of the coal dealers.   In 1881 the
steamboat Stamford, commanded by E. W. Davidson, began
to run regularly from Boston to Plymouth and back daily,
and continued to run uninterruptedly until 1895, under the
same command, except during a part of one season, when,
owing to some difficulty between Capt. Davidson and her owner, Nathaniel Webster of Gloucester, the former was temporarily displaced.   Capt. Davidson also ran the Shrewsbury
and Wm. Story each one season, and as a supplementary
freight boat after the close of one season the Shoe City of
Lynn.   Since 1897, or about that time, the following boats
have run on the route: The Lillie, Putnam, O. E. Lewis,
Henry Morrison, Plymouth, Cape Cod, Governor Andrew,
and Old Colony.   During one season the Stamford ran after
her name was changed to Endicott.   During the last three
seasons the Nantasket Steamboat Co. have had exclusive leases
of available wharves, and have run the Governor Andrew and
the Old Colony.   The latter is a new boat running in 1904
for the first time, and is recognized as the most convenient,
safest and most elegant excursion boat in the waters of Massachusetts.   The wharf is now, with three hundred feet of its
old timber and pile extension, owned by Charles I. and Henry
H. Litchfield of Plymouth who, having fitted it expressly for
steamboat purposes, keep it in excellent repair, and have leased
it to the Nantasket Steamboat Company.   The Pilgrim Society, owning Pilgrim wharf, refrain from leasing it to any
competing line, believing that the Nantasket Co. should be
encouraged in their efforts to establish a permanent and successful enterprise.

CHAPTER IX.

Allusion has been made to the embargo and to the Yankee shrewdness which evaded the watchfulness of government officers whose duty it was to prevent departures from port. The following narrative, for the incidents in which I am indebted to Capt Charles C. Doten, illustrates the shrewdness to which I referred.

During the Embargo, Plymouth's fishing fleet was laid up in the docks, and the owners found themselves cut off from the trade with the West India Islands. The catch of fish from the Grand Banks could not be sold to advantage for want of this market, and after being cured remained stored in the fish houses.

England and France then being at war their West India dependencies were subject to blockade, and as a consequence provisions which could be run into the ports of either nationality, commanded high prices. With such a temptation it was not strange that there were found adventurous men in fishing ports to hazard the loading of vessels with dry fish, and disregarding embargo penalties of our own government, surreptitiously depart "for the West Indies and a market."

Plymouth was not lacking in this sort of enterprise, and the writer proposes to sketch one or two of the "run-a-ways," to show the character of the men of those days who a little later did the country good service as "privateersmen" when the war between the United States and England was fought.

Anticipating that these attempts to break the embargo would be made in spite of stringent regulations, orders were given to the customs officers at every port to keep strict watch and prevent vessels from going to sea. Accordingly at Plymouth, Water street was nightly patrolled, and a guard boat well manned, and in charge of Capt. Joseph Bradford, was stationed in Beach channel to intercept any outward bound vessel which might succeed in getting away from the wharves. With these precautions it would seem to have been difficult to evade successfully the minions of the law and run out a cargo of fish in defiance of all the Federal government could do to prevent it, yet it was done.

The first schooner was the Hannah, lying at Hedge's, now known as Pilgrim wharf, which then had two or three warehouses on it, one of them containing fish.   On a dark night an industrious gang of men quietly loaded the vessel from the warehouse, but unluckily, before their work was completed, the tide fell so that the Hannah grounded, and could not get to sea that night as intended.   Next day the custom house officers noted that the vessel did not rise buoyantly with the tide, so going on board they lifted the hatches, and at once discovered "what was the matter with Hannah."

Felicitating themselves that they had caught their mouse, and determining that there should be no escape, they stripped the vessel "to a girtline," that is, they removed all her sails together with the running and standing rigging, leaving nothing aloft but a single block on each mast through which a line was rove for the purpose of hoisting a man when the craft was to be re-rigged.   All the gear was carted away, and, while the fish were left on board, the Hannah being absolutely reduced to bare poles, the officials were perfectly certain that they had made it impossible for her to take her cargo to the West Indies.   Of course the laugh went round town at the expense of the defeated owners, and the officials were "cocky" over their smartness.   Weeks went by and the incident passed out of mind, the deeply laden Hannah meantime lying in her berth and daily rising and falling with the tide. All the same her voyage to Martinique was made up, her captain and crew engaged, and the man who was to rig and take her out of dock had his gang picked for the purpose, and only awaited his opportunity.   This man was Capt. Samuel Doten, father of our townsmen, the late Major Samuel H. and Capt. Charles C. Doten, one of the most energetic shipmasters of his day, whom nothing ever daunted, and who liked nothing better than a bit of dare-devil business, being perfectly competent for anything pertaining to seamanship or calling for executive ability.   These qualities were well known in this town, so naturally he was "in it" with the Hannah.   Capt. George Adams, another old sea dog, was his right-hand man in the part he had to do, and there were two or three others, who could handle a marlinspike and make a knot or seizing as well in darkness as at noonday.

Capt. Doten lived at the foot of the Green, on what is now Sandwich street and kept a boat on the south shore near the place, where he afterwards built the wharf, now owned by Capt. E. B. Atwood. The long waited opportunity came one night with a howling southeast rain storm, from which the Water street watch sought shelter in one of the stores. There the officers with pipes and toddy made themselves comfortable, while right before their noses the Hannah's decks were alive with her own crew, and Capt. Doten's gang of riggers, who had come alongside in boats. A loft which contained the gear of another vessel, likewise clean stripped by her careful owner, so her rigging might not get weather worn in the months of the tie-up, was broken open and the shrouds and stays were carried on board the Hannah. Capt. Adams was the man to go aloft and put the eyes of the rigging over the mast heads, and Capt. Doten arranged for a system of wooden tags to be tied to the pieces as they went up, so that by feeling the notches cut in the tags, Capt. Adams would know whether what he received belonged on the starboard or port side. So it was also with the blocks and halliards, and all being understood, Capt. Adams took his place in the sling tied in the end of the girtline, and was soon hoisted to the crosstrees. The hours passed, but before daylight the Hannah was rigged, halliards rove fore and aft, and sails bent, though both rigging and sails were too large for her, belonging as they did to another vessel of greater tonnage. Capt. Doten had met this difficulty in the case of the standing rigging, which was too long, by turning up the ends of the shrouds over hand spikes used for shearpoles, and passing the lanyards from the deadeyes at the rail also over the handspikes, his deck men then setting taut with the watch tackles they had brought, and seizing all off securely. The sails were made smaller simply by putting in a reef.

All was now ready, and the Hannah cast off and dropped down to the end of the wharf. Capt. Doten, who was a good pilot for the harbor, took charge, and with the hoisting of the jib the vessel quickly fell off before the wind and ran directly along the shore for High Cliff, there then being no Long wharf in the way. This course was taken to avoid the guard boat which was supposed to be patrolling the channel along by the Beach, the usual way of leaving the port. It was the top of high water and there was little likelihood that with proper care the vessel would touch anything. At High Cliff Capt. Doten ordered the mainsail set and pointed the Hannah's nose for the open sea. Then giving the helm to her captain, whose name the writer unfortunately has never heard, he gave the course to steer, and the schooner went romping down by Beach Point at a pace which left no chance for the guard boat to intercept her, when from away up Beach channel Capt. Bradford descried the fleeting sail. Before getting far down the harbor Capt. Doten and his men wished the Hannah and her crew a successful voyage, and jumping into their boat towing alongside were, before the early morning, snugly stowed away in their respective homes. Of course there was great excitement when it was found the bird had flown, and instantly the conclusion was reached that "Sam Doten had run away with the Hannah," so the officers at once repaired to his house where his wife was unconcernedly getting breakfast, and Capt. Doten, having apparently just arisen, was leisurely dressing. The officers were greatly surprised at finding him and he equally surprised to learn from them that the Hannah had got away, nor did he hesitate to express his gratification that the custom house gang had been so thoroughly outwitted.

The Hannah made an excellent run to the West Indies and arrived safely at Martinique, where she sold her fish at $20 per quintal of 112 pounds and the vessel also was disposed of, the aggregate sum which ultimately got around to her owners being a very handsome one for the venture.

The Hope and the Cutter.

The brig Hope was the next Plymouth vessel to "run the embargo." She belonged to William Holmes of this town, and loaded a cargo of dry fish at Provincetown, where she was seized by the customs officers of that port, and anchored in the harbor, with a revenue cutter commanded by Capt. Thomas Nicolson of Plymouth lying near at hand to prevent her from going to sea. Under these circumstances her owner induced Capt. Samuel Doten, who had "assisted" in the Hannah adventure, to become the principal in "cutting out" the Hope from under the guns of the revenue vessel.

Selecting his crew, Capt. Doten took charge of the brig and waited for things to come around to his liking. What he wanted was a smart northeast gale, which is a fair wind out of Provincetown, though of course a pretty rough affair to contend with in the open bay, and against which he would have to work his vessel out past the Cape after getting clear of the harbor. No abler or more daring seaman ever trod a deck, and, whatever the chances, Capt. Doten was ready to take them, so when one night the weather shut in "nasty" with indications of the wished for gale the next day, he made his preparations. A mooring line was run out aft to keep the brig's head toward the harbor mouth, so that her square sails should immediately fill before the wind when hoisted. On the yards the gaskets keeping the furled sails in place were nearly cut off, so that while they still preserved the shape, they would part and allow the topsails to be hoisted without having to send men aloft to loose them as usual when getting under way, much depending on gaining a few minutes over the cutter at the start. Vessels of those days had hemp cables, and Capt. Doten meant to "cut and run" when the decisive moment came.

With the morning the gale was piping smartly, and it never occurring to the captain of the revenue cutter that a vessel would attempt to go to sea in such a blow, he took his gig with her crew and went ashore. The ebb tide left the boat on the beach while Capt. Nicolson and his men were up town, and meanwhile the sympathetic Provincetowners. ready to help the Hope, stole the thole pins and an oar or two. This was the favorable moment, while the cutter was disabled for want of her commander and several men, for whose return on board she would have to wait, so Capt. Doten cut his cable and stern mooring line, quickly hoisted and sheeted home his fore topsail, and was moving down the harbor before the lieutenant in charge of the cutter realized the situation. Seizing a musket he fired at Capt. Doten, who was at the Hope's helm, but made a bad shot. Then he let go a big gun at the brig, which also was poorly aimed, and did no harm. It served, however, as a signal for Capt. Nicolson to come on board, if he needed more than the evidence of his eyes. The town was immediately alive with excitement, for the sea-faring men took in the whole plan and shouted with delight over its boldness and sheer sailor-like daring. Men hindered more than they helped while pretending to assist in getting the boat down to the water, but at last, with her captain on board again, the cutter got into full chase, firing her bow guns at the brig in hope of crippling her spars if doing nothing more damaging. Provincetown has rarely seen anything more exciting than that running fight, and the story is told there even to this day, as the writer can vouch, having himself heard it from an old sea dog over there within a few years.

The Hope was a good sailer, and soon doubled round the long, sandy point at the harbor mouth, across which the cutter still continued firing, the shots sending the sand into the air in clouds as they skipped over the beach.

After getting outside, Capt. Doten made more sail for the better handling of his vessel, and one of his men, William Stacy of Boston, went aloft to loose a to'gallant sail. Just as he reached the crosstrees and gripped the shrouds for further ascent, a shot passed so close to him that, holding by his hands, the wind of it strung him out like a flag. Getting his footing again he yelled: "A good shot, try it again," and went on with his duty.

The cutter soon got into the open bay where the sea was so rough that her firing became entirely ineffectual, and she could only chase. Capt. Nicolson, however, was one of the plucky kind and meant to do his full duty by keeping the Hope in sight if he could do nothing more. The gale became fiercer, and the sea rougher as the two vessels got from under the lee of the Cape, and that night the cutter was forced ashore near Scituate and wrecked, but with no loss of life. Capt. Doten, with a loaded vessel under him, which he knew how to handle, made better weather of it, and succeeded in beating the Hope out past Cape Cod against the storm, and in a day or two was running for the West Indies, intending to make Martinique.

All went well until nearing his destination, when one afternoon a big British frigate poked her nose out from behind an island right across his path and fired a gun for him to heave to. There was nothing for it but to obey, and a boat with a boarding party was soon alongside. The officer wanted to know where the brig was bound, to which Capt. Doten replied, "West Indies and a market." "You mean Martinique, don't you?" said the officer, "and let me tell you that had you got in there the Frenchmen would have given you $25 a quintal for your fish; but you will do well as it is, for I'm going to send you into the English island of St. Lucia, and our people will give you $16." "Very well," answered Capt. Doten, "I'll go to St. Lucia then." "Yes," replied the officer, "I'm sure you will, as I'm going with you, for you Yankees are altogether too smart and slippery to be trusted alone, with $9 on a quintal of fish difference as to where you land them."

So the Hope went into St. Lucia, where Capt. Doten sold both fish and vessel, and later he found his way home with $25,000 in Spanish doubloons, a large part of the sum being sewed into his clothing, and the writer has heard the Captain's wife tell of letting him into the house at about two o'clock one morning, and of their sitting up in bed together, ripping out the gold pieces and tossing them into a shining pile, of which "Hope told a flattering tale."

CHAPTER X.

At the beginning of the Revolution the cod fishery of Plymouth was active and successful, and during the previous ten years had employed an average of sixty vessels. During the war it was of course seriously depressed, but after the declaration of peace its recuperation was rapid. In 1802 it had reached its maximum of prosperity, before the embargo and the war of 1812 again crippled it. In that year there were thirty-seven vessels engaged in it, employing two hundred and sixty-six men, and landing twenty-six thousand, one hundred and seventy-five quintals of codfish, or an average of seven hundred and seven quintals for each vessel. All but six of these vessels made two trips. The following list of the vessels engaged that year with their tonnage, the names of the skippers and the fare of each may be interesting to some of my readers.

Lucy, Thomas Sears, 75 tons, 800 quintals.
Old Colony, George Finney, 80 tons, 850 quintals.
Wm. Davis, Jr., Elkanah Finney, 90 tons, 1000 quintals.
Mary, Clark Finney, 75 tons, 450 quintals.
Swan, Thadeus Churchill, Jr., 60 tons, 895 quintals.
Polly, Amasa Churchill, 45 tons, 800 quintals.
Ceres, Wm. Brewster, 60 tons, 1,100 quintals.
Washington, Amasa Brewster, 90 tons, 840 quintals.
Swallow, Melzar Whiting, 50 tons, 900 quintals.
Benj. Church, Nathaniel Clark, 70 tons, 350 quintals.
Crusoe, Stephen Payne, 60 tons, 900 quintals.
Nightingale, Ansel Holmes, 35 tons, 700 quintals.
Union, Samuel Virgin, 70 tons, 850 quintals.
Rose, Barnabas Dunham, 55 tons, 710 quintals.
Dove, Wm. Barnes, 34 tons, 650 quintals.
Seaflower, Isaac Bartlett, 60 tons, 1,000 quintals.
— — — Nathaniel Sylvester, 80 tons, 800 quintals.
— — — Ansel Holmes, 60 tons, 500 quintals.
Phebe, John Allen, 75 tons, 700 quintals.
New State, Joseph Holmes, 50 tons, 700 quintals.
Drake, Barnabas Faunce, 44 tons, 550 quintals.
Columbia, Truman Bartlett, 70 tons, 700 quintals.
Neptune, Chandler Holmes, 55 tons, 600 quintals.
Esther, Seth Robbins, 45 tons, 600 quintals.

Lucy, Eben Davie, 50 tons, 600 quintals.
Caroline, Ellis Holmes, 60 tons, 800 quintals.
Hero, Joseph Doten, 60 tons, 600 quintals.
Industry, Joseph Ryder, 60 tons, 600 quintals.
Federalist, Finney Leach, 80 tons, 750 quintals.
Eagle, Jabez Churchill, 30 tons, 300 quintals.
Polly, Lemuel Leach, 70 tons, 700 quintals.
Leader, Job Brewster, 35 tons, 660 quintals.
Manson, Ellis Brewster, 105 tons, 450 quintals.
Rosebud, Andrew Bartlett, 40 tons, 580 quintals.
Hawk, Samuel Churchill, 60 tons, 700 quintals.
Seaflower, Ansel Bartlett, 40 tons, 790 quintals.
Rebecca, —— Codman, 50 tons, 700 quintals.

After the peace of 1815 the fishery entered upon a season of renewed activity, which continued with occasional periods of relaxation until its final extinction. The government having found during the revolution that fishermen made up a large share of naval enlistments, adopted the policy of aiding and encouraging the fishing industry, and in 1789 Congress passed an act granting a bounty of five cents per quintal on dried fish, and imposed a duty of fifty cents per quintal on imported fish. In 1790 the bounty of five cents was increased to ten, but on the 16th of February, 1792, the bounty of ten cents per quintal was discontinued, and an allowance was made to vessels employed in the cod fishery at sea for four months between the last day of February and the last day of November, according to the following rates: Vessels between twenty and thirty tons were to receive $1.50 per ton annually, and those of more than thirty tons, $2.50 per ton, but the allowance to any vessel was limited to $170. In 1797 the allowance was increased one-third; but in 1807 all bounties were abolished. In 1813 the bounty was revived and the allowance fixed as follows: To vessels from five to twenty tons, $1.60 per ton; to those from twenty to thirty, $2.40 per ton, and to those above thirty, $4, but no vessel was to receive more than $272. In 1819 an allowance was made to vessels from five to thirty tons of $3.50 per ton, and to those of more than thirty, $4 per ton, but vessels having a crew of ten men were to be allowed $3.50 per ton on a service of three months and a half. No vessel, however, was to receive more than $360. By an act passed in 1817, it was required in order to entitle a vessel to receive a

bounty that the master and three quarters of the crew should
be citizens of the United States, but in 1864 this requirement
was limited to the masters. By an act passed July 28, 1866,
bounties were abolished, and duties on salt used in curing fish
were remitted.

The abolition of bounties was a blow to the fishing interests,
which was destined to be followed by a more deadly one. It
cannot, however, be said that it was wholly undeserved, for
the requirement of four months' service at sea had been often
evaded. A very considerable number of the fishing fleet returned home before four months had expired, and anchoring
in beach channel by night and cruising in the bay by day, spent
the time in what was called bounty catching, until the expiration of the four months.

But a severer blow than the loss of bounty soon fell on the
fishery. In 1871 the treaty of Washington between the United
States and Great Britain provided that "fish oil and fish of all
kinds, except fish of the inland lakes, and of the rivers falling
into them, and except fish preserved in oil, being the produce
of the fisheries of the United States, or of the Dominion of
Canada, or of Prince Edward Island, shall be admitted into
each country, respectively, free of duty." This treaty went
into operation July 1, 1873, to remain in force for ten years,
and further until the expiration of two years after the United
States or Great Britain shall have given notice to terminate it.
• At the time of the repeal of the bounty law in 1866, the
product of the Plymouth fishery taking the returns from the
previous year as a basis of an estimate was as follows: Value
of fish, $261,053; value of oil, $24,530; bounties, $14,249, and
the number of men employed was 420. I am inclined to think
that the largest number of vessels ever employed was in the
year 1862, when sixty-seven were employed, but in 1873, the
year the treaty of Washington went into operation, there were
only twenty.

As nearly as I can judge the following is a correct list of
vessels engaged in the fishery since 1828:

Abby Morton	Albert
Abeona	Albion
Adelaide	Annie Eldridge
Adeline	Anti
Albatross	Arabella

Arno
Aurora
Austin
Avon
Banker
Ben Perley Poor
Betsey
Blue Wave
Black Warrior
Brontes
California
Caroline
Ceres
Challenge
Charles
Charles
Charles Augusta
Charles Henry
Christie Johnson
Clara Jane
Climax
Clio
Clifford
Cobden
Coiner
Columbia
Columbus
Conanchet
Confidence
Congress
Constitution
Cora
Costello
Deborah
Deliverance
Delos
Delta
Dolphin
Drake
Duck
Eagle
Elder Brewster
Eleanor
Eliza
Eliza Ann
Elizabeth
Ellis
Engineer
Enterprise

Essex
Experience
Fairplay
Fair Trade
Favorite
Fearless
Fisher
Flash
Flora
Fornax
Florida
Forest King
Fortune
Franklin
Fred Lawrence
Fredonia
Gentile
George
George Henry
Glendora
Glide
Grampus
Guide
Hannah
Hannah Coomer
Hannah Stone
Hattie Weston
Helena
Herald
Hercules
Hero
Hiram
Home
Horatio
Howard
Independence
Industry
Jane
John Eliot
John Fehrman
Joshua Bates
Juvenile
Latona
Leo
Leonidas
Lewis Perry
Linda
Linnet
Lizzie W. Hannum.

Louisa
Louise
Lucy
Lyceum
Malvina
Manchester
Manomet
Maria
Martha Washington
Mary A. Taylor
Mary Baker
Mary Chilton
Mary Holbrook
Mary Susan
Massachusetts
Matilda
May
Mayflower
May Queen
Medium
Molly Foster
Mona
Mountain King
Nahant
Naiad Queen
Nathaniel Doane
Neptune
N. D. Scudder
Oasis
Ocean
Old Colony
Olive Branch
Ontario
Orion
Oronoco
Pamlico
Perseverance
Philip Bridges
Pezarro
President
Profit
Rainbow
Reaper
Reform

Rescue
Resolution
Risk
Rival
Robert Roberts
Rollins
Roxanna
Sabine
Samuel
Samuel Davis
Sarah and Mary
Sarah E. Hyde
Sarah Elizabeth
Scud
Seadrift
Seaflower
Seafoam
Sea Witch
Seneca
Silver Spring
Speedwell
Storm King
Stranger
Sunbeam
Surprise
Susan
Swallow
Thatcher Taylor
Thetis
Three Friends
Traffic
Tremont
Vesper
Village Belle
Volant
Wampatuck
Wanderer
Wave
Wide Awake
Willie Lord
Wm. Tell
Wm. Wilson
Winslow

The following list of vessels employed in 1868 shows the gradual reduction of the fleet from sixty-seven in 1862 to twenty in 1873:

Abby Morton	Mary Taylor
Adeline	Mary Susan
Avon	Matilda
Charles	May Flower
Charles Augusta	May Queen
Clara Jane	Nahant
Climax	Naiad Queen
Cora	N. D. Scudder
Delos	Oasis
Dolphin	Ocean
Elizabeth	Olive Branch
Engineer	Oronoco
Favorite	Profit
Florida	Risk
Forest King	Samuel
George	Samuel Davis
George Henry	Seadrift
Glendora	Sea Witch
Helena	Silver Spring
Herald	Sunbeam
Joshua Bates	Surprise
Juvenile	Swallow
Linnet	Thatcher Taylor
Louisa	Tremont
Manomet	Volant
Manchester	Wave
Martha Washington	Wampatuck
Mary Chilton	Winslow

In 1869 there were fifty-four; in 1870, fifty-two; in 1871, forty; in 1872, twenty-six; in 1873, twenty; in 1874, twelve; in 1876, twelve; in 1878, eleven; in 1879, ten; in 1880, eight; in 1881, seven; in 1882, two; in 1883, two; in 1884, eight; in 1885, three; in 1886, one; in 1888, one, the Hannah Coomer, Capt. Nickerson, the last vessel to go to the Banks from Plymouth. In 1882 Prince Manter bought the Sabine, and Capt. James S. Kelley made seven trips in her in four summers, the last vessel to go to the Grand Banks, while the Hannah Coomer was the last to go to Quereau Bank.

The following is a list of fishing vessels lost since 1828, as complete as I am able to make it:

Abby Morton, Joseph Whitton, master, lost in Hell Gate, New York.

Adelaide, Capt. Joseph Sampson, was lost on the Banks.

Samuel, condemned in Nova Scotia.

Brontes, on a passage from Aux Cayes, to Boston, left

Holmes Hole December 31, 1862, and was never heard from. Her crew consisted of John E. Morton, captain; George Morey, mate, and Samuel Howland, Isaac Howland, Bartlett Finney and Josiah H. Swift.

Charles, Isaac Howland, master, was lost on Cape Cod.

Charles, Isaac Swift, master, left Plymouth September 29, 1868, on a fall fishing trip, and was never heard from.

Congress, owned by Samuel Doten, was lost.

Wampatuck, seized in Nova Scotia in 1870 or 1871.

Delos, sunk in Nantucket Roads in 1872.

Wm. Tell, sold before 1828, and lost on Grand Banks in 1829.

Christie Johnson, Solomon M. Holmes, master, was lost on the banks in 1874.

Ellis, was lost on Cape Cod in 1844.

Flash, Eli H. Minter, master, was lost in the West Indies in 1865.

Fred Lawrence was lost.

Herald, lost or sold in Nova Scotia in 1870.

Linnet, Wm. Langford, master, was lost with all hands, in September, 1870.

Martha Washington, Capt. Gooding, was lost in Nova Scotia in 1874.

Mary A. Taylor, Lewis King, master, was lost or sold in Nova Scotia in 1874.

May was lost in 1871.

Ocean, Jerry McCuskey, master, was lost in Nova Scotia in 1870.

Olive Branch was lost in 1869.

President, John Ellis Bartlett, master, lost in 1828, bound to Martinique.

President, Stephen D. Drew, master, was lost on Cape Cod in 1844.

Rollins, Charles Harlow, master, was lost on Cape Cod in 1868.

Seadrift was lost or sold in 1871 in Nova Scotia.

Speedwell was lost in the West Indies in 1865.

Swallow was lost or sold in Nova Scotia in 1871.

Thatcher Taylor, James Simmons, was lost or sold in 1871.

Fearless, Capt. George N. Adams, sailed from Boston for Aux Cayes, August 13, 1862, and was never heard from.

John Eliot, Francis H. Weston, master, sailed from Boston October 9, 1863, for Cape Haytien, and crew taken off November 21 by schooner Thrasher, and landed at Port Spain.

Mary Holbrook, was lost in the Gulf, January 25, 1831.

Joshua Bates was lost on Richmond Island in February, 1876.

Franklin was lost at the Western Islands in 1837.

George Henry, Lamberton, master, was condemned in West Indies, 1869.

Vesper, Capt. Burgess, sailed from New York, February 28, 1846, for Jamaica, and was lost probably in a gale March 2.

Flora, Benjamin Jenkins, master, was spoken August 8, 1846, with 15,000 fish; August 21, with 21,000; August 28, with 23,000; September 17, with 30,000, and was probably lost in a gale which occurred September 19, 1846.

Coiner, Samuel Rogers, master, was lost on a passage home from Inagua in 1865.

Stranger was lost at sea near St. Thomas, 1835.

Oronoco was lost in 1871.

Schooner Maracaibo, changed to a brig before she entered the whale fishery, has been earlier mentioned without any details of her loss. She sailed from Plymouth on a whaling voyage September 12, 1846. On the 19th, in latitude 38.22, and longitude 72.35, she was capsized, losing second mate, Wm. Tripp, of Tiverton, David Sylvia seaman, and George Ellis of Plymouth, also a seaman, who was drowned in the forecastle. The masts went by the board, and the brig righted, and Capt. Collingwood and eighteen men were lashed to the wreck ninety-six hours with only a barrel of sugar to eat. On the twenty-third they battered down the hatches and bailed the vessel out, and on the twenty-fourth set up jury masts. On the twenty-fifth they obtained from the bark Newton of New Bedford two spars and gear, and a quadrant, and finally, after being on the wreck twenty-one days, were taken off by the bark Clement.

The question is often asked, what becomes of all the vessels that have been built? Upon this question official records throw some light. The last accessible statistics show that during the ten years from 1879 to 1889, nineteen thousand one hundred and ninety United States vessels were wrecked on or near the coasts, or on the inland waters of the United States, and during the same period, sixty-six hundred and forty-one British vessels.

The following is an imperfect list of skippers since 1828:

Benjamin Nye Adams
George Adams
George N. Adams
John Allen
George Allen
Winslow Allen
Thomas Atwood
Wm. Atwood
Solomon Attaquin
Coleman Bartlett
Frederick Bartlett
Nathaniel Bartlett
Benjamin Bates
Braman L. Bennett
John Briggs
Frederick Burgess
Henry Burgess
James Burgess
Phineas F. Burgess
Horatio G. Camero
A. R. Carnes
John Chase
John B. Chandler
Samuel Chandler
Ephraim F. Churchill
Joseph Churchill
Lionel Churchill
Edward Clough
Isaac Connors
James Cornish
Thomas E. Cornish
Edward Courtney
Ichabod Davie
Lemuel Doten
Nathaniel Doty
Horace J. Drew
Stephen D. Drew
Daniel Eldridge
Barnabas Ellis
Stephen Finney
Henry Gibbs
Grenville W. Griffin
John Griffin

Wm. Grindle
Frew Gross
Thomas Hannagan.
Branch Harlow
Charles Harlow
Richard W. Harlow
Nathan Haskins
Robert Hogg
Gideon Holbrook
Barzillia Holmes
George Holmes
Solomon M. Holmes
Isaac Howland
John Howland
Lemuel C. Howland
Abiatha Hoxie
Nathaniel Hoxie
Robert Hutchinson
Benjamin Jenkins
Wm. Jordan
James S. Kelley
Lewis King
Robert King
William King
Wellington Lambert
Wm. Langford
Moses Larkin
Ezra Leach
Lemuel Leach
David Manter
David L. Manter
George Manter
Prince Manter
Owen McGahan
Jake McCarthy
Jerry McCluskey
Duncan McDonald
Eli H. Minter
George Morey
Wm. Morrisey
John Morse
Josiah Morton
Lemuel Morton

Levi P. Morton
Wm. Mullins
Grant C. Parsons
John Parsons
Ezra Pierce
Ignatius Pierce
Richard Pike
Calvin Raymond
Henry Rickard
Warren P. Rickard
Francis Rogers
George Rogers
David Robertson
Joseph Ross
Thomas Ryan
Andrew Sampson
Joseph Sampson
Nathan B. Sampson
Sylvanus Sampson
Angus Scott
Daniel Sears
Hiram B. Sears
Wm. Sears
Nathaniel Simmons

James Simmons
Wm. Stephens
Isaac Smith
Joseph Smith
Luther Smith
Peter W. Smith
Thomas Smith
— Sparrow
Isaac Swift
Philip Snow
Nahum Thomas
Lewis W. Thrasher
Oliver C. Vaughn
Perez Wade
John B. Walker
Robert Washburn
Solomon Webquish
John Whitmore
Samuel O. Whittemore
Joseph Whitten
Samuel M. Whitten
George R. Wiswell
Lemuel R. Wood
Edward Wright

There are several disconnected items which may be mentioned in this chapter. The Sunbeam, sold a few years ago, was employed in 1905 in carrying gravel from the Gurnet to Boston, and the Sabine, sold at the same time, is used as a house boat in Boston harbor by a Portuguese lobsterman. The Maria of Plymouth, and the schooner R. Leach of Bucksport, Me., were the first United States vessels to use, in 1859, trawls in salt fishing. It was a method of fishing introduced by the French, and until the above date was looked upon as an experiment. It may not be generally known that there is a Plymouth Rock on the banks. It is laid down in "Sailing Directions for the Island and Banks of New Foundland," etc., published in 1882, as one of the Eastern shoals, a group around Nine-fathom Bank, which latter lies in latitude 46.26.45 N. and longitude 50.28.06 W. Plymouth Rock has 15 fathoms of water, and was named in honor of Capt. Burgess, of the schooner Lyceum of Plymouth, who discovered it.

CHAPTER XI.

The following is a detailed account of the loss of the Plymouth bark · Charles Bartlett, which on the 27th of June, 1849, was run down and sunk by the Cunard steamship Europa. The incidents attending the disaster possess an interest in themselves, while the trial in the English law courts of a suit for damages brought by the owners of the bark in the early days of ocean steam navigation, was an important one, establishing as it did the duties of steam navigators and their liability in damages for a failure to perform them.

The Charles Bartlett was a bark of four hundred tons, built in Westbrook, Maine, and owned by Wm. L. Finney and others of Plymouth. She left the Downs on the 14th of June, 1849, bound for New York with a cargo of about four hundred and fifty tons of iron, lead, etc., and with one cabin passenger and one hundred and sixty-two in the steerage. Her officers and crew were William Bartlett of Plymouth, Captain; Thomas Parker of Charleston, S. C., first officer; Wm. Prince, second officer, and George Parsons of Portland, Me., Wm Rich of Gravesend, England, Isaac Hanson, James Fraser, John Bell, Joshua Carey, Levi Hunt, Wm. Perry, John Jordan, John Jackson and Harrison D. White, seamen. On the 27th of June, in latitude 50.48 N., longitude 29 W., in a thick fog, which gathered after the noon observation had been taken, the bark was heading northwest with the wind west by south, close hauled and all sails set. At half-past three the captain, who was standing on the weather side of the poop deck, caught sight of the steamship about one point forward of the beam, and about four hundred yards distant. He ordered his helm up and shouted to the steamer to port her helm. The officer of the deck on the Europa, however, ordered his helm put to starboard, which order was countermanded before the wheel had been turned one round. If the starboard helm had produced any effect, it was of course to make a collision the more sure, while if the helm had been at first promptly put to port there is room for doubt whether, as the bark was all the time going ahead, the steamer might not have slipped by her stern without causing serious damage. As it was, the Europa going at twelve and a half knots, struck the bark abreast of her main shrouds in one minute after she was first seen, and three minutes later the bark went down. The steamer's bow entered to within a foot of the after hatch, tearing away twenty feet of the bark's side, and suffering as her own damage only the loss of her head knees and her foretopmast. At the moment of the collision, about one hundred passengers were on deck, and it was estimated that about one half of them were killed by the impact. The captain and second officer and nine of the crew and thirty passengers were saved, all but ten of whom, who were picked up by boats, were saved by clinging to the bows of the steamer, and climbing on board.

The Europa had a full passenger list, and the excitement caused by the terrible scenes of the collision was followed by a serious anxiety for the safety of their own vessel, which only prompt investigations and the assurance of the officers that the hull was uninjured could allay. Among the passengers was Capt. Robert B. Forbes of Boston, who with that generous impulse and heroic courage which had always characterized him risked his life by leaping into the sea and aided in the rescue of his drowning fellow men. For the service rendered by him, a medal was presented to him by the Liverpool Shipwreck and Humane Society, and another by the Massachusetts Humane Society. The Cunard Steamship Company gave twenty pounds toward the relief of the survivors of the Charles Bartlett, and a free passage to America.

A suit was brought by the owners and underwriters to recover damages estimated at twelve thousand pounds, and tried in the English Admiralty Court, and the facts which I have stated were presented to the court by the plaintiffs. The responsive allegation in behalf of the Europa, claimed that the collision occurred in the usual track for steamers, but that it was two or three degrees to the north of the usual track of sailing vessels. It denied that there was a concentrating point in the Atlantic, and alleged that the noise of the paddle wheels might have been heard in the direction of the bark three or four miles, and that it was owing to some negligence that the bark was not therefore warned of the approach of the steamer.

It further alleged that though the third officer ordered the helm to be starboarded, before the order could be obeyed the order was revoked, and the wheel was directed to be put hard a port. The engines were stopped so that before the collision the steamer had come up to the wind a point and a half. It was still further alleged that the bark was going from five and a half to six knots an hour, having all possible sails set, and had neglected to fire guns, blow her fog horn or ring her bell at short intervals, so that those on board the steamer could be cognizant of her approach.

The presiding judge, addressing his brethren of the Court, said that these cases are becoming so numerous that it was for the interest of the owners of ships that they should be decided promptly. With regard to the burden of proof, it is of course necessary for the plaintiff to present all the evidence reasonably within his power, but that after he has done that it rests upon the other party to show that they have not been guilty of the acts attributed to them. With regard to the distance at which the vessels were seen by each other, and the time which elapsed before the collision, nothing is more difficult than to find consistent evidence. The conclusion of the allegation in defense is in substance that the collision was either the result of inevitable accident, or was the fault of those on board the Charles Bartlett. What is an inevitable accident? Inevitable must be considered as a variable term, and must be construed with regard to the circumstances of each case. In almost every case it is possible to avoid a collision by going at a slow pace, or lying to during a fog, but the import of the words "inevitable accident" is this, where a man is pursuing his lawful vocation in a lawful manner, and something occurs which no ordinary caution could prevent. Continuing, the presiding Judge said to his brethren of the Court, "It is very easy to define what is a lawful vocation, but it is not so easy to say what is a lawful manner. The test is the probability of injury to others, and that of course depends on circumstances, as for instance the time and locality where the occurrences take place. The object of our inquiry is whether in the case of the Europa going about twelve and a half knots an hour in so dense a fog that she could not see beyond one hundred and fifty or two hundred yards, and in latitude 50.48 and longitude 29, there was more than ordinary probability of meeting vessels. If there was a reasonable probability of a collision, then beyond all doubt she would be to blame. If, however, there was no reasonable probability of meeting vessels in the track pursued, she was nevertheless bound to take all necessary precautions to insure safety. One of the most important questions as to these precautions which we are to decide, is whether there was or was not a sufficient lookout on board the Europa. The law undoubtedly requires as a reasonable lookout the most ample that could be adopted. Was there such a lookout on board the steamer? According to the evidence the general practice on the Europa in dense fogs was as follows: first to station an officer on the foremost bridge; second, his junior at the Con; third, a quartermaster at the wheel; fourth, a second hand in the wheelhouse, and fifth and sixth, two lookouts on the top-gallant forecastle. There is some evidence also tending to show that a man was stationed in case of a fog on the lee side of the bridge, and also a man at the crank to convey orders to the engine room. Now, the actual watch when the collision occurred was as follows: Wardell, the second officer, was on the bridge; Coates, a quartermaster, on the topgallant fore-castle; White, at the wheel, and Fern, another quartermaster, at the Con, and I do not find any other person on the lookout. The second man is placed at the wheel so that in case of necessity it may be turned as promptly as possible. There is an entire absence of evidence as to whether at the time of the collision there was in operation any means of communicating orders to the engine room, or whether any orders were really communicated." Continuing, the presiding Judge said: "You will have to decide also whether there was more than one man at the wheel, and lastly, whether the order to starboard the helm, which is agreed on all hands to have been erroneous, did or did not produce any effect in the case. Looking at the rapidity with which the vessels were approaching each other, the last mentioned consideration is one of importance."

With regard to the Charles Bartlett the Judge said, "Was she carrying too much sail; was there a want of a sufficient look-out, and above all is it your opinion that she ought to have sounded a fog horn or rung a bell? Whether she ought to have heard the paddle wheels before she did, and neglected to take measures to avert a collision, is one of the questions for you to decide. But it is in evidence that even if she could have heard them, no fog horn could have been heard on board the steamer above the sound of the paddles."

The Court retired, and returning at the end of half an hour, Dr. Lushington, the presiding Judge, then said: "In conjunction with the gentlemen by whom I am assisted, we have considered all the points in this case, which I have suggested as necessary to be determined, and I trust that there has been no omission as to any one of them. We have come unanimously to the following determination: That no rate of sailing by steamers or other vessels can be said to be absolutely dangerous; but whether any given rate is dangerous or not, must depend on the circumstances of each individual case, as the state of the weather, locality and other similar facts. That the rate of twelve and a half knots an hour in a dense fog in the locality where this occurrence took place, must be attended with more risk than a slower pace; but assuming that it might be accomplished with reasonable security, and without probable risk to other vessels, such rate of going could not be maintained with such security, except by taking every possible precaution against collision. That proper precaution was not taken by the Europa: First, she had not a sufficient look-out; second, we think that no proper arrangement was made as to the engines; third, because no person was placed to report to the engineers the orders as to the engines; fourth, because no second person was placed in the wheel house; fifth, that the order to starboard the helm was erroneous. We are of the opinion that if proper precautions had been adopted, the accident might have been avoided, and that the collision took place for want of the proper precautions. With respect to the Charles Bartlett, we are of opinion that a good look-out was kept on board; that she discovered the approach of the Europa as soon as circumstances would permit; that she adopted all proper measures to avoid the collision by ringing the bell and putting the helm to port. Therefore, I must pronounce against the Europa in this case."

After the decision of the Court was read, Mr. Rothery, the proctor for the Europa, gave notice of appeal. All appeals from the Admiralty Court, which until the time of William

4th were made to the High Court of Admiralty, are now made to the King in council, and are referred to the Judicial Committee of the Privy Council, which committee is composed of the Chief Justice of the Court of King's Bench, the Master of the Rolls, the Vice Chancellor of England, and other ex-officio officers. The appeal in question was heard by Lord Justice Cranworth, Lord Justice Sir James Knight Bruce, Sir Herbert Jenner Fust, and Sir Edward Ryan, and judgment was delivered by Lord Justice Cranworth, December 1, 1851. It is unnecessary to relate the grounds of the judgment of the committee, as they were for the most part the same as those which entered into the decision of the Admiralty Court. There is one part, however, to which I wish to refer, because it lays down a rule for the guidance of ocean steam navigators, broader and more exacting than any suggested by the Admiralty Court. An important question in the examination of witnesses was whether it would have been possible to stop the steamer, or so far stop her as to enable her to get out of the way within the distance between the two vessels when they were first seen by each other. The preponderance of testimony was that she could not if going twelve and a half knots an hour. The peculiarity of this question is that an answer either in the affirmative or negative would bear against the Europa. If she could get out of the way and did not, she is to blame. If she could not get out of the way, the committee say that "it follows as an inevitable consequence that she was sailing at a rate of speed at which it was not lawful for her to navigate." The judgment closes as follows: "Their lordships have come to the opinion that the accident was without default on the part of the Charles Bartlett and was through the neglect of the Europa. The consequences will be that the appeal will be dismissed with costs."

In closing the narrative of this important case it is pleasant to remember the enconiums of the London press on the intelligence and general demeanor of our late townsman, Capt. William Bartlett, as displayed by him during the trial. The master mariners of New England were fortunate in having in a foreign land so worthy a representative.

CHAPTER XII.

The migration from New England and the middle states to California in 1849 and 1850, was one of the remarkable events in the history of the American Union.   It was one of those events, of which the history of the world furnishes many examples, accomplishing in the end results far removed from the purposes sought in their conception, and apparently carrying out the designs of an overruling providence, in which man has only served as its instrument.   It is a question worthy of consideration, whether the destiny of the American republic would have reached its present measure of accomplishment, without the inspiration which a mere thirst for gold served to excite. It was another of those incidents, of which the Pilgrim colonization was a striking example, whch reached its consummation through the aid of the merchants of London, who were looking merely for discoveries of ores of gold and silver to reward their enterprise.

On the 9th of February, 1848, while three Americans were at work repairing the race way of Sutter's Mill, on the American fork of Sacramento river, a little daughter of Mr. Marshal, the superintendent of the mill, picked up a lump of gold, and showed it to her father as a pretty plaything. The discovery was too important to be kept secret, and a letter written by Rev. C. S. Lyman appeared in the March number of the *American Journal of Science* announcing it to the world.   No news ever spread more rapidly.   In the New England states, and in Massachusetts, especially, a wave of migration set in, which was as strong in Plymouth as elsewhere.   The time was favorable; the supply of labor was just then greater than the demand, and the temptation to seek wealth in California became almost irresistible.   Those who at once made preparations to go were the bone and sinew of the town, carpenters, masons, painters and clerks, and for a time after their departure our streets seemed almost deserted.

Among the first to leave were those who sailed in the Brig Isabelle of Plymouth, Chandler Burgess, Jr. of Plymouth, master, which sailed from New York, January 14, 1849. Her passengers were: Ephraim Paty, Jr., James Burgess, Jr., Freeman Morton, Jr., Stephen Pember, Winslow Morton, George Morton of Plymouth, and twenty-one others.

The schooner Roanoke sailed from Boston, January 19, 1849, carrying Russell Bourne, John E. Sever and Frederick Morton of Plymouth.

The Capitol from Boston sailed in January, 1849, with Rufus Ball, Thomas Atwood, Thomas Wood, James A. Young, Jacob Hersey, James M. Thomas, Daniel Bickford, George E. Lugerder, Adam E. Stetson, George E. Burns, Tolman French and one hundred and eighty-four others.

The Rochelle sailed from Boston, February 7, 1849, with Daniel P. Bates, Wm. Churchill, Josiah Byram, David Gurney and John T. Pratt.

The bark Diman sailed from New Bedford, February 8, 1849, with Hiram Churchill and Samuel D. Barnes.

The bark Yeoman of Plymouth, James S. Clark of Rochester, master, sailed from Plymouth, March 18, 1849, with Geo. Collingwood of Plymouth, mate, and the following members of the Pilgrim Mining Company: Nathaniel C. Covington, president; Francis H. Robbins, secretary; and Robert Swinburne, Nathan G. Cushing, John E. Churchill, Henry Chase, Wm. Collingwood, Wm. M. Gifford, A. O. Nelson, Franklin B. Holmes, Nathan Churchill, James T. Collins, Nathaniel S. Barrows, Jr., Henry M. Hubbard, Henry B. Holmes, Alfred R. Doten, Ellis Rogers, Ellis B. Barnes, George P. Fowler, Wm. Saunders, Richard B. Dunham, Henry M. Morton, Caleb C. Bradford, Silas M. Churchill, Elisha W. Kingman, Ozen Bates, Chandler Dunham, James T. Wadsworth, Winslow B. Barnes, Thomas Rogers, Edward Morton, Wm. J. Dunham, Augustus Robbins, Sylvanus Everson, George A. Bradford, Seth Blankenship, John Clark, Thomas Brown and John Ward. The Yeoman was built as a brig in Plymouth, in 1833, and afterwards changed to a bark.

The Attila, Wm. W. Baker of Plymouth, master, sailed from Boston in March, 1849, with the following passengers: Timothy Allen, Charles H. Weston, Calvin Ripley, Samuel Lanman, Ellis H. Morton, William Randall, wood, Daniel F. Goddard, Charles T. Goddard, Isaac N. Har-

Manter, Allen Holmes, Joseph L. Weston, Ephraim Finney, Abner Sylvester, Samuel Doten, Thomas C. Smith, Winslow Bradford, Job Churchill, Samuel C. Chamberlain, Lewis Finney, George W. Virgin, Jr., Abram C. Small, Frederick Salter, Alfred N. Primes, Isaac R. Atwood, W. Bradford, Josiah Nichols, Charles W. Swift, John Leighton, Wm. Smith, Rufus Holmes, James Joyce, Lucien Winsor, Henry Holmes, Henry Lee, Samuel Alden, Benjamin F. Winslow, Frederick Bush, James Carey, John L. Nash and Ambrose Harmon.   The Attila was one hundred and seventy days on her passage to San Francisco.

The ship Mallory sailed from New York, February 28, 1849, with the following passengers, Thomas Rider, Richard T. Pope and Frederick W. Lucas.

The ship Frances Ann sailed from Boston in April, 1849, having as a passenger, John Haggerty.

The ship York sailed from Boston April 1, 1849, having as a passenger, John A. Spooner.

The ship New Jersey sailed from Boston in May, 1849, having Josiah Williams as a passenger.

The ship Iconium of Plymouth, Eleazer Stephens Turner, master, sailed from Boston, June 1, 1849, with Horace Jackson as a passenger.

The bark Helen Augusta sailed from Boston, August 15th, with James Gorham Hedge as a passenger.

The steamship Chesapeake sailed from New York, August 9th, 1849, for the Isthmus with Gideon Holbrook.

The ship Harriet Rockwell sailed from Boston, September 18, 1849, with Stephen P. Sears.

The ship Cordova sailed from Boston, September 26, 1849, having as passengers, Seth Morton, Jr., and wife; Mrs. Anna Bartlett and child, John B. Simmons, Daniel Williams, Wm. R. Lanman, Ichabod Harlow and George White.   The ship Persian of Plymouth, Robbins, master, sailed from Baltimore in May, 1849, with Charles Jackson as passenger.

The brig Sarah Abigail of Plymouth sailed from Plymouth, November 13, 1849, with the following passengers, Capt. Josiah Bartlett and wife, William Bartlett, Andrew Blanchard, Josiah Drew, Josiah C. Fuller, Ephraim Holmes, John B. Collingwood, Daniel F. Goodard, Charles T. Goodard, Isaac N. Harlow, Calvin Raymond, Eleazer H. Barnes, Joseph B. Hobart, Caleb Battles, Nathaniel Bradford, Thomas Diman, Wm. Bowen, Melzar Pierce, Clark Ellis, George Benson, Curtis Davie, Hira Bates, John P. Perry and Elisha Holbrook.

Steamer Ohio sailed from New York for the Isthmus, November 17, 1849, with George O. Barnes.

Steamer name unknown, sailed from New York for the Isthmus in December, 1849, with Joseph Cushman.

The ship Samuel Appleton sailed from New York at an unknown date in 1849, with the following passengers, Richard Pope, Wm. W. Pope, and John Lawrence.

The ship Regulus sailed from Boston in 1849, with Daniel Bradford, Thomas B. Bradford and Charles E. Bryant, and one hundred and twenty others.

The ship Cheshire sailed from Boston in 1849, with Joseph I. Holmes and Adoniram Bates.

The ship Sweden sailed from Boston in 1849, with Elisha Whiting as passenger.

The brig Reindeer of Plymouth sailed from New York in 1849, with Dr. Samuel Merritt, James M. Bradford, Wm. C. Bradford, Charles Randall, Henry Raymond, Mr. Warren and Laurence Cleales.

Steamer name unknown, sailed from New York for the Isthmus in 1849, with A. O. Whitmore, Samuel O. Whitmore, Cyrus Bartlett, Freeman Bartlett and Lewis Bartlett. By a route unknown, Frank Sherman sailed.

Of the above named persons, one hundred and seventy-seven in all, the following thirty-five were from other towns. Abington, James A. Young; South Abington, John L. Nash; Boston, Abram C. Small, Frederick Salter, Alfred N. Primes, Joseph Nichols, Charles W. Smith and John Leighton; Bridgewater, Benjamin F. Winslow; East Bridgewater, Josiah Byram, Frederick Bush, David Gurney, John T. Pratt, James Carey, James M. Thomas, Daniel Beckford, George E. Lugender, Adam E. Stetson, George E. Burns and Tolman French; Brooklyn, N. Y., John Ward; Duxbury, Daniel Bradford, Rufus Holmes, Samuel Joyce, Lucien Winsor, Henry Lee and Samuel Alden; Kingston, Thomas B. Bradford, Sylvanus Everson and George A. Bradford; Plympton, Charles E. Bryant; Pulaski, N. Y., Ambrose Harmon; Rochester, Mass., Seth

Blankenship, John Clark and Thomas Brown. Thus the number going from Plymouth was one hundred and forty-two, which number would doubtless be increased by those of whom I have no record. How many of those in the list of Plymouth men are now living I have no means of ascertaining, but of those who sailed in the Yeoman only two, George Collingwood and Wm. J. Dunham now survive. The last of the Yeoman's passengers to die was Alfred R. Doten, a brother of our townsmen, the late Major Samuel H. and Captain Charles C. Doten, who married in Nevada, and never returned to his native town.

Of Dr. Samuel Merritt, whose name is in the list of passengers on board the brig Reindeer, I have something to say. An account of the chief incidents in his career I had from his own lips. He was a native of Maine, and came to Plymouth in 1845, and established himself in the practice of medicine. He was a man six feet in height and large in proportion, frank and honest in speech, hearty, but rough in manner, possessing great will and energy, and calculated in every way to win the confidence of the people. He was a bachelor, and at first had an office on Main street, in the Bartlett building, where Loring's watchmaker's shop now is. After Union building was built on the corner of Middle street, he occupied two rooms on the lower floor at the corner, one for an office, and the other for a sleeping room.

When the California fever struck Plymouth it seized the Doctor with great virulence. Aside from the temptations of gold and sudden wealth, the idea of an expedition to the Pacific shores appealed to his adventurous spirit, and he at once determined to follow the wave of migration. Without a family to consult, he began his preparations. Collecting his professional bills, he invested his capital in the purchase of a snug and handy hermaphrodite brig of about one hundred and sixty tons, owned, I think, by Joseph Holmes of Kingston, which was then lying in New York. Having nearly finished loading her with such merchandise as according to the latest advices was bringing high prices, he found that he had about five hundred dollars unexpended. This amount, or a considerable portion of it, he determined to expend in tacks, so one afternoon he started to go to Duxbury and make the purchase at the tack factory carried on by Samuel Loring in that town. Before he reached

Kingston, he was overtaken by a messenger on horse back, summoning him to return at once, and attend a man, who, while engaged in painting the house of Capt. Nathaniel Russell at the corner of Court Square, had fallen from a ladder, and was thought to be seriously injured. As he had no time to spare to go to Duxbury after that day, he lost the opportunity of making a fortune in tacks, which he found on his arrival in San Francisco were selling at five dollars a paper.

With such a number of passengers as he could easily accommodate in the cabin, he sailed from New York in the summer of 1849, and reached his destination in the autumn. On the way up the Pacific coast a stop was made at Valparaiso, and while there it occurred to the Doctor that it would be a good plan to buy a lot of potatoes to fill up the hole which the passengers and crew had eaten in the cargo. Starting one day for the shore to make the purchase, a favorable wind sprung up, and the Captain signalled to him to return. Thus another good speculation was lost, for on his arrival at San Francisco there was not a potato in the market. To his dismay the bottom had tumbled out of the prices of nearly every other article in his vessel, following for instance the price of lumber, which had fallen from three hundred dollars a thousand to a price lower than it could be bought for in Bangor. After disposing of his vessel and cargo, and finding himself without capital, he opened an office and began a practice, which he hoped to have permanently abandoned. Doctors were fortunately as rare as tacks and potatoes, and within a year his medical and surgical receipts amounted to forty thousand dollars, a sum equivalent, perhaps, to five thousand dollars in the East.

One day a Maine Captain called at his office, who was acquainted with his family at home, and in the course of conversation, told him that he had a power of attorney to sell the brig which he commanded, and wished the Doctor would buy it. "No, I thank you," replied the Doctor, "I have had all the brigs I have any use for, and I think I will keep out of navigation." The captain called in occasionally afterwards, and the Doctor in the meantime thought, as the people of San Francisco suffered during the previous summer from the want of ice, that it might be a good speculation to go into the ice business in anticipation of the wants of the next summer. The next time the Captain called he asked him if he had sold his brig, and finding that he had not, he told him that he would buy her if he would go in her to Puget Sound and get a load of ice. The Captain agreed, and with a gang of men well supplied with axes and saws, the vessel sailed. In due time the Captain reported himself to the Doctor, who said, "Well, Cap., have you got a good load of ice?" "Ice, no" said the Captain, "not a pound; water don't freeze in Puget Sound; but I wasn't coming home with an empty hold, so I put my gang ashore and cut a load of piles." It so happened that piles were much needed on the harbor front, and the cargo sold at once at a big price, and the brig started off for a second load. By the time the second load arrived, which proved as profitable as the first, other vessel owners had got wind of the business, and the Doctor said, "now, Captain, we have had the cream of this business, I guess we will let these other fellows have the skim milk. You go up and get another load and carry it over to Australia and buy a load of coal." In due time again the Captain returned, but without a pound of coal, saying, that finding he would have to wait a long time for his turn to load, he thought it better to take his money for the piles and go down to the Society Islands for a load of oranges, six hundred thousand of which fruit he had on board. The orange market at that time was completely bare, and the profits of the voyage were heavy.

"Now, Captain, go up and get one more load, and carry it down to Callao, and sell out everything, brig and all, and we will close up our business, and you can go home." Thus by good luck, aided largely by the shrewdness of his captain, Dr. Merritt laid the foundations of a multi-millionaire's fortune. It is needless to say that he closed his office and sought favorable investments for his money. He bought land in Oakland across the bay, laid out streets, built houses, and in time became mayor of the city, whose foundation he had laid.

I saw the Doctor on his last visit East about six years ago, and he then boasted of nothing so much as of his yacht, which he said was the finest on the Pacific. I have recently read a journal of Mrs. Stevenson, the mother of Robert Louis Stevenson, of a six months' excursion in the Pacific for the benefit of her son's health in the yacht Casco, belonging to Dr. Merritt.

Her account of an interview with the Doctor illustrates his personalty and deportment which had more of the *fortiter in re* than the *suaviter in modo*. She says, "Dr. M. has just been here to settle the final business arrangements. He had heard that Louis had a mother, and was not at all sure of allowing an old woman to sail on his beloved yacht, so he insisted on seeing me before he left. When I came in I found a very stout man with a strong and humorous face, who sat still in his chair and took a good look at me. Then he held out his hand with the remark, 'You are a healthy looking woman.' He built the yacht, he told me, for his health, as he was getting to stout that some means of reduction were necessary, and going to sea had pulled him down sixty pounds. 'The yacht is the apple of my eye—you may think (to Fanny) your husband loves you, but I can assure you that I love my yacht a great deal better.' "

Dr. Merritt died three or four years ago, and the last I heard of his affairs was that his will was in litigation.

CHAPTER XIII.

In an earlier chapter I gave a list of the streets, squares, lanes and alleys, which existed in my boyhood, with the promise to say something concerning the changes, which they had gone through, and the houses and people and incidents associated with them.   I have since taken a passing glance at Court, Main, Middle and North streets with the intention of referring to them again.   In my treatment of Water street I have dwelt in detail on its buildings and occupants.

The next street in order is Leyden street, the most interesting of all the streets, associated, as it is with the first winter of the Pilgrims, with the Common House, the store houses, and the seven cottages, which with their walls of plank, their roofs of thatch, and windows of paper, served as hospitals for the sick and shelter for all.   How far east and west the original street extended is conjectural.   It is probable that on the west it extended at least as far as the fort, which in 1622 was built near the top of burial hill, and that within a year or two habitations for single families were constructed on both sides of the street. The easterly end of the original street is more doubtful.   It must be remembered that what we call ropewalk pond was a part of the harbor, a broad cove or bay with a wide entrance extending from a point on the south near the southerly corner of the present foundry, to a point on the north near the southerly end of the Electric Light building.   It is probable that this cove extended so far west that it felt the flow of the tide for some distance above the present arch of Spring hill.   It will therefore be seen that this bay furnished an excellent boat harbor protected from the ocean blasts, and, being in close proximity to the store houses, was undoubtedly used as a landing place for boats, plying to and from the Mayflower during her stay in the harbor.

In view of these conditions it is probable that the original street extended no farther east than the narrow way which may still be seen on the easterly side of the house with a brick end opposite the Universalist church, a way which is referred to in ancient deeds, and which in my opinion led to the landing place, and was used by the Pilgrims in reaching or leaving their settlement by water. The first official laying out of Leyden street was made in connection with Water street in 1716, and is entered in the town records under date of February 16, 1715-16 old style, or February 26, 1716 new style. It is signed by Benjamin Warren, John Dyer, John Watson and Abial Shurtleff, selectmen, and reads as follows: "Then laid out by us the subscribers, Town Wayes (viz) as followeth A street Called first street beginning att a stone sett into ye Ground att ye Corner of Ephraim Coles smiths shop, from Thence to rainge East 21 Degrees northerly To John Rickard's Corner bounds at The brow of The hill, & from thence To a stone att ye foot of the hill on the same Rainge The sd street is: 40: ffoots in Weadth att The bounds first mentioned, and to carrey its width till it comes to The Northerly Corner of Capt. Dyer's house There being a stone sett into ye Ground & from Thence To Rainge East Two Degrees Northerly To a stone sett into the Ground att The foot of The hill a little above Ephraim Kempton's house being the westerly corner bounds of the way That leads over the Brook and from Thence Northeast: 16: Degrees Easterly 40: foots to A stone sett into The Ground a little above John Rickard's upper Ware house, and from Thence To Extend Northeast: 6: Degrees Northerly one hundred and Three foots to a stone sett into ye Ground being 16 Degrees Southeasterly 30 foots from a stone sett into ye Ground at ye foot of the hill Neere or upon The Sootherly Corner of John Ward's land on ye westerly side of The Way That leads To ye New street Thence from sd stone To Extend Northeast 5 Degrees Northerly 29 foots To another stone sett in ye Ground in John Wards land & from Thence To Extend North 20 Degrees Easterly To a stone sett into ye Ground att ye North East Corner of Mr. John Watson's cooper's shop, and from Thence to Extend North 7 Degrees Easterly to a stone and poast sett into ye Ground above Thomas Dotyes Coopers shop, and from Thence to Extend North 21 Degrees westerly to a stone and poast sett in ye Ground above Thomas Doten's cooper shop, and from Thence to Extend North: 25: Degrees Westerly to a stone and stake sett into ye Ground Within The easterly corner bound of new street said stake and stones being

West, & eleven Degrees Northerly 36 foots from the Northerly
part of A Grat Rock yt lyeth below ye Way The sd Way from
ye stone att ye foat of ye hill neere the Southerly Corner of
John Ward's land is : 30 : foot in width Till it comes to ye stake
and stones at ye Easterly Corner of ye New streete." This
laying out is especially interesting as mentioning Plymouth
Rock.

A part of the smith shop of Ephraim Cole, at the corner of
which the above laying out began, is still standing, and may be
seen in the rear part of the express office on the corner of Main
street. The corner of John Rickard's land was at a point on
the stone wall opposite the middle of the alley next to the house
of Wm. .W. Brewster. Capt. John Dyer's house stood where
the brick end house stands, and the Ephraim Kempton house
stood about thirty or forty feet from the present street on the
lot now occupied by Mr. Blackmer's stable. It is probable
that the land in front of the house was kept open, and that the
way across the brook began at the corner of the narrow way
above mentioned just below the Dyer house, and crossing the
open space diagonally, passed east of the Kempton house to the
fording place. All through my boyhood the Kempton house
was occupied by Mrs. Wm. Drew, who married for a second
husband in 1833, Isaac Morton Sherman, the father of Leander
L. Sherman, formerly the janitor of the Central Engine house.
Its removal many years ago marked one of the changes which
have occurred in Leyden street within my recollection.

Until, perhaps twenty-five or thirty years ago, there was an
ancient footway leading from Cole's Hill at a point nearly opposite the south front of the house of Henry W. Barnes, next
to the Universalist church, to Leyden street, directly opposite
to the way to the fording place above mentioned. That footway doubtless ante-dated the opening of a way between Cole's
Hill and the water, and served to enable those who were occupying lots on North, then New Street, to make a short cut
over the hill to Leyden street, and thence to either the boat
harbor landing or across the ford to the south side of the settlement.

The John Rickard land referred to in the laying out of Leyden street included all the land between LeBaron's alley on the
west, Leyden street on the south, and the footway on the east,

and extended to Middle street. It was occupied for one hundred and eighty-seven years by a house built in 1639 by Robert Hicks, which was taken down in 1826, when the Universalist Church was erected on its site. If it were standing today, as it stood when I was four years of age, it would be the oldest house in New England, and invaluable as a relic of the Pilgrims. It was reached by a path or private way leading from Leyden street, and this way was never laid out as a public way until 1827, after the Universalist church was built. A picture of this house may be seen in Mr. Wm. S. Russell's Pilgrim Memorials, where in accordance with tradition it is called the Allyne house, after Joseph Allyne, who never owned it, but merely occupied it a short time as a tenant. It is often the case that a passing and perhaps trifling incident fastens on a spot or house a name, which has no rightful claim. I remember an illustration of this, which made Hon. Isaac L. Hedge very indignant. He was born in the house now occupied and owned by Wm. R. Drew on Leyden street, and lived there until he was married, the house remaining in the possession of his father until his death in 1840, and of his mother until her death in 1849, and of their heirs until 1854, when it was sold. For a short time after 1854, before it was sold to Mr. Drew, Zaben Olney occupied it as a hotel. Mr. Hedge became entirely blind, and employed John O'Brien to take his arm and walk with him about the streets. One day in walking down Leyden street he said: "Where are we now, John?" "Right by the old Olney house," John replied. Alas! "how soon are we forgot." The names of the wharves are gone, and Jackson, Hedge, Davis, Nelson and Carver have given way to Long, Pilgrim, Atwood, Millar and Craig, to be christened again by succeeding owners and occupants.

So far as the bounds of Leyden street are concerned, there has been no change in my day except the widening mentioned in a previous chapter at its junction with Water street. The changes in houses have been numerous. The Turner house above the old blockmaker's shop and Turner's Hall, has been removed, and its site occupied by the Electric Light Co. Nearly in front of it, a little below, near the westerly end of the blacksmith's shop of Southworth and Ichabod Shaw was a public well, on which the neighborhood relied for good drinking water.   The aqueduct water delivered through wooden logs from questionable sources, led our people to depend largely on pumps or wells.   These were scattered all over the town, either public or private, and even to the private wells householders were permitted free access.   There were public wells at the foot of North street, and below the bank at the foot of Middle street, and there was the town pump at the foot of Spring hill. Besides these there were the county well, a well between the old Lothrop house and Judge Thomas' house opposite the head of North street, another between John Gooding's and Dr. Bartlett's houses on Main street, another in the yard of Capt. Wm. Rogers on North street, another in the rear of Jacob Jackson's house on what is now Winslow street, which was known as Jacob's well, and there was still another near the sidewalk on Sandwich street, opposite the Green, between the Elkanah Bartlett and Rogers houses.   The wells on North street and below Middle street were liable to be fouled by drains, and their water was not used for drinking or cooking. Before the introduction of South Pond water, the whalemen and fishermen filled their water casks at a pump in the yard of John Tribble's paint shop on Water street.   But the well in Leyden street was the one to which I was often sent when a boy with two pails and a hoop to get our daily supply.

There was another old house near the so-called Allyne house, which I well remember.   It stood on the bank with its front door on what is now Carver street, nearly opposite the easterly side of the house of Henry W. Barnes, and was reached by the way from Middle street.   It was for many years owned and occupied by Wm. Holmes, the father of the three captains, Samuel Doten, Truman Cook and Winslow Holmes, and after his death, by his daughter Hannah, the wife of Laban Burt.   It was taken down forty or fifty years ago.   The Universalist church, and the parsonage east of it, stand on land bought of Barnabas Hedge in 1826, with the agreement on the part of Mr. Hedge that the bank opposite the church, which still belongs to his heirs should never be built on.   The Universalist Society was incorporated in 1826, and the church was dedicated December 22, in that year.   The sermon on the occasion was preached by Rev. David Pickering of Providence.   On the afternoon of the same day, Rev. James H. Bugbee was ordained pastor, the ordaining sermon being preached by Rev. John Bisbee of Hartford. Between the time of the organization of the church, March 10, 1822, and the ordination of Mr. Bugbee, Messina Ballou and Rev. Mr. Morse and others, preached to the society in one of the town halls. Mr. Bugbee was followed by Albert Case and Russell Tomlinson, who resigned in 1867, and was followed by A. Bosserman, Alpheus Nickerson, George L. Swift, A. H. Sweetzer and W. W. Hayward and others remembered by my readers. The parsonage house was at one time owned by Jeremiah Farris, and its sale by him to Roland Edwin Cotton, unaccompanied by whittling or dickering, was somewhat characterstic of the purchaser. Mr. Farris meeting Mr. Cotton in the street one day was asked by him what he would sell his house for next to the Universalist church. Mr. Farris named a price, taking care to name one high enough to allow for a discount, and Mr. Cotton, without taking breath, promptly said, "Too much by half, I'll take it."

The house next above the Universalist church, long known as the Marcy house, reminds me of a gentleman at one time its occupant, who for many years filled a large space in the social and official life of Plymouth, and performed elsewhere distinguished service in behalf of the state. Jacob H. Loud, born in Hingham, February 5, 1802, graduated at Brown University in 1822 and after studying law with Ebenezer Gay of Hingham, was admitted to the bar at the Common Pleas Court in Plymouth in August, 1825, and at once began practice in our town. His first office was in the building at the corner of Spring Hill and Summer street, which was taken down a few years ago, from which place he moved in 1827 to No. 3 Town Square, then called Market Square, which afterwards became the post office when Bridgham Russell was appointed postmaster in 1832. He married May 5, 1829, Elizabeth Loring Jones of Hingham, and occupied for a time the Marcy house above mentioned. From there he changed his residence to the house next below Mr. Beaman's undertaking rooms on Middle street, but in 1832 he bought a part of the Lothrop lot opposite the head of North street, and built and occupied the house now owned and occupied by Mrs. F. B. Davis. After the death of Beza Hayward, Register of Probate of Plymouth County, which occurred June 4, 1830, he was appointed to succeed him, and held office until 1852. In 1853, 1854 and 1855, he was chosen by the legislature state treasurer. From 1855 to 1866 he was president of the Old Colony Bank, State and National, Director of the Old Colony Railroad from 1845 to 1850, and again from 1869 until his death, Representative in 1862, Senator in 1863 and 1864, State Treasurer again by a vote of the people from 1865 to 1871, and actuary of the New England Trust Co. of Boston until his retirement in 1879. In 1871 he bought the house now owned and occupied by Father Buckley, and occupied it during the summer months until his death, which occurred in Boston, February 2, 1880.

The next house built by James Bartlett, Jr., in 1832, has been referred to in a previous chapter. It occupies a part of the land given by Bridget Fuller and Samuel Fuller, the widow and son of Dr. Samuel Fuller of the Mayflower, in 1664, to the Church of Plymouth for the use of a minister. The easterly boundary of the land was the middle of the alley, long known as LeBaron's alley. The house which up to 1832 stood on the site now occupied by the house built by Mr. Bartlett, was built by Lazarus LeBaron, and in my boyhood was occupied by Dr. Isaac LeBaron, the grandson of Lazarus. Land for the alley was thrown out by Lazarus LeBaron and James Rickard, the owner of the adjoining estate, and was laid out as a town way, September 7 and 10, 1832. At the time of the Fuller gift there was a house standing on the lot which was once owned by Rev. John Cotton, the pastor of the First Church, and which afterwards was displaced by the house built by Lazarus LeBaron.

The next house immediately west of the James Bartlett house, stands on the site of a house built by Return Waite, which when the present house was built not many years ago, was removed to Seaside, and now stands a tenement house on the easterly side of the road on land belonging to the heirs of the late Barnabas Hedge.

As I have stated the land on Leyden street extending from the estate of Wm. R. Drew to the centre of LeBaron's alley, was given in 1664 by Bridget Fuller, widow of Dr. Samuel Fuller of the Mayflower, and her son Samuel, to the church in Plymouth for the use of the minister. A parsonage was built on the easterly end of the lot, which was finally sold to Rev. John Cotton, the pastor of the church. The house built by Lazarus LeBaron on the site of the parsonage, which was in turn succeeded by the house built in 1832 by James Bartlett, Jr., and now occupied by Wm. W. Brewster, and also the house adjoining the Bartlett house have been referred to, leaving to be considered of the original Fuller land only that part which is now occupied by the house of the late Harvey W. Weston. When Rev. Chandler Robbins was settled over the Plymouth Church in 1760, the Parish agreed to pay him a salary of one hundred pounds, to give him the privilege of cutting wood on the parish lot, and to build for him a parsonage. The Weston house is the parsonage, built at that time. It was occupied by Mr. Robbins until 1788, when he built a house on the other side of the street, which he occupied until his death, June 30, 1799.

Rev. James Kendall, the successor of Mr. Robbins, was ordained January 1, 1800, and occupied the parsonage until his death, which occurred March 17, 1859, and it was sold the next year to Mr. Weston. Of Dr. Kendall, whose pastorate extended through a period of sixty years, I cannot forbear to speak, as his life was one of the most important passages in the history of our town. It is difficult to realize that more than a generation has been born, and has lived to nearly midlde age, without a knowledge of his personality and a daily observation of his character and virtues. He was born in Sterling, Mass., in 1769, and after graduating at Harvard in 1796, occupied the position of tutor in Latin at Harvard until he received an invitation to settle in Plymouth. At his ordination the sermon was preached by Rev. Mr. French of Andover, and the other parts of the ceremony were performed by Rev. Dr. Peter Thatcher, Rev. Dr. Tappan, Rev. Mr. Shaw and Rev. Mr. Howland. In 1825 he received the degree of Doctor of Divinity from Harvard, by whose government he was esteemed one of the distinguished incumbents of the ministry. I was in my early youth impressed by the benignant traits in his character and the purity of his life, as it was my fortune when nine years of age to be for a few weeks a member of his family, while my mother was passing a summer with her father in Nova Scotia. I remember him sitting in his study in the back west room, where if I happened to enter I was always greeted with a kindly smile and a cheerful word; I remember him in the front east room on a chilly day sitting by a Franklin stove, and often in the garden, which he tended with loving and faithful care. There was a vein of humor in his composition, which, unlike that I have often seen repressed on the Sabbath by ministers of the olden time, was too much the overflow of a contented and joyful spirit to be concealed on a day to him the happiest of the week. As long as I can remember he always carried a cane, which had descended to him through James, his father, James, his grandfather, and Samuel, his great-grandfather; from Thomas, son of Francis, who was born in 1649 in Woburn. This cane is now owned by his grandson, Arthur Lord of Plymouth, and represents an ownership by seven generations of the same family.

I remember him in the old meeting house, which was taken down in April, 1831, officiating in black gloves with a sounding board hanging over the pulpit, which I was in constant fear would fall on the dear man's head. I remember well the church itself, a large, square building with doors on three sides, and a steeple surmounted by a copper rooster, the like of which I have never seen since the day when in April, 1831, while workmen pulled the steeple over, it slipped off the spindle and took its unaided flight to the ground. I remember the square pews with seats, which were turned up in prayer time, and let down with a slam when the prayer was over, and I especially remember the spokes in the pew rails which we boys turned in their dowels and made to squeak when we thought that James Morton, the sexton, sitting at the head of the pulpit stairs, was either not looking or was asleep. And then there was the choir, with Webster Seymour leading the singing, and I can see even now Simeon Dike, father of the late Mrs. Samuel Shaw, drawing his bow across the bass viol, which I think, with the violin and clarinet performed the instrumental music.

Of Dr. Kendall, it may be appropriately said as was said of another:

"Pure was his walk, peaceful was his end;
We blessed his reverend length of days,
And hailed him in the public ways,
With veneration and with praise,
Our father and our friend."

The custom of wearing black gloves in the pulpit referred to above, which had once been universal, was abandoned before the middle of the last century, and I do not feel sure that Dr. Kendall wore them in the new meeting house, built in 1831.

With the estate of William Ryder Drew, some interesting incidents are associated beyond the memory of most of my readers. It was from his marriage in 1789 to his death in 1840, the residence of Barnabas Hedge, whom I remember well. He was the last man in Plymouth to wear small clothes, in winter with boots and tassels, and in summer with buckled shoes. I remember only two gentlemen in Boston, Nathaniel Goddard, who lived on Summer street, and a gentleman at the south end, whose name was Wheeler, who wore small clothes as long as Mr. Hedge. I am glad to see some indications of a return of a fashion too handsome and becoming to have been permitted to go out. Mr. Hedge was one of the founders of the Plymouth Bank in 1803, a Director from that date, and President from 1826 until his death in 1840. The house in question remained in the possession of the Hedge family until 1854, when it was sold to Zaben Olney.

One of the most interesting features of the celebration on the first of August, 1853, of the anniversary of the departure of the Pilgrims from Delfthaven, was the visit of the New York Light Guard with Dodsworth's band to Plymouth, and their participation in the parade of the day. As the Hedge house was then unoccupied it was made their headquarters. The celebration took place on Monday, and the arrival of the Light Guard, Sunday afternoon, and their march through Court and Main and Leyden streets presented a spectacle which so far as known, caused no protest from the spirits of the Pilgrims against such an unusual observance of the Lord's Day. Though I was Chief Marshal of the celebration, I have no knowledge of the ceremonies at the headquarters, but as the commander had a chaplain on his staff, it is to be presumed that they were interesting and appropriate. Before the sale of the house to Mr. Drew in 1858, Mr. Olney occupied it for a short time as a hotel, which during the winter months when the Samoset was closed, as was the custom in its earlier years, was well patronized.

CHAPTER XIV.

Of the occupants of the houses not yet referred to on the south side of Leyden street at various times within my memory, the first to be mentioned is Robert Roberts, who built the house on the brow of the hill, now owned by Wm. S. Robbins. Mr. Roberts was for many years a substantial merchant, engaged in navigation and foreign trade, and was one of the founders of the Plymouth Bank, of whose Board of Directors he was a member from the time of its organization in 1803, to his death in 1825. His sister Mary married John Clark, whose daughter, Eliza Haley Clark, occupied the house in question many years, and died December 23, 1882. I remember hearing when young a story about the source of a part of Mr. Roberts's wealth which may have been, like so many stories about others, without any foundation in fact. The story was that one of his vessels, either under command of himself or of another, was in a French port at one period of the French revolution and had taken on board the wealth of some refugees who had planned to escape from the persecution of the revolutionists, and sail for America, but that they were arrested and guillotined, and that their property never claimed by its owners, fell into the possession of Capt. Roberts and other owners of his vessel.

The only change within my recollection in the occupation of the next house, which has been for many years in the possession and occupancy of Salisbury Jackson, and his children and grandchildren, was the conversion in 1835 of one of the rooms on the street floor by Mr. Jackson into a store, which he opened in that year after having occupied for some years a store in the Witherill building on the corner of Main street and Town Square. In later years the store was abandoned, and the building restored to its original condition. I associate an old lady by the name of Johnson, who I think about 1830 occupied one or two rooms in the Jackson house, with a bonnet called the Navarino bonnet, which had a great run for a time among females everywhere, old and young. I wonder if

any of my readers remember as I do the Navarino bonnet?
The battle of Navarino, which secured Greek independence,
was fought October 20, 1827, in which the Turkish and Egyp-
tian navies were destroyed by the combined fleets of England,
Russia and France, and so great an interest was felt at that
time in Greek affairs that some ingenious originator of fashion
invented a bonnet made of paper resembling cloth, and of the
prevailing shape, with a crown a little turned up behind, and
a front, which entirely concealed the face and chin from a side
view, to which in order to attract attention and sales he gave
the name of the battle. Every woman bought one, and every
woman wore one, the streets were full of them, and in the
meeting houses they were in their glory. But alas, they were
fair weather bonnets, and like the feathers of a rooster, wore
a most bedraggled and flopping appearance when exposed to
the rain. The fashion was short lived, and went out like that
of hoop skirts, as rapidly as it came in, while the world still
wonders what became of them. If any one of my readers has
one of these relics of bygone days, I would be glad to have it
to help my memory in recalling the appearance of my sisters,
when one day they reached home in a drenching rain.

Of Capt. James Bartlett, the occupant of the next house
west of the Jackson house from 1801 to his death in 1840,
and of Leander Lovell, his son-in-law, the next occupant, by
whose heirs it was sold in 1880, to recent owners, mention has
been made in previous chapters.

The site of the next house, owned and occupied by Mr. Wm.
H. H. Weston, is an especially interesting one. For its early
history, which it is unnecessary to repeat, my readers are referred to page 164 of the first part of "Ancient Landmarks of
Plymouth." On that spot James Cole kept an ordinary, for
which he was licensed in 1645. Judge Samuel Sewall refers
to it in his diary under date of March 8, 1698, in which occurs
the following entry: "Got to Plymouth about noon. I lodge
at Cole's; the house was built by Governor Winslow, and is
the oldest in Plymouth." The present house was built in 1807
by General Nathaniel Goodwin, and was occupied by him
until his death, March 8, 1819. In 1827 it was sold by his
heirs to Thomas Russell, who made it his residence until his
death, September 25, 1854.

General Goodwin was born in Plymouth in 1749, and while engaged many years in iron manufactures, was more widely known as an officer in the militia and military superintendent for Plymouth county during the revolution. In the latter capacity he kept a record of enlistments in many of the towns in the county, including Plymouth and Kingston, which is more complete than the lists in the archives of the Commonwealth. This record was given to me some years ago by his grandson, the late Captain Nathaniel Goodwin, and has been given by me to the Pilgrim Society. After the battle of Saratoga, fought on the 7th of October, 1777, General Burgoyne and his army taken prisoners of war by General Gates, were marched to Cambridge and placed in barracks on Winter and Prospect hills, while Burgoyne himself was quartered in the Borland house in that town. General Goodwin was detailed under General Heath to command the guard having charge of the prisoners, and the following Plymouth men were enlisted to form a part of the guard:

Nathaniel Barnes	Eleazer Holmes, Jr.
Wm. Bartlett	Samuel Holmes
Wm. Blakeley	Daniel Howland
Wm. Cassady	Edward Morton
George Churchill	Josiah Morton
Israel Clark	Levi Paty
James Collins	Ebenezer Rider, Jr.
Thomas Dogget	Benoni Shaw
Lemuel Doten	Nathaniel Torrey
Stephen Doten	Benjamin Weston
Thomas Ellis	John Witherhead
John Harlow, Jr.	

General Goodwin and General Burgoyne became friends, and as a memento of their friendship, Burgoyne gave to General Goodwin his rapier, which was also given to me by his grandson, and is now a loan from me in the cabinet of the Pilgrim Society. General Goodwin was like Mr. Roberts and Mr. Hedge, an original subscriber to stock in the Plymouth Bank in 1803, and was a Director from the date of its organization until his death in 1819.

General Goodwin, I have always heard, was a man of fine figure and bearing, and vain of his appearance, especially when in uniform. His grandson, Capt. Nathaniel Goodwin, told me the following story about him and his negro servant Pompey, a freed slave, which illustrates the familiarity of the slaves with their old masters and the characteristic vanity of the General. One muster day morning the General, wearing his regimentals, said: "Pompey, how do I look?" "You look like a lion, massa." "Lion, Pompey; you never saw a lion." "Yes I have, massa; massa Davis hab got one." "That isn't a lion, you fool, that is a jackass." "I don't care, massa, you look just like dat er animal."

Thomas Russell, who bought the above mentioned Goodwin house in 1827, and occupied it until his death, was a brother of Captain John Russell, mentioned in a previous chapter as an enterprising ship owner, and married in 1814 Mary Ann, daughter of William Goodwin, and their children were Elizabeth, born in 1815, Lydia Cushing, 1817, who married Hon. Wm. Whiting; Mary, who married Benjamin Marston Watson of Plymouth; William Goodwin, 1821, Thomas, 1825, and Jane Frances, who married Abraham Firth of Boston. Of these children Mrs. Watson alone survives. Mr. Russell was for many years the treasurer and manager of the Cotton Mill at Eel River, established in 1812. After his retirement from that position, he was often the trusted adviser in the settlement of estates, and in 1837 Mr. Barnabas Hedge, supposing himself seriously involved in the liabilities of the Tremont Iron Works in Wareham, in which he was largely interested, made an assignment to his son-in-law, Charles H. Warren and Mr. Russell for the security of his indebtedness. Mr. Hedge was, however, under the management of his assignees extricated from his embarrassments, and was left with a handsome fortune. In accordance with the provisions of law then in force, Mr. Russell was chosen by the legislature in 1842 Treasurer and Receiver General of the Commonwealth, and again in 1844. It is worthy of mention that within eighty-five years from the adoption of the constitution in 1780 to 1865 three citizens of Plymouth should have served as treasurer during a period of fourteen years. These were Thomas Davis, from 1792 to 1797, Thomas Russell in 1842 and 1844, and Jacob H. Loud in 1853 and 1854, and from 1866 to 1871. If the term of Hon. Nahum Mitchell of East Bridgewater of five years from 1822 to 1827 be added, the county of Plymouth was represented in the treasurer's office more than a quarter of the time.

The various occupants of the site on which the Baptist church stands, are deserving of notice. The house, taken down when the church was erected in 1865, was built in 1703 by Dr. Francis LeBaron, who was a passenger in a French vessel wrecked on Cape Cod in 1694, and settled in Plymouth. A family tradition says that he was a Roman Catholic, and was buried with a cross on his breast, but Mrs. James Humphrey of New York told me that her grandmother, Elizabeth wife of Ammi Ruhama Robbins of Norfolk, Conn., who was a granddaughter of Dr. LeBaron, told her that the Doctor was a Huguenot. It is a singular fact that one hundred years later in 1794 or 1795, another French vessel was wrecked on Cape Cod, on which there was a passenger named LeBaron, whose descendants are living in one or more of the southern states. From Francis LeBaron the house descended to his son, Dr. Lazarus LeBaron, who sold it in 1765 to Nathaniel Goodwin, the husband of his daughter, Lydia. From Nathaniel Goodwin it descended to his son, General Nathaniel Goodwin, who occupied it until, in 1807, he built and occupied the W. H. H. Weston house. The General leased the house to John Bartlett and William White, who occupied it as a tavern. I have no knowledge as to who John Bartlett was, but William White came from New Bedford, having married Fanny Gibbs of Wareham, and was the father of Arabella White, who married the late Capt. Nathaniel Goodwin. I have no means of knowing precisely when Bartlett and White terminated their lease, but it is certain that in October, 1818, John H. Bradford kept a tavern in the house, as on the 9th of that month George Cooper, clerk of the Standish Guards, notified the members of the company to meet on the 21st at the house of John H. Bradford. At first the tavern was called as above, "the house of John H. Bradford," but later it came to be called Bradford's Tavern, and was so called until it was sold in 1857. It was a stately mansion. Its broad front, its spacious doorway, its broad hall, and its large wainscotted rooms, told the story of its ancient grandeur. There the "daughters of Lazarus" reigned as queens, and the fashion of the town engaged in the minuet of the olden time.

John Howland Bradford, or Uncle Johnny, as he was affectionately called, the landlord during a period of forty years, perhaps more widely known than any landlord of his time, was born in Plymouth, July 14, 1780, and never married. He was an interesting character, such as only an old New England town could produce, with only an ordinary public school education, but under the moral influences of an enlightened Christian home, he grew into manhood with habits of truth, industry, kindness of heart, and correct living, which no wordly influences could weaken. No better man has within my observation ever lived. His sphere of life was narrow, but he filled it full. Let every man do this and the machinery of social life will run without friction or jar. I never knew of his attendance at any church, and I do not believe that any theological question ever presented itself to his mind. His character, however, was such as Christianity seeks to form, and as long as it is formed, it is not worth while to ask whether it be the result of the lessons of Christianity acting directly on the man, or on those under whose ministrations his habits have been formed. When he died, December 7, 1863, we may be sure that the promise made to the pure in heart was kept that "they shall see God."

The hostess of Bradford's Tavern was Mrs. Abigail (Leonard) Hollis, wife of Henry Hollis and daughter of Thomas Leonard, of Plymouth. Mr. Hollis came from Weymouth and married his wife in 1819. He died March 9, 1838, and his widow died September 27, 1859. Two of their children were John Henry, a merchant in New York at the time of his death, and our late townsman, William T. Hollis. I have no recollection of Mr. Hollis, or his occupation, but I have no doubt that he was connected in some capacity with the tavern. His wife was a strong minded, vigorous woman, and was the mainstay in everything connected with the domestic concerns of the house. Her oldest son, John Henry, was my schoolmate in the High school, and I can testify to the care she bestowed on his moral and intellectual instruction. The inscription on her gravestone:

"Whosoever liveth and believeth in me shall never die," was not only intended as the statement of a general truth, but also as a recognition of its truth as specially applicable to her.

Among the guests at Bradford's Tavern the memory of

some lingers in my mind. When I was quite young, perhaps about the year 1830, a stranger arrived at the tavern on the evening stage from Boston, who was destined to keep the tongue of gossip wagging for some time. He was somewhat portly, but moderate in height, and dressed in linen and broadcloth of immaculate neatness and fashionable in style. His name was Surrey, but the register contained no place of residence. Occasional visitors for a day or two were not uncommon, and excited no remark, but when this stranger remained for a week or more with neither acquaintance nor business to protract his stay, the gossips began to wonder who he was, whence he came, to what nationality he belonged, and what the purpose of his visit could be. In suitable weather he took his morning and evening walk about the town, making no visits, entering no store or church or public meeting, and asking no questions concerning the town or people. From his dignified bearing he won the name of Lord Surrey, and was never referred to by any other name. He made occasional excursions to Boston, where apparently he received funds, and bought new clothes. He paid his board promptly, and his habits and demeanor were beyond criticism. At the end of a year he left town and gossips were left to wonder where he had gone, whether he was a refugee from abroad, or whether he was merely an eccentric man who was floating about the world at the dictate of a capricious will.

I remember another visitor at the tavern quite as mysterious, a man of gentlemanly appearance, who could not speak a word of English, and who remained six months without disclosing his nationality, and went as he came, a stranger in a strange land. Mr. Salisbury Jackson, whose humor led him to speak of every day incidents in a manner to amuse his hearers, in describing a visit to the unknown, said that he tried him in French, but found that he was not a Frenchman. He then tried him in Spanish, but he was not a Spaniard. He then tried him in German, but he was not a German. He then, after failing to make him out an Italian, tried him in the original tongue and fixed him. No efforts of available linguists could fix his nationality more successfully than the humor of Mr. Jackson, and he went as he came, and was for a long time remembered as the mysterious stranger.

In 1857 the tavern house was sold to Wm. Churchill, who sold it to Wm. Finney, who resold it to Mr. Churchill, from whom it was bought by the Baptist Society in 1862. From 1857 to the date of his death, December 7, 1863, Mr. Bradford boarded with Jacob Howland, who occupied chambers in the Witherell building on the corner of Main street and Town Square.

I have spoken of Pompey, a colored servant, once a slave of General Nathaniel Goodwin, with whom he lived in the old tavern house. He died within my recollection, and I think he was the last of the old slaves living in Plymouth. I remember his living with Nathaniel Goodwin, Cashier of the Plymouth Bank, who lived in what was called the bank house, which stood on Court street, where the Russell building now stands. Prince, whom I also remember, was once a slave of Dr. Wm. Thomas, and lived until his death, after the death of Dr. Thomas, with his son, Judge Joshua Thomas, who died January 10, 1821, and afterwards with his widow, in the house now occupied as an inn, called the Plymouth Tavern. There is no reason to doubt that the institution of slavery was recognized, and as firmly upheld in Plymouth as in other considerable towns in the northern states. So far as the slave trade was concerned, though it was abolished by an act of Congress in 1808, there is reason to believe that in the town of Bristol, R. I., within the limits of the original Plymouth Colony, until by a Royal Commission in 1751, that town was taken from Massachusets and added to Rhode Island, it was pursued until 1820. In that year Congress declared the trade to be piracy, and Captain Nathaniel Gordon, engaged in the trade, was in November, 1861, convicted and executed in New York. It was the generally entertained belief that one or more citizens of Bristol were engaged in the trade, which led Mr. Webster to make the following denunciatory reference to the trade in his memorable oration delivered in Plymouth on the celebration in 1820 of the anniversary of the Landing of the Pilgrims. "It is not fit that the land of the Pilgrims should bear the shame longer. I hear the sound of the hammer; I see the smoke of the furnace where manacles and fetters are still forged for human limbs. I see the visages of those who by stealth and midnight labor in this work of hell foul and dark, as may become the artificers of such instruments of misery and tortures. Let that spot be purified, or let it cease to be of New England. Let it be purified or let it be set aside from the Christian world; let it be put out of the circle of human sympathies and human regards, and let civilized man henceforth have no communion with it."

Slavery existed in Massachusetts until the adoption of its constitution on the 15th of June, 1780. Article first of the "declaration of the Rights of the Inhabitants of the Commonwealth" declared as follows: "All men are born free and equal, and have certain natural, essential and unalienable rights, among which may be reckoned the right of enjoying and defending their lives and liberties; that of acquiring, possessing and protecting property; in fine, that of seeking and obtaining their safety and happiness."

Whatever may have been the intent of the framers of the constitution in constructing the above article, the Supreme Court of Massachusetts decided as early as 1781 in the case of Walker vs. Jennison that slavery was abolished in Massachusetts by the declaration of rights, and that decision has been repeatedly confirmed by later ones. But singularly enough, notwithstanding these decisions a slave was sold by auction in Cambridge as late as 1793. Precisely how many slaves there were in Plymouth when the constitution was adopted, I have no means of knowing, but it is certain that, as elsewhere at the North where soil and climate and public opinion were unfavorable, the number had been for some years gradually lessening. The growth of slavery at the south was however astonishing. It has been estimated that at various times forty million slaves were taken from the shores of Africa, and at the first census in 1790, there were 697,897 slaves in the United States. This number increased to 893,-041 in 1800, to 1,191,369 in 1810, to 1,538,022 in 1820, to 2,-009,043 in 1830, to 2,487,455 in 1840, to 3,204,313 in 1850, and to 3,953,760 in 1860.

I have seen an assessor's record for the year 1740, which states that in that year there were thirty-two slaves in Plymouth between the ages of twelve and fifty, from which it may be fair to assume that there were at least fifty of all ages. The following were the owners in the above year:

Robert Brown, one; Samuel Bartlett, one; Timothy Trent, one; James Hovey, one; Hannah Jackson, one; Samuel Kempton, one; Isaac Lothrop, four; Thomas Jackson, two; Lazarus LeBaron, two; John Murdock, one; Thomas Murdock, one; Job Morton, one; Ebenezer Spooner, one; Haviland Torrey, one; David Turner, one; James Warren, one; John Watson, one; James Warren, Jr., one; Rebecca Witherell, one; Seth Barnes, one; John Bartlett, one; Stephen Churchill, one; Wm. Clark, one; Nathaniel Foster, two; Sarah Little, one; Joseph Bartlett, one.

The following slaves are mentioned in the town records at various dates:

Cæsar, Hester, Eunice, Philip and Esther, slaves of Edward Winslow in 1768; Cato and Jesse, slaves of John Foster in 1731; Britain, slave of John Winslow in 1762; Cuffee, slave of Isaac Lothrop in 1768; Nanny, slave of Samuel Bartlett in 1738; Hannah, slave of James Hovey in 1762; Cuffee, slave of George Watson in 1768; Dick, slave of Nathaniel Thomas in 1731; Phebe, slave of Haviland Torrey in 1731; Dolphin, slave of Nathaniel Thomas in 1731; Flora, slave of Priscilla Watson in 1731; Eseck, slave of George Watson in 1757; Rose, slave of William Clark in 1757; Prince, slave of Wm. Thomas in 1771; Plymouth, slave of Thomas Davis in 1753; Nannie, slave of Deacon Foster in 1741; Jane, slave of Thomas Jackson in 1760; Jack, slave of Thomas Holmes in 1739; Patience, slave of Barnabas Churchill in 1739; Pero and Hannah, slaves of John Murdock in 1756; Quamony, slave of Josiah Cotton in 1732; Kate, slave of John Murdock in 1732; Quash, slave of Lazarus LeBaron in 1756; Phillis, slave of Theophilus Cotton in 1751; Silas, slave of Daniel Diman in 1772; Venus, slave of Elizabeth Edwards in 1772; Pompey, slave of Nathaniel Goodwin in 1775; Cæsar, slave of Joshua Thomas in 1779; Venus, slave of Elizabeth Stephens in 1772; Quba, slave of Barnabas Hedge in 1775; Plato, slave of unknown in 1779; Ebed Melick, slave of Madame Thatcher of Middleboro.

Besides Pompey and Prince, Quamony Quash, an old slave, commonly called Quam, lived within my remembrance, and died April 18, 1833. Most of the slaves emancipated by the constitution, accepted their freedom, and so far as I know, only

Pompey and Prince continued as servants of their old masters. A few of them squatted on land belonging to the town of Plymouth, which on that account took the name of New Guinea. Among these were Quamony, Prince, Plato and Cato, but it is probable that Prince divided his time between his home at New Guinea and the house of his old master, where I remember him a faithful servant of the widow of Judge Joshua Thomas.

It is not improbable that Plymouth was associated with the first claim made on a citizen of Massachusetts for the restoration of a slave to his master. Information concerning it I found among my grandfather's papers. In 1808 the brig Thomas, Solomon Davie master, at some port in Delaware, received on board a slave who had deserted from his master, David M. McIlvaine, and until 1812 remained in my grandfather's service, receiving wages as a hired man. In 1812 Mr. McIlvaine found the slave on board the brig in Baltimore, and a claim for his restoration being made, he was given up. In the meantime the slave who called himself George Thomson, bought a small house on the brow of Cole's Hill, and in a settlement of a suit to recover wages, which my grandfather had paid to Thomson, Mr. McIlvaine, in consideration of the money paid, conveyed to my grandfather the house, and the following articles of personal property, which were in the keeping of a colored woman, named Violet Phillips, and were the property of Thompson—a blue cloth coat, fine; a black cloth coat, fine; one pair of ribbed velvet pantaloons; one black bombazet trousers; one white shirt; one white waistcoat; one black bombazet waistcoat; one black silk waistcoat; three yellow marseilles waistcoats; one pair white cotton stockings; two checked shirts; one new fur hat; one chest, and one trunk in which were the title papers to his house, and one silver watch.

Of many stories about these old slaves I have room for only one. When the use of biers, instead of hearses was universal, occasionally two of these freedmen would be hired as bearers. On one occasion, when Quamony and Plato were employed, they had heard that gloves were given to the bearers, and just as the procession was about to start, Quamony said to Plato, "Hab you hab'm glub?" "No," said Plato, "I no hab'm no glub." "Nor I hab'm glub nudder," said Quamony, "We no bare widout glub, let the man in the box carry hisself."

CHAPTER XV.

The house adjoining the Baptist church, now occupied by the Custom House, recalls next to the house on Cole's Hill, in which I was born, the pleasantest associations, and the dearest memories.   In that building my grandfather William Davis, born July 15, 1758, lived from 1781, the year of his marriage, until January 5, 1826, the date of his death.   He was the son of Thos. Davis, and one of a family of one daughter and six sons, Sarah, Thomas, William, John, Samuel, Isaac P. and Wendell. Sarah, born June 29, 1754, married LeBaron Bradford of Bristol, son of William Bradford, United States senator from the state of Rhode Island.

Thomas Davis, born June 26, 1756, was a representative from Plymouth, senator from Plymouth County, senator from Suffolk County, treasurer and receiver general of the Commonwealth from 1792 to 1797, and president of the Boston Marine Insurance Company from 1799 until his death, January 21, 1805.   I have on my walls the barometer which hung in the insurance office at the time of his death.

John Davis, born in Plymouth, January 25, 1761, graduated at Harvard in 1781, and entered the legal profession.   He was the youngest member of the convention on the adoption of the state constitution, and in 1796 was appointed by Washington comptroller of the United States Treasury.   In 1801 he was appointed by John Adams, Judge of the United States Court for the district of Massachusetts, and continued on the bench forty years.   He was treasurer of Harvard College from 1810 to 1827, a Fellow of Harvard from 1803 to 1810, and President of the Massachusetts Historical Society from 1818 to 1843. He died in Boston, January 14, 1847.

Samuel Davis, born March 5, 1765, was a well known antiquarian, a learned linguist, and a recognized authority on questions relating to Indian dialects.   He was a member of the Massachusetts Historical Society, recipient of an honorary degree from Harvard in 1819, and died in Plymouth, July 10,

1829.   He is worthily commemorated by the following inscription on his gravestone on Burial hill:

"From life on earth our pensive friend retires,
His dust commingling with the Pilgrim sires;
In thoughtful walks their every path he traced,
Their toils, their tombs his faithful page embraced,
Peaceful and pure and innocent as they,
With them to rise to everlasting day."

Isaac P. Davis, born October 7, 1771, was for many years an extensive manufacturer in Boston, owning a rope walk on the mill dam, now Beacon street, and perhaps was more widely known socially in Boston than any man of his time.   He was a friend of artists, and a patron of art, whose judgment and taste were freely consulted by purchasers.   Stuart, the portrait painter, was his intimate friend, and the horse in the Faneuil Hall picture of Washington, is a portrait of a horse owned by Mr. Davis.   After the completion of the picture he presented the study from which it was painted, to Mr. Davis, a picture about 20 by 24 inches, which after the death of Mrs. Davis was sold by Josiah Quincy, and myself, her executors, to Ignatius Sargent, for three thousand dollars.   The friendship between Mr. Davis and Mr. Webster may be judged by the following affectionate dedication to him of the second volume of Mr. Webster's works, published in 1851.

My dear Sir:

"A warm, private friendship has existed between us for more than half our lives interrupted by no untoward occurrence, and never for a minute cooling into indifference.   Of this friendship, the source of so much happiness to me, I wish to leave, if not an enduring memorial, at least an affectionate and grateful acknowledgment.   I dedicate this volume of my speeches to you.   DANIEL WEBSTER."

Wendell Davis, the youngest brother of my grandfather, born February 13, 1776, graduated at Harvard in 1796, and was clerk of the Massachusetts senate from 1802 to 1805.   He studied law with his brother John, and settled in Sandwich. He served by appointment of the Governor as sheriff of Barnstable county, and died, Dec. 30, 1830.   He was the father of Hon. George T. Davis of Greenfield, whom Thackery declared the most brilliant conversationalist he had ever met.

My grandfather, William Davis, born July 15, 1758, was trained in the business of his father, Thomas Davis, who was largely engaged in navigation and foreign trade, and with whom he became associated. After the death of his father, March 7, 1785, he continued the business of the firm of Thomas and William Davis with marked success until his death. Notwithstanding the depressing effects of the embargo, and the war of 1812, from which many suffered, I have been unable to discover in his files of business letters any indications of serious injury to his vessels or his trade. My father, William Davis, who died March 22, 1824, at the age of forty-one, was for some years associated with his father in business. My grandfather was representative and member of the executive council, and twenty-five years a member of the board of selectmen. It is perhaps worthy of mention that the services of members of four generations of my family as selectmen, cover a period of fifty-two years. Mr. Davis was also one of the founders of the Plymouth Bank, and its President from 1805 until his death, and one of the founders of the Pilgrim Society, and its first Vice-president.

Before leaving my grandfather's family I trust that I may be excused for referring to his daughter Betsey, or Elizabeth, as she was called late in life. She was born in the house under discussion, October 28, 1803, and until thirteen years of age attended private schools in Plymouth. After that time for three years, until she was sixteen, she attended the school of Miss Elizabeth Cushing, in the family of Deacon Wm. Cushing of Hingham. Miss Cushing's school was probably not surpassed by any ladies' school in the country, and there a solid foundation was laid, which served my aunt so well as the wife of Mr. Bancroft, during his services as minister at London and Berlin. History, geography and public affairs were her special subjects of study, and while in London it was said by Englishmen, that she was so familiar with English politics as to be able to discuss them, and hold her own with the leading statesmen of the Kingdom. To show the extent of her early reading, when a girl, or a young woman, she listened one Sunday to a sermon preached in the Plymouth pulpit by a minister of a Plymouth County town exchanging with Dr. Kendall, which was much admired. It seemed to her that she had read it somewhere, and on going home, succeeded in finding it in a volume of sermons by Rev. Newcome Cappe, an English clergyman, who became pastor of a dissenting congregation in York and served from 1756 to near the end of the century. After looking the sermon over and verifying her suspicions of a wholesale plagiarism, she laid the book down on the centre table with the title in plain sight. In the evening the clergyman called at the house, and during his visit, much to the embarrassment of the hostess, and doubtless to his own bewilderment, sat with the book at his elbow, and the title staring him in the face. I prefer not to mention his name, but my older readers may identify him when I say that invariably when he preached in Plymouth, as he often did, he selected for one of his hymns that from Peale Dabney's collection, with the familiar verse:

"Mark the soft falling snow,
  And the diffusive rain;
To heaven from whence it fell,
It turns not back again;
But waters earth through every pore,
And calls forth all her secret store."

She married in 1825, Alexander Bliss, law partner of Daniel Webster, who died July 15, 1827, and in 1838, married George Bancroft, the historian, who found in her efficient aid in the performance of his duties as secretary of the Navy, under President Polk, as minister to England from 1846 to 1849, and later as minister to Berlin.

It was my fortune to be in London in the month of February, 1847, during her residence there, and to receive from her and Mr. Bancroft many acts of kindness. It was during the Irish famine, and a benefit was planned to be held at Drury Lane Theatre, to add to the Irish charitable fund. There was no public sale of tickets, but a committee took the house from parquette to ceiling, and sent tickets for whole boxes to such members of the nobility as were available, and to the diplomatic corps, with prices affixed, which of course were taken regardless of cost in the nature of subscriptions, and tickets for the parquette to such single persons as they thought expedient. Mr. Bancroft's box containing four chairs, was occupied by himself and Mrs. Bancroft, Henry H. Milman, then distinguished as an historian, poet and dramatic writer, and Professor of poetry at Oxford, but later known as Dean of St. Paul's, and myself. In the dramatic world Mr. Milman was known as the author of the tragedy of Fazio, which I have seen played at the old Tremont theatre by Forrest and the elder Booth. The royal box, directly opposite in the same row, was occupied by Queen Victoria, Prince Albert, and the Duke of Cambridge. In the box next to the royal box were the Duke of Wellington and the Marchioness of Douro, while others whom I remember in other boxes were the Duke of Devonshire, the Earl of Westminster, the Duke of Norfolk, Hon. Mrs. Norton, Sir Robert Peel, Lord John Russell, Lord Lyndhurst, Macaulay, Hume, and Lord George Bentinck. I was undoubtedly the only American in the house, and probably the only one in the audience whom the society reporter of the *Times* could not call by name.

At a dinner at Mr. Bancroft's, I had an opportunity of meeting Thomas Carlyle, and I was astonished at his bitter denunciation of men and events, and his almost brutal speech. While the Irish question was under discussion, Duncan C. Pell of New York, one of the guests, asked him what he would do with the Irish, and bringing his hand down roughly on the table he growled out, "I would shoot every mother's son of them." I could not help contrasting his coarseness with the sweet and gentle spirit of Ralph Waldo Emerson, his friend on our side of the ocean.

Through the kindness of Mr. Bancroft I had an opportunity of seeing most of the above named statesmen in their seats in Parliament during a discussion on the corn laws, with the addition of Daniel O'Connell, who upon the whole, I think, was the most striking looking man I saw in England. During the discussion to which I have referred, Lord George Bentinck, who was well known for his fondness for horses, and the race course, made a speech which placed him on the side of the protectionists against Sir Robert Peel, whom he had before ardently supported. Sir Robert in a reply full of sharp invective said, "It is far from my intention to charge the honorable member with inconsistency, when he is universally known as a man of stable mind."

After the death of my grandfather in 1826 my grandmother continued to occupy the family mansion until 1830, when she removed to Boston, where she died, April 1, 1847.   For a year or more after her departure, the house was occupied by her son, Nathaniel Morton Davis, while his house on Court street, now owned by the Old Colony Club, was undergoing alterations and repairs.   In 1832 it was sold to Wm. Morton Jackson, who moved into it from his former residence in North street on the corner of Rope Walk lane, where the house of Isaac M. Jackson now stands.   Mr. Jackson fitted the front west room for a store, and removed his business in dry goods from the building on the corner of Summer street and Spring Hill, which was taken down about 1890.   In 1851 Mr. Jackson, who had been collector of the port from 1845 to 1849, sold the estate to Mrs. Sarah Plympton, and removed to Boston, where he engaged in the wholesale grocery business on State street, nearly opposite Merchants' Row.   During its ownership by Mrs. Plympton, it was occupied as a boarding house at various times by Ephraim Spooner, Mrs. Wm. H. Spear and Mrs. Ephraim T. Paty, and was sold in 1878 by her executor to George F. Weston, Charles O. Churchill and Samuel Harlow, with whose ownership and the erection of the Rink in 1884 my readers are familiar.

As long ago as I can remember, the next estate on the west, on which the store of W. H. H. Weston stands, was occupied by a building in the lower story of which Zaben Olney and Jas. E. Leonard kept a flour and grain store, established by them in 1827, and in the upper story of which the Custom House was located.   In 1831 Harrison Gray Otis Ellis, succeeded Olney and Leonard in the store, but in 1832 gave up business, and the building was sold to the Old Colony Bank, then recently organized.   The Custom House continued to occupy the second story until 1845, when Gustavus Gilbert occupied it for a time as a law office.   In 1846 Steward and Alderman, who had bought the building of the Bank in 1842, sold it to Wm. Rider Drew, who moved the building back, and added a new front, as the building stands at the present time.

In 1845 the Custom House was located in a room on the north side of the house at the corner of North and Main streets, where it remained through the administrations of Mr. Jackson, Thomas Hedge and Edward P. Little, until 1857.

James Easdell Leonard, the partner of Zaben Olney, was a

Plymouth man, the son of Nathaniel Warren Leonard, and married Abby, daughter of John Bishop, and step daughter of Ezra Finney, and lived for a time in the southerly half of the double house, recently owned and occupied by the late George E. Morton. Zaben Olney came from Rhode Island, and what his occupation was before he entered into partnership with Mr. Leonard, is not within my remembrance. He married in 1816, Rebecca Morton, and in 1862, Olive P. Wolcott. For some years after 1837, he kept the Old Colony House in Court Square, and for several years after 1854, a hotel in the old Barnabas Hedge house on Leyden street, now owned and occupied by Wm. Rider Drew.

Harrison Gray Otis Ellis, who succeeded Olney and Leonard, came to Plymouth, from Wareham, but was in business here not more than a year, during which time he married Margaret D., daughter of Jeremiah Holbrook. He removed to Sandwich, where I think he kept for a number of years a dry goods and clothing store. Steward and Alderman, who owned the building from 1842 to 1846, and Alderman and Gooding kept during that time dry goods stores in it.

Most of my readers will remember that in 1883 the corner of Market and Leyden streets was cut off by the county commissioners. At that time the old building on the corner was moved down Market street, and the present brick building put up on the new line of the street. As long ago as I can remember, in 1829, the old house was kept as a hotel by Wm. Randall. Built by William Shurtleff in 1689, it had twice before been used as a hotel, once in 1713 by Job Cushman, and again in 1732 by Consider Howland. In 1831 Mr. Randall occupied a part of the house as an auction room, and in 1832 he established with Lucius Doolittle a line of stages to Boston, which preceded the famous line established by George Drew. The stage office was in the corner room, and the stable was on the corner of School street and Town Square. In 1835 James C. Valentine had a harness shop on the corner, and later was succeeded by Martin Myers and Wm. Hall Jackson in the same business. Chandler Holmes and Lysander Dunham occupied the store until the building was moved. After William Randall, the residential part was occupied, at various times by Dr. Andrew Mackie, Sylvanus Bramhall, Wm. Rider Drew, James Thurber,

David Drew, Isaac B. Rich and Mrs. M. J. Lincoln, the author of the Boston Cook Book. Wm. Hall Jackson, above mentioned, died February 3, 1869.

The occupants of the buildings on Market street, and the changes in the line of the street, which have been made within my recollection, come next in order. There was no change in the boundaries after 1715 until December 30, 1873, when the street was widened on the easterly side from the present bake house south. It was again widened November 5, 1883, by cutting off the Leyden street corner. Again on the first of January, 1890, it was widened on the westerly side of Spring Hill by the removal of the building there situated. At the time the Leyden street corner was cut off, the building next to the corner was taken down, and the corner building moved into its place. A new brick building was put on the corner with the history of which my readers are familiar. The house now standing next to the brick one has already been discribed as the house on the corner. As long ago as I remember the house which stood next to the corner, and was taken down in 1883, was built by Benjamin Bramhall, and was called the green store. In 1827 it was occupied at times by William Z. Ripley, who kept a dry goods store, Rufus Robbins, who kept what was called the Old Colony bookstore, Benjamin Hathaway, who kept a harness store, and Sylvanus Bramhall, silversmith. In 1833 it was occupied by James G. Gleason barber, in 1851, by James Kendrick, and later, by George A. Hathaway, bookseller, and Benjamin Churchill.

The next building was occupied in my boyhood by Deacon Nathan Reed, who had at an earlier date kept a store in the next building on the south. He owned a barn in School street, which was burned in January, 1835, and I remember that the only house taking fire from flying embers was his own dwelling on Market street. He died, January 12, 1842, and in 1856 his widow sold the house to Barnabas H. Holmes, who converted its lower rooms into a store, and occupied it for a tailor's shop. It was later occupied by Benjamin Cooper Finney, as a store, and in 1883 was removed to the rear of the Brewster building on Leyden street, where it has since been used as a dwelling house with its old front room restored.

The next building was long known as the Shurtleff tavern

and, before the revolution, was partially occupied by General Peleg Wadsworth for a private school. General Wadsworth's daughter Zilpah married Stephen Longfellow, the grandfather of the poet. As long ago as I can remember its upper story was occupied by Robert Dunham, who owned a large stable in the rear, the entrance to which was through the yard on the south of the building in question. Mr. Dunham was connected with stage lines to Boston and Taunton in connection with George Drew, and died in 1833. He had three daughters, one of whom, Mary Ann, married Thomas Long, second cousin of Gov. John D. Long, and kept a milliner's store on Summer street in the house which was afterwards occupied by the late Benjamin Hathaway.

The lower part of the Dunham building was divided into two stores. The northerly one was a candy store, kept by two ladies, who were known only as Nancy and Eliza. I wish to embalm their memories in gratitude for the satisfaction my youthful taste often received at their hands. They were, Nancy, a maiden lady, daughter of James and Bethiah (Dunham) Paulding, and Eliza (Rogers) Straffin, wife of George Straffin. They were succeeded by Stephen Rogers, who carried on the same business, and died, May 18, 1868. The other store was occupied by Lazarus Symmes, who had succeeded Nathan Reed, and who died, Dec. 25, 1851. After the death of Robert Dunham, the upper part was occupied by Daniel Deacon, who married, Mary, daughter of Thomas Torrance, and died March 13, 1842. The building in question was taken down, and the present building, recently owned by the estate of Zaben Olney, was erected on the northerly part of the lot, and on the southerly part the present bake house was erected by Samuel Talbot and George Churchill, bakers.

In my youth a building standing on the south side of the entrance to Dunham's stable, was owned by Antipas Brigham, who occupied it as a dwelling house and store. Mr. Brigham died, August 6, 1832, and was succeeded in the occupancy of the store by William Barnes in 1832, and later by Stephen Lucas, Ephraim Bartlett, and Wm. Henry Bartlett. In 1827 Harvey Shaw, accountant, occupied the upper part for a time, and in 1845 Alvah C. Page occupied it for a writing school. The building in question was partially burned about 1870, and taken down, and in 1876 a building which had been occupied by Wm. Bishop and others, on the Odd Fellows' lot on Main street, was moved to its site.

This last building, after its removal was occupied for a time by Thomas N. Eldridge as a dry goods store.

The next building has had its front altered into a store, but in other respects it remains as it was in my youth, when owned and occupied as a dwelling house by John Macomber. In 1874 it came into the possession of Josiah A. Robbins, and the store now standing on its south side was moved from the present site of the store of Christopher T. Harris.

The next house built in 1832 by Capt. Isaac Bartlett, came into the possession of John B. Atwood in 1855, who fitted up a store on its northerly side, and occupied the remainder as a dwelling. Capt. Isaac Bartlett was a shipmaster for many years, and made many voyages in the Havana trade between that port and Plymouth, in the brig Hannah, owned by Barnabas Hedge. I have distinct and agreeable memories of his arrivals with loads of molasses, some of which I licked from sticks introduced into hospitable bung holes, without money and without price. Captain Bartlett died, May 3, 1845. By his second wife, Rebecca, daughter of Caleb Bartlett, he had a son, Robert, born in 1817, and a daughter, Rebecca, born in 1819, both remarkable for minds capable of unlimited development and cultivation. Robert Bartlett, of whom I wish particularly to speak, was fitted for college in Plymouth by George Washington Hosmer and Addison Brown, both graduates of Harvard in the class of 1826; and graduated in 1836. He was tutor in Latin at Harvard from 1839 to 1843, when his early death destroyed the promise of a brilliant career. Aside from being a fellow townsman, I had an opportunity afforded by being a fellow boarder with him two years in Cambridge, of estimating his character and learning. I do not feel that I am violating any rules of propriety in speaking of a passage in his career, which gave me as a young man my first insight into the romances of life. He became engaged to my cousin, Elizabeth Crowell White, a daughter of Capt. Gideon Consider White, a lady of about his own age, and as remarkable as he in literary culture. After the death of her father and mother she was a member of my mother's family until her death. In 1842, on a visit to relatives in Nova Scotia, she broke off her engagement with Mr. Bartlett, and soon after contracted a new engagement with an English gentleman. The blow to Mr. Bartlett was a severe one, and I remember well the visit which he made to our house on the afternoon of the day he received his letter of dismissal. After her return from Nova Scotia I was not long in discovering that her heart was still in the possession of her former lover, though she endeavored to conceal the fact. At this time an inherited tendency to a disease of the lungs began to show itself, both in her and in Mr. Bartlett, and in both cases, consumption rapidly performed its fatal work. She was soon confined permanently to the house, and he was obliged to abandon his college work, and return home to become like her a prisoner in his chamber and bed. He was brought from Boston in the steamboat, then running, and she, knowing that he was coming, sat by the chamber window on the north side of our house on Cole's Hill, evidently anxious to catch a glimpse of one whom she had mistakenly cast off, but whom she still loved with all her heart. I remember well the tears she shed as he was carried up the street, and she saw him for the last time. Both failed rapidly. He died at his home, September 15, 1843, and she on the 7th of the next month, and both are buried in Vine Hills cemetery, united at least in spirit, where "they neither marry nor are given in marriage."

It is not worth while to consider the occupancy of the remaining estates between the Isaac Bartlett house and the brook. It will be sufficient to say that the first building next to the Bartlett House was at one time occupied by Oliver Keyes, and again by Martin Myers, who kept a harness store on the corner of Leyden street. Two stores have been erected in front of the building which are occupied by C. T. Harris & Son, and by the Co-operative store. In 1828 a man named Joseph D. Jones. kept a tinman's shop on Market street, but its precise location I cannot define. He advertised bulbous roots for sale, and we boys, always ready to adopt nicknames, called him bulbous Jones. He deserved a better name, for he was one of the best of men, conscientious in all his dealings, and a valuable citizen. At a later date he moved to a one story building on Main street, where Leyden Hall building now stands, after Dr. Isaac LeBaron, apothecary, had moved from

it to the corner of North street.   Rev. Adiel Harvey, pastor
of the Baptist Society from 1845 to 1855, and superintendent
of public schools from 1853 to 1859, married his daughter.
About forty years after he left Plymouth I met him one day
in Boston, and instantly recognizing him, called him by name,
and had a pleasant conversation with him.   Of course he
failed to recognize me, but he expressed great pleasure at meeting some one from Plymouth, who could tell him about the doings in the old town.   Twelve or fifteen years ago I was advertised to deliver an address before the Young Men's Christian
Union, and the old man considerably over ninety years of age,
seeing the advertisement, came escorted by his daughter to
hear me.   He died not many years ago at the Old Men's
Home, on Springfield street, where he had been for some time
an inmate, nearly if not quite, a centenarian.

CHAPTER XVI.

On the opposite side of Spring Hill there was until 1890 a building with a front on Summer street, but there was a tenement on its easterly end which must be considered in connection with Market street.   This tenement in my youth was occupied by Clement Bates, a native of Hanover, who came to Plymouth and married Irene Sanger, daughter of Thomas Burgess, the keeper of the Plymouth lighthouse, who, because he always wore a red thrum cap, was called Red Cap Burgess. He married in 1824 Betsey Burgess, a sister of his first wife. He was a caulker, and graver by trade, and in 1831 was chosen sexton by the town, whose duty it was to conduct funerals, take care of the town house, and ring the town bell at such hours, morning, noon and night, as were specified by the town.   After his relinquishment of the management of funerals, which had been taken up by private undertakers, he told me that he had buried thirty-two hundred and fifty persons.   He performed the other duties of his office until his death, July 13, 1885.   It is an interesting fact that after so long a period of business dealings with the material bodies of the dead he became a confirmed believer in the doctrines of Spiritualism.

In my early youth a wooden building standing on the north corner of Market and Summer streets, was occupied as a store by Bridgham Russell, until he was appointed postmaster in 1832.   Mr. Russell was the son of Jonathan and Rebecca (Turner) Russell of Barnstable, and was born in 1793.   He. married in 1822 Betsey, daughter of Jeremiah Farris of Barnstable, and died March 29, 1840.   He was the second Captain of the Standish Guards, succeeding Captain Coomer Weston. The store which Mr. Russell had occupied, was taken down in 1832, and replaced by the present brick building, which was occupied by Alexander G. Nye, and for many years by Samuel and Thomas Branch Sherman.   Samuel Sherman was Town Treasurer from 1835 to 1856, serving one year after I entered, for the first time, the office of selectman, and died October 20, 1857.

The next building was occupied as long ago as I can remember by Osmore Jenkins, who kept a jeweller's store as early as 1830, and after leaving Plymouth became distinguished in his profession. He was born in Mt. Vernon, N. H., September 4, 1815, and died in Melrose, Mass., December 19, 1904. Mr. Jenkins was succeeded by Wm. Morey, who occupied the store many years in making and selling boots and shoes. In those days, especially in winter, it was the universal custom to wear boots, the common close legged boots, in contra distinction to the top boots worn with small clothes. In 1831, when I was nine years old, Mr. Morey made my first pair, and if school hours had not interfered I think I should have watched every stitch and peg in their construction. These boots, now little worn, were first introduced into the peninsular army by the Duke of Wellngton, and are to this day in England called Wellingtons. Why Congress boots, which have largely taken their place, should be so called, is somewhat strange, as similar laced boots have been for many generations worn in Ireland under the name of high-lows and brogans.

Wm. Morey had seven sons, William, born in 1813, John Edwards, 1815, Thos., 1817, Cornelius, 1820, Charles, 1825, Edwin, 1827, and Henry, 1833. Of these Edwin lives in Boston, a successful and well known merchant; Thomas was in 1899 the head of a thriving printing house in Greenfield, and of John Edwards I know nothing, while William, Charles and Henry have been dead some years, and Cornelius died in infancy.

The building extending from the Morey building to High street, was in my youth divided into two tenements. The southerly part was owned and occupied by Samuel Talbot, who bought it in 1826. Mr. Talbot, son of George Talbot of Milton, was born in that town in 1791, and came to Plymouth about 1820. In 1825 he formed a partnership with John Calderwood Holmes in the bakery business in the building in Summer street now occupied by the Misses Rich. Mr. Holmes died May 17, 1826, and Mr. Talbot became associated with George Churchill in the business. I have often seen the room, now a parlor, full of sea biscuit, waiting to be packed in casks and placed on board the whalemen. I remember, too, the two wheeled green baker's cart with America Rogers driving, and the round, warm biscuit which he left at our house nearly every morning, the size and color of which varied with the price and quality of flour. Mr. Churchill was a man of humor, and in speaking one day of the readiness of Plymouth people to catch at new ideas he said, "Yes, Plymouth people will swallow anything. I know that by experience, for I have stuffed them with poor bread a good many years." Nevertheless, those warm biscuits were good, but America Rogers' buns and election cakes were better. Mr. Talbot d'ed September 28, 1883. The northerly part of the building was owned and occupied in my boyhood by John Kempton, a caulker and graver by trade, as a dwelling house and store.

The building on the northerly corner of High street, recently owned by Chas. T. Holmes, was in 1832 the property and home of Samuel Robbins, and later of his son-in-law Robert Cowen. Until June 25, 1870, its southerly end extended about eight feet south of the general line of High street, but on that date the projection was taken by the town and the street line straightened. This projection was occupied in 1831, and later by Albert Leach as a shoemaker's shop, and still later by Eleazer H. Barnes as a candy shop. Outside of the northerly end of the building, was a covered stairway and passage leading to a store in the rear of the main building in which Mr. Robbins kept a store until his death, which occurred July 27, 1838, at the age of eighty-six. It must have been about 1830 that he dislocated his thigh. At that time the means of reducing dislocations were crude, and I remember hearing in the street the terrible groans of the old gentleman while under the hands of the Boston surgeon, who had been sent for to manage the case.

The next building, which belongs to the estate of the late Charles T. Holmes, was occupied as long ago as I can remember on the front by Wm. Brown for the post office on the street floor, while he held the office of postmaster from 1822 to 1832, after which it was occupied by Edward Hathaway for a harness store, and finally by Amasá and Charles T. Holmes. The cellar under the post office was occupied at various times by Henry Flanders, who died May 8, 1835, and later, by James Barnes and others as an oyster shop. In 1829 H. H. Rolfe taught a private school in the room over the post office, and in 1832, Cephas Geovani Thompson, a portrait painter, and native of Middleboro, occupied for a time the same room where he painted portraits of Rev. Dr. Kendall, Capt. Nathaniel Russell and my mother. His son of the same name, was a highly esteemed portrait painter in Boston many years. The Old Colony Hall, a part of the estate in the rear of the main building, was through my youth occupied for various purposes. The Universalist Society after its formation, held services there from 1822 to 1826, when their church was built on Carver street. In 1833 Hiram Fuller taught a private school in the Hall, and many times in my boyhood I attended lectures and exhibitions there, among which were those of Harrington, the ventriloquist. At a later period the hall and the upper part of the main building were occupied by Stephen P. and Joseph P. Brown for a furniture shop and show room. William Brown, above mentioned, died May 9, 1845.

In speaking of Main street in an early chapter I referred to the physical changes which it had undergone within my memory. I propose now to say something about the occupants of its houses. As far back as I can remember the building on the corner of Main and Leyden streets contained a store in the lower story on Main street, a large room or hall on the corner over the store, and a tenement with an entrance on Leyden street. The store was occupied as early as 1825 as a hardware store by James and Ephraim Spooner, who dissolved partnership in 1832, Ephraim continuing in the business. In 1839 John Washburn and William Rider Drew were established in the store in the same business. In 1846 Messrs. Washburn and Drew separated, the former taking a store on the west side of the street, and the latter establishing himself as has been stated in the building on Leyden street, which had been occupied by Steward and Alderman, and Alderman and Gooding. The store after Washburn & Drew left it was divided into two and the corner one was occupied at various times by Benjamin Swift in the watch and clock business, and Edward W. Atwood. The other was occupied by Edward Hathaway and Edward Bartlett, Reuben Peterson and Rich and Weston's express. At a later time both stores were occupied by Weston's express succeeded by their present occupant, the New York and Boston Despatch Express.

It is worthy of notice as showing one of the steps in the progress of the temperance movement that the Plymouth Temperance Society in 1825 placed in the hands of Ephraim Spooner a quantity of intoxicating liquors to be by him given without charge to persons presenting the written prescription of a physician. Mr. Spooner was appointed postmaster in 1840, and again in 1842, after an interval of one year, during which Joseph Lucas held the office. He died April 10, 1887.

The large room over the store was occupied as a school room in 1831 and 1832 by George Partridge Bradford, who taught a mixed school of boys and girls, of whom I was one, and by Wm. Whiting, also, as a school room in 1833. It was later used by private teachers, and often as political campaign headquarters. The tenement was in those days occupied by Oliver Wood, the father of the late Oliver T. and Isaac L. Wood.

Mr. Bradford was the son of Gamaliel Bradford of Boston, and graduated at Harvard in 1825. He prepared for the ministry, but never sought a settlement, devoting himself to the profession of a teacher. Concord was frequently his home, and he possessed that mental temperament which made him a congenial companion of Emerson and Alcott. He died in Cambridge in 1890 at the age of 80.

Mr. Whiting graduated at Harvard in 1833, and while preparing himself for the bar taught a school in Plymouth, and, like the teachers who had preceeded him, George Washington Hosmer, William Parsons Lunt, William H. Lord, Isaac N. Stoddard, Nathaniel Bradstreet, Benjamin Shurtleff, Horace H. Rolfe and Josiah Moore, married a Plymouth wife. Charles Field another teacher, died while his marriage engagement to a Plymouth lady was pending. Mr. Whiting married Lydia Cushing, daughter of Thomas Russell, and became a distinguished leader at the Boston bar. Miss Rose S. Whiting of Plymouth is his daughter. During the Civil war he was for a time the solicitor of the War Department, and published a very able paper on "War Powers under the Constitution," which was taken as a guide in many doubtful questions arising during the war. He died at his home in Roxbury, June 29, 1873.

The next one story building was occupied as far back as my memory goes by Thomas May as a shoe store. He occupied it until 1845, when Henry Howard Robbins took the store and occupied it as a hat store, and was succeeded by Harrison Finney, who occupied it many years for the sale of shoe kit and findings, until his death, July 27, 1878.   Mr. Robbins died December 19, 1872.

The next store now occupied by Benjamin L. Bramhall, was before 1830 occupied by Ezra Collier, who kept a bookstore and circulating library.   In 1829 he formed a partnership with William Sampson Bartlett, under the firm name of Collier and Bartlett, which was dissolved the next year.   Mr. Collier came to Plymouth about 1820, and married in 1823 Mary, daughter of Thomas and Mehitable (Shaw) Atwood, and I think removed from town after the dissolution of his partnership.

Mr. Bartlett continued the business in the same store until 1840, when he moved into the store built by him now occupied by Finney's pharmacy in the building owned by Dr. Benjamin Hubbard. Anthony Morse succeded Mr. Bartlett, and occupied it for a grocery store.   It was later occupied by Benjamin Bramhall for a short time, and by William L. Battles for a year, when it was again occupied by Mr. Bramhall, who was succeeded by his son, Benjamin L., its present occupant. Benjamin Bramhall died August 15, 1882.

The next store was occupied by Thomas and George Adams as a hat store from 1828 until the dissolution of their partnership in 1830.   Thomas Adams continued the business until 1832, when he gave up business, and not long after was employed as a salesman in the hat store of Rhodes on the corner of Washington and Court streets in Boston.   He was a son of Thomas and Mercy (Savery) Adams, and married Eunice H. Bugbee of Pomfret, Vermont.   He was not open to the charge of promoting race suicide as the following record of his children shows, to wit: Mary E., born in 1832; Thomas H., 1834; Frederick E. and Frank W., twins, 1836; Luther B. and Ellen, twins, 1837; Miranda B., 1839; Harriet E., 1841; James O. and another twin, 1841; David B., 1845; Walter S. and another twin, 1848, Adelaide V., 1849.

George Adams, brother of Thomas, removed to Boston, and became the well known and successful founder of the Boston directory.   He returned to Plymouth in 1846, and occupied the old store.   He married in 1829 Hannah Sturtevant, daughter of Ephraim Harlow, and had George W., 1830, who married

Mary Holland of Boston; Hannah, 1832, who married Dr. Edward A. Spooner of Philadelphia; Sarah S., 1840, and Theodore Parker, 1845, who married Ellen B., daughter of Joseph Cushman. He died October 4, 1865, at the age of fifty-eight.

In 1835 Henry Howard Robbins moved his hatter's business to this store, and it was later occupied by John Perkins & Reuben Peterson, hatters, Weston & Atwood, clothiers, and Wm. F. Peterson and others.

My first recollection of the OLD COLONY MEMORIAL was when it was located in one or both rooms over the two stores just mentioned. James Thurber was then the publisher, and Benjamin Drew was one of the type setters. The paper was ready for the press by seven o'clock every Friday evening, and I remember well how much I enjoyed as a boy the permission to go to the office after supper and help fold the papers. The machine used in printing was the old Washington hand press which, tended by two men, could print one side at the rate of two or three hundred in an hour. Today a Hoe press is furnished with a roll of paper more than four miles long, and will print fifteen thousand complete newspapers in an hour.

The next store was in 1834, occupied by James G. Gleason as a barber's shop, to which was attached a small room for the sale of soda and ice cream. Up to 1828 the barber shop of Jonathan Tufts, which stood on Church street, where the office of Jason W. Mixter, now stands, was the gathering place where the gossips of the town exchanged their news of the latest scandal. His shop had been for many years the place of deposit for curiosities which shipmasters collected in various parts of the world. Both the gossip and the curiosities were inherited by the Gleason shop, and finally descended to the shop of Isaac B. Rich and John T. Hall, Mr. Gleason's successors.

Sometimes practical jokes were played in the shop more entertaining to the lookers on than to the victims. One of the habitues was William Bradford, a manufacturer of cotton bats, a man of humor, always ready to play a part in any prank. One day while Mr. Bradford was in the shop, Mr. Gleason went out on an errand and a countryman came in to be shaved. Bradford with a wink at the crowd said, "All right sir, your turn next, sit right down." He gave the man a bountiful lather, and pulling off the towel said to him, "This is all we do in this department, you will have to go into the next shop to get your shave.   When you go in don't mind the old fellow in the front room, for he is a queer chap, a little off in his head, but go right through into the back room where they do the shaving."   Daniel Gale, the tailor, occupied the next shop, using the front room for cutting out work, and the back room for the sewing women.   Mr. Gale was astonished, and so were the women, but when the angry countryman returned, Bradford had left, and Gleason had to bear the brunt of his mischief. Mr. Hall occupied the store until he purchased the Dr. Warren house on the west side of Main street, which he occupied until his death, September 21, 1885. Among those who have since occupied the store were, Mrs. Mary F. Campbell and Frederick L. Holmes.

CHAPTER XVII.

The last chapter closed with a mention of the various occupants of the building on the east side of Main street, formerly occupied by John T. Hall, and now occupied by a provision store.

The next store was a one story building, which was occupied during my early youth by Deacon Solomon Churchill for a crockery store, and for some reason, good man as he was, the boys selected him as a victim of many of their mischievous acts. They would, after tying his door handle, throw gravel against his windows, throw a cat dead or alive into his store, or capturing one of their comrade's caps, toss it inside his door, where a good spanking was the only condition of its release. Deacon Churchill, son of Amaziah and Elizabeth (Sylvester) Churchill was born in Plymouth in 1762, where he married Betsey Bartlett, and died in Perry, Ohio, April 10, 1835. Daniel Gale, the tailor, already referred to, succeeded Deacon Churchill, and occupied it many years. Further mention will be made of him as an occupant of a house on the west side of the street.

The next store standing by itself was also a one story building, in my youth occupied as an apothecary shop by Dr. Isaac LeBaron until 1835, when he moved to the corner of Main and North streets. Dr. LeBaron was succeeded by Joseph D. Jones, tinman, who has been already referred to in connection with Market street. The above two one story buildings occupied the sites of the present Leyden Hall building, and the Hubbard building.

After the erection of Leyden Hall building its early occupants were, Joseph Cushman, Alderman & Gooding, on the North side, and Jameson & Company and Benjamin O. Strong on the South side. Mr. Cushman, son of Joseph and Sally (Thompson) Cushman of Middleboro, came a young man to Plymouth and opened a dry goods store on the corner of Main street and Town Square, whence he removed to the Leyden hall building, and continued in business there some years. In December, 1849, he sailed from New York for California, and became a permanent resident on the Pacific coast. He finally settled in Olympia in Washington territory, where he engaged in the lumber and general mercantile business, and held the position of receiver of public moneys. He married in 1835 Sarah Thomas, daughter of Barnabas and Triphena (Covington) Hedge of Plymouth, and died in Olympia, February 29, 1872. Two of his daughters, Mary A., widow of Alfred E. Walker of New Haven, and Ellen Blanche, who married Theodore Parker Adams, live in Plymouth.

The firm of Alderman & Gooding consisted of Orin F. Alderman and George Gooding. They had previously occupied a store where John E. Jordan's hardware store now is. Mr. Alderman came to Plymouth from some town unknown to me, and married Eliza Ann, daughter of John and Deborah (Barnes) Gooding of Plymouth, and sister of his partner. After closing his business in Plymouth, he removed to Framingham, where he and his wife are still living.

George Gooding, son of John and Deborah Gooding, above mentioned, was born in Plymouth in 1822. He was my playmate and schoolmate, and I may say my comrade in arms, as we were members of a boys' military company, of which he was captain, and I was lieutenant. In our Saturday afternoon parades with drum and fife, we flattered ourselves that we excited the admiration of the misses in their teens, but we failed to be appreciated by our fellow citizens, for to their shame, be it said, they did not even offer us a thirty thousand dollar armory for our use. Mr. Gooding married Eliza Merrill of Concord, N. H., and died in Plymouth, March 5, 1850.

Mr. Jameson, the head of the firm of Jameson & Co., came to Plymouth from one of the Bridgewaters and died in 1854.

Benjamin Owen Strong, son of Ely and Betsey (Baldwin) Strong was born in Granville, Mass., February 25, 1832, and came to Plymouth in the autumn of 1851, when nineteen years of age. He first held the position of clerk in the Mansion House at the corner of Court and North streets, then conducted by N. M. Perry, but in May, 1852, he became a clerk in the dry goods store of Jameson & Company. On the death of Mr. Jameson in 1854, Mr. Strong assumed control of the store. He later bought out the establishment, and from that time to this has carried on the dry goods business with honor and success. He married Betsey J. Chute of Newburyport, and again, February 17, 1891, Elizabeth H. Snow of Orleans. His son, Charles Alexander, became his partner in 1884. As the Nestor of the merchants of Plymouth, I make an exception of him among the living, and award to him a special notice.

The next building was erected by Wm. Sampson Bartlett in 1840, and the store on the lower floor was occupied by him as a book store until 1846, when he removed to Boston. Dr. Benjamin Hubbard has since that time occupied the tenement in the building as his home, and has also until a very recent date occupied the store as an apothecary shop.

The next building was occupied from 1826 to 1832 by Isaac Sampson as a dry goods store, and the late James Cox was his assistant. Mr. Sampson was the son of Benjamin and Priscilla (Churchill) Sampson of Plymouth, and married in 1822, Elizabeth, daughter of William Sherman. The late George Sampson of the firm of Sampson and Murdock, publishers of the Boston Directory, was his son. He died May 7, 1832, forty-two years of age. After the death of Mr. Sampson the store was occupied by various tenants, among whom were Reuben Peterson, who kept a hat store, Calvin Ripley, James Barnes, Stephen Lucas and Charles H. Churchill, who preceded D. Flanzbaum, a tailor, the present occupant.

A part of the store was set off as a separate room, and has been occupied at various times by Winslow S. Holmes and others. Calvin Ripley died May 1, 1874.

The next building was occupied for some years previous to 1852 by Thomas Davis and Wm. S. Russell, under the firm name of Davis & Russell, who kept a general store for the sale of dry goods and crockery. The importation of the Pilgrim plates was due to their enterprise. The tradition that they were manufactured expressly for use at the dinner in 1820 on the anniversary of the "Landing" is not correct. Messrs. Davis & Russell, impressed with the idea that an invoice of Pilgrim china would prove a profitable venture, ordered of Enoch Wood & Sons of Burslem, England, a considerable quantity of large sized plates and two sizes of pitchers. Happening to arrive not long before the celebration, they were hired for the dinner, and afterwards sold as mementoes of the occasion. They took so well with the public, and brought such high prices, that the firm ordered an additional invoice, which included in all six sizes of plates and the same two sizes of pitchers, and the pieces have been scattered far and wide, the market value in bric-a-brac stores being twelve dollars for the large plates, and fifteen and ten dollars for the two sizes of pitchers, while the small sized plates are unobtainable. There is a group of these various sizes owned by a collector in New York, a photograph of which may be seen in Pilgrim Hall. At this time it is impossible to distinguish . the pieces originally imported from those which came afterward.

Davis & Russell were succeeded by John S. Hayward in 1827, who continued in the dry goods business until 1831. The store was afterwards occupied by the Plymouth Institution for savings, the Old Colony Insurance Co., and a reading room, until 1842, and was bought in 1847 by Jason Hart, who moved his dry goods business from Summer street, and occupied the store until 1856, when Leander Lovell and John H. Harlow, under the firm name of Lovell & Harlow, became its occupants. John H. Harlow and Albert Barnes succeeded Lovell & Harlow, they in turn being succeeded by Wm. Atwood, clothier, the predecessor of H. H. Cole, the present occupant. Jason Hart died February 20, 1874, at the age of seventy-one. The room over the store was occupied at various times by Joseph W. Hodgkins, tailor, Wm. Whiting and Wm. G. Russell, teachers of private schools, Wm. Davis, attorney-at-law, and Stephen Lucas and others, photographers. William Davis died, February 19, 1853, and Mr. Hodgkins died, May 11, 1872.

William G. Russell was the son of Thomas and Mary Ann (Goodwin) Russell, and graduated at Harvard in 1840. He studied law with Wm. Whiting, his brother-in-law, and became an eminent member of the Boston bar. He married in 1847, May Ellen, daughter of Thomas and Lydia (Coffin) Hedge, and died in Boston, February 6, 1896.

The next building was divided into two stores as long ago as I can remember it, and the southerly one was occupied by John Bartlett 3d, as a dry and West India goods store from 1827 to 1846, and the late Joseph Holmes, brother of Mrs.

William Bartlett, was his assistant. Mr. Bartlett was the son of John and Polly (Morton) Bartlett, and married, 1829, Eliza, daughter of Ezra Finney, and lived in the northerly part of the house on Court street, next south of the present house of Capt. Edward B. Atwood. He afterwards removed to Boston, and engaged in the grocery business on the corner of Federal and Purchase streets, and died in 1862. He was the fourth Captain of the Standish Guards, and our townsman, J. E. Bartlett, who lives on Clyfton street, is his son. The next occupant of the store was Bradford & Gardner's express, which suggests a word concerning the Plymouth and Boston expresses. Samuel Gardner, a former driver on the Boston line of stages, was the father of the Plymouth express business. In January, 1846, two months after the opening of the Old Colony Railroad, he started Gardner's express with a booking office in the Pilgrim House on the corner of Middle street. In March, 1846, Edward Winslow Bradford, a former master of the packet Hector, started Bradford's express with an office at No. 4 Main street. After the burning of the Pilgrim House in June, 1846, Bradford and Gardner formed a partnership, and established Bradford & Gardner's express, and occupied the John Bartlett store. After a few years Harvey W. Weston bought Gardner out, and for a short time the firm name was Bradford & Weston. In the meantime Isaac B. Rich started an express with an office in Town Square. Mr. Rich next bought Bradford out, and the firm name became Rich & Weston, being succeeded by Weston alone, who finally sold out to the present company, the New York and Boston Despatch Express. Mr. Rich had immediately before the establishment of his express kept a flour and grain store on Water street. He died March 18, 1874.

Another express was started before the war by Allen Holmes, with an office first in Market street, and later in the old brick building on the corner of Court street. Mr. Holmes sold to Wait, who sold to Snow, who sold to Hubbard, who finally sold to Fowler, who had an office on Middle street. G. A. Holbrook ran an express a short time at an unknown date.

Edward Winslow Bradford, the old partner of Gardner, again started an express about 1870, which continued until his death, December 27, 1874. Still another express was started by Guilford Cunningham, and a man named Cook, which passed into the hands of Frederick W. Atwood.

Nathaniel Bradford, son of Edward Winslow Bradford, formed a partnership in the express business with Freeman E. Wells, who sold out to Simmons & Torrence, the predecessors of the present Torrence express. Benjamin H. Crandon ran an express for a short time with an office on Middle street in the easterly end of the building on the corner.

I know of no occupant of the John Bartlett store after Bradford & Gardner, until William H. Smoot occupied it as a restaurant. Mr. Smoot stuttered badly, as did our townsman, Anthony Morse, but neither knew the other's defect in speech. Not long after he began business Mr. Morse came one day into the shop and said, "Mr. Sm-o-o-t have you any ice cr-r-eam?" "Y-y-y-es—have s-s-ome?" "D-d-d-amn your ice c-r-r-eam," said Morse, very indignant at such an insult, and went out shutting the door with a slam. The more recent occupants, Jas. E. Dodge, who died February 20, 1888, Mr. Richards, Mr. McCoy, Martin Curly, and Manley E. Dodge, are well known to my readers.

The small store on the corner was occupied as a boot and shoe store by Bartlett Ellis from 1824 to 1831. I remember as a boy seeing in his store a box of India rubber shoes packed in sawdust, the first ever seen in Plymouth, having been imported in Boston in small quantities in the rough state from Para. This was before the process was discovered of making the rubber pliable, and the shoes were as stiff as iron, requiring to be warmed before a fire before they could be put on. Mr. Ellis was succeeded by Ephraim Bartlett, and Henry Mills, both in the same business, and later by E. D. Seymour, tailor. The more recent well known occupants have been Caleb Holmes, who died June 21, 1878, Charles H. Snell, Harrison Holmes, and the recent occupant, Henry C. Thomas, in the market business. The room over the store was occupied by the *Old Colony Democrat* in 1833, conducted by Benjamin H. Crandon and Thomas Allen, and in 1834 by *We The People*, conducted by C. A. Hack and Horace Seaver.

On the corner of Main and Middle streets there stood as long ago as I can remember the Plymouth Hotel, built by George Drew about 1825, and kept certainly in 1827, and perhaps earlier by James G. Gleason. I remember the hotel in 1828, when my aunt, Mrs. Gideon C. White was boarding there with her four children, while her husband was at sea in command, I think, of the ship Harvest, belonging to Barnabas Hedge. In the summer of the above year a small circus came to Plymouth and performed in a tent pitched in the stable yard on Middle street. Mrs. White's children were going to the circus, attended by William Paty, a brother of the landlord's wife, and I a boy of six years, was permitted by my mother to go with them. While the horses made no impression on my memory, I have a lively recollection of the monkey riding the pony's back. Mr. Gleason, who was the third captain of the Standish Guards, kept the Plymouth Hotel until 1830, when he was succeeded by Ellis Wright, who kept it until 1834.

Capt. Gleason was a portly, jovial landlord, who, I think, came to Plymouth from Middleboro and married in 1816 Lucy T., daughter of Joshua Bartlett, and second in 1820, Asenath, daughter of John Paty. He was at different times landlord of the Plymouth Hotel, hairdresser on Market street, barber on Main street, landlord of the Mansion House on the corner of Court and North streets, and a purveyor of oysters and clam chowder in various places. He was a man of humor, always ready with an answer turning the laugh away from himself. In those days the price of a common drink at the bar was four pence half penny, or six and a quarter cents, but a drink of brandy was nine pence, or twelve and a half cents. One day a stranger called at the bar for a glass of brandy and Gleason in the American fashion gave him the bottle to help himself. To the astonishment of Gleason he filled his tumbler nearly full, and with a little water, drank it with gusto, and placed on the counter a nine penny piece. Gleason gave him back four pence, half penny, and the stranger said: "I thought that brandy was nine pence. "It is," said Gleason, "but we sell half price by wholesale." The stranger took the hint, and insisted on paying a quarter for the extended drink. At another time, while keeping the Mansion House, a passenger by the stage arrived for supper and left after breakfast the next morning. On calling for his bill he found the charge to be five dollars. "Good gracious" said the traveller, "I never paid such a bill as that before." "No," said Gleason, "and I don't suppose you

ever had the honor of stopping at the Mansion House before."
Mr. Gleason died Oct. 6, 1853.

A few days after the Old Colony Railroad was opened
Gleason went down to the railroad station to gratify his curiosity, and seeing a locomotive on a track he climbed on, and while
fumbling about the rods and bars he turned on the steam and
away the engine went.   Gleason hopped off, but fortunately an
engineer on another locomotive attached to a train about to
start for Boston, unshackled his machine and caught up with
the runaway, and brought it back.   "Hem! didn't she whiz,"
said Gleason in telling the story.

Ellis Wright, who succeeded Capt. Gleason, was a Plympton
man, son of Isaac and Selah (Ellis) Wright, and after leaving
Plymouth removed to Boston.   The hotel had a good hall in
the second story, which was much used for dancing schools
and cotillion parties and exhibitions of various kinds.   I attended my first dancng school in that hall, and have danced
there at many cotillion parties since.

In 1834 Danville Bryant became the landlord, and from that
time until it was burned, the hotel was called the Pilgrim
House.   Whence Mr. Bryant came, or where he went, I have
no means of knowing, but he continued in the hotel until 1840.
His daughter, Abigail, married Horace B. Taylor.   It was
during his administration, and that of Mr. Wright, that the famous line of stages to and from Boston was established, and
continued until the opening of the Old Colony Railroad in 1845.
As I remember it the line consisted of an accommodation and a
mail stage.   The accommodation left Plymouth at six or seven
o'clock each day, and returning left Boston at two, going
through West Duxbury, Pembroke, Hanover, West Scituate,
Weymouth Landing, Quincy and Dorchester.   The mail
stage left Boston at five o'clock in the morning, arriving at
Plymouth at ten-thirty, when a return stage took passengers
from the Cape, arriving by the stage driven by Wm. Boyden,
and the Boyden stage took the passengers bound to the Cape.
The route of the mail stage would be one day the same as that
of the accommodation, and the next it would turn off at West
Scituate and go through Hingham to Quincy, and so into
Boston.   The mail stage carried two pouches, one containing the through mail from the Cape, and the other containing

the way mail, which would be thrown off at the various post offices to deliver and receive the mail to and from that office.

I remember the various lines of stages running every day into and out of Boston, and I can say that no better horses or better drivers could be seen than those on the Plymouth line. There were in Boston various stage houses, Wilde's on Elm street, Doolittle's City tavern on Brattle street, the Washington House on Washington street, and others. The Plymouth stage office was in the City Tavern on Brattle street, and there orders were left for calls by the stage for passengers. The business on the line was good, and extra stages were frequently required to meet the demand. It was a busy scene in front of the Pilgrim House about half past ten on the arrival and departure of the Boston and Cape stages, and Geo. Drew, the manager of the line, might be seen here and there with a red bandana handkerchief hanging from his teeth, giving directions and orders.

The drivers were as good as the horses. There were Capt. Woodward, Granville Gardner, Samuel Gardner, Benjamin Bates, John Bates, Asa Pierce, Phineas Pierce, Mr. Burgess, Mr. Orcutt, and I think at one time, Jacob Sprague. John Bates was perhaps the king of the line, wearing in suitable weather, a white beaver hat, a brown suit of clothes, well polished boots, and neat gloves. He was no more proud of his team than the team was of him. After the line was broken up by the railroad he drove for some years what was called a Roxbury hourly, running with its alternate mate from that part of Washington street between State street and Cornhill, to the Norfolk house and back. He always drove four horses, and his omnibus was not far from twenty feet long, and to reach his Boston station he would drive up Court street and down Cornhill. Mr. Bates married in 1827 Hannah S., daughter of John Faunce of Plymouth, but I know neither the place or date of his death.

Another estimable and much respected driver was Phineas Pierce, the father of Phineas Pierce, now a retired merchant in Boston, and a recent member of the School Committee in that city, and a trustee of the Boston Public Library. He married in 1829 Dorcas M., daughter of Caleb Faunce of Plymouth, and died August 10, 1841. His death was a sad one.   He stopped at Hanover to take a passenger, and in strapping the trunks on the rack of the stage he stood on the hub of the hind wheel, and throwing himself back with his whole weight on the strap, the strap broke, and falling to the ground, he was instantly killed.

There were other lines of stages within my recollection running to New Bedford, Middleboro and Bridgewater, with headquarters at Bradford's and Randall's taverns in which Oliver Harris, Theophilus Rickard and Henry Carter and others were employed as drivers.   Mr. Carter, who drove the Bridgewater stage some years, married in 1833, Maria Bartlett Banks, and for many years before his death he was the Plymouth station master of the Old Colony Railroad.   Mr. Harris came from New Bedford and married in 1835 Ruth Rogers (Goddard) Fish, widow of Samuel Fish, and daughter of Benjamin Goddard of Plymouth.   Our late townsmen, Capt. Wm. O. Harris and Christopher T. Harris, were his sons.

The dancing school which I attended in the Plymouth Hotel, was kept by F. C. Schaffer in 1833 and 1834.   There were no local dancing masters in those days, and professionals occupied the field, and as the lawyers say, followed the circuit. They would arrange schools in different towns for five afternoons and evenings in the week, and drive from one to another, reaching their homes on Saturday.   There were other professionals who preceded and followed Mr. Schaffer, among whom were S. Whitney in 1828, and Lovet Stimson in 1830, who taught in Burbank's hall on Middle street.   At the rear end of the Burbank house, which stood immediately above the present house of Winslow S. Holmes, there was a two story projection, the lower part of which was occupied by Samuel Burbank's bake house, above which was the hall in question. All I remember of the schools in that hall is that on the closing night of the term in one or the other, when pupils were permitted to dance until twelve o'clock, and invite their friends, a terrific thunder storm set in before midnight with heavy rain and fearful lightning, which continued so that pupils and parents, my mother with the rest, were unable to reach home until the small hours of the morning.   In those days it was the fashion for women to wear as stiffeners in their corsets busks made of wood or whalebone or steel, and doubtless on that as on similar occasions, those who wore steel drew them deftly from their waists, and put them where the lightning would fail to find them.

While Danville Bryant was keeping the Pilgrim House, men more or less generally adopted the fashion of wearing skin tight trousers spreading closely over the instep and fastened with a strap under the foot. The most conspicuous persons in Plymouth to adopt this fashion were Mr. Bryant and Capt. Simeon Dike. Of course the trousers and boots had to be put on and off together, thus making the fashion too trouble-some to last, and by a process of evolution the cloth or leather gaiters followed. It is as true in dress as in other things that one extreme follows another, and so the next fashion for men was for loose trousers with full plaited or gathered bodies.

In 1840 the Pilgrim House passed into the hands of Francis J. Goddard, who kept it two or three years, and was succeeded by Stephen Lucas, who again was succeeded in 1845 by Joseph White. Of course Mr. Goddard, son of Daniel and Beulah (Simmons) Goddard, is remembered by most of my readers. Mr. Lucas was a man of varied occupations during his long life. A wheelwright by trade, he kept several kinds of stores later, a stable on School street, the Pilgrim House, a photo-graph saloon, and last a fruit store, as the predecessor of Charles H. Churchill on Main street. He was the son of Sam-uel and Jemima (Robbins) Lucas of Carver, and married in 1820 Rebecca Holmes of Plymouth, and died November 23, 1888. Joseph White, previous to his taking the hotel, had a stall in the Plymouth market. The Hotel was burned June 20, 1846, and Mr. White left Plymouth and carried on a board-ing house in Boston on the corner of Bedford and Lincoln streets.

The Pilgrim House was burned as I have stated, June 20, 1846. I was in Europe at the time, but my letters from home told me about the midnight fire, and about the appearance on the scene of Dr. Wm. J. Walker, a director of the Old Colony Railroad, in his drawers. He was occupying for the summer the house on North street now occupied by the Misses Russell.

After the Masonic building, then called the Union building, was built on the site of the Pilgrim house, one of its first ten-ants was Dr. Samuel Merritt, already fully referred to in a former chapter, who occupied the two rooms on the corner, one for his office, and one for his sleeping room.   After Dr. Merritt went to California in 1849, the rooms were occupied successively by Dr. F. B. Brewer, dentist, Dr. Robert D. Foster, and Dr. Sylvanus Bramhall, also dentists, and by Dr. James L. Hunt.   Winslow S. Holmes at one time occupied a barber shop in a rear room on Middle street, and also at one time, Charles T. May and Lysander Dunham had shops in the northerly Main street room.   The other occupants of the street floor and basement, many of whom will be recalled by my readers, have been too numerous to mention.   The corner room upstairs was occupied in 1850 by Wm. H. Spear, attorney-at-law, and the other room, together with the hall, called Union Hall, was used by the Standish Guards.   Until 1869, when the building came into the possession of the Masons, the hall was used for miscellaneous purposes, including dancing schools kept by Wm. Atwood and others, cotillion parties, lectures and exhibitions.

The next site, on which the engine house stands, was occupied farther back than 1830 by a dwelling house, in which lived on the south side Dr. Nathan Hayward, and on the north side two of my great aunts, Miss Hannah White, who died Jan. 3, 1841, at the age of ninety-four, and her sister, Mrs. Joanna Winslow, who died in May, 1829.

Dr. Hayward was the son of Nathan and Susanna (Latham) Hayward of Bridgewater, and in 1793-4 was a surgeon in the United States Army, under Major General Anthony Wayne in the war against the western Indians.   In 1795 he married Anna, daughter of Pelham and Joanna (White) Winslow, and settled in Plymouth.   He was at one time in partnership with Dr. James Thacher, and with him was instrumental in establishing the first stage line to Boston in 1796.   He was my mother's family physician, and I have a vivid recollection of his administration to my rebellious stomach of senna and salts, tincture of rhubarb and castor oil, and also of that instrument fearfully and wonderfully made with which he occasionally extracted a tooth.   He was appointed in 1814 by the Governor sheriff of Plymouth county, and continued in office until 1843.   His youngest son, George Partridge Hayward, now living in Boston, was named after his predecessor in office, George Partridge of Duxbury. Dr. Hayward in 1831 formed a professional partnership with his nephew, Dr. Winslow Warren, and died June 16, 1848.

Pelham Winslow, the husband of Mrs. Joanna Winslow, was a son of General John and Mary (Little) Winslow, well known as the officer in command of the expedition for the removal from Acadia of the neutral French, and married in 1770 Joanna, daughter of Gideon and Joanna (Howland) White. He graduated at Harvard in 1753. In 1768 he and James Hovey of Plymouth were the only barristers at law in Plymouth County, thus holding a position at the bar above that of either Attorney-at-law or counsellor. At the coming on of the revolution he adhered to the crown, and after the evacuation of Boston, joined the British Army in New York, where he was appointed paymaster general. He died on Long Island in 1783, leaving in Plymouth his widow and two daughters, Anna above mentioned, who married Dr. Hayward, and Mary, who married Henry Warren. With little means of her own, and wishing to do what she could to maintain herself and family, her father, Gideon White, who owned the house in question, built an addition, coming out to the sidewalk, and fitted up the lower story for her store. The last time I saw the old lady she and her sister, after taking tea at our house, fitted out for home with a lantern, which in those days everybody carried on dark evenings, as there were no street lights of any kind. An incident which occurred many years after in one of the financial panics, recalled her to my mind. Mr. Wm. R. Sever, county treasurer, came to me one day in great distress, because he was unable to borrow at any of the banks ten thousand dollars to meet county obligations coming due, and asked me to help him. I went to Boston, and, knowing that it would be useless to apply at any bank, went to see Mr. Ebenezer Francis, living in Pemberton Square, who with Abbot Lawrence, Robert G. Shaw and Peter C. Brooks, were the only persons in Boston rated at a million, while now you can't turn a corner without running against a millionaire. "No, Mr. Davis, I cannot loan the money to the county," Mr. Francis said in answer to my application. "I am a poor man. I have one hundred thousand dollars lying in the old Boston bank, drawing no interest." "But," said I, "here is a good opportunity to place a portion of it at interest." "But I don't like the security, I can't put every man in the county in jail." "May I ask what you call good security" I rejoined. "Yes, sir," with an emphasis which showed his business training at a time when commercial honor was more potent than law—"a note based on a business transaction signed by the buyer and endorsed by the seller." But I got my money much to the joy of Mr. Sever, and the obligations of the county were paid.

Before I left he asked me if I had ever heard of a Mrs. Joanna Winslow, and he was interested to learn that she was my great aunt. More than fifty years ago he said he kept a store on Washington street, where she bought for her store pins and needles and ribbon, buttons and laces for her stock in trade. "She was very much of a lady," he added, and was remembered by him always with pleasure. It was a surprise to him to learn that Judge Charles Henry Warren, whom he knew very well, was her grandson.

The interview presented to my mind two transitions in the shifting scenes of life—one from the home of gentle blood to the little store, and the other from the little store to the mansion of the millionaire.

After the death of Miss Hannah White in 1841, William S. Russell moved into the part of the house which had been occupied by her and made it his home with his family until his death, and after the death of Mrs. Dr. Hayward the house was occupied for a time by the Old Colony Club, until it was bought by the town. The little store was abandoned by Mrs. Winslow after a few years' occupancy, and used as a store by James LeBaron. As far back as I can remember it was occupied by John Thomas, attorney-at-law, who was succeeded by Gustavus Gilbert, also an attorney, who occupied it until 1845. In that year William S. Russell occupied it as a grocery store, followed by Miss Priscilla Hedge with a circulating library. Capt. Eleazer Stevens Turner then occupied it as a grocery store, succeeded by Pelham Winslow Hayward, who had his office there until the town bought the estate.

Gustavus Gilbert was a son of David Gilbert, an attorney-at-law in Mansfield, who graduated at Harvard in 1797. Mr. Gilbert came to Plymouth not far from 1830, and married Caroline Eliza, daughter of Dr. Isaac LeBaron. He practiced law in Plymouth many years, and died September 1, 1865.

William S. Russell was a son of James and Experience (Shaw) Russell, and married in 1820 Mary Winslow, daughter of Dr. Nathan Hayward. After the firm of Davis & Russell in Plymouth, of which he was a member, was dissolved in 1827, he moved to Boston, and for a time was in the wholesale dry goods business in Central street, the senior member of the firm of Russell, Shaw & Freeman. After the dissolution of the partnership in 1829, he formed a partnership with Wm. Sturtevant in the same business, which continued two years, when he continued the business in partnership with Andrew L. Russell. When the last firm discontinued business he went to Illinois as the representative of parties in Plymouth and Boston, owners of land in that state, and after his return settled in Plymouth. In 1846 he was chosen Register of Deeds for Plymouth County, and continued in office until his death. He was a careful student of Pilgrim history, and by the publication in 1846 of a "Guide to Plymouth and Recollections of the Pilgrims," and in 1855 of "Pilgrim Memorials and Guide to Plymouth," made valuable contributions to Pilgrim literature. He died in Plymouth, February 22, 1863.

CHAPTER XVIII.

I remember the occupants of the building north of the engine house as far back as 1828. On the 9th of July in that year, I was playing on the sloping cellar door, while the funeral procession of Henry Warren was forming in front of the next house. The house in question was occupied on the north side by David Turner, and on the south side down stairs by Mrs. Grace (Hayman) Goddard, and her sister, Abigail Otis, and up stairs on the south side by Betsey Morton Jackson, and her sister, Maria Torrey Jackson, daughters of Woodworth Jackson. Betsey Morton Jackson died June 10, 1827, and her sister Maria became one of the family of my grandmother, after her removal to Boston, and died in Boston, May 18, 1856.

David Turner was a son of David and Deborah (Lothrop) Turner, and married in 1793 Lydia Washburn. I remember him well with his military walk and bearing. His pew was in the northwest corner of the old church, and I can see him now entering by the north door and marching up to his seat with a soldierly air and step.   .

Mrs. Goddard and Miss Otis were daughters of John and Hannah (Churchill) Otis of Plymouth. Grace Hayman married in 1796 John Goddard, a surgeon in the United States Navy, who while serving on board the sloop of war Boston, died at Gibralter, June 15, 1802, at the age of thirty-two years. She had two daughters: Harriet Otis, born in 1797, who married Abraham Jackson, and Mary, who married Arthur French of Boston. Mrs. Goddard, as long as I knew her, kept a little store in the southerly corner room now occupied by a furniture store, which was once the law office of James Otis, the patriot, and died February 8, 1851, and her sister Abigail died February 11, 1857.

Not many years after the death of David Turner, his part of the house was occupied some years by James Thurber, who came to Plymouth in 1832, and conducted until his death, the OLD COLONY MEMORIAL. That paper, under his management, had able contributions to its columns, and held a high position among the country newspapers of the state. Mr. Thurber was an ardent Whig, and during the political campaigns of the period, exerted a potent influence on the voters of Plymouth county. I knew him well, and from the time when as a boy I assisted on Friday evenings in folding newspapers in his office, until his death I enjoyed his friendship. He married in 1831 Elizabeth, daughter of Asa Danforth of Taunton, and sister of Allen Danforth of Plymouth, and had Elizabeth 1832, and in 1839 James Danforth, Treasurer of the Plymouth Savings Bank. He moved into the house in question from the house where he had lived some years on the corner of Leyden and Market streets. Mr. Thurber died May 20, 1857. Among the tenants of the house in later times were Wm. H. Spear, John Perkins, John Morissey and Mrs. Thomas Atwood, and the stores have been occupied by Keith and Cooper, pharmacists, J. W. Cooper, pharmacist, the Loring pharmacy, by Baumgartner, James B. Collingwood & Sons, and W. N. Snow, all furniture dealers.

On the south side of the dwelling house on the corner of North street, was a yard with a chaise house and stable in its rear. In 1839 Allen Danforth bought the yard and outbuildings and built the house now occupied by the post office in which he lived until his death.

He was a son of Asa and Deborah (Thayer) Danforth of Taunton, where he was born, January 18, 1796, and married December 30, 1818, Lydia Presbry, daughter of William Seaver of that town. In 1821 he established in Taunton the *Old Colony Reporter*, edited by Jacob Chapin, the first number of which was issued April 4, in that year. In the spring of 1822 he came to Plymouth and established the OLD COLONY MEMORIAL, the first number of which was issued to two hundred and twenty-three subscribers, May 4, in that year. In its early years the MEMORIAL occupied a chamber in Market street, over the store of Antipas Brigham. In 1836 he gave up the management of the paper to his brother-in-law, James Thurber, the printing office being then located on Main street.

The Plymouth Institution for Savings, whose name was changed in 1847 to the Plymouth Savings Bank, and with which Mr. Danforth was for forty-three years identified, was incorporated June 11, 1828, and on the 25th of July Barnabas

Hedge was chosen President, and Benjamin Marston Watson, Treasurer. On the first of August, 1829, the same officers were chosen, but Mr. Watson declining, Mr. Danforth was chosen in his place. The place of business of the bank was at first in the Plymouth Bank on Court street, and as its annual meetings were held in various places, sometimes at the Plymouth Bank, sometimes in the reading room, and again at the Old Colony Bank—it is difficult to locate for some years its actual resting place. I am quite sure, however, that for a time its office was in the room on Main street, in which John S. Hayward had kept a store where H. H. Cole is now in business.

The Old Colony Insurance Company was incorporated March 6, 1835, with a capital of $50,000, and organized with Jacob Covington, president, and Mr. Danforth secretary, and shared an office with the savings institution. On the 2d of June, 1841, the institution for savings jointly with the Plymouth Bank, the Old Colony Bank, and the Old Colony Insurance Company, bought of Thomas and William Jackson a vacant lot on Main street, and erected a building into which those institutions moved in 1842. Mr. Danforth retired from the office of secretary of the Insurance Company in 1853, and subsequently its charter was surrendered.

At the time of the establishment of the Savings Bank, such institutions were comparatively new and general confidence in their soundness had not been established. Facilities for reaching Plymouth were imperfect, and consequently the early growth of the bank was slow. The custom of hoarding, however, was soon abandoned, and the integrity of Mr. Danforth, and his discreet management of the Bank soon attracted a rapidly increasing business. Its deposits, which at the end of five years, had only reached one hundred thousand dollars, amounted according to the last statement made by Mr. Danforth in December, 1871, to $1,759,189.97, while since that time about three-quarters of a million have been added.

Mr. Danforth was a man possessing traits of character which fitted him for the responsible position in which he was placed. He was eminently a man of a judicial mind, and if he had been bred to the law he would have been a leader at the bar, or a distinguished judge. No statute or decision touching financial matters escaped his notice, while court reports, recent or old, relating to banks and banking, were familiar to him. During his life he devoted himself to the welfare of the institution under his care, neither seeking office nor accepting it, except twice as representative, and twice as a member of the board of selectmen. While repeatedly solicited to act as executor or administrator or trustee, he was only in few exceptional cases willing to assume their distracting responsibilities. Mr. Danforth's death was a sad one. He was taken with smallpox, and before many of his fellow citizens were aware of his sickness, he died May 28, 1872. Death came near the midnight hour, and before morning he was buried, unattended, except by those who were immune. A funeral service was held in the Unitarian church, Sunday, June 2, and a fitting tribute was then paid to his memory.

The Warren house on the corner of North street was occupied as long ago as I can remember by Henry Warren, the son of James Warren, of the revolution, whose wife was Mercy Otis, sister of James Otis, and who lived in the house in question. Mr. Warren was born in 1764, and married in 1791 Mary, daughter of Pelham and Joanna (White) Winslow. He was the collector of the port from 1803 to 1820, and died July 6, 1828. He had two daughters and seven sons. Of these James died young, and Mary Ann died unmarried. Marcia married in 1813, John Torrey, and was the mother of Henry Warren Torrey, late professor of history at Harvard. Winslow, born in 1795, graduated at Harvard in 1813, and fitting himself for the practice of medicine settled in Plymouth, where as early as 1831 he became a partner of Dr. Nathan Hayward. His office was for some years at the corner of North street, and there in 1832 I was examined by him as chairman of the School Committee for admission into the High School. He married in January, 1835, Margaret, daughter of Dr. Zacheus and Hannah (Jackson) Bartlett, and after the death of Dr. Bartlett, which occurred December 25, 1835, he moved into his office and occupied it until his death, June 10, 1870. Dr. Warren was not only learned and skillful in his profession, but was also a man of mental culture, familiar with the world's affairs, and decided in his opinions on the great questions of the day; a man of moral culture, conscientious to the last degree; a man of social culture, a true gentleman. Pelham Winslow Warren, born in 1797, graduated at Harvard in 1815, and from 1822 to 1831 was the clerk of the Massachusetts House of Representatives, holding also in 1829 the office of collector of the port of Plymouth, and living in the Warren house. During the last few years of his residence in Plymouth he was the superintendent of the Sunday school in the old church. The general lessons given by him I remember well. They were not mere platitudes, such as are often addressed to children, but interesting and instructive in language adapted to young minds on the handiwork of God in sea, earth and sky. Under his ministrations I became for the first time conscious of a power to think. When the Railroad Bank in Lowell was incorporated he was appointed its cashier, and lived some years in that city. When he retired from the Bank he removed to Boston, and engaged in the banking and brokerage business until his death. He married at Clark's Island in 1825, Jeanette, daughter of John and Lucia (Watson) Taylor, and died in Boston, October 6, 1848.

Charles Henry Warren, born September 29, 1798, graduated at Harvard in 1817. He studied law with Joshua Thomas of Plymouth and Levi Lincoln of Worcester, and settled in New Bedford first as a partner of Lemuel Williams, and later of Thomas Dawes Eliot, and from 1832 to 1839 was District Attorney for the five southern counties of Massachusetts. In 1839 he was appointed Judge of the Common Pleas Court, continuing on the bench until 1844, when he removed to Boston and associated himself with the law firm of Fiske and Rand, composed of Augustus H. Fiske and Benjamin Rand. He appeared as counsel for the defendant in the memorable trial of Rev. Joy H. Fairchild, charged with adultery, and secured his acquittal. Experiencing premonitions of heart disease he abandoned practice, and in 1846 was chosen president of the Boston and Providence railroad, remaining in office until 1867. He was president of the Massachusetts Senate in 1851, and president of the Pilgrim Society from 1845 to 1852. He married Abby, daughter of Barnabas and Eunice Dennie (Burr) Hedge of Plymouth, and died in Plymouth, June 29, 1874. As no monument or stone marks the place of his burial, I think it proper to say that the bodies of both himself and wife were deposited in the Warren tomb.

Richard Warren was born in 1805, and in early manhood embarked in business in Boston and failed, settling with his creditors for a percentage on their claims. He afterwards removed to New York, where he engaged successfully in an auction commission business, confined chiefly to cargo sales of teas, sugar, coffee and other importations. As soon as his recuperated financial condition warranted, he discharged principal and interest the old indebtedness from which he had been formally released. He was president of the Pilgrim Society from 1852 to 1861, and the two great celebrations of the anniversary of the embarkation of the Pilgrims on Monday, the first of August, 1853, and Tuesday, the second of August, 1859, owe their inspiration largely to him. He married first Angelina, daughter of Dr. Wm. Pitt Greenwood of Boston, and sister of Rev. Francis Wm. Pitt Greenwood of King's Chapel, and second, Susan Gore of Boston, and died in Boston, April 12, 1875.

George Warren, born in 1807, in early manhood made several voyages as supercargo in the Havana and Russia trade. The ship Harvest belonging to Barnabas Hedge, in which I think he sailed when bound with sugar, to Russia, would put into Plymouth to obtain a clean bill of health before completing her voyage. He afterwards went to New York and formed a partnership with Ebenezer Crocker, a native of Barnstable, under the firm name of Crocker & Warren. The firm owned the following ships: Alert and Talisman, commanded by Capt. Gamaliel Thomas of Plymouth; Queen of the East, commanded by Capt. Truman Bartlett, Jr., of Plymouth; Raven, commanded by Capt. Bursley of Barnstable; Archer, commanded by Capt. Henry, and the Skylark, commanded by Capt. Bursley. Capt. Thomas made seven voyages to Calcutta and California in their employ, and Mr. Warren told me once that his accounts were always so complete and accurate that he could settle with him a nine months' Calcutta voyage in fifteen minutes. In the great fire which occurred in New York, December 23 and 24, 1835, which burned six hundred and seventy-four houses between lower Broadway and the East River, Crocker & Warren had five hundred bags of saltpetre stored in a warehouse burned, and the cause of repeated explosions which occurred, was for a time a mystery, leading to the often repeated question—will saltpetre explode? It was finally determined that while saltpetre alone is not explosive, the carbon furnished by the burned bags formed an explosive mixture. He married Elizabeth, daughter of Barnabas and Eunice Dennie (Burr) Hedge, and died in New York, November 20, 1866.

Edward J. Warren, born in 1809, was in business in New York many years, a part of the time associated with his brother Richard. Of ready wit and quick eye, and with a familiarity with prices he was one of the most attractive and efficient salesmen in New York. He married Mary, daughter of Wm. G. Coffin, the official head for many years of the Massachusetts land office, and died in New York April 27, 1872.

Soon after Henry Warren died, Madam Warren removed to Boston and lived some years on Allston street, but later returned to Plymouth and occupied successively until her death, the house on Middle street, next to Mr. Beaman's undertaking rooms, and the house on Main street, where the new bank building stands. In 1833 Dr. Isaac LeBaron moved into the Warren house, and in 1836 occupied the apothecary's shop, which Dr. Warren had vacated. I not only remember the gilded pestle and mortar over his door, but also the sugar baker's molasses, which he kept in stock furnished to him by the father or brother of his wife, who owned a sugar refinery in Leverett street, Boston. Almost as dark colored as tar, and nearly hard enough to cut with a knife, it was like the witch's gruel, "thick and slab," and those who now eat buckwheat cakes with honey or syrup, have little idea how good they were eaten with that sugar baker's molasses. Dr. LeBaron died January 29, 1849.

At various times the Warren house was occupied by Mrs. Wm. Spooner, the family of Capt. Wm. Bartlett, and in still later times by the Young Men's Literary Institute, the Public Library, the Custom House, and stores of Wm. Babb, John Churchill, Pratt & Hedge, James C. Bates, Davis and Whiting, N. M. Davis, Edgar Seavey, Allen Holmes and Edward Baker and Allen T. Holmes. Among the transient residents were Mrs. Ann Boutelle, widow of Dr. Caleb Boutelle, and her daughter Anne Lincoln, boarding with one of the permanent families in the house. The south front chamber is hallowed in my memory, for there on the 5th of December, 1835, Anne Lincoln Boutelle, one of my playmates and schoolmates, died in consumption, one too sweet and pure and frail to tread the rough paths of life. I saw her a day or two before she died, with a little table by her bed side laden with gifts of fruit and flowers, which loving friends had sent, and to which I added my own. I never go into the printing office, which includes the chamber in which she died, without recalling her saintly face, her saintly voice, and her saintly spirit, joyous at the thought of journeying home. A memorial of her life and character was published, written by Mary Ann Stevenson, a niece of Mrs. Judge Joshua Thomas, a copy of which if one can be found, I am anxious to obtain.

The Odd Fellows' lot on the corner of Main street and Town Square, included as long ago as I can remember the sites of two houses, one on Main street and one on the square. In this chapter only the occupants of the former will be considered. In 1829 there were two stores on the lower floor facing Main street, and two tenements above. The store on the corner was occupied by Salisbury Jackson, who removed in 1835 to a store, which he had fitted up in his house on the south side of Leyden street. He was succeeded by Joseph Cushman, who has been already noticed.

Mr. Cushman was succeeded by J. M. Perry, agent, and Mr. Perry by Henry Orson Steward and Eleazer C. Sherman in the grain business. Mr. Steward, who previously was a member of the firm of Steward and Alderman, carrying on a dry goods store on Leyden street, came to Plymouth from Connecticut, and married Bethiah, daughter of Samuel West and Lois (Thomas) Bagnall. He finally removed from Plymouth, and after a second marriage, died in Framingham. Mr. Sherman later carried on the business alone, removing to a store at the head of Hedge's wharf, where he remained as long as he continued business in Plymouth. He later became a wholesale dealer, receiving in Plymouth and Boston constant shipments of corn, which were sold in the various markets of the state. He was President of the Old Colony Bank for a time, a member of the executive council, and finally, until his death, President of the Commonwealth National Bank in Boston. He was a son of Levi and Lydia (Crocker) Sherman of Carver, and was born in 1817. He married first Louisa Jane Gurney of North Bridgewater, now Brockton, and second in 1878 Mary

L. (Perkins) Thayer, widow of Edward D. Thayer of Boston, and died in Boston.

Mr. Sherman was succeeded by Thomas Loring, who occupied the store many years. Mr. Loring was son of Ezekiel and Lydia (Sherman) Loring of Plympton, and married Lucy, daughter of Jonathan Parker of Plympton, and died in Boston a few years ago.

The next store was occupied at various times by Bridgham Russell, Jeremiah Farris, Benjamin Hathaway, Henry Howard Robbins, Edward Bartlett, Reuben Peterson, Lewis Peterson, and Wm. F. Peterson. Mr. Russell has already been referred to. Mr. Farris was a son of Jeremiah and Lydia (Eldridge) Farris of Barnstable, and was born in that town in 1810. He married in 1832 Mary, daughter of Nathaniel and Betsey (Woodward) Carver of Plymouth, and settled in Plymouth. He first formed a partnership in the dry goods business with Benjamin Hathaway, and after the partnership was dissolved Mr. Hathaway continued in business, and added the business of making neck stocks. Not long after Mr. Farris joined with Oliver Edes in the manufacture of rivets in North Marshfield, and Plymouth, and finally established the Plymouth Mills, which is still in active business as a corporation under the management of his son-in-law, Wm. P. Stoddard. Mr. Farris was the sixth captain of the Standish Guards. Mr. Hathaway afterwards continued the stock business in other locations, and the first time I ever saw Chief Justice Albert Mason, he was at a bench in Mr. Hathaway's shop cutting out material for stocks. Nothing in the career of Mr. Mason as artisan, lawyer, soldier and Judge, impressed me as much as his resolve while working at his bench to change the current of his life. The flow of the tide never specially impresses me, but when I see the buoys change their slant from East to West, I begin to wonder.

Mr. Mason was the son of Albert T. and Arlina (Orcutt) Mason, and was born in Middleboro, Mass., Nov. 7, 1836. He came to Plymouth in 1853, and after working a short time in Mr. Hathaway's stock factory, he studied law in Plymouth with Edward L. Sherman, and was admitted to the Plymouth bar Feb. 15, 1860. In July, 1862, I was requested to raise two companies to be attached to the 38th Regiment, and recommend

their officers, and in accordance with that request I raised
Companies D and G, and recommended Mr. Mason for the post
of second lieutenant of Company D. He was duly commissioned, and afterwards promoted to be first lieutenant, Captain
and Assistant Brigade Quartermaster. At the close of the
war he resumed practice in Plymouth, and in 1874, removing
to Brookline, was appointed by Governor Washburn a member
of the Board of Harbor Commissioners. In 1879 he was appointed a member of the Board of Harbor and Land Commissioners by Governor Talbot; Judge of the Superior Court by
Governor Long in 1882, and Chief Justice in 1890 by Governor
Brackett. He married November 25, 1857, Lydia F., daughter
of Nathan and Experience (Finney) Whiting of Plymouth.
In 1893 he received from Dartmouth the degree of LL. D.,
and died in Brookline January 2, 1906.

Henry Howard Robbins was the son of Rufus and Mar-
garet (Howard) Robbins, and was born in Plymouth in 1811.
He was a hatter by trade, and at various times occupied other
stores on Main street. My first recollection of him was as a
member of the old Plymouth Band, organized soon after 1830.
The members of the band, according to my recollection, were
Bradford Barnes, leader, clarinet; William Atwood, trom-
bone; John Atwood, serpent; Eleazer H. Barnes, cornopean;
James M. Bradford, bassoon; Samuel H. Doten, clarinet; John
N. Drew, trombone; Nathaniel D. Drew, bugle; Edward Hath-
away, bass drum; Albert Leach, bugle; Thomas Long, fife;
Seth Morton, snare drum; Edmund Robbins, orphicleide;
Henry Howard Robbins, clarinet; Albert Finney, bugle, and
Ellis Rogers, bass drum.

The orphicleide, one of the instruments above mentioned,
had a short career, and has not only gone out of use, but also
almost out of memory. I have been unable to find any one besides myself who remembers it. The proprietor of the music
store in Plymouth never heard of it. No one in the store of
John C. Haynes & Co., of Boston, remembers it, and the leader
of the band in Cambridge on Commencement Day told me that
he had no recollection of it. I remember it distinctly, a brass
instrument about three feet long and six inches in its largest
diameter, and with a curved mouthpiece, resembling somewhat
that of the bassoon. The snare drum, which in its oblong form

stood the test of four hundred years, has since my youth de-generated into the present instrument, which resembles in shape and size a generous Herkimer county cheese. The trombone, probably the ancient sackbut, has held its own, and is the oldest musical instrument now in use. Mr. Robbins married Mercy Morton, daughter of John Eddy, and died December 19, 1872.

Reuben Peterson was the son of Elijah and Abigail (Whittemore) Peterson of Duxbury, and was born in that town about 1788, and married in 1812 Mary, daughter of Benjamin White of Hanover. He was a hatter by trade, and he, as well as his son Lewis, who died October 5, 1878, and grandson, William F., now living, are remembered by my readers.

Edward Bartlett was a harness maker, and occupied this as well as other stores. He was the son of Stephen and Polly (Nye) Bartlett, and was born in Plymouth. He married Betsey Beal of Kingston, and died within the memory of many readers.

Mr. Hathaway above-mentioned, retiring from active business, became a director of the Plymouth National Bank and devoted himself to the care of his ample property. He married in 1828 Hannah, daughter of William Nye of Plymouth, and second in 1857, Sally Barnes, daughter of George W. Virgin, and died July 15, 1880.

In my early youth the second story was occupied by Mrs. Francis Leonard Maynard and Dr. Hervey N. Preston. Mrs. Maynard, the daughter of Major William and Anna (Barnes) Jackson, was born in Plymouth in 1789, and married February 5, 1821, Samuel Maynard. She occupied the whole front of two rooms on Main street, and one room on the northerly side of the building separated from the other two by a narrow entry to which access was had by an outside flight of stairs leading from Main street. The corner room on the square she occupied as a schoolroom, in which she taught boys and girls from about six to ten years of age. I was one of her pupils, and must have entered the school as early as 1828, because I remember seeing the engines go by on their way to the fire which burned the anchor works in that year. Among my fellow pupils I can recall Jane Elizabeth Bartlett, daughter of James Bartlett, who married Thatcher R. Raymond; Mary Holbrook, daugh-

ter of Jacob Covington, who married George H. Bates of
Brooklyn, N. Y., and her sister Martha, Betsey Foster Ripley,
daughter of Deacon Wm. Putnam and Elizabeth Foster (Morton) Ripley, Priscilla and Barnabas Hedge, children of Isaac
L. Hedge, and Francis L. and George Maynard, children of
the teacher. Mrs. Maynard was at that time a widow and an
ideal schoolmistress. She was an accomplished lady, and
taught not only the ordinary branches of a school education, but also sewing and, above all, good manners. I carried away from her school as evidence
of my industry and skill a section of a patchwork bed quilt,
and I trust also some of the fruits of her lessons in deportment.
I may incidentally say that the wife of Rev. Dr. Mann of Trinity church in Boston is a grandchild of Mrs. Bates, one of the
pupils above mentioned. I think that Lucy Ann Jackson, a
granddaughter of Benjamin Crandon, was also a pupil, and
much the oldest girl in the school, who is now remembered
because I recall the dinners she brought to eat at the noon recess. Mrs. Maynard's daughter Frances married a lawyer in
St. Louis, and her son disappeared from my memory soon
after my schoolboy days. The chief punishment in the school
was standing in the corner wearing a foolscap, and one
girl who was exemplary and conscientious in after life, scarcely passed a day without suffering this punishment.

The chambers in the westerly end of the house occupied by
Dr. Preston, were reached by a door with a projecting porch
on the southerly side of the building eight or ten feet from the
town tree, which stood on what is now the gutter in the square.
The stairway from the outside door led to a broad hall above
which separated the school room from Dr. Preston's sitting
room. These two rooms had broad folding doors which were
used when the building was a hotel, and called after its owner,
the Witherell tavern. John Howland, who died in Newport
not many years ago at the age of 97, said in his diary, "that at
the Pilgrim celebration, December 2, 1803, the dinner was held
in a large old house, in which the partitions in the chambers
had been removed to make room for the tables." He doubtless
took it for granted that what were really doorways were open-
ings made for the occasion. I remember well the folding
doors. Dr. Preston came to Plymouth in 1829. He was the

son of Amariah and Hannah (Reed) Preston, and was born in
Bedford, Mass., June 21, 1806. He married a Miss Sargent,
and practiced in Plymouth until his death, which occurred in
Boston July 14, 1837.

The later occupants of the second story were Thomas Loring, Augustus Deming, Lydia Keyes, who died June 30, 1873,
at the age of 75 years, and Jacob Howland, who died June 3,
1876, at the age of 82 years.

The building in question stood ten feet or more back from
the southerly line of the lot, while the building above it on
the square, came out to the sidewalk.   When Odd Fellows'
Hall was built the open space was built upon. About 1850
Mr. Isaac Brewster, representing the owners of the lot, erected
a two story building in the yard on its northeast corner, which
was occupied below for many years by Wm. Bishop, as early
as 1845, as the Old Colony bookstore, and later by Charles
C. Doten, and above by William Davis as a lawyer's office, and
by Benjamin Whiting and Wm. S. Robbins, photographers.
In 1876 it was moved to a lot on Market street, below the bake
house, where it now stands. Odd Fellows' building had three
rooms on Main street. That in the corner was occupied many
years by the postoffice. The next was occupied by Stevens M.
Burbank, H. N. P. Hubbard, and Hathaway and Sampson,
and the third by Z. F. Leach, H. W. Dick, Alfred S. Burbank
and Hatch & Shaw.   The building was destroyed by fire
January 10, 1904.

CHAPTER XIX.

There stood where the Sherman block stands until that block was built a few years ago a two story wooden building occupied in my boyhood by George W. Virgin at the south end, and by Deacon Wm. P. Ripley at the north end. These stores were at various times also occupied by Samuel Shaw & Co., Henry Tilson, Wm. Z. Ripley, Wm. T. Hollis, Southworth Barnes, Stevens M. Burbank, Thomas Holsgrove, Jacob Howland and Albert N. Fletcher.

Samuel Shaw, a son of Southworth and Maria (Churchill) Shaw, was born in Plymouth in 1808, and married Mary Gibbs, daughter of Simeon Dike, and died May 28, 1872. Mr. Virgin, the son of John and Priscilla (Cooper) Virgin, married in 1816, Mary, daughter of Isaac and Lucy (Harlow) Barnes, and died April 19, 1869. Henry Tilson, who died in January, 1835, and Wm. P. Ripley have been already referred to. William Z. Ripley, the son of William P. and Mary (Briggs) Ripley, was born in Plymouth and married Adeline B. Cushman. He finally removed to Boston. William T. Hollis, as already mentioned in connection with the Bradford tavern, was the son of Henry and Deborah (Leonard) Hollis, and was born in Plymouth in 1826. He was jointly with Thomas Prince, proprietor and editor of the OLD COLONY MEMORIAL from 1861 to 1863, and of the *Memorial and Rock* after the *Memorial* was consolidated with the *Plymouth Rock*, jointly with Thomas Prince and George F. Andrews, from 1863 to 1864. He died unmarried at the Plymouth Rock Hotel only a few years ago. Southworth Barnes, son of William and Mercy (Carver) Barnes, was born in Plymouth, and married in 1833, Lucy, daughter of John and Lydia (Mason) Burbank. After his death, which occurred October 29, 1861, his store was taken by Stevens Mason Burbank, nephew of his wife, who married in 1851, Cornelia, daughter of Samuel and Rebecca (Bradford) Doten. The rooms over the stores in the building in question were occupied by various persons at various times for miscellaneous purposes. Among the occupants were the Plymouth Anti-Slavery Society, Thomas May, Benjamin F. Field and Abel D. Breed, tailors, Benjamin Hathaway, manufacturer of neck stocks, Clary and Burr, barbers, Dr. Sanborn, dentist, the *Plymouth Free Press*, newspaper, P. T. Denney, and N. A. T. Jones, tailors, Thomas B. Drew and Thomas D. Shumway, dentists.

The occupant of the next house from 1828 to 1837 was Daniel Gale, a tailor whose shop on the other side of Main street has been already mentioned. He was a son of Noah and Rebecca Gale, but where he was born and when, I do not know. He married Elizabeth, daughter of Edward Winslow of Duxbury, and probably about 1837 moved away from Plymouth, as I find no record of his death. Like all men in his line of business in localities too small for keeping an assortment of cloth, he was only a tailor, and not a draper. Customers furnished their own cloth, and by an unwritten law the tailor was entitled to the remnants from which in time considerable profit accrued. These remnants were universally, in Plymouth at least, called cabbage. Hence the word cabbage as applied in the sense of stealing or, to use a milder phrase, of taking possession of. Mr. Gale, after a residence of some years in Plymouth, built the block of houses between Sandwich street and the Mill pond, which in my boyhood was known as Gale's Cabbage, implying that it was built from the profits of his remnants.

Another house somewhat pretentious in style, received a name suggested by a practice more reprehensible than one which custom permitted. The owner was often employed as a surveyor to run out large lots of woodland into smaller lots for sale. In doing this work certain strips and gores of land would be omitted, and in time sold as his own. The house took the name of Strips and Gores, as having been built from the proceeds of these sales. I mention neither the house nor the name of its owner, because like many other stories, the charge may have no foundation in fact, and I have no desire to taint his memory. The next occupant of the house in question was Dr. Levi Hubbard, the brother of our townsman, Dr. Benjamin Hubbard, and father of Hervey N. P. Hubbard, the librarian of the Pilgrim Society. He was succeeded in 1841 by John Washburn, who occupied a hardware and tin shop on the street floor and the tenement above, many years. Harlow

& Barnes, a firm engaged in the same business, consisting of John C. Barnes and Samuel Harlow, succeeded Mr. Washburn, and were themselves succeeded by Harlow & Bailey, the firm consisting of Samuel Harlow and H. Porter Bailey, and by H. P. Bailey & Bro., the predecessors of the firm now occupying it.

Dr. Levi Hubbard, son of Benjamin and Polly (Walker) Hubbard, was born in Holden, Mass., and after graduating at the medical college of Pittsfield, settled in Medfield, whence he moved to Plymouth in 1839, and occupied the house in question until May 29, 1841, when he moved to the north side of Town Square. In January, 1844, in consequence of a fire in the house he occupied on the square, he removed to the house above the town house, where he remained until November, 1844, when he removed to New Bedford. From New Bedford he went to Chicopee, and in 1849 to California in the ship Edward Everett, sailing from Boston. Returning in 1851 after short residences in Dutchess and Saratoga counties in New York State, he removed to Iowa, and died in Glenwood in that state in 1886. He married in 1837, Luzilla, daughter of Roger Haskell of Peru, Mass., and his son, Hervey N. P. Hubbard was born in the house under consideration, in 1839.

The site of the house next north of the store of Bailey Bros. is memorable as the site of the Bunch of Grapes Inn in the middle of the eighteenth century.

The house now standing was built by Joseph Avery, a bookseller and book binder, who had branch establishments in Worcester and Portland. In school book binding his concerns were extensive and profitable. He came to Plymouth in 1807, and up to 1816 occupied for his business one of the one story buildings on the east side of Main street already referred to. On the 29th of July, 1822, while superintending the erection of the building he incautiously stepped on a loose board and fell from the upper story to the street floor, suffering injuries which resulted in his death on the fourth of the following month at the age of forty-two years. In 1826 the house was sold to Dr. Zacheus Bartlett, who occupied it both for his business and home until his death, which occurred December 25, 1835. Dr. Bartlett was born in South Plymouth, September 20, 1768, and graduated at Harvard in 1789. He studied medicine with Dr. Ezekiel Hersey of Hingham, and settled in his native town. He served his fellow citizens as their Representative in the General Court one or more years, was one of the founders of the Pilgrim Society, and its vice-president from 1828 to 1835, and by invitation of the Town, delivered the oration on the Pilgrim anniversary in 1798. He married in 1796 Hannah, daughter of Samuel and Experience (Atwood) Jackson, and up to the time of his occupancy of the Main street house lived in a house on North street, easterly of the house now occupied by Miss Lydia Jackson. All through my boyhood there was a one story building in the southeast corner of the yard which I have always supposed was his office. As I remember the house it was still owned by Dr. Bartlett, and occupied by various tenants, and the office building was occupied by Thomas Maglathlin, who lived alone. Dr. Bartlett had four children, Sydney, the eminent lawyer who married Caroline Louisa Pratt of Boston, and for many years was recognized as the leader of the Boston bar; Margaret, who married Dr. Winslow Warren, Dr. George Bartlett of Boston, who married Amelia, a daughter of Dr. Wm. Pitt Greenwood of Boston, and Caroline, who married James Pratt of Boston. It is worthy of mention that three Plymouth men, Richard Warren, George Bartlett and Charles L. Hayward, married daughters of Dr. Wm. Pitt Greenwood. The occupation of this building by John T. Hall and others, is too recent to require notice. John T. Hall, son of Eber and Elizabeth (Burgess) Hall, was born in Plymouth and married in 1843 Betsey, daughter of Joab Thomas, and at various times kept a barber shop, a fancy goods store and engaged in insurance business.

The occupation of the site on which the store of George Gooding stands with a tenement over it, possesses unusual interest. About the year 1750 James Shurtleff built a house on the site which in 1789 came into the possession of Caleb Leach, who came to Plymouth from Bridgewater and projected the Plymouth water works, the first water works built in the United States. The company was chartered in 1796, the year after a company was chartered in Wilkesbarre, Penn., but the Plymouth works were constructed before the works of that town. The pipes were yellow or swamp pine logs, ten to twelve feet long, and ten inches in diameter, clear of sap, with a bore from two to four inches in diameter, and sharpened at one end, the other end bound with an iron hoop to prevent splitting when driven into the bore. During the latter years of the company iron connections with a flange in the middle were used.

In 1800 the house came into the possession of Asa Hall, who came from Boston, and fitted up its lower room for a watchmaker's shop. From that time to this, a period of one hundred and six years the site has been identified with the watch making business. In 1802 John Gooding, who came to Plymouth from Taunton, succeeded Mr. Hall in the shop, and in 1805 married Deborah, daughter of Benjamin Barnes. In the next year Mr. Barnes bought the house, and his son-in-law, Mr. Gooding, continued to occupy it, finally receiving in 1836 a deed of the property from Mr. Barnes. Not many years after Mr. Gooding obtained possession, he took down the old house and built the present one. I remember the old house well. The shop door was divided across the middle, the lower part wood, the upper part glass, and in suitable weather, the upper part was swung back. The other doors which I remember like this, were in the harness shop of Barnabas Otis on the south side of Summer street, the second or third above Spring street, the office of Dr. Amariah Preston, next north of the Gooding house, in the old house where Davis building now stands, and in the Solomon Churchill shop on the east side of Main street. Mr. Gooding was the son of Joseph and Rebecca (Macomber) Gooding of Taunton, and was born in 1780. His father was a watchmaker, and he had at least one, and I think two brothers, who followed the same trade. His brother Josiah and nephew Josiah, kept within my recollection a watchmaker's and jeweller's store in Joy's building on Washington street, in Boston, many years. A member of one of the branches of Jos. Gooding's family, Mr. A. W. B. Gooding, married Mary Woodward Barnes, a daughter of Bradford Barnes. Mr. Gooding was a member of the Board of Selectmen from 1825 to 1831, inclusive, a Director of the Plymouth Bank from 1839 to 1865, inclusive, and died September 25, 1870, at the age of ninety years. He had seven children, Deborah Barnes, who married Aurin Bugbee, John, 1808, who married Betsey H., daughter of Ephraim Morton, and became a well known master of the Bark

Yeoman, William, 1810, who married Lydia Ann, daughter of Putnam Kimball, Benjamin Barnes, 1813, who married Harriet, daughter of Charles Goodwin, Eliza Ann, 1818, who married Orin F. Alderman, George Barnes, who married Eliza Merrill of Concord, N. H., and James Bugbee, 1823, who married first, 1851, Almira T., daughter of Henry Morton of Plymouth, and second, Rhoda Ann White of Worcester.   Benjamin Barnes Gooding succeeded his father in business in the same store, and died June 28, 1900, at the age of 87.   Two sons of Benjamin Barnes Gooding, Benjamin W. and George, succeeded their father and continued until the spring of 1905, when their partnership was dissolved, George continuing in the business.   Thus for 103 years, three generations of the Gooding family have carried on the business of watch making on the same site, and as Earl W. Gooding, the son of George, has become associated with his father, it may with some degree of certainty be predicted that a fourth generation will continue the business.   What I have said does not tell the whole story.   James Bugbee, the youngest son of John Gooding, learned the watchmaker's trade, and established himself in Worcester, finally becoming connected with the Waltham watch factory.   His ingenuity and skill soon gave him a leading position in that concern and improvements invented by him in watchmaking machinery for which numerous patents were secured, enabled him to leave at his death a substantial property for his widow and son, who are still living.   The upper part of the building in question is occupied by Dr. E. E. Fuller.

The next house is occupied by two stores and a tenement. As long ago as I can remember, the small store now occupied by Mr. Loring as a watchmaker's shop, was the office of Dr. Amariah Preston, the father of Dr. Hervey N. Preston, previously mentioned.   Dr. Preston was born February 5, 1758, and entered the army in 1777.   After the war he lived a short time in Uxbridge, Mass., and Ashford, Conn., and then removed to Dighton, Mass., to learn a trade.   In 1785 he began the study of medicine, and in 1790 settled in Bedford, where he married October 18, in that year, Hannah Read, and second, May 15, 1796, Ruhamah Lane.   After practising in Bedford forty-three years, he removed in 1833 to Plymouth, and occupied the office in question. He practised in Plymouth until 1845, eight years after the death of his son, and in that year at the age of 87 went to Billerica to live with another son, Marshall Preston, and finally removed with him to Lexington, where he died, October 29, 1853, at the age of ninety-five. I remember well the kindly manner of the old gentleman when I went frequently to his shop to buy gamboge to paint the pictures in my geography.

After the departure of Dr. Preston from Plymouth in 1845, his office was taken by Dr. Samuel Merritt, who has been already noticed in connection with the exodus to California in 1849. After the removal of Dr. Merritt to the Union Hall building, after its erection in 1848, Dr. Ervin Webster succeeded to the office and occupied it until his sad death, and that of his son, Olin E. Webster by drowning in Billington Sea, August 28, 1856. Since that time the office has been occupied by Charles C. Doten, Ichabod Carver, Edward W. Atwood, Benjamin H. Crandon, Sarah Morton Holmes, and B. D. Loring, its present tenant.

The store on the north corner of the building was taken by Bartlett Ellis, for the sale of fancy goods, and for a circulating library, after he gave up his shoe store on the corner of Middle street in 1831, and was occupied by him many years. His successors in the store I think, have been a Mrs. Richards, and the present occupant, Miss F. F. Simmons both in the millinery business.

The tenement above the stores was occupied until 1831 by John Churchill, and after his death, George Churchill, his son, sold the building to Thomas Burgess Bartlett, who occupied it until his recent death. Thomas Burgess Bartlett married Bethiah, a daughter of John Churchill, while Bartlett Ellis, the occupant of the store, married in 1821 for his second wife, Hannah, another daughter of Mr. Churchill.

During my boyhood the house which stood on the site of the Plymouth Savings Bank, was occupied by two brothers, Thomas and William Jackson, substantial merchants for many years, Thomas occupying the southerly part, and William, the northerly. Thomas, called Thomas, Jr., born in 1757, was the son of Thomas and Sarah (Taylor) Jackson, and married in 1788 Sally May. They had three children, Thomas, Edwin and

Sarah, but I have no recollection of any child in their family. He was one of the founders of the Plymouth Bank in 1803, and a subscriber for thirty shares of stock, and was a director from 1826 until his death, August 8, 1837. William Jackson, known as Major Jackson from his rank in the militia, was born in 1763, and married in 1788, Anna, daughter of David Barnes of Scituate, and had Francis Leonard in 1789, who married Samuel Maynard, Leavitt Taylor, 1790, and David Barnes, 1794. He married second in 1795, Mercy, daughter of John and Mercy (Foster) Russell, and had Frederick William, 1798, Anna, 1799, and William R., 1801. He married third in 1804, widow Esther (Phillips) Parsons. Mr. Jackson was one of the founders of the Plymouth Bank, a subscriber for twenty-seven shares of stock, and a director from 1803 to 1815, and again from 1827 to 1836. He died in Plymouth, October 22, 1836.

There was a vacant lot belonging to the Messrs. Jackson with two cellars, the remains of houses taken down long before my remembrance, and in the Jackson yard there was a Jackson apple tree, from which in season apples would fall upon a shed and roll into the vacant lot, and in recess there was a race to capture such apples as might have fallen during school hours. What has been the fate of the Jackson apple trees of my youth, and where have they gone? It was a red, juicy, early summer apple, a fit prize for the race, and where have the queen apple trees gone, only one of which is left in Plymouth.   That in the yard of Wm. Rider Drew was cut down during the last year, leaving the one in the yard of Mrs. Lothrop, solitary and alone.   And where are the June Eatings, a name corrupted into Jenitons, of which I think there is only one left in the yard of Miss Lydia Jackson in North street.   And I must not forget those favorites with the boys, the button pears. Not especially prized by their owners we boys were permitted to take all we could find on the ground.   With our trouser's pockets bulging with the little fellows, we would find our way to school, little suspecting that we were paying dearly for them in the cost of a doctor's visit, and a dose of picra.

In the vacant lot above mentioned, the most conspicuous feature was a large sty in which Major Jackson kept his hogs. So far from such appurtenance being considered a nuisance in those days, a family without one or more hogs was an exception. In earlier times they were permitted to run at large, though not within my day in Plymouth, but it may surprise my younger readers to know that in New York and Washington, as late as the civil war, they roved about the streets as freely as dogs. As late as 1721 it was voted by the inhabitants of Plymouth that they might run at large that year if properly ringed and yoked, and hog constables were annually chosen to see that the condition was complied with. The custom of keeping hogs was so universal in my day that perhaps a dozen times during the season a dealer would buy in the Brighton market a drove of hogs and drive them home over the road, selling them on the way. When a sale was made the drivers would tie the four legs of the hog and raise it to a pair of steel-yards, hanging from a bar supported by their shoulders, and thus find the weight. While this operation was going on the drove would roam at their own sweet will, nosing up the gutters and sidewalks in every direction. I remember James Ruggles of Rochester, the donor to the county of the fountain in front of the Court house, and Swift, one of the members of the firm of pork packers in Chicago; driving their hogs from house to house. Until a very recent date, more in deference to an old custom, than to any necessity, hog-reeves were chosen each year by the town, and recently married grooms were selected for the honor.

The occupants of the house in question after the Jacksons were, Madam Mary Warren and Wm. F. Peterson, in the southerly part, and Susan, Sarah and Deborah L. Turner, daughters of Lothrop Turner, and Miss Deborah L. Turner, Dr. Alexander Jackson, and Hannah D. Washburn, milliners, and Sarah M. Holmes and Mrs. Charles Campbell, in the northerly part, until the house was taken down, and the present building was erected in 1887, the occupants of which are now the Old Colony National Bank, Plymouth Saving's Bank, the Black & White Club, Dr. Schubert and Dr. Lothrop, and the Natural History Society. After the Jackson house came into the posession of the Savings Bank, a one story building was erected on the northerly line of the lot, which was occupied at various times by the Public Library, and by Arthur Lord and Albert Mason, attorneys-at-law, and finally removed to the Hathaway land on Middle street.

Before speaking of the occupants of the two houses which stood north of the vacant lot on which the Bank building was erected in 1842, I will state that in 1851 a slice fifteen or twenty feet deep was cut from the two lots, including the front yard of the Thomas house, now the Plymouth Tavern, and enough from the lot south of it to make the present line to which Davis building when soon after erected, was made to conform. As long ago as I can remember, the old house which stood on the site of Davis building was occupied by Timothy Goodwin, a tinman by trade, who occupied for his tinshop the upper story of a projection in the rear of the main building. I have an impression that he was club footed, and that he had two sons older than myself, who with their father must have moved from Plymouth not far from the year, 1835.

The old fashioned tinman's trade which flourished in Mr. Goodwin's day when all the tinware in use was made in the local shops, has practically disappeared, leaving only the manufacture of hot air furnace pipes to remind us of the resonant clatter of a tinshop once so familiar to the ear. Mr. Goodwin was born in 1779, and was the son of Timothy Goodwin, who came from Charlestown and married Lucy, daughter of Abiel Shurtleff of Plymouth. His father, who was associated with the earliest postal system of Plymouth, deserves a passing notice. Up to 1775 no post office had ever been established in Plymouth, and at that time there were only seventy- five post offices in the colonies, and eighteen hundred and seventy-five miles of post routes. In the above year Benjamin Franklin was appointed Postmaster General, and on the 12th of May William Watson was appointed postmaster of Plymouth, and in 1790 was commissioned by Washington. On the appointment of Mr. Watson in 1775, a horseback mail route was established from Cambridge to Falmouth, through Plymouth, and Timothy Goodwin and Joseph Howland were appointed post riders, making the trip down and back once in each week. They left Cambridge Monday noon, and arrived at Plymouth at four o'clock, Tuesday afternoon; and leaving Plymouth at nine o'clock Wednesday morning, reached Sandwich at four o'clock on that day, and Falmouth at eight o'clock Thursday morning. Goodwin and Howland divided the route, making the exchange at Plymouth.

Until 1816 the rate of postage remained unchanged as follows: for a single letter under forty miles, eight cents; under ninety miles, ten cents; under one hundred and fifty miles, twelve and a half cents; under three hundred miles, seventeen cents; under five hundred miles, twenty cents; over five hundred miles, twenty-five cents. In 1816 the rate was fixed for a single letter not over thirty miles, six and a quarter cents, over thirty miles and under eighty, ten cents; over eighty and under one hundred and fifty, twelve and a half cents; over one hundred and fifty, and under four hundred, eighteen and three quarters cents; over four hundred, twenty-five cents, with an added rate for every additional piece of paper, and if the letter weighed an ounce, the rate was four times the above. The newspaper rate fixed at the same time was one cent under one hundred miles, or within the state; over one hundred miles, and out of the state, one and a half cents, magazines and pamphlets one and a half cent a sheet under one hundred miles, if periodicals, two and a half cents a sheet over one hundred miles, but if not prepaid, four and five cents.

The above was the rate of the postage during my youth, and until I was twenty-three years of age, when gradual reductions began to be made, the result of which has been the postal rates as they stand today. The rates above mentioned indicate the kind of currency prevailing at the time. Articles on sale were priced at so many cents, or a four-pence happenny (six and a quarter cents), nine pence (twelve and a half cents,) a shilling (sixteen and two-thirds cents) a quarter of a dollar, two and three pence (thirty-seven and a half cents) a half a dollar, three and nine pence (or sixty-two and a half cents) four and six pence (or seventy-five cents) and so on to a dollar. Finally Mexican coins were eliminated from our currency, and the genuine American decimal coinage exclusively prevailed. Until the year 1855, prepayment was optional, but with the introduction of postage stamps, prepayment was required, and when after the establishment of expresses, it was found that they engaged in the carriage of letters the practice was forbidden unless the letters were stamped.   If under the old system letters were not prepaid, it was by no means unusual for persons to whom they were addressed, to refuse to receive them and pay the high postage due. It goes without saying that persons known to be going to Boston or New York were pretty well loaded, as I have often been with letters to be delivered not only to friends, but also to men in business.

If cheap postage is a blessing, it may be doubted whether it is an unalloyed one.   As one of its penalties, letter writing has become a lost art.   A three-line note or a postal card, or what is worse, a dictation by a stenographer from which the last vestige of communion of friend with friend is completely extinguished, has taken the place of the welcome epistles which our grandmothers and aunts wrote with care, and filled full not only with gossip and family news, but also with instructive comments on events of the day.   How much future readers will lose by the absence of such volumes of correspondence as have graced our literature during the last hundred years!

In connection with letters it may be well enough to say for the benefit of my young readers that until 1840 envelopes were unknown, and letters were universally folded and sealed either with sealing wax or wafers.

There was an expression of deliberation and composure investing such correspondence which is lost in the correspondence of today.   Now and then some impecunious person found sealing wax and even wafers unnecessarily extravagant. I was told many years ago by a man who called on the late Joshua Sears who left his millions to a son, recently deceased, that he found him splitting wafers.   Since the days of envelopes I have known an officer of one of our institutions to save all his letters, and turn the envelopes for future use.

CHAPTER XX.

William Watson, the first postmaster of Plymouth, was the son of John and Priscilla (Thomas) Watson, and was born in Plymouth, May 6, 1730, and graduated at Harvard in 1751. In addition to the office of postmaster, he was appointed in 1782 naval officer for the port of Plymouth, and in 1789 he was commissioned collector by Washington. In 1803 he was removed by Jefferson from both the office of postmaster and collector, and died April 22, 1815. In 1765 he bought the lot of land in Court street, on which the Old Colony Club house stands, and there can be no doubt that he built the house now standing, and occupied it until his death. After the death of Mr. Watson, the estate was bought by my grandfather, William Davis, and occupied by my uncle, Nathaniel Morton Davis from the time of his marriage in 1817 until his death, when its occupancy passed to his son, Col. Wm. Davis.

The story of the life of the mother of Wm. Watson is full of romantic interest. She was Priscilla Thomas, a daughter of Caleb and Priscilla (Capen) Thomas of Marshfield. She became engaged to Noah Hobart, a divinity student, who was at the time teaching scnool in Duxbury. John Watson of Plymouth, who had married in 1715, Sarah, daughter of Daniel Rogers of Ipswich, lost his wife, and not knowing of the engagement of Miss Thomas, made through her father, an offer of marriage. As Mr. Watson was a man of high standing and abundant means, Mr. Thomas was favorably impressed by the offer, and said that he would consult his wife and daughter. A family council was held, into which Mr. Hobart was called, and it was finally decided with the assent of Mr. Hobart, who was ready to make any sacrifice to secure a happy establishment for life for one whom he sincerely loved, to accept Mr. Watson's offer. Thus with a tearful parting two loving hearts were separated apparently forever. In 1729 John Watson and Priscilla Thomas were married, and the first act of a new romance of John and Priscilla was performed. In 1732 Mr. Watson died, and at that time his son, Elkanah, was a nursing infant.   At about the same time the wife of Isaac Lothrop died, leaving also a nursing infant. As the families were intimate, Mrs. Watson offered to nurse Mrs. Lothrop's infant with her own.   The natural consequence of the family relations was an offer of marriage from Mr. Lothrop, which was unhesitatingly accepted.   The alliance was an eligible one.   Mr. Lothrop was one of the Justices of the Court, and was possessed of a large estate.   The marriage took place in 1733, and he died April 26, 1750, having by a life illustrating the highest qualities of the human character deserved the following inscription on his gravestone:

"Had virtue's charms the power to save
Its faithful votaries from the grave,
This stone had ne'er possessed the fame
Of being marked with Lothrop's name."

In the meantime it may be interesting to learn what had become of Noah Hobart, the old time lover. He in due time entered the ministry, and was settled over the church in Fairfield, Conn. Though he had never held communication with Priscilla by letter or otherwise, by the wireless ways which lovers have, he had kept himself informed of the varied scenes in her life. He knew of the death of her first husband, and her second marriage, as well as the two families of children which had grown up around her. He had heard also of the death of her second husband, while with a wife and two children of his own, a veil not wholly impenetrable obscured the remembrance of his early days. About seven years after the death of Mr. Lothrop her second husband, the wife of Mr. Hobart died, and after a becoming period of mourning, his old love, which time had not obliterated, speedily revived at the thought that both he and his early love were free. Without delay he, as was the fashion of the time, drove in his chaise to Plymouth, and presented himself as suitor at the Lothrop mansion. It is unnecessary to disclose the interview. A further sacrifice was needed before in the fullness of time God should join together whom man had put asunder. She had promised her husband on his death bed that as long as his mother lived, then eighty years of age, she would like a real daughter care for her and promote her happiness.

Again there was a parting which seemed to be one forever. On his way home Mr. Hobart stopped over night with his friend, Rev. Mr. Shute of Hingham, and attended with him the next day a religious service in the church held every Thursday, which was sometimes called the Thursday lecture, and sometimes the Preparatory lecture. On their way home from church a friend passed them on horseback, who said that he had ridden from Plymouth. In answer to the inquiry for news in the old town he said that just as he left he was told that old Mrs. Lothrop was found dead in her bed that morning. It is needless to say that the continuance of the journey to Fairfield was postponed, and a return to Plymouth was made. After the funeral and a due publication of the bans, the marriage took place under date of 1758, and the seventeen years which she passed in Fairfield with her third husband, were the happiest years of her life. Mr. Hobart died in 1775, and she returned to Plymouth, where the remainder of her days was spent until her death, June 23, 1796, in the 90th year of her age.

John Sloss Hobart, son of Rev. Noah Hobart, by his first wife, became United States Senator from New York, and his daughter, Ellen, married Nathaniel Lothrop, a son of Mrs. Hobart by her second husband, Isaac Lothrop.

Returning to the old house where Davis building stands, of which in my wanderings I have almost lost sight, its later occupants whom I can remember were Capt. Woodward, the driver for many years of the Boston mail stage, his son-in-law Bradford Barnes, John R. Davis and George Churchill. All of these except Mr. Davis have been noticed in other chapters. Mr. Davis was a ropemaker by trade, but when the Robbins Cordage Company discontinued work he sought other means of livelihood, chiefly that of restaurant keeper. He was a good man, of a deeply religious spirit, who carried his religion into every day life. He not only believed in the fatherhood of God, but also in the brotherhood of man. It would have been impossible to provoke him to the utterance of an angry or unkind word, and his kindly words often appeared more kind with the touch of humor in which they were uttered. His kindness of heart and gentleness of speech, and his humor as well, were illustrated when a man after eating at his lunch counter left without paying. Instead of running out to the sidewalk and calling out to the man in the hearing of passers-by "to come back and pay his bill," he said in the mildest tone of voice, "Mr., did I give you the right change?"

The house now occupied as a public house, and called the Plymouth Tavern, was for many years identified with the family of Joshua Thomas. He bought the house in 1786, and occupied it until his death, January 10, 1821. He married in 1786 Isabella Stevenson, of Boston, who continued to occupy it until her death. Few families displayed more earnest patriotism than the family to which he belonged. His father, Dr. William Thomas, born in Boston in 1718, practised medicine in Plymouth many years, and died September 20, 1802. He was on the medical staff in the expedition against Louisburg in 1745, and at Crown Point in 1758. He had four sons born in Plymouth, Joshua, Joseph, Nathaniel and John. Joshua was born in 1751, and graduated at Harvard in 1772. After some time spent in teaching, and in theological studies, he became especially interested in public affairs, and in 1774 was adjutant of a regiment of militia organized in Plymouth County, in view of the threatening war clouds appearing above the horizon. In 1776 he served on the staff of General John Thomas on the Canadian expedition, in which General Thomas died, and soon after returned home where he studied law, and henceforth devoted himself to his profession. Having served as a member of the committee of correspondence and as Representative and Senator, he was appointed in 1792 Judge of Probate, and continued in office until his death. He was also President of the Plymouth and Norfolk counties Bible Society, the first president of the Pilgrim Society, and Moderator of town meetings twenty-eight years. He lay on his bed of death during the celebration of December 22, 1820, when Daniel Webster delivered the oration, and John Watson was selected to preside on that occasion. Judge Thomas had three sons, John Boies, 1787, William, 1788, and Joshua Barker, 1797. John Boies graduated at Harvard in 1806, and married Mary, daughter of Isaac LeBaron. He was a member of the bar, a member of the Board of Selectmen, from 1831 to 1840, inclusive, moderator of town meetings from 1829 to 1841, inclusive, President of the Old Colony Bank and Clerk of the Plymouth County Courts from 1811 to his death, December 2, 1852. William Thomas, the second son of Joshua, graduated at Harvard in 1807, and was at the time of his death, September 20, 1882, the oldest living graduate. He practiced law in Plymouth, was in 1852 sheriff of the county, and married in 1816 Sally W., daughter of John Sever of Kingston. Joshua Barker, the youngest son of Joshua, was also a member of the bar, but never practised. Though not fitted by temperament for the labors of his profession, he was a man of culture, and a conversationalist, whom it was always agreeable to meet. Much younger than his brothers, he was always an indulged and petted son. I heard when I was young of an amusing effort to send him to a boarding school. His father and mother, with great reluctance, and only from a sense of duty, decided to send him to a school known as the Wing school in Sandwich. So they started one morning with their boy in a chaise, and a trunk strapped to the axle. After leaving him in the hands of Mr. Wing they regretfully bade him goodbye and left for home. They drove into their yard, landing at the rear door, and going into the house, found Joshua sitting by the fire, having ridden home on the axle and entered the house at the front door before them. They were overjoyed to see him, and embraced him with as much fervor as if he had returned from a long term at school. He died in Plymouth unmarried, March 7, 1873.

After the death of the widow of Judge Thomas, the house was occupied for some years by Allen and S. D. Ballard as an eating saloon, with lodging rooms to let. The Ballards were succeeded by Mr. Holbrook, and under the name of the Central House it was occupied by Charles H. Snell. Mr. Huntoon and Mr. McIntire and St. George and Manley E. Dodge followed, who were succeeded by Mr. Shaw, Mr. Minchen, and Bruce and Abbot Jones followed, and then Jones alone, who was succeeded by McCarthy and Buckman, and the recent proprietor, Mr. McCarthy. The name was changed to Plymouth Tavern by Mr. Bruce. Joseph Thomas, a brother of Judge Joshua Thomas, born in 1755, was in the early part of the revolution a Lieutenant of Artillery, and later,

Captain and Major. He died in Plymouth unmarried, Aug. 19, 1838. Nathaniel, another brother, born in 1756, was a Captain in the revolution, and died in Plymouth, March 22, 1838. He married in 1781 Priscilla Shaw, and second in 1796, Jane (Downs) widow of Isaac Jackson. John, a third brother ot Judge Joshua Thomas, born in 1758, was on the medical staff during the revolution, and after the war settled in Poughkeepsie. Some of his descendants are living in Cleveland, Ohio.

As long ago as I can remember the house next to the store of Moore Bros., on the north was occupied by Benjamin Marston Watson, and was built by him on a vacant lot in 1811. He was a son of John and Lucia (Marston) Watson, born in 1774, and married in 1804 Lucretia Burr, daughter of Jonathan Sturges of Fairfield, Conn. His only children remembered by me were Lucretia Ann, who married Rev. Hersey B. Goodwin, and was the mother of Professor William Watson Goodwin of Cambridge; and Benjamin Marston. His son, Benjamin Marston Watson, born January 17, 1820, graduated at Harvard in 1839, and married in 1846, Mary, daughter of Thomas Russell, and died February 19, 1896. He was a lovable man, whose companionship I prized; a man of culture, who enjoyed the friendship of Emerson and Alcott and Thoreau; a man in whose presence ordinary ambitions appeared insignificant and mean; a lover of nature with its fruits and flowers, who received in return from nature's hand congenial occupation and support.

Mr. Watson, senior, was a merchant in Plymouth, President of the Plymouth Aqueduct Company, one of the founders of the Pilgrim Society, and for many years its recording secretary. He was also chosen treasurer of the Plymouth institution for savings at the time of its organization in 1828, but declined a re-election in 1829. As a boy I remember him well looking over into the trench of the aqueduct and cleaning perch at a South Pond picnic and putting wood on the parlor fire, in doing which he had a way inherited by his son of standing with his limbs straight from feet to hips, and his body at a sharp angle straight from hips to head without a lounge or a bend. He died while on a visit to Fairfield, November 10, 1835. In 1845 his widow sold the house to William Thomas, who has been already noticed, and it is now owned and occupied by his grandchildren, children of William H. Whitman, who married his daughter Ann.

Captain William Bartlett, whose widow occupies the next house, has been already noticed in connection with the loss of the bark, Charles Bartlett, of which he was master. The house has, however, other interesting associations. In the middle of the eighteenth century it was owned and occupied by Ansel Lothrop. Mary Lothrop, daughter of Ansel, had a son born in the house, who received the name of his father, Elkanah Cushman, and was brought up and educated by him. The son was at one time engaged in business as a member of the Boston firm of Cushman & Topliffe, and lived in various places in Charlestown, and in the north end of Boston. Among his places of residence was a wooden house on Richmond street, now called Parmenter street, between Hanover and Salem streets, and there Charlotte Cushman, his daughter, was born, July 23, 1816. It is a little singular that John Gibbs Gilbert, the distinguished actor, should have been born six years before in an adjacent house. Mr. Cushman attended with his family the Second Church on Hanover street, between Richmond and North Bennet streets, of which Henry Ware, Jr., Ralph Waldo Emerson and Chandler Robbins were pastors before new places of worship were found in Bedford street, and finally in Copley Square. The site of the Cushman house is now occupied by a school house erected in 1866, and named after the distinguished actress, the "Cushman School." Miss Cushman early displayed creditable vocal talent, and was one of the choir in the Second Church. On Thursday evening, March 25, 1830, she appeared at a concert given at No. 1 Franklin avenue, by Mr. G. Farmer, her music teacher, when she sung, "Take this Rose," "Oh, merry row the bonny bark just parting from the shore," and "Farewell, my love." Until 1835 she continued to sing in church, and in April of that year, while J. G. Maeder and his wife, who was Clara Fisher, were producing English opera at the Tremont Theatre, the contralto fell ill, and Miss Cushman was selected to sing the Countess Almaviva in Mozart's "Marriage of Figaro" in her place. The next part she sang under the Maeders was Lucy Bertram in "Guy Mannering," and thus she was early brought into association with the dramatization, in which she became famous. Being shortly afterwards engaged to sing in English operas in New Orleans, she made a sea voyage to that city, during which, as I have always heard, she lost her voice in consequence of the change of climate. Rev. J. Henry Wiggin, whose family were acquainted with the Cushmans at the Northend, and to whom I am indebted for many of the facts in this notice, attributes the loss of voice to the overstraining to which she subjected it after her arrival in New Orleans. Further effort as a singer was of course hopeless, and returning to New York she served three years as a stock actor in the old Park Theatre, under Manager Simpson. It is unnecessary to follow her distinguished career further than to speak of one passage in it, which came under my direct notice. During the winter of 1843 and 1844, which I spent in Philadelphia, she was the lessee and manager of the Chestnut Street Theatre, where I saw her repeatedly in Macbeth, Julia in the Hunchback, Juliana in the Honeymoon, Queen Katherine, Meg Merrilies, Oberon, Bianca in Milman's Fazio; Lady Gay Sparker, Shylock and Beatrice. In 1847 I saw her at the Haymarket Theatre in London, and I remember how my patriotism was stirred by the rapturous applause her acting elicited. During the Philadelphia winter, to which I have alluded, Miss Cushman, with her father and a brother, whom she was educating at the Pennsylvania Medical School, was a regular attendant morning and evening, at the Unitarian Church, of which Rev. Dr. Furness was pastor.

Miss Cushman had a younger sister, Susan, whose beauty presented a marked contrast to her own masculine plainness. In early life Susan married at the Northend a tailor by the name of Merriman, after whose death Charlotte introduced her to the stage, and as Romeo to Susan's Juliet, played Romeo and Juliet in London one hundred nights. On the 9th of March, 1848, Susan married in Liverpool Dr. James S. Muspratt, Professor of Chemistry, in that city, and died there May 10, 1859. Charlotte Cushman died in Boston, February 18, 1876, and was buried from King's Chapel on Washington's birthday.

Until 1858 a dwelling house stood on the south corner of

Court square, which in that year was removed for the purpose of widening the square. All through my youth that
house was owned and occupied by Captain Joseph Bartlett.
He bought the house in 1800, of Nathaniel Thomas, having
up to that time, after his marriage, lived in Wellingsley on an
estate which had previously belonged to his father-in-law,
Joseph Churchill. Captain Bartlett, through life, kept up the
Churchill farm, the entrance to which was through a gate at
Jabez Corner. Warren avenue, when it was laid out, followed
the cartway, which led through his farm. More than once
Captain Bartlett took me in his chaise over to his farm at
Poverty Point, as it was called, and I have a vivid recollection of the apples with which I filled my pockets, and the
sweet corn which the old gentleman gave me to carry home
to my mother. His chaise was one with an iron axle, and
its loud rattle in his comings and goings always indicated
his latitude and longitude. For many years he was an enterprising and successful ship owner and merchant, and in 1803
bought the lot on the north corner of Court square, and built
and occupied the brick house now occupied by William Hedge.
His losses were so severe during the embargoes and the war
of 1812, that in 1820 he moved back to his old home, and continued to occupy it until his death. He was a son of Samuel
and Betsey (Moore) Bartlett, and was born June 16, 1762,
and married in 1784, Rebecca Churchill, and had William,
1786, Rebecca, Susan, 1795, Joseph, Augustus, John, Samuel,
Benjamin and Eliza Ann. He married second in 1821, Lucy,
daughter of Charles Dyer, and died March 4, 1835. His
son, William Bartlett, married in 1814, Susan, daughter of
Dr. James Thatcher, and had Susan Louisa, 1815, who married Charles O. Boutelle, Elizabeth Thatcher, 1818, John,
1820, and Eliza Ann, 1825.

John Bartlett, son of William and Susan (Thatcher) Bartlett, became distinguished in both commercial and literary
life, and deserves a special notice. He was born in Plymouth, June 14, 1820. When his grandfather, Joseph Bartlett,
removed in 1820 to his old home, his son, William, the father
of John, who had been occupying his father's house since his
marriage in 1814, moved into the brick house and kept it as
a public house under the name of the Old Colony Hotel. Ex-

actly how long William Bartlett kept the house I have no means of knowing, but he was succeeded in a year or two, by William Spooner, who was in turn succeeded by Ezra Cushing until 1827, when the house was bought by Nathaniel Russell, and became his residence. I have a letter from Judge John Davis of Boston, dated September 23, 1820, to my grandfather, William Davis, disclosing a plan, proposed by William Sturgis and others, friends of the Pilgrim Society, in Boston, to purchase the house for a memorial edifice, dedicated to the Pilgrims. The plan was to have it kept as a hotel, where meetings of the society might be held, and dinners and balls provided for on anniversary days. Judge Davis was opposed to the scheme, and finally a committee of Boston gentlemen was appointed to aid the trustees of the society in erecting such a memorial as might be agreeable to them. The gentlemen appointed as the committee were Lemuel Shaw, Francis C. Gray, Harrison Gray Otis, Isaac P. Davis, James Savage, George Bond, Benjamin Rich, Francis Bassett, John T. Winthrop and Nathan Hale.

Returning now to John Bartlett, who was born June 14, 1820, the year in which at an unknown date his father moved into the brick house, it is impossible to determine in which house he was born. He was educated in the public schools of Plymouth, and was my schoolmate and playmate. In the autumn of 1836 he entered the bookbinding establishment connected with the University Bookstore in Cambridge, of which John Owen was the proprietor. In the next year, 1837, he became a clerk in the bookstore, and at once displayed remarkable aptitude for the business. He was an extensive reader, and possessed a wide knowledge of authors, and was soon recognized as an expert in the preparation of books for the press. In August, 1846, Mr. Owen failed, and he continued as clerk with his successor, George Nichols, until 1849, when he bought out Mr. Nichols. In 1859 he sold out his store to Sever & Francis, having published a number of books for various authors. He had also published three editions of his "Familiar Quotations," the first of which was issued in 1856. In 1861 he prepared a few books for publication, but transferred them to Sever & Francis. In 1862 he served as volunteer paymaster nine months on board Admiral

Du Pont's despatch boat. In August, 1863, he entered the publishing house of Little, Brown & Co., as clerk, with the promise that at the expiration of eighteen months, when the existing partnership would terminate, he would be taken into the firm. In 1864 Little, Brown & Co. published the fourth edition of his "Familiar Quotations," and an edition de luxe of "Walton's Angler," edited by him. In February, 1865, he became a partner in the firm, and the literary, manufacturing and advertising departments were assigned to him, all of which he retained during his connection with the firm. In 1882 Little, Brown & Co. published his Shakespeare "Phrase Book," and in February, 1889, having been several years senior partner, he retired from the firm in order to complete his "Shakespeare Concordance." The fifth and sixth editions of "Quotations" were published by Little, Brown & Co., the seventh and eighth by Routledge of London, and the ninth by Little, Brown & Co., and Macmillan & Co. of London, and of all these editions, more than two hundred thousand copies, have been sold.

In 1891 Macmillan & Co., of London, offered to publish his "Shakespeare Concordance" at their own risk, and it was issued by them in 1894. In recognition of his literary service, he was made in 1892 a member of the American Academy of Arts and Sciences; in 1871 was awarded by Harvard an honorary degree of Master of Arts, and in 1894, he was made an honorary member of the Phi Beta Kappa Society. He married, June 4, 1851, Hannah, daughter of Sydney Willard, Professor of Hebrew at Harvard from 1805 to 1831, and granddaughter of Joseph Willard, President of Harvard from 1781 to 1804, and died in Cambridge, December 3, 1905.

I have spoken of the occupants of the brick house on the north corner of Court Square, before 1827, when it came into the possession of Nathaniel Russell, who occupied it from that time until his death, October 21, 1852. He was the son of John and Mercy (Foster) Russell, and was born April 6, 1769, in the house on the west side of Main street next north of Mr. Gooding's watchmaker's store, where his father lived from 1759 to 1776. After reaching manhood he was engaged for a time in business in Bridgewater, removing to Plymouth not long after the year 1800, and occupying the house which until recently stood on the lower corner of Middle street and LeBaron's alley. About 1808 he removed to the house on the north side of Summer street next to the house on the corner of Ring Lane, and made that his home until he bought the house on the corner of Court Square. He was extensively engaged many years in iron manufactures in connection with William Davis and Barnabas Hedge, and after 1837, as the head of the firm of N. Russell & Co. He was a man who always had at heart the welfare of his native town, and joined in every movement to elevate its social and moral condition. A Lyceum in 1829, of which he was President; a Temperance Society at about the same date, with which he was connected; a Peace Society in 1831, and affairs of the church, of which he was a member, always commanded his aid and support. He married, June 18, 1800, Martha, daughter of Isaac Le-Baron, and had Nathaniel, Mary Howland, Andrew Leach, Mercy Ann, Francis James, LeBaron and Lucia Jane. He was always known in my day as Captain Nathaniel Russell, having been commissioned by Governor Samuel Adams, May 25, 1795, Captain in the Fourth Regiment, first brigade and fifth division of the State Militia. Nathaniel Russell, Jr., born in Bridgewater, December 18, 1801, graduated at Harvard in 1820, and became associated with his father in business. He married, June 25, 1827, Catherine Elizabeth, daughter of Daniel Robert and Betsey Hayward (Thacher) Elliott of Savannah, Georgia, and died February 16, 1875. He will be further mentioned later.

Mary Howland Russell, born October 22, 1803, died January 12, 1862.

Andrew L. Russell, born May 16, 1806, graduated at Harvard in 1827, and was engaged at one time in the dry goods' jobbing business in Central street, Boston, in partnership with William S. Russell, and later with N. Russell & Co. in Plymouth. He married, May 3, 1832, Laura Dewey, and, second, October 5, 1841, Hannah White, daughter of William Davis, Jr. He has been already noticed in connection with the rows of elms planted by him on Court street, which if not consigned to death by the concrete sidewalks, will serve as a lasting memorial of his service to his native town.

Mercy Ann, born August 16, 1809, died September 18, 1832.

Francis James graduated at Harvard in 1831, and died September 6, 1833.

LeBaron graduated at Harvard in 1832, and died August 19, 1889.

Lucia Jane, born November 22, 1821, married Rev. Dr. George W. Briggs, November 5, 1849, and died November 1, 1881.

LeBaron Russell, above mentioned, studied medicine in Boston and Paris, and established himself in Boston. Indisposed to active labor in his profession, he devoted himself to literary pursuits, and by his interest in the schools and charities of the city, led a useful and beneficent life.

The house itself, so long identified with the Russell family, deserves special notice. It is a fine example of the style of domestic architecture which had its origin in the middle of the eighteenth century. It has been suggested by some that it was designed by Charles Bulfinch, but I lived from 1849 to 1853 in a block of houses on Franklin street in Boston, designed by him, and I remember nothing in their exterior or interior to suggest his handiwork. I am inclined to think that it was modelled after the designs of Peter Harrison, an English architect, examples of whose work may be found in Salem, which were followed more or less closely in later times in that city, and in Marblehead and Portsmouth. Harrison came to Newport, R. I., in 1829, in the ship with Bishop Berkley and Smibert, the distinguished portrait painter, and before his death, which occurred in Boston, designed the Redwood library in Newport, King's chapel in Boston, and Christ's church in Cambridge. Symmetry and proportion were the characteristics of his work, and no better illustration of these exquisite qualities can be found than in his original efforts and their faithful copies. The beautiful old porch of the house in question, rounded in shape and supported by clover leaf columns, harmonizing with the windows beneath and above it, was replaced by the present one about 1840.

CHAPTER XXI.

To break the monotony of personal reminiscence, I shall recall some of the games which prevailed in my youth. When the April showers and the dog days come year after year at their appointed times, we are satisfied with the explanation that they are following the order of nature. When in their seasons the robins build their nests, and the blackbirds gather in flocks preparatory to their autumn flight, we are content with the statement that they are guided by instinct. But we have no answer to the question—why we boys, as if in obedience to a mysterious edict issued by a secret council, each year simultaneously in all our towns brought from their winter quarters our alleys and taws, and snapped our marbles on every available sidewalk. After the marble fever had run, like measles, a certain number of days, the scene suddenly changed, and driving hoop was the order of the day. The hoop was not one of those toy hoops we see in these days, galvanized iron rings, with an attachment to push them with, but the genuine hoop from an oil cask, one from the bilge for the larger boys, and one from the chine for the smaller ones. When we gathered at twilight, and either in single or double file, made the circuit of the town, we made the welkin ring literally to beat the band.

After the hoop came, as now, the ball games, skip, one old cat, two old cat, hit or miss, and round ball. We made our own balls, winding yarn over a core of India rubber, until the right size was reached, and then working a loop stitch all around it with good, hard, tightly spun twine. Attempts were occasionally made to play ball in the streets, but the by-laws of the town forbidding it were rigidly enforced. There were four gangs of boys, the North street gang, which played in the Jackson field in the rear of North street; the Court street gang, which played in Captain Joseph Bartlett's field, where the easterly end of Russell street and the adjoining buildings are; the Summer street gang, which played in Cow Hill Valley, and the "tother side gang," which played on Training

Green, sometimes to the detriment of neighboring windows.

While the days were longest the street games were next in order, hare and hounds, prison bar, leap frog, Tom Tiddler's ground, Red Lion in his den, I spy, hide and seek, nine holes, back side in the way, and follow the leader.

> Over hill and dale,
> Through bush, through briar,
> Over park and dale,
> Through flood, through fire.

Wherever the leader went we must follow, over fences, off stone walls, in and out of houses, astonishing families, and if the boot of the head of the family was in order, coming out a little more expeditiously than we went in. The members of the North street gang, to which I belonged, were besides myself and brother, Augustus H. Tribble, the Collingwood boys, John J. Russell, Richard W. Bagnall, Lewis Weston, the Jackson boys, Thomas Cotton, Charles Cotton, George Maynard, George Gooding and Charles T. May.

Football came next in the early autumn, with a ball made of an ox bladder inserted in a leather case of our own making. We bought the bladder at the slaughter house, and put it in pickle until it was ready to be used, and then when the case was made we put it through a slit, and blowing it up with a quill tied a string around the nozzle, laced up the slit, and the game began. In those days all the boys wore boots, and consequently little damage was done to our shins.

With the coming of the first cool nights we hunted in the morning for strips of ice in the gutter, and spent the hour before school in sliding, boys and girls together, the girls, I never knew the reason why, giving a little hop at the beginning of their slide. And then came our sliding down hill, the larger boys with George P. Hayward and William Rider Drew and Jesse Turner at their head. Mr. Hayward's Constitution, painted green, and having round steel spring runners, taking the lead, would slide from the top of Burial Hill down through a wide open gate between the high schoolhouse and the Unitarian church, along Leyden street, down Turner's hill to the end of Barnes' wharf. The smaller boys would spend the afternoons of Saturday perfectly happy on the short slide from the bottom of the Middle street steps to

Water street. All our sleds were made to order, scorning as we would if they had been purchasable, the toy sleds which can now be bought for a song, and are high at the price. There was a sled of domestic manufacture in my day which, considering its cheapness and simplicity, was a quite satisfactory sled in the minds of those who could afford no better. It was made of six white oak cask staves, three above and three below, with the convex on the outside, and a cleat at each end between the staves, to which it was nailed. With a little less speed, perhaps, than other sleds, yet in humpy dagger and belly hacker in wearing out boot toes, and heels, they were as efficient as any. With skating and its accompaniment hocky, the winter passed away, and the year came to an end. Of course many out of door games now in vogue were not known in my early days. Cricket was little played, while croquet, tennis, and golf had not made their appearance. To these modern innovations doubtless before long curling and lacrosse will be added. The game of ten pins was a familiar one, but its enjoyment was limited by the almost entire absence of alleys until the Samoset alleys were built in 1845. There was a poor, short alley on Billington Sea Island, but rarely used except on the occasion of picnics. It was by no means an uncommon thing in the college vacation to go as far as Holmes' Tavern, near Harrub's corner, and roll in the alleys of Mr. Holmes, whose lame back we sorely tried by his efforts to act as ball boy, and sometimes we went as far as an alley near the Cushman cotton factory, beyond Plympton Green. Carriage hire in those days was so low that such an afternoon expedition could be had without extravagance. We could hire for a half a day at George Drew's stable in Middle street, for a dollar, either Dolly or Little Jack, or the Eastern mare, or the Peabody horse with a chaise, or for a dollar and a half, Bob sorrel with a carryall. I say chaise, a name derived through the English word chair, from the French chaire, because buggies were unknown in Plymouth in my youth. Buggies were introduced from India, where in Hindustani they were called baggi or bagghi, four wheeled carriages with hoods, and our wagon is derived from the Dutch word wagen. Every family owning a horse had a chaise, and carriage houses were universally called chaise houses, as they are still by myself, and older persons. The fronts of these houses were always made with curved tops, and I know of only three now left in town, those of Mrs. Lothrop, Father Buckley and William Rider Drew. The first buggy in Plymouth was brought from Boston by my uncle, Nathaniel Morton Davis in the 1830's, and was owned ' by John Harlow of Chiltonville at the time of his death a few years ago.

Of the indoor games of my youth, battledore and shuttlecock and the graces have gone out. The other games of the young were as they are now, blind man's buff, scandal, cribbage, backgammon, commerce, whist, chess, checkers, vingtun, all fours, bragg, loo and euchre. The gambling game of bridge was unknown, as it ought to be today. Quadrille was played by older people, and Boston, after a disappearance for many years, was again introduced in 1844. Piquet, the ancient game of ombre adapted to four instead of three persons, and played also by older persons, was immortalized by Pope in the following lines:

> Belinda when thirst of fame invites,
> Burns to encounter two adventurous knights,
> At ombre singly to decide their doom,
> And swells her breast with conquests yet to come.

In the selection of leaders and sides in the out of door games, what were called "countings out" were used, very curious doggerels, whose origin is as mysterious as that of language itself. They are used in every town in every state in our Union, and have been found in more than twenty languages, including English, French, Spanish, German, Russian, Dutch, Gallic, Turkish, Hindustani, Japanese, Hawaiian, Irish, Romani, Cornish, etc. There is a vein of similarity running through them, though changes and additions and corruptions have been the result of their adoption into various dialects. In closing this chapter I subjoin the following list of such as my own memory, and that of others have furnished me, and such as I have found in print.

> Eena, meena, mony my,
> Tuscalona, bona sty,
> Hulda, gulda, boo.
> Out goes you.   (United States.)

Eena, meena, mona my,
Tuscalona, bona stry,
Tin pan, maska dary,
Higly, pigly, pig snout,
Crinkly, cranky, you are out.

(New Hampshire.)

Eeny, meeny, mony my,
Barcelona, stony stry,
Eggs, butter, cheese, bread,
Stick, stock, stone dead.   (England.)

Eeny, meeny, mony mo,
Catch a nigger by the toe,
If he squeals, let him go,
Eeny, meeny, miny mo.   (Scotland.)

Eena, deina, dina doe,
Catch a nigger by the toe,
If he screams, let' him go.
Eena, deena, dina doe.   (Ireland.)

Ena, mena, bona mi,
Kisca, lana, mora di,
Eggs, butter, cheese, bread,
Stick, stock, stone dead.   (Ancient.)

Allem, Bellem, Chirozi,
Chirmirozi, fotozi,
Fotoz girden, magara,
Magarada, tilki bush,
Pilki, beni korkoostdi,
Aallede, shovellede, edimeda,
Divid bushe,
Den Olayen, kehad bashi.   (Turkey.)

Anery, twaery, duckery, seven,
Alama crack, ten am eleven,
Palm, pom, it must be done,
Come lettle, come total, come twenty-one.   (Druids.)

One-ery, two-ery, ziccary zan,
Hollow bone, crockabone, ninery tan,
Spittery, spot it must be done,
Twiddle-um, twaddle-um twenty-one.   (England.)

Ekkeri, akaisi, you kaiman,
Fillisin, follasy, Nicholas Jan,
Kivi, Kavi, Irishman,
Stini, stani, buck.   (Romani.)

Eena, meena, mona, mite,
Basca, lora, hora, bite.   (Cornwall.)

Eena, tena, mona, mi.
Pastor, lone, boni strei.   (German.)

Eena, meener, mulker,
Porceleiner, stutker.   (Dutch.)

Hickory, hoary, hairy, Ann,
Busybody, oven span,
Pare, pare, virgin, mari.   (Guernsey.)

One ery, two ery, Dickey Davy,
Hulleboo, cracker, gentle Mary,
Dixum Dandy, merrigo hind,
Fersumble-du, tumble-du, twenty-nine.   (Ireland.)

Eena, deena, dina dust,
Calita, meena, wina, must,
Spin, spon, must be done,
Twiddledum, twaddledum, twenty-one.
O. U. T. speels out,
With the old dish clout,
Out boys, out.   (England.)

One is all, two is all, Zick is all zan,
Bobtail, vinegar, little tol tan,
Harum, scarum, Virginia merum,
Zee, tan, buck.   (New Hampshire.)

One-ezzoll, two-ezzoll, ziggle, zol zan,
Bobtail vinegar, little tall tan,
Harum, scarum, virgin marum,
Zinctum, zanctum, buck.   (Delaware.)

Intry, mintry, cutry, corn,
Apple seed, and briar thorn,
Wire briar, limber lock,
Three geese in a flock,
One flew east, and one flew west,
And one flew over the cuckoo's nest.

Delia Domna, Nona dig,
Oats floats, country notes,
Hy, born tusk,
Hulali, Gulala, goo,
Out goes you.

One is all, two is all,
Zick is all zeven,
Arrow bone, cracker bone,
Ten or eleven.

Six and four are ten,
Chase the red lion to his den.

Intry, mintry, cutry corn,
Apple seed and briar thorn,
Wire, briar, limber lock,
Six geese in a flock,
Set and sing by a spring,
My grandmother lives on the hill,
She has jewels, she has rings,
She has many pretty things,
O. U. T. spells out you go.

Hunt the squirrel through the woods,
I lost him, I found him;
I sent a letter to his son,
I lost him, I found him.

Fe, fi, fo, fum,
I smell the blood of an Englishman,
Be he live, or be he dead,
I'll have his bones to make my bread.   (Plymouth.)

Eggs, cheese, butter, bread,
Stick, stock, stone, dead,
Hang him up, lay him down,
On his father's living ground.   (Plymouth.)

Een, teen feather pip,
Sargo, larko, bump.   (Plymouth.)

Inditie, Mentitie, Petitee, Dee,
Delia, Delia, Dominee,
Oacha, Poacha, Domminnicher,
Hing, Ping, Chee.   (Plymouth.)

Henry, pennery, pit for gold,
Had a louse in his head,
Seven years old.
Seventy, seventy on to that,
This old logy will grow fat,
Hinchiman, pinchiman, make his back smart,
If ever I catch him, I'll sling him to my heart;
Sling, slang, chattery bang—out.   (Plymouth.)

Intry, tentry, tethery, methery,
Bank for over Diman Diny,
Ant, tant, tooch,
Up the causey, down the cross.
There stands a bonnie white horse,
It can gallop, it can trot,
It can carry the mustard pot,
One, two, three, out goes she.   (Scotland.)

Eeny, teeny, other feather hip,
Satha, latha, kedarthun deck,
Een dick, teen dick, ether dick, fether dick, bunkin,
Een bunkin, teen bunckeen, either bunkin, fether bunkin
    digit.   (Indiana.)

Eenity, feenity, fickety, fig,
El del, dolman egg,
Irby, birky, stony rock,
An tan toosh Jack. (Scotland.)

Hinty, minty, cutry corn,
Apple seed and briar thorn;
Wire, briar, limber lock,
Three geese in a flock;
One flew east, and one flew west,
One flew over the cuckoo nest.

Up on yonder hill,
There's where my father dwells.
He has jewels, he has rings,
He has many pretty things,
He has a hammer with two nails,
He has a cat with two tails.
Strike Jack, lick Tom,
Blow the bellows, old man. (New England.)

      Onerie, twoerie,
      Hahbo crackaro,
      Henry Lary,
      Guacahan Dandy,
      Bullalie Collilie,
      Forty-nine.

Onery, youery, eckery Anna,
Phillicy, pholocy, Nicholas John,
Queeby, quoby, Irish Mary,
Tinkerlam, Tarkerlum buck.

One ezzol, two ezzoll, zichara zan,
Bobtail vinegar, little tall tan,
Harum, scarum, virgin marum,
Zinctum, zanctum buck.

      Tit, tat toe,
      Here I go,
      And if I miss
      I pitch on this.

Rumble, rumble in the pot,
King's nail horse top,
Take off lid.

Fe, fi, fo fum,
I smell the blood of an Englishman.
Be he live, or be he dead,
I'll have his bones to make my bread.

Een, teen, feather pip,
Sarco, larco, bump.

Akaha, ou oi, ha,
Paele, kakini,
I kana, hoole pa;
Mai, no alaee
Ohu, memona kapolena,
Kaide, wilu.   (Hawaii.)

Een, twee, koppie thee,
Drie, vier, glaas ge beer,
Vzl zes bitter in de flesch,
Ziyen acht san op wacht,
Negen teen, ok hit diener gezzen.   (Dutch.)

Ene tene mon emei,
Pastor Loni bone strei.
Ene funi, herke berke,
Wer-we-wo-was.   (German.)

Eggs, cheese, butter bread,
Stick, stone dead,
Stick him up and stick him down,
Stick him in the old man's crown.   (United States.)

Ink, pink, papers, ink,
Am pam push.   (Scotland.)

Ink, mink, pepper stink,
Sarko, Larko, Bump.   (Plymouth.)

Hink, spink, the puddings stink,
The fat begins to fry,
Nobody at home but jumping Joan,
Father, mother and I.   (English.)

One, two, three,
Out goes she.

One, two, three,
Nanny caught a flea,
The flea died, and Nanny cried,
Out goes she.   (United States.)

One-ery, two-ery, eckeery Ann,
Phillisy. phollisy, Nicholas John,
Queebe, quarby, Irish Mary,
Sinkum, sankum, Johnny go buck.   (Cambridge.)

Winnery, ory, accury han,
Phillisy, Phollisi, Nicholas Jan,
Queby, quorby, Irish Mary,
Sink, sunk, sock.   (England.)

Eeny, meeny, mony mi,
Pastalony, bony sty,
Harby, darby, walk.   (Michigan.)

Great house, little house, pig sty, barn.
Rich man, poor man, beggar man.

The last two were used in Plymouth in the ball game of skip.   One of the two boys who chose sides tossed the bat to the other who caught it and held it.   Then the two alternately grasped it hand over hand, and if there was enough of the bat left for the next one to hold it, and throw it over his head, he had the first choice of players.

CHAPTER XXII.

I will add in this chapter some additional memoranda relating to marine matters, before proceeding with the regular order which I had prescribed for my memories.   In connection with the account of vessels built and owned in Plymouth, it will not be inappropriate to speak of those in Kingston and Duxbury, of which I have any recollection, or of which I have been able to obtain an account.   All of these in entering or leaving their port passed through the waters of Plymouth.

Ezra Weston & Sons owned more vessels than any other firm in New England, except William Gray of Salem, and, perhaps, more than any other in the United States, with the above exception.   The following is a partial list of their vessels built in Duxbury with their tonnage as far as ascertained, for which I am indebted to Major Joshua M. Cushing of Duxbury.

> 1800, Brig Rising Sun, 130 tons.
> 1800, Brig Sylvia, 130 tons.
> 1800, Schooner Ardent.
> 1801, Schooner Maria.
> 1801, Schooner Berin.
> 1801, Schooner Union .
> 1802, Schooner Volant.
> 1802, Schooner Laurel.
> 1802, Schooner Prissy.
> 1803, Schooner Sophia.
> 1803, Schooner Phœnix.
> 1803, Sloop Fame.
> 1803, Sloop Jerusha.
> 1803, Sloop Pomona.
> 1803, Brig Federal Eagle, 120 tons.
> 1804, Ship Julius Cæsar, 300 tons.
> 1804, Brig Admittance, 128 tons.
> 1805, Schooner Rising States.
> 1805, Schooner Fenelon.
> 1806, Schooner Salamis, 160 tons.
> 1806, Brig Ezra & Daniel, 125 tons.
> 1806, Brig Gershom, 136 tons.
> 1807, Ship Minerva, 250 tons.
> 1807, Brig Warren, 120 tons.

1807, Sloop Apollo.
1808, Ship Camillus, 350 tons.
1809, Ship Admittance, 300 tons.
1809, Sloop Linnett, 50 tons.
1810, Schooner Flora.
1811, Schooner George Washington, 50 tons.
1813, Brig Golden Goose, 130 tons.
1813, Schooner Copack.
1815, Brig Despatch, 125 tons.
1816, Ship Brahmin, 339 tons.
1816, Brig Messenger, 135 tons.
1816, Schooner Collector, 70 tons.
1816, Sloop Exchange, 60 tons.
1817, Schooner St. Michael, 120 tons.
1817, Sloop Diamond, 50 tons.
1818, Brig Despatch, 130 tons.
1818, Schooner Angler, 60 tons.
1819, Brig Two Friends, 240 tons.
1819, Schooner Franklin, 60 tons.
1820, Brig Margaret, 185 tons.
1820, Brig Baltic, 212 tons.
1821, Schooner Star, 20 tons.
1821, Schooner Panoke, 60 tons.
1822, Brig Globe, 214 tons.
1823, Brig Herald, 162 tons.
1825, Ship Franklin, 246 tons
1825, Brig Pioneer, 231 tons.
1825, Brig Smyrna, 162 tons.
1825, Bark Pallas, 209 tons.
1826, Brig Levant, 219 tons.
1826, Brig Ganges, 174 tons.
1826, Schooner Dray, 86 tons.
1826, Schooner Triton, 75 tons.
1826, Ship Lagoda, 340 tons.
1827, Brig Malaga, 150 tons.
1827, Brig Ceres, 176 tons.
1827, Schooner Pomona, 84 tons.
1828, Ship Julian, 355 tons.
1828, Sloop Reform, 53 tons.
1828, Schooner Virginia, 73 tons.
1829, Sloop Glide, 60 tons.
1829, Brig Neptune, 196 tons.
1829, Schooner Seaman, 70 tons.
1830, Ship Renown, 300 tons.
1831, Ship Joshua Bates, 316 tons.
1831, Ship Undine, 253 tons.
1832, Schooner Seadrift, 90 tons.
1832, Schooner Ranger, 32 tons.

1832,   Brig Angola, 220 tons.
1832,   Ship Minerva, 291 tons.
1833,   Schooner Volunteer, 109 tons.
1833,   Ship Mattakeesett, 356 tons.
1833,   Ship St. Lawrence, 356 tons.
1834,   Brig Messenger, 213 tons.
1834,   Schooner Liberty, 92 tons.
1834,   Ship Admittance, 426 tons.
1835,   Ship Vandalia, 432 tons.
1835,   Brig Trenton, 226 tons.
1836,   Ship Eliza Warwick, 530 tons.
1837,   Brig Oriole, 218 tons.
1837,   Schooner Maquet, 80 tons.
1839,   Brig Lion, 235 tons.
1839,   Brig Smyrna, 196 tons.
1839,   Ship Oneco, 640 tons.
1841,   Ship Hope, 880 tons.
1842,   Sloop Union, 63 tons.
1842,   Brig Vulture, 140 tons.
1843,   Ship Manteo, 600 tons.
1844,   Schooner Angler, 86 tons.
1844,   Schooner Mayflower, 24 tons.
1845,   Schooner Ocean, 103 tons.
1846,   Schooner Express, 93 tons.

Ezra Weston, son of Ezra and Salumith (Wadsworth) Weston of Duxbury, was born November 30, 1771. He married Jerusha Bradford, and died August 15, 1842. His sons, living until manhood, were Gershom Bradford, born August 27, 1799; Alden Bradford, 1805, and Ezra, 1809.

Besides the ship yards of the Westons there were the yards of Samuel Hall, Joshua Cushing and Joshua Cushing, Jr., the Drews and of Paulding and Southworth, in which many vessels were built.

The following is a list of vessels built and owned by Joseph Holmes of Kingston, between 1801 and 1862, the year of his death, for which I am indebted to Mrs. H. M. Jones of Kingston:

1801,   Brig Two Pollies, 250 tons.
1802,   Brig Algol, 220 tons.
1804,   Ship Lucy, 208 tons.
1805,   Schooner Alexander, 100 tons.
1806,   Brig Trident, 130 tons.
1806,   Brig Brunette, 180 tons.
1807,   Schooner Dolly, 106 tons.
1809,   Brig Roxanna, 200 tons.

1812, Ship Elizabeth, 300 tons.
1813, Ship Chili, 300 tons.
1814, Schooner Milo, 100 tons.
1814, Brig Lucy, 140 tons.
1816, Schooner Ann Gurley, 100 tons.
1816, Brig Indian Chief, 150 tons.
1817, Schooner Celer, 64 tons.
1817, Schooner Paraclite, 95 tons.
1818, Schooner Hope, 70 tons.
1818, Ship Rambler, 320 tons.
1820, Schooner Edward, 40 tons.
1821, Ship Columbus, 320 tons.
1822, Ship Horace, 53 tons.
1822, Ship Kingston, 325 tons.
1822, Brig Sophia and Eliza, 200 tons.
1823, Brig Leonidas, 180 tons.
1824, Schooner Cornelius, 35 tons.
1824, Schooner Pamela, 75 tons.
1824, Brig Deborah, 165 tons.
1825, Schooner Wm. Allen, 88 tons.
1825, Schooner Five Brothers, 76 tons.
1825, Brig Edward, 239 tons.
1825, Schooner Eveline, 75 tons.
1826, Schooner Industry, 72 tons.
1827, Bark Truman, 267 tons.
1827, Brig Galago, 160 tons.
1828, Schooner Hunter, 12 tons.
1828, Schooner January, 64 tons.
1828, Schooner February, 88 tons.
1828, Schooner March, 90 tons.
1828, Brig Roxanna, 140 tons.
1829, Brig Two Sisters, 130 tons.
1829, Schooner April, 64 tons.
1829, Ship Helen Mar, 290 tons.
1830, Bark Turbo, 280 tons.
1830, Ship Ohio, 300 tons.
1831, Bark Alasco, 286 tons.
1834, Schooner December, 50 tons.
1834, Ship Rialto, 460 tons.
1837, Schooner July, 48 tons.
1837, Schooner August, 117 tons.
1838, Schooner September, 119 tons.
1838, Brig Belize, 164 tons.
1838, Ship Herculean, 540 tons.
1839, Schooner October, 110 tons.
1840, Schooner Honest Tom, 115 tons.
1840, Schooner November, 107 tons.
1843, Ship Raritan, 499 tons.

1843,   Schooner May, 92 tons.
1843,   Schooner June, 92 tons.
1843,   Brig Gustavus, 153 tons.
1845,   Brig Edward Henry, 164 tons.
1848,   Schooner Risk, 94 tons.
1848,   Ship Nathan Hannum, 512 tons.
1849,   Schooner Cosmos, 108 tons.
1849,   Bark Ann and Mary, 210 tons.
1850,   Schooner Clark Winsor, 127 tons.
1851,   Ship Joseph Holmes, 610 tons.
1852,   Schooner Ocean Bird, 118 tons.
1852,   Bark Fruiter, 290 tons.
1853,   Schooner Kingfisher, 116 tons.
1855,   Bark Sicilian, 320 tons.
1855,   Bark Abbv. 178 tons.
1856,   Bark Neapolitan, 320 tons.
1858,   Brig Bird of the Wave, 178 tons.
1859,   Bark Fruiterer, 320 tons.
1860,   Bark Egypt, 547 tons.
1863,   Bark Lemuel, 321 tons.

Mr. Holmes was in many respects a remarkable man. He was born in Kingston in 1771, and died in that town in 1862. On the 27th of May, 1821, he went to Bridgewater and collected materials for building a vessel, hiring a yard near the Raynham line and laid the keel of the brig Two Pollies. After launching the brig Trident in 1806, she took all the spare materials in the yard, and carried them to Kingston, where all his vessels were built except the Two Pollies, Algol, Lucy, Alexander and Trident, which were built in Bridgewater. He stated in a letter written July 1, 1859, that he kept a vessel on the stocks nearly all the time, and sometimes two, and once built three in a year, all of which he built, fitted and sent to sea, except two, on his own account and risk. In that letter he said that at the age of 87 years and 7 months, he was about to lay the keel of a vessel of two hundred tons, and that he was writing the letter without spectacles. I knew him well, and often called at his house on the corner of Main street. He did his bank business in Boston, leaving only at the Plymouth Bank a deposit made up chiefly of his bank dividends, and I was a little amused by a incident which occurred somewhere between 1859 and 1862, for which I never saw an explanation, though I think it may have been intended as a personal compliment. One day while in the bank he said, " I don't suppose you would lend me any money if I wanted it." Knowing very well that he was never in want of money, I said, "Mr. Holmes, make out your note payable to your own order for such an amount and on such a time as may be agreeable to you, and endorse it, and you can have the money." He signed a note for $5,000 on four months, and told me to place the money to his credit. I did so, and the money remained untouched until the note became due.

The following vessels were built and owned by his son Edward Holmes of Kingston:

1864, Schooner Anna Eldredge, 139 tons.
1865, Schooner Fisher, 105 tons.
1866, Bark Solomon, 600 tons.
1867, Schooner Lucy Holmes, 137 tons.
1868, Bark Hornet, 330 tons.
1869, Schooner Mary Baker, 139 tons.
1874, Brig H. A. Holmes, 320 tons.
Sloop Roxanna, 60 tons.
Sloop Leo, 70 tons.
Sloop Rosewood.

Besides the above the ship Matchless was built in Boston, and owned by James H. Dawes of Kingston, and the ship Brookline, with others, was owned by John and James N. Sever of Kingston.

The following is a list of Kingston captains in the merchant service within my memory, for which I am indebted to Capt. John C. Dawes of Kingston:

William Adams, Frederick C. Bailey, Justus Bailey, Otis Baker, George Bicknell, Calvin Bryant, Cephas Dawes, James H. Dawes, John C. Dawes, Paraclete Holmes, Edward Richardson, Benjamin T. Robbins, James W. Sever, Charles Stetson, William Symmes, Peter Winsor, William Winsor.

The following is a partial list of vessels wrecked within my memory in Plymouth waters:

The earliest wreck in Plymouth waters of which I have any recollection, was that of the brig Sally Ann, Captain Caulfield, in January, 1835, bound from Porto Rico to Boston. She was owned by Charles W. Shepard of Salem, and after striking on Brown's Island became a total wreck on the beach. No lives were lost, and Martin Gould, one of the crew, became a permanent resident of Plymouth, and married in 1836 Ruth (Westgate) widow of William Barrett.

The next wreck within my memory was that of the brig Regulator of Boston, Phelps master, on Brown's Island, February 4, 1836. She was bound from Smyrna to Boston, and with rudder and rigging frozen, and the vessel unmanageable, she came into the bay in a gale from east, northeast, and bore away for Plymouth to find an anchorage in Saquish Cove, where she saw a brig lying. She dropped her anchor at the entrance of the channel in three fathoms of water, and in the heavy swell struck hard. At eight in the evening she floated with the tide, and held on until seven o'clock the next morning, when she drifted into the breakers, and the captain cut away his foremast, which carried with it the main mast, and the main yard. At half-past eight she began to break up, and George Dryden, an Englishman, Daniel Canton of New York, and Augustus Tilton of Vermont, who took to the long boat, capsized fifty yards under the lea of the brig and were lost. John Smith, a Swede, and a Greek boy, were killed by the wreckage, and the remainder of the crew retreated to the main rigging, and their final safety was due to the presence, in the channel, under the Gurnet, of the brig Cervantes of Salem, Kendrick, master, which bound into Boston from Charleston, had succeeded in finding a safe anchorage. The crew of the Cervantes, after six hours of heroic work, took off the men and carried them to their own vessel. The cargo of the Regulator consisted of four hundred and sixty bales of wool, twenty-five cases of opium, twenty-five cases of gum Arabic, twelve bales of senna, two thousand drums of Sultana raisins, five packages of cow's tails, one case of saffron flower, four hundred sacks of salt, and five tons of logwood. The men saved were Captain Phelps, Martin Adams, first mate; James Warden, second mate; Elijah Butler, and Louis Almeira.

On the 20th of November, 1848, the schooner Welcome Return, from Charlottetown, bound for Boston, went ashore in a gale at Rocky Hill. She had as passengers, John and Mary Burns and six children: Ellen, 11; Catherine, 9; Henry, 7; Mary, 5; Rose, 3; and Sarah, six months old. The father and mother and infant were saved, and all the others lost. The father and mother died in Taunton, and the infant, Sarah A., is living in Plymouth, the widow of John H. Parsons.

The next wreck I remember occurred on Friday, January 25, 1867, at Gunners' Point at Manomet. A gale with snow set in Wednesday night, and the railroad was so blocked that no trains ran through to Boston until Sunday, and the train from Boston Wednesday night reached no further than Halifax, where the passengers were supplied with refreshments. The flag staff in Shirley Square was blown down, as well as those at Pilgrim Hall and at the Cordage Factory, and also the store house of the Cordage Works. Considerable damage was done at the wharves, and the schooner Thatcher Taylor was capsized, and her masts were carried away. The bark Velma from Smyrna, October 18th, Zenas Nickerson of Chatham, master, entered the bay on Thursday morning, and during the early part of the gale, headed northeast with the wind southeast, and finally struck at two o'clock Friday morning, a half a mile off shore. Beating over the ledge she came within twenty rods of the beach, and swung round with her head to the sea. The crew took to the mizzen rigging. A little before daylight the steward, unable to longer hold on, fell overboard, carrying with him another of the crew, and both were lost. The main mast soon fell, carrying also the mizzen above the men, and through the forenoon the survivors succeeded in holding on. At two o'clock in the afternoon Henry B. Holmes, Paran Bartlett, James Bartlett, James Lynch, Henry Briggs, Otis Nichols, Robert Reamy and Octavius Reamy, reached the vessel and saved the remainder of the crew as follows: Zenas Nickerson of Chatham, master; Starks Nickerson of Chatham, first mate; John G. Allen of New Bedford, second mate; Augustus L. Jenkins of Portsmouth, John Florida of New York, John Perry of Lisbon and Joseph Sylvia of Boston. The names of the two men lost were William Sampson, England, and Manuel Gustres of Pico, Western Islands. The men were carried to the Manomet House, and when stripped, one called Jack was found to have on seven undershirts and four pairs of stockings. Dr. Alexander Jackson of Plymouth, and Dr. C. J. Wood of Chiltonville, the father of Gen. Leonard Wood, who was then practicing in Chiltonville, attended the men, and performed a number of necessary amputations. While they were under treatment I visited them several times and rendered such assistance as I was able. The vessel belonged to G. W. Bisbee, and her cargo consisted of 1245 cases of figs; 1120 boxes do; 7,937 drums, do; 3,527 mats, do; 1,340 drums of Sultana raisins; 7 casks of prunes; 108 bales of wool; 180 bags of canary seed; 6 cases of gum tragacanth; 3,070 pieces of logwood; 50 cases of figs; 8,407 cases, and 1,587 drums, do, the consignees of which were Baker & Morrell, Ryder & Hardy, and the captain.

In the same gale the schooner Shooting Star, Captain Coe, with corn from Newcastle, Delaware, for Salem, went ashore at Saquish, and was lost.

In 1873 the schooner Daniel Webster, loaded with iron, went ashore on Brown's Island, and was a total loss.

The brig John R. Rhodes, loaded with corn, was wrecked in the outer harbor in the winter of 1850-1. The wreck was bought by John D. Churchill and others, and after repairs in Boston was sold.

In previous chapters I have mentioned Samuel Doten in connection with the escape of Plymouth vessels from the embargo, but I have not by any means done with him. He was the son of Samuel and Eunice (Robbins) Doten, and was born in 1783. His father had three wives, and twenty-three children, the oldest of whom was Samuel, born in 1783, and the youngest, James, born in 1829. Captain Doten in early life was an enterprising shipmaster, later a builder and owner of vessels engaged in the grand bank fishery, and finally a lumber merchant on Doten's yard and wharf, the latter of which he built not far from 1825. He was a man of commanding figure, judicious, active, and prompt, selected many times to serve as chief marshal at celebrations of the Pilgrim Society and town. He married in 1807 Rebecca, daughter of Nathaniel Bradford, and died September 8, 1861. Two of his sons, Major Samuel H. and Captain Charles C., will be noticed in a later chapter in connection with the civil war. Captain Doten was engaged in the privateer service during the war of 1812, and the following narrative of some of his experiences in that service may be interesting to my readers. For its incidents, and for extracts from his log and diary, I am indebted to Captain Charles C. Doten, his son.

CHAPTER XXIII.

During the war of 1812, as in that of the Revolution, the government of the United States issued "letters of marque," giving authority to private individuals to build, arm, and man vessels, for the purpose of making reprisals upon and destroying the enemy's commerce. While these "privateers," as they were called, were entirely outside of and unconnected with the regular naval force of the country, they became one of the most potent weapons wielded on the high seas in behalf of the government. Their destructiveness to English commerce made them the dread of the ocean, for the daring men who engaged in privateering enterprises were the best shipmasters and seamen of their day, perfectly familiar with all coast ports and the highways of the sea, so they knew where to strike most effectively for their own advantage. A vessel captured under the English flag, became, with her cargo, the lawful prize of her captors, and the proceeds of sale were divided under established rules among the owners, officers and men of the privateer, the business in many instances being very profitable. The English commercial vessels likewise armed for defence, and quite often there were spirited engagements before the English Jack would be lowered to the Stars and Stripes flown by some saucy, fast sailing Yankee brig, or long, low, rakish schooner of the Baltimore clipper type.

France being friendly to the United States, her ports were open to our privateers and their prizes, so the English channel itself, right under the nose of Great Britain, was a tempting cruising ground where our letters of marque made many a successful venture and some of them came to grief in capture by the English men-of-war.

As has been previously said in this series of reminiscences, Plymouth had her full number of adventurous spirits, and her "men of the sea" on board the many privateers, sailing from southern and northern ports. On two vessels, however, the "Leo" and the "George Little," fitted at Boston, the crews were largely made up of Plymouth men, so they may be regarded as the "Plymoutht privateers" of 1812. Of the "Leo's" career we have no detailed knowledge, but it has been told us that Captain Harvey Weston, Captain Robert Hutchinson, Captain John Chase, Captain Nat Bartlett and others from this town whose names are not known, were members of her company, and that she took several prizes before she herself was forced to surrender over on the English coast. Her men were imprisoned for the rest of the war period, some of them being sent to the horrible Dartmoor prison of England, of which history says that the dreadful tales of suffering and death in the "black hole" and massacre by the guards are all too truthful, but the "Leo's" men were not there when the prison was at its very worst.

The "George Little" was a smart hermaphrodite brig, mounting ten guns and a "chaser," and was owned and fitted at Boston. Her commander was Captain Nathaniel Spooner; first lieutenant, Captain Samuel Doten; second lieutenant, William Holmes, and third lieutenant, — Turner, all of Plymouth. The crew list contained the names of many of our townsmen, but as it was not preserved, only those of Jacob Morton, William Hammatt and William Stacy are now remembered. A private log book of the voyage was kept by first lieutenant Doten, and is now in possession of his son, Captain Charles C. Doten, the first entry being: Monday, December 26, 1814, at 2 p. m., passed Boston light, fresh gale, north by east, and extreme cold. At 3 p. m. chased by one of His Majesty's gun brigs, and outsailed her with ease."

At that time there was a fleet of British men-of-war cruising along the American coast from Maine to Virginia, several frigates and gun brigs making rendezvous at Provincetown, and often coming over near the Gurnet, thence running up off Boston and along the Cape Ann shore. It was from one of these brigs that the "George Little" so easily escaped and got to sea. The log has daily entries, that of January 7, 1815, recording that William Stacy fell from the top gallant mast head, sending down royal yard, by the royal mast pitch poling, and was saved on topsail yard." "January 12, at 6.25 a. m., made a sail four leagues away, and set chase. At 11.30 she fired a lee gun—11.40 fired another, and set English colors—11.55, seeing American colors she fired her stern chasers in good direction for us, but without effect, they falling short, and in a moment struck. Proved to be the ship "Mary," six guns and eighteen men, James Bags, master, from New Foundland with fish for Lisbon. 13th took some articles from the prize, put Mr. Turner and nine men on board, and ordered her to proceed for first port in the United States."

It may here be stated that the "Mary" arrived safely at Marblehead, where with her cargo she was sold, yielding to the "George Little's" owners and men a good amount of prize money. The "Mary's" crew, being two to one of the "Little's" men put on board, attempted to retake her, but after a severe fight were driven below, and Jacob Morton of Plymouth, who was a powerful man, drew the companion slide over them, and upon it placed a large anchor, lifting alone the weight which two ordinary men would have found a test of their strength.

The "George Little" held on her course across the ocean, intending to cruise in the English channel and take her prizes, if any were there secured, into French ports. Off the Azores or Western Islands, January 21st and 22d, she chased a vessel but lost her. January 28 she overhauled the Prussian schooner "Ferwarhting," from St. Michael's for Hamburg with fruit, and put Captain Bags, his son and mate of the "Mary" on board.

"February 2 overhauled Prussian brig, "Ann Elizabeth," from London to St. Michael's, in ballast. Put four prisoners on board and ordered her to proceed. Lost both boats boarding, but saved all the men."

February 4th and 5th the privateer brig was in chase of a sloop, which escaped in the darkness of the second night, and the next day the "George Little" met her own fate, the log reading as follows: "February 6, made a sail on our lee bow, which gave chase at 8.30. Bore away, made all sail, supposing her to be a frigate. At 9 she fired her bow chaser, which fell short. At 10 her shot went over us. At 11.30, finding no means of escape, we reluctantly struck our colors to His Majesty's ship "Granicus" of 36 guns, Captain William Furlong Wise. So was lost the "George Little," in my opinion for the want of those necessaries to induce one and all to do their best to save her, as we were short of bread, beef—poor rum—generally spirits sunk—this is the effect of too much economy privateering. So ends these 24 hours, rainy, and overpowering all with heavy hearts."

The closing remarks above would indicate that the owners of the "George Little" had not been liberal in fitting out the vessel, and in consequence some discontent had existed on board. The "Granicus" took the prisoners to Gibraltar, where they were placed with others on hulks anchored in the harbor, and kept during March. On the 26th of that month "His Majesty's ship Eurylaus from the Chesapeake, arrived with news of the ratification of peace between the United States and Great Britain," and on the 29th the prisoners were embarked for England in the "Eurylaus," arriving at Plymouth April 16th. Captain Doten's memorandum becomes personal after that date, and relates that on the 17th he was sent on board the "Ganges" 74, and on the 21st "had intelligence of the arrival of the Mary at Marblehead, by an American paper of February 24." April 24, he says he "obtained permission to go on shore from the Ganges," and May 3d, "smuggled myself on board the 'Royal Sovereign,' Captain Spence, bound to Boston as a cartel"—a vessel commissioned to exchange prisoners. The "Royal Sovereign" had 400 prisoners, and as she was coming direct to Boston, Captain Doten, not being included in the list, took his chances as a stowaway. The vessel sailed from Plymouth, England, May 4th, and arrived in Boston after a passage of 35 days. In crossing the Grand Banks the schooner "Almira" of Provincetown was spoken, 25 days from home, with 10,000 fish.

A personal expense account appended to Captain Doten's journal of the "George Little's" cruise shows that at Gibraltar he spent $51.25, among the items being $15.25 for provisions, and $1.00 for liquor, a proportion which certainly was very moderate for those days. On board the "Ganges" his expenses were $14.95, and at Plymouth, $105.63, mostly for clothing, and passage home. The latter, seven pounds, was probably paid to Captain Spence for not finding him on board until the "Royal Sovereign" was at sea. The total of $171.83 paid out on account of capture, was recouped with a fair margin of profit from his share of the prize money of the "Mary."

The lack of facilities for quick transmission of news at that time, is strikingly illustrated by the fact that the treaty to end the war was signed at Ghent, December 24, 1814, two days before the "George Little" sailed from Boston, so her entire cruise was made in a period of unknown peace. The battle of New Orleans, in which the British were defeated with a loss of 2,000 men, including the death of their commanding general, Edward Pakenham, was fought January 8, 1815, two weeks after the agreement on articles of peace, which at the present time would have been known all over the world within a few minutes of their adoption.

It was a custom for old shipmasters and seamen, after their seafaring days were over, occasionally to meet in Captain Doten's counting room at the head of what is now Captain E. B. Atwood's wharf, and while a wild northeaster howled outside they would toast their shins at a good fire, smoke their pipes, and spin yarns of privateering days, or their experiences in various voyages to the West Indies or ports across the ocean. There could be no keener enjoyment to those of younger generations than to sit while all was blue about them from the tobacco exhalations, and listen to these "tales of the sea" from men who were veritable actors in the scenes so vividly recalled. Two incidents pertaining to Captain Doten's cruise in the "George Little," as her first lieutenant, thus came out, not written in his journal. When at the time of her capture by the "Granicus" the American flag was hauled down on the "George Little," Lieutenant Doten was not only chagrined, but wrathy, and swore that he wouldn't surrender his sword to any Englishman, so he broke it across his knee. The boarding officer from the "Granicus" on finding him without side arms to give up, at once declared him not entitled to consideration, and ordered him ironed. This was done, and in that condition, with Captain Spooner, he was taken to the "Granicus." To the great surprise of the boarding officer who had thus thought to humiliate him, he was greeted by Captain Wise of the frigate as he stepped on the deck with, "Hallo, Sam! what have you got those on for?" "Because I was a fool and broke my sword," was the response, at which Captain Wise laughed and called the master-at-arms to relieve him of the "bracelets," bidding him go to the private cabin. There

Captain Wise soon joined him, and over a bottle of the best, they renewed the acquaintance of some years before, when Captain Doten, then master of the brig "Dragon" of Plymouth, Mass., had sailed for three years in succession under convoy of Captain Wise, engaged in carrying naval stores up the Baltic from Plymouth, England, the "Dragon" having been chartered by the British government among other merchant vessels for that purpose. This service brought Captain Doten into quite intimate relations with many of the English naval officers, so that when he was a prisoner at Gibraltar, he was allowed many privileges. Among these was shore going almost daily, and passage through the batteries to the top of the Rock, where he could spend the time more agreeably than on the prison hulk. One day in going up he found Lieutenant Daly, who was in charge of one of the batteries, unshotting the guns, and was told by him that some ships in the offing were from America and signalled that the British had won a great victory, in honor of which he was ordered to fire a salute when the details were known. Much depressed in spirits, Captain Doten listened during the day for the salute, but it was not fired. Returning in the afternoon, Daly was then engaged in reshotting the guns, and explained that when the ships got nearer, the fortress had learned that there indeed had been a great battle "at a place called New Orleans," but it had resulted in a tremendous defeat for the British arms, and General Pakenham had been "sent home in a hogshead of rum." Daly—who of course was an Irishman—added at a low breath, "and I'm glad of it." Captain Doten told the great news to his fellow prisoners on the hulk, and that night after they had been confined below the gratings one of their number, a ship carpenter, who had located where a barrel of beer rested on the deck, bored up through the planks and bilge of the cask, inserting an improvised tube or pipe, and drew off the contents. Of course a great deal ran to waste, but enough was secured to make all hands feel mighty "merry," and they hilariously celebrated the victory of New Orleans, taunting the guard so outrageously, singing "Yankee Doodle," and bandying epithets, that they were only partially quieted by the gratings being removed, the guard drawn up around the hatchways with muskets pointed down into the crowd, and the threat made to fire if the disturbance did not cease. Undoubtedly there would have been shooting, but the English officers had heard rumors of peace, and under such circumstances the killing of unarmed prisoners would have been deemed murder. They "made a night of it," and the next day, when the loss of the beer was discovered, the cause of their high spirits was explained, while the shrewd manner in which they had obtained the liquid for the jollification, was characterized by the commander of the hulk, as "another d—d smart Yankee trick."

During the passage of the Royal Sovereign bringing home 400 prisoners, she was caught in a heavy gale near the Grand Banks, but Captain Spence, her commander, was a good seaman, and made a safe arrival at Boston.

CHAPTER XXIV.

During my youth the house now occupied by Miss Perkins, the daughter of the late John Perkins, was owned and occupied by George Drew, who has already been noticed. He built the hotel which stood on the corner of Middle street, and besides conducting a stable on that street, was largely engaged in the management of the Boston line of stages. Among other children he had a son, John Glover Drew, who was one of my playmates and schoolmates. John Glover was afflicted at times with a singular infirmity which like paralysis of the vocal organs would for the space of fifteen minutes disable him from uttering a word. I remember once his receiving a flogging for not answering a question put to him by the teacher the first time an attack occurred in school. I had a classmate at Harvard who for a time was affected in the same way, but in both cases the infirmity finally disappeared.

George Drew had a brother, Thomas, known as Dr. Drew, though I never knew of his practicing medicine, who for many years rendered important service in the educational field in Plymouth. Besides teaching a private school, he was in conjunction with Benjamin Drew, a teacher in the school in town square, and, when what was called the town school was established in 1827, and a school house built in that year for its accommodation in School street, opposite the rear land of the Davis building lot, he was selected as its teacher. He was also town clerk from 1818 to 1840, succeeding Deacon Ephraim Spooner in that office. He had a son, Thomas, three years older than myself, one of the old boys in the High school when I entered it in 1832. Tom was a bright fellow, and for many years performed valuable service as a journalist in the offices of the Worcester *Spy* and the Boston *Herald*. While William H. Lord was the teacher of the High school, a gentleman, by the way, very popular with the boys, and one who always enjoyed a joke, it was the custom at the opening of the school in the morning for the scholars to rise in turn and repeat a verse of scripture. On the morning after it became known that the teacher was engaged to Miss Persis Kendall, the daughter of Rev. Dr. Kendall, Tom rose in his place and said, "Salute Persis, the beloved of the Lord."

John Perkins, a later occupant of the house under consideration, son of John and Sarah (Adams) Perkins of Kingston, married in 1825 Adeline Tupper of Kingston, and established himself as a hatter in Plymouth, where he ever after made his home. He was many years a constable of the town, and Deputy Sheriff, and in the year 1856 he was Sheriff of Plymouth county. While constable and deputy, I have reason to know, as chairman of the Board of Selectmen during a long period, that he performed his duties with firmness, and at the same time with great discretion. For instance in arresting men for drunkenness, especially in cases where the offence was unusual or perhaps accidental, he was careful not to disgrace them by a public exhibition of their weakness, and often led them by circuitous routes to their homes, exacting the promise of a reform which rougher treatment would have tended to prevent. On one occasion, however, his usual discretion failed him. It was during the civil war when it was feared that confederate emissaries gathered in Canada might by secret invasion of our towns cause widespread damage by extensive conflagrations. While in Boston one afternoon I was informed by Alexander Holmes, President of the Old Colony Railroad, that he had been notified by the chief of police of Boston that an invasion of our coast towns was expected that night, and that extraordinary precautions had been ordered for the protection of public buildings and lumber yards, wharves and freight houses. As I had an appointment in Boston that evening and could not return home, I telegraphed to Mr. Perkins to place a dozen or fifteen watchmen in various places, stating my reason, but telling him to say nothing about it for fear of a popular alarm. When I came home the next day I was a little mortified to find that the story had been told, and that the whole town had been through the night in a fever of excitement, and consternation. I consoled myself, however, with the belief that I had done my duty and would have been unable to justify myself if I had failed to act on the information received, and any untoward act had occurred. The same precautions were taken in the cities on the coast, but with less notoriety. Mr. Perkins died August 20, 1877.

There was another alarm which occurred in 1871 or 1872, which it may be well to mention here of which nothing was known except by those immediately concerned. A letter was received from New York at the Plymouth Bank, of which I was president, in which the writer stated that he had overheard a plan to enter and rob the bank on or about a certain night, and advised that proper precautions be taken. Watchmen were placed in my house, and in that of the cashier, and extra watchmen in the bank. In those days it was frequently the plan for bank burglars to secure the officers having the keys, and carrying them to the bank to force them to open the safe. The bank watchmen were consequently instructed to admit no one to the bank on any pretense, even if accompanied by the officers themselves. After I think the second or third night of watching, the writer of the letter appeared at the bank, and said that the plan had been given up. The men in New York had either heard from their pal, who had been some time in Plymouth, that he had discovered indications of unusual precautions on the part of the bank, or for some other reason had decided to abandon the scheme. If the writer of the letter had demanded or asked for money, his story might have been thought a fake, but as he betrayed no wish for compensation, and was perfectly satisfied with the payment of twenty-five dollars for his expenses, I came to the conclusion that he was a stool pigeon, under pay from the New York police, and neither asked nor expected pay from the bank.

An actual entry of the bank occurred on the 13th of January, 1830. Pelham Winslow Warren, brother of the late Dr. Winslow Warren of Plymouth, about to leave town for a season to attend to his duties as clerk of the Massachusetts House of Representatives, deposited for safe keeping his silver and plate in the vault in the basement of the bank, whose place of business was at that time the southerly end of the building which stood where the Russell building now stands. The deposit consisted of nine silver table spoons, twelve silver teaspoons, two silver ladles, one pair of silver sugar tongs, one silver toast rack, one silver fish knife; and these plated articles, one coffee pot, one teapot, one sugar dish, one cream pot, one cake basket, and two pairs of candlesticks, all of which were marked J. T., the initials of Jeanette Taylor, the maiden name of Mr. Warren's wife. All of the above articles were stolen, and the entry was made through a back window by means of a short ladder, evidently cut from a longer one, the other part of which was afterwards found in the back yard of a resident of the town. None of the property of the bank was missing, except a roll of twenty ten cent pieces, which happened to be in the basement vault. It was evident that the burglar knew of the deposit of the silver, and was probably a Plymouth man, as no attempt was made to enter the safe in the banking room. Strong suspicions were entertained of a man, whom I remember very well, but no arrest was ever made.

For many years the two houses next but two north of the Perkins house, were at different times owned and occupied by Johnson Davee, who was a son of Solomon and Jedidah (Sylvester) Davee. He was a mason by trade, and married in 1823, Phebe, daughter of Ephraim Finney. He was one of the water commissioners who made a contract with the Jersey City cement pipe company to lay the pipe for the Plymouth water works. In the performance of his duties as commissioner he rendered important service to both the town and the company by following with trowel in hand the laying of the pipe and assuring himself that every foot had a sufficient covering of cement properly mixed and laid. He was a man of brains, and used them so that he often found himself encountering public opinion, which was said by Carlyle to be the opinion of fools. He died December 25, 1882. Ezra Johnson Davee, his son, born in 1824, entered about 1840 the counting room of Langdon & Co., a Boston house in the Smyrna trade, and after a few years, on the death of the Smyrna bookkeeper he was sent out to take charge of the business until another man could be sent out to take his place. He has been there ever since either managing the affairs of Langdon & Co., or his own for more than forty years, visiting his family in Plymouth about once in five years. I made a passage with him in 1895 in the Cephalonia on his return from one of these visits, and now in 1905 he has just sailed August 1, in the Ivernia for Liverpool, at the age of eighty-one, with the vigor of middle life scarcely impaired.   He married in Smyrna Betsey Ghout and Amelia Marion Ghout, the latter accompanying him on his late visit home.

The northerly house of the two owned by Mr. Davee was kept as a public house, under the name of the Old Colony House for some years prior to 1871, by N. M. Perry, who was a native of either Norfork or Worcester county. He had previously kept the Mansion House on the corner of North and Court streets, and later after living in Whitman a short time, he returned to Plymouth and kept what is now the Plymouth Rock House, called by him the Old Colony House, where he died July 17, 1877.

Coomer Weston of whom I next speak, was the son of Coomer and Patty (Cole) Weston, and was born in 1784. He was the keeper of the jail some years, which position he resigned in 1829, and moved into the house now occupied by Mrs. Wm. S. Danforth, where he lived until 1839 or 1840, when he built a house on the corner of Court street and Faunce's lane, now Allerton street, where he died July 7, 1870.   He was the first captain of the Standish Guards. During the last thirty years of his life he was interested in raising fruit, especially apples and pears, and in horticulture. He married in 1804 Hannah, daughter of Jabez Doten, and had Coomer, 1805, who was also at one time captain of the Standish Guards; Francis Henri, 1807, an enterprising shipmaster; Hannah Doten, 1809; Ann Maria, 1813; Lydia, 1818; Thomas, 1821, a clergyman settled at various times in various towns, and our townsman, Myles Standish Weston.

In 1849 Lemuel Bradford opened a store called the North end grocery, where the Cold Spring Grocery store now stands, and up to that time there were only three stores where there are now twenty-seven between North street and the Kingston line.   At the date above mentioned there were two hotels in the town, while now there are six open all the year, and four more open only during the summer.   As an indication of the extension of the town towards the North, it may be stated that while in 1880 the center of population was in the center of Leyden, Market and Summer streets, it was in 1900, at the house of Capt. E. B. Atwood on Court street.   It is probable that it will be found under the last census to be still further North.

In a modest house a little beyond the North end grocery on the east side of the street there lived for many years one of the uncles of the town. Every town has its uncles, and wherever you find them they are sterling, upright men, who have a kindly and affectionate word for and from everybody. Peter Holmes was the man known only as Uncle Peter, a shipmaster in his early days who sailed for my grandfather, and whose letters written from foreign ports, which I have read, show him to have been skilful and trusted in his profession. My young readers will be fortunate if they find as worthy a man as my old Uncle Peter. He died July 17, 1869. He married in 1801 Sally, daughter of Lazarus Harlow, and had five sons, one of whom was our late townsman, Peter Holmes, who lived in the house now occupied by Dr. Brown on North street, and six daughters, two of whom married our venerable townsman, William Rider Drew.

There was another uncle, Uncle Lem, sailmaker by trade, whose soul was as white as the canvas on which he worked. He was the son of Lemuel and Abigail (Pierce) Simmons, and was born in 1790. He married in 1818 Priscilla, daughter of Thomas Sherman, and died December 6, 1863. No truer inscription was ever cut on a gravestone than that which says in simple, unaffected words that, "he was universally beloved and respected; honest and upright, with a cheerful, pleasant manner, and a kind, benevolent heart. To know him was to love him."

There was still another uncle of whom I am glad of an opportunity to say a word as the tribute of a friend to his memory. Uncle Ed. Watson, the Lord of the Isle, was in many respects a remarkable man. Born and bred on Clark's Island at the entrance of Plymouth harbor about four miles from town, and eighty acres in extent, he there spent his life a sailor and fisherman when occasion demanded, always a farmer familiar with the secrets which nature is ready to disclose to her lovers, a poet of no mean acquirements, and above all a student of the events of the world, a philosopher who acted his philosophy without preaching it, and who as much deserves the title of sage as some who in a broader field won a more notorious name. He did not talk philosophy as Hawthorne described Emerson and Thoreau talking it, leaning on their hoes in the garden with Alcott sitting on the fence discoursing on the "Why and the Wherefore," but as he laboriously tilled the soil he recognized in every stone and worm and blade of grass the prodigality of nature, and in every annual bloom of the buttercup and rose a lesson of obedience to the laws of God. He said to me once, "Oh, Mr. Davis, if all were as obedient to the divine will as the blossoms on yonder apple tree, by Geo. Germain, what a world this would be." In his island home he was hospitable to the last degree. Visitors came to his grounds as if they were public, and if friends were among them he dropped his hoe or spade or scythe to entertain them when his labor in the field could ill be spared, and perhaps invited them to partake of his noonday meal, but like Sir Roderick:

> "Yet not in action, word or eye,
> Failed aught in hospitality."

I was one day at Plymouth Rock with Wm. E. Forster, who had recently distinguished himself by his efforts in parliament in favor of the educational bill, when Mr. Watson came up the wharf with a kinnerkin in one hand, and a pair of chickens in the other. I introduced him to Mr. Foster as a member of the English parliament, and he asked if the gentleman was Wm. E. Forster—Forster, with an "r," and when assured that he was, he said, "I am glad to see you. I know all about you, that last education speech you made hit the nail on the head." The two then engaged in conversation on English affairs, and after they separated I pointed out to Mr. Forster the island on which Mr. Watson was born, and had always lived, having had only a schooling of three months in all his life. "You astonish me," he replied, adding, "why, that man knows more about English politics than three-fourths of the members of parliament."

To give him his full name, Edward Winslow Watson, son of John and Lucia Marston Watson, was born December 17, 1797, and died where he was born, August 8, 1876. His funeral was unique and impressive. The green bottom lap streak boat in which many hundreds of times he had stemmed the winds and tide was the catafalque which bore him to town, while the boats of his island and Saquish and Gurnet friends, like white-winged angels, attended him to his rest.

In closing this notice of my friend I will quote from his little book of poems lines illustrating the serious thought which his mind evolved from the most trifling incidents of life:

"Dear Jennie, that nice cranberry tart,
You gave to me bedecked with paste,
Lies like a bleeding, broken heart,
Whose inner life has run to waste.

You placed it on the basket top,
In paper coverings still it lay,
Mid rolling seas a lurch it got.
And bled its inner life away.

Its fate, how like the buoyant heart
That o'er life's billowy ocean springs
Till disappointment tips the bark,
And overstrained, snap go the strings."

CHAPTER XXV.

I speak next of the Samoset House estate, not for the purpose of following its title, but for the purpose of speaking of its occupants at various times. As long ago as I remember the estate extended from Court street up Wood's Lane to what is now Allerton street. Its Court street line extended by the line of the present gutter, the street being widened afterwards by cutting off a strip of that and adjoining estates on the north. There was a high, close board fence along the street, which I remember because when a boy I brought up against it a runaway horse which I was riding. The house on the estate was what is now the old part of the Samoset, and was owned and occupied by Mrs. Betsey H. Hodge and her father, Dr. Jas. Thacher, until 1827. It faced the south, and was reached by a driveway from Wood's Lane, and its spacious yard was bounded on the southwest by a carriage house and barn, a handsome lawn lying along Court street. The estate called Longwood was altogether the most aristocratic one in town, and at the above date, with the exception of the old Merrick Ryder house on the southeast corner of the Mixter lot, and an old red house on the corner of Lothrop Place, no houses were in sight at the north. In 1827, Dr. Thacher moved into the easterly part of the Winslow house on North street, and the estate was sold to Charles Sever, who married in that year Mrs. Hodge's daughter Jane. Mr. Sever was a Kingston man, brother of Col. John and James N. Sever, and as I have no recollection of his connection with any business in Plymouth, I think he must have been associated with his brothers in navigation and foreign trade. In 1833 Mr. Sever sold the estate to John Thomas, and moved temporarily into the house on Middle street next below Mr. Beaman's undertaker's establishment, while he was building the Sever house on Russell street, which he did not live to occupy, but which was occupied by his family until the recent death of his daughter Catherine.

In 1837 Mr. Thomas sold the estate to Jason Hart, and removed to New York. His business connections in that city, and his death in Irvington, have been referred to in a previous chapter. Mr. Hart has been already noticed as a member of the firm of Hart and Alderman, and in business alone where the store of H. H. Cole on Main street now stands.

In 1844 the Old Colony Railroad corporation then building their road from Boston to Plymouth, bought the estate and built and furnished the Samoset House, which was opened in 1845, under the management of Joseph Stetson, who was employed by the road for the purpose. Mr. Stetson was succeeded by James S. Parker and Henry C. Tribou, under the firm name of Parker & Tribou, who kept it under the direction of the railroad until 1850. In that year the house and furniture were sold to the Samoset House Association, who leased it until 1878, at various times to the following persons in the order named: Granville Gardner and Henry C. Tribou, under the firm name of Gardner & Tribou, James S. Parker, A. & N. Hoxie, Comfort Whiting and Peleg C. Chandler. In 1878, while Mr. Chandler was lessee, he bought the estate, and in 1882 his widow sold it, exclusive of house lots at its westerly end to T. F. Frobisher. In 1883 Mr. Frobisher sold the above remaining estate to Daniel H. Maynard, who sold it a few years ago to the present proprietors, James S. Clark and the late Edward E. Green doing business under the firm name of Clark & Green.

While I am wandering about the North part of the town, let me speak of Bourne Spooner, who having been dead thirty-five years, cannot be remembered by any of my readers who are much less than fifty years of age. Few are aware to whom the town was indebted, for the establishment of the Plymouth Cordage Co., a corporation filling so large a place among the industries of the town, and which with its growing proportions promises to stand many years as a conspicuous and deserved monument to his memory. He was a son of Nathaniel and Mary (Holmes) Spooner, and was born in Plymouth, February 2, 1790. After receiving the education which our public schools could furnish, he went to New Orleans, where he spent ten years engaged in rope making, but in what capacity I have no means of knowing. It is probable that the material used in the manufacture was Kentucky hemp, as its transportation from the hemp fields by the Mississippi river was easy and cheap. It is doubtful whether sisal from Mexico was much used in those days and Russia hemp and Manilla could be obtained in Boston more expeditiously and cheaper than in New Orleans. The unprofitableness of slave labor employed in that city appealed to his Yankee spirit of thrift, and he conceived the idea of establishing if possible a cordage factory in his native town. Returning home he kept for a time a store opposite the Green, and later conferred with a number of gentlemen in Boston, who looked favorably on the scheme of a Plymouth factory, and on the 12th of July, 1824, an act of incorporation was granted by the Massachusetts legislature to Bourne Spooner, William Lovering, Jr., John Dodd and John Russell, and their associates, as the Plymouth Cordage Company, with power to hold real estate not exceeding twenty thousand dollars. The location decided upon for the factory was in the north part of Plymouth, on a stream supplied by two brooks, one of which was called Nathans brook, after Nathan Holmes, the grandfather of Gideon F. Holmes, the present treasurer of the company, the capacity of which was twenty horse power. Thus it seems evident that any very considerable growth of the establishment was not anticipated. The part of Plymouth selected for the factory was called in Pilgrim days, "Plain Dealing," but in my boyhood, Bungtown, and a little later, North Town. When the Old Colony Railroad established a station there they unwittingly adopted practically the old Pilgrim "Seaside," as "Plain Dealing" meant a plain by the sea. The growth of business set in at a very early day, and up to 1883, when the capital stock of the company was increased to half a million of dollars, only forty-four thousand dollars had been paid in, and all the remainder of the half million had been furnished by the profits of the company. In 1894 the capital was still further increased to a million, all of the increase being furnished by the stockholders. To meet the growth of the factory business the original water power was supplemented by steam engines in 1837, 1839, 1850, 1868, 1888, and 1900. The last two of these are of 1500 and 1600 horse power. In 1827 the sales of cordage amounted to 601,023 pounds, and in 1899 to 19,597,644 pounds. In addition to the above, while the first lot of binding twine sold in 1882 amounted to 384,820 pounds, the sales of the same in 1899 amounted to 27,905,981 pounds, and the entire product of the factory is estimated to be about one-seventh of the product of all the Cordage companies in the United States. Of the large cables made by the Company I have personal knowledge of one of fifteen or fifteen and a half inches. About the year 1865, an English steamer, named, I think, "Concordia," was wrecked on Cape Cod and bought by Boston parties. The cable, to which I refer, was ordered for the purpose of hauling her off shore. I was told by Osborne Howes, one of the purchasers that within forty-eight hours after it was coiled on the beach the junk men cut it up and carried it off. The steamer was got off and towed to Boston, where she was lengthened and refitted for service.

I have said thus much concerning the Cordage Company for the purpose of illustrating the sagacity, energy, good judgment and integrity of Mr. Spooner, who was until his death, during the career of the company, its agent, and after 1837, its treasurer. He did his business so unostentatiously, that I think few of his fellow citizens realized the great work he was doing in building up an industry which has done so much in promoting the growth and welfare of Plymouth. Next to his interest in the affairs of the company intrusted to his care, was his interest in the anti-slavery cause. How, and exactly when he enlisted in the cause, I never knew. His life in New Orleans probably opened his eyes to the evils of the institution of slavery, but I do not think that he entered the anti-slavery ranks until after the visit of George Thompson to Massachusetts, and the Garrison mob in Boston in 1835. Among the earliest in Plymouth to engage in the movement, according to my best recollections were, Lemuel Stephens, William Stephens, Ichabod Morton, Edwin Morton, Ephraim Harlow, Kendall Holmes, George Adams and Deacon Wm. Putnam Ripley, and I think Johnson Davie and their families. Nearly all of these, except the Ripleys, lived on "tother side," as it was called, like "l'autre cote" of Paris the other side of the Seine, as our "tother side" is the other side of Town Brook. The merchants, professional men, including ministers, and the politicians in both the whig and democratic parties, were either too timid to join the anti-slavery ranks, or were decidedly hostile to the anti-slavery movement.

An anti-slavery meeting was held on the evening
of July 4, 1835, in the Robinson church, which was disturbed
by an incipient mob which contented itself with breaking a few
windows, and afterwards smearing with tar the dry goods
sign of Deacon Ripley.   Though the OLD COLONY MEMOR-
IAL contained a paid advertisement of the meeting, its columns were silent concerning its doings and the disturbance.
It is of little consequence how or when Mr. Spooner became
interested in the movement. He became one of the most prominent men in the state, supporting it, and undoubtedly furnished to it material aid not exceeded in amount by the contributions of any other in its ranks.   He was a constant friend
and supporter of Garrison, Phillips, Quincy and Douglas, all
of whom frequently enjoyed the hospitalities of his home.

Mr. Spooner was widely known, especially by fellow travel-
lers on the railroad, as an expert and entertaining story teller,
and skilful in the art.   He knew how to tell a story, omitting
details, careful never to say that he had a capital story, being
willing to leave its quality to the judgment of his listeners,
never laughing until he had finished, and then when his companions began to laugh he would join with them as heartily
as if he had never told the story before.   He told many stories
about his great uncle, Deacon Ephraim Spooner, which seemed to amuse some persons, the humor of which I never could
see.

But he had a nearer kinsman, his own uncle, Thomas
Spooner, who was a man of both wit and humor, from whom
he must have acquired his own delicate sense of these qualities.   Thomas Spooner was at one time town treasurer, and
many years a constable.   One evening he was called upon to
serve a precept, and while making his way in the dark through
a private yard he encountered a clothes line, and then a second
one which knocked off his hat. "By George," said he, "I
never knew before what the Bible meant by 'precept upon
precept; line upon line.'"   He was an ardent whig, and when
returning home one day after an absence of a couple of days,
he found posted on the town tree a notice for a democratic
meeting. "By thunder," said he, "can't I leave town twenty-
four hours without there being the devil to pay?" and he pulled the notice down.

Mr. Bourne Spooner, not only as occasion offered, repeated stories which his tenacious memory had treasured up, but he found satire and humor in the incidents of every day life, which he often used to point a moral, as for instance, the case of the old lady who had a husband somewhat addicted to profanity, and who when rebuked by a sister of the church then attending revival meetings because she bestowed so much care on her husband, who she said was a bad man, replied, "I know sister, my husband is a very bad man, and has little to expect in the next world, so I feel it my duty to do what I can for his comfort and happiness in this."

Mr. Spooner was a tender hearted man, especially towards his workmen and their families. An instance of his tender feelings once came under my own observation. The Cordage Company did their banking business in Boston, discounting once a month at the Old Colony Bank a note to obtain bills for the monthly pay roll. During one of the financial panics when money was almost impossible to obtain, he came one day into the Plymouth Bank in despair. He said that he could not get a dollar in the Old Colony Bank, and Mr. Dodd, his Boston director, could not obtain a dollar in Boston. He had put off the settlement of his payroll two or three times, and he was afraid to go home and meet the disappointed looks of his men, whose families were in absolute need of their wages. As he said this, I noticed the tears trickling down his cheeks. It so happened, either by good luck or good lookout, we had for some time been confining our discounts to short paper, and our maturities were keeping us well supplied with funds. We gave him the money, charging him only 7 per cent, while as the following incident will show, money was worth more than double that rate. A day or two afterwards I met on Water street, Boston, the President and Treasurer of a large manufacturing concern in Taunton, who asked me if I would let him have ten thousand dollars. I told him that I would, and should charge him for it on a four months' note, fifteen per cent. He turned on his heel and left me. An hour after I met him in the National Bank of Redemption, and he asked me if my offer held good. I told him it did, and the loan was made then and there.

Mr. Spooner married in 1813, Hannah, daughter of Amasa and Sarah (Taylor) Bartlett, and died July 21, 1870.

All through my boyhood there were two brothers living on adjoining estates on the easterly side of Court street, Leavitt Taylor Robbins and Nathan Bacon Robbins, sons of Charles and Mary (Bacon) Robbins. The former lived in the house now owned by Miss Elizabeth N. Perkins from the time of his marriage in 1831, until his death, owning a large estate of from fifteen to twenty acres extending from Court street to the shore. He built a wharf and established a lumber yard about 1831, which he carried on forty years or more, until his death, and which was afterwards carried on by his son, Leavitt Taylor Robbins, Jr., until his recent death. During that long period it was carried on by father and son under the same name seventy-five years, always with the highest credit and probably longer known on the Kennebec and Penobscot than any other lumber yard in Massachusetts. Mr. Robbins, born in 1799, married in 1831, Lydia, daughter of Ephraim Fuller of Kingston, and had Lydia Johnson, 1833, who married Noah P. Burgess; Elizabeth Fuller, 1834, who married Nathaniel Morton; Leavitt Taylor, 1837, who married Louisa A. Bradford, and Mrs. Anna V. (Wright) Southgate, Lemuel Fuller, 1839, Helen F., who married Edward G. Hedge, and Sarah B., and died September 24, 1871. Nathan Bacon Robbins owned and occupied the house now owned and occupied by Mrs. Frederick N. Knapp, and was a shipmaster by profession, sailing I believe, chiefly in the employ of John and James N. Sever of Kingston. One of the ships commanded by him was the Brookline. Born in 1797, he married in 1819, Lucia W., daughter of George Rider, and second in 1830, Lucia Ripley, of Kingston, and died December 24, 1865.

CHAPTER XXVI.

I trust that I may be pardoned if I speak of my brother, Charles G. Davis, of whose early life, though only two years have elapsed since his death, most of my readers know little or nothing. The son of William Davis, Jr., and Joanna (White) Davis, he was born May 30, 1820, in the house now known as the Plymouth Rock House on Cole's Hill. After receiving a common school education in Plymouth, he was fitted for college, under the direction of Hon. John A. Shaw of Bridgewater, and graduated at Harvard in 1840. He studied law in the office of Jacob H. Loud of Plymouth, at the Harvard Law school, and in the office of Hubbard and Watts in Boston, and was admitted to the bar in Plymouth at the August term of the Common Pleas Court in 1842, establishing himself in practice in Boston, where he remained until 1853. During his nine years residence in Boston, he was at various times in partnership with William H. Whitman, George P. Sanger and Seth Webb. In 1848 he was one of the prominent organizers of the Free Soil Party, and was a delegate to the Buffalo Convention, which nominated Martin Van Buren for President, and Charles Francis Adams for Vice President.

In 1851 he was tried before Benjamin F. Hallet, U. S. Commissioner, for complicity in the rescue of Shadrach, a fugitive slave. The charge was that as he was entering the court room, Shadrach was going out, and that he held the door in such a way as to make the escape effectual. Though he was acquitted, I never knew how much or how little, if at all, he aided the negro in his flight. In 1853 Mr. Davis was a member of the state constitutional convention, and in that year changed his residence to Plymouth, and building a house, established there his permanent home. In 1856 he was appointed a member of the State Board of Agriculture, and in the same year chosen President of the Plymouth County Agricultural Society, retaining the latter office until 1876. In 1859 he was chosen an overseer of Harvard University. In 1861

he was appointed by Gov. Andrew on a commission to propose
a plan for a State Agricultural College, and after the establishment of that institution, served as one of its trustees many
years. In 1862 he represented his town in the General Court,
and in the same year was appointed under the U. S. Revenue
law assessor for the first District, holding that office until
1869. In 1874 he was appointed Judge of the 3d District
Court, and remained on the bench until his death. He loved
his native town, and was always recognized as a public spirited man, who would make a liberal response to every call aim-
ing at its welfare. He built Davis building in 1854, the brick
block at the corner of Railroad avenue in 1870, and was for
many years the largest individual holder of real estate in the
town. He married November 19, 1845, Hannah Stevenson,
daughter of Col. John B. Thomas and Mary (LeBaron)
Thomas, and has two children living, Joanna, wife of Richard
H. Morgan, and Charles S. Davis, a graduate at Harvard in
1880, and now practicing law in Plymouth.

As thirty-seven years have elapsed since the death of Robert B. Hall, I am inclined to think that three-quarters of my
readers know no more concerning him than that his widow
was until her recent death a much respected resident in Plymouth. Mr. Hall was the son of Charles and Catherine Hall,
and was born in Boston, January 12, 1812. He had not as far
as I know a collegiate education, but prepared for the Congregational ministry at the Yale Divinity school. After leaving the school he spent two years in Europe, where he grati-
fied his taste not only by literary pursuits, but also by the
study of art in its various forms. He served also during his
absence as an agent of the American Anti-Slavery Society.
In 1837, soon after his return, he was settled over the Third
Society in Plymouth, whose place of worship was on Pleasant
street, opposite Training Green. In that year he delivered an
address before the Pilgrim Society on the anniversary of the
Landing of the Pilgrims, and in 1839 on the same occasion an
address before the Third church. In 1841 he delivered an address at the dedication of Oak Grove cemetery.

In 1840, largely through his influence, the present church
on the north side of Town Square was built under the name
of the Church of the Pilgrimage, and a new society was
formed called the Society of the Pilgrimage.

In 1844 Mr. Hall became Episcopalian in faith, and at his house on the 15th of November in that year, the present Episcopal Society was formed, and on the 3d of October, 1846, the church on Russell street was consecrated with Theodore W. Snow, rector, who had been chosen on the 13th of the previous April. At about that time Mr. Hall was called to St. James' Episcopal church in Roxbury, where he remained several years. In 1849 he returned to Plymouth, where he preached for a time in the Robinson church, and soon after built the house on the corner of Lothrop Place, which he made his home until his death. In 1855 he joined the Know Nothing movement, and was chosen State Senator, and in 1856 he was chosen by the Know Nothings, member of Congress: In 1858 on the termination of the Know Nothing party, he was sent back to Congress by the Republicans, thus serving two terms in Washington. After his retirement from public life he devoted himself to literary pursuits, and in 1864 delivered the oration at the dedication of the Masonic building in Boston on the corner of Tremont and Boylston streets.

Mr. Hall married in 1841 Abby Mitchell, daughter of Nathaniel Morton Davis, and died April 15, 1868.

I suppose that few of my readers know that Jonathan Walker, the man with the branded hand, ever lived in Plymouth. About fifty years ago, or perhaps a little earlier, he lived in the house now standing in what is called the Nook at the head) waters of Hobb's Hole brook. I do not remember to have ever seen him, but I recall the time when he was complained of for shingling his house on the Sabbath. He was born in Harvard, Mass., March 22, 1799, and at the age of seventeen went to sea. When quite young he assisted Benjamin Lundy in colonizing slaves in Mexico, and for a time lived with his family in Florida. In 1844 he assisted four slaves to escape by water, but was overtaken and captured with his companions by a Revenue Cutter, which was sent in pursuit. He was carried to Pensacola, and after trial for his offense was sentenced to stand one hour in the pillory, to pay a fine of one hundred and fifty dollars, and be branded on the hand with the letters S. S., signifying slave stealer. It is creditable to Southern humanity that a blacksmith refused to heat the instrument of torture. He remained in prison eleven months in default of

payment of the fine, and was then by the aid of Northern
friends released. After his release he delivered lectures in
various Northern towns, and then settled down in Plymouth.
In 1863 he bought a farm in Lake Harbor, Michigan, and
carried on the business of raising fruit until his death, April
30, 1875. He left behind him in Plymouth a son John, whom
I knew very well, and whom it fell to me once to aid during
a pecuniary embarrassment. His father had neglected his
education, but he was a noble fellow in whose presence I always felt that I was in the presence of a man.

I think he was one of not more than twenty men whose personality during my long life has impressed me. He always
called me William, and I always called him John. I would
have trusted to him my life in any emergency, for I knew
that he would have risked his own to save the life of a fellow
man. He held a commission as pilot for some years, and in
appearance an ideal pilot he was. With his broad Scotch face,
almost buried in hair and whiskers, it was easy to imagine
him in his tarpaulin and oil clothes beating his pilot lugger
up channel in a heavy sea. About eight years ago he went to
Michigan to live with a sister on a farm which his father had
occupied, and a few months ago I heard of his death.

I have spoken of Joseph Bartlett, who lived on the corner
of Court street and Court square, but there was another
Joseph Bartlett of whom probably few of my readers have
ever heard. He was a man of diversified talents, of diversified traits of character, and led a diversified life. He was
author, poet, orator, lecturer, lawyer, merchant, gambler, prisoner for debt, and generally an adventurer. He was son of
Sylvanus and Martha (Wait) Bartlett, and was born in Plymouth in 1761. His father was a well to do merchant, who
owned real estate in the neighborhood of the present junction
of High and Russell streets. He had a sister, Sophia, who
married Benjamin Drew, the father of our late deceased friend,
Benjamin Drew, and I have always supposed that our friend
inherited his brilliant talents from his mother's side of the
house. Mr. Bartlett graduated at Harvard in 1782, and
studied law in Salem, and was recommended to be sworn as
attorney in 1788. Soon after the close of the revolution he
went to England, and in London, attracted by his eccentri-

cities and wit much attention. One evening at the theatre during the performance of a play in which American soldiers were caricatured as cobblers, tailors and tinkers, he stood up in the pit and called for cheers for the army of cobblers, tailors and tinkers who had defeated the British. The interference so far from being resented, was taken in good part, and the young Londoners took him into their companionship and invited him to the clubs where he was for a time made much of. He afterwards fell into gambling habits, and finally was imprisoned for debt. He wrote a play, and from the proceeds of its sale obtained a release, after which for a short time he appeared on the stage. After his return home he opened a law office in Woburn, and painted it black, calling it "the coffin" to attract notice. He afterwards removed to Cambridge, and in 1799 delivered a poem before the Harvard Phi Beta Kappa Society on "Physiognomy," in which some of his allusions, like the following, were believed to be personal:

"First on the list observe that woman's form,
Who looks a very monster in a storm.
Her skinny lips, her pointed nose behold,
And say if nature's marked her for a scold;
Observe her chin, her every feature trace,
And see the fury trembling in her face;
By nature made to mar the joys of life;
And damn that man who has her for a wife."

In 1823 he delivered a Fourth of July oration in Boston, and recited a poem entitled, "The New Vicar of Bray." At one time in his varied career he was a member of the Maine legislature, and at another had a law office in Portsmouth, N. H. In 1823 he published a collection of "Aphorisms on men, manners, principles and things," and also an essay on "The blessings of poverty," prefaced by the following lines:

I tell thee Poverty that you and I
Have friendly met together;
Thou art the soul of minstrelsy
In every kind of weather.
Through all life's journey thou hast not
From me an hour departed;
Thou never hast my track forgot,
Which proves thee most true hearted.

I have two letters from Mr. Bartlett to my grandfather, William Davis, soliciting aid, and one to my grandfather from

President Kirkland of Harvard University, inclosing thirteen dollars contributed by a few Cambridge gentlemen with the request that he would use it for Mr. Bartlett's benefit. He married Anna May, daughter of Thomas Witherell of Plymouth, and died in Boston, October 21, 1827.

Of Perez Morton, a Plymouth man, and one of the most distinguished members of the Massachusetts bar in the latter part of the eighteenth century, and the first half of the nineteenth, probably few of my Plymouth readers have ever heard. He was son of Joseph and Amiah (Bullock) Morton of Plymouth, and was born October 22, 1750. He graduated at Harvard in 1771, and was recommended to be sworn as attorney in 1774. In 1786 he was made a Barrister, and on the 7th of September, 1810, he was appointed Attorney General. At the time of the appointment of Mr. Morton as Attorney General, the office of Solicitor General was occupied by Daniel Davis, who had been appointed January 20, 1802, under an act passed March 4, 1800, reviving the office which had been discontinued for a time after the revolution. In 1821 it having been the general feeling for some time that the two offices were unnecessary, the legislature, while unwilling on account of the respect entertained for their incumbents, to abolish either, passed an act providing "that whenever the office of Attorney General or Solicitor General shall become vacant by death, resignation or otherwise, the salary annexed to the office, which shall first so become vacant as aforesaid, shall thenceforth cease and determine." As neither death nor resignation occurred, an act was passed March 14, 1832, to take effect June 1, abolishing both offices and establishing the office of Attorney General for the Commonwealth. On the 31st of May, therefore, 1832, Mr. Morton went out of office, and James T. Austin was appointed under the new law, Attorney General of the Commonwealth. Sarah Morton, the wife of Perez, was an authoress of some repute. She wrote a book entitled, "The power of Sympathy," a copy of which is in the library of the Pilgrim Society, which is claimed to have been the first American novel. Mr. Morton died in Boston, October 14, 1837.

I cannot pass by Court Square without a notice of Mrs. Nicolson's boarding house, which stood many years on the north side of the Square. Thomas Nicholson, son of James, came into possession of the house after the death of his father in 1772. He married for a second wife about 1790, Hannah, daughter of John Otis, and sister of Mrs. Grace Heyman Goddard, already noticed as the mother of Mrs. Abraham Jackson. Thomas Nicolson was a shipmaster, and I believe was for some time before his death in the United States Revenue Service, and died on the island of Gaudaloupe, February 9, 1798.

He was also during the revolution commander of the privateer sloop America, carrying six swivels and seventy men, owned by William Watson, Ephraim Spooner and others. Capt. Nicolson had by his first wife Sarah Mayhew, nine children: Sarah, 1771; Hannah, 1773; Polly, 1775; Elizabeth, 1777; Lucy Mayhew, 1778; Nancy, 1780; Thomas, 1782; James, 1784, and Anna. Of these Hannah married John Morong; Polly married John Allen of Salem, and Anna married John D. Wilson of Salem. Lucy Mayhew died in Boston, January 21, 1858. By his second wife, Hannah Otis, he had Samuel, 1791, who married Sarah Brinley, and died in Boston, January 6, 1866; Hannah Otis, 1793, who married William Spooner; Daniel, 1796, who died March 6, 1815; Caroline, 1798, who married Edward Miller of Quincy.

The estate when Capt. Nicolson died extended from the present yard of Mr. Hedge to the line of Mr. Bittinger, and consisted of the main house and a range of outbuildings which included a woodshed, chaise house, ice house and barn, with a large garden in the rear. After Capt. Nicolson's death, but precisely when I do not know, Mrs. Nicolson fitted up her house as an inn, and called it the Old Colony House. The Pilgrim House was the stage house, and Mrs. Nicolson's house was the lawyer's house. The judges, however, sought private lodgings, and I remember that Chief Justice Shaw always occupied a front parlor in the house opposite Court square, which was the residence of Ichabod Shaw, where the Methodist church now stands. Among the regular boarders in the Old Colony House whom I remember were Samuel Davis, Ebenezer G. Parker, cashier of the Old Colony Bank, Gustavus Gilbert, attorney, Eliab Ward, student at law, Isaac N. Stoddard and Hiram Fuller, teachers. During the sessions of the court it was the gathering place of the lawyers who, without railroad conveniences, made a week of it under Mrs. Nicolson's roof. There might be found Charles J. Holmes of Rochester, Seth Miller of Wareham, Zachariah Eddy of Middleboro, Williams Latham of Bridgewater, William Baylies and Austin Packard of West Bridgewater, Welcome Young of East Bridgewater, Kilborn Whitman of Pembroke, and Ebenezer Gay of Hingham. To these were sometimes added James T. Austin, Attorney General, Franklin Dexter and Rufus Choate. Timothy Coffin of New Bedford generally attended the Plymouth court, and was sought for in many cases on one side or the other to make the argument to the jury. If he could find anybody to play a game of cards he would play nearly all night, and come into court in the morning looking as fresh as a rose. The house was a rambling one with sleeping rooms arranged in such a way that it was difficult to find them. There was one in particular through which it was necessary for the occupants of the other rooms to pass. This room was assigned on one occasion to Mr. Choate, whose habit it was to retire early. In the morning when he appeared at the breakfast table and was asked how he had slept, he answered, "Very well, I thank you, considering I slept in the highway." As the lawyers sat by the fire in the evening, Mr. Eddy in a dressing gown, and Mr. Latham securing a seat near the spittoon, occasionally some one would say, "Packard, are we there?" To understand this question, a story must be told. In the early days of the Old Colony Railroad, just after what was called the Abington branch was built, the lawyers I have named met at Bridgewater to take the train for Abington to meet the last train to Plymouth to attend the usual session of the court. When the branch train reached East Bridgewater, Packard, who thought he knew all about the road, jumped up and said, "Warl guntlemen, here we ar," and they all got out to find the train going on, and themselves in a dreary station, on a cold and dark November night, seventeen miles from Plymouth. There was only one thing to do, to hire an omnibus, which they promptly did, and they reached their destination about half past ten, cold, hungry and cross. Hence the inquiry, "Packard, are we there?" All the gentlemen named are dead, and were doubtless met by Packard on the further shore with "Warl gentlemen, here we ar." I hope he has not landed them at the wrong station.

In 1836 Mrs. Nicolson gave up the public house, and moved to Boston to live with her daughter, Mrs. Miller, and died in that city, June 22, 1844. The Old Colony House was kept afterwards by Zaben Olney and William Randall, and after a further occupation as a private residence by Moses Bates and Theodore Drew, was sold in 1835 to Mary Howard Russell and taken down.

On the south side of Court square on the corner of School street, there lived until 1839 a worthy old man, who for some years was stone blind. He was Joseph Barnes, the great-grandfather of our townsman, bearing the same name. He carried, extended out in front of him, a staff about eight feet long, with which he tapped the sidewalk constantly, and directed his steps without any other guide or support. It was his privilege to live in days when bicycles, automobiles and trolley cars had not been invented to endanger the lives of even the far-seeing and wary. As I remember him he walked alone through the various streets of the town, and if occasional aid became necessary in avoiding some new obstruction, both old and young were ready to lend it. His wife kept a little candy shop, if so it may be called, in the front room on the east side of the front door, and there children who thought it too far to go to Nancy and Eliza's shop on Market street, patronized her. It was a queer kind of a shop, showing as its only furniture a bed and chairs, and looking glass and table. Under the bed three or four spice boxes were placed in a row, containing in tempting neatness assortments of candy comprising the usual twisted parti-colored sticks, and kisses and Salem Gibralters. How these last received their name, and why their manufacture should have been confined to Salem, I never knew, but there they were made, and there they are made today, and if any of my young readers never saw them, they had better induce their grocer to send for some and keep them in stock. Their makers are welcome to this gratuitous advertisement. Mr. Barnes died January 28, 1839, and the house in which he lived was occupied some years by Nathaniel Cobb Lanman, and finally removed to Lothrop street, when Court square was widened in 1857.

CHAPTER XXVII.

Through all my boyhood Nathaniel Morton Davis occupied
the house on Court street, now owned by the Old Colony
Club, except for a year, when, while repairing the house, he
occupied for a year or more the house on Leyden street, which
his mother had occupied before her removal to Boston. The
house at that time had its front door on the southerly side
where an arch may now be seen in the front hall. On the west
side of the front door there was a good sized parlor, which
reached within about three feet of the street. What is now
the library, lapped far enough by the above parlor to admit
of a door from one to the other, and was the law office of Mr.
Davis, with an outside entrance north of the parlor above
mentioned.

Mr. Davis was the son of William and Rebecca Morton
Davis, and was born in Plymouth March 3, 1785. He graduated at Harvard in 1804, and after studying law with Judge
Joshua Thomas, was admitted to the bar in Plymouth. He
was appointed early in his career Judge Advocate, with the
rank of Major, which title he bore through life. In 1821 he
was appointed Chief Justice of the Court of Sessions, and
served until the court was abolished in 1828. He was at various times representative and senator, and was a member of
the executive council from 1841 to 1843. He was a director
of the Plymouth Bank from 1826 to 1839, and from 1840 to
1848, and President from 1840 until his death. He was a
man of commanding presence, an impressive speaker, and was
selected on several public occasions to act as presiding officer.
The first time I saw him in the President's chair was at a
whig county celebration on the Fourth of July, 1840, when
the chief address of the day was made by Robert C. Winthrop.
His speech and his toasts calling up the speakers were unusually happy. Martin Van Buren, who had succeeded Andrew Jackson as President, and was a candidate for re-election, had many times boasted of following in the footsteps of
his illustrious predecessor, and Mr. Davis gave as one of the
sentiments, "Martin Van Buren, he has followed so fast in the

footsteps of his illustrious predecessor, that he has accomplished his journey in half the time."

Mr. Davis married, July 8, 1817, Harriet Lazell, daughter of Judge Nahum Mitchell of East Bridgewater, and his children were William, born May 12, 1818, who married December 2, 1849, Helen, daughter of John Russell; Abby Mitchell, born November 9, 1821, who married in 1841 Robert B. Hall, and Elizabeth Bliss, born November 8, 1824, who married Henry G. Andrews. Mr. Davis died at the United States Hotel in Boston, July 29, 1848.

In 1849, William Davis, previous to his marriage, cut off the westerly end of the house in question, and it was moved to a lot on Court street, opposite the foot of Cushman street, where it now stands the property of Charles B. Bartlett. I have never known a more complete mutilation of a house than that caused by the alteration to which I have referred. .

Before leaving Mr. Davis I must tell a story about his dog Ponto, which illustrates the intelligence often found in the canine race. He was an ordinary black and white cur, which, as is often the case with favorite dogs, was equally a delight to his master, and a nuisance to everybody else. He was in the habit of following the family to church, and after being kicked out by the sexton, he would slyly find his way in, and going up the broad aisle, scratch at the family pew door. In order to stop this habit, orders were given to keep him confined to the house on Sundays, to which Ponto demurred. After suffering confinement two Sundays he circumvented the orders and through the first door or window which happened to be opened, every Sunday morning at the earliest opportunity he left the house and fled to the house of Nathaniel Holmes, on School street, who did the family chores, and there passed the day, returning home in the evening. He knew when Sunday came by symptoms, which he easily discovered, and while never going to the Holmes house at any other time, he kept up his weekly visits for many months, until sickness or accident ended his career.

Ponto reminds me of another dog which belonged to John J. Russell, when he lived in the Cotton house, which stood where Brewster street enters Court street. Mr. Russell bought of Warren Douglas of Half Way Pond one of a litter of hound pups with the agreement to take him when he became old enough to be of use. When he thought it about time to bring him home he went for him, and it being a rainy day he held the pup by a chain between his feet beneath the boot which excluded all sight of the road over which he had never before travelled. At the end of a fortnight, thinking that the pup had been chained to his kennel long enough to become domesticated, he unfastened his chain with the intention of giving him his breakfast. Preferring, however, freedom to breakfast, the pup hopped over the fence, and was last seen running up Court square. Mr. Russell, thinking he might have found his way to Half Way Pond, drove there the next day, and there was the pup. On comparing notes with Mr. Douglas, it was found that the little fellow had travelled ten miles in less than two hours. So much for the instinct of Ponto and the hound pup. If we ask what instinct is, it might be correct to say that it is the gift of God unimpaired by education. The homing pigeon has it when she finds her way to her distant nest. The Indian has it somewhat qualified by civilization when he laughs at the white man who needs a watch to show the lapse of time. The Christian has it, beyond the realm of reason, a divine teacher assuring him of a life beyond the grave, a belief in which the device of human education has done much to impair if not destroy. But without further suggestion I submit these mysteries to the investigation of my readers and pass on.

The Old Plymouth Bank building stood until recently where the Russell building now stands. It was bought by the bank at the time of its incorporation in 1803, and a brick addition was erected at its southerly end for the accommodation of the bank. William Goodwin, who had served as cashier from the foundation of the bank, died July 17, 1825, and Nathaniel Goodwin was chosen to succeed him. He moved at once into the bank house, and continued to occupy it until his resignation as cashier in 1845, when he moved into the house on the corner of Middle and Carver streets, where he died February 13, 1857. In early life he carried on the manufacture of rope in Nantucket, and later in Beverly. He was the son of General Nathaniel Goodwin, and was born in 1770 in the house on Leyden street, owned and occupied by his father, and afterwards long kept as a hotel by John Howland Bradford, and known as Bradford's tavern. He married in 1794 Lydia, daughter of Nathaniel Gardner of Nantucket, and had seven children, only four of whom I remember, Lydia Coffin, 1800, who married Thomas Hedge; Albert Gardner, 1802, who married 1831 Eliza Huzzey of Nantucket, and 1840 Eliza Ann, daughter of Joseph Bartlett, and Nathaniel, 1809, who married, 1833, Arabella, daughter of William White of New Bedford. Mr. Goodwin was the last person in Plymouth to wear a cue. Mrs. Goodwin was a quakeress, always wearing the garb of her faith, which was further illustrated by her gentle spirit and kindly words.

That part of the house used for a dwelling was occupied at various times after Mr. Goodwin moved to Middle street by Samuel Lanman, George F. Andrews, and Frank A. Johnson, the last of whom kept a public house under the name of the Winslow House. The old banking room was used by Daniel J. Jane and Samuel Merriam, shoe manufacturers; Charles F. Hathaway, for a general store; Joseph P. Brown, cabinet maker, and Frank A. Johnson in connection with his hotel. It is only necessary to say further in connection with the old bank building that it was taken down and the Russell building erected on its site in 1892.

Daniel J. Lane manufactured one hundred thousand pairs of boots and shoes annually, and gave employment to about one hundred and sixty hands. There were other manufacturers of shoes about the same time, of whom it will be well to speak: S. Blake & Co., who made one hundred and twenty thousand pairs, employing about two hundred hands, having their headquarters in Leyden hall building; John Churchill, Benjamin Bramhall, William Morey, Henry Mills and Nathaniel Cobb Lanman, in whose shop on Allerton street William L. Douglas was a workman.

George Gustavus Dyer came to Plymouth with Mr. Blake from Abington, and after serving as bookkeeper for his company, was elected cashier of the Old Colony Bank. Mr. Dyer was the son of Christopher and Mary (Porter) Dyer of Abington, and married in 1852 Mary Ann Bartlett, daughter of Schuyler Sampson. After some years' service as cashier of the Old Colony Bank, he was chosen President, and died January 9, 1891.

The shoe business in the days to which I have referred was conducted very differently from the methods in vogue today. The headquarters not necessarily extensive, were used for the reception of stock, the cutting of the leather, the shipment of shoes and the business office. When the leather was cut shoemakers would call periodically for packages of uppers, and linings and heels, and making the shoes at home would bring them to the office and carry home a new supply. They would furnish their own tools and thread and nails and pegs, and consequently the need existed of local stores, such as that which was kept on Main street by Harrison Finney for shoe kit and findings. These shoemakers did their work at home, and there was scarcely a house in the smaller towns which did not have its small shop on the premises where the cut material was converted into shoes for the more or less distant manufacturer. In consequence of the change above mentioned, the local kit stores were abandoned, and there was a gradual flow of population from the farming towns where the little workshops were located to the large towns, Abington, Brockton, Rockland, Plymouth and Whitman, where the factories were built. This is one of the causes of the falling off of population in the smaller towns, and of the rapid growth of the larger ones. There are indications now of a reflex tide, as a result of the facilities afforded by trolley cars for workmen to seek distant homes where the cost of living is moderate, and where in dull seasons farming can be carried on with profit.

The building which stood on the corner of Court and North streets, which was taken down and replaced by the Howland building in 1888, was occupied as long ago as I can remember by Dr. Rossiter Cotton. He was the son of John and Hannah (Sturtevant) Cotton, and was born in 1758. He married in 1783 Priscilla, daughter of Thomas Jackson, and had nine children, of whom I only remember two, Charles, born in 1788, and Rowland Edwin, born in 1802.

Dr. Cotton practiced medicine in Plymouth about twenty years, and retired from his profession in 1807. He seems to have inherited the right to hold county offices. His grandfather, Josiah Cotton, was Register of Deeds and County Treasurer from 1713 to 1756; his father, John Cotton, held

both offices from 1756 to 1789, and he held the same offices
from 1789 to his death, August 12, 1837. His son, Rowland
Edwin, continued in the office of Register from 1837 to 1846.
Thus the office of Register was held in the family through
four generations, one hundred and thirty-three years, and the
office of Treasurer through three generations, one hundred
and twenty-four years. Dr. Cotton was an antiquarian, and I
find on the records many of his memoranda and plans, which
aid materially in elucidating matters which without them it
would have been difficult to understand. His son, Charles
Cotton, graduated at Harvard in 1808, and settled as a physician in Newport, where he married a Miss Northam, and
had a family of children, of whom I only remember four, Rossiter, Thomas, Charles and Sophia. He removed to Plymouth
in 1831, occupying the house under consideration, where he
practised until his father's death in 1837, when he returned
to Newport, where he died. The three boys attended the
high school with me, and must have been all within two years
of my age. I remember two incidents of our school days, with
which they are associated. I have referred in a former chapter to the rule, while Mr. William H. Lord was the teacher,
for each boy to repeat at the opening of the school in the
morning a verse from the bible. One day Rossiter received a
flogging for some offense, and the next morning he repeated
in his turn, "For whom the Lord loveth, he chasteneth." The
other incident occurred while Mr. Isaac N. Stoddard was
teacher. Dr. Cotton thought his son Charles had been either
unjustly or too severely whipped, so arming himself with a
whip he went to Mrs. Nicolson's hotel where Mr. Stoddard
boarded, with the intention of flogging him. But he reckoned
without his host, and when he raised his whip, Mr. Stoddard,
seizing him by the collar, laid him on the floor, and taking his
whip away sent him home.

In 1833 scarlet fever prevailed extensively in Plymouth,
and was very fatal. In a population of 5,000 the number of
deaths during the year was one hundred and sixty-seven, of
which sixty-seven were of children under ten years of age.
Taking the population of Plymouth in 1904 of 11,118, and
the number of deaths in that year, one hundred and fifty-seven,
as a basis, the normal number of deaths in the population of

five thousand in 1833, would have been less than seventy. I remember that a daughter of Dr. Charles Cotton, either Sophia or another whose name I do not recall, died of the prevailing disease, and that I was one of the pall bearers at her funeral. It was the invariable custom in those days, never varied from, to have pall bearers for old and young, and in cases of funerals of children, Clement Bates, the sexton, would call at the High school and ask for a detail of six boys for service at one or more of the funerals on that day. As well as I can remember, no precautions were taken to prevent the spread of the contagion, and funerals were attended as usual, and no quarantine was established. I have no doubt that during the visitation of the sickness I served as pall bearer at least a dozen times.

Some years later I narrowly escaped serious inconvenience arising from municipal precautions against contagious diseases. In February, 1857, I had a schooner in the West India trade, and when after her departure from Boston in the early part of that month I thought her well on her way towards her destination, I received a telegram from Thomas Everett Cornish, her master, that she had been caught by the ice in the bay soon after leaving Boston, and driven by the prevailing northwest gales into Truro Bay, where she was in the ice jam a week, during which she had received damages which she was now repairing in Provincetown. I at once drove to Sandwich, and taking the cars for Yarmouth, then the terminus of the Cape Cod Railroad, drove to Truro, reaching there about midnight. The next morning I hired a conveyance to Provincetown, reaching there for dinner. After dinner I boarded the schooner, where carpenters were at work getting out new stanchions for the damaged bulwarks. While talking in the cabin with Capt. Cornish, who was bald, and had taken off his hat, I noticed some pustules on his scalp which I saw at once were the pustules of varioloid. Fearing that he might become sick and would require a substitute for the voyage, I called on Dr. Stone, who fortunately was an old friend, and took him to see the Captain, whom he at once declared suffering from a mild attack of varioloid, which, however, would not prevent his prosecution of the voyage. He said that he was the port physician, and that it would be his duty to report the case to the board of health. Fortunately I had said nothing at the hotel concerning my business, or my connection with the schooner, and I exacted a promise from Dr. Stone to say nothing about me. Not long after the departure of the Doctor we heard while sitting in the cabin a hail from the head of the wharf commanding the captain to haul at once into the stream and have no communication with the shore. A watchman was placed at the head of the wharf by the board of health, and I began to wonder how I was to escape a quarantine. I waited until after dark and then giving the captain directions to proceed to Boston with the first favorable wind, I went ashore, and sneaking up behind a store house with only the cap log of the wharf to walk on, I found an opening between two buildings about four feet wide, and came out on the street unobserved. As I walked to the hotel I found the town in a panic, and groups were standing here and there discussing the situation. I spoke to no one but on reaching the hotel gave orders to be called to take the six o'clock mail chaise, and went to bed. At six o'clock I was off and reached home the same day. It was eight days before my vessel was able to reach Boston, and thus I narrowly escaped a prolonged confinement on board, and the watchfulness of the Provincetown board of health. In view of my experience I advise my readers in visiting a town, to follow my example, and say nothing and keep open the avenues of retreat.

After the death of Dr. Rossiter Cotton in 1837, and the return of his son to Newport, the house in question was kept as a hotel named the Mansion House for some years by James G. Gleason, succeeded by Benjamin H. Crandon and N. M. Perry. In still later years the post office occupied the corner room down stairs for a time, and the Custom House a room upstairs, until finally the whole upper part of the building and the northerly and easterly part below were occupied by newspaper offices, and the corner by Charles P. Morse for a drug store, until the building was taken down in 1888. Since the mention of N. M. Perry in a previous chapter, I have learned that he was a native of Holliston.

There are several estates on the west side of Court street, whose occupants have not been noticed. Opposite the head of North street there was in my youth the Lothrop estate, on

which a house stood, which was occupied by Dr. Nathaniel
Lothrop, until his death, October 10, 1828. Dr. Lothrop was
the son of Isaac and Priscilla (Thomas) (Watson) Lothrop,
and was born in the house in question in 1737. His mother
married in 1758, Noah Hobart of Fairfield, Connecticut, who
had a daughter Ellen by a previous wife. This daughter,
Ellen Hobart, married Nathaniel Lothrop, and thus Nathaniel
Lothrop married his mother's step-daughter, and Ellen Hobart married her father's step-son. I leave my readers to determine the relationship between them. In 1831 the Lothrop
house was taken down, and while its demolition was going
on, I a boy of nine years of age, saw quantities of papers
thrown out of the garret windows, and picking up many of
them carried them home. I found them on examination to be
official papers with autographs bearing date from 1675 to 1700.
These I arranged in an album, and have recently presented
them to the Pilgrim Society. In 1832 the northerly part of
the lot was sold to Jacob H. Loud, who built the house now
owned and occupied by Mrs. Francis B. Davis.

The southerly part of the lot was sold in 1839 to Nathaniel
Russell, Jr., who built the house now occupied by Col. William P. Stoddard, and occupied it until his father's death in
1852, when he moved into the brick house on the corner of
Court Square, which had been his father's home. At his
removal the house was left furnished, and was occupied during
the summer of 1853 by Richard Warren and family of New
York. From the autumn of 1853 to the autumn of 1854, the
house was occupied by myself, and there in the summer of
1854 my oldest child was born. Not long after I left the
house, it was occupied by Rev. George S. Ball, during his pastorate as colleague of Rev. Dr. Kendall. In 1857 the house
was sold to Jeremiah Farris, whose son-in-law, Col. Stoddard,
now occupies it.

Mr. Russell was as has been before stated, the son of Nathaniel and Martha (LeBaron) Russell, and was born in
Bridgewater, December 18, 1801. He graduated at Harvard
in 1820, and married, June 25, 1827, Catherine Elizabeth,
daughter of Daniel Robert and Betsey Hayward (Thacher)
Elliott of Savannah, Georgia, and died February 16, 1875.
Until 1837 he was associated with his father in the manage-

ment of the iron industries belonging to the firm of N. Russell & Co., composed of Nathaniel Russell, William Davis and Barnabas Hedge. After the retirement of the Davis and Hedge interests from the firm, Mr. Russell became a member of the firm of N. Russell & Co., and so continued until the death of his father, October 21, 1852, after which he continued the business until the sale of the Summer street works in 1866 to the Robinson Iron Co.

During the exciting period of anti-masonry which extended from 1828 to 1835, an anti-masonic political party sprang up in many of the Northern states, and candidates were generally nominated for State and National offices. The party had its origin in the belief that William Morgan of Batavia, New York, a former mason, who was reported to intend publishing the secrets of the order of free masons, had been kidnapped and drowned in Lake Ontario. It was believed that the masonic oath disqualified those in the higher degrees from serving as jurors in cases where members of the same degrees were parties. The anti-masonic party originated in New York in 1828, and in 1830 Francis Granger, its candidate for Governor, received 128,000 votes. In 1831 a National Anti-masonic convention nominated William Wirt of Maryland, and Amos Ellmaker of Pennsylvania, for President and Vice-President. Vermont was the only state which threw its electoral vote for the anti-masonic candidates. The anti-masonic excitement reached Plymouth, and for one or more years Mr. Russell was chosen a member of the legislature on the anti-masonic ticket. I am not a mason, but as a somewhat close observer of public affairs for nearly seventy years, and many times a successful candidate for public office, I feel bound to say that I have never suspected any masonic participation either collectively or individually in the selection of nominees to office, or the election of candidates.

In 1840 after the death of Barnabas Hedge, Mr. Russell was chosen to succeed him as President of the Plymouth Institution for Savings, which was incorporated in 1828, and continued in office until his death. In 1847, during his incumbency, the name of the institution was changed to the Plymouth Savings Bank.

CHAPTER XXVIII.

The house in North street occupied by Dr. Brown, stands on the site of a house, which in my youth, was owned and occupied by Stephen Marcy. The old house was during the revolution kept as an Inn by Thomas Southworth Howland, and there on December 22, 1769, the Old Colony Club for the first time celebrated the anniversary of the landing of the Pilgrims. On that occasion at half-past two a dinner composed of the following dishes was served: "A large baked Indian whortleberry pudding, a dish of sauquetach, a dish of clams, a dish of oysters, and a dish of cod fish, a haunch of venison, a dish of sea fowl, a dish of frost fish and eels, an apple pie, a course of cranberry tarts and cheese."

The pudding alone preceded the meat, and the dessert was as now the last course. This custom went out before my day, but it was no more strange than that now in vogue, of beginning a breakfast with fruit and oatmeal.

I remember the house well with a front door near its westerly end, and an office door near its easterly end opening into a room which in its last days was occupied by Dr. Robert Capen. In 1833 Jacob Covington bought the estate and built the house now standing.

The Covington family was not one of the old Plymouth families. Thomas Covington came to Plymouth a few years before the revolution, and married in 1771 Sarah, daughter of Joseph Tribble. Jacob Covington, son of Thomas, was no doubt a shipmaster in early life. He was evidently trained in a business school, and was repeatedly placed in positions of trust by his fellow-citizens. He was the first President of the Old Colony Insurance Company, and of the Old Colony Bank, holding both positions until his death. He was among the first to enter the business of the whale fishery, and was among its most energetic and competent managers. The enterprise of building Long Wharf, and putting the steamboat General Lafayette on the line between Plymouth and Boston, was chiefly due to him and James Bartlett. He married in 1816, Patty, daughter of Gideon Holbrook, and had Elam, 1817, who died in California; Mary Holbrook, 1820, who died in East Orange; Martha Ann, 1822, who died in Plymouth; Edwin, 1825, who died in Boston; Harriet, 1827, who died in Plymouth; Helen, 1830, still living; Jacob, 1832, who died in Providence, and Leonard, 1834, who died in Dorchester.

Mary Holbrook Covington married George H. Bates, a native of Farmington, Maine, and the wife of Rev. Dr. Mann, the present rector of Trinity church in Boston, is her granddaughter. Capt. Covington died May 28, 1835, at the age of forty-four. After the death of Capt. Covington the house in question came into the occupancy of Josiah Robbins, who has already been noticed, and later of Thomas Prince, who occupied it as a boarding house. The next occupant was Peter Holmes, who was the son of Peter and Sally (Harlow) Holmes, and was born in 1804. Mr. Holmes was engaged many years in Boston in the cork manufacture, returning to Plymouth and becoming the owner of the house under consideration. He died October 14, 1880, and the house came into the possession of Nathaniel Morton in 1881, who owned and occupied it until Dr. W. G. Brown not many years since came into its possession. Mr. Morton moved into a new house which he built on Union street, and died July 18, 1902, at the age of seventy-one years, one month and twenty-one days.

The lot next below the Covington house was all through my boyhood, as late as 1830, an outlying barn yard, belonging to Henry Warren, who lived on the corner of North street. I remember well the large barn on the rear of the lot, and the extensive hog stye and hog yard on its easterly side. In 1830 the widow of Henry Warren sold the lot to Rev. Frederick Freeman, who built the house now occupied by Dr. Helen Pierce. Mr. Freeman was descended from early Plymouth Colony ancestors, who for many generations lived in Sandwich, where Mr. Freeman's grandfather was born. His father, George W. Freeman, settled in North Carolina and married Ann Yates Ghobson, and was for a time an instructor in Raleigh, where he became rector of Christ Church, later accepting the position of Rector of Emanuel Church in Newcastle, Delaware. He received in 1839 the degree of Doctor of Divinity from the University of North Carolina, and October 26, 1844, was consecrated Bishop of the southwestern diocese, including Texas, Arkansas and the Indian Territory. He died at Little Rock, Arkansas, April 29, 1858.

Rev. Frederick Freeman, son of George Ward and Ann Yates (Ghobson) Freeman, was born in Raleigh, December 1, 1799, and was there ordained as an evangelist. He was settled in 1824 over the Third Church of Plymouth, whose place of worship was on the corner of Pleasant and Franklin streets, and built the house in question in 1830. In 1830 some disaffection arose in his church, which resulted in the secession of a considerable number of its members, and the establishment of the Robinson Congregational church in 1831, and the erection of its place of worship on the corner of Pleasant street, and a street which has since been laid out and named Robinson street. No hint is given so far as I know by any historian as to the cause of the dissension in the church, but there are reasons to believe that, brought up in the Episcopal church, he was never a full fledged Calvinist, and that the secession above referred to and his final resignation in 1833 were due to this fact. The visit of his father to Plymouth in 1832, and his holding an Episcopal service for only the second time in the history of the town, tends to confirm this view of the case. My impression is very strong that sooner or later after he left Plymouth he became a member in full standing of the Episcopal church. He afterwards became a citizen of Sandwich, his ancestral town, and devoted some years to the preparation and publication of a history of Cape Cod, which is a valuable contribution to Old Colony Historical literature. I have a distinct recollection of his personality, a strongly built man with black hair and a Websterian type of head and face, who could not pass in a crowd without observation. He married December 26, 1821, Elizabeth, daughter of George Nichols of Raleigh, who died in Plymouth March 12, 1833. He married second, April 20, 1834, Hannah, daughter of Frederick W. Wolcott of Litchfield, Conn., and third, November, 1841, Isabella, daughter of Hartwell Williams of Augusta, Maine, but I do not know the date of his death. A sister of his married Weston R. Gales, mayor of Raleigh, and hence the name of our late townsman, Weston Gales Freeman of Summer street.

In 1833 Mr. Freeman sold the house to Daniel Jackson,

who has already been noticed in these memories. After the death of Mr. Jackson and the removal of his widow to Boston, Dr. Alexander Jackson became the occupant of the house in 1860, and was succeeded by Dr. Edgar D. Hill in 1880, whose occupancy last year gave way to that of Dr. Pierce, the present occupant.

Dr. Alexander Jackson was a descendant in the fifth generation from John Jackson, who came from England and died in 1731. He was the son of Isaac and Sarah (Thomas) Jackson, and was born in Winthrop, Maine, May 18, 1819. His father moved to Boston when he was a boy, and Alexander was educated at the Boston Latin School, where he fitted for college. He graduated at Amherst in 1840, and took his medical degree from the Harvard Medical School in 1843, having been associated during his three years' course with the Boston Dispensary, and the Boston Eye and Ear Infirmary. Not long after receiving his degree he began the practice of his profession in Chiltonville, where he remained until October, 1858, when he moved to Main street, Plymouth, and occupied the house where the Plymouth Savings Bank now stands. In May, 1860, he moved to the house under consideration on North street, which he occupied until October, 1880, when he bought the house on Court street, now occupied by Father Buckley. In October, 1890, he retired from professional business, and moved to Boston. He married, June 14, 1849, Cordelia A., daughter of Nathaniel Reeves of Wayland, and had Isaac, 1850, who married Elizabeth, daughter of Edward Parrish of Philadelphia; Alexander, 1853, who married Abby Warren, daughter of William T. Davis of Plymouth; and Nathaniel Reeves, 1857, who married Hannah M., widow of George W. Brown, and daughter of Lyman Shaw. Dr. Jackson died in Boston, December 12, 1901.

Passing now to the house of Arthur Lord on the lower corner of Rope Walk lane, as it was called, its occupant in my boyhood was Mrs. William Sturtevant, the widow of William Sturtevant, who died December 15, 1819. She was the daughter of Benjamin and Jane (Sturtevant) Warren, and was born in Plymouth in 1769, and died December 5, 1838. Her husband was the son of William and Jemima (Shaw) Sturtevant, and was born in that part of Plympton, which is now Carver, in 1761. I have no means of learning what his business was, as I am unable to associate him with any enterprise, industry or profession. He was a member of the Board of Selectmen in 1817, but I find him in no other office. The inscription on his gravestone calls him William Sturtevant, Esq., and as it is certain that he was not a shipmaster or a lawyer, I am inclined to the opinion that he was a merchant, and like George Watson, who died in 1800, and William Jackson, who died in 1837, was called Esquire. Mr. Sturtevant was married in 1791, and had the following children, who survived infancy: Jane, 1794; Hannah, 1796; Sarah, 1799; Lucy, 1802; Rebecca W., 1805; and William, 1809. Hannah married Thomas J. Lobdell, a banker in Boston and died October 3, 1818; William was for a time a partner with William S. Russell in the dry goods jobbing business in Central street, Boston, and later a stock broker; Sarah died July 1, 1833; Lucy died August 7, 1807, and Jane died November 8, 1832. Rebecca W. married in 1831 Rev. Josiah Moore of Duxbury, and died April 7, 1838. Mrs. Moore makes the tenth Plymouth lady whom I remember who married husbands who came to the town to teach school. These were Nathaniel Bradstreet, who married Anna Crombie; Charles Burton, who married Sarah Stephens; George Washington Hosmer, who married Hannah Poor Kendall; William H. Lord, who married Persis Kendall; William Parsons Lunt, who married Ellen Hobart Hedge; Josiah Moore, who married Rebecca W. Sturtevant; Horace H. Rolfe, who married Mary T. Marcy; Benjamin Shurtleff, who married Sally Shaw, Isaac Nelson Stoddard, who married Martha Thomas, and William Whiting, who married Lydia Cushing Russell. Another might have been added to the list if a letter of which I was the innocent bearer, had received a favorable reply. I had no right to know the contents of the letter, but little pitchers have great ears, and mine were uncommonly great when I overheard the letter discussed. The marriage of another teacher, Charles Field to Elizabeth Hayward, was prevented by his death, August 22, 1838.

In 1839 the house in question was sold to Dr. Timothy Gordon, who occupied it until his death. Dr. Gordon came to Plymouth in 1837, but where he lived until he moved into the

Sturtevant house, I am not able to say. His ancestor, Alexander Gordon, a Scotchman, came to New England in 1651, and settled in New Hampshire. The Doctor was the son of Timothy and Lydia Whitmore Gordon, and was born in Newbury, N. H., March 10, 1795, and made several voyages as supercargo.

In 1823 he entered the office of his brother William in Hingham, and completed his studies at the Bowdoin College medical school, where he received a degree in 1825, and first settled in Weymouth. In 1837 he came to Plymouth, and in 1839 moved into the house in question. He was bold and successful as a practitioner, and skilful as a surgeon. For many years he was one of the chief supporters of the Third Church, and a liberal contributor to its funds, and both he and his wife made large gifts for the support of foreign missions. He was a trustee of the Pilgrim Society, and Vice President from 1872 to 1877; a Director of the Plymouth Bank and Plymouth National Bank from 1845 to 1877, and the recipient of the degree of Master of Arts from Amherst College in 1868. He married May 12, 1825, Jane Binney, daughter of Solomon and Sarah Jones, and had two children, Solomon Jones, September 21, 1826, and Timothy, April 19, 1836, the latter of whom died young. Dr. Gordon was a shrewd man, and would have made a good detective, as the following incident shows. He believed that the methods pursued in New York and Boston in detecting criminals by the aid of newspaper reporters was like hunting ducks with a brass band, and acted accordingly. He had a famous peach tree in his garden laden with luscious fruit, of which one night he was robbed. Neither he nor his wife mentioned the loss even to their servant, and no one knew of the robbery besides themselves and the thief. One day as the Doctor was sweeping his sidewalk a man came along and entered into conversation. Just as he turned to leave he said, "by the way, Doctor, did you ever find out who stole your peaches." "Yes, you rascal," the Doctor replied. "You stole them, and if you don't pay me five dollars instantly I will have you put in jail." The man confessed at once, and paid the money down.

Solomon Jones Gordon, the son of Dr. Gordon, was born in Weymouth, September 24, 1826, and graduated at Harvard in 1847. He studied law with Jacob H. Loud in Plymouth, and in the Harvard Law School, and was admitted to the Suffolk bar October 18, 1850. He soon after became associated with Orlando B. Potter, who was interested in sewing machine patents, and removed his office to New York, where he accumulated a handsome fortune. He married Rebecca, daughter of David Ames of Springfield, in which city he made his home until his death in 1890.

After Dr. Gordon, the house under consideration was successively occupied by Rev. A. H. Sweetser, pastor of the Universalist Society, and by Dr. Parker, and the last occupant before Mr. Lord, its present occupant, was Dr. Warren Pierce.

Perhaps I ought to offer an excuse, for the continuance of these personal reminiscences which may have become wearisome to some of my readers. There is a legend that myriads of sombre birds have periodically flown from the Black Sea to the beautiful sea of Marmora, and after hovering over the cypress shades of the cemetery at Scutari have retraced their flight without food or drink, never touching the earth. The Turks are said to believe that they are condemned souls denied the peaceful quiet of the grave, visiting the tombs of others. I trust that my wanderings among the scenes of the past will not be attributed to the restlessness of a condemned soul, but rather to a love of my native town, and of those in whose footsteps I am daily walking, and in whose vacant homes I recall blessed memories.

The house on North street, now owned by John Russell, the occupants of which have been only incidentally alluded to, was built by Samuel Jackson soon after the revolution and passed from him to John Russell, who married his daughter Mary. From John Russell it passed to his son, John, who owned and occupied it through my boyhood until his death in 1857, from whom after his widow's death it passed to his son, John Jackson Russell, the father of the present owner. John Russell, whom I remember as the occupant of the house, was the son of John and Mary (Jackson) Russell, and was born in 1786. In early life he followed the sea, and soon became master. He sailed some years in the employ of my grandfather, Wm. Davis, and I have seen many letters from him in various ports in the North of Europe, which show him to have been a skilful navigator, and an intelligent, shrewd business man. He gave up the sea before my day, and jointly with Thomas Davis of Plymouth, and Wm. Perkins and Sydney Bartlett of Boston, owned the ships Massasoit, Sydney, Granada and Hampden, of which he was manager. As far as I know his masters were Robert Cowen, Nathaniel Spooner, Wm. Sylvester, and Henry Whiting, the latter making a single voyage to California in the Hampden in 1849. Not long after giving up the sea he became interested in town affairs, and could always be relied on to oppose extravagant measures. He was a member of the Board of Selectmen from 1841 to 1844 inclusive, and in the years 1846, 1851, 1853 and 1854. He was also one of the corporators of the Plymouth Cordage Company in 1824, and a director I think until his death. It was during his service as shipmaster that the political lines began to be drawn between the advocates and opponents of a protective tariff, the manufacturers asking for protection, and the ship owners opposing any measures tending to check importations. His attitude on this question carried him into the ranks of the Democratic party a constant opponent of a tariff which, drawn chiefly for protection purposes, he believed to be unconstitutional. In 1844 the ship Hampden was in New Orleans loading cotton for Amsterdam, and either for the benefit of his health or the relief of Capt. Cowen, he concluded to take command of her for the voyage. Sending for his son John, who was teaching school in Barnstable to be his companion, they joined the ship and made the voyage to Amsterdam and back to Boston or New York, I think with a load of iron.

Captain Russell married in 1816 Deborah, daughter of Nathaniel and Mary (Holmes) Spooner, and had Mary Spooner, who married James T. Hodge, John Jackson, Helen, who married Wm. Davis and Wm. H. Whitman, and Laura. He died February 6, 1857.

John Jackson Russell, son of the above, who became the next occupant of the house in question, was born July 27, 1823, and graduated at Harvard in 1843. After teaching school in Barnstable and making a voyage to Amsterdam with his father in the ship Hampden in 1844, he studied law with Jacob H. Loud in Plymouth, and Allen Crocker Spooner in Boston, and was admitted to the Suffolk bar in 1848. Returning to Plym-

outh in 1850, after practising law for a time, he was appointed
Assistant Treasurer of the Plymouth Savings Bank, and after
the death of Allen Danforth in 1872 treasurer, which position
he held until his death.   He was also a director of the Plymouth National Bank, and in 1878, a short time its President.
He married in 1855 Mary A., daughter of Allen Danforth, and
had Helen, 1857, John, 1860, and Lydia, 1863.   He died November 10, 1897.   The house in question in my judgment illustrates those admirable qualities in architecture, symmetry
and proportion, which are rarely found in the works of ar-
chitects of the present day.   It illustrates also the importance
of retaining the original color of a house intended by the architect to be built of brick in order to preserve its symmetry, for
it must be apparent that since the house was painted red the
symmetry has been restored, which a light color had previously
disturbed.

Until within five or six years a house stood on the easterly
side of the Russell house, which during my boyhood was occupied by Daniel Jackson until 1834, and by Isaac Tribble until
1846, both of whom have already been noticed.   In 1846 it
was bought by Anthony Morse, who occupied it until his death.
Mr. Morse was born in Gloucester in 1795, and was the son of
Humphrey and Lydia (Parsons) Morse of that city. He came
to Plymouth when a young man, and learned the trade of rope
making, working a number of years in the rope walk extending from the gardens of the North street houses along the rear
of the Court street lots to Howland street, and afterwards in
the works of the Robbins Cordage Company.   At a later time
he was an assistant in the store of Samuel Robbins on Market
street, and still later he kept a grocery store a short time on his
own account.   He was an ardent whig, and during political
campaigns he rendered valuable service to his party by setting
up a reading room, collecting campaign funds, and making
sure of the appearance of whig voters at the polls.   Colonel
John B. Thomas was the general adviser of the party, and no
measures were adopted without his approval.   One election
morning Col. Thomas was awaked before daylight by a loud
rapping at his door.   Opening the window and asking what
was the matter, Morse appeared out of the darkness and called
out, "C-Co-Colonel, rains like h-hell, shall I engage all the h-

horses?   The Colonel said Yes, and went back to bed.   As a
reward for his party services he was appointed Deputy Collector in 1841.   Mr. Morse married in 1837 Nancy, widow of
Branch Johnson, and daughter of William Atwood, and had
Charles P., 1830, who kept an apothecary's shop some years
at the corner of Court and North streets, and later in the house
of his father, to which he succeeded.

Mr. Morse was a man of the strictest integrity, and conscien-
tiousness was the most marked feature in his character.   He
possessed a morbid conscience which kept him in constant fear
that he might be suspected of dishonesty.   He was a director
of the Plymouth Bank from 1844 to 1858, and he told me once
that on one occasion when the cashier left him during a temporary absence to keep the Bank he found a twenty dollar bill
behind a chair on the floor.   I found it impossible to convince
him that it had not been placed there to test his honesty.   The
morbid state of his mind intensified with age, and he committed suicide April 19, 1858.

Passing now to the house standing in the angle of Winslow
street, I am led to speak of its occupants for the purpose of
making appropriate mention of Dr. Charles T. Jackson, a distinguished son of Plymouth, who was there born June 21, 1805.
His father, Charles Jackson, married Lucy, daughter of John
Cotton, in 1794, and his children, whom I remember, were
Lucy, born, 1798, who married Charles Brown, Lydia, 1802,
who married Ralph Waldo Emerson, and Charles Thomas.
Mr. Brown, the husband of Lucy, lived many years in Con-
stantinople, and rendered laborious and self-sacrificing service
to the sick during a visitation of the plague in that city.   Dr.
Jackson studied medicine with Dr. James Jackson and Dr. Walter Channing of Boston, and graduated at the Harvard Medical
school in 1829.   In the same year he went to Europe, where
he remained three years studying in Paris, and returned in
1832.   For his scientific labors and researches he was made a
fellow of the American Academy of Arts and Sciences.

In 1836 he was appointed geologist of Maine, and was also
appointed by Massachusetts to survey her Maine lands.   In
1839 he was appointed geologist of Rhode Island, and in 1840
of New Hampshire.   In 1844 and 1845, he explored the
southern shores of Lake Superior, and opened mines of copper.

In 1847 he superintended for a time a survey of mineral lands
of the United States in Michigan.   When Professor S. F. B.
Morse secured a patent for the telegraph in 1840, Dr. Jackson
claimed that on board the ship Sully in 1832, in which he and
Morse were passengers, he suggested the possibility of correspondence by means of electricity, and explained to Mr. Morse
the method of applying electricity to telegraphic use.   It is in
my power to furnish to a certain extent a confirmation of Dr.
Jackson's claim, which, as far as I know, has not found its
way into the literature of the telegraph.   In 1846 I was a passenger from New York to Liverpool in the ship Liverpool, in
which a man by the name of Blithen was mate, who was also
mate of the ship Sully, in which Jackson and Morse were passengers in 1832.   He told me that he remembered well when
Dr. Jackson made the suggestion of the possibility of an electric telegraph, at the dinner table, and the interest with which
Mr. Morse listened, and his questionings concerning a possible
use of electricity in the manner proposed.   Mr. Blithen said
that it was evident that the subject was a new one to Mr.
Morse, bearing on matters entirely outside of the profession of
painter to which he belonged.   The controversy upon the
respective claims of Morse and Jackson never reached a definite settlement, except *sub-silentia* by public opinion in favor
of Morse.

Dr. Jackson made another claim, resting on a more substantial basis, on which both scientific and general opinion have
been and probably always will be divided.   The question
whether he or Dr. W. T. G. Morton was the real discoverer of
anasthesia, will never be settled, and perhaps the only solution
it will reach is that which gives both jointly the credit of the
great discovery.   A memorial was presented to Congress in
1852, signed by one hundred and forty-three physicians of Boston and vicinity, ascribing the discovery exclusively to Dr.
Jackson.   The French Academy of Science decreed a Mont-
yon prize of 2,500 francs to Jackson for the discovery of ether-
ization, and one of the same amount to Morton for the application of the discovery to surgical operations.   Dr. Jackson received orders and decorations from the governments of France,
Sweden, Prussia, Turkey and Sardinia, but what the final ver-
dict of history, the court of last resort, will be, it is too early
to say.

Dr. Jackson was a man of broad and deep scientific learning, and in exploring the mysteries lying in the field of science he found so much that his frank and open nature would not permit him to conceal, that those who knew him were not surprised at the disputed claims which marked his career. He knew too much, and too many things for him to develop, and by his own labors to apply to practical use. His mind was like a garden so crowded with vegetation of his own planting that none or few reached perfect bloom and seed. But the passerby attracted by one or another, though ignorant of botany, would pluck a slip or a root, and setting it in his own grounds, by unremitting care nurse it into vigorous growth and a perfected life. Without the garden which the gardener had planted, the passerby would never have found the plant, and without the act of the passerby the plant would have died and the labors of the gardener would have been in vain. Thus it is true that one soweth another reapeth. Dr. Jackson married Susan Bridge of Charlestown, and died in 1880.

At the time the controversy between Jackson and Morton was going on, Horace Wells, a dentist in Hartford, made a claim that prior to the use of ether he had used in his profession nitrous oxide gas to prevent pain. In the autumn of 1846 he went to Europe to lay his discovery before the medical profession in Paris, and in March, 1847, on his return, he was my fellow passenger on board the steamship Hibernia, and shared my stateroom. He was a landsman, unfamiliar with the sea, and easily frightened by the noises of the ship. He was especially frightened on a dark night in a northwest gale surrounded by broken ice off the Flemish cap, the northeast edge of the grand banks. As we entered the field ice Capt. Harrison deemed it prudent to stand to the southward and escape it. We were constantly feeling the huge blocks of ice, thumping against us, and with the windows of the dining saloon which was on the main deck, well shuttered, it was about as dismal a prospect as passengers not yet fully satisfied of the seaworthiness of sidewheel ocean steamships had ever experienced. In those days the trumpet was used by the officers on the deck in giving orders at night or in a storm to the men at the wheel, and about ten o'clock the few of us who were not sick, sitting in the saloon, heard the order, "hard a

port." Of course we ran to the door, but before reaching it
heard the order, "hard a starboard." I saw on the port side
perhaps a quarter of a mile distant the glisten of an iceberg,
and those on the starboard side saw the glisten of another about
the same distance away, and as we went wallowing along in
the trough of the sea we sailed between them. We turned
in soon after, but there was not much sleep for the poor Doctor after the fright he had received.

About midnight we were awakened by the crash on our
decks of a gigantic wave, which enveloped the ship, filling the
dining saloon sill deep, and pouring down into the cabin, en-
dangering the lives of several passengers whose stateroom
doors were broken open, and who were washed out of their
berths. The Doctor was out and off in an instant, returning
in about ten minutes telling me to get up as the ship was sink-
ing. As I never was easily rattled, I remained in my berth,
either taking no stock in his outcry, or thinking that a speedy
death in my stateroom would be better than a lingering one
among floating cakes of ice. In the morning we were clear of
the ice, and once more on our course. The troubles to which
Dr. Wells was subjected in endeavoring to substantiate his
claim, affected his brain, and he committed suicide in New
York, January 24, 1848. A statue has been erected to his
memory in the park at Hartford, his native city.

Another distinguished Plymouthean was a resident on North
street. Dr. James Thacher lived from 1817 to 1827 in what
is now called the old part of the Samoset House, which he
named Lagrange in honor of Lafayette, and moved from there
into the Winslow house on North street, which he occupied until he built the house until recently occupied by Dr. Thomas
B. Drew in or about 1832. I remember him in the Winslow
house, but it was chiefly in the house built by him which he
occupied until his death that I knew him intimately. His
family and my mother were close friends, and I made frequent
visits to his house to talk with him and learn from him tales
and incidents of the past. I always found him sitting at his
desk in the northwest corner of the westerly parlor ready to
talk with a young man who was sufficiently interested in early
days to visit an old man. He was as long ago as I knew
him very deaf, and sometimes, though not always, I talked

with him through an ear trumpet. Like all deaf persons, his hearing depended much on the tone in which he was addressed, not necessarily a loud one, but distinct, clear cut, and from the throat rather than the lips. His wife, whose voice was low and soft, but clear, conversed with him with ease. He was a short man, stoutly built, though not fleshy, and always as long as I knew him, walked with a cane. He was a jovial man, ready to laugh at a good story, or at a joke on a friend or on himself. He was an ardent friend of temperance, full of religious sentiment, but owing to his deafness he was while I knew him, a rare attendant on church worship. Before my day he had abandoned the practice of his profession, and was devoted to literary pursuits.

Dr. Thacher was born in Barnstable, February 14, 1754, and was the son of John and Content (Norton) Thacher of that town. He attended the public schools until he was eighteen years of age, when he was apprenticed to Dr. Abner Hersey for the study of medicine, completing his apprenticeship at the age of twenty-one soon after the battle of Bunker Hill. He at once presented himself for examination for medical service in the army, and being accepted was appointed surgeon's mate in the hospital at Cambridge, under Dr. John Warren. In February, 1776, after another examination, he was assigned to Col. Asa Whitcomb's regiment as mate to Dr. David Townsend, and went with his regiment on the expedition to Ticonderoga. In November, 1778, he was appointed surgeon of the First Virginia State Regiment, and in 1779 he exchanged into the First Massachusetts Regiment commanded by Col. Henry Jackson, and was present at the execution of Andre. In July, 1781, he was appointed surgeon in the Regiment, commanded by Col. Alexander Scammel, and was present at the siege of Yorktown, and the surrender of Cornwallis. Retiring from service in January, 1783, he settled in the following March in Plymouth, where he resided until his death. His large experience in the army, and his well known skill as a surgeon, gave him a large and lucrative practice, from which he would have acquired a handsome property, had not his investments and ventures been disastrous. He established with his brother-in-law, Dr. Nathan Hayward in 1796, the first stage line between Plymouth and Boston, which with other enterprises, no more successful, wasted the savings from his practice. While carrying on his practice he had in his office a number of students, among whom were Dr. Perry of Keene, N. H., Dr. Nathaniel Bradstreet of Newburyport, and Dr. Benjamin Shurtleff of Carver and Boston. In many things he was always a little in advance of his generation, and was inclined to adopt new ideas before they were sufficiently tried, though in others he was the successful pioneer. He introduced the tomato into Plymouth, and with my mother, was the first to set up a coal grate, and use anthracite coal for domestic purpose.

In 1810 Dr. Thacher published "The American Dispensatory," and in 1812 "Observations on Hydrophobia." In 1817 he published "The Modern Practice of Physic," in 1822 the "American Orchardist," and in 1823 "A Military Journal during the Revolutionary War," in 1828 "American Medical Biography," in 1829, "A Practical Treatise on the Management of Bees," in 1831, "An Essay on Demonology, Ghosts, Apparitions and Popular Superstitions," and in 1832 a "History of the Town of Plymouth." Of some of these books second editions have been published; some are standard works, and all are rare. The suggestion I have made that he was in advance of his time is confirmed by his work on hydrophobia, in which more than a hint is given that methods of prevention or cure might be successfully adopted, such as Pasteur has in recent years advocated. In that work the following passage may be found:

"Experiments made upon the canine poison in brutes might be considered as an arduous and hazardous undertaking, but it is not to be deemed altogether impracticable, and I will suggest the following project for the purpose. In the first place dogs when affected with madness, instead of being killed, should be confined and secured that the disease may run its course, and for the ascertainment of many useful facts connected with its several stages. If experiments on dogs should be deemed too hazardous let other animals of little value be selected, provided a sufficient number can be procured. Having provided for their security in some proper enclosure, let them be inoculated with the saliva of the mad dog. With some the inoculated part might be cut out at different stages to ascertain the latest period at which it may be done successfully. To others, various counter poisons and specific remedies might be applied to the wound and administered internally. In fact it would be difficult to determine *a priori*, the extent of the advantages of this novel plan if judiciously conducted. You may smile at my project, but however chimerical and visionary it may appear, I would rejoice to be the Jenner of the proposed institution; though I might fail in realizing my thousands I could pride myself in being the candidate for the honor, and the author of an attempt to mitigate the horrors attending one of the greatest of all human calamities."

Dr. Thacher received from Harvard the honorary degrees of Master of Arts and Doctor of Medicine in 1810, and from Dartmouth in the same year, and was made a Fellow of the American Academy of Arts and Sciences. He married Susanna, daughter of Nathan Hayward of Bridgewater, and sister of Dr. Nathan Hayward of Plymouth, and had Betsey Hayward, 1785, who married Daniel Robert Elliott of Savannah, Georgia, and Michael Hodge of Newburyport; Susan, 1788, who died in infancy; James, 1790, who also died in infancy; James Hersey, 1792, who died in 1793; Susan, 1794, who married Wm. Bartlett, and Catherine, 1797, who died in 1800. Dr. Thacher died May 26, 1844, and his wife died May 17, 1842.

CHAPTER XXIX.

James Thacher Hodge, another distinguished son of Plymouth, was associated with North street, where he had his home for some years with his mother and his grandfather, Dr. James Thacher. His father, Michael Hodge of Newburyport, a graduate of Harvard in the class of 1799, married in 1814 Betsey Hayward, widow of Daniel Robert Elliott of Savannah, Georgia, and daughter of James and Susannah (Hayward) Thacher of Plymouth, and James Thacher Hodge, his only son, was born in Plymouth in 1816. Mr. Hodge graduated at Harvard in 1836, and at once applied himself to the study of chemistry, mineralogy and geology, a field of science in which he was destined to become distinguished. Among his early labors were those performed with Dr. Chas. T. Jackson, also a native of Plymouth, on the geological survey of Maine, and with Professor Henry D. Rogers on the geological survey of Pennsylvania. He was afterwards engaged in testing and utilizing the mineral wealth of Lake Superior lands, and the explorations and reports made by him largely aided in developing the mining interests of the northwest.

In later times, as one after another, new state and territory extended our limits in the west, he was among the first to discover beneath their surface the rich tribute they were ready to pay as they entered the gates of the union. I believe that science will find no step treading its paths more vigorous than his, and no keener eye exploring its mysteries. After a season's work on the southern shore of Lake Superior he left Marquette in the steamer Colburn on the 12th of October, 1871, and on her passage to Detroit the steamer foundered in a gale and he with others was lost. He inherited from his grandfather the firmness of nerve which had distinguished him in his surgical practice, and from his father, a fearlessness amounting at times to rashness. Mr. Hodge in preparing his reports was a careful writer, preferring a criticism for undue caution to a final discovery of extravagant statements leading unwary investors to failure and misfortune. Within the field of his literary efforts must be included some hundreds of articles on scientific subjects contributed to the American Cyclopædia.

Mr. Hodge married in 1846 Mary Spooner, daughter of John Russell of Plymouth, and had Elizabeth Thacher, who married George Gibbs of Riverside, Kentucky; John Russell, 1847, who married Harriet, daughter of Seth Evans of Cincinnati; James Michael, 1850, and Mary, 1854.

I cannot leave North street without a word in memory of the house in which I was born, March 3, 1822, now occupied as an Inn, known as the Plymouth Rock House. After my father's death in 1824, my mother continued to occupy the house until 1845, when she moved to the house now occupied by the Misses Russell, near the head of the street. The succeeding occupants in their order were Rev. Henry Edes, who kept a young ladies' boarding school; Mrs. Sarah Jenkins, Simon R. Burgess and Charles H. Snell. As long as it was occupied by our family it had a stable at the westerly end of the garden on Carver street, and a chaise house opening on Cole's Hill, which long since gave way to an enlargement of the dwelling house.

There have been so many alterations and enlargements in the house since my mother left it in 1845, that there is little left as it was in my boyhood. The middle kitchen, as it was called, with its dresser containing articles in pewter, such as hot water plates, candle moulds, syphons, etc., and its sink with a pewter ewer and bowl where I washed my hands when coming from play, and the long buttery leading out of it where the flour and sugar barrels and common china and the last batch of pies were kept, is now an indistinguishable feature of the house. The large kitchen, too, with its box seat, the meal chest with compartments for Indian meal, white meal and rye meal, the coffee grinder on the wall, the mantel with its row of two wicked brass lamps always clean and bright, the fireplace with its high andirons, and a four foot stick for a forestick, a crane with pothooks and a tin kitchen before the fire, has gone with the rest. Only one room remains as it was of old, the northeast corner parlor, a room that is historic, for there the first grate in Plymouth was set in 1832 for burning anthracite coal for domestic use.

Dr. Thacher and my mother each had a grate set at the

same time, but as his house was not yet finished the fire was kindled in ours first with coal bought by Capt. George Simmons in Boston, and brought to Plymouth in the packet sloop Splendid. Outside of the house the old garden is gone with its lilac tree announcing by its bloom the advancing step of summer.

> How well I remember that old lilac tree,
>   Which stood in the garden near our back entry door;
> No lily nor rose seemed ever to me
>   As sweet as the blossoms that lilac tree bore.
> How gladly it welcomed the warm airs of spring,
>   As out of the west they swept down the vale;
> How responsive it seemed, how eager to fling
>   Its banners of purple to the ravishing gale.
> Like the honey bee sipping the sweets of a flower,
>   How oft and how richly my sense was regaled,
> While sitting beneath my ivy clad bower
>   I drank in the perfume its blossoms exhaled.
> The garden is gone, and the old lilac tree
>   Stands no longer by the back entry door;
> But its fragrance remains, reminder to me
>   Of a home once beloved—but now no more.

What changes time has wrought in the scenes of my youth. One feature of these scenes is left to remind me of my Cole's Hill home, which years have failed to erase. In my earliest youth nearly four score years ago a bed of bouncing betts bloomed on the grassy bank opposite our home, and it is blooming still as if contesting with me a race for the longest life. I visit it every year to make sure that it has not given up the contest, and when I stand by it it seems to say, "Ah, old fellow, I will beat you yet." I hope you will, dear friend of my youth, and bloom on for generations to come, reminding others as you do me of my childhood days.

I have spoken of N. Russell & Co., and Jeremiah Farris and Bourne Spooner as connected with manufacturing interests in Plymouth. There are two others among those who have passed away, whom I ought to notice, Oliver Edes and Nathaniel Wood. Mr. Edes was the son of Oliver and Lucy (Lewis) Edes, and was born in East Needham, November 10, 1815. At the age of sixteen he began to learn the trade of nail making at works on the Boston mill dam owned by Horace

Gray. He afterwards ran a tack machine in the works of Apollos Randall & Co., in South Braintree, and at the age of twenty-two invented a machine for cutting rivets from drawn wire. Before that time rivets had been made by hand, and it was difficult to make the trade believe that any but handmade rivets would meet the wants of mechanics. In 1840 he entered into a partnership with Andrew Holmes under the firm name of Holmes, Edes & Co., with a factory at North Marshfield. At the end of three years the firm was dissolved and a new one formed between Mr. Edes and Jeremiah Farris, under the firm name of Edes & Co. At the expiration of a year, in 1844, the firm moved their business to Plymouth. In 1850 Mr. Edes, having disposed of his interest, formed with Nathaniel Wood the firm of Edes & Wood, and began the manufacture of zinc shoe nails and tacks, and soon after the rolling of zinc plates at Chiltonville. In 1859 he bought out Mr. Wood, and in 1880, with his son Edwin L. Edes, the partnership of Oliver Edes and son was formed. In 1883, a partnership was formed consisting of Oliver Edes, Jason W. Mixter, Edwin L. Edes and T. E. Heald of Knoxville for the development of zinc mines in Virginia and Tennessee, and for the manufacture of zinc metal. He married October 7, 1836, Susan, daughter of Ebenezer and Lydia (Curtis) Davie, and had William Wallace, 1847, who married Ellen M., daughter of Calvin H. Eaton, Lydia Curtis 1851, who married Jason W. Mixter, and Edwin L., 1853., who married Mary E., daughter of Edgar C. Raymond. Mr. Edes died February 21, 1884.

Nathaniel Wood of Dedham married Rhoda Colburn, and came to Plymouth in the early part of the last century, and had six children, after 1810, among whom was Nathaniel, who was born November 25, 1814. The son, Nathaniel, learned the nail cutter's trade at the works on the Mill dam in Boston, owned by Horace Gray, father of the late Horace Gray, associate justice of the United States Supreme Court. He worked for some years in the nail factory of N. Russell & Co., and for a time on his own account in cutting zinc nails and tacks, and in 1850 formed a partnership with Oliver Edes, under the firm name of Edes & Wood, in a factory which stood on Forge pond brook in Chiltonville, where the business was carried on of making zinc shoe nails and tacks and rolling zinc plates. In 1859 he sold out his interest to Mr. Edes, and with Charles O. Churchill, under the firm name of N. Wood & Co., continued the business in a factory farther down the stream on the road leading from the Sandwich road to the old Manomet road at what was called the Double Brook dam. At a later time he ran a small factory on Little Brook. He married in 1837 Angeline, daughter of Lewis and Betsey (Weston) Finney, and had Warren Colburn, 1840, and Florence A., 1847. He married second, 1854, Betsey R., daughter of Charles and Abigail (Russell) Churchill, and had Nathaniel Russell, 1856, and died April 26, 1888.

Allen Crocker Spooner, whom I knew intimately, was a brilliant man, who was cut off by death at the threshold of an especially promising career. He was the son of Capt. Nathaniel and Lucy (Willard) Spooner, and was born March 9, 1814, in the house on the southerly side of High street, next west of the house on the corner of Spring street. He graduated at Harvard in 1835, and was admitted to the Suffolk bar, September 3, 1839. He belonged to a coterie of scholarly and jovial men, who met at the eating house of General Bates once a week, and over their bitter ale were legitimate successors of the Fleet street club of Johnson and Garrick and Goldsmith. The members of this coterie were Fay Barrett of Concord, James Russell Lowell of Cambridge, George W. Minns, Nathan Hale, Allen Crocker Spooner and John C. King of Boston and Benjamin Drew of Plymouth. All of these were Harvard men except King, who was a sculptor, and Benjamin Drew, a journalist, connected with the Boston *Post*. Their jokes on each other, though sometimes rough, were always taken in good part. One evening Minns and Spooner were walking into town from Cambridge and feeling a little dry in the throat, Spooner said: "Minns, have you got any money about your clothes, for I spent my last cent in paying toll?" "I've got just twelve and a half cents," said Minns, a sum which was the silver nine pence of that period. Peter B. Brigham kept a drinking saloon in the old concert hall building on the corner of Hanover and Court streets, and his drinks were of two prices, those like Deacon Grant and Dr. Pierpont, named after distinguished temperance men, were nine pence, and all other common drinks were six and a quarter cents or four pence half penny. They marched into Brigham's as if they were rolling in riches, and as they came to the counter, Minns said, "Spooner what are you going to have." Spooner answered, "I think I will have a Deacon Grant, what are you going to have?" "Well, I don't feel very dry, I guess I won't take anything." Mr. Spooner was sought as a guest on many public occasions, where he was sure to entertain his audience by either a graceful speech, a bit of humor, or an appropriate poem. I remember that on one occasion he was invited to join the Boston underwriters in their annual excursion down Boston harbor. A little while before, Capt. Jas. Murdock, commanding the packet ship Ocean Monarch, had run his ship ashore at Cohasset or Scituate in a fog, though fortunate enough to get her off. At the lunch of the party on board the excursion steamer, Mr. Spooner assumed the position of toastmaster, and calling up the guests one after another, answered the toasts himself, adopting the personality of each. Among others he toasted Capt. Murdock, who was present, and kept the company in a roar by claiming a discovery in the science of navigation by which he had found that the use of the lead was an obsolete practice, only persisted in by those who had not yet learned that ships were constructed to navigate the ocean and not the land. Capt. Murdock, I believe, was a cabin window Captain, a fine looking man, jolly good fellow, popular with his passengers, but not a sailor in the truest sense of the word. Afterwards in coming down the English channel, his ship was destroyed by fire off Holy head, and a passenger whom I knew by the name of Southworth, told me that Murdock was the first of the ship's company to reach Liverpool with news of the disaster.

About the year 1845 Mr. Spooner went to England, a passenger in the packet ship Devonshire, Capt Luce, the same Captain Luce who commanded the Collin's steamship Arctic, which was run into by the Brig Vesta, near Cape Race, Sept. 24, 1854, and sunk with the loss of three hundred and fifty lives. Capt. Luce, whom I afterwards met, told me that when the ship went down he stood on the paddle box holding his little boy by the hand and that he thought he would never stop going down. He had no sooner reached the surface, still holding his little boy by the hand, than a spar loosened from the wreck, came up with great force, and striking his son, killed him instantly. He succeded in reaching a fragment of the wreck, and was picked up by one of the brig's boats.

On his return home, Mr. Spooner told the Boston Old Colony Club, of which I was a member, that in running into the harbor of old Plymouth as he lay on deck basking in the sun, he saw a vessel coming out, which he pictured in his mind as the Mayflower starting on her voyage to the new world. His surprise was great when, as the vessel passed, he read on her stern the name of the Pilgrim ship the Mayflower.   My wonder at the time whether his eyesight was not blurred by an exuberant imagination was modified at a later time by an incident within my own experience. On the 19th of August, 1895, in crossing the English channel from Queenboro to Flushing in Holland, I saw coming from a northern port a small steamer crossing our course diagonally, almost exactly the course which the Speedwell steered in August, 1620, in running from Delfthaven to Southampton, where she joined the Mayflower. As she passed our stern I was a little startled as I read the name Speedwell on her bow. I was talking at the time with two passengers, and calling their attention to the name of the vessel, I told them the Pilgrim story. Lest I might be suspected like my friend Spooner of an exuberant imagination, I examined the British marine register, after my return home, and found one of the three Speedwells whose size agreed with the vessel I saw. She belonged in Ipswich, and I wrote to the owner asking him to advise me of the whereabouts of his steamer on the 19th of August, 1895. Unable to find in Boston a Victoria stamp, I was obliged to send my letter without a return stamp enclosed, and I attribute to that circumstance my failure to receive a reply. The incident was especially interesting, as I had just visited Scrooby for the purpose of placing a bronze tablet on the site of Scrooby Manor, in which the Pilgrim church was formed, and was on my way to Leyden, the Pilgrims' home in Holland.

I shall at this point in my narrative devote some space to notices of such Plymoutheans as have distinguished themselves in other localities without regard to the houses with which by birth or otherwise they may have been associated.

To these will be added notices of a few who were residents of Plymouth, but who have been in preceding chapters only incidentally alluded to.

William G. Russell was the son of Thomas and Mary Ann (Goodwin) Russell, and was born in Plymouth, November 18, 1821. After attending the public schools he was fitted for college by Hon. John A. Shaw of Bridgewater, and graduated at Harvard in 1840. After teaching in a private school in Plymouth a short time, and in the Dracut Academy a year, he studied law in the office of his brother-in-law, Wm. Whiting, and at the Harvard Law School, receiving from the latter the degree of LL. B. in 1845, and being admitted to the Suffolk bar July 25, 1848. He was at once associated with Mr. Whiting as a partner, and while the latter was holding the position of solicitor of the War Department from 1862 to 1865, the business of the firm devolved on him. After the death of Mr. Whiting in 1873, George Putnam joined him as a partner, and at a later period, Jabez Fox was added to the firm. After the death of Sydney Bartlett he was universally recognized as the leader of the Suffolk bar, and was offered a seat on the bench of the Supreme Judicial Court, both as associate and chief justice. He was a member of the Massachusetts Historical Society, and at various times held the positions of President of the Union Club, the social library association, and the Suffolk bar association; vice president of the Pilgrim Society, director of the Mount Vernon National Bank, and the Massachusetts Hospital Life Insurance Co., and Harvard overseer from 1869 to 1881, and from 1882 to 1894. He married October 6, 1847, Mary Ellen, daughter of Thomas and Lydia Coffin Hedge of Plymouth, and died in Boston, February 6, 1896.

Thomas Russell, brother of the above, was born in Plymouth, September 26, 1825, and graduated at Harvard in 1845. He studied law with Whiting & Russell in Boston, and was admitted to the Suffolk bar November 12, 1849. He was appointed Justice of the Police Court of Boston, February 26, 1852, and in 1859 on the establishment of the Superior Court was appointed one of its associate justices. While he was on the bench a number of cases of garrotting and robbery occurred on Boston Commons, which for a time made the Common dangerous to cross in the evening. The first person charged with the offence was tried before Judge Russell, and convicted, and the severe sentence imposed by him put an end to the commission of the crime. In 1867 he resigned his seat on the Superior bench, and on the accession of General Grant to the Presidency, was apointed collector of the port of Boston. During General Grant's second term he resigned the collectorship, and was appointed minister to the Republic of Venezuela, where he remained several years. He was a Harvard overseer from 1855 to 1867; a Trustee of the State Nautical School several years, and in 1879 was chosen President of the Pilgrim Society, holding that position until his death. The judge was an ardent republican, and being a ready speaker, was always in demand on the political stump. He was occasionally selected for the delivery of formal orations, the most notable of which ocurring to me were a fourth of July oration before the Boston City Government, and a eulogy on General Grant delivered in Plymouth. He married in 1853 Mary Ellen, daughter of Rev. Edward T. Taylor of Boston, and died in Boston, February 9, 1887.

Henry Warren Torrey, born in Plymouth, was the son of John and Marcia Otis (Warren) Torrey. He graduated at Harvard in 1833, and studied law in the office of his uncle, Charles Henry Warren in New Bedford. He was at the same time co-operating with Frederick Percival Leverett in preparing what is known as Leverett's latin lexicon, published in 1837. While engaged in that work his eyes became seriously affected, and practice in the profession of law was abandoned. I remember that at the time of the great whig celebration in Boston on the 10th of September, 1840, he was living in New Bedford, and on that occasion the New Bedford delegation carried a banner with an inscription of which he was the author. On the banner a whale ship was painted with a whale alongside in the process of stripping, and the fires under the try pots smoking on deck, and beneath was the inscription: "Martin VanBuren—we have tried him in, and now we will try him out."

In 1844 Mr. Torrey was appointed tutor at Harvard and .instructor in elocution, and served until 1848. My impression is that from 1848 to 1856 he lived in Hamilton

Place, Boston, and with his sister, Elizabeth, taught a young ladies' school. In 1856 he was appointed McLean Professor of Ancient and Modern History at Harvard, serving until 1886, when on his resignation he was appointed Professor Emeritus, serving until his death. In 1879 he received the degree of LL. D. from Harvard, and from 1888 until his death, he was a Harvard overseer. He was also a member of the Massachusetts Historical Society, and a fellow of the American Academy of Arts and Sciences. He died in Cambridge in 1893.

Lemuel Stephens, son of Lemuel and Sally (Morton) Stephens, was born in Plymouth, February 22, 1814. He belonged to a sturdy race, and I well remember his grandfather, William, who was born in 1752. His father, Lemuel and his uncle William, occupied the two Stephens' houses between Union street and the shore, but I am inclined to think, while Lemuel built the house he occupied, that the house William occupied was built by his father. Lemuel and William, the father and uncle of the subject of this notice were engaged many years in the grand bank fishery, and Stephens' wharf, which since the abandonment of the fishery has gradually crumbled away, presented once a busy scene when the Jane and Constitution and the Duck and the Industry were fitting out in the spring, and washing out in the autumn. The Stephens brothers were men of brains, and consequently men of ideas, men who were called pessimists because they looked out for weak spots in government and society, and sought to correct them. The optimists on the other hand flattered themselves that everything was right when everything was wrong, and that the ship was tight, though leaking a thousand strokes an hour. They were the earliest abolitionists in the town, the earliest advocates of temperance reform, the earliest promoters of a well maintained education of the people, while the optimists as long as they were making money said, "All is well, let things be."

Lemuel Stephens of whom I specially speak, the son of Lemuel, graduated at Harvard in 1835, and soon after graduation went to Pittsburg in Pennsylvania, where for a time he taught in a private school. After leaving Pittsburg he went to Germany for study, spending three years in Heidelberg and

Gottingen.   On his return he was appointed Professor of
chemistry in the western University of Pennsylvania, where
he remained until 1850, when he was appointed professor of
chemistry and physics in Gerard College, continuing in
service until 1885.   He married Ann Maria Buckminster of
Framingham, · Mass., a relative of Rev. Dr. Joseph Stevens
Buckminster, once pastor of Brattle street church in Boston,
and died in Philadelphia, March 25, 1892.

Another Plymouth man, of whom I must speak, was Winslow Marston Watson, of whom few of my readers ever heard.
The son of Winslow Watson he was born I think on Clark's
Island in 1812, and graduated at Harvard in 1833.   His
mother, Mrs. Harriet Lothrop Watson, was a close observer
of persons and families, their traits of character and their
relations to each other, and was the first genealogist whom I
ever saw.   Her son, Winslow, inherited her powers of observation, and her remarkable memory, which in a broader sphere
of life made him a reconteur of wide reputation.   He early
entered the profession of journalism, and in 1842 I found him,
while on a visit to Troy, the editor of the Troy *Whig*.   He
later removed to Washington, where for some years he rendered valuable service as correspondent of leading newspapers
in New England and New York.   His artistic taste and literary ability attracted the attention of Mr. Corcoran, the
wealthy banker and patron of art, and in his service he performed appreciative work.   I doubt whether any man ever
lived in Washington who came in contact with more persons
of distinction, and could portray their characters and habits
more thoroughly, than Mr. Watson.   For nearly forty years
I never failed to see him when visiting Washington, and if
he had followed my advice to publish a book of reminiscences
he would have made a valuable contribution to the literature
of Washington life.   His personality was striking, of medium height and weight, with a fair complexion and large pro-
tuberant blue eyes, with that sad, patient, placid, yet protest-
ing expression which Homer recognized who called the celes-
tial queen the ox-eyed Juno.   He married in 1852 Louisa
Gibbons, and died in Washington in 1889.   He was a cousin
of the late Benjamin Marston Watson, of whom I have already spoken, and to whom it occurs to me to refer again

by inserting the following lines, which I inscribed in a book presented to him on his last birthday, and which better than my earlier reference to him, illustrate the beauty of his character and life:

> A placid stream, with flowers on either hand,
> And meads beyond, tempting the eye of art;
> With here and there a ripple as it runs
> Against opposing winds, or flows triumphant
> Over hidden shoals, with lips upturned
> And smiling in the noonday sun.
> Such, my dear friend, has been thy life.
> 'Twere vain to wish it ever thus to be,
> For every stream must some time reach the sea.

There lived in my youth on the lower corner of Summer and Spring streets an elderly gentleman of kind words and gentle speech, who, though living a distance from my home, early attracted me and found a lasting place in my memory. From 1806 to 1819, he had been treasurer of the town, and was some years a teacher in what was later called the high school. His name was Benjamin Drew, and he was the father of my long time friend, Benjamin Drew, who died in 1903. He was something of a poet, and his son told the story that one time when asked to contribute an inscription to be placed on the gravestone of his brother-in-law, Barnabas Holmes, he composed the following:

> By temperance taught, a few advancing slow,
> To distant fate by easy journeys go;
> Calmly they lie them down like evening sheep,—
> On their own woolly fleeces softly sleep.

Objection was made to the inscription by the family of Mr. Holmes, it appearing too personal, as Mr. Holmes had been a dealer in mutton. Like most emasculated poetry the substitute adopted was tame—as follows:

> By temperance governed, and by reason taught,
> The paths of peace and pleasantness he sought;
> With competence and length of days was blest,
> And cheered with hopes of everlasting rest.

He married in 1797 Sophia, daughter of Sylvanus and Martha (Wait) Bartlett. His son, Benjamin, of whom I especially speak in this notice, was born in Plymouth, November 28, 1812. He was educated at the public schools, leaving the high school about four years before I entered it. After leaving school he entered the office of the *Old Colony Memorial* to learn the printer's trade, and there laid the foundation of his reputation as an expert in typography. About the year 1835 he began his career as teacher, and during a period of twenty-five years taught in the Phillips, Otis, Mayhew and Glover schools in Boston. While living in Boston his companionship was prized by scholarly men, and he was one of a group of social fellows already referred to who met at a saloon in Cornhill square, called the Shades, kept by General Bates, a Scotchman. There the group would frequently meet in Bohemian fashion to exchange witticisms and criticisms and enjoy a mug of ale. These occasional opportunities to give vent to his sense of humor were not sufficient to exhaust his flow of wit and under the cognomen of Ensign Stebbins he often wrote for the "carpet bag," and was always a welcome contributor to the humorous columns of the *Boston Post*. I remember reading a squib of his in the *Post* sixty years ago, representing a showman explaining and describing to his audience the various features of his exhibition, as for instance:

"This, ladies and gentlemen, is the zebra, it measures ten feet from head to tail, and eleven feet from tail to head, has twelve stripes along its back and nary one alike."

"This is the hippopotamus, an amphibious animal, what dies in the water and can't live on the land."

"This, ladies and gentlemen, is the shoved over of the scalper's art, the statute of Apollos spoken of in the acts of the Apostles, where it says that Paul doth plant and Apollos water, and to illustrate the text more fully I have appended to his left hand a large, tin watering pot, which I bought of a tin peddler for thirty-seven and a half cents."

About 1860 Mr. Drew went to St. Paul, where he taught school a year, and then for some years he performed the duties of proof reader in the Government printing office in Washington. In 1881 he made a journey around the world, spending a short time on the way with his son Edward Bangs Drew, a Mandarin in the Chinese Imperial Customs Service, with headquarters at Tientsin, where he passed his 70th birthday. On his return he settled permanently in his native town, recalling the scenes and friends of earlier days, and roaming among the haunts of the fathers of the town. He published during his life a book entitled "Pens and Types," a standard work on typography, and another entitled, "The North side of slavery," and after his final return to Plymouth he published a valuable descriptive catalogue of the gravestones and inscriptions on Plymouth Burial Hill. He married Caroline Bangs of Brewster, and died in Plymouth July 19, 1903, at the age of ninety years, seven months and twenty-one days.

Zabdiel Sampson, son of George and Hannah (Cooper) Sampson, was born in Plympton in 1781, and graduated at Brown University in 1803. He studied law with Joshua Thomas, and settled in Plymouth. In 1816 he was chosen member of Congress, and in 1820 was appointed collector of the port of Plymouth to succeed Henry Warren. At that time political lines were in a comparatively subdued and inactive state. The loose constructionist or federal party was still in existence, but declining in strength and power. Monroe, a strict constructionist or Democratic Republican, was re-elected with practical unanimity, while the campaign of 1824 was rather a personal contest between John Quincy Adams and Andrew Jackson, than a party struggle. During the administration of Adams the name National Republican took the place of Federalist, and the Democratic Republican party assumed the name of Democrat. Thus parties remained until the campaign of 1832, when the National Republicans assumed the name of Whigs. Thus the two great parties continued until 1856, when the Republican party was born. There were splinters from these parties at various times, such as the anti-masonic party in 1830, the liberty party in 1839, the free soil party in 1848 and the American party in 1852, as there are now splinters from the Democratic and Republican parties like the temperance and labor parties.

Mr. Sampson was undoubtedly when appointed collector in 1820 a Monroe strict constructionist, or in other words a Democrat, but retained the office through the Adams administration because during that period party lines were loosely drawn. He died while in office, July 19, 1828. He was a member of the board of selectmen eight years, during five of which he was its chairman. He married in 1804, Ruth, daughter of Ebenezer Lobdell of Plympton, and had ten children, neither of whom I think has descendants living in Plymouth.

I have said that the presidential contest in 1824 was a personal one between Adams and Jackson. Then began the hostility between these two men, which was never placated. General Jackson died June 8, 1845, before the days of the telegraph, and rumors of his death drifted to the East several times before the event occurred. Rev. Dr. Wm. P. Lunt, Mr. Adams' pastor in Quincy, told me that while in Boston one day, authentic news of Jackson's death was received, and on his return home he though it proper for him to call at Mr. Adams' house and communicate to him the sad news. As he entered the library Mr. Adams was standing with his back to the door, looking over some papers on a window seat. He said, "Mr. Adams, I heard in Boston this afternoon the sad news of the death of General Jackson, your successor in the presidential chair." Mr. Adams, without looking round or stopping in his work exclaimed, "Umph, the old rascal is dead at last, is he?"

Schuyler Sampson, brother of the above mentioned Zabdiel, was born in Plympton in March, 1787, but moved with his father to Plymouth when young. I am inclined to think that he and his brother lived for some years in the house which until recently stood on the corner of Summer street and Spring hill. All through my boyhood, however, and until his death, he owned and occupied the house on the northerly side of Summer street, next westerly of the house for many years occupied by Benjamin Hathaway. He was for several years a member of the board of selectmen, and in 1828 was appointed to succeed his brother as collector of the port. He served in the latter office during the administrations of Jackson and Van Buren, and in 1841 succeeded Ebenezer G. Parker as cashier of the Old Colony Bank. He married in 1823 Mary Ann, daughter of Amasa Bartlett, and had Mary Ann Bartlett, 1825, who married George Gustavus Dyer. He married second, 1827, Sarah Taylor (Bartlett) Bishop, sister of his first wife, and widow of Wm. Bishop. By his second wife he had Sarah Taylor Bartlett, 1829, George Schuyler, 1833 and Hannah Bartlett, 1835, who married Rev. Isaac C. White. The late Wm. Bishop of Boston was the son of the second wife by her first husband. Mr. Sampson died in Plymouth May 10, 1855.

During my boyhood Truman Bartlett lived on the notherly side of High street, west of Spring street. He was a tall, robust man, weighing I should judge about two hundred and twenty-five pounds, and I remember him well with his plaid Camlet cloak which he wore in the winter, reminding me of the outer cold weather garment worn by the watchmen in Boston before the police patrol was established in that city. He was the son of Samuel and Elizabeth (Jackson) Bartlett, and was born in Plymouth, March 10, 1776. He was a shipmaster for many years, and sailed for my grandfather, Wm. Davis and Barnabas Hedge. He married in 1798 Experience, daughter of Robert Finney, and had William, Josiah, Flavel, Charles, Stephen, Truman, Azariah, Ann, Lucia and Angeline. Of these Angeline died at the age of twenty, April 24, 1838, and Charles died in childhood in 1826; Lucia died October 3, 1841, at the age of twenty-eight, and of Ann I know nothing. The remaining six sons all became shipmasters, and formed a group of merchant captains, such as no other Plymouth family can match. Of William, who commanded the Charles Bartlett, and Truman, who commanded the Queen of the East, I have already spoken, but of the others I have no reliable record. Captain Bartlett died August 18, 1841.

Ezra Finney, called Captain, lived on the northwesterly corner of Summer and Spring streets from 1822, until his death. He was the son of Ezra and Hannah (Luce) Finney, and was born in Plymouth July 5, 1772. He may have been a shipmaster in his early days, and his connection with the Old Colony Insurance Company, of which he was at one time President, as well as his ownership and management of navigation, renders such an occupation probable. He was a member of the board of selectmen three years, and the absence of his name in connection with the whale fishery suggests a conservatism in business affairs which precluded investments over which he could have no personal supervision. In navigation he was enterprising and successful, but as far as I know never engaged in the grand bank fishery. He married in 1797 Lydia, daughter of Andrew Bartlett, and had Lydia Bartlett, 1799, who married Capt. Lemuel Clark, Ezra, 1804, who married John Bartlett. He married second 1808, Betsey, widow of John Bishop, and daughter of Eliphalet Holbrook, Eliza, and

had Betsey Bishop, 1809, who married William Sampson Bart-
lett; Mary Coville, 1811; Caroline, 1814; Ezra, 1817; Mary
Coville, 1819, who married Henry Mills; and Caroline, 1822.
Abby, daughter of Captain Finney's second wife by her first
husband, John Bishop, was born in 1801, and married James
E. Leonard and Henry Mills.

It was the custom under what was called the Suffolk Bank
system, when banks were forbidden by law to pay out any
bills but their own to send every two or three days all foreign bills received by the banks to the Suffolk
bank in Boston and receive from that bank their own bills in
return.   As expresses were not established in Plymouth until
after 1845 packages of bills to or from the Suffolk bank were
entrusted to any friend of the Plymouth or Old Colony Bank,
as they were to myself even when a boy.   On one
occasion Mr. Finney received from the Suffolk bank a package of the bills of the Old Colony Bank. Chilled by his ride
from Boston in a stage sleigh, it was not until he had thawed
out by the home fire that the package was brought to his mind.
It was not in his pockets, nor was it to be found anywhere in
the house.   As a last resort he hurried to the stage stable,
where his anxiety was relieved by the discovery of the package
hidden by the straw with which the floor of the sleigh was
covered.   This incident was far from being indicative of
carelessness on his part, for he was a methodical business man,
and one as thoughtful of the interests of others as of his own.
On another occasion he proved himself a thrifty trustee of the
Savings Bank.   Mr. Danforth, the treasurer, having occasion
to leave town for a day or perhaps two, left Mr. Finney in
charge of the bank, and among the contents of the safe was
a strapped package of counterfeit bills which had been collecting for some time, and had been charged off to profit
and loss. On Mr. Danforth's return, not finding the package, he asked Mr. Finney if he had seen the bills, and Mr.
Finney replied that he had, and not doubting them genuine,
had paid them out.   The bills were never heard from afterwards, and their amount was in due time credited back to
profit and loss. Captain Finney died February 5, 1861.

Andrew Bartlett, son of Andrew and Sarah Holbrook Bartlett, was born in Plymouth, October 20, 1806, and lived in

High street, near his kinsman, Truman Bartlett. He was a shipmaster, possessing those qualities which made him not only a skilful navigator, but a prudent, economical and trustworthy business man. He told me once that during his career as master, he had never lost a man or a spar. While this fact speaks well for his seamanship, it was due largely to the models of vessels in his day, and the absence of those hasty methods of doing business which characterize our times. A blunt bow and a full counter made it easy to encounter a head sea, and to leave a following one, while there was enough left of the old kettle bottom to check the shift of even a cargo of railroad iron, which, however securely braced, is always ready to start with the kick of a rolling sea. Safety to ship and cargo, not speed, was the great consideration sought. When Capt. Fox in the brig Emerald, after a thirteen days' passage from Liverpool, rounded to off Long wharf and was hailed with the question, "When did you leave Liverpool, Capt. Fox," his reply was, "Last week, damn you, when do you think?" He did not say how many sails he had lost, nor whether his cargo in the forehold was dry. I think Capt. Bartlett sailed for a combination of owners of whom Ezra Finney, Wm. Nelson and Benjamin Barnes were the chief.

After abandoning the sea his interests in seamen led him to devote his life to their service in connection with the sailors' Bethel and Home in Boston. He married in 1830 Mary, daughter of William Barnes of Plymouth, and had Victor A., 1841, Mary E. 1843 and Andrew P., 1848. He married second, in 1866, Phebe J. Tenney, who had been for a number of years a school teacher in Plymouth. Captain Bartlett died February 4, 1882.

William Nelson, son of William and Bathsheba (Lothrop) Nelson, was born in Plymouth, September 29, 1796, on the old Nelson farm near Cold Spring, which had been in the Nelson family from the time of its first American ancestor, William Nelson, who married Martha, daughter of widow Ford, who came to Plymouth in the ship Fortune in 1621. I think Mr. Nelson lived on High street until 1841, when he built and occupied until his death the house on Summer street, which in 1867 was sold to Barnabas Churchill. He had a sister, Mary Lothrop Nelson, who married Jesse Harlow, and he with Mr. Harlow, under the firm name of Nelson & Harlow, was engaged some years in navigation, with a counting room on the westerly side of Water street, opposite to Nelson's wharf. He was a director in the Old Colony Bank, and in the Old Colony Insurance Company, a prominent member of the Orthodox Congregational church, and a liberal contributor to its support. He married in 1821 Sarah, daughter of Josiah Carver, and had William Henry, 1830, who is noticed at the end of this chapter; Thomas Lothrop, 1833, who married Susan A. Warren of Exeter, N. H., and Mary Stratton of Atchison, Miss.; and Sarah Elizabeth, who married Wm. K. Churchill. Mr. Nelson died October 6, 1863.

There is one whom I omitted in my wanderings in the northerly part of Court street, of whom I shall be glad to speak. I heard much of him in my youth, though he died before my birth, and of the disappointment which his premature death caused to be felt by his friends. Isaac Eames Cobb, the son of Cornelius and Grace (Eames) Cobb, was born January 19, 1789, in the old Nehemiah Savery house, still standing south of Cherry street, a little back from Court street. He graduated at Harvard in 1814 a leading scholar in his class, and began the study of law. A disease of the lungs obliged him to abandon a profession in which there was every reason to believe that he would have a successful career. He entered into business with Messrs. Isaac L. and Thomas Hedge, but died a victim of consumption January 14, 1821. He married in 1816 Elizabeth, daughter of Thomas Bartlett, whose house occupied the site on which that of Gideon F. Holmes now stands. His daughter Elizabeth, the widow of Joseph Holmes, lives in a house standing on what was a part of her grandfather Bartlett's estate. The following inscription is on his gravestone on Burial Hill:

> Possessed he talents, ten or five or one,
> The work he had to do—that work was done;
> Informed his mind, in wisdom's ways he trod,
> Reluctant died, but died resigned to God.

No man was better known in Plymouth in his day than Joseph Lucas. He was a son of Joseph and Ruby Lucas of Plympton, and was born in that town in February, 1785. He learned the nail cutter's trade, and worked at it many years in the works of N. Russell & Co. His work was something more than perfunctory, for it not only led him into a study of machinery with its needed improvements, but it gave him also an opportunity to ponder over worldly affairs beyond the horizon of his daily occupation. His ingenuity suggested useful improvements in nail cutting machines, which proved profitable to both his employers and himself. Mr. Lucas was an ardent whig, and as a manufacturer was a supporter of the tariff policy of his party, little thinking that within thirty-five years of his death the tariff policy which he advocated would by the imposition of high duties on coal and iron wipe out of existence the nail cutting business of New England.

Mr. Lucas was often sought to represent the town in the General Court, and in the house of representatives his name was as much identified with Plymouth as that of Kellogg with Pittsfield; Banning with Lee; Lawrence with Belchertown, or Lee with Templeton. In his day it was not the custom as it is now, to nominate one of two or three who set themselves up as candidates, but the voters selected the men they wanted for representatives, believing that laws to be respected must be enacted by men of good judgment and superior intelligence. Mr. Lucas married in 1823 Lydia, daughter of William and Lydia (Holmes) Keen, and had Augustus Henry, 1824; Catherine Amelia, 1825, and Frederick William, 1831. Mr. Lucas died January 13, 1871.

Before crossing Town Brook I must speak of Joseph P. Brown and Wm. H. Nelson, though they are not associated with the remote history of our town. Mr. Brown was the son of Lemuel Brown, and was born December 12, 1812. His father was a cabinet maker who came to Plymouth with a wife, Sarah Palmer of Cambridge, and established himself in business with a shop in the rear of the house next west of the present residence of the Misses Rich on Summer street. He did good work, and I know many mahogany chairs of his workmanship still doing good service in the parlors of some of my friends. His two sons, Stephen P. and Joseph P., learned the trade of their father, and in later years carried on business on the south side of High street, and in the building, a part of which is occupied by the provision market of C. B. Harlow on Market street. At a still later time Joseph P.

carried on the same business in the old Plymouth bank building on Court street. Joseph was on the board of selectmen with me from 1856 to 1860, inclusive, and I am glad of the opportunity to attest his usefulness and fidelity in the management of town affairs. He was a man of dry humor, and had many a story to tell, often provoking a laugh against himself. He chewed tobacco freely, and was obliged before speaking to deliver himself of the saliva which had been accumulating. I remember that one autumn afternoon when the board had been visiting the south end of the town, we stopped at the house of David Clark, a member of the board, to leave him, and went into the house to warm ourselves. As we sat around the wood fire I noticed a couple of herrings roasting in the ashes for supper. Before Mr. Brown could answer a question I put to him he was obliged to relieve his mouth of its contents, and he discharged them squarely upon the herrings, completely covering them. Nothing was said, and I did not suppose that any one but myself noticed the catastrophe. After we had started for home, Mr. Brown turning to me said, "Good heavens, Davis, did you see me baste those herrings?"

He told me once of an expedition to Sandwich to bring home his wife's invalid sister, who had been visiting there. He started one November morning about four o'clock, and after driving two hours he came to a cross road, and seeing a light in a house, stopped to inquire the way. On rapping at the door a man appeared with a lamp in his hand, whom he recognized as John Harlow, an old resident of Chiltonville. "What are you doing, John, down here in Sandwich," he asked, and John replied, " I guess, mister, your morning toddy was a little strong, I am in Chiltonville, not Sandwich." Then for the first time recognizing his visitor, he added, "Why, Mr. Brown, what are you doing here at this time in the morning?" "Why, John, I started for Sandwich, but at the rate of progress I have made I don't think I shall get there much before night." The trouble was that his horse, following the track which suited him best, had after leaving the Cornish tavern, borne constantly to the left and traversed the Beaver Dam road, and the road over the Pine Hills until he reached the Harlow house, four miles from his starting point two hours before. Mr. Brown married in 1837 Margaret, daughter of George Washburn, and died June 23, 1877.

William H. Nelson was the son of William and Sarah (Carver) Nelson, and was born August 13, 1830. After leaving school he was a clerk for a time in the hardware establishment of Cotton, Hill & Co., in Boston, but eventually established himself in business in his native town. As well as I can remember he first embarked in the grand bank fishery, supplemented by the mackerel fishery. Gradually enlarging his fleet, and also the size of his vessels, he extended his business operations by either chartering some of his vessels to Boston merchants engaged in the West India trade, or engaging himself in that trade. Building from time to time still larger vessels which were employed entirely under charter, his fishing interests became a secondary matter. By prudence and sagacity, his business was made successful and profitable, and as he won the confidence of his fellow citizens, he was sought for in the management of institutions and public affairs. He was a director of the Old Colony National Bank many years, and after the death of George Gustavus Dyer for a short time, until his own death, its President. His chief service, and one which made him respected, and his trustworthiness relied upon by his fellow citizens, was that rendered by him on the board of selectmen, of which he was a member for twenty years, and chairman sixteen years. As manager of town affairs he was conservative and faithful to his trust, never hasty in the support of new schemes, but sure in the end to support them when satisfied of their merit. He married Hannah Coomer, daughter of Coomer Weston, Jr., and died July 18, 1891.

CHAPTER XXX.

I have thus far in my wanderings omitted to mention any member of the Harlow family, scarcely one of whom can be found on the north side of Town Brook. But in crossing the brook I am at once confronted by three Harlow houses, standing like sentinels to guard what may be considered their family domain. These are the houses which in an earlier generation were occupied by Ephraim, Sylvanus and George Harlow. In my study of family names I have often found them confining themselves within certain town bounds. For instance there are the names of Stetson, Gray and Willis in Kingston; Sprague, Weston, Winsor and Soule in Duxbury; Lobdell, Harrub and Parker in Plympton, and of Ransom and Vaughan and Murdock in Carver, all like the clans of Scotland, keeping within their own borders. Nor were the limits within which the various names were found always as broad as the bounds of the towns. As for instance there were on the north side of the brook the Jacksons, Russells, Hedges, Spooners, Cottons, etc., and on the south side the Harlows, Dotens, Stephens and Barnes, representatives of each succeeding generation, settling among the familiar scenes of their youth. A hundred years, or perhaps more, ago, it was the custom in town meeting to divide the house in voting on important questions, the affirmative voters gathering on the north side, and the negative on the south. On one occasion after the division, but before the count, the moderator called out—a Ponds man on the wrong side of the house. When I see the sign of C. B. Harlow on Market street I am tempted to say, a Harlow man on the wrong side of the brook. In 1851 I was riding from Halifax, Nova Scotia, to Shelburne, and stopped at the inn in Liverpool for dinner. While eating alone, the landlord came into the dining room and entered into conversation. I asked him his name, and he said, Bradford Harlow, and in answer to my inquiry where he came from he said, " You may guess a hundred times and you will not guess right." "Well," I said, "I will venture to say that either you or your father came from Plymouth in Massachusetts." "By George," he exclaimed, pounding his hand down on the table, "You have guessed right the first time." I then told him I was a Plymouth man, and I did not believe such a combination of names could be found in any other town. His father was a ship carpenter, who after the Revolution moved down to Liverpool to work at his trade, and made that town his future residence. For some reason, which I cannot satisfactorily explain, there was at that time quite a migration of ship carpenters from Plymouth to Nova Scotia, which was made practicable by the frequent resort of Plymouth vessels bound to the fishing banks, to the harbors of Shelburne and Barrington and Liverpool. Among them were William Drew, who went to Liverpool, and James Cox, who went to Shelburne, the latter of whom married there Elizabeth Rowland about the year 1800, and continued there until his death. The late William Rowland Cox of Chiltonville, a son of James, and a well known master carpenter, came to Plymouth as long ago as I can remember, and Martha Taylor, a daughter, also came and married Ephraim Bartlett, whose daughter Martha Ann, widow of the late Geo. E. Morton, is a much respected resident of Plymouth.

Ephraim Harlow, above mentioned, was the son of Sylvanus and Desire (Sampson) Harlow, and was born in 1770. He was somewhat extensively engaged in navigation and real estate. In navigation he not only built one or more vessels on his own account, but he was also associated with James Bartlett, Jr., and others, in building the bark Fortune in 1822 for the whale fishery, and at a later period in building the schooner Maracaibo, for the same business. In the early part of the last century he owned in connection with his brother Jesse, Nathaniel Carver, and Benjamin M. Watson all the land on the west side of Pleasant street, between the brook and Jefferson street extending back to the poor house land, the northeasterly part of which, after sundry sales and divisions, came into his sole possession. On this part he built the house which he occupied until his death, on Robinson street in the rear of the old Robinson church. In the rear of his house he opened a Court in 1825, and built a house which was occupied by James Morton, sexton of the Unitarian church, whom

I remember sitting during the service at the head of the south pulpit stairs. Mr. Harlow was a man of tried probity and intelligence, receptive of various measures of reform, such as anti-slavery and temperance measures, which both he and his family did much to support. He married in 1794 Jerusha, daughter of Thos. Doten, and had Jerusha Howes, Ephraim, Thos. Doten and Jabez. He married second, Ruth, daughter of William Sturtevant of Carver and had Jane, 1808, who married Atwood L. Drew, Hannah Shaw, 1810, who married George Adams, Ruth Sturtevant, 1815, whose early death was lamented by a large circle of friends; Zilpha Washburn, 1818, who married Nathaniel Bourne Spooner, and Desire Sampson, 1821. He died December 15, 1859.

The house on the corner of Pleasant and Sandwich streets, now occupied by William H. Harlow, was built by his grandfather, Jesse Harlow, not long after the Revolution, and in my early days was occupied by David Harlow, the father of the present occupant, who kept a store there for many years. David Harlow married in 1823, Eliza Sherman, daughter of Lewis and Betsey (Weston) Finney, and had David L., who married Lucy Cook of Kingston; Isaac Newton, who married Catherine Weston; Henry M., who married Sarah F. Cowen; Ezra, who married Catherine Covington; Ann Eliza, Hannah, Pelham W., who married Etta H. Mayo; Edward P., who married Nancy Sanford of Taunton, and William H., who married Annie Gibbs of Providence. David Harlow died July 22, 1859.

The house on Sandwich street, next but one to the David Harlow house, was built in 1825 by George Harlow, who bought the lot on which it stands, in that year from the heirs of Thomas Doty. George Harlow was the son of Samuel and Remembrance (Holmes) Harlow, and was born in 1789. He was in my day chiefly engaged in the Grand Bank fishery. He married in 1813, Lydia, daughter of Nathaniel Ellis, and had Nathaniel Ellis, 1813, who married Julia A. Whiting of Bangor; Lydia, 1819, who married Albert Tribble; Esther, 1821, who married John Henry Hollis; George Henry, 1823, who married Sarah E. Morton, and Samuel, who married Mary H. Bradford. Mr. Harlow died May 9, 1865.

I must not wander far beyond the brook without a notice

of Rev. Adoniram Judson, the distinguished Baptist missionary, who was a citizen of Plymouth from 1802 to 1812, and who always, until his death, considered it his American home. His father, Rev. Adoniram Judson, was born in Woodbury in 1751, and graduated at Yale in 1775. After settlements in Malden and Wenham he was settled, May 12, 1802, the first pastor of the third Plymouth church near Training Green. Before coming to Plymouth he married Abigail, daughter of Abraham Brown of Tiverton, and had four children, Adoniram, Elnathan, Abigail Brown and Mary Alice. Elnathan, born probably in Wenham in 1795, was a surgeon in the United States Navy, and died in Washington May 8, 1829. Of Mary Alice I know nothing. Abigail Brown was born in Malden March 21, 1791, and died in Plymouth, where since 1802 she had always lived, January 25, 1884. I remember her well, and many times called at her home to talk with her about her brother, Adoniram, and his missionary service. She was a calm, placid woman, with a saintly face, and in everything but speech resembled a Quakeress. The last time I saw her she was crossing Town Square on a hot summer day, wearing a green calash pulled down by the ribbon loop attached to its front, to protect her face from the rays of the sun. The father continued his pastorate until 1817, when becoming a Baptist he resigned, and after preaching for the Plymouth Baptists, then worshipping in Old Colony Hall, previous to the erection of their meeting house on Spring street in 1822, he removed in 1820 to Scituate, where he died November 28, 1826. During his Plymouth pastorate he became the owner of all the lots of land on the west side of Pleasant street, which for a time was called Judson street, from the lot now owned by Chas. P. Hatch to Jefferson street inclusive. On the Hatch lot he built and occupied the house, which with considerable alteration is now standing, and in 1808 sold it to his daughter, Abigail, who made it her home until her death in 1884. Rev. Adoniram Judson, the missionary, son of Rev. Adoniram and Abigail (Brown) Judson, was born in Malden, August 9, 1788, and graduated at Brown University in 1807. After leaving college he taught a private school two years in Plymouth, where he published the "Young Ladies' Arithmetic," and a work on English Grammar. Until 1810 his religious views were unsettled, but in that year he joined his father's church, and after a short time at the Andover Seminary was admitted to preach by the Orange Association of Congregational ministers in Vermont. Having determined to enter the missionary service, he sailed for England with the view of making the necessary arrangements, and was captured by a French privateer, and after a short imprisonment at Bayonne, reached England, returning in 1811, and being ordained as missionary at Salem, February 6, 1812. He married February 5, 1812, Ann Hazeltine, of Bradford, Mass., and daughter of John and Rebecca Hazeltine, and sailed for Calcutta on the 19th of that month. Soon after reaching India he became a Baptist, and severing his connection with the American Board he was baptized by Dr. Carey, the English missionary at Serampore. When the war broke out between the East India Company and the Burman Government, Dr. Judson was arrested for alleged complicity with the English, and suffered a long imprisonment, during which a child, Maria E. B. Judson, was born, who died April 24, 1827, at the age of two years and three months. Mrs. Judson died at Amherst, Burman Empire, October 24, 1826. In 1834 he married Sarah Hall Boardman, widow of Rev. George Dana Boardman, and daughter of Ralph and Abiah Hall of Alstead, N. H., who died on her way to America at St. Helena, September 1, 1845. In the autumn of that year Dr. Judson made his first and only visit to the United States, where he remained until July, 1846. During that visit it was my privilege to meet him. At that time the mail stage for Boston, leaving Plymouth at half past ten, met the accommodation stage leaving Boston at eleven o'clock, and the passengers dined together at the half way house in West Scituate, and there I met and sat next to him at the dinner table. He was rather above the average height, had brown hair, a smooth face, and an expression indicative of a life of serious thought and sad experience. He reminded me of portraits of Charles the First, and also of the portrait now in Pilgrim Hall of Governor Josiah Winslow, in both of which is depicted the expression to which I have referred. During his visit he married in June, 1846, Emily Chubbuck, a native of Eaton, N. Y., known in the literary world as Fanny Forester, and sailed with her for India in the following month.

By his second wife his children were Adoniram, Elnathan, Henry, Edward and Abby Ann, and by his third wife, a daughter, Emily, who married a Mr. Hanna. Dr. Judson died at sea April 12, 1850, and his widow returning to America in 1851, died June 1, 1854. His great literary works were a Burmese translation of the Scriptures, and a Burmese English dictionary.

Ichabod, son of Ichabod and Sarah (Churchill) Morton, was born in Plymouth in ´ January, 1790. He always lived in Wellingsley, but precisely where he was born I am unable to say. His father built the house now owned by the heirs of Edwin Morton, when Ichabod was a year old, and there he lived until he bought in 1829 the house in which he died. For many years he kept with his brother Edwin, a general store in a building which was erected and occupied as a dwelling house by Eleazer Churchill. The firm of I. & E. Morton early added to their business that of the Grand Bank fishery, and also built vessels engaged in coatwise and foreign trade. They were the earliest traders in Plymouth to abandon the sale of intoxicating liquors, and among the first to join the movement against the institution of slavery. Mr. Morton became also much interested in the cause of education, and in town meetings strongly advocated increasing appropriations for the support of public schools. When the policy was adopted by the state of establishing Normal schools, he only needed the co-operation of the leading men in Plymouth to make his own earnest efforts successful in securing the location here of the school which was established in Bridgewater. Horace Mann publicly recognized in him one of his ablest coadjutors in the cause of education. For a short time his business was interrupted by his association with the Brook Farm enterprise, but the dreams of that social experiment soon gave way to the practical pursuits of business life. He married Patty, daughter of Coomer Weston, and had November 22, 1821, a daughter, Abigail, who married Manuel A. Diaz. He married second Betsey, daughter of Gideon Holbrook, and had George E., 1829, Nathaniel, 1831, Ichabod, 1833, Austin, 1834, and Howard, 1836, and died May 10, 1861. Mrs. Diaz, well known as a writer, died in Belmont in the spring of 1904, and was buried at Mount Auburn.

One of the measures in which at one time Mr. Morton was much interested, was that for a division of the town. In 1855, at the time when the construction of town water works was decided, it was supposed by many in the south part of the town that the pecuniary burden which the enterprise would impose on the town, it was their duty to adopt every means to escape. Henry W. Cushman, who had been Lieutenant Governor of Massachusetts from 1851 to 1853, had expressed a desire for the incorporation of a town bearing his name, and it was understood that the christening might confer a financial benefit on the town so named. It was thought therefore that the time was a favorable one to have the southerly part of the town set off under the name of Cushman. If I remember rightly the dividing line asked for in the petition of Caleb Morton and others ran from the harbor, through Winter and Mount Pleasant streets. Favorable reports were made in both 1855 and 1856, but the bills recommended for passage were rejected. Mr. Morton took an active part in urging the division, but I suspect that neither he nor any person now living regretted the issue.

Two other attempts to divide the town have been made since Kingston was set off and incorporated in 1726. In 1783 ten heads of families representing themselves as composing one-sixth of the precinct of Manomet Ponds petitioned the General Court to have Cedarville and Ellisville set off to Sandwich. The petitioners who were given leave to withdraw were, Seth Mendall, Wm. Ellis, Thomas Ellis, Eleazer Ellis, Barnabas Ellis, Phineas Swift, Samuel Morris, Prince Wadsworth, Samuel Gibbs and Catherine Swift. Another movement in favor of a division was started in 1837, but when brought before the town it was defeated by a vote of 376 to 246.

While the question of the division was pending in 1855 and 1856, I was chairman of the Board of Selectmen, and of course was cognizant of all that was done to defeat the measure. In those days the members of the legislature remained during the week in Boston, or its immediate vicinity, only going home to spend the Sabbath. The board invited them to make an excursion to Plymouth on Fast Day, and entertained them at the Samoset House. It is needless to say that the argument was conclusive. A more difficult task awaited the board the next year to oppose a petition to change the shire to Bridgewater.

As soon as the legislature of 1857 came together, the board of which I was still chairman, placed printed remonstrances in the hands of reliable men in every town in the county, which poured into the legislature bearing, I think, the names of a majority of the voters of the county. A similiar petition was sent to the legislature at a time earlier than I can remember, headed by Col. Sylvanus Lazell of Bridgewater, who unfamiliar with the meaning of words, claimed that Plymouth had been a seaport long enough, and that it was Bridgewater's turn. At that time a resolve was passed by the legislature requiring the submission of two questions to the voters of the county: First, are you in favor of a removal of the shire, and second, in what town shall the shire be located. In answer to these questions a majority voted for a removal, and singularly enough, a majority also voted in favor of Plymouth for the location. With the erection of a Court house in Brockton, and the erection of a Registry in Plymouth, I think the crisis is passed, and that no further attempts will be made to remove the shire. The increasing population of Plymouth will serve to check the disturbance of the equilibrium of the county, which the growth of Brockton has heretofore caused.

CHAPTER XXXI.

The following professional men have not heretofore been mentioned in these memories:

Dr. F. G. Oehme, a German homeopathic physician, came to Plymouth about 1857, and occupied for a time the house on Middle street, now owned by Charles H. Frink, and later bought the house on Court street occupied in recent years by George E. Morton. He had an office at one time in the second story of the building on Main street, now occupied by H. H. Cole. He sold his dwelling house in 1873 to Martha T. Bartlett, the widow of Ephraim Bartlett, and removed to Long Island, from thence going to Portland, Oregon, where he died in 1905.

Dr. Ervin Webster, born in Vermont, January 25, 1828, came to Plymouth in 1850, and established himself as a botanic physician in the rooms on Main street, now occupied by Loring's watchmaker's store. With his son, Olin E., four years of age, he was drowned in Billington Sea, August 28, 1856.

Dr. George F. Wood, son of Isaac Lewis and Elizabeth (Robbins) Wood, was born in Plymouth, March 12, 1841. He married Sarah E., daughter of Sylvanus Harvey, and established himself as a physician in an office on the North side of Town Square. He died October 27, 1868.

Dr. Nathaniel Lothrop, son of Isaac and Priscilla (Thomas) (Watson) Lothrop, was born in Plymouth in 1737, and graduated at Harvard in 1756. He married first, Ellen, daughter of Noah Hobart of Fairfield, Conn., and second, Lucy, daughter of Abraham Hammatt of Plymouth, and died October 9, 1828.

Dr. Robert Capen taught a private school in Plymouth in 1828, and in 1830 was practising medicine with an office in the Marcy house, which stood on North street, where Dr. W. G. Brown's house stands. I do not know either the date or place of his death.

Dr. Mercy B. Jackson, widow of Daniel Jackson, belonged to the Homeopathic school and practiced in Plymouth and Boston, and died in 1877.

Dr. Isaac LeBaron, known in my day as an apothecary, was always called Doctor, but I do not know that he was educated as a physician. He lived through my early youth in a house standing on the upper corner of Leyden street and LeBaron Alley, and had his shop in a one story building on Main street, where Dr. Hubbard's house now stands. At a later time he lived in the house on the corner of North and Main streets, and had his shop in the same building. He married in 1811 Mary Doane of Boston, and died, January 29, 1849.

Dr. Parker came to Plymouth about 1882 and occupied for a short time the house now owned by Arthur Lord, but whence he came and where he went I do not know.

Dr. Warren Peirce succeeded Dr. Parker, and occupied the same house until it was sold to Mr. Lord, when he moved to the house at the lower angle of Carver street. He was born in Tyngsboro, Mass., Nov. 30, 1840, and graduated at the Harvard Medical School in 1869. He enlisted May 11, 1864, in Co. K First Regiment of Heavy Artillery of Massachusetts, and was appointed Hospital steward. After he received his degree he practised some years in Boylston or West Boylston. He was the son of Dr. Augustus and Alectia (Butterfield) Peirce. His father was born in New Salem March 13, 1803, and died in 1849. Dr. Warren Peirce died in Plymouth, July 10, 1898.

Dr. Francis B. Brewer had in 1850 an office at the corner of Main and Middle streets, but I do not know whether he was engaged in general practise or exclusively in that of dentistry. He was succeeded in the same year by Dr. Robert D. Foster, who advertised himself as having had "the most ample experience in operative surgery, both in England and the United States."

In September, 1855, Dr. James L. Hunt occupied the office which Dr. Brewer and Dr. Foster had occupied, but I know neither his specialty nor the length of his service in Plymouth.

Dr. Andrew Mackie, son of Dr. Andrew of Wareham, was born in 1799, and graduated at Brown in 1814. He came to Plymouth in 1829, and lived on the corner of Market and Leyden streets, and in the house next below the rooms of Mr. Beaman on Middle street. He removed to New Bedford soon after 1832.

Dr. John Flavel Gaylord, son of Ebenezer and Jane (Phelps) Gaylord, was born in Amherst, Mass., March 22, 1852. He fitted for college at the Hopkin's Grammar school and graduated at Yale in 1876. He took his degree from the Yale Medical school in 1878, and completed his studies in 1879 and 1880 at the University of Berlin, and at Heilbronn. On his return home he practised a few years in Cincinnati, and settled in Plymouth in 1889, where he married Susan, daughter of William Rider Drew, and died April 14, 1903.

Dr. Charles James Wood came to Plymouth in 1866 and settled in Chiltonville. He was son of Leonard Wood, and was born in Leicester, Mass., February 18, 1827, and was educated at the Leicester Academy. He practised in Barre, Chiltonville, Sandwich and Pocasset, in which latter place he died August 25, 1880. I remember him as attending with Dr. Alexander Jackson in Manomet Ponds, the sailors who were wrecked in the bark Velma in 1867. He was the father of General Leonard Wood, now in the Philippines, who attended school in Chiltonville.

Dr. John C. Bennett appeared in Plymouth in 1835, and advertised himself an eclectic physician "formerly professor of obsteric medicine and surgery." The various medicines prepared by him were claimed to be infallible ones for many diseases; and of a tooth extractor invented by him, it was said by an enthusiastic friend that it made the extraction of a tooth an operation of pleasure instead of pain. He married Sally, daughter of Job Rider of Plymouth, and lived and had his office on Summer street. The introduction by him of the Plymouth Rock breed of fowls gave him a reputation of a more substantial character than his medicines. In 1842 he published "The History of the Saints," an expose of Joe Smith and Mormonism.

Dr. John Bachelder, son of John and Mary Bachelder, was born in Mason, N. H., March 23, 1818, and graduated at Dartmouth in 1841. He began to practice in Monument in 1844, and married Martha Swift Keene of Sandwich, September 30, 1846, afterwards removing to Plymouth, where he died October 28, 1876.

Of Dr. Benjamin Hubbard I make an exception among the living physicians, and include in these memories a notice due

to his age and long practice in Plymouth. He was born in
Holden, Mass., November 25, 1817, the son of Benjamin and
Polly (Walker) Hubbard. He came to Plymouth in 1840 and
studied medicine with his brother, Dr. Levi Hubbard, and after attending one term at the college at Woodstock, Vt., graduated at the Pittsfield Medical college in 1844. After receiving his degree he practiced six months in South Weymouth,
and then came to Plymouth, succeeding his brother, who removed in the autumn of 1844 to New Bedford. Aside from
his practice he has been assiduous in his devotion to the welfare
of the Baptist Society, which owes him a debt which it grate-
fully acknowledges, but can never repay. He married June
29, 1844, Ellen Maria, daughter of Elisha Perry of Sandwich,
and is enjoying in a serene old age the love and respect of the
community, whom for more than sixty years he has faithfully
served.

William Davis, son of Nathaniel Morton and Harriet Lazell
(Mitchell) Davis, was born in Plymouth May 12, 1818. He
fitted for college at the Boston Latin school, and graduated
at Harvard in 1837. He studied law with his father, and at
the Harvard Law school, and was admitted to the Suffolk bar
January 18, 1841. In those days it was the custom in the
Harvard Law school to hold a moot court once each winter for
which the jury was drawn from the senior class in college, and
lots were drawn among the senior law students for the positions of senior and junior counsel on each side. William M.
Evarts was in the law school, and having come from Yale college with a high reputation for eloquence, it was taken for
granted that if unsuccessful in the drawing, one of the successful ones would surrender his place to him. Mr. Davis, one of
the successful ones, declined to give up his position as senior
counsel for the defendant, but a place was given to Mr. Evarts
as senior counsel for the plaintiff. As Mr. Davis lived in Boston with his grandmother, he was little known by his fellow
students, and when the trial came on the lecture room of the
school was crowded with law students and undergraduates to
hear the eloquent man from Yale. I was one of the jury, and
I remember well the astonishment with which the masterly
speech of Mr. Davis was received. Some years afterwards
Mr. Richard H. Dana, who was a member of the law school at

Dr. John Flavel Gaylord, son of E⸱ ⸱ool was
Gaylord, was born in Amherst, M⸱ ⸱arts was
fitted for college at the Hopkir⸱ ⸱sture and
uated at Yale in 1876. He⸱ ⸱an was who
Medical school in 1878, an⸱ ⸱ale.
1880 at the University o⸱ at the bar in-
return home he practi⸱ long sentences,
in Plymouth in 18⸱ ⸱ escape from his
William Rider Dr⸱ nominative. He
Dr. Charles J⸱ his rhetoric that in
tled in Chilto⸱ ⸱oner in the dock was the
born in Le⸱ ⸱ong sentences. He was a man
at the L⸱ ⸱retary of state in the cabinet of Presi-
ville, S⸱ ⸱ never had wine on his table no matter who
ust ⸱ ⸱uests, he said one day to a lady sitting next to him
ar ⸱ne state dinner, when the Roman punch was served—"Ah,
we have reached the life saving station." The next day when
a friend asked him how the dinner went off he said, "Splendid-
ly, water flowed like champagne."

Returning from this digression, Mr. Davis settled in Plymouth, and was appointed in 1844 aide with the rank of Lieutenant Colonel on the staff of Governor George N. Briggs, and in
1850, 1851 and 1852, was chairman of the Board of Selectmen.
From 1844 to 1852, he was Vice-President of the Pilgrim Society, and from 1848 to 1850 inclusive, a Director of the Plymouth Bank. He married December 2, 1849, Helen, daughter
of John and Deborah (Spooner) Russell, and had Harriet
Mitchell in September, 1850, who died in December, 1852, and
William, September 27, 1853. He died February 19, 1853.

William H. Whitman, son of Kilborn and Elizabeth (Winslow) Whitman, was born in Pembroke, January 26, 1817. He
studied law with Thomas Prince Beal of Kingston, and began
practice in Bath, Maine, where his sister, Sarah Ann, the wife
of Benjamin Randall lived. He moved to Boston in 1844,
where he practiced law until 1851, a part of the time a partner
of Charles G. Davis. In 1851 he was appointed clerk of the
Courts of Plymouth County, and continued in office until his
death. He married in 1846, Ann Sever, daughter of William
and Sally W. Thomas, and had Isabella Thomas, Elizabeth H.
and William Thomas. He married second, Helen, widow of

and daughter of John Russell, and had Russell,
Ann Thomas.   He died August 13, 1889.

Hayward was born in Thetford, Vt., August
luated at Dartmouth College in 1859.   He
sse E. Keith of Abington and Charles G.
and was admitted to the Plymouth bar
' practiced one year in Plymouth, then
finally moved to New York in 1865,

me to Plymouth from Roxbury
gn School, and while teaching, stud-
admitted to the Plymouth bar in 1848, and
ousiness in Plymouth until his death.   He married
y 1, 1831, Catherine Hinsdale, daughter of Nathan Allen of
Medfield and Dedham, but I find no record of his death.

William F. Spear, son of Wm. H. and Catherine H. (Allen)
Spear, was born in June, 1832, and was admitted to the Plymouth bar in 1853.   He married Caroline Augusta, daughter
of Elisha Whiting, and died in Plymouth, September 21, 1858.

There was an Edward L. Sherman practicing law in Plymouth about fifty years ago, but I know nothing about him.   He
may have been the Edward Lowell Sherman, a Harvard graduate of 1854, who was admitted to the Essex bar in 1856, and
was practicing in Boston in 1860, and until his death in 1893.

Isaac Goodwin, son of William and Lydia Cushing (Sampson) Goodwin, was born in Plymouth, June 28, 1786.   He
studied law with Joshua Thomas, and began practice in Boston,
afterwards removing to Sterling, and in 1826 to Worcester.
In 1825 he published a book entitled "The Town Officer," and
in 1830 another on the duties of a sheriff, which was followed
by a general history of Worcester County, written for the Worcester Magazine.   At the 150th anniversary of the destruction
of the town of Lancaster he delivered the oration.   He married in 1810, Eliza, daughter of Abraham Hammatt, and had
Lucy Lothrop, 1811; Elizabeth Mason 1813, Wm. Hammatt,
1817, John Emery, 1820, John Abbot, 1824, Mary Jane, 1834,
who married Loring Henry Austin of Boston, and was the well
known authoress.   He died September 10, 1832.

Rev. Dr. Joseph Sylvester Clark, son of Seth and Mary
(Tupper) Clark, was born in Manomet Ponds, December 19,

1800.   Dr. Clark was born in a house nearly opposite the residence of the late Horace B. Taylor.   His brother Israel, one of the purest of men, was on the board of selectmen with me in 1855, and lived at the time in the old homestead.

In 1818 Rev. Seth Stetson, the pastor of the Manomet church, became Unitarian, and in the temporary division of the church which followed, Dr. Clark's father was one of Mr. Stetson's followers.   As late as 1819 it seems to be certain that the son had not been able to believe in the divinity of Christ, and he did not become a member of the church until June 9, 1822, after which time he was a member in full standing of the Orthodox Congregational church.   At the age of seventeen Dr. Clark taught school in Manomet, and soon after in Hingham, and by his earnings as a teacher and the moderate assistance which his father could afford to render, he was enabled to enter the classical academy at Amherst on the 29th of July, 1822, and to enter Amherst college in September, 1823, where he graduated in due course with valedictory honors.   In 1827, after a short service as tutor at Amherst, he entered the Andover theological seminary, and after intervals spent in teaching school, graduated in 1831.   On the second of October, 1831, he preached at Sturbridge, Mass., and on the twenty-seventh was unanimously invited to become the successor of Rev. Alvan Bond in that town.   His ordination followed on the twenty-first of December.   On the twenty-eighth of May, 1839, he was appointed secretary of the Massachusetts Missionary Society, and severing his connection with the Sturbridge parish, he entered on the discharge of the duties of secretary continuing them until his resignation on the twenty-third of September, 1857.   In 1858 he published "A Historical sketch of the Congregational churches of Massachusetts from 1620 to 1858. Dr. Park said of him "his experience in the Home Missionary work convinced him that Congregationalists had sacrificed the spiritual welfare of their own churches to an ill-regarded zeal for harmony with other denominations.   They had cultivated such a dread of sectarianism as induced them to abandon their own distinctive principles for the sake of living in peace with sectarians who became the more exclusive as Congregationalists became the more liberal."

At the time of the formation of the Congregational Library

Association, he was chosen its Corresponding Secretary in May, 1853, and its financial agent in June, 1857, and soon after united with Rev. H. M. Dexter, and Rev. A. H. Quint, in publishing the Congregational quarterly, the first number of which was issued in January, 1859. To his unremitting labors was largely due the consummation of the project to buy for the Association the Crowninshield building, which it long occupied on the corner of Beacon and Somerset streets in Boston. In 1851 he received from his Alma Mater the degree of Doctor of Divinity, and in 1852 was chosen a trustee of the college. He married December 27, 1831, Harriet B., daughter of Joseph Bourne of New Bedford, and died at the home of his brothers, Israel and Nathaniel, at Manomet, August 17, 1861.

Rev. Ezra Shaw Goodwin, son of General Nathaniel and Ruth (Shaw) Goodwin, was born in Plymouth in 1787, and was settled as pastor of the first church in Sandwich. He married Ellen Watson, daughter of John Davis, and died in Sandwich, February 5, 1833.

Rev. Hersey Bradford Goodwin, son of William and Lydia Cushing (Sampson) Goodwin, was born in Plymouth, and graduated at Harvard in 1826. He graduated at the Harvard Divinity school in 1829, and was settled in Concord. He married in 1830, Lucretia Ann, daughter of Benjamin Marston Watson of Plymouth, and had Wm. Watson, 1831. He married second, Amelia Mackie of Boston, and had Amelia and Hersey Bradford, and died in 1836.

Rev. Thomas Weston, son of Coomer and Hannah (Doten) Weston, was born in Plymouth, August 30, 1821. He prepared for the ministry at the Meadville school in Pennsylvania, and was settled at various times over Unitarian societies in Northumberland, Penn., Bernardston and New Salem, Mass., Farmington, Maine, and Barnstable and Stowe, Mass. He married April 29, 1852 Lucinda, daughter of Ralph Cushman of Bernardston, and died in Greenfield, Mass., March 29, 1904.

Rev. James Augustus Kendall, son of Rev. Dr. James and Sarah (Poor) Kendall, was born in Plymouth, Nov. 1, 1803, and graduated at Harvard in 1823. He was settled in Medfield six years, and after spending a short time in Stowe and Cambridge, he removed to Framingham, where he married May 29, 1833, Maria B., daughter of Col. James Brown, and died May 16, 1884.

Rev. Sylvester Holmes, son of Sylvester and Grace (Clark) Holmes, was born in Manomet Ponds April 6, 1788, and was ordained as minister in 1811. He was for many years engaged in the service of the American Bible Society, especially in the South, where he was everywhere known among leading men of both church and state. From 1861, until 1866, he was settled over the church at Manomet Ponds, where he married in 1810 Esther Holmes. He married a second wife, Fanny Kingman of Bridgewater, and died in New Bedford at the house of Ivory H. Bartlett, November 27, 1866.

Rev. William Faunce, son of Solomon and Eleanor (Bradford) Faunce, was born in Plymouth about 1815. In 1840 he organized a Christian Baptist Society, and built a meeting house near the Russell Mills. After a long pastorate he removed to Mattapoisett, where he died about ten years ago. He married Matilda, daughter of Josiah Bradford, and had Matilda B., 1835, who married Weston C. Vaughan, William, 1837, and Ellen, 1840.

Rev. Lewis Holmes, son of Peter and Sally (Harlow) Holmes, was born in Plymouth, April 12, 1813, and graduated at Colby University. He had settlements at various times over Baptist Societies in Edgartown, Scituate, Leicester and other places. He married Lydia K., daughter of Pickels Cushing of Norwell, and died May 24, 1887.

Rev. Russell Tomlinson, son of David and Polly (Sherman) Tomlinson was born in Newtown, Conn., October 1, 1808, and after fitting for the ministry was settled pastor over a Universalist Society in Buffalo, N. Y. In September, 1838 he came to Plymouth, where he was settled in May, 1839, pastor of the Unversalist church as the sucessor of Rev. Albert Case. In 1867 he resigned his pastorate, continuing to live in Plymouth until his death, and devoting himself to the practice of homeopathy, and the advocacy of the cause of temperance. He married Harriet W., daughter of Charles and Mary Ann (Williams) May, and died March 4, 1878.

Rev. George Ware Briggs, son of William and Sally (Palmer) Briggs, was born in Little Compton, April 8, 1810, and graduated at Brown University in 1825. He graduated at the Harvard Divinity school in 1834, and was soon after settled in Fall River. In 1838 he was installed colleague pastor of Rev. Dr. Jas. Kendall of the First Church in Plymouth, continuing in that pastorate until 1852. January 6, 1853, he became pastor of the First Chuch in Salem. On the first of April, 1867, he resigned the Salem pastorate, and in that year became pastor of the Third Congregational Church in Cambridge, located in Cambridge Port, where he remained until his death, having a colleague in his later years. He married first Lucretia Archbald, daughter of Abner Bartlett, and second in 1849, Lucia J., daughter of Nathaniel Russell of Plymouth. He received the honorary degree of Doctor of Divinity from Harvard in 1855, and died in Plymouth, September 10, 1895.

Rev. Daniel F. Goddard, son of Daniel and Polly (Finney) Goddard, was born in Plymouth about 1828, and married in 1854 Mary E., daughter of Ellis Barnes. He studied for the ministry, and was settled in various places, including, I think, Harvard and Weymouth. He died in 1883.

Rev. Dr. Daniel Wooster Faunce, son of Peleg and Olive (Finney) Faunce, was born in Plymouth, January 3, 1829, and graduated at Amherst in 1850. He studied for the ministry at the Newton Theological Institute, and was ordained in 1853. He married, August 15, 1853, Mary P. Perry, and in 1871 Mary E. Tucker. He was settled in Washington, D. C., and Pawtucket, R. I., and was the author of a number of religious works. His home is now in Providence, near that of his son, Rev. Wm. Herbert Perry Faunce, President of Brown University.

CHAPTER XXXII.

Mention of Plymouth grave yards has been confined thus far
to a slight allusion to Cole's Hill. Of the many within the
limits of the town two are burial places of the aborigines,
Watson's Hill and High Cliff, and the numerous skeletons ex-
humed at those places from time to time, make it conclusive
that they were places set apart for the burial of the dead. The
grounds in and about the central town have been thoroughly
explored in laying out streets, in excavating cellars and digging
trenches for water, gas and sewer pipes, and not enough Indian
bones have been found to warrant the conclusion that any other
burial places were used by the Indians than those above mentioned. The discovery of the burial ground at High Cliff was
brought to my knowledge by an incident in my own experience.
I met one day in the autumn of 1844 on Court street a little
girl about six years of age, crying and bleeding at the mouth.
An older girl leading her told me that she had a pin in her
throat. I led her to her home on South Russell street, stopping on the way at Mr. Standish's blacksmith shop to borrow
a pair of pincers, and soon relieved her from her suffering.
The next day Mr. Orin Bosworth, learning that I was his little
daughter's friend, gave me as a reward for my service a stone
pipe, which he said a gang of laborers, of whom he was fore-
man, had found in the railroad cut at High Cliff. I visited
the spot at once, and found that seven or eight skeletons had
been found, indicating an extensive burial ground, undoubtedly
antedating the days of the Pilgrims. Some years afterwards,
after the establishment of the Agassiz Museum in Cambridge,
the pipe was examined by the experts of the Museum and
pronounced of European workmanship, probably brought over
and given to the Indians, either by European fishermen, or
by one of the early adventurers like Champlain, John Smith
or Thomas Dermer. It is made of stone about eight inches
long, with a bowl about an inch square, and is in perfect order.
I have quite recently seen a drawing of a fragment of a similar
pipe which was found between the floor timbers of the Spar-

row-hawk, wrecked on Cape Cod in 1626, the timbers of which have been put together, and are now in Pilgrim Hall. The burial ground in question owes its escape from forgetfulness to the pin in the throat of little Hannah Elizabeth Bosworth.

Passing by Burial Hill and Cole's Hill to be mentioned later, there are Oak Grove and Vine Hills cemeteries; the Catholic cemetery; two burial grounds in Chiltonville, one at Bramhall's corner, and one at the Russell Mills meeting house; three at Manomet, one where the first meeting house stood not far from the residence of the late Horace B. Taylor, one at the present meeting house, a modern Indian burial ground, on an Indian reservation on the westerly side of Fresh Pond; one at South Ponds, near the Chapel; one at the head of Half Way Ponds; one at the head of Long Pond; one near Bloody Pond, and one at Cedarville There are also burial places in the South part of the town, which have been devoted to family uses and single graves may be found near Hospital landing at Billington Sea, and on the South Pond road, where the old pest house stood. At the last place there is a headstone at the grave of Mary, wife of Thomas Mayhew, who died September 3, 1776, aged 54 years. She was a daughter of Thomas Witherell, and as her husband was one of the most prominent men in the town, it is probable that she died of small pox, and that the removal of her body to a grave among her deceased relatives was thought dangerous.

I take the liberty to suggest that the selectmen set up a bronze tablet in the Indian burial ground at Fresh Pond with the following inscription, including an extract from a poem by the Rev. Theodore Dwight;

"Indian Burial Ground."

"This tablet is erected in memory of the Indian tribes whose extinction, beginning in the Plymouth Colony, is now almost complete."

"Indulge my native land, indulge a tear,
That steals impassioned o'er a nation's doom;
To me each twig from Adam's stock is dear,
And sorrows fall on an Indian's tomb."

With regard to Cole's Hill, the impression has prevailed that burials there were confined to the winter of 1620 and 1621. After a somewhat thorough examination of evidence and probabilities, I have reached the conclusion that this impresssion is not correct. I have already stated that no record

exists of the discovery of the remains of white men except on
Cole's and Burial Hill. Pretty thorough explorations beneath
the surface of the ground, in or near the main town settlement, prove with reasonable certainty that one of these two
places was during the early years of the Plymouth Colony the
place of burial. It is an interesting fact that the Pilgrims,
unlike the Puritans, followed the English custom of burying
their dead in the church yard, a spot as near as possible to
their place of worship. In Duxbury the first meeting house
was built near the shore, not far from the base of Captain's
Hill, and the first burials were made immediately about it. In
Marshfield the first meeting house was built near the tomb
of Daniel Webster, and what is called the Winslow burial
ground, which incloses that tomb, was the church yard. There
is every reason to believe that the same custom prevailed in
Plymouth. The Common house was for many years used for
public worship, except in times of impending dangers when
resort was temporarily had to the fort, on what is now Burial
Hill, and Cole's Hill, sloping down to that house lying directly
at its base was the church yard. As long then as the Common House was the place of public worship, I cannot doubt
that Cole's Hill was the burial place, and that when the first
meeting house was built on the North side of Town Square,
Burial Hill sloping down to its walls, became the church yard
and the place for depositing the bodies of the dead.

In this view of the case it becomes important, in deciding
when burials ceased to be made on Cole's Hill, to ascertain
when the first meeting house proper was built. Upon this
question there has been a difference of opinion, some writers
saying 1637, and some 1647. Those fixing the time at 1647
have based their opinion, so far as I can discover, on the historic record that the town meeting held in May, 1649 was held
in the meeting house, and on the fact that the meeting house
was then for the first time mentioned as the place for holding
town meetings. The meeting held on the 10th of July, 1638, is
recorded as having been held in the Governor's house, and it is
asked by the advocates of the later date why should that meeting have been held in the Governor's house if the meeting
house was built in 1637. It must be remembered that the purpose of the meeting house was not to furnish a place for civic

meetings, but a place for religious worship, and that only the increasing numbers of the settlement in 1649 outgrew the capacity of the Governor's house, and rendered the use of the meeting house at that time one of necessity. And again it must be remembered that with the single exception of the meeting, July 16, 1638, no meeting place is mentioned until May 17, 1649, and for all that is known to the contrary, meeting after meeting before 1649 may have been held in the meeting house without any record of the meeting place. Mr. Goodwin in a foot note on page 231 of the "Pilgrim Republic," makes it appear that the record states that the meeting of May 17, 1649, was held in the *new* meeting house, but the word (new) is not in the record, and therefore adds no weight to the argument in support of the date of 1647. The question may be pertinently asked, "Why, if the meeting house was built in 1647 was its occupation for town meetings delayed until May 17, 1649?" and this question is as difficult to answer as the other, "Why was it not earlier devoted to civic uses if it was built in 1637."

The probabilities in favor of 1637 are too strong to be overcome. Until 1636, after the settlement of Duxbury was made, it was a mooted question whether the meeting house should not be built in some place midway between the two settlements. A decision was reached in that year, and at once the meeting house in Duxbury was built in 1637, making it probable that Plymouth followed and built its meeting house in the same year. It would be a severe reflection on the religious spirit and enterprise of the Plymouth people to suppose that Duxbury built its house of worship in 1637, and Marshfield in 1641, while the erection of the meeting house of the parent church of which Wm. Brewster was the Elder, was delayed ten years longer.

But we are not left alone to probabilities. In the will of William Palmer, executed in November, 1637, and probated in the following March, is a clause providing for the payment "of somewhat to the meeting house in Plymouth."

Thus then in my opinion Burial Hill became the church yard in 1637. It retained its name of Fort Hill many years, and under that name extended across what is now Russell street along the rear of the estates on the west side of Court street.

At a town meeting held on the 14th of May, 1711, it was voted to sell "all the common lands about the fort hills reserving sufficient room for a burying place." From that time Burial Hill has remained practically within its present limits. But it is asked why is the headstone of Edward Gray bearing the date of 1681 the oldest stone on the hill. The answer is to be found first in the undoubted fact that for many years it was not the custom to mark the graves with stones, and second, in the depredations to which stones were subjected by neglect and rough usage. In the early days of the Colony slate stone was not found within accessible distances, and when they were finally imported from England, their cost undoubtedly precluded their general use. Many of those imported were creased and opened to the weather, and finally were disintegrated by frost and broken up. I, myself, by the permission of the selectmen, and of course at the cost of the town, devised a kind of hood made of galvanized iron with which I have protected seventy or more from both the influence of frost and the no less destructive invasions of relic hunting vandals. So far as neglect of the hill is concerned, I can find no suggestion in the records of any proposition to protect the hill until 1757, when it was voted to fence it. Nothing was done, however, until 1782, when it was voted to permit Rev. Chandler Robbins to fence and pasture it with the right at any time to remove the fence and possess it as his own. Then for the first time the hill was fenced, and Mrs. Robbins, after the death of her husband petitioned the town to buy the fence. In 1800 it was voted to permit Rev. Dr. Kendall to pasture the hill and build a fence on condition that no horses be permitted within the inclosure. Before that time it is evident that horses were permitted to pasture it, and the treatment to which the stones were thus exposed, is easily imagined. In later times, decayed and fallen stones have been piled up behind the hearse house, where masons in want of covering stones have taken them at their pleasure. Of late years, however, the hill has had better treatment, and the stones which have fallen have been reset at the expense of the town. It is unnecessary to say that the most vigilant care on the part of the town should be used, for aside from all sentimental reasons, and aside from the duty of the town to realize that it holds the hill in trust for all our country, the hill and its stones form a commercial asset of incalculable value. An attempt was made in 1819 to plant ornamental trees on the hill, but either nothing was done, or the attempt to carry out the vote of the town proved a failure. In 1843 another more successful attempt was made, and a large number of trees were planted, and the duty of keeping them well watered was assigned to the scholars in the High school. Many of these survived, and others have at various times been added.

Among the conclusions to which I have been led by the foregoing review, is this, that Elder Brewster, Governor Bradford and John Howland, and the other Mayflower passengers who died in Plymouth after 1637, were buried on Burial Hill. With regard to the burial of the Elder, I am obliged to reverse the opinion heretofore expressed by me, that he was buried in Duxbury. There are on record two inventories of the property of Brewster, one of his house and its contents in Duxbury, and the other of his house and its contents in Plymouth. The contents of the former are so meagre and unimportant as to make it certain that the Duxbury house was only an occasional residence, while those of the latter, consisting of clothing and a full household equipment, prove that he died in Plymouth, and that there was his permanent home. Besides Brewster was the Elder of Plymouth church, and of course lived among his people, and further, Bradford says in his history, that Mrs. Brewster died before 1627, before the Duxbury settlement began, and of course was buried in Plymouth, near whose grave the Elder would have sought for himself a final resting place.

The inscriptions on the gravestones, though not quaint, are interesting to others besides the antiquary, and a few of them I shall include in this chapter without either alphabetical or chronological order as follows:

"Priscilla Cotton, widow of Josiah Cotton, born September 30, 1860, died October 4, 1859."

Mrs. Cotton lived and died in a house which was removed when Brewster street was opened, and now stands on the North side of that street. She told me that at the time of the Boston tea party in 1773 she attended a boarding school a little below the Old South Meeting house, and remembered some of the incidents attending the destruction of the tea. A man servant brought home some of the tea, but some of the scholars refused to drink it. After her husband's death in 1819, she bought an annuity at the office of the Massachusetts Hospital Life Insurance Company, which after forty years of payment was terminated, much to the satisfaction of the company.

"In memory of Samuel Davis, A. M., who died July 10, 1829."

> "From life on earth our pensive friend retires;
> His dust commingling with the Pilgrim sires;
>   In thoughtful walk, their every path he traced;
>   Their toils, their tombs, his faithful page embraced;
> Peaceful and pure, and innocent as they,
> With them to rise to everlasting day."

The above inscription and the following one were written by Judge John Davis.

"In memory of George Watson, Esq.,who died the 3d of December, 1800."

> "No folly wasted his paternal store,
> No guilt, no sordid avarice made it more;
>   With honest fame, and sober plenty crowned,
>   He lived and spread his cheering influence round.
>   Pure was his walk, and peaceful was his end,
> We blessed his reverent length of days,
> And hailed him in the public ways
> With veneration and with praise,
>   Our father and our friend."

"F. W. Jackson, obiit., March 23, 1799, aged one year, 7 days."

> "Heaven knows what man he might have been,
> But we know he died a most rare boy."

"In memory of Mrs. Tabitha Plasket, who died June 10, 1807, aged 64 years."

> "Adieu vain world, I have seen enough of thee,
> And I am careless what thou say'st of me;
> Thy smiles I wish not, nor thy frowns I fear,
> I am now at rest, my head lies quiet here."

"Died, Captain Simeon Sampson, June 22, 1789, aged 53 years."

Capt. Sampson was an early hero of the revolution, who commanded the Brig Independence, built in Kingston, and the first vessel commissioned by the provincial Congress.

An obelisk over the supposed grave of Governor William Bradford contains among other inscriptions a Hebrew sentence which translated is "Jehovah is the portion of mine inheritance."

"Here lyeth buried the body of that precious servant of God, Mr. Thomas Cushman, who after he had served his generation according to the will of God, particularly the Church of Plymouth for many years in the office of ruling elder, fell asleep in Jesus, December, ye 10, 1691, & in ye 84 year of his age."

Elder Cushman was brought to Plymouth in the Fortune, fourteen years of age, by his father, Robert Cushman, and was the second elder of the church.

"Here lyes ye body of Mr. Thomas Clark, aged 98 years, departed this life March ye 24, 1697."

The mate of the Mayflower was John Clark, and not the above Thomas. A part of the colony grant of land in Chiltonville to Thomas Clark was called by him Saltash. An outlying suburb of old Plymouth is called Saltash, and the name of Clark is common there.

"Here lyeth ye body of Edward Gray, aged about 52 years, & departed this life ye last of June, 1681."

The stone bearing the above inscription is the oldest stone on Burial Hill. Mr. Gray became a prominent business man and owned lands in Rocky Nook, some of which is still owned by his descendants.

"Here lyes the body of Mr. Thomas Faunce, ruling Elder of the First Church of Christ in Plymouth, deceased February 27. An: Dom, 1745-6, in the 99th year of his age."

   "The fathers where are they:
   Blessed are the dead who die in the Lord."

"Ruth D., wife of Edward Southworth, died May 8, 1879, aged 101 yrs., 10 mos., 13 days."

Mrs. Southworth's maiden name was Ozier, and she came from Duxbury. She lived all through my boyhood on the slope of Cole's Hill. I called on her on her hundredth birthday, and she told me that she had not worn spectacles for twenty years. Her son, Jacob William, is now living in Plymouth.

"Here lyes the body of Mr. Francis Le Barran, phytician, who departed this life August ye 18th, 1704, in ye 36 year of his age."

The above Francis LeBarran is the hero in the "Nameless Nobleman."

"In memory of James Thacher, M. D., a surgeon in the army during the war of the Revolution; afterwards for many years a practising physician in the county of Plymouth; the author of several historical and scientific works; esteemed of all men for piety and benevolence, public spirit and private kindness. Born February 14, 1754.   Died May 26, 1844."

"Gen. James Warren died November 28, 1808, aged 82."

General Warren succeeded Dr. Joseph Warren as President of Provincial Congress, and married Mercy, sister of the so-called patriot, James Otis.

There are also on the hill stones at the heads of the graves of James H. Bugbee, pastor of the Universalist Society who died May 10, 1834, aged 31 years; of James Kendall, who died March 17, 1859, aged 89 years, after sixty years' service as pastor of the First Church; of Ephriam Little, pastor of the First Church, who died Nov. 24, 1723, aged 47 years, two months and three days; and of Chandler Robbins, pastor of the First Church, who died June 30, 1799, at the age of sixty-one.

It may not be out of place to present to my readers by way of contrast with the foregoing somewhat sombre inscriptions a few of a quaint character to be found in grave yards in other towns. Omitting names of persons and places and dates, I give merely the inscriptions as follows:

Accidentally shot, as a mark of affection by his brother.

> Beneath this stone our baby lays,
> He neither cries nor hollers.
> He lived just one and twenty days,
> And cost us forty dollars.

She lived with her husband fifty years, and died in the confident hope of a better life.

> Under this stone lie three children dear;
> Two are buried in Taunton, and one lies here.

Here lies the body of Dr. Ransom, a man who never voted.   Of such is the kingdom of heaven.

> Underneath this pile of stones
> Lies all that's left of Sally Jones.
> Her name was Lord; it was not Jones,
> But Jones is used to rhyme with stones.

He did his damnedest.   Angels can do no more.

Wife, I'm waiting for you.
Husband, I'm here.

Stranger pause and shed a tear,
For Mary Jane lies buried here.
Mingled in a most surprising manner
With Susan, Maria, and portions of Hannah.

My father and mother were both insane.
I inherited the terrible stain.
My grandfather, grandmother, aunts and uncles,
Were lunatics all, and yet died of carbuncles.

Within this grave do lie,
Back to back my wife and I.
When the last trump the air shall fill—
If she gets up, I'll just lie still.

CHAPTER XXXIII.

During my youth, public entertainments were rare in Plymouth, especially in the winter. During that season, with unlighted streets and the houses lighted for the most part with oil lamps, the town, more particularly in a storm of rain or snow was gloomy, indeed. Families gathered around their wood fires and here and there groups of men would sit on the counters and boxes in the stores until the nine o'clock bell called them home. When any of the housewives ventured to have a party, candles with their candlesticks and snuffers were brought out and scattered about the parlors on mantels and tables. Occasionally instead of a formal evening party a lap tea was the entertainment, the guests arriving at half past six or seven. Those lap teas were glorious times for us boys, for there was something exciting in the preparation. An extra supply of cream was to be bought, the sugar loaf was to be divested of its blue cartridge paper covering, and chopped into squares, and sandwiches and whips and custards were to be made, of which we were sure to get preliminary tastes. And better than all we were permitted to carry around waiters loaded with cups of tea and plates and cream and sugar, and the various articles of food.

Music at these entertainments was uncommon. There were as long ago as about 1828 or 1830 only four pianos in town, and these were owned by Mrs. Pelham W. Warren, Mrs. Nathan Russell, Jr., Miss Eliza Ann Bartlett and my sister Rebecca. My sister's was given as part pay for a Chickering piano; Miss Bartlett's was sold to Joseph Holmes of Kingston and is now owned by his granddaughter, Mrs. H. M. Jones of that town; Mrs. Russell's is still owned by her daughter, Mrs. Wm. Hedge, and Mrs. Warren's went I know not where. The Russell piano is, as I remember the others were, of mahogany, ornamented with brass and with a scale of five and a half octaves. It was made by Alfred Babcock of Philadelphia, probably before 1825, for R. Mackey of Boston, who was not a manufacturer, but probably an agent for the maker. I say that it was probably made before 1825, because it is stated in histories of piano making that Mr. Babcock invented in that year the iron string board, which this one does not have.

At a party in a house where either of the above pianos was owned, one of the guests, probably a visitor from Boston, favored the guests, by request, with a song. I recall one occasion when a lady was invited to sing who was unable to pronounce the letter "s." She unhesitatingly consented, and taking her seat at the piano sang the song beginning with the words, "Oh ting tweet bird, oh ting." Though more than sixty years have elapsed I am often reminded when I hear a lady sing at the piano of the polite invitation of that lady to the tweet bird to ting.

Aside from the parties the entertainments were chiefly lectures by Rev. Chas. W. Upham on "Witchcraft;" by Rev. Chas. T Brooks on, "Education in Germany," by Mr. Emerson on "Socrates;" or lectures by other prominent men; exhibitions of ledgerdemain by Potter or Harrington, or of a mummy which walked "in Thebes' streets three thousand years ago"; or if nothing better offered an evening book auction. Occasionally a debating society would be formed of which Timothy Berry was always the organizer and patron, a man always ready to encourage the oratorical efforts of young men. I was permitted as a boy to attend the meetings of the society, and I remember the debaters well. As young as I was I could not help being amused at the seriousness with which the grandest subjects were attacked as if then and there their settlement depended on the merits of the debate. There was one gentleman who every evening, when the nine o'clock bell rang, rose impressively and said, "Mister President, many subjects not been teched on to-night, move we journ." The club accordingly adjourned, and the impressive gentleman left the hall, evidently feeling that he had been an active participant in the debate.

There was another society in my boyhood called the Plymouth Madan Society, but from whom it derived its name I never knew. It was a musical society, and occasionally gave concerts. The nearest approximation to the name I ever knew until recently, was the Scripture name of Medan, the son of Abraham. But that was evidently a misfit. I next found among the proper names in the Century dictionary, that of

Martin Madan, an English Methodist divine who published in
1780 a book called Telyphthora, advocating polygamy. But
as the Plymouth Madan Society gave concerts in the Universalist church, it is not probable that it was named in honor of
a polygamist. Having since met with the name of Madan in
the newspapers of a family in Marshfield, I wrote to Lot J.
Madan, living at Green Harbor, asking him if any of his family in past generations, either his father or grandfather, had
been musical. Mistaking my word musical for married, he
replied that if his father and grandfather had not been married he would not have been around in these days. In a subsequent letter he said he played on the violin, and was as far
as he knew the only musician in the family. For whom then
the society was named is a question still unsolved.

Among other societies within my day was one to aid in arresting horse thieves, and that was one of many formed in
various towns. The only surviving one within my knowledge
is in Dedham, which annually meets and elects its officers. I
have already alluded in another chapter to a temperance society which was formed in 1832, by whose efforts more was
done to promote temperance than by all other agencies combined from that time to this. The sale of intoxicating liquors was almost completely stopped, the family use of wines
was abandoned, and under the influence of Daniel Frost, whose
addresses were largely attended, more than a thousand names
were secured to pledges to abstain from the use of ardent
spirits.

An Anti-slavery society I have also referred to which was
formed in the Robinson church on the evening of the Fourth
of July, 1835, and occupied for some years rooms in the second story of the northerly end of the building which up to
1883 stood on the site of the Sherman block on the west side
of Main street. The seed of anti-slavery fell in Plymouth on
sandy soil, but watered by heavenly dew, it soon took root and
broke through the conservative crust which under the influence
of the commercial and financial interests of the town, for a
time obstructed its growth.

There was a peace society formed in 1831, but as we were
then at peace with the world, there does not appear to have
been at that time any special call for the organization. It

seems to have been a fashion of the times to form peace societies, but their influence was not sufficiently enduring to check the movements which resulted in the Mexican war not many years later. But it seems to be the way of our people to advocate peace in a time of peace, and when war threatens, to advocate war. The President of a Massachusetts Sunday-school Association preached in peaceful years as a minister of the gospel peace on earth and good will among men, but in 1898 I saw him marching with the first battery in all the panoply of war to join the murderers of his fellow men. Another prominent minister of the gospel who, when no war clouds darkened the horizon, permitted himself without protest to be called the apostle of peace, was as dumb as an oyster when the opportunity came to utter trumpet-tongued his protests against the war.

Bu it was not always so with the people of Plymouth. Ever after the close of the revolution they were advocates of peace, and when the war with Great Britain broke out in 1812 they uttered in no uncertain language their determined protest. A memorial to the President denouncing the war was passed unanimously in town meeting, the closing words of which were as follows: "Thus sir, with much brevity, but with a frankness which the magnitude of the occasion demands, they have expressed their honest sentiments upon the existing offensive war against Great Britain, a war by which their dearest interests as men and Christians are deeply affected, and in which they deliberately declare, as they cannot conscientiously, so they will not have any voluntary participation. They make this declaration with that paramount regard to their civil and religious obligations which becomes the disciples of the prince of peace whose kingdom is not of this world, and before whose impartial tribunal presidents and kings will be upon a level with the meanest of their fellowmen, and will be responsible for all the blood they shed in wanton and unnecessary war."

My only comment on the above memorial is that milder language was flippantly denounced as treasonable by some of the advocates of the recent war with Spain.

The various societies which I have thus far mentioned were temporary in their character, and had short careers. There

were, however, two others formed in the first quarter of the
last century, one charitable and the other historical, which have
continued to this day, and having been incorporated, will continue for an indefinite period. One of these, the Pilgrim Society, will be noticed in a later chapter in connection with the
celebrations of the anniversary of the landing of the Pilgrims.
The other, the Plymouth Fragment Society, having its origin
and inspiration in the heart of a benevolent lady a native of a
foreign land, with whom the ladies of Plymouth enthusiasti-
cally co-operated, has year after year for nearly ninety years, by
the kindly hands of each succeeding generation, dispensed
among the suffering poor a charity which, dropping like the
gentle rain from heaven, is twice blessed, for it blesseth him that
gives, and him that takes. It was founded by Madame Marie
de Verdier Turner on the 13th of February, 1818, for the
declared purpose of "relieving the wants of the destitute poor."
To meet legal requirements imposed by bequests to the So-
iety, it was incorporated March 14, 1877, with a capital not
estimated nor divided into shares.

The officers of the Society since its organization have been as
follows: Presidents, Mary Warren, Martha Russell, Joanna
Davis, Betsey F. Russell, Margaret Warren, Sarah M. Holmes,
Laura Russell, Martha Ann Morton, Caroline B. Warren,
Esther Bartlett.   Vice-presidents: Esther Parsons Hammatt,
Betsey Torrey, Elizabeth Freeman, Lucretia B. Watson, Re-
becca D. Parker, Mrs. Thomas, Sally Stephens, Mercy B.
Lovell, Ellen M. Hubbard, Helen Russell.   Secretaries: Betsey
H. Hodge, Rebecca Bartlett, Elizabeth L. Loud, Abby M. Hall,
Helen Russell, Jennie S. Hubbard.   Treasurers: Francis L.
Jackson, Phebe Cotton, Mary Ann Stevenson, Eunice D. Rob-
bins, Caroline E. Gilbert, Lydia G. Locke, Elizabeth W.
Whitman.   The amount expended in charity during the year
ending October 1, 1905, has been $883.93 for food, fuel and
clothing, and $360 in payments of $2 a month to eleven regu-
lar, and four special pensioners.

So little is known by the present generation of Madame
Turner, the founder of the Society, and of her romantic life
that I present to my readers a short sketch of her career for the
facts in which I am chiefly indebted to a paper read by Lois B.
Brewster as a graduating exercise in 1899, at the Plymouth

High school, the language of which I have in a measure adopted:

Mrs. Turner was a native of Sweden, born in Malmo in 1789. Her father was a retired officer in the Hussars, an accomplished gentleman, and her mother was connected with noble families from whom she inherited the prejudices of the aristocracy. She received an education which beside the ordinary branches taught in the schools, included music, embroidery and painting. Her father died when she was fifteen years of age, leaving her mother with only a little more than a government pension for her support. After removing with her family to Copenhagen, Madame de Verdier soon after died, never having recovered from the shock caused by the death of her husband. Marie became an inmate of the home of a rich merchant, who provided her with every luxury, and in whose house she often met guests of the merchant from foreign lands. Among these guests at dinner one day were Captain Robinson, an Englishman, and Captain Lothrop Turner of Plymouth, ship masters, whose ships were consigned to their host. It is needless to say that the handsome Captain Turner and the pretty Swedish maid fell deeply in love with each other before his ship was ready to leave, but as she could speak no English, and Swedish was to him an unknown tongue, their language of love was carried on by the tell tale eye and blushing cheek, except when Robinson lent his services as an interpreter. Marie, against the advice of her friends, yielded to the influence of her own head, and accepting his hand in marriage, the husband and wife after a marriage solemnized in April, 1812, sailed for her new home in New England. It was during the war of 1812, and in entering Massachusetts Bay, Capt. Turner barely escaped capture by an English frigate patrolling the coast, but finally reached Plymouth. The story of the romantic marriage had reached Plymouth before them, and on the day of their arrival the young friends of the captain were gathered to give a cordial welcome to his Swedish bride. Long before the arrival of the stage bearing them was due, numbers of women and children anxious to see the bride gathered on Cole's Hill, and from that vantage ground saw the blue-eyed, golden haired little woman as she dismounted and entered the house of Capt. Turner's father, which stood near the foot, and on the South side of Leyden street. It was a trying season for her among new friends whom she had never seen, imperfect in the use of the English tongue, and amid scenes to which she must become accustomed, as those of home. Not long after her arrival a daughter Maria was born, who died in infancy.

It now became her task to learn the language which she must make her own, but she was an apt scholar, and bravely and speedily fought her way through its intricate words and phrases. As she became acquainted with Plymouth people she was surprised that the pupils in school were not taught to paint and embroider, and as two sisters of her husband were teaching a private school she engaged in the instruction of their pupils in those accomplishments. She also formed classes of girls, and taught them music, besides painting and needlework. In her visits among the sick she came to realize the needy condition of many families suffering from the effects of the embargo, which were added to the sad conditions of the revolution from which they had not yet recovered. Throughout the early years of her life in Plymouth, she worked with zeal in enlisting the aid and sympathy of those in comfortable circumstances in charitable work, and while engaged personally in visits among the poor she conceived the idea of associated work in aid of the sick and destitute.

Her husband died in Havana, April 28, 1824, and she was left with little means of support, except that derived from her own labors. Friends in Boston offered her aid which she refused, believing it inconsistent with the character of a true American to accept assistance while able to support herself.

She opened a school in the house of a friend on Fort Hill in Boston, but after a short time felt a longing to return to her native land, and sailed for Sweden in a vessel owned by Capt. John Russell. She found, however, her country not as she had left it, rich and moral, but a decaying monarchy, its people intemperate, and without the political freedom enjoyed in America. She lived for a time in Stockholm as a friend of Countess Ferson, and there received an advantageous offer of marriage, which she declined, saying, "I have been the wife of a free citizen, I will not lower myself by marrying a subject." One day while riding with the Countess, she saw a ship flying an American flag, and exclaiming—"See the stars—see the stars," told the Countess that she must return in that ship to her adopted country. And this she did, declaring that she preferred a home of poverty in a free country to an abode of luxury under a monarchy.

Arriving in Boston in delicate health, with symptoms of pulmonary disease, after a season of suffering, she removed to New York, hearing of a place there where she could teach. Her disease, however, increasing, she went south, where she spent two years with friends, engaged in finishing a translation of "Waldermar, the Victorious," from the Danish of Ingerman, which she had begun while on her last voyage.

She had previously published with great success a work on "Drawing and Shadowing Flowers," with lithographic plates, executed by herself, and "The Young Ladies' Assistant in Drawing and Painting," and several stories for magazines. She returned to Boston in 1837, with the hope of continuing literary work, but her disease increasing, she was obliged to abandon the publication of her book, and told her friends that if it should be published after her death, she hoped that a sketch of her life might be prefixed, for she "believed that it would make the women of America more sensible of the inestimable value of their free institutions; more thankful for their religious privileges, and more American, when they read her story. I would do something for the country where I have found a Saviour for my soul, where I have had a home, and where I shall have a grave." She died at the Massachusetts General Hospital, March 15, 1838, and her body was removed to Plymouth and buried in Oak Grove cemetery. Her life and work should be remembered by something more enduring than an occasional allusion, and I suggest that a stone be erected over her grave with something like the following inscription:

> This stone is erected by the Plymouth Fragment Society in memory of its founder, Marie de Verdier Turner, a native of Sweden, who was born in Malmo, in 1789, and died in Boston, March 15, 1838.
> And Christ said: "Inasmuch as ye have done it unto one of the least of these, ye have done it unto me."

CHAPTER XXXIV.

I have said in an early chapter that after having attended Ma'am Weston's school on North street, Mrs. Maynard's in the second story room in the building on the corner of Main street and Town Square, and Mr. George P. Bradford's school in a second story room on the opposite corner of Main street, I entered the high school in 1832.   The high school house was situated on the north side of the Unitarian church between School street and the town tombs, and was a one story building about forty-five feet long and twenty or twenty-five feet wide, with a door on the southerly end.

. The situation of the house recalls these lines of Whittier:

"The town ne'er heeds the sceptic's hands,
While near her school the church tower stands;
Nor fears the bigot's blinding rule,
While near the church tower stands the school."

Standing on sloping ground the foundation of the house on the street side was high enough to admit of a cellar above the street level.   In the northerly end of the school room there was a platform, two steps above the main floor, with the teacher's area in the centre flanked on each side by three unpainted pine desks with lids, and with long seats to correspond, facing the area.   An alley led from the door to the platform with a row of desks and seats on each side, the row on the east side being broken by a space for a box stove for burning wood, the only fuel at that time used.

The house was built in 1770, and until 1826 was called the central or grammar school, but in that year it received the name of high school.   It had a belfry on its southerly end, and a bell with the rope coming down into a cross entry between the outer door and the schoolroom.   When the house was taken for an engine house the bell was placed on the Russell street school house, and when during some repairs, it was removed from that building and abandoned, I captured it for Pilgrim Hall, where it now is.   The first bells, as large as this one, made in the United States, were cast in Abington by Aaron Hobart in 1769, under the direction of a deserter from the British Army, named

Gallimore, a bell founder by trade. There can be little doubt that the bell in question was made by Mr. Hobart in 1769. It is not altogether gratifying that, with other customs of the past, the ringing of bells should be falling into disuetude. The Court bell no longer calls the liar to come to Court, the school bell is silent, the funeral bell is not heard, even the fire bell is giving way to the electric alarm, and I fear that the church bell will be the next to fall asleep under the soporific influence of fashion. But I trust that the day is far distant when the sweet voice of the Sunday bell shall become mute. Years ago when Julian, the great French composer of instrumental music was in the habit of bringing out his new pieces for the year, he played them for the first time at the series of mask balls, beginning each year at Christmas. I had been in Paris six months without hearing the church bell ringing its summons to service, and I have never forgotten the emotions stirred within me when I heard at the first ball in the series, sixty years ago, the piece entitled *"la dimanche au sonneur,"* the Sunday bells. The first time I saw the "Angelus" by Millet, the same emotions were revived, and the music of *"la dimanche au sonneur"* is still ringing in my ears.

While talking of bells, I wonder how many of my readers know how far church bells can be heard. I read a few years ago an article in the *Living Age* on the rut of the sea, or as it is better known, the roar of the ocean, which many persons think is caused by the surf on the shore after a storm. I discovered many years ago that this was not so, as I had often heard it when there was no storm, and when there was scarcely a ripple on the beach. The article referred to stated that the rut was the sound of a distant storm, perhaps hundreds of miles away, and illustrated the distance at which sounds can be heard at sea by the following incident. A ship bound into New York one Sunday forenoon was sailing close hauled on the wind on the starboard tack about eighty miles dead to leeward from Sandy Hook. The mate reported to the Captain that he could hear the New York church bells. The captain doubting it, went on deck and heard them distinctly. Putting his ship into the wind, and thus shivering her light sails, he lost the sound, but putting her off again the bells continued to be heard. The sound of the bells reached the upper sails, and

s prepared to credit the
,y grand bank fishermen that
CH⅃ ⅃ heard the paddles of an ocean

I have said in ar ..gression, let me say that in 1832 I
Ma'am Weston's ' ..e office of Dr. Winslow Warren, on the
second story re ⅃ North streets, chairman of the school com-
and Town S .amined for admission into the high school. The
second st ,ts were at that time, an age of ten years, an ability
tered t' ,well and spell, to write a fair round hand, a knowledge
situ ,burn's first lessons, and Robinson's arithmetic as far as
S, fractions, and ability to parse a simple sentence. I had
that time not only gone beyond the requirements in my studies, but had made a considerable advance in Latin. When I
entered the school it was kept by Samuel Ripley Townsend.
When he flogged a boy he did it neither in sorrow nor in anger,
but rather for the quiet fun it gave him. He wore spectacles,
and had a way of walking leisurely up the alley as if his
thoughts were far away from the school, and if any boy after
he had passed made a face behind his back, or threw a spit ball
at another boy, he would see the reflection in his spectacles, and
then going quietly to his desk, and taking out his cowhide,
would walk back apparently in an absent mood, and when he
walked by the boy he would bring the hide down smartly on his
back, and keep on his walk with an ill concealed smile on his
face as if he had played a joke on the offender.

Mr. Townsend, son of Samuel and Abigail Townsend, was
born in Waltham, April 10, 1810, and graduated at Harvard in
1829. After leaving Plymouth he engaged in business in Boston for a time, and afterwards taught the Bristol Academy
from 1846 to 1849, during which period he studied law with
Horatio Pratt, and was admitted to the Bristol bar in 1850. In
1853 he was chosen treasurer of Bristol County, serving three
years, and in 1858 was appointed Judge of the Police Court of
Taunton. After the dissolution of the court he practiced law
in Taunton, serving three terms as a member of the city council, and in 1882 was appointed City Solicitor. He married
June 29, 1837, Mary Snow Percival, and died September 27,
1887.

In 1833 Mr. Townsend was succeeded by Isaac Nelson Stod-

`n Upton, October 30, 1812, who graduated at Am-
He taught the school about two years, and then
Bedford, where he taught until 1837, when he
outh, and again had charge of the school until
er year he was appointed collector of the
, in office until 1845, when he was made cashier
,nouth Bank, continuing in office in that and its
.sor, the Plymouth National Bank, until 1879, when he
.,as made president.   He married in 1836, Martha Le Baron,
daughter of John B. Thomas, and died July 23, 1891.   He
fitted John Goddard Jackson and myself for college during the
first half of 1838, when we carried on our studies at home,
and went to Mr. Stoddard's house late each afternoon to recite.
While in New Bedford Mr. Stoddard became an intimate
friend of Judge Oliver Prescott, Judge of Probate of Bristol
county, and hence the name of our genial friend, Col. Stoddard.   The ordinary punishment to which the boys were subjected by Mr. Stoddard, was a squeeze of the ear between his
thumb and forefinger, but the punishment for high offences was
a flogging on the soft parts, while the victim lay across a chair.
Some of my readers will doubtless remember Bill Randall, and
the jolly way in which he did everything.   One day knowing
that Mr. Stoddard intended to flog him, he went to school prepared for the occasion.   When he was called out and told to
lie down he exhibited a protuberance never equalled by any
bustle of the dressmaker's art, and as he took the blows which
might as well have been inflicted on a bale of wool, he would
wink to the other scholars as much as to say, "go ahead old fellow if you enjoy it, go ahead."   Bill went to California, and
on a visit to Plymouth a few years ago he was the same old
Bill, and if he be living and sees these memories, he will have a
laugh over the flogging incident.

During Mr. Stoddard's absence in New Bedford the first
teacher was Leonard Bliss of Rehoboth, a scholarly man, who
published a history of Rehoboth, a valuable contribution to historical literature.   After leaving Plymouth he went to Louisville, Ky., and edited the *Louisville Journal.*   For some offensive remarks in the columns of his paper, he was shot dead
in his office.   He was a son of Leonard and Lydia (Talbot)
Bliss, and was born in Swanzey, December 12, 1811.

Wm. H. Lord succeeded Mr. Bliss, a native of Portsmouth, born September 10, 1812, and a graduate at Dartmouth in 1832. He graduated at Andover Academy in 1837, and was settled for a time over the Unitarian Societies of Southboro, Mass., and Madison, Wisconsin. At one time he edited a newspaper in Port Washington, and was Consul at St. Thomas from 1850 to 1853. He married Persis, daughter of Rev. Dr. James Kendall, and died in Washington in 1866. He was a popular teacher, and introduced a new feature into school government, which proved successful. At the opening day of his term he told his scholars that they might have the afternoon of that day to themselves in the school room for the purpose of enacting a code of rules for the management of the school, and reporting the same to him the next day, but he wished them to distinctly understand that when enacted, the rules were to be obeyed. It requires no deep knowledge of human nature to know that such a confidence in the good faith of the school would be conscientiously respected. I do not remember a single case of flogging under his administration.

Before the return of Mr. Stoddard to Plymouth in 1837 the school was kept a short time by Robert Bartlett of Plymouth of the Harvard class of 1836, and by LeBaron Russell of the Harvard class of 1832, but nothing occurred during their terms, especially worthy of notice, except the pranks usual in every school. One of these pranks was tried on each teacher in turn. In the cool days of autumn or spring, the fire in the box stove was not kept up continuously, so some morning when there was no fire, a bundle of seaweed was rammed down the chimney, and soon after the school opened the boys began one after another to shiver and ask for a fire. Of course, when the fire was kindled, the room would fill with smoke, and the usual result, the dismissal of the school, followed. There were no janitors in those days, and each Saturday two boys would be detailed to discharge during the next week a janitor's duties, including sweeping out, sawing wood, making fires and ringing the bell. I do not think such work ever did me any harm, indeed, I am sure that it taught me as much that was useful as is taught today in some branches of instruction included in the regular curriculum, for which special salaried teachers are employed.

A school called the town school, was kept in my day by Thomas Drew in a house built in 1827, which has been recently taken down. It stood also on School street, near the way up Burial Hill, a little distance south of the high school house. The boys attending that school were older and larger than the high school boys, and when there was snow on the ground there was scarcely a day without a pitched battle between the two schools. During my time our leader was Abraham Jackson, always cool and fearless, and generally leading his followers to victory, and driving the enemy into their school. He entered Harvard a year before I did, and on the Delta he was the same hero in the strife that he was on Burial Hill at home. More than once I have seen him there with ball in hand rushing through the crowd with an impetus which no obstacle could check, and heard the cry, "go it Jackson, go it Jackson," and then a cheer when he sent the ball home. I can conceive of no danger from which Jackson would have retreated, and of no act of daring which he would not if necessary have performed. He once saved a boy from drowning, who had ventured on thin ice in the middle of Murdock's pond and fallen through. While other boys were paralyzed with fear he kept his presence of mind, and did just the right thing. There was a pile of rails on the shore, and seizing two he dragged them side by side near the broken ice, and then lying down on them worked his way with his weight distributed over as much surface as possible, to the boy, and taking him by the collar, pulled him to the rails and to safety. He was always a hero, and in war would have been a Cushing in Roanoke river or a Hobson at Santiago.

A fuller history of Plymouth schools than I propose to give in these memories, may be found in my Ancient Landmarks of Plymouth, and I must content myself with saying that after the school became the high school in 1826, the teachers, omitting those already mentioned, were Addison Brown, Harvard, 1826, George W. Hosmer, Harvard, 1826, who married Hannah Poor, daughter of Rev. James Kendall, Horace Hall Rolfe, born in Groton, N. H., July 20, 1800, graduated at Dartmouth, 1824, married, 1828, Mary T., daughter of Stephen Marcy, and died in Charleston, S. C., February 24, 1831, Josiah Moore, Harvard, 1826, who married in 1831,

Rebecca W., daughter of Wm. Sturtevant, Charles Clapp, Mr. Jenks, Philip Coombs Knapp, Dartmouth, 1841, John Brooks Beal, Thomas Andrew Watson, Harvard, 1845, Samuel Sewall Greeley, Harvard, 1844, Wm. H. Spear, J. W. Hunt, Frank Crosby, Edward P. Bates, Admiral P. Stone, George Lewis Baxter, Theodore P. Adams, Harvard, 1867, Joseph Leavitt Sanborn, Harvard, 1867, Henry Dame, George Washington Minns, Harvard, 1836, Gilman C. Fisher, and Charles Burton, who was succeeded by teachers with whose names my readers are familiar.

There are two of the above of whom I am able to furnish meagre sketches. Charles Burton, son of Thomas and Elizabeth (Deane) Burton, was born in Wolverhampton, England, December 16, 1816, and about 1818 came to America with his widowed mother and one brother and four sisters, and settled in Pittsburgh, where in early life he learned the trade of pattern maker. In Pittsburgh he became acquainted with Lemuel Stephens, who was instructor there in Daniel Stone's private school, and about 1839 sailed with him for Germany in a vessel belonging to I. and E. Morton. After a year's study in Gottingen and Heidelberg, he returned home, and soon after came to Plymouth with messages from Mr. Stephens, whose sister Sarah he afterwards married. He taught first a private school on Watson's Hill in a building erected for the purpose, and for many years afterwards was associated with the public schools of Plymouth, either as principal of the high school or as superintendent of schools. He died November 25, 1894.

George Lewis Baxter, son of William W. and Ann E. (Weld) Baxter, was born in Quincy, Oct. 21, 1842, and graduated at Harvard in 1863. In 1864 he was principal of the Reading High School, and afterwards for three years principal of the high school in Plymouth. In 1867 he was appointed headmaster of the Somerville high school, in which capacity he is still serving with about four hundred and thirty scholars under his charge. In 1872 he married Ida F. Paul, and has a son, Gregory Paul Baxter, who graduated at Harvard in 1896.

I entered college at sixteen, the usual age at that time, while now it is eighteen. There are persons who believe that every-

thing is lovely in our day, and that our fathers were unedu-
cated, ignorant men. They claim that our public schools are
more efficient in instruction, and their pupils further advanced
than formerly. This I doubt. I began to study Latin at nine,
and I have no reasons to think that I was an exception. They
explain the advanced age of freshmen, by claiming that the
requirements for admission to college are greater, and this
claim I also doubt. They further claim that a higher scholar-
ship is reached by the graduate of the present time. But to
substantiate this claim, they should show first that the old instructors were inferior to the present, and second that the various activities of life are now represented by abler men than
ever before. But are Professor Felton in Greek, Professor Beck in Latin, Professor Channing in Rhetoric and
Elocution, Professor Pierce in Mathematics, and Professor Longfellow in French, outclassed by recent professors?
Then if we turn to the various professions we find among the
graduates of the earlier half of the last century in the ministry, Wm. Ellery Channing, James Walker, Frederick Hedge,
George Putnam, Wm. P. Lunt, Henry W. Bellows, and Edward Everett Hale; in law, Samuel Dexter, Lemuel Shaw,
Sidney Bartlett, Benjamin Robbins Curtis and William Whit-
ing; in literature, Wm. H. Prescott, George Bancroft, Jared
Sparks, Francis Parkman, J. Lothrop Motley, James Russell
Lowell, Oliver Wendell Holmes; in medicine, John Collins
Warren, Henry Bigelow and George H. Gay, and in states-
manship, John Quincy Adams, Josiah Quincy, Harrison Gray
Otis, Edward Everett, Charles Sumner and George F. Hoar;
in science, Benjamin Pierce, Asa Gray and B. A. Gould. Is
a comparison with recent graduates unfavorable to these men?
I was told not many years ago by a distinguished scholar, a
graduate of Harvard, and one of its professors, that in his
opinion Harvard did not graduate as good scholars as it did
fifty years before. If this be true, I think there is a reason
for it. Many persons mistake bigness for greatness, but I
believe that sixteen hundred undergraduates cannot be mould-
ed as well as four hundred. There is not that personal interest felt in the student by the instructors, which was once
felt. I am inclined to doubt whether in the faculty today
there is more than one member able to recognize and call by

name fifty students. In my day it was different, and to apply the *reductio ad absurdum,* there was Charles Stearns Wheeler, Greek tutor, the Pinkerton of the faculty, who boasted that if day or night he could see the heel of a student going round a corner he could give his name—*ex pede herculem.* Only a few incidents in my college career are worthy of mentioning. I think I am one of very few students whose pardon has ever been asked by a professor. One day while solving a problem in geometry before Professor Pierce, or Benny, as we called him, and performing my work with ease and rapidity, he stopped me suddenly and sent me to my seat, telling me to begin at the next recitation at the beginning of the text book, which we were then half through. At the next recitation he called me to the blackboard and asked me how far I was prepared. I told him, "Up with the class," and then he began to screw me, giving me three problems in different places in the book, which I solved with ease. He then said, "Take your seat, and remain after the class leaves the room." When we were alone he said, "Davis, I thought you were copying at the last recitation, but I am satisfied that you were not, and I beg your pardon." The students sometimes marked difficult points in the problems on their cuffs, and sometimes on a slip of paper, and the professor seeing me doing my work so glibly, thought I had an auxiliary somewhere about my person. He never alluded to the matter again, but he manifested his regret by inviting me very frequently to spend a part of a night with him, or his assistant in the observatory to aid in recording magnetic or astronomical observations.

No professor was more interesting to me than Edward Tirrell Channing, at the head of the department of rhetoric and elocution. I think he made a deeper and broader mark on the undergraduate mind than has been felt since his day. His custom was to take up the themes, which he had examined, and criticise them before the class. On one occasion, taking up mine he said, "Davis, I have only one thing to say to you, when you have written anything which you think particularly fine, strike it out." A member of my class published a book of poems during his college course entitled, "Pebbles from Castalia," which we boys called, "Brickbats from Kennebunk." On one occasion he wrote a theme in verse, and Channing taking it up said, "Mr. Blank, I see that in your theme every line begins with a capital, what is the reason?" "It is poetry, sir." "Ah, poetry, is it, I did not think of that, but hereafter, leave out some of your capitals."

In my day there were five degrees of punishment: expulsion, suspension, public admonition before the faculty, private admonition by the president, and mild censure by the professor, who had a room in college. There was a race course a little more than a mile from the college which the boys often attended to see trotting races under the saddle. One rider was easy and graceful in riding jockey hitch. At one time I was called before Professor Lovering who held the position above referred to, and told by him that I was reported for attending the race on the Wednesday before. I said, "Yes, I was there, and saw you there." "Well, how do you like jockey hitch," he asked, and after we had exchanged our views on that style of riding, he bade me good morning. This mild censure reminds me of a story told of Professor Felton, one of whose brothers, some twenty years younger than himself, was an undergraduate, and was reported for swearing in the college yard. The faculty requested the professor to speak to his brother, so sending a messenger for him to come to his recitation room he told him that he had been reported as above mentioned. "Yes," his brother said, "I plead guilty, but I do not often indulge in profanity." "Damnation, John, what do you mean by using the word profanity. There is no such word; profaneness, John, profaneness, not profanity— you may go."

Josiah Quincy, born in Boston, Feb. 4, 1772, a Harvard graduate of 1790, was president during my term. He had occupied the positions of member of congress, state senator, mayor of Boston, and Judge of the Boston Municipal Court, when he was chosen president in 1829, serving until 1845. He was sixty-six years of age, when I entered college, but appeared much older. He bore the reputation of being absent minded, but though many of the stories illustrating this mental condition, are probably untrue, an instance of it once occurred under my own eye and ear. He and Hon. Tyler Bigelow, the father of Chief Justice Geo. Tyler Bigelow, were intimate friends, and their families were also intimate. Meeting one day in the waiting room of the Old Colony station some years after the death of Mr. Bigelow's wife, Mr. Quincy asked him how Mrs. Bigelow was. Putting his hand to his ear, as he was very deaf, Mr. Bigelow said, "What did you say?" Mr. Quincy raising his voice said, "How is Mrs. Bigelow." Mr. Bigelow said, "Speak louder," and Mr. Quincy called out in his loudest voice, attracting the attention of every one in the room, "How is Mrs. Bigelow." "Dead, dead," said Mr. Bigelow, much to the amusement of the crowd. Mr. Quincy was a noble man. He loved Boston, and was devoted to its interests. The city owned what was called city wharf, opposite the Quincy Market, and when he was about eighty years of age the city government voted to sell it by auction. Mr. Quincy protested publicly against the sale of property which in his judgment would appreciate largely in value in the near future. No attention was paid to his protest, and the sale went on. He bought it, and then offered it to the city at the price he paid, but his offer was refused. I have heard his profits on the purchase put as high as a half a million of dollars. He died in Quincy, July 1, 1864, at the age of ninety-two.

CHAPTER XXXV.

As has been already stated, in the early days of the Plymouth Colony, town meetings were held in either the Governor's house, or the meeting house. The last meeting in the meeting house, so far as the record shows, was held July 6, 1685. In that year Plymouth County was incorporated with Plymouth, the shire, and though I can find no record of the event, it is probable that the County Court house, which stood on the site of the present town house, was built in that year, and that from that time it was the meeting place of the town. There are scattering records of town meetings held there before it was taken down in 1749, in which year the present town house was built by the county as a Court House. In anticipation of the erection of the present house it was voted by the town at a meeting held in the Court House, Oct. 10, 1748, "to give towards building a new house three hundred pounds old tenor, provided that the town shall have free use and improvement of the said building, as long as it stands, to transact any of the public affairs of the town in." On the 6th of March, 1749, it was voted "that the town will add to their former vote for building a Court House, the sum of seven hundred pounds old tenor   . provided that the Court of General sessions for this county at its next sessions shall order that the said Court House shall immediately be built, and that the town have the privilege of transacting their public affairs in the same so long as the said house shall stand."

At the next session of the court it was voted to accept the additional grant and a copy of the vote was attested by Edward Winslow, clerk.

In order that my readers may understand the meaning of old tenor money, let me say, that there were three issues of paper money by the Massachusetts province prior to 1750. The issues prior to 1737 were called old tenor, the issue made in that year was called middle tenor, and the issue of 1741, new tenor. When the province bills were redeemed in 1750, the old tenor was redeemed at the rate of one piece of a dollar for forty-five shillings of old tenor, which would make the

amount paid to the county a fraction over $444.44.   This
sum it must be remembered was in addition to the snare of the
cost of the building to be assessed on the town in its county
tax.

In 1749, then, the present town house, was erected.   A
somewhat doubtful tradition ascribes its design to Peter Oliver,
who in 1747 was appointed Judge of the Inferior Court of
Plymouth County; and a still more doubtful tradition states
that originally its entrance was on the easterly end and was
changed about 1786 to the north side, where it is now.   After a careful examination of the latter tradition, I have reached
the conclusion that it is erroneous.   A market was established
as early as 1722, and for more than a hundred years clerks
of the market were annually chosen by the town.   Having
examined every land title from Wellingsley to Cold Spring,
and found no mention of a market anywhere except under
the town house, I am satisfied that the basement of both the
old and new building contained a market from 1722 to the
time of its comparatively recent abandonment in 1858.   The
tradition therefore concerning the change of the entrance to
admit of the establishment of a market probably refers, not
to the present building, but to the old one in which a change
of plan may have been made to admit of the establishment
of a market in 1722.   There is no reason to doubt the statement that at one time there was a one story wooden projection as far out as the sidewalk to furnish larger accommodations for the market, but it was removed before my day, and
the market was confined to the basement alone.   The market
in my day was equipped with stalls, which were leased by the
clerk of the market to various persons, among whom I remember Elisha and Charles Nelson, Amasa Holmes, Joseph White,
Brackley Cushing and Maltiah Howard.   The interior arrangement of the town house was much the same as now, except that a safe has in later times been built, and the old Court
room occupied the whole of the second story.   The Court
room was provided with a raised desk for the judge, a desk
below for the clerk, a sheriff's box on one side, a court crier's
box on the other, the jury seats facing the judge, and separat-
ing the lawyer's area from the space for the public in the rear.
Such was the arrangement of the building until 1820, when a

new Court House having been built in Court Square, the building was sold to the town for the sum of two thousand dollars. It remained practically unchanged until 1829, when the Torrent No. 4, a suction hose engine was bought, and the room at the westerly end was fitted for its accommodation. For the supply of water to this engine, and the Niagara No. 1, which was at the same time changed to a suction engine, reservoirs were built in Shirley and Town Squares to be filled by the aqueduct. The specifications for these reservoirs required them to be sixteen feet in diameter in the clear, and fourteen feet deep from the spring of the arch. To complete the story of the reservoirs, that on Training Green was built in 1834, that at the crossing of High and Spring streets, and that opposite Pilgrim Hall in 1853, and one at the foot of Russell street at an earlier period.

All through my boyhood the Town House remained as I have described it until 1839, when all the equipments of the old Court room except the judge's desk were removed and substantial seats were built on a sloping floor, which necessitated three more steps on the stairs. In 1858, while I was chairman of the selectmen, the engine Torrent was removed to the basement, and the room and ante-room, recently occupied by the selectmen, were fitted for use by the board. As first arranged, a large, round table with five drawers was constructed around an iron column in the room, which was removed some years later. The hall above was used for meetings of the town until 1872, since which time they have been held in Davis Hall and Odd Fellows' Hall, and the Armory. At a later date it was occupied by the Public Library for a short time, and then divided into rooms, one of which was occupied until recently by the school committee, and the other is now occupied by the Assessors. It may be interesting to some of my readers to learn that Catholic mass was celebrated in Town Hall, April 4, 1849.

While this book is in press, the selectmen have remodelled the interior and built a new and larger safe.

My first connection with town affairs began in 1854, when I was chosen a member of the school committee. I had the previous year become a permanent resident of Plymouth, after some years residence in Boston, and until 1892, a period of thirty-eight years, I do not recall a year in which I did not hold a town office. In 1855 I was chosen a selectman with Jacob H. Loud, chairman, and Ezekial C. Turner, Israel Clark and Ezra Leach, my other associates. In 1856 I was chairman, associated with Joseph Allen, Joseph P. Brown, Bradford Barnes and David Clark, and 1857-8-9, the board remained unchanged. In 1860 I remained chairman with Joseph P. Brown, Ezekial C. Turner, David Clark and Thomas B. Sears my associates, and in 1861 my associates were Lysander Dunham, Hosea Bartlett, Thomas B. Sears and Ezekial C. Turner, the same board continuing in office until the spring of 1866, when I declined further service. I was again chosen in 1870 and 1881, but declined serving, and was finally chosen in 1888, '89, '90, serving the last year as chairman. At regular, adjourned and special meetings, and November elections, I served as moderator seventy-nine times.

During my first service as moderator, the men who took the most active part in discussions were Moses Bates, Wm. H. Spear, Ichabod Morton, Charles G. Davis, Wm. H. Whitman, Captain John Russell, Jonathan Thrasher, Nathaniel Ellis, Charles H. Howland, Barnabas H. Holmes, Samuel H. Doten and Chas. O. Churchill. Occasionally the debates were spirited and personal. Some of the above were remarkable men. Jonathan Thrasher born and brought up, and a life-long resident, at Long Pond, denied favorable opportunities of instruction, was a man of large brain, who under the sunlight of a higher education, would have been a formidable competitor in the arena of professional life. When he spoke he at once arrested attention by his calm and judicial manner, and well expressed arguments, which were the result of careful thought. Nathaniel Ellis of Ellisville, was also a man of mark, vigorous in mind and body, ready in speech, and at every opportunity keen in ridicule and satire. I remember the roars of laughter, elicited by his speech in opposition to an additional appropriation asked for by a school committee, in whom he had no confidence. He described one of their junkets, hiring a two horse carriage, stowing under the seats lemons and sugar and sandwiches and cold chicken and pickles, and the purpose of their service in behalf of the town, the conveyance of an inkstand to the Ellisville school of four scholars. He said it was the same committee which went on a similar junket to examine the Red Brook School, and learned from the teacher after their erudite examination was finished that Red Brook school was in Sandwich, and not in Plymouth. It is needless to say that the additional appropriation was defeated. Ichabod Morton on every question relating to schools was conspicuous in debate. He was an ardent advocate for larger appropriations for public schools, and though often subjected to ridicule by his opponents, he never lost his temper and waited patiently for time to prove in the end that one with a righteous cause was a majority. At the time to which I refer in 1855 and 1860, the appropriations for schools were $8,600, and $10,000, respectively, with a population of six thousand, while the appropriation for the present year is forty-nine thousand dollars, to which the interest on the school debt must be added, with little less than double the population.

In performing the duties of moderator many questions arise for which neither law nor parliamentary usage furnishes any solution. He possesses arbitrary power which he must be careful in exercising. Some of the questions which came up during my service in that office were sufficiently interesting to justify a reference to them. On one occasion an article in the warrant involved an appropriation to which the voters in the south part of the town were opposed, and after a full discussion the appropriation was defeated, and the town passed on to the consideration of other articles in the warrant. In the latter part of the afternoon, after the southern voters had left for home, a motion was made to reconsider the vote of rejection, and with no rule of law to guide me, but one of fair play and square dealing, I ruled the motion out of order. I stated that the person moving reconsideration failed to make it before other business was done, and not having made it or given notice that he intended to make it, before adjournment, the opponents of the measure had a right to consider the question settled for the day. Some complained of the ruling, but its fairness was afterwards conceded, and so far as I know has been adopted as a guide for other moderators.

On another occasion, while several articles in the warrant remained unconsidered, a motion was made to adjourn, which

I ruled out of order. It was claimed that a motion to adjourn was always in order, and was undebatable. That is undoubtedly true in any body or convention, which has regular sessions, for in that case an adjournment means merely an adjournment to the next session, and the business arrested by the adjournment can be resumed when the next session comes together. But in a town meeting, unless it has been voted that when the meeting adjourns, it shall adjourn to meet at a certain time, a motion to adjourn cannot be entertained. There were only two courses which the mover might have pursued. He might have moved as above that when the meeting adjourns it adjourn to a certain time, and then if the town so votes a simple motion to adjourn would have been in order; or he might have moved that the consideration of the remaining articles in the warrant be indefinitely postponed, and if the town so vote, he could have moved to dissolve the meeting. A motion to adjourn unless there is a fixed time to adjourn to is simply an absurdity.

Under the old system of voting for town officers each set of officers was chosen on a separate ballot, and the counting of each set of ballots before balloting for the next officers involved great labor and delay. In order to expedite matters, a motion was made at the annual meeting in 1882 to instruct the moderator to appoint tellers, and I ruled the motion out of order, as being in controvention of the law. Many towns had been in the habit of employing tellers and their example was quoted as sufficient precedents for my guidance. I stated in general terms that the law conferred on the moderator extraordinary powers, and imposed upon him responsible duties which he could no more delegate to another than a constable or an assessor could delegate to a substitute his powers and duties. At the adjourned meeting I gave my reasons in writing to the town, and a reporter for the Boston *Herald* being present, had it printed in full in the Sunday edition of that paper. The legislature was still in session, and the judiciary committee acknowledging the correctness of my ruling at once secured the passage of an act authorizing the appointment of tellers in town meetings.

The question has often been asked whether a moderator can participate in debate. I am clearly of the opinion that except for the purpose of explaining rulings and answering questions within certain limitations, he cannot with propriety engage in the discussion of any measure before the town. It is extremely doubtful whether if he takes a marked interest in a debate he can secure the confidence of the town in the entire impartiality of his rulings and acts. For the same reason I do not believe in the propriety of his leaving the chair to speak from the floor. If, however, he should do so, I am clearly of the opinion that he vacates his chair, and that the only business before the town is to choose a moderator pro tem. His powers and duties cease the moment he leaves the chair, and they cannot be assumed by another upon whom they are not conferred by the town by ballot, and the use of the checklist.

How far a moderator shall go in ruling on the illegality of a proposition contained in the warrant, it is difficult to lay down any rule. There are many moderators unfamiliar with the laws who would necessarily permit the consideration of the article, trusting to the meeting to decide on the arguments in which illegality is alleged whether the proposition shall be rejected. If in such a case an illegal vote is favored a remedy may be found on an application to the court for an injunction.

On the whole the ruling must be left to the judgment of the moderator, who would not hesitate to rule, for instance, out of order an article to see if the town will build a steamboat to run between Plymouth and Boston.

I cannot close this chapter without suggesting that, while the most stringent laws are in force to prevent illegal voting in the elections of officers, a law should be enacted either excluding non voters from the floor at town meetings, or prescribing such a method of voting on appropriations as shall preclude the possibility of illegal voting. If other methods are impracticable it might at least be provided that in voting on appropriations exceeding $5,000, voters shall pass between two tellers appointed by the moderator and standing in front of the platform, who shall count the votes and report to the moderator.

CHAPTER XXXVI.

Accounts of the celebrations which have been held in Plymouth within my memory, or described to me by those who witnessed them, are worthy of record. I shall first, however, give a list of Pilgrim celebrations conducted by the Old Colony Club, the town, the Pilgrim Society, the first and third parishes, the Robinson Society and the Fire Department, with the names of orators.

1770, Old Colony Club, Edward Winslow, Jr., of Plymouth.
1772, Old Colony Club, Rev. Chandler Robbins of Plymouth.
1773, Old Colony Club, Rev. Charles Turner of Duxbury.
1774, Town, Rev. Gad Hitchcock of Pembroke.
1775, Town, Rev. Samuel Baldwin of Hanover.
1776, Town, Rev. Sylvanus Conant of Middleboro.
1777, Town, Rev. Samuel West of Dartmouth.
1778, Town, Rev. Timothy Hilliard of Barnstable.
1779, Town, Rev. William Shaw of Marshfield.
1780, Town, Rev. Jonathan Moore of Rochester.
1798, Town, Dr. Zaccheus Bartlett of Plymouth.
1800, Town, Hon. John Davis of Boston.
1801, Town, Rev. John Allyn of Duxbury.
1802, Town, Hon. John Quincy Adams of Quincy.
1803, Town, Rev. John T. Kirkland of Cambridge.
1804, First Parish, Rev. James Kendall of Plymouth.
1804, Town, Hon. Alden Bradford of Boston.
1806, Town, Rev. Abiel Holmes of Cambridge.
1807, Town, Rev. James Freeman of Boston.
1808, Town, Rev. Thaddeus M. Harris of Dorchester.
1809, Town, Rev. Abiel Abbot of Beverly.
1811, Town, Rev. John Eliot of Boston.
1815, Town, Rev. James Flint of Bridgewater.
1816, First Parish, Rev. Ezra Shaw Goodwin of Sandwich.
1817, Town, Rev. Horace Holley of Boston.
1818, Town, Hon. Wendell Davis of Sandwich.
1819, Town, Hon. Francis C. Gray of Boston.
1820, Pilgrim Society, Hon. Daniel Webster of Boston.
1822, Pilgrim Society, Rev. Eliphalet Porter of Roxbury.
1824, Pilgrim Society, Hon. Edward Everett of Cambridge.
1826, Third Parish, Rev. Richard S. Storrs of Braintree.
1827, Third Parish, Rev. Lyman Beecher of Boston.
1828, Third Parish, Rev. Samuel Green of Boston.
1829, Third Parish, Rev. Daniel Huntington of Bridgewater.
1829, Pilgrim Society, Hon. Wm. Sullivan of Boston.

1830, Third Parish, Rev. Benjamin Wisner of Boston.
1831, Third Parish, Rev. John Codman of Dorchester.
1831, First Parish, Rev. John Brazier of Salem.
1832, Third Parish, Rev. Jonathan Bigelow of Rochester.
1832, First Parish, Rev. Converse Francis of Watertown.
1833, First Parish, Rev. Samuel Barrett of Boston.
1834, Pilgrim Society, Rev. George W. Blagden of Boston.
1835, Pilgrim Society, Hon. Peleg Sprague of Boston.
1837, Pilgrim Society, Rev. Robert B. Hall of Plymouth.
1838, Pilgrim Society, Rev. Thomas Robbins of Mattapoisett.
1839, Third Parish, Rev. Robert B. Hall of Plymouth.
1841, Pilgrim Society, Hon. Joseph R. Chandler of Philadelphia.
1845, Pilgrim Society, dinner with speeches.
1846, Third Parish, Rev. Mark Hopkins of Williamstown.
1847, First Parish, Rev. Thomas L. Stone of Salem.
1848, Robinson Society, Rev. Samuel M. Worcester of Salem.
1853, Pilgrim Society, dinner and speeches.
1855, Pilgrim Society, Hon. Wm. H. Seward of Auburn, N. Y.
1859, Pilgrim Society dinner and speeches.
1870, Pilgrim Society, Hon. Robert C. Winthrop of Boston.
1880, Pilgrim Society, dinner and speeches.
1885, Pilgrim Society, dinner and speeches.
1886, Fire Department, dinner and speeches.
1889, Pilgrim Society, Hon. W. P. C. Breckinridge of Lexington, Ky.,
   and a poem by John Boyle O'Reilly of Boston.
1895, Pilgrim Society, Hon. George F. Hoar of Worcester, and a poem
   by Richard Henry Stoddard of New York.

On the 24th of January, 1820, the Pilgrim Society was incorporated and a committee of arrangements consisting of Nathan Hayward, Wm. Davis, Jr., and Nathaniel Spooner was chosen for the celebration of the next anniversary of the Landing of the Pilgrims. It was determined to make the first demonstration of the Society a memorable one. It is creditable to the foresight of the society that they selected Mr. Webster for orator. He was only thirty-eight years of age, and had not so far as was generally known, reached the maturity of his powers. Before coming from Portsmouth to Boston in 1816, he had served two terms in the lower house of Congress, and was then practicing successfully at the Suffolk bar. He had, however, leaped into fame by his argument in the United States Supreme Court in 1818 in the Dartmouth College case. In 1769 a corporation called the "Trustees of Dartmouth College" was chartered to have perpetual existence, and power to hold and dispose of the lands for the use of the college, and the right to fill vacancies in their own body. In 1816 the New Hampshire legislature changed the corporate name to "The trustees of Dartmouth University," and made the twelve trustees, together with nine others to be appointed by the Governor and council, a new corporation with the property of the old corporation, with power to establish new colleges and an institution under the control of twenty-five overseers. After a transfer of the property had been made the old trustees brought an action of trover to recover it on the ground of the unconstitutionality of the act. The act of the legislature was declared constitutional by the Superior Court of New Hampshire, and by a writ of error the case was carried to the United States Supreme Court in 1818, where, in 1819, the decision of the New Hampshire Court was reversed, and the act of the legislature declared unconstitutional. Mr. Webster's argument had never before been equalled, and has never since been surpassed.

At the time of the celebration, whoever, within an easy distance from Boston, could secure accommodations in Plymouth availed himself of the opportunity. I have letters addressed to my grandfather, written in August, asking him to engage lodgings of some sort. There were three hotels in Plymouth, all of them crowded with guests, and every spare bed in town was secured. On the day of the celebration, by stage, by private carriage, and public hack, visitors came on a two days' trip in the dead of winter, fortunate if able to obtain a whole or a part of a bed, while the drivers slept in their carriages. But fortunately the day of the celebration was as mild as Indian summer. I was told many years ago by a man who remembered it, that he sat through a part of the day by an open window in his shirt sleeves. There has been preserved by the Pilgrim Society a parchment containing the autographs of all who attended the dinner, so that the array of distinguished men who listened to Mr. Webster is not left to the imagination. Among the visitors were, Rev. John T. Kirkland, President of Harvard, Professors Edward Everett, Geo. Ticknor and Levi Hedge, Rev. Abiel Abbot, Rev. Abiel Holmes, Rev. John G. Palfrey, Rev. John Pierce, Rev. Converse Francis, Rev. James Flint, Rev. Alexander Young, Rev. Charles Lowell, Rev. Francis Parkman, Rev. Wm. P. Lunt, Judge John Davis, Isaac P. Davis, Thomas H. Perkins, Francis C. Gray,

Levi Lincoln, Stephen Salisbury, Timothy Bigelow, Laban W. Wheaton, Martin Brimmer, Benjamin Rotch, Amos Lawrence, Thomas Bulfinch, Theron Metcalf, Nahum Mitchell, Wm. S. Otis, George A. Trumbull, Augustus Peabody, Henderson Inches, Francis Baylies, Willard Phillips, Henry Grinnell, Samuel A. Eliot, Isaiah Thomas, Dudley A. Tyng, Isaac Mc-Clellan, Amos Binney and others of no less distinction. No such an assembly had ever before gathered in New England as that which filled the church of the First Parish on that memorable day. The scene was worthy of the best efforts of the painter's art. The galleries reserved for the ladies, seemed with the mingling of colors in dress and hats and fans like banks of summer flowers mellowing the sombre garb worn by the society and their guests on the floor below. Mr. Webster wearing small clothes and buckles and shoes, and over all a silk gown, stood on a raised platform in front of the high oak pulpit and began his oration with words to which his audience was in the spirit to heartily respond, "Let us rejoice that we behold this day."

Perhaps that part of the oration which gave to it its chief distinction, was that denunciatory of the slave trade. A law was passed by Congress in 1808 abolishing the trade, but it had slumbered on the statute books until Mr. Webster twelve years later, breathed into it the breath of life. In a town, which was in early days within the Plymouth colony, the trade was still carried on, and by this fact the scathing words of the oration were inspired. "I hear the sound of the hammer. I see the smoke of the furnace where manacles and fetters are still forged for human limbs. I see the visages of those who by stealth and at midnight labor in this work of hell, foul and dark as may become the artificers of such instruments of misery and torture. Let that spot be purified, or let it cease to be of New England."

There was another passage, never more needed than to-day to be impressed on the public mind, relating to military achievements. "Great actions and striking occurrences having excited a temporary admiration often pass away and are forgotten. * * Such is frequently the fortune of the most brilliant military achievements. Of the ten thousand battles which have been fought; of all the fields fertilized with carn-

age; of the banners which have been bathed in blood; of the
warriors who have hoped that they had risen from the field
of conquest to a glory as bright and as durable as the stars,
how few that continue to interest mankind. The victory of
yesterday is reversed by the defeat of today; the star of military glory rising like a meteor, like a meteor has fallen; disgrace and disaster hang on the heels of conquest and renown;
victor and vanquished presently pass away to oblivion, and the
world goes on in its course with the loss only of so many lives,
and so much treasure."

A dinner was served in the Court House, then building, by
John Blaney Bates of Plymouth, who also served the supper
for the ball held in the same place. I have a letter addressed
to my grandfather in the summer of 1820, showing that an
invitation to Mr. Everett to deliver a poem after the oration
was contemplated, and that Mr. Everett said he would accept
such an invitation. But wise counsels prevailed, and it was
thought best to give to Mr. Webster alone the honors of the
day.

In 1822 Rev. Eliphalet Porter of Roxbury delivered an address before the Pilgrim Society, but no record of the ceremonies of the day have been preserved.

In 1824 Edw. Everett was the orator of the Pilgrim Society,
and on Wednesday, the 22d of December, a crowd of strangers
visited the town to hear the eloquent orator. Mr. Everett,
after graduating at Harvard in 1811, was settled pastor of the
Brattle street church in 1813, to succeed Rev. Joseph Stevens
Buckminster, who died in 1812. In 1814 he was chosen
Eliot Professor of Greek at Harvard, and from 1815 to 1819,
he spent in study and travel in Europe preparing for his duties
as Professor. In 1819 he returned and entered upon his office,
resigning in 1824, in which year he delivered an address before
the Phi Beta Society, and was chosen member of Congress.
His oration was a splendid effort, and I was told by Rev. Samuel K. Lothrop, who was present, that it was repeatedly said
at the time that his oration came fully up to the Webster standard. But time failed to justify the comparison. Beauty of
imagery, and a grace of delivery, captivated for the hour, but
like the elusive tints of the rainbow, they were forgotten,
when the thunder and lightning which had preceded it were

recalled. After the oration, a dinner was served in Pilgrim Hall, the cornerstone of which was laid on the first of the previous September, and which was finished in time for the celebration.

The celebration in 1829 was the first of which I have any recollection. I was then seven years of age, but I remember being carried up North street and along Main and Court streets to see the illumination of the town on the evening before the celebration. Even that I should perhaps have failed to remember had I not got something in one of my eyes and gone home crying. Hon. William Sullivan of Boston delivered the oration, the son of James Sullivan, who was Governor of Massachusetts in 1807. Mr. Sullivan was one of the leaders of the Boston bar, but as far as I know this was the first opportunity to display his powers as an orator. During a winter's residence in Philadelphia in 1844, I became intimate with his son, John T. S. Sullivan, a man of more varied accomplishments than any man I ever personally knew. He was a master of the Spanish, French, Italian and German languages, was an excellent singer, a skilful performer on the piano, guitar, banjo and harp, and a story teller who would put Depew and Choate to the blush.

On Monday, December 22, 1834, Rev. George W. Blagden of the Boston Old South church, was the orator of the Pilgrim Society, and in the absence of the President, Dr. Zaccheus Bartlett presided, assisted by Judah Alden of Duxbury, Wilkes Wood of Middleboro, Wm. W. Swain of New Bedford, Henry J. Oliver of Boston, John Thomas of Kingston, and Josiah Robbins of Plymouth. Samuel Doten was chief marshall, and the dinner in Pilgrim Hall, as well as supper for the ball in the same place, was furnished by Danville Bryant of the Pilgrim House. During the year preceding the celebration a handsome glass chandelier fitted for candles was hung in Pilgrim Hall, and the present wooden portico was built. During the day Dr. James Thacher, then eighty years of age, was knocked down and run over by a carriage, but not seriously injured.

Rev. Dr. George Washington Blagden, son of George and Anne (Davies), Blagden, was born in Washington, D. C. October 3, 1802 and graduated at Yale in 1823 and at the

Andover Theological Seminary in 1827. He was ordained in Brighton, Mass. in 1827, installed in the Salem street church in Boston in 1830 and in the Old South church in Boston, in 1836. He was made Doctor of Divinity by Yale in 1843, by Union College in 1849 and by Harvard in 1850. While *pastor emeritus* of the Old South, he died Dec. 17, 1884.

On Tuesday, December 22, 1835, an oration was delivered before the Pilgrim Society by Hon. Peleg Sprague of Boston. Mr. Sprague, son of Seth and Deborah (Sampson) Sprague of Duxbury, was born April 27, 1793, and graduated at Harvard in 1812. He studied law at Litchfield law school, and was admitted to the Plymouth bar in 1815, and settled in Augusta, Maine, removing at the end of two years to Hallowell. He was Representative in 1820-1; member of Congress from 1825 to 1829; United States Senator from 1829 to 1835, when he moved to Boston. He was Judge of the United States District Court from 1847 to 1865, and died in Boston, October 13, 1886. On that occasion Samuel Doten was chief marshal, assisted by John Tribble, Sylvanus Harlow, Eliab Ward, John Washburn, Ichabod Shaw and Nelson Holmes. At the dinner Alden Bradford, the president of the society presided, assisted by Jos. Tilden of Boston; Wilkes Wood of Middleboro: Phineas Sprague of Duxbury; Dr. Samuel West of Tiverton; Samuel A. Frazier of Duxbury, and Benjamin Rodman of New Bedford. Hon. Edw. Everett of Boston was one of the numerous speakers, and Miss Harriet Martineau, who was the guest of Dr. Zaccheus Bartlett, was present at both the dinner and ball. She was very deaf, and conversation with her was difficult. I was a boy of thirteen, but I remember standing near her accompanied by Mrs. Dr. Winslow Warren, when Judge Warren as he joined the group was asked if he did not wish to be introduced to her. The air of the hall was thick and heavy with dust, which together with the music of the band made the ear sensitive to sounds, and as the Judge replied that he could not make her hear he was surprised to hear her say "I think, Judge, that you will have no difficulty." I had once very much the same experience. I called on a friend who had a guest who had been stone deaf many years, and had learned the art of reading what was said, in the motion of the lips. I did not know this, and when my host left the room temporarily, I asked her to return soon, as it would be embarrassing to be left with a person with whom I could not engage in conversation, and was astonished to hear the lady say she thought we could talk well enough together. Though I wore a moustache her eye read what her ear could not hear.

In 1837 an address was delivered before the Pilgrim Society by Rev. Robert B. Hall, a notice of whom may be found in a previous chapter, to which I take this opportunity to add that in 1849, after his return to Plymouth to take up a permanent residence, he accepted an invitation to preach for a time in the Robinson church.

In 1838 Rev. Thomas Robbins of Rochester delivered an anniversary address before the Pilgrim Society. Mr. Robbins, son of Ammi Ruhamah and Elizabeth (LeBaron) Robbins, was born in Norfolk, Conn., August 11, 1777. He entered Yale College in 1792, and in 1795 removed to Williams College, where he graduated in 1796. Immediately after his graduation he returned to Yale and graduated there in the same year. He spent two years in teaching in Sheffield, Mass., and Torringford, Conn., and in studying for the ministry. In 1798 he was licensed to preach by the Litchfield North Association, and engaged in missionary service until 1809, when he was settled in East Windsor, where he remained until 1827. After a year at Stratford, Conn., he was settled in that part of Rochester, Mass., which is now Mattapoisett, where he remained until 1846. He gathered a valuable library, which he gave to the Connecticut Historical Society, with the understanding that he should be appointed librarian with a suitable salary, and he continued in that office until his death, which occurred at Colebrook, Conn., September 13, 1856.

At the celebration, December 22, 1841, Hon. Joseph Ripley Chandler of Philadelphia, delivered the oration. A dinner was served in the lower Pilgrim Hall, at which Hon. Nathaniel Morton Davis, president of the society, presided, assisted by Abraham Hammatt of Ipswich, Pelham Winslow Warren of Lowell, Joshua Thomas Stevenson of Boston, Gershom B. Weston of Duxbury, Thomas Prince Beal of Kingston, and Barnabas Churchill of Plymouth. Among the speakers were Samuel M. Burnside, President of the American Antiquarian Society, and Rev. John L. Russell. Mr. Chandler was born

in Kingston, August 25, 1792, and early became a clerk in
Boston, soon after teaching school, and about 1815 removing
to Philadelphia.   In that city he and his wife engaged in teaching a school, and in 1822 he became connected with the
United States Gazette, and from 1826 to 1847, was its editor.
He was a member of the city council from 1832 to 1848, a
delegate to the state constitutional convention in 1836, a member of Congress from 1849 to 1855, and travelled in Europe
from 1855 to 1858, in which latter year he was minister to the
two Sicilles.   He died in Philadelphia, July 10, 1880.

In 1845 the Pilgrim Society departed from their usual custom, and omitting an oration, celebrated the twenty-second
of December by a short service in the First church, at which
Rev. Dr. Francis Wayland, president of Brown University,
and Rev. Dr. James Kendall officiated, and a dinner in the
passenger station of the Old Colony Railroad, which had been
closed in and floored over for the purpose   On that occasion Pelham W. Hayward was chief marshal, and as one of
the marshals, I then began in an humble way, a participation
in the celebrations of the Pilgrim Society, which has continued in the various positions of chief marshal, member of the
committee of arrangements, and presiding officer without in-
terruption down to the present time.   At the dinner Hon.
Charles Henry Warren, president of the society, presided, assisted by Col. John B. Thomas of Plymouth, Henry Crocker,
Abbot Lawrence and David Sears of Boston, and John H.
Clifford of New Bedford.   The dinner was served by J. B.
Smith of Boston, and was contributed to by a baron of beef
from Daniel Webster, and a turbot and saddle of mutton
brought from England in the Cunard Steamer Acadia, from
S. S. Lewis, the agent of the Cunard Company.   The speak-
ers were Josiah Quincy, president of Harvard, Rufus Choate,
George S. Hillard, Edward Everett and Nathaniel Morton
Davis, ex-president of the society.   Dr. Oliver Wendell
Holmes read a poem, written for the occasion, entitled "The
Pilgrim's Vision."

The speech of Mr. Everett is worthy of special comment
as showing how thoroughly he had studied the art of oratory.
Before the dinner he sent a message to the caterer, Mr.
Smith, asking him to place an orange by the side of his plate.

At the close of his speech, after refuting the charge that the Pilgrims were narrow and bigoted he said, "But by their fruits ye shall know them; not by the graceful foliage which dallies with the summer breeze; nor by the flower which fades and scatters its perfume on the gale; but by the golden, perfect fruit (seizing the orange, and lifting it above his head) in which the genial earth, and ripening sun have garnered up treasures for the food of man, and which in its decay leaves behind it the germs of a continued and multiplying existence."

The next celebration conducted by the Pilgrim Society occurred August 1, 1853, the anniversary of the departure of the Pilgrims from Delfthaven.   On the 16th of June in that year a committee of arrangements was chosen by the trustees consisting of Richard Warren of New York, president of the society, Timothy Gordon, Andrew L. Russell, Eleazer C. Sherman and Wm. S. Russell of Plymouth; Nathaniel B. Shurtleff, Charles Henry Warren and James T. Hayward of Boston.   I was appointed Chief Marshal, and I appointed Samuel H. Doten and John D. Churchill, aids and the following assistant marshals;   Wm. Atwood, Wm. Bishop, Charles O. Churchill, Winslow Drew, John H. Harlow, Barnabas Hedge, George H. Jackson, Thomas Loring, John J. Russell, Edward W. Russell, Nathaniel B. Spooner, George Simmons, Jeremiah Farris, Samuel Shaw, B. H. Holmes, Isaac Brewster, Wm. R. Drew, George G. Dyer, Daniel J. Lane, Wm. H. Nelson and George Bramhall of Plymouth; Waterman French of Abington; Phillip D. Kingman of Bridgewater; Matthias Ellis of Carver; Charles Henry Thomas, Wm. Ellison and George B. Standish of Duxbury; James H. Mitchell of East Bridgewater; James H. Wilder of Hingham; Perez Simmons of Hanover; Nathan Cushing of Hanson; Robert Gould of Hull; Joseph S. Beal of Kingston; Harrison Staples of Lakeville; J. Sampson, Jr., of Middleboro; W. N. Ellis of Marion; George M. Baker of Marshfield; G. W. Bryant of North Bridgewater; Zacheus Parker of Plympton; George F. Hatch of Pembroke; Theophilus King of Rochester; Wm. P. Allen of Scituate; Albion Turner of South Scituate; Thomas Ames of West Bridgewater; Lewis Kenney of Wareham; LeBaron Russell, Rufus B. Bradford, Solomon J. Gordon, George P. Hayward, Thomas Russell, Isaac Winslow and Pelham W. Hayward of Boston.

A large number of guests was invited, including the President of the United States; members of the cabinet; the Governor of Massachusetts; members of Congress and U. S. Senators from Massachusetts; the Mayor of Boston; President of the Massachusetts Senate, and Speaker of the House of Representatives; Wm. H. Seward, John J. Crittenden, Nathaniel P. Banks, Charles H. Warren, Robert C. Winthrop, Abbott Lawrence, Josiah Quincy, Judge Peleg Sprague, George Bancroft, John P. Kennedy, the presidents of Harvard, Yale, Williams, Brown, and Amherst colleges, Jared Sparks, John P. Hale, Edward Everett, Oliver W. Holmes, the Plymouth Church, Southwark, England, the authorities of Delfthaven, Leyden, Southampton and old Plymouth, the New England societies of New York, Brooklyn, Philadlephia, Charleston, Pittsburg, Cincinnati, Louisville, St. Louis, New Orleans, Detroit, San Francisco and Washington, and many others, too numerous to mention. The New York Light Guard, which had been invited to attend the celebration with the New England Society of New York, arrived in the afternoon of Sunday, and with Dodworth's band marched to their quarters provided in the old Hedge house in Leyden street, which happened at that time to be vacant, and was fitted up for their accommodation. The town was profusely decorated; arches were erected on Court, Main, North, Summer and Pleasant streets, and every building was decorated with flags and mottoes. The inscription in large letters on the house of Wm. Brewster Barnes, opposite Pilgrim Hall, "August 1, Forefathers' Day Thawed Out" attracted much attention. The features of the day were a religious service in the First Church in the early forenoon, a procession and a dinner. The service consisted of Scripture reading by Rev. Dr. George W. Blagden of the Old South Church in Boston, a prayer by Rev. Dr. James Kendall, preceded and followed by the singing of appropriate hymns, and a benediction by Rev. Chas. S. Porter of Plymouth. The dinner was provided by John Wright of Boston in a mammoth tent, which covered more than the easterly half of Training Green, with the speaker's platform in the middle of the westerly side, and was set for twenty-five hundred persons. The procession with its head near the chief marshal's headquarters, which were located on the Samoset House lawn, marched north to Lothrop street, then countermarching and proceeding through Court, Main, Leyden, Water, Market, High, Summer and Pleasant streets to the tent which was completely filled, about seven hundred ladies having been admitted before the arrival of the procession to seats on one side of each table. The order of the procession was as follows: Escort, Boston Brigade Band, The Standish Guards, Abington Artillery, Samoset Guards, Halifax Light Infantry, Plymouth Band, Chief Marshal and Aids. President and officers and committee of arrangements of the Pilgrim Society, Governor of Massachusetts and staff, attended by the Corps of Independent cadets, and Adjutant General, South Abington band, presidents of New England societies, and of the Cape Cod Association, United States Senators, members of Congress, president of the State Senate, United States District Attorney, Attorney General of Massachusetts, invited guests, New England Society of New York, attended by the New York Light Guard and Dodworth's band, Pilgrim Society, town officers, clergy, school teachers, South Bridgewater band, and the Plymouth fire department. At the President's table sat at his right and left Rev. Dr. James Kendall, Rev. Dr. George W. Blagden, Hon. Edward Everett, Governor John H. Clifford, Hon. Chas. H. Warren, Hon. Chas. Sumner, Hon. John P. Hale, Hon. H. A. Scudder, Hon. Richard Yeadon, Hon. Chas. W. Upham, Rev. Sam'l Osgood, Rev. Chas. S. Porter and Hiram Fuller. The speeches were of a high order, elaborate and eloquent. Governor Clifford in his speech rebuked the reckless spirit which proclaims manifest destiny as our National guide in the following words: "But what is the manifest destiny doctrine of our day with which we are constantly stimulating our national arrogance and self conceit? . . I believe the most recent and authoritative exposition of it is that it is one of the inexorable conditions of our country's existence, "to march, march, march" in the path of Pagan Rome as restless as the eternal tramp of the Wandering Jew . . till its mission is accomplished. Sir, are we content to abide by the example of our fathers? Which will you carry from this scene of joyous festivity and pious commemoration—a prayer that the forward march of the country you love, and in which your

children' are to live shall be symbolized by the Wandering
Jew or by the Christian Pilgrim."   Governor Clifford was
then forty-four years old, and consequently he was not uttering the sentiments of over caution which sometimes characterize old age.   If any of my readers think that he was, they
will be pleased with the following eloquent passage in the
speech of Mr. Everett, which followed.   In speaking of the
great work of the Pilgrims not yet finished he said: "The
work—the work must go on. · It must reach at the North to
the enchanted cave of the magnet within never melting bar-
riers of Arctic ice; it must bow to the Lord of day on the altar
peaks of Chimborazo; it must look up and worship the
Southern cross.   From the Eastern most cliff on the Atlantic
that blushes in the kindling dawn, to the last promontory on
the Pacific which receives the parting kiss of the setting sun
as he goes down to his pavilion of purple and gold it must
make the outgoings of the morning and evening to rejoice in
the gladsome light of morals and letters and arts."   This was
a poetic sentiment of great beauty illustrating the art of eloquence which Mr. Hale turned into ridicule in his later speech
when he said, "I find that the boldest tropes that ever rung
beneath the dome of your Federal capitol are tame to the con-
ceptions which have been poured forth from Pilgrim lips upon
Pilgrim ears today.   We heard there of men whose powers of
digestion were so capacious that the idea of swallowing Mexico
at a meal did not alarm them.   Today in the most eloquent
language we have had the genius of our country taking her
seat at the center of magnetic attraction swallowing Chimborazo for supper, and kissing sunset with an affectionate em-
brace."

The other speakers were Mr. Sumner, Dr. Blagden, Charles
W. Upham, Richard Yeadon, Henry A. Scudder, Rev. Sam-
uel Osgood and Hiram Fuller.   In the evening there was a
brilliant display of fireworks, music by the Brigade band in
Town Square, and a reception at the house then occupied by
President Warren, now the home of Colonel Stoddard.

John Henry Clifford was born in Providence, January 16,
1809, and graduated at Brown in 1827.   After studying law
he settled in New Bedford and began his public career as Representative in 1835.   He was Attorney General from 1849 to

1853, and from 1854 to 1858, having been chosen governor in 1852. He received in 1849 from Harvard a degree of LL. D., and died in New Bedford, January 2, 1876.

John Parker Hale was born in Rochester, N. H., March 31, 1806, and graduated at Bowdoin in 1827, and was admitted to the bar in Dover and settled there. He was a representative in 1832, and United States District Attorney from 1834 to 1841, member of Congress from 1843 to 1845. In 1846 he was speaker of the New Hampshire House of Representatives and United States Senator from 1847 to 1853, and from 1855 to 1865. He was minister to Spain from 1865 to 1869, and candidate of the Liberty party for president in 1852. He died in Dover, November 19, 1873.

Charles Sumner was born in Boston, January 6, 1811, and graduated at Harvard in 1830. The only political office he ever held was that of United States Senator, to which he was chosen in 1851, remaining by successive elections in office until his death, which occurred in Washington, March 11, 1874.

Charles Wentworth Upham, son of Joshua Upham, a noted loyalist, was born in St. John, N. B., May 4, 1802, and graduated at Harvard in 1821. In 1824 he was settled as colleague pastor of Rev. John Prince of the First Church in Salem. In 1844 he relinquished preaching on account of a partial loss of voice, and thenceforth devoted himself to literature and politics. In 1852 he was Mayor of Salem, and after serving some years as Representative, was President of the Senate in 1857 and 1858. He was a member of the State Constitutional Convention in 1853; a member of Congress from 1853 to 1855, and died in Salem, June 14, 1875.

Rev. Samuel Osgood was born in Charlestown, August 30, 1812, and graduated at Harvard in 1832. After leaving the Cambridge Divinity school in 1835 he was settled in Nashua, N. H., in 1838, and in 1841 over the Westminster Unitarian church in Providence. In 1849 he became pastor of the Church of the Messiah, Unitarian, in New York, where he remained until 1869. In 1870 he was ordained deacon in the Episcopal church, and continued in that faith until his death, April 14, 1880.

Hiram Fuller was born in Halifax, Mass., at a date unknown by me, but probably about 1807. I remember hearing him say that the first time he ever came to Plymouth he rode on a charcoal cart. He opened a private school in Plymouth in 1832, keeping it at various times in Robbin's Hall on Middle street or Paine's hall, as it was later called, and in Old Colony Hall in the rear of the present market of C. B. Harlow. He went from Plymouth to Providence about 1835 or 1836, where he taught school for a time, and afterwards opened a bookstore. He went from Providence to New York, where he became associated with N. P. Willis and George P. Morris in the editorship of the *New Mirror and Home Journal*, retaining his connections with those papers during a period of fourteen years. Under the name of Belle Brittan he published a volume of brilliant letters, and devoted much of his time to miscellaneous literary labors. When the Civil War came on his sympathies were enlisted in behalf of the South, and finding New York an uncongenial residence, went to England, where he remained until his death. At one time he had an editorial connection in London, with a newspaper called the *Cosmopolitan*, but I have reason to believe that the issue of the war and the consequent loss of English interest in the Confederate cause, left him stranded and reduced in a foreign land.

In 1855 the anniversary of the Landing was celebrated on the 22nd of December, on which occasion Hon. Wm. H. Seward of Auburn, N. Y., delivered an oration in the First Church. The incident which I remember more distinctly than any other in connection with the oration, was Mr. Seward's lighting a cigar the moment the benediction was pronounced as he stood on a raised platform in front of the pulpit. He was a confirmed smoker, and like too many other confirmed smokers of our day had little regard for the time and place for the indulgence of his habit. The dinner was prepared by J. B. Smith of Boston in Davis Hall, and Richard Warren, president of the Pilgrim Society, presided. The speakers were: Mr. Seward, Hon. George S. Boutwell, Rev. John S. Barry, Wendell Phillips, Rev. Thomas D. Worrell of London, Rev. Dr. George W. Briggs and Hon. B. F. Butler of New York. The last named gentleman sharing with the Massachusetts General a distinguished name, was born in Kinderhook, N. Y., Dec. 15, 1795, and on his admission to the bar became in 1817 partner of Martin Van Buren. He was Attorney General of the United States, under Andrew Jackson, from 1831 to 1834, acting secretary of war under Van Buren, and from 1838 to 1841, U. S. District Attorney for the Southern District of New York. He died in Paris, France, Nov. 8, 1858.

William Henry Seward, the orator of the day, was born in Florida, N. Y., May 16, 1801, and graduated at Union college in 1820. He was admitted to the bar in 1822, and settled in Auburn, and in 1830 was chosen State Senator on the anti-masonic ticket. In 1838 he was chosen Governor, and re-elected in 1840, and in 1849 was chosen U. S. Senator. In 1861 he was appointed by President Lincoln secretary of state, and continued in office until the close of President Johnson's term. He died in Auburn, October 10, 1872.

CHAPTER XXXVII.

In 1859, the necessary arrangements having been concluded for beginning work on the canopy over the Rock and on the National Monument, it was decided by the Pilgrim Society to lay at once the corner stones of those structures with suitable ceremonies. The anniversary of the embarkation was again selected for celebrating the event, but as the first of August would fall on Monday, it was thought best to have the celebration on Tuesday, the second. The following committee of arrangements was appointed, by whom I was again appointed Chief Marshal, Richard Warren, Timothy Gordon, Wm. T. Davis, Samuel H. Doten, Charles O. Churchill and George G. Dyer. A committee on the ball was appointed, consisting of Edward W. Russell, Edward B. Hayden, Charles C. Doten of Plymouth, Austin C. Cushman of New Bedford, and Wm. S. Huntington of North Bridgewater. The chief marshal appointed as aides, Admiral P. Stone, Wm. Atwood, Samuel H. Doten, Charles Raymond, Leavitt Finney, John H. Harlow of Plymouth, James H. Beal of Boston, James Bates of East Bridgewater. He also appointed twenty-eight assistant marshals from Plymouth, and ten from other places.

The committee decided on the following plan for the celebration: The laying of the cornerstone of the canopy by the Masonic order; a procession; the laying of the cornerstone of the National Monument with Masonic ceremonies; a dinner provided by J. B. Smith of Boston in a tent, capable of holding twenty-five hundred persons, pitched in the field below the present store of Wm. Burn's, now occupied by three dwelling houses, owned by Mr. Emery; fireworks, and a ball in the evening in Davis Hall. At ten o'clock a Masonic procession was formed on Main street, consisting of the Massachusetts, Boston and DeMoley encampments of Knights Templar, under command of John T. Heard, and marched to the Rock, where addresses were made by President Warren and Mr. Heard, and a hymn was sung, composed by John Shepard. At half past eleven the grand procession, whose various divisons had been forming while the ceremony at the

Rock was going on, started from the headquarters of the
chief marshal near the Samoset House, and proceeded through
Court, Main, Market, High, Summer, Pleasant, Green, Sandwich, Market, Leyden, Water, North, Court and Cushman
streets to Monument hill. The procession marched in the following order: Mounted police, Boston brigade band, Standish
Guards, New Bedford City Guards, Braintree Light Infantry,
So. Abington Infantry, New Bedford brass band, chief marshal and aids mounted, president of the Pilgrim Society and
invited guests, St. Paul's lodge of South Boston, lodge of
Cambridge, Liberty lodge of New Bedford, Star of the East
lodge of New Bedford, King Solomon lodge of Charlestown,
Boston brass band, Washington lodge of Roxbury, the Plym-
outh lodge, Plymouth brass band, Royal Arch chapter of New
Bedford, Boston encampment of Knights Templar, Royal
Arch Chapter of South Abington, South Abington band, De-
Moley encampment, Grand lodge of Massachusetts, American brass band, Odd Fellows, New England Society of New
York, Massachusetts Historical Society, American Antiquarian
Society, Historic Genealogical Society, Cape Cod Association,
Finney's band, Plymouth Fire Department, Campello Engine
company, North Bridgewater band, and six groups on flats rep-
resenting the Landing, Indians, advance of civilization, the
thirty-three states, different nations, and the marine interests
of Plymouth.

After addresses at the monument by President Warren, and
the ceremony of laying the cornerstone, conducted by the
Grandmaster, John T. Heard, the invited guests were escorted
to the dining tent, where Rev. Edward H. Hall, pastor of the
First Church asked a blessing. Besides the president the
speakers were, Gov. Banks, Salmon P. Chase, Wm. Maxwell
Evarts, Gov. Buckingham of Conn., John P. Hale, Francis
P. Bair, Jr., Anson Burlinghame, Gov. Kent of Maine, George
Sumner and Rev. Mr. Waddington of Southwark, London.
I have room for notices of only a few of these speakers.
Nathaniel Prentiss Banks, born in Waltham, Mass., January
30, 1816, was a boy in a factory, editor of a local paper, rep-
resentative in 1849, speaker of the Massachusetts House of
Representatives, 1851 and 1853, chairman of the Massachus-
etts constitutional convention, 1853, member of congress,

1853 to 1857, and speaker of the National House of Representatives from 1855 to 1857. He was chosen governor in 1857, serving three years; after which he was chosen president of the Illinois Central railroad, made Major General in 1861, serving until 1864, again member of Congress from 1865 to 1877, excepting one year, when he was a member of the Massachusetts Senate, and finally United States Marshal in Boston in 1879. He died in Waltham, Sept. 1, 1894.

Salmon P. Chase was born in Cornish, N. H., January 13, 1808, and graduated at Dartmouth in 1826. He taught school in Washington, where he was admitted to the bar in 1830. He was later Senator, Secretary of the Treasury, and Chief Justice of the U. S. Supreme Court, and died in New York, May 7, 1873.

William Maxwell Evarts was born in Boston in Feb., 1818, and graduated at Yale in 1837. He studied law at Cambridge and settled in New York, and was counsel for President Johnson on his impeachment trial. Attorney General under Grant in 1868, Secretary of State under Hayes, and later U. S. Senator. He died in New York, Feb. 28, 1901.

Edward Kent was born in Concord, N. H., January 8, 1902, and settled as a lawyer in Bangor in 1825. In 1827 he was made chief justice of the Court of Sessions for Penobscot County, in 1829 was chosen Mayor of Bangor, and was Governor from 1838 to 1840. He was made U. S. Consul at Rio by President Taylor, and in 1859 Associate Justice of the Supreme Court. He died in Bangor, May 19, 1877.

William Alfred Buckingham, born in Lebanon, Conn., May 28, 1804, was a merchant and manufacturer, and Governor of Connecticut from 1858 to 1866, and in 1869 was chosen U. S. Senator. He died in Norwich, February 3, 1875.

Anson Burlingame was born in New Berlin, N. Y., Nov. 19, 1822, and studied law at the Harvard Law school and in Boston, where he was admitted to the bar. He was a member of the Massachusetts Senate in 1852, a delegate to the Massachusetts Constitutional Convention in 1853, and member of Congress from 1856 to 1861, in which latter year he was appointed minister to Austria. From 1861 to 1867 he was minister to China, and while in the service of China, died in St. Petersburg, February 23, 1870.

George Sumner was a brother of Charles Sumner, born in Boston, February 5, 1817, where he died October 6, 1863. He published memoirs of the Pilgrims in Leyden, and delivered the Fourth of July oration in Boston in 1859.

Francis P. Blair, Jr., son of Francis Preston Blair, and brother of Montgomery Blair, was born in Lexington, Ky., February 19, 1821, and graduated at Princeton in 1841. He studied law and began practice in St. Louis. During the Mexican war he enlisted as private and served until 1847, when he returned to St. Louis and resumed practice. In 1848 he was a Free Soiler, and edited the *Missouri Democrat*. In 1852 and 1854 he was a member of the Missouri Legislature, and in 1856 was chosen member of Congress, and again in 1860 and 1862. He was commissioned Colonel in the army in 1861, and Brigadier General and Major General in 1862. In 1866 he was appointed Collector of Customs at St. Louis. In 1868 he was the candidate of the Democratic party for Vice-President. In 1870 he was chosen U. S. Senator from Missouri, and died in St. Louis, July 8, 1875.

In 1870 the Society voted to celebrate the 250th anniversary of the Landing of the Pilgrims on the 21st of December, and to establish that day for the first time and forever as the true day, instead of the 22d. Without entering upon any detailed explanation of the error leading to the observance of the 22d, it is sufficient to say that in 1620 the difference between the Julian calender, and the Gregorian calender, now used, was ten days, and that consequently an almanac made up in accordance with the latter, would have marked the 11th of December the day of the Landing, as the 21st. It follows, of course, that what was then the Gregorian 21st, must be the 21st for all coming time.

I was then Vice-President of the Pilgrim Society, and at a meeting of the trustees held on the 7th of September, it was voted that the committee of arrangements for the celebration be appointed, of which the Vice-President should be chairman. The committee as appointed consisted of Wm. T. Davis, Wm. H. Whitman, Eleazer C. Sherman, Charles G. Davis and Wm. S. Danforth, by whom subsequently the following additional members were appointed, John Morissey, Albert Mason, Samuel H. Doten, Nathaniel Brown of Plymouth, Thomas

Russell and George P. Hayward of Boston, and Richard Warren of New York. Albert Mason was appointed chief
marshal, and Wm. S. Danforth, treasurer. A finance committee was also appointed, and to the committee of arrangements as managers of the ball, the following honorary managers were added, Richard Warren of New York, Thomas
Russell, Wm. G. Russell, James T. Hayward, Benjamin W.
Harris of Boston, James H. Harlow of Middleboro, James
H. Mitchell of East Bridgewater, Wm. Savery of Carver,
Wm. L. Reed of Abington, George W. Wright of Duxbury,
C. B. H. Fessenden of New Bedford, and Charles F. Swift
of Yarmouth. The following were selected as floor managers, Henry G. Parker of Boston, Dwight Faulkner, Francis H. Russell, B. M. Watson, Jr., Benjamin O. Strong, Wm.
P. Stoddard, James D. Thurber, Robert B. Churchill, Ed-
ward W. Russell and Isaac Damon.

The committee of arrangements voted to have a public din-
ned in the Old Colony Railroad station, the use of which had
been tendered for the purpose, and that L. E. Field of Taunton be engaged to furnish both the dinner, and the supper
at the ball. The Standish Guards were invited to perform
escort duty, as the guests of the Society, and Gilmore's band
of Boston, and the Plymouth brass band were engaged for the
occasion. At an early meeting of the trustees of the society
held before any arrangements had been entered upon, it was
voted to invite Hon. Robert C. Winthrop to deliver an oration,
and it was after his acceptance that the plans for the celebration were perfected. A large number of guests were invited
to attend the celebration, including one hundred and twenty-
two men of distinction, and fourteen historical, and New England Societies, but it is only necessary to mention those who
were present. At eleven o'clock a procession was formed at
Pilgrim Hall, under the direction of Albert Mason, chief
marshal, assisted by his aids, Capt. Charles C. Doten and
Major James D. Thurber, and by twelve marshals, and under
escort of the Standish Guards, and with the music of the
Plymouth brass band, and Gilmore's band of Boston, marched
through Court, North and Leyden streets to the First Church.
As it passed Plymouth Rock a National salute was fired on
board the U. S. Revenue Cutter Mahoning, Capt. R. A. Fen-

gar, who was a guest of the society. Seats reserved for ladies in the church were occupied previous to the arrival of the procession, and seats reserved for the press were occupied by representatives of two Plymouth journals, one Abington, one Hingham, one North Bridgewater, one Middleboro, one New Bedford, one Weymouth, one Yarmouth, one Northampton, one Hartford, one Chicago, one Mexico, N. Y., three New York, and nine Boston.

The services in the church were as follows: Voluntary, prayer from "Moses in Egypt," by Gilmore's band, ode, "Sons of Renowned Sires"; scriptures read by Rev. Dr. Frederic H. Hedge; hymn; oration; prayer, by Rev. Dr. Joseph P. Thompson of New York; hymn; benediction, by Rev. Frederic N. Knapp; voluntary, "Selection from Il Trovatore," by Gilmore's band. The choir was a double quartette, consisting of Mrs. Winslow B. Standish and Miss Olive M. Collingwood, sopranos; Mrs. E. W. Atwood and Miss Lina Rich, contraltos; Joseph L. Brown and Dr. Thomas B. Drew, tenors; Chas. H. Richardson and James M. Atwood, bassos.

In arranging for the celebration, Hon. Edward S. Toby, president of the Pilgrim Society, stated to the committee that he should be necessarily absent during most of the time at the dinner, and I, as vice president, consequently presided in his place. After my opening address, the following gentlemen made speeches: Hon. Edward S. Tobey, Major General O. O. Howard, Hon. Robert C. Winthrop, Hon. Henry Wilson, Hon. George S. Hillard, Hon. John H. Clifford, Rev. Joseph P. Thompson, Hon. Charles S. Bradley, Hon. Marshal P. Wilder, Hon. Nathaniel B. Shurtleff, Hon. T. Sterry Hunt, and Hon. George T. Davis. Mr. Clifford spoke as chairman of the board of overseers of Harvard, Mr. Shurtleff as Mayor of Boston, Mr. Bradley as Chief Justice of the Rhode Island Supreme Court, and Mr. Hunt as President of the Montreal New England Society. Mingled with the speeches, was a poem read by Mr. William Everett. In the evening a brilliant ball was held in Davis Hall.

Hon. Robert Charles Winthrop, son of Thomas Lindall and Elizabeth (Bowdoin) Winthrop was born in Boston, May 12, 1809, and graduated from Harvard in 1828. His father was Lieut. Governor of Massachusetts from 1826 to 1833.

He studied law with Daniel Webster, and was admitted to the Boston bar in 1831. He was a member of the legislature from 1835 to 1840, being speaker of the House of Representatives the last two years. He was a member of Congress from 1840 to 1842, and from 1844 to 1850, serving two years as speaker. When Daniel Webster left the Senate to become secretary of state in 1850, he was appointed to fill out his term. In 1851 he was the Whig candidate for Governor, and though receiving a plurality vote, failed to receive a majority, as then required by the law. The election then went to the legislature, and George S. Boutwell was chosen. He published the "Life and Letters of Gov. John Winthrop," and delivered many speeches and orations, which have been published in a book form, the most notable of which were his Pilgrim oration of Plymouth in 1870, and his oration on the Anniversary of the surrender of Cornwallis in 1881. He died in Boston, November 16, 1894.

Rev. Joseph Parrish Thompson was born in Philadelphia, August 7, 1819, and graduated at Yale in 1838. He became pastor of the Chapel street church in New Haven in 1840, and from 1845 to 1872 was pastor of the Broadway Tabernacle in New York. He was a prolific writer, and in 1856 received from Harvard the Degree of Doctor of Divinity, and died in Berlin, Sept. 21, 1879.

Major General Oliver Otis Howard was born in Leeds, Me., Nov. 8, 1830, and graduated at Bowdoin in 1850, and at West Point in 1854. In 1861 he was Colonel of a Maine Regiment, and commanded a brigade at Bull Run. He was made a Brigadier General in 1862, and lost his right arm at Fair Oaks. After the battle of Antietam he commanded a division, and was made Major General of volunteers Nov. 29, 1862. On the 27th of July, 1864, he took command of the army of the Tennessee, and commanded the right wing of Sherman's army in his march to the sea. He was appointed brigadier general on Dec. 21, 1864, and brevet major general, March 13, 1865, and is still living.

Thomas Sterry Hunt was born in Norwich, Conn., September 5, 1826, and after studying medicine was in 1845, a student in chemistry with Prof. Benjamin Silliman, Jr., in New Haven, and later his assistant in the Yale laboratory.

In 1847 he was made chemist and mineralogist to the geological survey of Canada, and held that position until his resignation in 1872. After retiring from his position in Canada, he succeeded Prof. Wm. B. Rogers in the chair of geology in the Massachusetts Institute of Technology. He published in 1874 a volume containing his collected scientific essays, and received from Harvard the honorary degree of LL. D., and of Sc. D. from the Universities of Montreal and Quebec. He was made a fellow of the Royal Society of London in 1859, and of the National Academy of the United States in 1873, receiving also an appointment as officer in the French order of the legion of honor. He died in New York, Feb. 12, 1892.

Hon. Henry Wilson was born in Farmington, N. H., Feb. 16, 1812. In 1829 he was authorized by the New Hampshire legislature to change his original name of Jones Colbath to that by which he was known through his public life. From 1822 to 1833 he was employed by a farmer in his native town, during which time he received only twelve months' schooling. About 1833 he walked from Farmington to Natick, Mass., where he worked as shoemaker two years, and then returning to New Hampshire attended the academies at Stafford, Wolfeboro and Concord. In 1838 he returned to Natick and continuing shoemaking, entered politics in 1840, as a stump speaker in behalf of Harrison for President. He was three years a representative from Natick, and a state senator in 1850 and 1851, and president of the senate. He was a member of the state constitutional convention in 1853, and in 1855 was chosen U. S. Senator, and by re-election continued in that office until he was chosen vice-president of the United States in 1872, and died in Washington, Nov. 22, 1875.

George Stillman Hillard was born in Machias, Me., Sept 22, 1808, and graduated at Harvard in 1828. He was admitted to the bar in Boston in 1833, and mingled with his professional labors literary pursuits. He was United States District Attorney from 1867 to 1870, and died in Boston, January 21, 1879.

Dr. Nathaniel Bradstreet Shurtleff was born in Boston, June 29, 1810, and graduated at Harvard in 1831. His father born in Carver, Mass., studied medicine with Dr. James

Thacher of Plymouth, and settled in Boston.   Dr. Nathaniel Bradstreet of Newburyport was a fellow student, and for
him Dr. Benjamin Shurtleff named his son.   The son abandoned practice and devoted himself to historic pursuits.   He
was a prolific writer, and one of his most important works
was a topographical History of Boston.   He also edited the
publication of the Plymouth Colony and Massachusetts Records, and was mayor of Boston in 1768-'69-'70.   He died in
Boston, October 17, 1874.

The Pilgrim Society again celebrated the anniversary of the
Landing, on Wednesday the 21st of December, 1880.   No attempt at display was made, and the observance was largely a
domestic one.   A simple service was held in the First Church,
followed by a dinner in Davis Hall, furnished by George E.
Patterson of Boston.

Thomas Russell, president of the Society, presided, and
speeches were made by Hon. John D. Long, Hon. Alexander
H. Rice, Hon. Thomas D. Eliot, Rev. Dr. McKensie, General
Armstrong of Hampton College, President Drehan of Roanoke College, and Rev. Dr. Geo. W. Briggs.   The next celebration held on Monday, December 21, 1885, was of the same
character.   A service was held in the church, and a dinner in
Davis Hall, at which Thomas Russell, President of the Society
presided.   The other speakers were: Rev. Dr. George E.
Ellis, James Russell Lowell, Rev. Dr. Henry M. Dexter, Hon.
Charles L. Woodbury, Hon. Oliver Ames, Rev. Dr. J. T. Duryea, Rev. Adoniram J. Gordon, Rev. Dr. Brooke Hereford,
Justin Winsor and Rev. Dr. A. A. Miner.

At a meeting of the trustees of the Pilgrim Society held
March 23, 1889, a committee of twelve was appointed to
make arrangements for a celebration of the completion of the
National Monument on the first of August.   The committee
consisted of John D. Long, President of the Society, and Wm.
T. Davis, Wm. S. Danforth, Charles G. Davis, Wm. H. Nelson, James D. Thurber, Charles C. Doten, James B. Brewster
Arthur Lord, Daniel E. Damon, Wm. Hedge and Winslow
Warren.   At a town meeting held April 2, the sum of $1,500
was appropriated in aid of the celebration, and it was voted
that the Board of selectmen be joined to the committee of
arrangements in the expenditure of the money.   As Mr. Nel-

son and myself were already members of the committee, the other three members of the board, Everett F. Sherman, Leavitt T. Robbins and Alonzo Warren were added. At a meeting of the committee it was voted as the president would be unable to attend its meetings, that Wm. T. Davis be appointed vice chairman. At a subsequent meeting it was voted that the celebration consist of a procession and dinner and ball. Hon. W. C. P. Breckinridge of Lexington, Kentucky, was invited to deliver an oration, and John Boyle O'Reilly of Boston to deliver a poem, and both accepted. Myron W. Whitney was also invited to be a guest of the Society, and to sing the ode of Mrs. Heman's. Col. Wm. P. Stoddard was appointed Chief Marshal who subsequently appointed Major George B. Russell, U. S. A., chief of staff, and Dr. James B. Brewster, Capt. Andrew H. Russell, U. S. A., William H. Drew, Dr. Warren Peirce, Wm. Hedge, Albert E. Davis and Elmer E. Sherman, marshals of divisions. Other marshals appointed were, George L. Osgood, George Russell Briggs, Dr. H. F. Copeland, Arthur Braman, H. L. Hayden, S. L. Parks, Isaac S. Brewster, Dr. Edgar D. Hill, Henry A. Atwood, Wm. F. Atwood, Capt. James L. Hall, Charles S. Davis, Col. Benjamin S. Lovell, Capt. James D. Thurber, D. Clifton Freeman, Charles A. Strong, Frank H. Holmes, Henry H. Fowler, Edward Manter, Joseph T. Collingwood, John W. Herrick and C. E. Small.

Other committees were appointed consisting of a committee on transportation, committee on decorations, committee on fireworks, committee on the dinner, committee of reception and committee on the ball, the last consisting of Wm. Hedge, George B. Russell, Howland Davis, Thomas Russell, Richard H. Morgan, Benjamin M. Watson, Jr., Charles S. Davis, Edwin S. Damon, Alfred S. Burbank, Wm. B. Thurber, Edward S. Emery, Henry H. Fowler, Joseph T. Collingwood, James Mullins, George R. Briggs, Harold Whiting and Charles B. Stoddard. Invitations were sent to the various Plymouth organizations of Masons, Odd Fellows, Standish Guards, Good Fellows, Pilgrim Fathers, Iron Hall, Good Templars, Royal Arcanum and the Fire Department, and liberal appropriations were made by the committee to enable them to entertain guests. The Independent Corps of Cadets of Boston and Battery A of Boston were invited to participate in the parade and accepted.   A contract was made with A. Erickson of Boston for a tent two hundred and fifty feet long and eighty feet wide, which was pitched in the meadow between the house of Mrs. J. R. Lothrop and Water street, and arrangements were made with Harvey Blunt of Boston and David H. Maynard of Plymouth to furnish the dinner, and also the supper for the ball.   It is unnecessary to mention the various associations and guests invited by the committee, but, including Masonic bodies, Odd Fellows, Military Companies and associations and individuals, they numbered about one hundred and fifty.   It was arranged that a salute should be fired by Battery A at six o'clock a. m., and that at 9.30 a. m. the M. W. Grand Lodge should dedicate the monument, and that at 11 o'clock the procession should proceed through Court, Allerton, Cushman, Court, North, Water, Leyden, Market, Summer, High, Russell, Court, Brewster, Water, North, Main, Market, Pleasant, South Sandwich and Water, streets to the tent.   From three to five o'clock it was arranged to have concerts in Shirley Square by the Lynn Cadet Band, on Training Green by the Plymouth Rock Band, on Cole's Hill by the Silver Fife and Drum Corps, and on the Samoset lawn by Lindall's band. The fireworks were planned for Monument hill, an electric illumination of the Monument, and a concert in Shirley Square from nine to ten by the Plymouth Band.   With a ball in the Armory with music furnished by the Germania Band of Boston, seventeen pieces, the festivities were to close.

The order of the procession is too long to include in this narrative.   It is sufficient to say that it included three companies of Infantry, Battery A, twelve bands, five Grand Army Posts, delegations from ten societies and associations, five commanderies of Masons, ten Masonic Lodges, two Encampments of Odd Fellows, six lodges of Odd Fellows, and three Fire Departments.   It was planned that the seventh division of the procession, composed of five hundred school children, should be seated on the slope of Cole's Hill, and join in singing appropriate hymns, while the procession passed.

The dinner tent holding two thousand, was full to the last seat.   Governor John D. Long, the president of the Pilgrim

Society, had on his right Lieut. Governor Brackett, Adjt. General Samuel Dalton, John Boyle O'Reilly, Grand Master Henry Endicott, Hon. Wm. Cogswell, Hon. Frederic T. Greenhalge, Hon. Charles S. Randall, Hon. Wm. G. Russell, Hon. Wirt Dexter, Wm. T. Davis and Myron W. Whitney, Esq., and on his left, Hon. W. C. P. Breckinridge, Hon. Geo. F. Hoar, Hon. Henry Cabot Lodge, Hon. John W. Candler, Hon. Elijah A. Morse, Hon. Henry B. Pierce, Hon. Wm. W. Crapo, Roland Mather, Esq., Rev. Joseph H. Twichell of Hartford, Hon. William E. Barrett and Hon. Charles F. Choate. Among others seated on the platform were the Mayor of Boston, the Mayor of Brockton, the chairmen of the Boards of Selectmen of Plymouth, Kingston, Duxbury and Plympton, Rev. Samuel Hopkins Emery of Taunton, Hon. Stephen Salisbury of Worcester, Hon. John Winslow of Brooklyn, Justin Winsor, Abner C. Goodell, Samuel C. Cobb, Hon. John E. Russell, Hon. Albert Mason, Prof. Lemuel Stephens, Prof. E. N. Horsford, Lt. Col. Thomas F. Edmunds, Major Dexter H. Follett, Lt. Frederick I. Clayton, Francis Bartlett, Esq., and Rev. Charles P. Lombard. A blessing was asked by Mr. Lombard, and after an opening address by Hon. John D. Long, President of the Pilgrim Society, the oration by Mr. Breckinridge, and the poem by John Boyle O'Reilly followed. After the poem an address of welcome was made by myself, which was followed by speeches by Lt. Gov. J. Q. A. Brackett, Hon. George F. Hoar, Hon. Henry Cabot Lodge, Hon. Wm. Cogswell, Hon Elijah A. Morse, Hon. Frederick T. Greenhalge, and by the singing of "Breaking Waves Dashed High" by Myron W. Whitney, Esq., and by a musical selection rendered by the Temple Quartette Club of Boston. The decorations along the route of the procession exceeded in appropriateness and good taste any ever before seen in Plymouth, and the five arches on Court, North, Leyden, Summer and Pleasant streets were pronounced by competent critics as models in proportion and adornment. The press was represented on the occasion by two members from Plymouth, one from Brockton, one from Burlington, Vt., one from Troy, ten from Boston, five from New York, and by the Associated Press. The number of visitors was estimated at fifteen thousand, and as compared with the celebrations of

1853 and 1859, was from three to five thousand larger than that at either.

In writing chapters of Plymouth memories it seems unnecessary to include a celebration as recent as that in 1895, but a complete record of the observances conducted by the Pilgrim Society may aid future historic explorers and writers.   In the above year the Society held its celebration on the 21st of December.   Arthur Lord was then President of the Society, and he and Wm. T. Davis, James D. Thurber, Wm. S. Danforth, Charles C. Doten, Charles B. Stoddard and Gideon F. Holmes, were appointed a committee of arrangements. Col. Wm. P. Stoddard was appointed Chief Marshal, with Winslow B. Standish and Wm. Hedge as aids, and a committee on the ball was appointed, consisting of Edgar D. Hill, Charles A. Strong, James Spooner, Henry J. W. Drew, Alfred S. Burbank, W. C. Butler, A. E. Lewis and E. A. Dunton.   Hon. Geo. F. Hoar and Richard Henry Stoddard, who had been invited to deliver respectively an oration and poem, accepted their invitations.   The Society met at Pilgrim Hall, and with the orator and poet and invited guests proceeded to the Armory, where exercises were held, consisting of an overture by the Plymouth Band, anthem by the Plymouth Musical Club, prayer by Rev. Charles P. Lombard, ode, "Sons of Renowned Sires," poem by Richard Henry Stoddard, ode, "Breaking Waves Dashed High," sung by Myron W. Whitney, oration by Hon. Geo. F. Hoar, ode, "The Pilgrim Fathers Where are They," benediction by Rev. Ernest W. Shurtleff.

The trustees of the Society, with the chief marshal and aids and members of committees and guests dined at the Samoset House, where speeches were made by Lt. Gov. Roger Wolcott, Hon. Winslow Warren, Hon. Samuel R. Thayer, and Hon. Robert S. Rantoul, and the dinner closed with a song sung by Myron W. Whitney.

In addition to the above the anniversary of the Landing was celebrated by the Plymouth Fire Department, Dec. 21, 1886, by a procession, dinner and a ball, at which the Boston Cadet band furnished the music.   John C. Cave and Henry Harlow were chairman and secretary of the committee of arrangements, and I was invited to preside.   After my address speeches were made by Chas. H. Howland, Chas. G. Davis, Rev. F. N. Knapp, Rev. W. P. Burnell, Daniel E. Damon, Albert E. Davis, Wm. H. Nelson, James Morton, John C. Ross, Edward B. Atwood.   Other celebrations not already mentioned in these memories have been the following, of which I have space for only superficial notices.   The Fourth of July, 1825, was celebrated by the citizens of Plymouth. Hon. Wm. Davis presided, assisted by Joseph Thomas, Coomer Weston, Pelham W. Warren, Bridgham Russell, Joseph Allen, and Samuel Doten, vice presidents, and an oration was delivered in the First Church by Wm. Thomas, Esq., of Plymouth.   In 1826 the Fourth of July was again celebrated. Hon. John Thomas of Kingston presided, and an oration was delivered by Hon. Charles Henry Warren of New Bedford, a native of Plymouth.   A ball in Pilgrim Hall closed the observance of the day.   The Fourth of July, 1828, was again celebrated by citizens, with Hon. Nathaniel M. Davis president of the day, assisted by Nathan Hayward, Ezra Finney, Abraham Jackson, Isaac L. Hedge, James G. Gleason of Plymouth and Jonathan Parker of Plympton.   Hon. John A. Shaw of Bridgewater delivered an oration, and a dinner and ball were held in Pilgrim Hall.   In 1832 Washington's birthday was celebrated with an oration by Hon. Solomon Lincoln of Hingham.   Capt. Samuel Doten was chief marshal, and Hon. Isaac L. Hedge was president of the day, assisted by Jacob H. Loud, Nathaniel Wood, Thos. Paty and John Bartlett as vice presidents.   In 1865, Independence day was celebrated by the citizens, the features of the celebration being morning salutes, the ringing of bells, and a march of the ancient and horribles, followed by a procession, and an oration by Rev. George H. Hepworth of Boston.   Hon. Jacob H. Loud presided, and Thomas Loring was chief marshal, assisted by John T. Stoddard and Albert Hedge as aids, and Barnabas Hedge, George G. Dyer, Thomas Pierce, Warren Macomber, Frederic W. Robbins, Charles Burton, George L. Baxter, B. H. Holmes, T. B. Atwood, Aaron Cornish, Gustavus D. Bates and Nathaniel C. Lanman, marshals.   Among the features of the procession were the Plymouth Lodge of Masons, the Mayflower Lodge of Odd Fellows, a car of liberty, and the army and navy, represented by Ignatius Pierce,

Jr., M. A. Diaz, Jr., Wm. W. Brewster and Herbert Morissey, and five hundred public school scholars. The services were held on the grounds of the Samoset House, and at their close the scholars enjoyed a collation at Goddard's grove, the general public in Samoset house orchard, the Odd Fellows at Pilgrim Hall, and the Masons at the Winslow House on Winslow street.

On the 9th of July, 1869, the dedication of the Soldiers' monument on Training Green, was celebrated under the direction of the Soldiers' Monument Association. As President of the Association I presided at the ceremonies. A large tent was erected around and over the monument, and there after my own address, an oration was delivered by Hon. Joshua L. Chamberlain of Maine. Hon. John Morissey was chief marshal, assisted by Albert Mason and Charles H. Drew as aids, and the following marshals of divisions, Charles Raymond, James D. Thurber, Charles B. Stoddard, Alvin Finney, Henry W. Loring, Thomas B. Atwood, assisted by Wm. E. Barnes, Elkanah C. Finney, Stephen C. Drew, B. A. Hathaway, George Finney, Charles Mason, J. Frank Churchill, A. Merritt Shaw, Robert B. Churchill and Alexander Atwood. Among the invited guests present were: Governor Claflin of Massachusetts, Governor Stearns of New Hampshire, Lt. Gov. Tucker of Massachusetts, Hon. James Buffington, Thos. Russell, General Benham and members of the executive council. Among the associations were Collingwood Post G. A. R., the McPherson Post, the Old Colony Encampment of K. T., the Samoset Chapter of Masons, the Mayflower Lodge of Odd Fellows, the Bay State Lodge of Lynn, the Palestine Encampment of Lynn, and the Fire Department. The Standish Guards and the Bay State Guards of Carver performed escort, and the music was furnished by the North Bridgewater Band, the Weymouth Band, the Abington Band, the Lynn Band, and the Plymouth Band.

The reception at Plymouth of Louis Kossuth, May 12, 1852, though not a celebration, may properly be recorded here. The committee of arrangements were Capt. John Russell, Andrew L. Russell, E. C. Sherman and Moses Bates, and Mr. Bates presided with John D. Churchill, chief marshal. At a dinner at the Samoset House, after the address made by Kossuth in the First Church, speeches were made by Mr. Bates, Gov. George S. Boutwell, Stephen H. Phillips, and by M. Pulzzly and M. Kocielski.

There was a celebration in 1849, which though not a public one, I may be permitted to include in my narrative. A party of gentlemen, all of whom were special friends of Daniel Webster, came to Plymouth and dined at the Samoset on the anniversary of the departure of the Pilgrims from Old Plymouth. The departure occurred on the 16th of September, but as that day in 1849 fell on Sunday, Monday was the day of the dinner. The dinner was proposed by Mr. Webster, and he presided. The occasion was a memorable one, including among its guests leading professional and business men of Boston, New York, Providence and New Bedford. At that time I was living in Boston, and through the kindness of my uncle, Chas. Henry Warren, who made up the party, I attended the dinner, the youngest man at the table, and now the only one living. Such men as Josiah Quincy, Rufus Choate, Edward Everett, John H. Clifford, George S. Hillard, Benjamin R. Curtis, Sidney Bartlett and Nathan Appleton were there renewing allegiance to him from whom some had been alienated by his patriotic refusal to leave the cabinet of John Tyler, and others by his reluctant support of the nomination of Zachary Taylor for the presidency. Mr. Webster's speech was eloquent and pathetic, feeling as he did, with the increasing infirmities of age, that it might be the last time he should address those who had put their trust in him, and on whom he had leaned for support. It was my privilege to hear Mr. Webster probably more times than any man now living, and of the thirteen speeches I have heard from his lips, this was the most tender and eloquent. Nathaniel P. Willis, in a letter to his journal in New York said in describing it, that, "it was the most beautiful example of manly pathos of which language and looks could be capable. No one who heard it could doubt the existence of a deep well of tears under that lofty temple of intellect and power."

Before closing the account of celebrations I ought to say that the old Standish Guards, which was organized in 1818, made its first public parade as an escort to the procession on the 22d of December in the above year. They continued to perform escort duty at the Pilgrim celebrations until they were disbanded in 1883.   After the change was made in 1870 of the celebrations from the 22d to the 21st of December, the company continued its celebration, not of the anniversary of the Landing, but of the anniversary of the company's first public parade.   From 1883 to 1888, there was no military company in Plymouth, but in the latter year the present company was chartered, not as Co. B, third Regiment, like the old company, but as Co. D, 5th Regiment, having no more connection with the old Standish Guards than the present Old Colony Club on Court street has with the Old Colony Club which was organized in 1768, and went out of existence at the beginning of the Revolution.   There seems, therefore, to be no reason why the present company should keep up the observance of a day with which it has no connection, as the 22d of December is neither the anniversary of the landing, nor of its first public parade, which occurred in 1888, and not in 1818.

CHAPTER XXXVIII.

In my memories of the Civil War I shall confine myself as closely as possible to events which I saw, and in an humble way, a part of which I was. When on the 18th of April, 1861, the train bearing the Sixth Massachusetts Regiment to Washington, halted at the Trenton station in New Jersey, the Governor of that state walking in a thoughtful mood up and down the platform, was asked by a friend, what he was thinking about. He replied, "I am thinking about that damned little state of Massachusetts. Here she is two days after the call for troops, with seven states between her and Washington, half way to that city with a full regiment armed and equipped, bearing the first relief to our beleagued capital. How could she do it?" My answer to the Governor's question is that Massachusetts had an executive who knew how to do things, and a people accustomed to take the initiative in important emergencies. Governor John A. Andrew was inaugurated on the 5th of January, 1861, and before he slept that night he despatched confidential messages to the Governors of the other New England states urging preparations for the crisis, which he believed to be impending. Realizing also that the 8th of January would be the anniversary of Andrew Jackson's victory in the battle of New Orleans, though Massachusetts had not been in the habit of celebrating that day, he seized the opportunity to arouse the spirit of patriotism among the people and ordered a hundred guns to be fired on the noon of the 8th on Boston Common, and national salutes to be fired in Charlestown, Lexington, Concord, Waltham, Roxbury, Marblehead, Newburyport, Salem, Groton, Lynn, Worcester, Greenfield, Northampton, Fall River and Lowell. The guns fired on that day were the first guns of the war, and, as a note of defiance to South Carolina, which had voted itself out of the Union, they sent a thrill through every loyal heart, and turned the minds of the people into channels to be gradually familiarized with thoughts of war. On the 16th of January, eleven days after the inauguration, he directed the promulgation of an order requiring the commanders of all volunteer militia companies to take immediate steps to fill their ranks with men ready to respond to the call of the commander-in-chief, discharging any who were not so ready, and supplying their places with those who were.   At a later date the Governor by contracts afterwards confirmed by the legislature, ordered six thousand yards of cloth, a yard and a half wide at $1.37 per yard, two thousand military overcoats at $2.15 each, two thousand knapsacks of the army pattern at $1.88 each, one thousand pairs of blankets at $3.75 a pair, two thousand haversacks at 75 cents each, coat buttons costing $740, two hundred thousand ball cartridges at $14 a thousand, and three hundred thousand percussion caps.   The legislature adjourned on the 11th of April, having appropriated one hundred thousand dollars as an emergency fund, twenty-five thousand dollars for overcoats and equipage, and having so far amended the existing militia law which limited the active militia to five thousand men, as to give the Governor authority to organize as many companies and regiments as the public exigency might require.   Such, your Excellency, the Governor of New Jersey, was the condition of Massachusetts, when the first call for troops was made on the 15th of April, and thus is your question answered.   Massachusetts was ready with her toe on the line when the call to arms was sounded.

On the 15th of April, Company B, 3rd Regiment, the Standish Guards of Plymouth, was without a captain.   Charles C. Doten, 1st Lieutenant in command, was at that time in charge of the telegraph office, in the rooms now occupied by Mr. Loring's watchmaker's-shop on Main street.   In the early evening of that day he received a despatch from David W. Wardrop of New Bedford, Colonel of the Third Regiment, ordering him to report with his company to him on Boston Common the next forenoon.   A messenger bearing an official order reached Plymouth during the night.   The news of the order spread like the wind through every street, and into every house and home.   The excitement was intense.   Every store was vacated by its loungers, every meeting was dissolved, and every family circle gathered around the evening lamp was broken up, and the armory of the Guards in Union Building on the corner of Main and Middle streets, became at once the meeting place of the citizens. One after another of the members of the company who were accessible, reported himself, every man ready to respond to the call. As chairman of the Board of Selectmen I gave the men assurances, which were reinforced by prominent citizens, that their families would be provided for during their absence, and ready hands were offered to take up and finish any work which they might leave uncompleted. The call was for three months' service, and at nine o'clock the next morning nineteen members of the Company marched to the station, escorted by a large procession of citizens, and embarked for Boston. With the addition of two members joining at Abington, and two others joining in Boston, the company was quartered that night in the hall over the Old Colony Railroad station, and Wednesday morning received nineteen recruits from Plymouth. In the afternoon of that day the Company embarked on the steamer S. R. Spaulding, which hauled into the stream, and anchored for the night. After the steamer had left the wharf, seventeen additional recruits reached Boston, and quartering in Faneuil Hall, joined their comrades aboard ship on Thursday morning. On Thursday the 18th, the steamer sailed for Fortress Monroe with sixty men in the ranks of the company.

I do not propose at this stage of my memories to follow the Plymouth soldiers to the front, but shall at a later point in my narrative include a list of their names, and as far as possible an account of their services in the field. While in Boston with the Plymouth Company, I offered to the Governor on Wednesday in behalf of the Plymouth bank, of which I was President, the use of twenty thousand dollars as a contribution to an emergency fund to meet expenditures which must at once be made. I have every reason to believe that this was the first contribution made by the banks of Massachusetts to a fund, which when an extra session of the legislature convened on the 14th of May, had reached the sum of thirty-six hundred thousand dollars. This fund was necessary, as when the extra session met the amount of the emergency fund provided for at the regular session, had been exceeded by expenditures and liabilities by the sum of four hundred and fifty thousand dollars. On my return home the Selectmen called an informal meeting of the citizens to meet on the afternoon of Saturday the 20th to consider ways and means to provide for the families of the soldiers.   At that meeting it was voted, "That the Selectmen be requested to apply and distribute at their discretion a sum not exceeding $2,000 towards the assistance of those families who by the sudden departure of the troops are left in need of pecuniary aid—such sum to be raised in the name of the town, or in such other way as the Selectmen shall deem expedient."

On Wednesday, April 24th, I was in Philadelphia, and after concluding the business which had called me there, I made up my mind that if possible I would run on to Washington. General Butler had left Philadelphia on Saturday the 20th, and at Perryville on the north bank of the Susquehanna River, had with the 8th Massachusetts Regiment embarked on board the ferry boat Maryland for Annapolis, as the railroad between the river and Baltimore had been obstructed, and the bridges burned.   The 7th New York Regiment, at the same time took the steamer Boston at Philadelphia and started for Annapolis by the way of the Delaware river and the sea.   Going to the Philadelphia, Wilmington and Baltimore station in Broad street, I asked Mr. Felton, the President of the road, if it were possible to reach Washington.   He told me that there was no communication by rail or wire with any point south of the Susquehanna, and that nothing was known of the movements of the Maryland since she left Perryville on the previous Saturday.   He said that Major T. W. Sherman's Battery was at Elkton on the line of the road awaiting an opportunity to go to Washington, and that when the Maryland returned from Annapolis he should despatch a train, with the view of following in the wake of Gen. Butler.   After waiting in his office an hour or two, he told me that the boat had arrived, and that he should start a train for Perryville at four o'clock.   At that hour the train started, made up of a single passenger car, a combination car, and a platform car, carrying two guns protected by a portholed sheet iron casemate.   There were only three or four on board, and not wishing to be discommoded by impedimenta on a somewhat doubtful excursion, I left my valise at the hotel.   Arriving at Perryville in the early evening with the Battery which we found waiting at Elkton, we embarked on the Maryland for the trip down the Susquehanna River and Chespeake Bay outside of Baltimore to Annapolis, which we reached about midnight. On our way we passed over the anchorage ground where Francis Scott Key, while a prisoner on board of a British man of war in the war of 1812, witnessed the bombardment of Fort McHenry, and wrote the "Star Spangled Banner." As we sailed over the spot the Battery men gathered on deck and sang the song with the very scene in view which had original-ly inspired it. Lying at the entrance of Annapolis harbor until we had communicated by rockets with the town, we fin-ally reached the wharf, passing the frigate Constitution on the way, which with sails bent by members of the Marblehead companies in the eighth regiment was about to be taken for safety to New York, manned with the Marblehead men. At Annapolis we learned that when General Butler arrived with the 8th Massachusetts, the rebels had torn up the track of the branch road connecting Annapolis with the Baltimore and Washington railroad, and disabled the locomotives. But the General was equal to the emergency, and with mechanics in his command he relaid the track, with machinists also in the ranks he repaired the locomotives, and also with his Marble-head soldiers he bent sails on the Constitution. The day be-fore he had marched on to the junction, and was then with the 7th New York artillery at the junction, or in Washington.

We arrived in Washington about daylight on Thursday morning, the 25th, and while registering my name at Wil-lard's hotel, I heard the cry of fire, and going out found a fire well started in a building on the avenue next to the hotel. The efforts of the firemen seemed to be unavailing, with lad-ders too short, and no means of reaching the roof of the build-ing. Directly cheers and the rattle of wheels were heard up the avenue, and the Ellsworth Zouaves appeared on the scene. They were quartered in the Capitol, and hearing the alarm had jumped out of the windows, and breaking open an unused en-gine house in which was stored an old engine, they dragged the machine down the avenue at a double quick, and were at once the chief actors in the scene. They were nearly all New York firemen, and hence were called the Fire Zouaves, and shinning up the water spouts they were soon on the roof, where I saw two of them hang a comrade by his legs over the eaves so that he could reach the hose held by a ladderman, and be pulled up with it to the flat roof above. What was mere play for them was done in the presence of a cheering crowd, and the fire was soon extinguished.

There were then four Regiments in Washington, the Sixth Massachusetts, the Ellsworth Fire Zouaves, the Seventh Regiment of New York and the First Rhode Island commanded by Colonel Ambrose E. Burnside. The two first were in the capitol, the Rhode Island Regiment was quartered in one of the public buildings, and the Seventh Regiment was encamped. All of these Regiments, except the 6th Massachusetts, had reached Annapolis by the sea, and the 8th Massachusetts Regiment was still encamped between Annapolis Junction and Washington. I called on Col. Jones of the Sixth, and visited the quarters of the other regiments. The tale told by Col. Jones of his passage through Baltimore, and his reception in Washington, was pathetic, indeed, and aroused a feeling of pride in my state, which I had never so completed experienced before. This feeling was intensified by the tales told me by men of Washington who with tears in their eyes described the march up the avenue of the regiment on the nineteenth, and the sudden transformation from despair to hope, from despondency to joy, from the fear of the capture of the city to an assurance of its safety, the tale always ending with the exclamation, "God Bless old Massachusetts." Wherever it was known, whence and how I came to Washington, I found everything wide open. In the evening I returned to Annapolis, and so on to Philadelphia, and reached home on Saturday.

After my return the Selectmen issued a warrant for a town meeting to be held on the 11th of May to further provide for soldiers' families, and to appropriate money for uniforms and equipments. At that meeting it was voted to confirm the vote passed at the informal meeting on the 20th of April, and in addition it was voted to pay six dollars per month to each soldier with a family, who shall enlist for the war, and four dollars per month to each unmarried soldier during the term of one year from the first of May. It was also voted to appropriate $1,500 for equipping volunteers for three years'

service, who might be citizens of Plymouth. At the special
session of the legislature convened on the 14th of May, the
state adopted the monthly pay to the soldiers, and it became
henceforth what was called state aid. Before the 6th of May
Samuel H. Doten had been authorized to recruit a company
for three years' service, and had promptly enrolled sixty-seven
men, including himself, whose enlistment papers bore the
above date. By authority of the Selectmen, acting under the
vote of the town, passed on the 11th of May, the ladies of
the town at once bought materials, and in Leyden Hall, met
daily for the purpose of making uniforms. The company was
equipped at an expense of $1,025.49, and on the 18th of May
left for Boston. They marched directly to the State House,
where they were drawn up in Mt. Vernon street some hours
awaiting acceptance, and a supply of muskets and equipments,
including overcoats, blankets, knapsacks, and haversacks. The
acceptance of the company was delayed by the interference of
Hon. Henry Wilson, who had arrived that morning from
Washington, and was urging upon the Governor a stoppage
of enlistments. When I went to the Governor's room to report the arrival of the company, I met Mr. Wilson at the door,
and he said, "Davis, carry your company home, we have got
all the men we want, and more, too;" but notwithstanding
he was chairman of the committee on Military Affairs on the
part of the United States Senate, Governor Andrew disregarded his opinion, and finally in due form accepted the company and ordered the necessary arms and equipments. On
the 1st of January, 1861, the state owned ten thousand ser-
viceable muskets and twenty-five hundred Springfield rifles,
and after ineffectual efforts of myself and Capt. Doten, to secure the rifles, the company was obliged to take up with the
inferior arms. On that afternoon, the 18th of May, the company went on board the steamer Cambridge, and sailed for
Fortress Monroe, where it was attached to the Third Regiment
during that Regiment's three months' service.

After the departure of the Standish Guards, Plymouth was
left without a military company, and to meet any possible
emergency it was thought advisable to organize a Home
Guard. Its ranks were at once filled, and meetings were held
for drill in Davis Hall, which continued for several months.

Nathaniel Brown, who in earlier days was skilled as a drill master in the volunteer militia, was chosen captain, and I held the position of 1st Lieutenant.   As chairman of the Board of Selectmen I urged the formation of the company, believing that it would serve as a preparatory school for military instruction, which would in due time develop a military spirit, and promote enlistments.   Such proved to be the effect of the organization as of those who were at various times its members, nearly all joined the army.

At the time of which I am speaking wage earners in Plymouth found little to do, and the monthly pay to soldiers' families was proving inadequate to meet their necessities.   The wives and mothers of the soldiers were anxious to add to their means of support if work could be furnished them.   In order to do what I could to help them I made arrangements with a clothing house in Boston to send me such quantities of cut out clothing as they were able, which was eagerly taken and made up, and sent back to Boston.   For some weeks my house looked like a clothing store, with cases packing and unpacking, and applicants for work coming and going with bundles of garments either cut out or made up.

In the last week of May, Governor Andrew asked me to visit the Massachusetts soldiers at their various camps, and report to him in writing concerning their condition and needs, and any complaints they might make of their treatment in the service.   These troops consisted of the 3rd, 4th, 6th and 8th Massachusetts Regiments, already referred to, to which the 5th Regiment, Cook's Battery and the Third Battalion of Rifles had been added.

On the 4th of March, 1861, the day of the inauguration of President Lincoln, the government was without money and without credit.   Howell Cobb of Georgia, secretary of the treasury, under Buchanan, had before resigning looted the treasury, and placing about six millions where it could be used by the projected Confederacy, had left the government chest with not enough money to pay for a single day's supply of stationery.   John B. Floyd of Virginia, secretary of war, had before resigning, disarmed as far as possible the free states, transferring from the arsenals at Springfield, Mass., and Watervliet, New York, to arsenals in the slave states, one hundred and fifteen' thousand arms, and a large amount of cannon, mortars, balls, powder and shells.   Isaac Toucey of Connecticut, secretary of the navy, a northern man with southern principles, had performed his part of the great conspiracy, by so dispersing the national war vessels as to render them ineffective in the hands of the government.   Of a fleet of ninety vessels, carrying 2,415 guns, five were sent to the East Indies; three to Brazil; seven to the Pacific; three to the Mediterranean, and seven to the coast of Africa, leaving, besides dismantled ships, only two, the steamer Brooklyn, 25 guns, and the storeship Relief, two guns, in northern ports. These men should not have been permitted to escape punishment, not because they became secessionists, but because, while holding office under a government which they had sworn to support, they had been guilty of treason.

The well laid plan of the Confederates was to first weaken the hands of the government while strengthening their own, and then as soon as Sumter fell to seize Harper's Ferry, Washington and Fortress Monroe, the three outposts of the slave states, and to hold them against any forces which the north might be able to raise in time for their recovery.   But they calculated without their host.   They failed to take into account the rapidity with which Yankees act in an emergency, and they believed that before the militia of the north could be prepared to move, their own initiatory steps would have been successfully taken.   They little thought that within five days after the fall of Sumter the state of Massachusetts would occupy Fortress Monroe with two regiments, and Washington with two more.

In the early movements of the government the depleted state of the treasury made it necessary to seek the aid of the states in carrying on the war.   The first attempt to raise money by a loan resulted in bids from bankers running from 85 to 40 for six per cent. bonds, all of which were rejected. In this emergency Massachusetts as usual came to the front, and buying two steamboats, the Cambridge and Pembroke, kept them busy for many weeks in transporting from Boston to Annapolis, Fortress Monroe and Washington soldiers, provisions and camp equipage.   As the rebel batteries on the Potomac rendered for some time a passage to Washington by the river impracticable, at first the trips of these steamers were chiefly confined to Fortress Monroe.   As the Cambridge was to sail on Friday, May 31, for the Fortress, Governor Andrew asked me to go out in her and visit the Massachusetts troops there, and if practicable in the neighborhood of Washington, also, and as already stated, report to him their condition, sanitary and otherwise, with the view of allaying the anxieties of soldiers' families from whom he had received earnest inquiries.   With Hon. John Morissey as a companion, I left Boston at 4 o'clock, Friday afternoon, having also as fellow passengers, General Ebenezer W. Pierce, with the members of his staff, one of whom was Col. Wm. C. Lovering, our present member of Congress.   There were on board twenty carpenters and twenty-nine sappers and miners, and our cargo consisted of lumber, provisions and camp equipage of various kinds.   During the trip I spent much of my time in the pilot house, and having kept a pretty close run of our courses and distances, by a sort of instinct, I guessed from time to time our position.   About eight o'clock on Sunday evening, while smoking my cigar in the pilot house, I said to Capt. Matthews, "You, of course, know your own business better than a landsman, but it seems to me that if you keep on this course much longer you will go ashore."   His smile indicated that he did not think much of a landsman's reckoning, and not long after I went below and turned in.   I was soon awakened by the stoppage of the engine, and directly a steward rapped at my door and said that the steamer was ashore, and the captain wanted all hands on deck.   On reaching the deck I found the propellor churning the water with a full back, without any movement of the vessel.   The two howitzers, which had been on the forward deck, had been moved aft, and all hands were jumping.   It was fortunately a dead calm, with scarcely a ripple on the shore, and after a while we succeeded in backing into deep water.   We had crossed a sand bar just rubbing it, as we went, and had gone onto Hog Island twenty-five or thirty miles north of Cape Charles.   After sending out a boat to sound a passage for recrossing the bar, we reached about daylight the open sea, and were on our way to the Fortress which we reached about ten o'clock Monday forenoon.   Some excuse may be found for the blunder of the captain, in the fact that all the lights from Maryland to Texas, except those at Key West, Tortugas and Rosas Island, had been put out by the rebels, and possibly there may have been a current setting to the north at that time. I believe, however, that in navigation, as in many other matters, there is something in instinct, or what you feel in your bones, as old women say, which should not be disregarded.

When we landed at the Fortress, some of the Plymouth boys were on the wharf expecting boxes from home, and they were, of course, glad to see us. We loaded them down with packages, of which a box of tea was the most prized, as tea was not included in the regular rations. The Fortress is surrounded by a moat, which is crossed by four bridges. Entering the main gate after crossing the bridge leading to it, I found myself in an area about seventy acres in extent, with casemates on the right, barracks on the left, a parade ground of about seven acres in the centre, and in the distance a two story brick building, the headquarters of General B. F. Butler, who was the commander at the post. Calling at once on the General, with whom I was intimate, having been with him in the senate two years before, he received us with courtesy, and invited us to make his house our home as long as we remained at the Fortress. He introduced us to his nephew, Capt. John Butler, and Major Haggerty, members of his staff, and to his military secretary, Major Theodore Winthrop, the last of whom was our constant companion during our visit. He and I seemed to have found our affinities, and I do not think on so short an acquaintance I ever formed so strong an attachment. When at the end of the week we left for Washington, he came down to the steamboat to bid us good-bye, and I little thought that on the next Tuesday, the 10th, he would meet his death on the battlefield of Big Bethel. He was born in New Haven, September 22, 1828, and in 1848 graduated at Yale. He began the practice of law in St. Louis, but removed to New York, where he acquired reputation as the author of Cecil Dreeme, John Brent and other popular books. He went to Washington with the New York seventh regiment, and was selected by General Butler as a member of his staff.

There were thirteen Massachusetts companies in the For-

tress: The Halifax Company, Captain Harlow; Plymouth
Standish Guards, Capt. Charles C. Doten; Plymouth Rock
Guards, Capt. Samuel H. Doten; Freetown Company, Capt.
Marble; Plympton Company, Capt. Perkins; Carver Com-
pany, Capt. McFarlin; New Bedford Company, Capt. Ingraham; Cambridge Company, Capt. Richardson; Sandwich
Company, Capt. Chipman; East Bridgewater Company, Capt.
Leach; Lynn Company, Capt, Chamberlin; Boston Company, Capt. Tyler; and Lowell Company, Capt. Davis.
Of these companies two, the Boston and Lynn, belonged to the 4th Regiment, which was encamped at Newport
News, and the Lowell company was attached to the post, the
remaining ten forming the 3d regiment.   The officers were
quartered in the casemates, and the privates in various buildings, the Cambridge and Halifax companies in the carriage
shop, the Plympton company in a room overhead, the two
Plymouth companies in the forge, which had been floored
over, the East Bridgewater, New Bedford, Sandwich and
Lowell companies in other buildings, and the remainder of the
Massachusetts companies in tents.   The health of the men
was good, only ten being in the hospital, and twenty off duty
all told in the thirteen companies.   I made a note of the rations for eleven days allowed to a company of seventy men,
which included 352½ pounds of pork; 352½ pounds of salt
beef; 45 quarts of beans; 47 quarts of rice, 103½ pounds of
coffee; 155 pounds of sugar; 10½ gallons of vinegar; 12¼
pounds of candles; 41 pounds of soap; 20½ quarts of salt;
352 pounds of fresh beef, a fresh supply of bread every day,
and an allowance of potatoes and chocolate.   The East
Bridgewater Company had not received the new uniforms, the
Plympton Company was without overcoats, and none of the
companies had canteens or rubber blankets, all of which,
however, were supplied later.   On the Hampton camping
ground outside of the Fortress, there were five New York
regiments, commanded by Colonels Duryea, Allen, Townsend,
Carr and McChesny, and General Pierce had his headquarters
in the Hampton female seminary.   The troops I have mentioned, with a few regulars made up the force at and about
the Fortress during my visit, which extended from the third
to the seventh of June.

On Tuesday, June 4th, we went seven miles or more up the bay to Newport News at the mouth of James River, where the 4th Massachusetts Regiment was in camp. We went up in the Steamer "Cataline," a spelling of the name of the old Roman, for which the author may have had the excuse of Major Ben Russell, the editor of the *Columbian Centinel* who, when printing his first number, having no capital S, substituted C, and having begun with that letter, always continued its use. At Newport News there were encamped all of the Fourth Massachusetts Regiment except the two companies, which were at the Fortress, the Steuben Rifles of New York under Col. Bendix, and a Vermont regiment under Col. Washburn, the whole under the command of Colonel Phelps of Vermont. Newport News is a peninsula, bounded on one side by the bay and on the other by James River, and an earthwork had been constructed a half mile long, extending across it. Three hundred and thirty of the Fourth were without tents, and occupying huts made of rails covered with branches. For several days tents had been lying piled up on the wharf at the Fortress, but owing to inefficiency, or red tape, they were not delivered until the sixth of June. The hospital was in charge of F. A. Saville of Quincy, and from the three regiments it had only three inmates. Henry Walker, now a lawyer in Boston and the Commander of the Ancient and Honorable Artillery Company on its late visit to England, was Adjutant of the Fourth, and a friend whom I was glad to see.

On Monday, the tenth of June, the next week after our visit, General Pierce was ordered by General Butler to take five companies of the Fourth, the Steuben Rifles, and Col. Washburn's New York Regiment, and go up the peninsula from twelve to twenty miles and dislodge a force of rebels at Little and Big Bethel. By a sad blunder Col. Washburn's Regiment was fired upon by the Steuben Rifles and eleven men were killed, thus breaking up the expedition in which before its retreat Major Winthrop and three of the Fourth Massachusetts were killed.

The Sloop of War Roanoke under the command of Commodore John Marston, the Steamer Vanderbilt, which had been given to the government by Cornelius Vanderbilt, and the

Revenue Cutter Harriet Lane temporarily attached to the navy, were anchored between the Fortress and Newport News.   Commodore Marston was well known in Plymouth by the Watson family, to whom he was related, and during a winter spent in Philadelphia, where he lived, I was intimate with him and his family.   Both as an old friend and as a Plymouth man, he extended to me every courtesy.   The Harriet Lane was commanded by Capt. John Faunce, a Plymouth man, first cousin of our townsman, Richard W. Bagnell, their mothers having been sisters, and daughters of Ebenezer Sampson.   John was one of the boys, as fearless as Paul Jones or Farragut, and would have enjoyed nothing better than to have a good ripping sea fight for our entertainment. While we were at Newport News he ran across the mouth of the James and banged away at a batttery on Pig Point until he was called off by the Commodore.   He was glad enough to see a Plymouth boy and while I was on his vessel I was given the "freedom of the ship."

General Ebenezer W. Pierce who went to the Fortress with me in the Cambridge and who had command at Big Bethel, had been detailed to command the three months' men in Southern Virginia.   He was born in Freetown, Mass., April 5, 1822, and in the Massachusetts militia, before the war, had occupied various positions from Captain to Brigadier General.   After he was mustered out July 22, 1861, at the expiration of three months' service, he again entered the army and December 31, 1861, he was mustered in as Colonel of the Massachusetts 29th Regiment, serving until his resignation November 8, 1864.   He was an eccentric man but patriotic and brave.   At the battle of White Oak Swamp June 30, 1862, I have been told that when he was ordered to take his regiment into the fight his order was—"by the right flank up the hill; God damn you, forward march."   Within five minutes a ball from a rebel battery took off his right arm at the shoulder.   After the wound had been partially dressed under fire he was left on the field within the rebel lines until night, when he crept to cover and found his way to a union camp. Within thirty days he reported for service again and continued in commission until his resignation November 8, 1864.   He died in Freetown, August 14, 1902.

On Friday, the 7th of June, the despatch boat Mt. Vernon arrived from Washington, and General Butler gave us passes for her return trip that night. The boat, besides her captain, had two river pilots, and as the lights on the Potomac had been extinguished by the rebels we were guided through its tortuous channels entirely by the lead. Besides the bearer of despatches there was on board a guard of ten men of the 71st New York Regiment, and under deck there was a half a ton of powder. All but one of the rebel batteries on the river were passed in the night, and as we approached them we slowed down so as to make little noise and put out all the lights on board. One battery remained to be passed after daylight, but as we rounded a point and brought it in sight we saw the gunboat Powhattan anchored in the stream, having silenced it since the down trip of the despatch boat. The bearer of despatches was one of those fellows which war would be likely to bring to the surface, apparently a German Jew, about twenty-five years of age, bragging of his exploits as secret messenger from Gen. Butler at Annapolis to Gen. Scott in Washington, and distrusted by the guard, who called him the mysterious cuss. Every step he took and every movement he made was carefully watched, lest he might by a match or some other signal inform the batteries of our passage. I learned on a later visit to Washington that he came to grief as a suspected rebel spy.

Arriving at the Navy Yard at Washington about ten o'clock, after breakfast at the hotel we visited the 5th Massachusetts Regiment, of which my friend, George H. Brastow was Major. They were encamped near Alexandria, and with the 5th Pennsylvania, 1st Michigan and the Ellsworth Zouaves formed the Union outpost near Shooter's Hill, between Alexandria and the Fairfax seminary. The next day, Sunday, I went out to the Relay House at the junction of the Harper's Ferry and the Baltimore and Washington Railroads, where were encamped the 6th and 8th Massachusetts Regiments and Cook's Massachusetts Battery. I spent the night with Col. Hincks of the 8th, whose commissary of the post was Dexter F. Parker of Worcester. The Colonel was a clerk in the office of the Secretary of State when I was in the Senate in 1858 and 1859, and Commissary Parker was a

brother Senator in 1859. Their camp was delightfully situated on the grounds of Dr. Hall overlooking the Valley of
the Patapsco River.   On Monday I went down to Baltimore
and rode round to Fort McHenry, where the 3d Massachusetts
Battalion of Rifles, under Major Charles Devens was quartered.   This Battalion consisted of the Worcester City Guards
and the Holden Rifles, to which were attached the Emmet
Guards of Worcester and a Boston Company, raised after
the call for troops was issued. I found General Banks at the
Fort, and on our way back to Baltimore together he criticised
the limitation of the President's call to 75,000 men, feeling
assured that the war was to be a long one.   He was wise in
his anticipation of a long war, but I think he was mistaken
as to the call.   The delay in raising a larger number of three
months' men would have disheartened the North and encouraged the South, and a larger call for short service would have
interfered with enlistments for a long one. On the whole it
seems to me that the early war measures were conceived and
executed by wise, far-seeing men.   From Baltimore I returned
home and made a report to the Governor.

CHAPTER XXXIX.

I have spoken in the last chapter of being intimate with Commodore John Marston and family during a winter I spent in Philadelphia. There was another Commodore whom I knew there. I lived four months next door to Commodore James Barron, who in 1820 killed Commodore Stephen Decatur in a duel. Before the war of 1812 Barron was in command of the Ship Chesapeake, from which, under a claimed right of search, a British frigate had taken several sailors, alleged to be British. For his conduct in that affair he was tried and sentenced to five years' suspension without pay. After the war he returned from Europe where he had lived some time, and his application for employment in the navy was opposed by Decatur on the ground that he had been disloyal to his country in not returning to fight her battles. A challenge followed, and a duel was fought on the historic field of Bladensburg. Both fired together, Decatur receiving a mortal wound in the breast, and Barron a wound in the thigh which he thought was also mortal. As they lay on the ground bleeding, the scene was a pathetic one. Barron said, "I hope, Decatur, when we meet in heaven that we shall be better friends than we have been here." Decatur answered, "I have not been your enemy, but tell me, Barron, why you did not come home and fight for your country." Barron replied, "I had been living many years in Europe, and had contracted debts which I could not run away and leave unpaid." "Ah," said Decatur, "If I had known that, we should not be lying here awaiting death." Barron recovered, and was again employed in the service. His life was saddened by the event, but he never alluded to the melancholy scenes attending it. "If I had known that," said Decatur! Alas, how many duels might have been averted if the parties had come together and heard in a personal interview reasons and explanations. Yes, and in the broader field of national honor if nations had sent their representatives to discuss dispassionately their complaints and differences, how many thousands of lives might have been saved and how many millions of treasure.

After returning from a visit to the Massachusetts troops at
the front I was kept busy during the summer of 1861, enlisting
men in Plymouth, and Kingston and other neighboring towns.
I was several times in Washington on business in the war and
navy departments.   Simon Cameron was secretary of war
from the 4th of March, 1861, until January, 1862, when he
was succeeded by Edwin M. Stanton.   I have nothing of interest to say concerning the former, but later I shall tell a story
of my interview with the latter in October, 1862.   The secretary of the Navy was Gideon Welles of Connecticut, but
Gustavus Vasa Fox, the assistant secretary, was really the
right hand of the department.   Mr. Fox I had known for
many years, my acquaintance beginning when a midshipman
he came, I think in 1838, to Plymouth in the practice brig Ap-
prentice, commanded by Lieut. Moore, and anchoring in beach
channel, remained over a Sunday and attended church.   He
was a remarkable man, thought by some to be the strongest
man connected with the administration during the war.   He
was born in Saugus, Massachusetts, June 13, 1821, and was
appointed midshipman January 12, 1838.   In 1856 he resigned
with the rank of first lieutenant, and was appointed agent of
the Bay State Mills in Lawrence.   In March, 1861, he was
sent by President Lincoln to Charleston to confer with Major
Anderson about sending him aid at Fort Sumter, and was
soon appointed assistant secretary of the Navy.   To him was
due the plan for the capture of New Orleans, and the selection
of Farragut for the command in which he distinguished himself.   His sound judgment and earnest advice led to the construction of the Monitor, and he established and perfected the
blockade.   After the war he was assigned to the duty of carrying the ram Miantonomah to the Baltic, which had been
sold to the Russian government, and he was at the same time
made a bearer of despatches conveying the congratulations of
our government to Emperor Alexander 2nd, on his escape
from assassination on the 16th of April, 1866.   The Miantonomah was the first iron-clad to cross the ocean, and Capt. Fox
reported her a comfortable craft, which instead of pitching
and rolling in heavy weather, took the seas across her deck,
and remained comparatively on an even keel.   On his return
home he was appointed manager of the Middlesex Mills in

Lowell, and died in New York, October 29, 1883. In my communications with him, concerning appointments in the service, I never failed to receive a favorable response. I was the more careful therefore in making requests. In one instance I recommended a man for ensign, and hearing something soon after leading me to doubt his competency. I immediately wrote to Mr. Fox withdrawing my recommendation, and the applicant now dead, failed to receive an appointment. Sometimes at a later period of the war I was often asked to intercede in behalf of some soldier for a furlough. I remember the case of an officer, now dead, who was quite successful in obtaining furloughs on his own account, and who was in the habit while at home of criticising the conduct of the war. On one of his visits an old lady said, "lah, that—is home again—this is the curiousest war that ever I see, if they don't like the percedings they come home." In quoting the quaint remark of the old lady I do not intend to suggest any doubt of the fidelity of a brave and efficient officer who probably had good and sufficient reasons for his furloughs.

The Standish Guards returned home after their three months' service, on the 23d of July, and were received at the railroad station by the Home Guard, and in the evening at a festival in Davis hall. The officers of the company chosen after their arrival at Fortress Monroe, were Charles C. Doten, captain, and Otis Rogers and Wm. B. Alexander first and 2nd lieutenants, respectively. Lemuel Bradford, 2nd, who went out with the company as 4th lieutenant, was not permitted to be mustered, as only two lieutenants were allowed to each company. I have always understood that four lieutenants were mustered in the companies of the 5th, 6th, and 8th Massachusetts Regiments in and about Washington, where for some unknown reason a different rule prevailed.

In August, 1861, a second three years' company was recruited by Capt. Joseph W. Collingwood to be attached as Co. H. to the 18th Massachusetts Regiment. All the men of this company were enlisted in the recruiting office established by the Plymouth Selectmen. Thirteen Plymouth men were enlisted in Co. H, and eight in other companies of the 18th Regiment. The Regiment was mustered into service August 24, and on the 26th left Readville, where they had been in camp, for Washington, joining the army of the Potomac at Hall's Hill near that city.

In September, 1861, Capt. Wm. B. Alexander was authorized to raise a company to be attached as Co. E to the 23d Regiment, and ninety-seven men were enlisted at the Plymouth office, of whom sixty were Plymouth men. This company, with Wm. B. Alexander, Capt., and Otis Rogers, and Thomas B. Atwood, respectively, first and second lieutenants, went into camp at Lynfield, and November 11 left for Annapolis.   Three other Plymouth men later joined Co. E as recruits, and three Plymouth men joined other companies in the 23d regiment.

In December, 1861, Lieutenant Josiah C. Fuller aided in recruiting Company E for the first Battalion of Massachusetts, which was finally recognized as the 32d Regiment, and twenty men were enlisted in Plymouth. · Twenty more were enlisted for Company F, and four more for other companies in the same regiment, and three recruits were added later to Company E. This regiment was organized for garrison duty at Fort Warren in Boston harbor with Josiah C. Fuller, Capt. of Company E, and Edward F. Phinney second lieutenant of Company F, and May 20, 1862, left for Washington.

On the 7th of July, 1862, an order was issued at headquarters, stating that Massachusetts had been called on for fifteen thousand men, of which number Plymouth was required to furnish sixty. The Governor asked me to raise two companies to be designated as Companies D and G in the 38th Regiment, and to select officers for them. I first enlisted men for Company D, and soon filled its ranks with thirty men from Plymouth, and the remainder from neighboring towns.   I first recommended Chas. H. Drew for captain, Cephas Washburn and Albert Mason, first and second lieutenants, respectively. Charles H. Drew was then first lieutenant in Company H, 18th Regiment, and the war department refused to muster him out to enable him to receive his commission. I then filled the ranks of Company G with thirty-one from Plymouth, and the remainder from neighboring towns, and recommended Charles C. Doten for captain and George B. Russell, second lieutenant. The town's quota was completed by one enlistment for the 13th Regiment, one for the 20th and one for the

35th. The 38th Regiment went into camp at Lynfield, and September 24, 1862, left for Baltimore, where it went into camp near the city and left November 9th in the steamer Baltic for Ship island. I went with the Plymouth companies to Lynfield and spent a week with them under canvas to aid in making requisitions for equipments, and looking generally after the comfort of the men. My classmate, Wm. Logan Rodman of New Bedford, was commissioned Major of the Regiment, and later before it left, lieutenant colonel. When the commission as lieutenant colonel was offered to him he asked my advice about accepting it, as he knew nothing about military matters, but he was finally commissioned, and in the absence of Col. Ingraham, went to Baltimore in command of the regiment. Poor fellow, he was killed at the siege of Port Hudson in May, 1863. He was lying down with his command behind logs, and lifting his head was instantly killed by a rebel sharpshooter. During my stay at the Lynfield Camp, I for the first time was christened with a high military title. Patrick Maguire of Company D was found one night outside the camp somewhat under the influence of liquor, and carried to the guard house. When asked what regiment he belonged to he said, "by gorrah, I don't belong to no regiment at all, I belong to Davis's brigade."

In August, 1862, a call was made for 300,000 nine months' men, of which the quota of Plymouth was thirty-seven. Every organized militia company in the 3d Regiment was authorized to recruit up to the standard, but as it would be impossible to fill the Standish Guards and the Carver and Plympton companies, it was agreed that the three companies should recruit together as Company B, the letter of the Standish Guards, under a Carver Captain, and with a first lieutenant from the Guards, and a second lieutenant from the Plympton company. Under this arrangement Thos. B. Griffith was made captain; Charles A. S. Perkins of Plymouth, first lieutenant, and Wm. S. Briggs of Middleboro, second lieutenant. Thirty men enlisted in Plymouth, including John Morissey, who was appointed Major. The regiment went into camp at Lakeville, and October 22, 1862, sailed from Boston in the steamships Merrimac and Mississippi for Newbern, North Carolina. Twelve other nine months' men were enlisted in

Plymouth for the 4th, 6th, 44th, 45th and 50th Regiments. Thirty-five of the nine months' men received a bounty of one hundred dollars in accordance with a vote of the town.

After the defeat of General Pope by General Lee at the second Bull Run, the rebel army crossed the Potomac at Noland's ford, and reached Frederick in Maryland on the 6th of September, 1862. In the meantime General McClellan had been restored to the command of the army of the Potomac, and crossing the Potomac in pursuit of Lee, entered Frederick on the 12th, two days after its evacuation by the rebel army. On the 13th the union army passed through Frederick and overtook the rebel army at South mountain, where they fought a victorious battle on the 14th. The pursuit was kept up through Boonesboro and Keedysville, until Antietam river was reached, where the rebel army was strongly entrenched. Without intending to write a history of the battle, I think I can say as a result of my frequent studies of the conflict, that the Massachusetts troops acquitted themselves with special bravery. The battle was won, but while Burnside on the left was fighting desperately to hold a position, the loss of which would have involved the defeat of the army, and was calling on McClellan for aid, the 18th corps, under Fitz John Porter, to which the 18th and 32d Massachusetts belonged, was held fifteen thousand strong in reserve, and had no share in the battle. With the light we now have it is easy to see that if the reserves had been put in at the critical moment, as they were put in by Wellington at Waterloo, when he shut his field glass with a snap and gave the order, "Up guards, and at them," the rebel army would have been destroyed before it recrossed the Potomac. The only excuse for McClellan was his belief that the battle was only suspended, not terminated, when night set in, and that on the morrow the army with fresh troops would win.

In the two battles, of South Mountain on the 14th of September, and Antietam on the 17th, the Massachusetts regiments suffered severely. In the first the 12th, 13th, 21st and 28th regiments, and the 1st and 8th batteries were engaged, and in the last the 2nd, 12th, 13th, 15th, 19th, 20th, 21st, 28th, 29th and 35th regiments, and two batteries. The 12th had seventy-four killed and 165 wounded, the 15th had 108 killed,

and the 29th, 9 killed and 31 wounded, while the others suffered in various degrees between the highest and lowest as
above. The most severely wounded were carried to hospitals
on the field, and to temporary hospitals in Sharpsburgh and
Frederick, while those less severely wounded were carried to
Washington, Baltimore and Philadelphia, and some sent to
their homes. Governor Andrew asked me to go out and visit
the Massachusetts men, wherever they might be found in the
hospitals. They needed no supplies, for they were abundantly
furnished by the commissariat and the sanitary commission
with everything from bedding and underclothing to wines and
canned fruits and preserves. But there was something which
neither of these agencies could supply, something to remove
the depression of spirits which a sick man feels away from
home, and which is the greatest obstacle to recovery. I have
often seen the pallid cheeks of a soldier furrowed with pain,
light up with a smile as he opened his eyes and found standing by his bedside a messenger from home.

Reaching Baltimore at night, I met at the hotel Dr. LeBar-
ron Russell, and the next morning we went together by rail to
Frederick, where we passed the night. Every available public building, including churches, had been converted into a
hospital, and in one of these I remember finding Barnabas
Dunham of Plymouth, a member of the 29th Regiment. In
one of the church hospitals, I found Dr. Theodore Cornish in
charge, brother of the late Aaron H. Cornish of Plymouth,
who I think was either surgeon or assistant surgeon in a
Rhode Island regiment. He gave us much information about
the condition of the wounded in Frederick, and their dispersion to other places. About five years ago I met him on the
steamboat coming to Plymouth, never having seen him since
our interview in Frederick, and called him by name. He
failed to recognize me until I reminded him of my encountering him in the hospital dressing the wound of a soldier who
had been operated on by an excision of a section of the humer-
us to avoid amputation The next morning we hired a conveyance to Boonesboro, a small village, through whose streets
both armies had passed from South Mountain gap, where
the battle of September 14th had been fought. The shat-
tered trees and levelled fences and trodden down fields told

their story of the conflict. We passed the night at Boones-
horo, finding no Massachusetts wounded there. I was amused
at a custom prevailing in that neighborhood disclosed to me
by the landlady, when to a mild complaint of sleeping on a
blanket, she answered that nobody thought of putting more
than one sheet on the bed. The next morning we rode on
to Keedysville, a straggling village of five hundred inhabitants, where nearly all the houses contained wounded men.
There was a provost marshal stationed there, and going to
his office we were surprised to find him to be Capt. Joseph W.
Collingwood. His company was attached to Fitz John Porter's Corps, held in reserve, and consequently had not been in
the battle. Taking Capt. Collingwood into our carriage we
drove to the Locust Spring hospital, containing under canvas
about two hundred and fifty severely wounded men. Here
Charles Henry Robbins, son of Heman C. Robbins of Plymouth, died from a wound received in the battle. I saw his
nurse, a fine woman from Chicago, named Mary Everingham,
who expressed great interest in him, and I visited his grave
in a pleasant field marked with a head and foot stone by a
soldier named Keith of North Bridgewater, from which I took
a stone to carry to his mother. Mr. Robbins belonged to
Company H, 35th regiment, and enlisted in Weymouth. The
next field tent hospital which we visited was at Smoketown,
less than a mile from the extreme right of the Union line of
battle, where hard fighting was done under Hooker in the
early part of the day. This hospital contained about four
hundred and fifty patients, under the charge of Dr. Vander-
keefe, a Hollander, who had served in the Crimea. His hospital was a model in care, cleanliness, distribution of comforts,
and surgical skill. The work done by the sanitary commission was wonderful. At the first sign of a battle it despatched many wagons loads of sheets, coverlids, beds, towels,
handkerchiefs, preserved meats, stockings, drawers,
shirts, bandages, wines, etc., which reached the vicinity of the battle field before a gun was fired, and was ready
for work when the wounded were carried to the rear. From
this point we rode over the whole battle field, four miles in
length, from Hooker's cornfield to Burnside's bridge, by the
sunken road and the Dunker church, still littered with the

debris of battle, and reached Sharpsburg late in the afternoon, on our way visiting Porter's camp, and calling on Captains Charles H. Drew and Wm. H. Winsor of the 18th Massachusetts regiment. Late in the evening we reached Harper's Ferry, where after a supper of ham and eggs we found sleeping quarters in an attic room, lighted and ventilated by a broken glass scuttle, and equipped with a bed with broken slats, leaving us to sleep on the floor, with our heads and feet on the rails of the bedstead. The next morning we went out to Boliver Heights, and visited the camps of the 15th, 19th, 20th and 29th Massachusetts regiments, the last having returned the night before from an expedition to Charlestown, and in the evening went by rail to Washington.

During my stay in Washington I visited all the hospitals, beginning with Lincoln Hospital. While passing through one of the wards I heard my name called by an occupant of one of the beds. Responding to the call I found a young man whom I had enlisted in Plymouth a few months before as a recruit for Col. Lee's 20th Regiment. His name was Erik Wolff, a Swede of good education, who came to America to learn to become a soldier, and thought that promotion would be sure and speedy. His father, a merchant in Gottenburg, had had some years before business relations with Capt. John Russell, and having letters of introduction to Capt. Russell's family he came at once to Plymouth on his arrival. He was now very sick with typhoid fever, and in his anxiety to be discharged, was so depressed in spirits that the surgeon said his recovery was hopeless, unless his discharge was secured. Col. Lee's efforts had been unavailing, as at that time every application of the kind was rejected by the department. I told him that I would see what I could do, and jumping into a horse car, rode at once to the war department, reaching there before the office of the secretary was open. A long line of men and women stretched down the hall, all with anxious faces, evidently waiting to ask some favor of the secretary. When the door was opened the line shortened up so rapidly that I felt sure that short work was made of the applications. When I reached the door Mr. Stanton was standing at a small standing desk, and turning off the applicants right and left. I had never seen him before, and had no reason to believe that he had ever seen or heard of me. When my turn came I told him my story in as few words as possible, that I enlisted Wolff, that he was a foreigner, on whose service we had no claim, and was in the Lincoln hospital. Not a word was spoken by the secretary, not a single question asked, but as soon as I finished he touched a hand bell, to which an officer responded, and the secretary said, "Mr. Davis, if you will follow Major Hardee, he will make out the discharge." Within two hours from the time I left the hospital I returned with the discharge to gladden the young fellow's heart. He recovered after a protracted confinement, and returned to Massachusetts, receiving later from Governor Andrew a captain's commission in the 5th Massachusetts Cavalry Regiment. On my way home I visited the hospitals in Baltimore and West Philadelphia, carrying with me a realizing sense of the terrible incidents of war. I have told the story of my interview with Secretary Stanton to show the injustice of the charge that he was destitute of sympathy for the soldiers whom he used merely as a part of the machinery of war.

Proceeding in my narrative in chronological order, in the winter of 1862 and 1863, strenuous, but unavailing efforts were made by Governor Andrew to have the exposed harbors of the state properly protected. Finally it was determined to construct earthworks on the Gurnet and Saquish, and the work was entered upon at once under the direction of the Selectmen at the expense of the Commonwealth. I obtained from Mr. Fox, assistant secretary of the Navy, an order on Commodore Hudson in command at the Charlestown Navy Yard for seven guns for Fort Andrew, and five for Fort Standish, and had carriages made in Plymouth. These forts were completed in the early summer of 1863, and Governor Andrew was advised by the selectmen of their intention to name that on the Gurnet, Fort Andrew, and that on the Saquish, Fort Sandish. On the 16th of March I received from the Governor the following letter:

Dear Sir.—No fort as yet bears the name which your board of selectmen has so generously proposed for the larger fort now in progress in Plymouth harbor, nor had any ambition of my own ever suggested to my mind the possibility of becoming in that manner associated with such a work. I am deeply sensible of the honor; and while I feel that it does not properly belong to me, I can only leave to you and your associates the final decision, with a single suggestion that it would seem to be more fitting the occasion to connect the name of the first Governor of the Plymouth Colony with one of the fortifications of the harbor of Plymouth than the name you propose, even if I were a hundred times more worthy than I know myself to be."

Notwithstanding Governor Andrew's modest estimate of his public services, the fort received his name.

In 1862 I became quite intimate with Capt. James Birdseye McPherson of the United States Engineers. He was undoubtedly one of the ablest officers in the army, and his early death closed a career of great brilliancy. It was widely believed in the army up to the time of his death, that if Grant had died or resigned, he would have been his successor. During several years of the war I was obliged to spend much time in Boston, and while there I made the Tremont House my home. There were five or six regular bachelor boarders who occupied a table by themselves, one of whom was Capt. McPherson. He was born in Sandusky, Ohio, November 14, 1828, and graduated at West Point first scholar in the class of 1853. He rose rapidly, and while serving as an engineer in California, he became acquainted with General Halleck. When the war came on, having been promoted to a captaincy he was sent to Boston to mount guns on Fort Warren, and it was at that time that he boarded at the Tremont House, and at the table where he sat I was always when in town offered a chair. No one could meet and talk with him without being struck with his clear eye, his thoughful face and thoroughly trustworthy deportment. One afternoon while I was at the Hotel, Captain Paraclete Holmes of Kingston, boarding there took up the *Transcript* and read aloud a news paragraph stating that Capt. McPherson had been ordered west to join the staff of General Halleck. When the Catpain came in he was shown the despatch, and said that he knew nothing about it. When, however, he received his evening mail, his orders reached him. As he was ordered to report at once, we arranged a parting supper for the next evening, for which I remember, by the way, I ordered a gallon of oysters, which had been bedded on the Plymouth flats by S. D. Ballard, and which were pronounced by the supper party as the best they had ever tasted. When I bade the Captain good bye he said, "I shall have an opportunity now to see whether I have mistaken my profession." The sequel demonstrated that he had not. He was soon promoted to be Major General of volunteers, and transferred to the staff of General Grant as Chief Engineer, serving with him at the battles of Fort Henry, Fort Donelson, Shiloh, Corinth and Iuka. He later commanded the right wing of Grant's army, and at the siege of Vicksburg commanded the 17th Army Corps. After Grant assumed command of the army of the Potomac, he joined Sherman, under whom he was in command of 30,000 men. At the siege of Atlanta he was killed, July 22, 1864, at the age of thirty-five.

I was again in Washington visiting the hospitals after the battle of Fredericksburg, on the 13th of December, 1862, and after the death of Capt. Collingwood on the 24th, I sent a despatch to Andrew L. Russell, who informed his family and friends. I was on a visit to the College hospital in Georgetown, when Capt. Charles H. Drew was brought in severely wounded in the Fredericksburg battle. It fell to me while in Washington, during the battles of the Wilderness, to send a despatch to Mr. Russell, informing him of the death of Lemuel B. Morton, killed at the battle of Spottsylvania Court House, May 12, 1864.

On the 17th of July, 1863, as the result of a draft, one Plymouth man commuted, thirteen found substitutes, and three entered the service. In the autumn of 1863, under a call for 500,000 men, the quota of Plymouth was fixed at one hundred and seventeen. After the selectmen reported that the quota had been filled they were notified that in consequence of a delay in crediting enlistments for the army and navy, there existed a deficiency of twenty-five men, which must be filled by a draft. One man was held under the draft who found a substitute, and before another draft was ordered the selectmen had filled the quota by the purchase of recruits in Boston. A vote had been passed by the town offering to recruits a bounty of $125, and a committee of citizens were appointed to raise such funds to increase the bounty to such an amount as

the selectmen might think advisable. The committee raised
the sum of $3,776.25, and with this sum and the bounty, voted
by the town, the selectmen secured twenty-two recruits for
the army and four for the navy. Another call for 500,000 men
was made July, 1864, and with money raised by the above committee to wit, $5,011.00, the selectmen obtained twenty-six re-
cruits, who with the credit for the men in the navy hertofore
withheld, and one representative recruit purchased by a citizen,
filled the quota of the town.

On the 19th of November, 1864, seven Plymouth men were
mustered into the 20th unattached company, stationed at
Marblehead for one year's service, and on the 11th of December, forty-two more were mustered into the 26th unattached
company raised to garrison Forts Andrew and Standish, but
which finally was stationed at Readville, where it remained
until it was mustered out. Until a late period in the war, the
recruiting office in Plymouth was kept up by the selectmen,
and at various times ninety-eight were enlisted in Plymouth
and other places for the 1st, 7th, 11th, 12th, 13th, 16th, 17th,
18th, 20th, 24th, 28th, 30th, 34th, 41st, 55th, 58th, Massachusetts Regiments, 1st, 4th, 5th Massachusetts Cavalry, 2nd
Massachusetts Heavy Artillery, 3rd, 5th, 7th, 12th Massachusetts
Batteries, 2nd Massachusetts Sharpshooters, 3rd Rhode Island
Cavalry, 5th, 8th New Hampshire Regiments, 3rd, 10th, 99th,
New York Regiments, 10th Pennsylvania Regiment, 8th Illinois Regiment, the Signal Corps, President's Guard, Veteran
Reserve Corps and California Cavalry. In addition to the
above, six were recruited by the commission appointed to recruit in rebel states, and credited to Plymouth, and the following re-enlistments were also credited to the town—six in Co. E,
29th Massachusetts Regiment, one each in companies C, E
and H, 18th Regiment, twelve in Co. E, 23rd Regiment, eight
in Co. E, 32nd Regiment, five in Co. F, 32nd Regiment, four
in other companies in the 32nd Regiment, two in the 1st Cavalry, one in the 58th Regiment, one in the Rhode Island Cavalry, one in the 17th Regiment, one in the 30th Regiment, one
in the Regular Army, and one in the Corps D'Afrique. On
the first day of February, 1866, all the above soldiers enlisted
and re-enlisted to the credit of the town had been mustered
out except Brevet Major Geo. B. Russell, Provost Marshal

of the District of Columbia, and Philander Freeman and
Stephen M. Maybury in the regular army.   Before closing this
record of the Plymouth soldiers in the war it should be stated
that on the 26th day of May, 1862, a telegram was received by
Governor Andrew from the war department urging him to send
at once all the militia force of the state, as General Banks had
been driven from the Shenandoah Valley, and Washington was
in danger. On the 27th in obedience to an order from the Governor, Capt. Charles C. Doten reported in Boston with the
Standish Guards of fifty-seven men. Fear for the safety of
the Capital, however, was soon dissipated, and the company
returned home without being mustered into the service.

In order to complete the roll of men furnished by Plymouth
for the war, it only remains to say that the enlistments in the
navy were three acting lieutenants, six ensigns, ten masters,
two acting masters, seventeen mates, one assistant paymaster,
three assistant engineers, one sailmaker, and sixty-five seamen.

One of the most troublesome features of the service which
the selectmen were called on to perform, was that regulating to
filling the towns quotas with purchased men.   There were
private recruiting offices in Boston, where men were furnished,
and to a great extent the recruits offering themselves were
bounty jumpers as we called them.   Unless a sharp eye was
kept on these recruits, and the bounty withheld until they were
examined by an army surgeon in Faneuil hall, and receipts
given for them by the Provost Marshal, stating age, date of
enlistment and Regiments for which they were enlisted, they
would take up with a higher bid, or steal away with the
bounty and receive another elsewhere. I landed all my men,
but I knew of a number of cases where unwary selectmen lost
their bounty and their men.   Many recruits who failed in their
efforts to evade service after they had received their bounty,
deserted their regiments and enlisted where they could safely
do so with another bounty.

The whole number of men furnished by Plymouth for the
war was 653 soldiers and 111 naval officers and seamen, which
number filled all the quotas and left a surplus of 28 to the
credit of the town.   The cost to the town for all purposes connected with the war was a little more than $28,000, to which
should be added $8,787.25 subscribed by the citizens for
bounties.

CHAPTER XXXX.

The following record contains the names of Plymouth men in the army and navy during the war, and as far as possible an account of their service.

The Third regiment enlisted for three months with Chas. Raymond, lieutenant colonel, Company B. Chas. C. Doten, 1st lieutenant, captain; Otis Rogers, 2nd lieutenant, 1st lieutenant; Wm. B. Alexander, 2d lieutenant, and the following men:

Sherman Allen
Thomas B. Atwood
Timothy S. Atwood
Charles E. Barnes, 2d
George R. Barnes
Wm. E. Barnes
Amasa M. Bartlett
Ellis B. Bramhall
Caleb N. Brown
Wm. S. Burbank, Jr.
David L. Chandler
George H. Chase
Robert B. Churchill
Charles C. Crosby
Lyman Dixon
Charles H. Drew
Stephen C. Drew
Lemuel B. Faunce, Jr.
Solomon E. Faunce
George H. Fish
Augustus H. Fuller
Theodore S. Fuller
Thomas Haley
Azel W. Handy
Sylvanus R. Harlow
John F. Harten

Eliphalet Holbrook
Charles H. Holmes
Isaac T. Holmes
Daniel D. Howard
Charles Jones
Charles N. Jordan
Franklin S. Leach
John S. Lucas
Charles Mason
Job B. Oldham
Henry Perkins
Charles W. Peirce
Charles M. Perry
Henry Ripley
Francis H. Robbins
James H. Robbins
Leander L. Sherman
Winslow B. Sherman
Edward Smith
Jacob W. Southworth
James C. Standish
John Swift
John Sylvester
James Tribble
John B. Williams

Company B arrived at Fortress Monroe, April 20, 1861, and was sent at once to Norfolk in the U. S. Steamer Pawnee to destroy the Navy Yard, and on its return, was on the 22d mustered into the service for three months. Lemuel Bradford, 2nd, who went out as 4th lieutenant of Company B, was not mustered in, as only two lieutenants were recognized, but remained during the three months at Old Point at work in the

Government Foundry, and returned home with the Company. On the 30th of April Lieutenant Colonel Charles Raymond, who had remained behind on recruiting service, arrived at the Fortress with the following recruits:

Levonzo D. Barnes
Nathaniel F. Barnes
David W. Burbank
Albert E. Davis
Josiah R. Drew

Alexander Gilmore
Frederick Holmes
Daniel Lucas
Harvey A. Raymond

All the above three months' men remained in the Fortress during their service, except during the last two weeks, when they were quartered at Hampton, and embarked for Boston in the steamer Cambridge, arriving at Long Island in Boston harbor, July 19th, where they were mustered out July 22nd.

The only other three months' Plymouth man was George W. Barnes, who was quartermaster's sergeant in the 4th regiment.

Company E, 29th regiment, 3 years:

Samuel H. Doten, capt. Bt., major; John B. Collingwood, 1st lieutenant, adjutant; Nathaniel Burgess; 1st lieutenant; Thomas A. Mayo, 2nd lieutenant; Horace A. Jenks, 2nd lieutenant; John Shannon, 2nd lieutenant; Edward L. Robbins, principal musician.

John K. Alexander
John M. Atwood
Charles C. Barnes
Ellis D. Barnes
Moses S. Barnes
Winslow C. Barnes
Simeon H. Barrows
Lawrence R. Blake
Andrew Blanchard
Cornelius Bradford
George F. Bradford
Benjamin F. Bumpus
George F. Burbank
Nathaniel Burgess
Sylvanus L. Churchill
Thomas Collingwood
Barnabas Dunham
Henry F. Eddy
Ichabod C. Fuller
Philander Freeman
Timothy E. Gay
Wm. P. Gooding
John F. Hall

Samuel H. Harlow
Thomas W. Hayden
Alexander Haskins
James S. Holbrook
Orin D. Holmes
Seth L. Holmes
Wm. H. Howland
Henry W. Kimball
Charles E. Merriam
George S. Morey
Wm. Morey, 2d
John E. Morrison
John A. Morse
Isaac Morton, Jr.
Lemuel B. Morton
Wm. T. Nickerson
Seth W. Paty
John H. Pember
George F. Pierce
Wm. H. Pittee
Albert R. Robbins
Henry H. Robbins
Albert Simmons

Frank H. Simmons
Patrick Smith
Miles Standish
Winslow B. Standish
James E. Stillman
Wm. Swift
Francis A. Thomas

Samuel D. Thrasher
Francis H. Vaughn
Leander M. Vaughn
George E. Wadsworth
Alfred B. Warner
Joseph B. Whiting
Wm. Williams

The above company was mustered into the service at Fortress Monroe, May 22, 1861, and attached to the 3rd regiment. After the expiration of the term of the 3rd regiment, it was attached, as Co. E to the 1st Massachusetts Battalion, and sent to Newport News. On the 13th of December it was joined as Co. E to the 29th regiment, and sent from Newport News to Norfolk, Suffolk and White House Landing. At various periods in 1862, the following recruits joined the company.

Benjamin F. Bates
Thomas B. Burt
Elisha S. Doten
Justus W. Harlow

Charles E. Kleinhans
George F. Peckham
Charles E. Tillson

The 29th regiment was engaged in the various battles on the peninsula, and from the peninsula went into Maryland and fought in the battle of Antietam, September 17, 1862. It was at the battle of Fredricksburg, went to Vicksburg and Knoxville, and finally joined the army of the Potomac, and continued with it until its term of service expired. The following Plymouth men re-enlisted:

Benjamin F. Bates
Nathaniel Burgess
Orin D. Holmes

Wm. T. Nickerson
John Shannon
Charles E. Tillson

The following Plymouth men were in the 29th regiment, besides those in Co. E:

Edward L. Daniels, Co. H
Curtis Eddy, Co. C

Ephraim T. Lucas, Co. H
Darius Perry, Co. H

Company H, 18th regiment, three years.

Joseph W. Collingwood, captain; Charles H. Drew, 1st lieutenant, captain; Stephen C. Drew, 1st and 2nd lieutenants.

James S. Bartlett
John Duffy
John Duffy, Jr.
Thomas Haley
John M. Harlow

John F. Harten
John F. Hogan
George P. Hooper
Frederick W. Robbins
Horatio N. Sears

Members of other companies in 18th regiment were Wm. H. Winsor, 1st lieutenant, captain.

Ezra Burgess
George W. Burgess
Winslow T. Burgess
Winslow Churchill

Zenas Churchill
J. Q. A. Harlow
S. M. Maybury

This regiment was engaged in the peninsula battles, the second Bull Run, Fredericksburg, Chancellorsville, Gettysburg and the Wilderness. The following re-enlisted: Winslow T. Burgess, Co. E; John Duffy, Jr., Co. H; J. Q. A. Harlow, Co. C.

Company E, 23rd regiment, three years.

Wm. B. Alexander, captain; Josiah R. Drew, 2nd lieutenant, 1st lieutenant; Otis Rogers, 1st lieutenant, captain.

Charles H. Atwood
Thomas C. Atwood
William T. Atwood
Ichabod P. Bagnall
George Bailey
Henry Baker
Henry C. Bartlett
Winslow Bartlett
Edward Bassett
Albert Benson
George Benson
Wm. T. Besse
Edward D. Brailey
John R. Brailey
Homer Bryant
Asaph S. Burbank
David W. Burbank
Wm. S. Burbank, Jr.
James K. Burgess
John Burns
John E. Burt
Augustus T. Caswell
Thomas Chandler
Joseph L. Churchill
Wm. E. Churchill
Francis E. Davis
George H. Dunham
George Feid

Walter H. Finney
Theodore S. Fuller
Warren Gibbs
Henry Gould
Samuel W. Holmes
Hiram J. Lanman
Charles H. Long
Henry Marshall
Perez McMahon
Seth Mehuren, Jr.
James W. Page
Daniel H. Paulding
George O. Paulding
Isaac H. Perkins
N. B. Perry
John D. Ryder
Thomas S. Saunders
Andrew T. Sears
Edward Smith
Jacob W. Southworth
James C. Standish
Charles C. Stevens
Edward Stevens
James H. Stillman
George W. Swift
Wm. A. Swift
John Taylor
Benjamin Westgate

The following recruits joined the company while in the field: John Quinlan, Harvey A. Raymond and Horatio N.

Sears. The following were members in other companies in the 18th regiment:

John Carline

Seth Mehurin

H. I. Lucas

James Ryan

The following members of Co. E re-enlisted.

Charles H. Atwood

Seth Mehurin, Jr.

Icabod P. Bagnall

James W. Page

Edward Bassett

Isaac H. Perkins

John Burns

Andrew T. Sears

George H. Dunham

Charles C. Stevens

Henry Gould

James H. Stillman

The 23rd regiment sailed from Annapolis to Hatteras Inlet, Jan. 6, 1862, was at the reduction of Roanoke Island and other battles in North Carolina. In January, 1863, it went to Hilton Head, and in February returned to Newbern, and in October went to Fortress Monroe and Newport News. In May, 1864, it joined the army of the Potomac, and in September returned to Newbern.

Company E, 32d regiment. Josiah C. Fuller, 1st lieutenant, captain.

James H. Allen

Anthony L. Pierce

Arvin M. Bancroft

Weldon S. Pierce

George W. Bartlett

Henry L. Raymond

George H. Blanchard

Eleazer Shaw

George B. Brewster

Wm. H. Shaw

John R. Davis, Jr.

David A. Taylor

George M. Heath

Perez C. W. Vaughn

Adoniram Holmes

Weston C. Vaughn

Wm. M. Lapham

Seth Washburn

Henry Morton, Jr.

Company F. Edward F. Finney, 2nd lieutenant.

Robert B. Barnes

Moses Hoyt

George B. Beytes

Augustine T. Jones

Albert F. Green

Charles W. Pierce

George F. Green

Alexander Ripley

Gustavus C. Green

Wm. S. Robbins

Richard F. Green

Nehemiah L. Savery

Wm. H. Green

Winsor T. Savery

Charles H. Holmes

Edward S. Snow

Joseph Holmes

Charles F. Washburn

John F. Hoyt

In other companies of 32d regiment.

Patrick Downey

John E. McDonald

Melvin C. Faught

Patrick McSweeney

Abner Lucas

James Rider

Patrick Manehan

The 32nd regiment went from Capitol Hill to Alexandria, Harrison's Landing, Williamsburg, Yorktown, Newport News, Fredericksburg and to Antietam, where it was in the reserve at the time of the battle. It was in the battles of Fredericksburg and Gettysburg. The following Plymouth men in the 32nd regiment re-enlisted:

George W. Bartlett
George H. Blanchard
John R. Davis, Jr.
George F. Green
Gustavus C. Green
Adoniram Holmes
Abner Lucas

Nehemiah L. Savery
Anthony L. Pierce
Wm. H. Shaw
David A. Taylor
Perez C. W. Vaughn
Weston C. Vaughn

The following re-enlisted men from other places were credited to Plymouth:

George W. Allen
George C. Drown

Elliott Pierce
Henry W. Roberts

38th regiment, three years, Co. D.

Albert Mason, 1st lieutenant, captain, assistant quartermaster, U. S. Volunteers; Francis Bates, musician; Charles Mason, 1st lieutenant, 2nd lieutenant.

James E. Barrows
Gustavus D. Bates
James A. Bowen
Timothy Downey
Benjamin F. Durgin
Solomon E. Faunce
George H. Fish
Thomas Gallagher
Albert F. Greenwood
Benjamin Harvey
Benjamin A. Hathaway
John H. Haverstock

George B. Holbrook
James Kimball
Daniel Lovett
Wm. W. Lanman
Patrick Maguire
Charles S. Peterson
Bernard T. Quinn
Frederick R. Raymond
George B. Sawyer
Thomas G. Savery
Israel H. Thrasher
James T. Thrasher

Company G, 38th regiment. Charles C. Doten, captain; George B. Russell, 2nd lieutenant, 1st lieutenant, captain V. R. Corps, 1st. lieutenant regular army, captain, major, lieutenant colonel; Sanford Crandon, 2nd lieutenant; Albert T. Finney, chief musician.

Charles E. Barnes
Joseph A. Brown
Job C. Chandler, Jr.
Timothy T. Eaton
Lemuel B. Faunce, Jr.
James Frothingham
Edward E. Green

Frederick Holmes
Thomas Haley
Isaac T. Hall
Wm. N. Hathaway
Isachar Josselyn
John Edgar Josselyn
Bernard T. Kelley

Charles W. Lanman
Joseph McLaughlin
Wm. Perry
Christopher A. Prouty
Heman Robbins
Levi Ransom
Adrian D. Ruggles

Horatio Sears
Otis Sears
Joseph F. Towns
Charles C. White
John M. Whiting
Charles T. Wood

At the time the 38th regiment was enlisted the following were also enlisted: James D. Thurber, Co. A, 13th Massachusetts regiment, afterwards 2nd lieutenant, 1st lieutenant, captain, brevet major U. S. Vols. in 55th Massachusetts regiment.

Erik Wolff, private, 20th Massachusetts regiment, 2nd lieutenant, 5th Massachusetts Cavalry. In January, 1865, Edward Allsworth credited to Plymouth was added to the 38th regiment, and transferred to the 119th U. S. Cavalry, and commissioned 2nd lieutenant.

The 38th regiment went to Ship Island in November, 1862, and to Carrolton, near New Orleans, then to Bisland, then to Alexandria and Port Hudson. From Port Hudson the regiment went to Baton Rouge, Alexandria, Morganza Bend, Algiers, and Fortress Monroe, where it arrived in July, 1864. It then went to Harper's Ferry, and the Shenandoah Valley, where it was engaged in the battles of Opequan Creek, Fisher's Hill and Cedar Creek. In December, 1864, it went to Savannah, Newbern and Goldsboro, where it joined Sherman's army. In May, 1865, it went to Savannah, and embarking for Boston, June 30, reached Boston July 6, and was discharged July 13, 1865.

Third regiment, nine months. John Morissey, major; Charles A. S. Perkins, 1st lieutenant; Edward L. Robbins, sergeant major.

Benjamin F. Barnes
Amasa M. Bartlett
Ebenezer N. Bradford
John F. Chapman
Charles S. Cobb
George H. Doten
Harvey B. Griffin
Isaac S. Holmes
Nathaniel Holmes
Samuel N. Holmes
Ivory W. Harlow

George F. Jackson
Benjamin F. Jenkins
Charles W. Johnson
James Neal
Job B. Oldham
James T. Paulding
Charles M. Perry
Charles C. Place
Isaac H. Place
Samuel R. Raymond
Herbert Robbins

James H. Robbins   Thomas Smith
James F. Sears   Wm. F. Spooner
Leander L. Sherman

This regiment sailed from Boston for Newbern, N. C., Oct. 22, 1862, and engaged in the battles of Kinston, Whitehall and Goldsboro. After various expeditions it returned to Newbern, and June 11th, returned to Boston.

Other Plymouth men in the nine months' regiments were:

Schuyler S. Bartlett, 44th   Wm. Hedge, 44th, 1st Lieut.
James B. Brewster, 44th hospital   James R. McLaughlin, 50th
  steward   Joseph H. Sears, 6th
Wm. Burt, 4th   Winslow B. Sherman, 4th
George H. Cobb, 50th   Wm. Stevens, 4th
Edward H. Hall, 44th chaplain   Sylvester R. Swett
Horace Holmes

Under the call of July, 1863, Wm. Ross, commuted, Horace P. Bailey, Jesse Harlow, George A. Whiting, Francis H. Russell, Alfred Maybury, Edward W. Atwood, Wm. J. Dunham, Charles F. Ellis, John T. Stoddard, Lemuel B. Bradford, Lorenzo M. Bennett, Charles F. Harlow and Gustavus G. Sampson, found substitutes, and the following entered the service:

Jedediah Bumpus, Co. C, 9th   Thomas Dexter, 55th regiment.
  regiment   Charles E. Wadsworth, 12th regt.

Under the call of January, 1864, Walter L. Gilbert was held and found a substitute, and the following recruits were obtained in Boston:

Dennis Bassingham, unattached   James McDonald, unattached
  Co.   Gustavus A. E. Miller, 20th regt.
Wm. G. Blythe, 28th regiment   Wm. Mullens, 2nd regiment
Thomas Coogan, unattached   Thomas Nolan, 2nd regiment
David Dow, 2nd regiment   John Purdy, 2nd regiment
John Ely, 2nd regiment   Elbridge Reed, unattached
Robert Henry, 5th cavalry   John Slocum, 2nd regiment
Wm. Johnson, 5th cavalry   Edwin Terry, 2nd cavalry
I. Lang, 2nd regiment   James White, 2nd cavalry
Peter H. Mara, 2nd regiment   Charles E. Williams, 5th cavalry
Michael Malony, 2nd regiment   George Williams, 2nd cavalry

Under call of July, 1864, the following recruits were obtained in Boston:

James F. Andrews, 61st regiment   Thomas Foley, 23d regiment
Thomas Bacon, 2nd regiment   Edward H. Forbes, 2nd cavalry
Charles Brooks, 26th regiment   Patrick Hogan, V. R. C.
William Burns, 2nd regiment   Alvin H. Henry, 2nd cavalry
John Clark, 2nd regiment   John A. Keefe, unattached
Henry Crosley, 5th cavalry   Patrick Kelley, 2nd regiment

Edward Kenney, 2nd, H. A.
John Leach, V. R. C.
Wm. Lee, 2nd regiment
John Lyden, 2nd H. A.
Michael I. Menagh, 35th regiment
John O'Brien, 2nd H. A.
Joseph O'Brien, V. R. C.

Abraham Page, 5th cavalry
Edward Paine, 2nd cavalry
Thomas Paine, V. R. C.
John Riley, 2nd regiment
Lewis Paszaut, 2nd cavalry
Henry Robinson, 33d regiment
Frank Smith, 27th regiment

Daniel E. Damon bought a representative recruit. 20th un-attached company.

Joseph L. Bartlett
John F. Chapman
John C. Chase
Nathaniel M. Davis

Abner Leonard, Jr.
Frank C. Robbins
Wm. Waterson

24th unattached company, Francis E. Davis, 2nd lieutenant.

Charles D. Badger
Edward D. Badger
George Bailey
Alexander J. Bartlett
Jesse T. Bassett
John R. Bradley
John Brown
Charles W. Bump
Albert L. Burgess
John E. Burt
Wm. B. Burt
Eugene Callahan
Wm. H. Churchill
Charles F. Drake
Samuel N. Dunham
Sylvester Dunlap
Wm. Dunlap
Thomas H. Ellis
George Green
Wm. T. Harlow
Charles G. Hathaway

Isaac K. Holmes
Seth L. Holmes
Sumner Leonard
Stephen M. Maybury
Michael McCrate
Thomas M. Nash
Simeon L. Nickerson
Stephen P. Nightingale
Wm. T. Pierce
Obed C. Pratt
Charles Remington
Thomas Ryan
Barnabas E. Savery
Leander M. Vaughn
Charles A. Washburn
Daniel S. Wells
Samuel A. Whitten
John B. Williams
Philip H. Williams
Albert S. Wood

The following is a list of Plymouth soldiers in the war in addition to the lists already mentioned:

Charles B. Allen, 5th cavalry
Sherman Allen, 2nd sharp shooters
Frederick Atwood, 7th regiment
George H. Atwood, V. R. C.
Mason B. Bailey, 7th battery
Luther R. Barnes, 58th regiment
Ansel Bartlett, 58th regiment
John W. Bartlett, 7th regiment
Temple H. Bartlett, 58th regiment
Otis L. Battles, 24th regiment, 3d
  R. I. cavalry

Orin Bosworth, 2d regiment
Ellis E. Brown, 5th cavalry
Daniel A. Bruce, 99th N. Y.
Henry Bryant, 3d R. I. cavalry
Frederick W. Buck, 4th cavalry,
  4th Lt., 5th cavalry
Luke P. Burbank, 34th regiment
C. B. Burgess, 24th regiment
Joseph W. B. Burgess, 8th regt.,
  N. H.
Phineas Burt, 58th regiment

Horatio Cameron, 1st cavalry
Nathaniel Carver, 12th regiment, 58th regiment
John S. Cassidy, 58th regiment
James H. Chapman, 11th regiment
James E. Churchill, 99th N. Y.
John Cunningham, 9th and 32d regiments
John Daley, 16th regiment
Isaac Dickerman, 99th N. Y.
Josiah M. Diman, 10th Pennsylvania cavalry
Maurice Dooley, 28th regiment
Wm. L. Douglass, 58th regiment
John Duffy, 2nd H. A.
Wm. Duffy, 1st cavalry
Seth W. Eddy, 58th regiment
Wm. Edes, 11th regiment
Samuel Eliot, 28th regiment
Frank Finney, Sig. Corps
Walter H. Finney, 2nd H. A.
Philander Freeman, U. S. Army
Henry Gibbs, 99th N. Y.
Phineas Gibbs, 24th N. Y.
Thomas Gibbs, 3rd N. Y.
Amos Goodwin, 5th cavalry
Edwin F. Hall, 58th regiment
George A. Hall, 5th cavalry
Christopher T. Harris, 12th regt.
Sylvanus K. Harlow, 20th regt.
B. F. Harten, 11th regiment
Allen Hathaway, 99th N. Y. regt.
Allen T. Holmes, Signal Corps
Edwin P. Holmes, Davis Guards, Lowell
Samuel N. Holmes, 3d R. I. cavalry
Wm. C. Holmes, President's Guard
Daniel D. Howard, 58th regiment
Charles H. Howland, 34th regt., Lieutenant Quartermaster
Wm. H. Jackson
Henry A. Jenkins, 5th battery
George H. Jenness, 5th regiment, N. H.
John K. Kincaid, 58th regiment
Wm. King, 13th regiment
Wm. W. Lanman, 3d R. I. cavalry

Melvin G. Leach
James A. Lovell, 2nd H. A.
John Matthews, 12th battery
Stephen M. Maybury, 18th regt., 24th infantry, 17th U. S. A.
Wm. McGill
Lewis S. Mills, 5th cavalry
John Monk, 2nd H. A.
Charles P. Morse, 17th regt., hospital steward
Gideon E. Morton, 7th regiment
Howard Morton, 30th regiment, 2nd Lt. Corps, d'Af.
James O'Connell, 28th regiment
J. S. Oldham, 24th regiment
J. T. Oldham, 24th regiment
Frank W. Paty, 2nd H. A.
Edward H. Paulding, 58th regt.
John Perkins, 10th N. Y.
Alonzo H. Perry, 58th regt.
R. W. Peterson, 1st regiment
Wm. A. Pittee, 2nd H. A.
Albert D. Pratt
James H. Pratt, 58th regiment
Thomas Pugh, 5th cavalry
Charles Raymond, 7th regiment, Lt. Col.
Samuel B. Raymond, 3 R. I. cavalry
Edmund Reed, 58th regiment
Edward L. Robbins, 2nd Lt. H. A., 2nd Lieutenant
Herbert Robbins, 3d R. I. cavalry
Augustus Sears, 7th regiment
George A. Shaw, 8th Illinois
Winslow B. Sherman, 2nd H. A.
Albert Simmons, 2nd H. A.
George A. Simmons, 2nd H. A.
James C. Standish, 2nd H. A.
Charles B. Stoddard, 41st regiment, 1st Lt. Q. M. 3rd cavalry, 1st Lt. A. Q. M.
John Sylvester, 1st cavalry
John Taylor, 58th regiment
Wallace Taylor, 24th regiment
J. Allen Tillson, 7th regiment
Alexander J. Valler, 30th regt.
David R. Valler, 58th regiment

Taylor J. Valler, 17 regiment
Ansel H. Vaughn, 4th cavalry
Edward N. H. Vaughn, 99th N. Y.
Benjamin Weston, California cavalry
Benjamin F. Whittemore, 58th regiment
Wm. B. Whittemore, 58th regt.
John B. Williams, 3rd battery
Erik Wolff, 5th cavalry, 2nd lieutenant

The following Plymouth men entered the service during the war as officers in the navy:

Sherman Allen, mate
Alexander B. Atwood, mate
Edward Baker, master, acting lieutenant
Winslow B. Barnes, mate
Cornelius Bartlett, ensign
Francis Burgess, master
Victor A. Bartlett, sailmaker
Charles H. Brown, master, acting lieutenant
Charles Campbell, mate
Robert B. Churchill, 3rd, assistant engineer
John F. Churchill, mate
Wm. R. Cox, mate, ensign
Francis B. Davis, ensign, acting master
Wm. J. Dunham, 3d assistant engineer
Alvin Finney, master
Elkanah C. Finney, mate
George Finney, master
Robert Finney, mate
Augustus H. Fuller, mate, ensign
Ichabod C. Fuller, mate, ensign
Ezra S. Goodwin, master
Nathaniel Goodwin, acting lieutenant
Eliphalet Holbrook, mate
George H. Holmes, master
Charles H. Howland, mate
Lemuel Howland, Jr. mate,
Wm. H. Howland, mate
Wm. H. Hoxie, mate
Franklin S. Leach, mate
Phineas Leach, master
Wm. W. Leonard, mate, ensign
Everett Manter, mate
John Morissey, ensign
Frank T. Morton, assistant paymaster
Thomas B. Sears, Jr., master
Amasa C. Sears, master
Merritt Shaw, 3d assistant engineer
E. Stevens Turner, master in com.
Frank W. Turner, mate
Adoniram Whiting, mate
Benjamin Whitmore, master
Henry C. Whitmore, mate
John Whitmore, master

Plymouth seamen in the service during the war:

Wm. Archer
Albert Ashport
Richard Atwell
Edward A. Austin
Hiram F. Bartlett
Temple H. Bartlett
Jesse T. Bassett
Wm. Brown
Caleb Bryant
Henry Burns
John B. Chandler
Charles W. Chickering
Solomon H. Churchill
James Cook
Ephraim Douglass
Atwood R. Drew
B. F. Dunham
Robert Dunham
James L. Field
John Fisher
George B. Foley
Henry C. Gage
Arthur M. Grant
James Gray
James Halpin
Allen Hathaway

Edward W. Hathaway
Samuel Haskins
Charles H. Hollis
Thaxter Hopkins
Wm. Horton
Edward Howland
George H. Jenness
Benjamin Kempton
Walter S. King
Josiah Leach
Amos Lonnon
James B. Lynch
Wm. H. Maxey
Owen McGann
Bache Melex
John A. Morse
John F. Morse
Patrick Murphy
Sylvester Nightingale

Hiraim S. Purrington
George Rice
Orin W. Ring
Francis Roland
Wm. C. Russell
Martin H. Ryder
Harvey C. Swift
Wm. Slade
Albert Swift
Francis Sylvester
Wm. H. Sylvester
Auguste Thomas
James E. Thomas
E. F. Townsend
George Tully
Henry Vail
James Welch
Joseph Weston
Joseph Wright

Plymouth men killed during the Civil War:

John K. Alexander, at Spotsylvania Court House, May 12, 1864.
Lawrence R. Blake at Antietam, Sept. 17, 1862.
Edward D. Brailey at Newbern, April 27, 1862.
Jedediah Bumpus, June 30. 1864.
Nathaniel Burgess, wounded at Fort Steadman, March 25th, 1865, died of wounds in July, 1865.
Joseph L. Churchill at Newbern, March 14, 1862.
Joseph W. Collingwood, at Fredericksburg, December 13, 1862, died December 24.
Edwin F. Hall, at Coal Harbor, June 3, 1864.
Frederick Holmes, at Port Hudson, June 14, 1863.
Orin D. Holmes, at Fort Steadman, March 25, 1865.
Thomas A. Mayo, at Gaines Mill, June 27, 1862.
Lemuel B. Morton, at Spotsylvania Court House, May 12, 1864.
Isaac H. Perkins, at Coal Harbor, June 3, 1864, died June 26.
Harvey A. Raymond, at Whitehall, Dec. 16, 1862.
Edward Stevens, at Whitehall, Dec. 16, 1862, died Jan. 19, 1863.
David A. Taylor, at Petersburg, June 22, 1864.
Israel H. Thrasher, at Port Hudson, June 14, 1863, died June 29.
Benjamin Westgate, at Whitehall, Dec. 16, 1862.
John M. Whiting, Opequan Creek, September 19, 1864.

Plymouth men who died in the service.

Wm. T. Atwood, at Newbern, July 20, 1862.
George W. Barnes, at Harrison's Landing, August 3, 1862.
Victor A. Bartlett, at Salisbury, March 25, 1864.
Wm. Brown, on Ship Constellation, Dec. 24, 1864.
George W. Burgess, Falmouth, March 8, 1863.

Joseph W. B. Burgess, at Washington, December 9, 1864.
Thomas B. Burt, at Washington, October 31, 1862.
John Carline, at Roanoke Island, October 14, 1864.
John B. Collingwood, at Cincinnati, August 21, 1863.
Thomas Collingwood, Camp Parks, Kentucky, August 31, 1863.
Isaac Dickerman, near Fortress Monroe, November 12, 1863.
Benjamin F. Durgin, Baton Rouge, August 8, 1863.
Seth W. Eddy, Readville, March 13, 1864.
Wm. Edes, Andersonville, August 30, 1864.
Melvin C. Faught, Windmill Point Hospital, Va., Feb. 5, 1863.
Lemuel B. Faunce, Jr., Goldsboro, April 23, 1865.
Theodore S. Fuller, Rebel Prison, probably Oct. 1, 1863.
Edward E. Green, Baton Rouge, July 11, 1863.
Thomas Haley, St. James Hospital, La., April 5, 1863.
Justus W. Harlow, near Ft. Monroe, September 17, 1862.
Wm. N. Hathaway, Washington, Feb. 23, 1863.
Thomas W. Hayden, Crab Orchard, September 4, 1863.
George M. Heath, Harrison's Landing, July 30, 1862.
Horace A. Jenks, Mill Dale Hospital, Mississippi, July 24, 1863.
Charles E. Merriam, Harper's Ferry, November 12, 1862.
Gideon E. Morton, Fredericksburg, May 3, 1863.
J. T. Oldham, Newbern, 1863.
Louis Payzant.
George T. Peckham, Knoxville, Nov. 1, 1863.
William Perry, New Orleans, June 5, 1863.
Thomas Pugh, at sea, November 18, 1865.
Albert R. Robbins, Plymouth, March 5, 1864.
Henry H. Robbins, Washington, December 4, 1863.
Thomas S. Saunders, Roanoke Island, March 11, 1862.
Otis Sears, Plymouth, January 5, 1864.
Wm. H. Shaw, Plymouth, August 6, 1865.
Edward Smith, Annapolis, May, 1862.
John Sylvester, Andersonville, December 16, 1864.
Wallace Taylor, Newbern, November 23, 1862.
Frank A. Thomas, Camp Hamilton, September 14, 1862.
Charles E. Tillson, Andersonville, July 14, 1864.
E. S. Turner, Rio Janeiro, August 5, 1864.
David R. Valler.
Charles E. Wadsworth, Salisbury, Nov. 29, 1864.
George E. Wadsworth, Camp Parks, Ky., August 30, 1863.
John Whitmore, at sea, August, 1862.
David Williams, Camp Dennison, Ky., September 14, 1863.

Plymouth men wounded in the service.

John K. Alexander, Antietam.
Simeon H. Barrows, Hampton, July 14, 1861.
Benjamin F. Bates, May 30, 1864.
Charles H. Drew, Fredericksburg.

John F. Hall, Newport News, 1862.
James S. Holbrook, Wilderness.
Charles E. Kleinhans, Fair Oaks.
Charles E. Merriam, Malvern Hill.
Seth W. Paty, Newport News and siege of Knoxville.
John Shannon, Antietam.
Samuel D. Thrasher, Wilderness.
George E. Wadsworth, White Oak Swamp.
Wm. H. Winsor, Fredericksburg.

CHAPTER XXXXI.

In speaking of the changes, in habits and customs, which have occurred in my day, it will be difficult to draw the line between those, which only my older readers will remember, and those more recent ones, which will be recalled by the young. In noting these changes I shall not confine myself to Plymouth, but shall as far as possible include those which have elsewhere come under my observation. The population of Plymouth in 1820, two years before my birth, was 4,384. Its growth to 11,017, in 1905, is one of the least remarkable changes in the history of the town during that period. Turning, however, to the nationality of the population, we find a change which has kept pace with the growing facilities of international communication, and the restless tide of migration, which characterized the 19th century. This change in nationality began to show itself about the time of my birth. Up to that time the population was not only practically wholly American, but also largely of Plymouth nativity. There are records showing that in 1813 there were two Irishmen, John Burke and Michael Murphy, living in Plymouth, and there are reasons for believing that they and their families were the only persons of Irish birth in the town. It is possible that the above two men were servants, or employees of Judge Joshua Thomas, who lived in the house on Main street, now called the Plymouth Tavern. At any rate, Judge Thomas must have felt a special interest in them, as in the year above mentioned, 1813, Bishop Cheverus, by his invitation, came down from Boston and celebrated mass for their benefit in the parlors on the southerly side of his house. It is undoubtedly true that Bishop Cheverus was the most distinguished Divine who ever visited Plymouth. He was born in Mayenne, France, Jan. 28, 1768, and came to Boston in 1796, where he became associated with the Catholic mission. In 1803 he raised by subscription money to build the Catholic church in Franklin street, the site of which is now occupied by Devonshire street, and more than $3,000 of the sum raised was subscribed by Protestants, of whom John Adams headed the list. The esteem in which he

was held in Boston was further shown by the gratuitous services of Charles Bulfinch, the distinguished architect, who furnished the design for the church, and by the gift of a picture
of the crucifixion by Henry Sargent, a Boston artist, to place
on its walls. Among the subscribers to the church fund were
Harrison Gray Otis, Benjamin Crowinshield, Theodore Lyman, Thomas H. Perkins and Samuel Dexter, and General
E. Hasket Derby gave the church a bell.   While in Boston
Bishop Cheverus accepted invitations to preach in Protestant
churches, following as he said, the example of Christ, who
preached in the synagogues. In 1810 he was consecrated in
Baltimore the first Bishop of Boston, and in 1818 his associate,
the Abbé Mantignon, died, at whose funeral the body was
borne to the grave through the streets of Boston with the
Bishop wearing ecclesiastical garments, and a mitre, presenting
a novel scene to the eyes of New England people. In 1823, the
Bishop was called to France to take charge of the Bishopric of
Montauban, and in 1826 was nominated to the Metropolitan
See of Bordeaux.   In 1828 he was made councillor of state,
and in 1830 commander of the order of the Holy Ghost. In
February, 1836, he was made a Cardinal, and on the 9th of
March received from Louis Philippe the Cardinal's hat. He
died July 2d, 1836.

Until ocean steamers were built of sufficient size to accommodate steerage passengers, immigration was chiefly confined to
the Irish, who came in the packet ships plying between London
or Liverpool and New York, Philadelphia, or Boston. There
were the Cambridge, Devonshire, London, Henry Clay, York-
shire, Liverpool, Ashburton and Hottingeur, coming to New
York; the Daniel Webster, North America, Anglo Saxon and
Ocean Monarch coming to Boston, and the Tuscarora and
Shenandoah to Philadelphia, and for some years their steerages
were crowded with Irish immigrants. With the coming in of
the steamers the numbers largely increased. It was during the
period from 1835 to 1855, that the Irish element began to be
perceptible to any considerable extent in Plymouth. Within my
day the first Irishman to come to the town was John Cassidy,
about 1820 or 1830. He had been living for a time in
Boston, and there his son, John S., our townsman, was born.
He was a blacksmith by trade, and a man of striking appear-

ance. He had two daughters, whom I knew very well, fine women; Elizabeth, who married Gridley T. Poole, and Ellen, who married a Mr. Southmayd of Campton, New Hampshire. There was a Michael McCarthy who came not long after Mr. Cassidy, whose daughter was the mother of our late townsman, Timothy Downey. Quite a number came both before and soon after 1850, including Timothy and John Quinlan in 1849, John O'Brien in 1851, and not far from those dates Jeremiah Murray, John Murray, Timothy Regan, Wm. O'Brien, Timothy Lynch, James Ready, Timothy Hurley, James Lynch, James Burns, Barney Sullivan and others. For many years the number of Catholics in Plymouth was insufficient to maintain a church, and father Moran of Sandwich, where the glass works had gathered a considerable Irish population, was in the habit of holding service once or twice in each month in the town hall and Davis Hall, and elsewhere, until the Catholic church was erected in 1874.

After the advent of the Irish there was for some years quite a large German immigration, which found occupation in the Cordage works at Seaside. The German population, however, was rather a changeable one, and after a few years of savings, it largely found its way west, and was followed in Plymouth by the Italians, French and Portuguese, who, added to the Irish, now make up nearly one quarter of the population of the town. The Portuguese have drifted here chiefly from New Bedford and Provincetown, to which places they found their way in vessels bringing the first catch of oil landed at the Western Islands by whale ships from those ports. The effect of this immigration on Provincetown has been remarkable. The first time I ever went to that town was in 1836, when I was permitted as a boy of fourteen to join a party of older persons in the sloop Thetis, going one day and returning the next. At that time its population was about two thousand, nearly all of whom were Cape Cod people, who had moved there to either engage in the whale or cod fishery, or to keep stores for the sale of ship chandlery and supplies of all kinds to vessels making harbor there. A man by the name of Lothrop from some up Cape town, kept a hotel, and by the aid of loam brought from distant towns, he was cultivating the only garden in town. The only street was parallel with the shore, and from

fence to fence it was a bed of loose sand, through the middle
of which everybody waded, the women I have heard it said,
having a way of kicking their heels in walking by which they
kept the sand out of their shoes.   One of our party asked the
landlord if he could have a horse and ride through the village.
"My dear sir," said Mr. Lothrop, "there is not a horse owned in
town, but the mail chaise will arrive about six o'clock, and perhaps the driver will let you have his horse."   During the administration of Andrew Jackson not only was our National
debt extinguished, but a very considerable surplus revenue
grew up, which in 1836 was divided among the states in the
form of a loan, each state giving its obligation to repay the
loan if ever called for.   Massachusetts distributed its share
among the towns, and Provincetown spent her portion in building plank sidewalks.   At the present time the Portuguese con-
stitute a majority of the population of the town.   At the beginning of the civil war one of the measures proposed for the
relief of the financial straits of the government was a call on
the states for the payment of the loan above mentioned.   It
has been stated by Mr. L. E. Chittenden, Register of the Treasury under President Lincoln, that it was found at that time
that the obligations of the Rebel states had mysteriously disappeared.

One of the important results of the foreign immigration in
Plymouth County, and probably elsewhere has been the solution of the problem concerning the future of our abandoned
farms.   These foreigners, more especially the Portuguese and
Italians, have picked them up one after another, and are pros-
pering, where their former native owners failed. It must not be
forgotten, while considering changes in population and occupation, that the abandonment of the fisheries has caused a great
change in the industries of our town.   With seventy-three vessels engaged in the Grand Bank fishery, as there were thirty-
five years ago, our wharves and flake yards presented busy
scenes.   The large increase, however, of our coal and
lumber trade, amounting now in the former, to thirty thous-
and tons annually, has helped materially to prevent any recent
depreciation of wharf property.

I propose now to speak of the changes which have occurred
within my recollection in carriages and in general methods of

travel. I have in an early chapter referred to buggies and wagons, giving the derivation of their names, and the countries where they were originally used. The introduction of the carry-all in Plymouth occurred within my time, and as far back as I can remember there were only two, one in the stable of George Drew in Middle street, and the other owned by Bourne Spooner. It is generally supposed that its spacious interior gave rise to its name which, however, is really only a corruption of the name of the French Carriole. A vehicle called a cab, which is simply an abbreviation of cabriolet came quite extensively into use in Boston about 1840, but never reached Plymouth, and in the city has now largely given way to a four wheeler, which retains the old name. The carriage known as a hack, brought to America from London, and receiving the name which there applied to the horse alone, was never introduced into Plymouth until 1870. At the celebration of the dedication of the Soldiers' Monument on Training Green in 1869, the committee of arrangements borrowed one from Geo. W. Wright of Duxbury, and hired another in Boston. There is probably no city in the world in which the hack has been for more than a hundred years in such general use as in Boston. The superior quality for which Boston hacks have long been distinguished, has been probably due to the fact that wealthy families have patronized hack stables rather than keep carriages of their own, and they wanted the best. I can well remember when there were not more than four private carriages and coachmen in Boston, and when nothing in livery was seen on its streets. About 1850 Mr. Deacon, who built an elegant mansion at the south end after the style of a French Chateau, surrounded by a high brick wall, set up a livery, and when his flunkey first appeared sitting like Solomon in all his glory on the box, he was followed and hooted at by the boys. The vehicle for many years in general use was in Boston, as elsewhere, the chaise. Lawyers and doctors and merchants constantly used them, and always drove themselves, while before the days of street cars business men drove every morning into the city from suburban homes, and put up their horses for the day in some central stable. I remember stables in Cambridge street, Bowdoin Square, Howard street, Elm street, Brattle street, Devonshire street, Franklin street, Federal street, School street, Bromfield street, Bedford street, West street and Charles street.   With the introduction of street cars leading to neighboring towns, the livery business gradually disappeared, and the high price of central city lots has left the older sections of the city with scarcely a place where a horse can be put up for a night.   These stables first found a new resting place in the extension of Chestnut street on the river side of Charles street, which Tom Appleton, the Boston wit, called Horse Chestnut street, but they have gradually extended to localities farther west.   In the process of evolution the wheel has now turned, and the suburban business men are deserting the street cars, and, coming to Boston in their automobiles, instead of chaises, put them up for the day in the grand garage in Park Square.   Again referring to the general use of chaises, I remember that such men as President Quincy, Lucius Manlius Sargent, Ebenezer Francis and Jeremiah Mason were frequently seen driving their chaises, and Mr. Webster often rode in one over the road from Marshfield to Boston, holding the reins himself, and having a trunk lashed to the axle.   Mr. Mason, above mentioned, the distinguished lawyer, one day when riding in his chaise, turned from Washington street into Spring Lane, and met a truckman coming up with his team. He was six feet six inches in height, but he always sat in his chaise so bent as not to appear to be a tall man.   The truckman called out to him to back out, which Mr. Mason was not inclined to do, as he would have to back up hill, while the truckman could more easily back down.   Mr. Mason said nothing, but the truckman finally began to swear at him, and showed a disposition to fight.   Mr. Mason becoming a little angry, began to straighten up and show his size, much to the astonishment of the man with the team, who called out, "for God's sake, Mr., don't uncoil any more, I'll get out of the way."

The stage derived its name, which it took from the stage coach of England, from the word stage, meaning a section or the whole of a road route.   The name, however, reached New England many years before the arrival of the English coach, and was applied to a carriage of very different construction. The New England stage in the early part of the last century was a long covered wagon hung on leather thorough-braces,

and contained seats without backs, which were reached by
climbing over the seats in front.   In 1801, according to the
Farmer's Almanac, there were twenty-five lines of coaches running out of Boston, most of which started from the King's Inn
on the corner of Exchange street and Market Square.   The
stages running to Cambridge and Roxbury and Brookline,
made each two trips a day, and the stage to Plymouth made
three trips a week by the way of Hingham, being ten hours on
the road.   The South Boston and Dorchester turnpike running as far as Neponset River, was incorporated, March 4,
1805, and the Braintree and Weymouth turnpike running from
Quincy to Queen Ann's Corner in West Scituate, was incorporated March 4, 1803.   Thus a new route was opened by the
last named turnpike, over which the fast line ran every day,
while the mail line ran every alternate day through Hingham.
Until the Old Colony Railroad was opened these turnpikes
were toll roads.   After a few years the clumsy stage gave way
to the well known English coach made with the addition of
a middle seat with an adjustable back strap.   With the exception of the English post carriage a sort of a barouche
drawn by two horses, one of which was ridden by a uniformed postilion, I have never found a more comfortable and attractive traveling carriage.   In 1846 I rode
with the coachman on one of these coaches from Glasgow to Carlisle, ninety miles, in nine hours, with the four
horses on the gallop, and never leaving the centre of the track.
The red coated guard occupying a seat at the back of the coach,
warned with his horn every team to clear the road, and when
passing a post office he threw off a mail pouch and took another from a hooked rod, held up by the master of the post.
On approaching a station for change of horses, the guard
gave notice with his horn, and the coachman halting in the
middle of the road, dropped his reins right and left, and four
hostlers, two to unhitch, and two to hitch, would have a new
team ready with a delay of not more than two minutes, the
coachman leaving his seat but once in the nine hours.   During
the last years of these coaches the schedule time of a trip from
London to Edinburgh, four hundred miles, was forty hours.
The hansom, which for more than fifty years has been used
in London, has found a difficult entrance into Boston, but is

now gradually finding its way into use.   The fares charged for them are much lower in London than in Boston.   In 1895 I took one at the railway station and rode with a fellow passenger to Morley's hotel at Trafalgar Square, nearly three miles, and paid two and six pence for the two, while in Boston the charge would have been from two to three dollars.

The introduction of omnibuses in Boston, first used in London, was very gradual.   Having an aunt living in Cambridge, one of my excursions during my vacation visits in Boston was to her home, and thus I became early familiar with the methods of communication with that town.   As long ago as I can remember these omnibuses, taking the place of the old coaches, made only two or three trips a day, in answer to calls entered on a slate at the office in Brattle street, picking up passengers at their houses, and dropping them at their destinations.   As business increased, passengers were obliged to take the omnibuses at the office, starting at every hour, and thus they became known as hourlies.   Their business was partially interrupted for a time by the construction of a branch of the Fitchburg railroad, which had a station about where the law school is now located, but it was soon abandoned, and the track was taken up.

As I have begun to speak of matters connected with Boston, I may as well speak of the changes in that city since my early boyhood.   For this digression I ask to be excused.   I was almost as familiar with Boston, when a boy, as I was with Plymouth, as I spent nearly every vacation there with my grandmother who lived in Winthrop Place, which, with Otis Place, formed a circuitous avenue, entering from and returning to Summer street.   Summer street during my early life was distinguished, not only for its beautiful shade trees and elegant houses, but also for its notable residents.   Among the latter whom I remember were, Dr. Jacob Bigelow, Robert C. Winthrop, Dr. Putnam, Edward H. Robbins, Nathaniel Goddard, John Wells, Horace Gray, John P. Cushing, Benjamin Buzzey, Charles Tappan, Edward Everett, Rev. Dr. Nathaniel Langdon Frothingham, John C. Gray, Benjamin Rich, Rev. Dr. Alexander Young, Wm. Sturgis, Joseph Bell, Benjamin Loring, James W. Paige, and Daniel Webster.   There also were Trinity church on the north side, and the Octagon church, Unitarian, at the junction of Summer and Bedford streets, while in Winthrop and Otis Place lived Rufus Choate, Abel Adams, Wm. Perkins, Samuel Whitwell, H. H. Hunnewell, George Bond, Henry Cabot, Joshua Blake, George Bancroft, Nathaniel Bowditch, and Israel Thorndike.

When that neighborhood was changed from a residential to a business one, Winthrop Place was extended across Franklin street to State street, the whole taking the name of Devonshire street. From Franklin to Milk street the nucleus of the extended street was Theatre Alley, so-called, because in the alley was the stage entrance of the Federal Street Theatre. The Catholic church, which stood on the south side of Franklin street, was taken down to make way for the extended street. Ma'am Dunlap's famous cigar, snuff and tobacco store, which every gentleman in Boston knew, partly on account of the quality of her goods, and partly on account of the beauty of her daughter Rachel, stood on the west side of the alley. Boston has always been famous for its alleys, at least fifteen of which I remember. They furnished very convenient cut shorts for those who were in a hurry, or did not wish to encounter undesirable friends. Mr. Choate, whose office was on the southerly corner of Court and Washington streets, lived at different times at the United States hotel, in Edinboro street and Winthrop Place, and in going home he invariably went down State to Devonshire street, and thence through Theatre Alley and Catholic Church Alley. The Alley from State street to Dock Square, now called Change Alley, was formerly called Flagg Alley, taking its name from its pavement of flaggstones, which again took their name from Elisha Flagg, who about 1750 opened a quarry in Grafton, and furnished Boston and some other New England towns with slabs of that description. For some unknown reason alleys seem to have been peculiar to seaport places like Provincetown, Salem, Marblehead, Newburyport and Plymouth, in the last of which were in my day, Thomas's Alley, Cooper's Alley, LeBaron's Alley, Spooner's Alley and Clamshell Alley, all of which remain except Thomas's Alley on the south side of the estate of Col. Wm. P. Stoddard, which was closed some years ago, under an agreement with the town.

On the south side of Franklin street, until about 1800, known as Barrell's pasture, extending from the Catholic Alley, now Devonshire street, up to Hawley street, there was a single block called the Tontine block, such as we ought to see more of in Boston today. It was designed by Charles Bulfinch, and contained sixteen dwelling houses, with a front curved to correspond to the curve of the street, and built with a palace front, two houses at each end projecting about six feet, and the centre carried up higher than the rest of the building, and built over three arches, a central arch for a street called Arch street to pass through, and one smaller arch on each side over the Arch street sidewalks. A door under the arch led up to the old Boston Library, which is still in existence with a home in Boylston Place. The block was built on the Tontine plan, with a certain number of owners, the property descending to the survivors. After some years its tontine feature was abandoned and the property divided among the survivors.

All through my boyhood, Franklin, Federal, Atkinson, now called Congress, Pearl, High, Purchase, South, Lincoln, Summer, Arch, Winter, Tremont, West, Bedford, Chauncy, Boylston, Essex and Kingston streets, Otis Place, Winthrop Place and Fort Hill were occupied by dwelling houses. Fort Hill, which rose about twenty-five or thirty feet above Pearl street, was cut down in 1865, and High street extended across it. Pemberton hill, the residence of Gardner Greene, was cut down in 1835 to its present level, and Pemberton Square laid out for houses. The estate covered by Pemberton hill was a famous historic estate. It was occupied by Sir Harry Vane in 1636, by Rev. John Cotton and his son Seaborn, John Hull, Wm. Vassall, Madame Hayley, the society leader in Boston, Jonathan Mason, and Gardner Green. The house of Mr. Green, which was taken down in 1835, was built by Mr. Vassall in 1760. When the hill was levelled, a rare tree called the Gingko, brought from China, was removed to the Common, slips from which are now standing on the grounds of Jason W. Mixter and B. F. Mellor in Plymouth.

When the city government decided to remove the hill Patrick T. Jackson, in behalf of the city, made a contract with Asa G. Sheldon of Wilmington to perform the work and fill the flats north of Causeway street. Mr. Sheldon moved the Gingko tree to a spot on the Common near the Beacon street mall on a stone dray drawn by oxen, driven by Waterman Brown of Woburn.

Washington street, once called the Neck, was until 1786 the only way in and out of Boston.   South Boston, then a part of Dorchester, could only be reached by the way of Roxbury; and Cambridge could not be reached except by ferry, only by going through Roxbury and Brookline.   The Charles River Bridge Company was incorporated March 9, 1785, and built the old Charlestown bridge, which was opened June 17, 1786. This bridge furnished a new and convenient route to Cambridge.   The West Boston Bridge Company was incorporated March 9, 1792, and built the bridge extending from Cambridge street, which was opened November 23, 1793.   These two bridges continued as toll bridges until January 30, 1858. Dorchester Neck, now known as South Boston, was annexed to Boston, March 6, 1804, then having only ten families, and on the same date the South Bridge Co. was incorporated.   The Dover street bridge was built by that company, and opened Oct. 1, 1805, and was sold to the city April 19, 1832, and made free, tolls having been charged up to that time.   Canal bridge now Craigie's Bridge, a toll bridge, leading to East Cambridge, was built by a company incorporated Feb. 27, 1807, and after its purchase by the state, was made free January 30, 1858.   On the 14th of June, 1814, Isaac P. Davis, Uriah Cotting and Wm. Brown, and their associates, were incorporated as the Boston and Roxbury Mill Corporation, who built the mill dam leading from Beacon street to Brookline, over which a road was opened July 2, 1821.   This was a toll road, and during my college life the toll gate was located a little east of Arlington street, and tolls were collected until it was laid out as a highway, Dec. 7, 1868.   The Boston Free Bridge Corporation was incorporated March 4, 1826, and built the South Boston Bridge, which crossed Fort Point Channel at Sea street, and was bought by the city September 16, 1828, and called Federal street bridge.   The Warren Bridge Corporation was incorporated March 11, 1828, and opened Dec. 25, in that year. It was assumed by the state in 1833, and made free in 1858.

Between the toll gate on the Mill Dam and Brookline there were no houses, and what is now called the Back Bay extended from the Mill Dam to Washington street.   In this connection the statement may be interesting that in 1830 the pasturage of cows on the Common was for the first time forbidden by a city ordinance.

When I was ten years old, my great uncle, Isaac P. Davis, who was born in 1771, and who as one of the corporators of the Mill Dam, was familiar with that neighborhood, took me one day down to the corner of Boylston street and Charles street, and said to me, William, here was the original bank of Charles River, and on this spot the British embarked for Charlestown on the morning of the battle of Bunker Hill. I was also told by one of the building committee of Trinity church, that in driving piles to support the foundation, the bed of an old channel was found where hard bottom could not be reached, and the expedient was adopted of clearing away the earth between the piles several feet down and filling the space with cement, thus holding them from the top instead of supporting them at the bottom. On this foundation, containing either five thousand piles at a cost of $7 each, or seven thousand at a cost of $5, I have forgotten which, the structure stands without a crack, to show any settling. If an X ray could penetrate the sub-surface of the Back Bay, it would disclose thousands of piles with a composite between, of old hats, bonnets, shoes, hoop skirts and tomato cans on which stand the domiciles of wealth and fashion. Perhaps, however, such a foundation is as genuine and real as that on which stands fashion itself. In my youth the South Bay, east of Washington street, was open to the harbor through Fort Point channel, only obstructed by the Dover street, and the old South Boston bridges. At that time the yards of the houses in Purchase street extended to the water, and Atlantic Avenue, north of Dewey Square, was built along the harbor margin. Thus within in my recollection, there have been added between the Mill Dam and Washington street, Boylston street, Huntington, Columbus, Atlantic, Shawmut and Harrison avenues, all built where once was water, and adding more than eight hundred acres of made land to the old peninsula of Boston, which contained only six hundred and ninety. Until 1852 the Commonwealth owned 2,453,730 square feet of land in the Back Bay, which in that year it began to have filled with the view of selling it. At that time it was estimated that the land was worth, less the cost of filling, $906,516.00. The conservatism of this estimate is shown by the fact that in 1872 $3,551,514 had been received from sales, or $2,044,294 taking out the cost of filling, and 500,000 square feet remained unsold, valued at $750,000, leaving a profit to the Commonwealth of $1,887,178. In view of the probably speedy and profitable sales of this land, the question came up in the legislature of 1859, when I was a member of the Senate, whether it would not be well to devote a part of the proceeds of these sales to educational purposes, and petitions were presented looking to this end, which were referred to the committee on education, of which I was chairman. After several hearings I drew up a report at the request of the committee, and after I submitted it to the legislature, the daily papers paid it the unusual compliment of printing it in full. Resolves accompanied the report, giving $100,000 to the Museum of Natural History and Comparative Zoology in Cambridge, fifty thousand dollars to Tufts college, and $25,000 each to Amherst and Williams colleges, and the Wilbraham academy, and in addition a substantial amount to enlarge the school fund of the state. Against some opposition the Resolves were passed by both branches of the legislature, and it has always been a source of satisfaction to me that I was in some degree instrumental in prosecuting to a successful issue a measure so plainly conducive to the best interests of the state.

One of the most striking changes in Boston within my time, has been the change in the location of meeting houses from those localities where they were once marked features, to the newer parts of the city. While many of the meeting houses which stood sixty years ago in Purchase street, Summer street, Hollis street, Cambridge street, Chambers street and Hanover street, have been abandoned, and others in Federal street, Franklin street, Summer street, Washington street and Essex street have been replaced by new, no less than twenty-five have been built in sections which in 1840 were covered by water. Thus the money changers, instead of being driven out of the temple, have driven the temples away from the haunts of trade.

In recalling these recollections of Boston, to which I have merely glanced, it seems to me that I have witnessed its growth from youth to age. There are other evidences of its

growth than those to which I have alluded. I was told many
years ago by Edwin Rice, a resident in East Boston, which now
contains a population of thirty thousand, that when he settled
there its population did not exceed a hundred. I recall sitting
one calm summer afternoon nearly seventy years ago on the
grassy bank of Noddles Island, as East Boston was called,
now covered with a dense population, and listening to the roar
of the city across the harbor. I do not remember to have
heard it before or since. The experience was an interesting
one. There was no single distinguishable sound, but the rattle
of wheels on the pavement, the footfall of horses on the bridges, the hammer on the anvil, the drum of a passing band, the
cries of street venders, and, perhaps the rustle of trees and
the voices of boys at play, all mingled in a continuous rumble
of a busy, populous city. It has been stated that during the battle of Waterloo the people of Brussells heard neither the rattle
of musketry, nor the booming of cannon, but both were combined in an unbroken roar of the battle field. In recalling that
summer afternoon at East Boston, I have thought that the
voices of the past, not the voice of this man or that, performing
his part in the drama of life, but the voices of all good and
great men who have lived and died need time and distance
to be blended as a harmonious whole in the grand symphony of
civilization.

In 1832 the whole of East Boston, containing 663 acres of
upland and marsh with the flats contiguous thereto and one
house, was bought by Wm. H. Sumner, Stephen White, Francis J. Oliver and others for about $80,000, and the East Boston
corporation was soon after formed. From that time it rapidly grew, attracting a large population, and becoming a hive of
industry. Before the civil war two hundred and thirty or
more vessels had been built on its shores, with a measurement
of more than two hundred thousand tons. Ship builders
were drawn there from the shallow waters of Duxbury, the
North river and other places, among whom the chief were
Samuel Hall, Donald McKay, Daniel D. Kelly, A. & G. T.
Sampson, Jackson & Ewell, Paul Curtis, Jarvis Pratt, Brown,
Bates & Delano, Robert E. Jackson, Andrew Burnham, Brown
& Lovell, Hugh R. McKay, G. & T. Boole, Wm. Hall, Pratt &
Osgood, Samuel Hall, Jr., Joseph Burke, Wm. Kelly, Otis

Tufts, Burkett & Tyler, C. F. & H. D. Gardiner; E. & H. O. Briggs. There Donald McKay built the fleet of ships which made his name famous. The following is, I believe, a correct list of his vessels:

Anglo Saxon,	894	tons	Star of Empire,	1635	tons
Ocean Monarch,	1301	tons	Romance of the Seas,	1500	tons
Washington Irving,	751	tons	Challenger,	1400	tons
New World,	1404	tons	Lightning,	2083	tons
Moses,	700	tons	Great Republic,	4556	tons
Anglo American,	704	tons	Champion of the Seas,	2447	tons
Az,	700	tons	James Baines,	2526	tons
Jenny Lind,	533	tons	Commodore Perry,	1964	tons
Plymouth Rock,	960	tons	Santa Claus,	1256	tons
Helicon,	400	tons	Benin,	692	tons
Reindeer,	800	tons	Blanche Moore,	1787	tons
Parliament,	998	tons	Japan,	1964	tons
Moses Wheeler,	900	tons	Adriatic,	1327	tons
Antarctic,	1116	tons	Mastiff,	1030	tons
Daniel Webster,	1187	tons	Zephyr,	1184	tons
Staghound,	1534	tons	Defender,	1413	tons
Flying Cloud,	1782	tons	Donald McKay,	2594	tons
Staffordshire,	1817	tons	Abbott Lawrence,	1497	tons
North American,	1469	tons	Amos Lawrence,	1396	tons
Sovereign of the Seas,	2421	tons	Minnehaha,	1695	tons
Westward Ho,	1650	tons	Harry Hill,	568	tons
Bald Eagle,	1704	tons	Baltic,	1720	tons
Empress of the Seas,	2200	tons	L Z,	897	tons

The total tonnage of the above, forty-six ships, was 67,041, averaging 1,457. The greatest achievements of these vessels were the passage of the Flying Cloud, Capt. Cressey, from New York to San Francisco in 89 days, and the run by the Sovereign of the Seas of 430 geographical miles in 24 hours.

Some of the customs prevailing in my youth and early manhood may be as interesting as the topographical changes in Boston. There was no day police established in Boston until 1854, and old Constable Derastus Clapp stationed in and about State street, was the only officer ever seen. In the above year a police force, under the direction of a chief, was established, but not uniformed until 1856. I remember that the newspapers on a day after the 4th of July, commented with pride on the quiet and peaceful dispersion of the crowd on the Common, witnessing the fireworks the evening before, without a police officer to keep them in order. There were only night watchmen with their rattles who cried the hour with "All is well." They

wore in cool weather plaid camlet cloaks, and as there was a
city ordinance forbidding smoking in the streets, which by the
way has never been repealed, I have many a time when meeting
them concealed my cigar until they were out of sight.   My
readers may not be aware that a by-law was adopted in Plymouth in 1831, which is still in force, forbidding smoking in any
street, lane or public square, or on any wharf in the town.

Ringing the bell at various hours during the day and evening for the convenience of the inhabitants, has so far as Plymouth is concerned, been confined to the town sexton.   Since,
however, the ringing has been detached from the duties of a
sexton proper, who was an officer of the church, the name sexton in our town is now given to the bell ringer, who continues
to be chosen by the town every year, though he has now no connection with the church.   The first mention of a sexton in the
town records is under date of 1712, when Eleazer Rogers was
chosen "to ring the bell, sweep the meeting house, keep the
doors and windows of said meeting house shut and open for
the congregation's use upon all occasions, and carefully look
after said house as above said."   In 1714 he was required
to ring the bell at nine o'clock every evening.   From
that time to this a town sexton is chosen each year, who since
the severance of the First Church from the town no longer
rings the bell for church, while each church has its own sexton for that duty.   The custom in Plymouth is to ring the
Town bell as follows at 7 a. m., 12 noon, 1 p. m. and nine p. m.,
all the year; 6 p. m. when the sun sets after that hour, and on
Saturdays 5 p. m., instead of 6.   This custom of bell ringing
existed in Boston, as well as other places, and I have heard
it stated that the Old South Church bell was rung as late as
1836 at 11 a. m. to announce "the grog time o' day."   The
nine o'clock evening bell had its origin in the ancient curfew
bell, which derived from the French words, *"couvre feu,"*
was rung at an hour when the fires in houses should be covered
up. It was adopted in New England merely to indicate the
hour.

There was a method in Boston of lighting the street lamps,
which was primitive. The city was divided into districts, and
a lamplighter was appointed for each district. The lamps
were all oil lamps until 1834, and each lighter would start from

home in the morning carrying a ladder, a can of oil, and a filled and trimmed lamp. He would take the old lamp out of the first lantern, putting the fresh one in its place. He would then fill and trim the lamp he took out and go on to the next lantern, and so on through his district. There was another custom, so far as I know peculiar to Boston, where domestic life was less extravagantly and luxuriously enjoyed than in New York, Philadelphia and Baltimore. Few families kept men servants, and many gentlemen, rather than impose the work of blacking boots on servant girls, or have blacking in the house, fell in with a plan suggested by the Brattle street negroes. For many years the shops on the south side of that street were chiefly occupied by shoe blacks and negro dealers in second hand clothing. Some of these negroes went about on the first of January and secured lists of subscribers for their work for the year as a milkman or an ice man would for his milk or ice. If, for instance, he was a beginner in the industry, he would start out early in the morning with two rods about eight feet long, and an inch or more in diameter, and calling at the house of the first subscriber, take his boots and stringing them by the tugs on a rod like herrings on a stick, go the rounds of his subscribers, and the next morning exchange the clean boots for soiled ones. A more general employment of men servants, and finally boot black shops and stands put an end to this custom.

CHAPTER XXXXII.

The changes in the militia system of Massachusetts within my memory have been great, but in my judgment not materially for the better. There are always those who are anxious to tinker existing methods of doing things and

> "Who are apt to view their sires
> In the light of fools and liars,"

and the organization of the militia has not escaped their meddlesome hand. Under the militia law in force when I was a boy, every man between the ages of eighteen and forty-five was enrolled, and was required to appear at an annual inspection and drill. The volunteer militia and some specified persons, were exempted from this service. These enrolled men were called militia men, and on the day fixed by law those in Plymouth appeared on Training Green, and after being duly inspected, were generally dismissed. But this was not invariably the case. I remember one year when a newly chosen captain determined to exact of his company all the duties, which the spirit, if not the letter, of the law required. Much to the discomfort of his men he marched them through town and nearly out to Seaside, and made it known that the legal fine would be imposed on all delinquents. I have a distinct recollection of their march up North street, their line extending in single file from Water to Court street. The younger men in the ranks enjoyed the fun, each carrying his musket as was convenient to himself, and some wearing knapsacks of domestic manufacture, displaying devices intended to excite the applause of the accompanying crowd. Apples and peanuts were freely indulged in, while long nine cigars and pipes of extraordinary proportions left a trail of smoke like the steam from a locomotive. It was not, however, the law, but the method of enforcing it, which made the annual inspection a farce, and if it be necessary to inculcate a martial spirit in the community and maintain a volunteer militia, it would be well to revive the old law and re-establish the old militia from which volunteers could be drawn.

Under the old system, the volunteer militia was in a healthy condition, and was at the height of its glory when the Civil War broke out.. It was divided into divisions, brigades and regiments, and for many years there were in Plymouth an infantry and an artillery company; an infantry and artillery company in Abington, and infantry companies in Carver, Plympton, Halifax, Middleboro, Bridgewater, and I think Hingham. There were in those days annual brigade or regimental musters, and the musterfield in Plymouth was what is now the Robbins' field, opposite to the house of Gideon F. Holmes. Those musters were great occasions for the boys, and we were always on hand, not caring whether school kept or not. We carried out our programme for the day to the minutest detail. We were on hand in Town square when the Carver company abandoned their wagons and began their march to the tented field. We then inspected the caparisoned horses of Col. Thomas Weston of Middleboro and his staff in the yard of Bradford's tavern, and when under escort of the Standish Guards and the Plymouth Artillery, they marched to the music of the Plymouth Band, we followed, and perhaps reached the field in time to witness the arrival of the Halifax Light Infantry and the Plympton Rifle Rangers. A few cents in our pockets were sufficient to carry us through the day. The company drills, the dress parade and the sham fight received our careful attention, and the casualties in the last were on one occasion less than they would have been had not a ramrod fired by a careless soldier found a target in a distant barn. When I recall my experience at muster I am reminded of a remark made by Edward Trowbridge Dana, a brother of the late Richard H. Dana, after a service at the old Trinity church in Summer street, in Boston, in which Bishop Eastburn officiated. The Bishop was an Englishman, a handsome man, and splendid horseman, whom I have often seen riding in Boston streets wearing top boots, and looking as if he had been accustomed to following the hounds. He was as showy in the pulpit as in the saddle, and impressed his hearers more by his voice and gestures than by the matter of his discourse. On the occasion referred to, Dana, when asked by a friend on coming out of church, how he liked the Bishop, replied, "I feel as I used to when a boy on the muster field, belly full of watermelon, and head full of bass drum." It was at one of the musters above referred to held in Dedham that a new, slangy name was introduced. It was when the temperance movement was active, and the sale of intoxicating liquor was kept as much as possible out of public sight. One of the side show tents at the muster in question exhibited over its entrance a large canvass bearing a picture of a striped pig, which could be seen for a fee of ninepence. This new zoological specimen attracted great attention, and crowds learned novel lessons in Natural History. The exit from the tent was in the rear, and it was observed that every zoological student came out wiping his lips, while a large number returned for a second sight of the "critter."

I have said that at the time the Civil War broke out the volunteer militia was in its prime. Under the law each company furnished its own uniforms, while the state furnished to the privates arms and equipments. Such men as George T. Bigelow, afterwards Chief Justice of the Supreme Judicial Court, Lincoln Flagg Brigham, afterwards Chief Justice of the Superior Court, Ivers J. Austin, John C. Park, and Elbridge Gerry Austin, attorneys at law, Newell A. Thompson, merchant, and Charles O. Rogers, editor of the Boston *Journal*, were captains of companies. With a population in the state of less than thirteen hundred thousand, the militia force was 5,593 officers and men, while in 1905, with a population of three millions, it is no larger, which is equivalent to a falling off of fifty per cent. The idea underlying the plan of the reformers of the militia was to bring it up to the standard of the regular army, which any practical man must see cannot be done, with volunteer enlistments, small pay and an exaction of service which busy men cannot afford to render. The first blow struck at the life of the militia by the meddlers, was to make the regiment instead of the company the unit of organization, and have all the companies in the regiment uniformed alike.

Under this system the individuality of the company was lost at once, its pride and *esprit de corps* were extinguished. Even the names of company commanders became practically unknown, and as galley convicts are known by their number, the companies were only known by their letter. Before the war every boy in Boston knew the New England Guards, the City Guards, the Boston Light Infantry, and the Fusileers,

and as each paraded in the streets, every man was ambitious
to have his company excel in numbers, in dress, and in march.
On one occasion the Boston Light Infantry with Dodworth's
Band marched up State street one hundred and seventeen
strong,and the next day the City Guards with the Brigade Band
marched up the same street with one hundred and eighteen in
the ranks. The flourishing condition of the Independent Corps
of Cadets, shows what the Volunteer Militia might have been
without the so-called reform to which I have alluded. The
death blow to the volunteer militia was struck when the present armory law was enacted. The requirement that towns, in
which companies are chartered, shall furnish armories, has extinguished the militia in the towns, in only five of which, out
of three hundred and twenty-one, companies now exist. To
make the army law the more destructive in its effect on the militia, the most extravagant demands were made by the authorities for accommodations,in many instances including the equipment of club houses, which towns with a due view to economy
were not disposed to meet. Aside from all other considerations
the armory law is not only oppressive in its operations, but it
violates the underlying principles of our constitution, to wit:
equality of taxation and the enactment of equal laws, inasmuch
as it imposes for the support of a state institution, burdens on
a few towns and exempts all the rest. It is not an answer to
this objection to say that towns incurring armory expenses receive certain reimbursements from the state, inasmuch as the
reimbursement ceases with company disbandments, and towns
losing it are left with an armory on their hands for the erection
of which they have incurred large expense; and inasmuch,
also, as the towns maintaining armories, are also taxed for
their share of the reimbursements. It is not a rash prophecy
that if the present militia laws continue in operation, not many
years will elapse before militia organizations will be confined
to the cities of the Commonwealth. In closing the foregoing narrative concerning the militia, it will be proper to refer
more particularly to the Plymouth volunteer companies. The
Plymouth Artillery was organized January 7, 1777. Thos.
Mayhew was the first commander, and as far as I have been
able to ascertain, it was commanded afterwards until its disbandment about the year 1850 by the following captains: Geo.

Drew, 1804-09; Wm. Davis, 1810-15; Southworth Shaw, 1816-20; John Sampson, 1821-24; Nathaniel Wood, 1825; Joseph Allen, 1826-29; David Bradford, 1830-32; Eleazer Stephens Bartlett, 1833-35; Wm. Parsons, 1836-39; Ephriam Holmes, 1840-41; David Holmes, 1842; Wendell Hall, 1843-45; Samuel West Bagnall, 1846-47; Ebenezer S. Griffin, 1848; and Lt. Robert Finney, 1849. The field pieces furnished to the company by the state were kept for many years in a gun house located by permission of the town on the northeast corner of Training Green, which on the disbandment of the company was sold to Henry Whiting, Jr., who made of it the house in which he lived and died on the east side of Sandwich street, next to the south corner of Winter street.

The Standish Guards was chartered in 1818, and its commanders up to the time of its disbandment in 1883 were: Coomer Weston, Bridgham Russell, James G. Gleason, John Bartlett, Wm. T. Drew, Jeremiah Farris, Coomer Weston, Jr., Barnabas Churchill, Benjamin Bagnall, Sylvanus H. Churchill, Charles Raymond, Joseph W. Collingwood, Charles C. Doten, Josiah R. Drew, Stephen C. Phinney, Herbert Morissey and Joseph W. Hunting. The present Plymouth company was chartered in 1888, and attached as Company D to the Fifth Regiment. In 1770 a powder house was built by the town at the northwesterly end of Burial Hill, which was removed within the memory of the present generation. It was intended as a place of deposit for powder belonging to the town, but a vote was passed by the town requiring all powder brought into town by any person to be placed in it, excepting amounts not exceeding fifty pounds in the hands of any trader, and twenty pounds in the hands of any other inhabitant. The tablet containing an inscription, which was originally placed in the wall of the building is now in Pilgrim Hall.

I do not intend to say much more concerning Boston, but as every eastern Massachusetts person looks on that city as his own, I have ventured to say more than I otherwise would. Until about the time of the Revolution there were no sidewalks in the city, and most of the streets were paved with cobble stones and sloped toward the centre, thus forming a surface drain. That style of street was rather Dutch than English, and may still be seen in Holland. It was universal in New

York until the middle of the eighteenth century, when Madam Provost laid down flagstones called walking-sides, for the convenience of visitors to her business offices. The surface drainage above referred to was universal in Plymouth until after South Pond water was introduced in 1855, when the numerous wells in town were converted into cesspools, and initiated the first step in the present sewage system of the town.

Before leaving Boston a few words about its theatres and its harbor and navigation will not be out of place. The first theatre was established in 1792 in Hawley street, but though its representations were advertised as moral lectures, it was suppressed as violating the law. The law was repealed in the same year, and on the 3rd of February, 1794, the Federal street theatre, on the corner of Franklin and Federal streets was opened, and burned in 1798. It was at once rebuilt and reopened in the same year, continuing until 1833, under various managers as a popular resort. During its career Edmund Kean, Macready, J. B. Booth, and John Howard Payne, appeared on its stage, and in 1832 I attended a performance there by the Ravels in a play called "The Skaters of Smolenska," of which I have a vivid recollection. In later years I had the pleasure of an intimate acquaintance with John Howard Payne, who at the age of twenty created a sensation in the theatrical world under the soubriquet of the youthful Roscius, and who later was the author of "Sweet Home." He was born in Easthampton, Long Island, June 9, 1792, and appeared at the Park theatre in New York, February 24, 1809, as "Young Norval." On June 4, 1813, he appeared at the Drury Lane Theatre in London. He left the stage after a few years, but remained in London engaged in writing plays, among which were "Brutus," which still holds its place on the stage, "Therese" and "Charles the Second." He also wrote "Clari, or the Maid of Milan," which was produced as an opera, and contained the song which gave him special distinction. In 1832 he returned to the United States, and in 1841 was appointed Consul at Tunis. On his removal from office by Polk in 1846, he started for home, but lingered in Paris while efforts were making for his restoration to the Consulate. In the autumn of that year I formed an acquaintance with him, which became intimate. We were in the habit of dining together frequently at Tavernier's restaurant in the Palais Royal, and one day while we were strolling through the quadrangle of the Palais where fountains were playing, bands performing, and children amusing themselves, he called my attention to a round window in the rear attic of the Palais, where, separated from the main building, rooms were let for various purposes, and said, "In that room with a scene like this before my eyes, I wrote 'Home Sweet Home.'" He further said that he had come over from London discouraged, in want and almost in despair, and with the thought of home the words came to his lips and were uttered like a sigh for the scenes of his youth, which he feared he should never see again. He was restored to his Consulate, and died in Tunis, April 10, 1852. How easy it is to imagine him looking from that window on the gay scenes below and uttering the words:

"An exile from home, pleasure dazzles in vain,
Ah, give me my lowly thatched cottage again;
The birds, singing sweetly that came to my call,
Give me them and that peace of mind dearer than all."

His body was brought home and buried, I think, in Washington.

In 1827 the Tremont theatre was built and opened on the 24th of September. In 1842 it was sold to the Baptist Society, of which Rev. Dr. Colver was pastor. In 1831 a building on Traverse street, known as the American amphitheatre was built by W. and T. L. Stewart, which was opened in July as the Warren Theatre, but replaced in 1836 by the National Theatre, which was burned in April, 1852. It was again rebuilt, and finally destroyed March 24, 1863. In January, 1836, the Lion Theatre was opened on Washington street, on the site of the present Keith's Theatre, and later as the Melodeon, was the scene of performances by Macready, Charlotte Cushman and others. In 1841 the Eagle Theatre was built on the corner of Haverhill and Traverse streets, but was soon abandoned. In 1841 the Boston Museum was established on the corner of Tremont and Bromfield streets, and in 1846 was removed to the site which it recently occupied north of King's Chapel Burial ground. During the Millerite excitement in 1843, the Miller Tabernacle was built on Howard street, and converted into the theatre called the Howard Athenæum, in 1845. It was opened October 13 in that year, and was burned in February, 1846, in which year the present Howard Anthenæum was built. In 1848 the Beach Street Museum was erected, but had a short life. The present Boston Theatre was built in 1854, and at that time was exceeded in capacity by only six theatres in the world. To return to the Federal street theatre, which I have said was abandoned for dramatic purposes in 1833, the building passed in 1834 into the possession of the Academy of Music, and was called the Odeon. In 1846 it was leased for a time again as a theatre, and was afterwards occasionally used for short seasons by Italian Opera companies, by the Central Church, and by the Lowell Institute, until it was taken down in 1852.

In connection with the theatres it will not be out of place to speak of Concert Hall, which once stood on the corner of Hanover and Court streets, built about 1750, and taken down a few years ago to widen the first mentioned street. Before and during and after the Revolution it was a famous place for concerts, balls and other entertainments. I have a card of invitation issued by the officers of the French fleet, then in Boston harbor, to a ball to be held there. It is printed on the back of a playing card, showing the straits to which Boston was reduced during the Revolution. In my boyhood I saw there an exhibition by Maelzel of his famous diorama of the "Conflagration of Moscow," and of his "automaton chess player," which beat Boston's best players, but was finally discovered to have a small humped-backed dwarf concealed inside. There, also, I saw an exhibition of legerdemain by a colored man named Richard Potter, who also exhibited in Pilgrim Hall about 1831. He was born in Hopkinton, Mass., on the estate of Sir Harry Frankland, one of whose slaves named Dinah, and brought from Guinea, was his mother. After attending school he went to England with a Mr. Skinner of Roxbury, and there learned the magician's art. In 1836 Concert Hall was taken by Peter B. Brigham, and occupied as a hostelry, where could be found the best oysters and the most famous drinks. He was notable for the concoction of new alcoholic mixtures, to which he gave such names as "Tip and Ty," "I. O. U.," "Paris White," "Fiscal Agent," "Free Soiler," "Same Old Coon," "Clay Smash," "Webster eye-opener," and "Deacon Grant." He made a

fortune, a large part of which was bequeathed for the erection
of a hospital now building.

It may be asked how, before the introduction of railroads,
the producers in remote sections of New England found a
market. Every valley and hillside yielded bountiful crops,
and every water privilege had its little mill, and of course
the farmer and manufacturer depended for returns from their
labor on the markets of the seaboard. The market gardeners of
Waltham and Brighton and Cambridge found no difficulty in
supplying daily the markets of Boston, and the brigs, schooners and sloops, plying as packets between Boston and the various ports along the shores of New England, brought to the
metropolis the products of a considerable territory lying along
the banks and head waters of the Penobscot, the Kennebec,
Merrimac and Connecticut rivers. But the large district beyond the reach of these outlets was obliged to largely depend
on teams and baggage wagons for transportation. While I
was in college, from 1838 to 1842, there was a ceaseless procession of these teams passing through Cambridge from Vermont, New Hampshire and distant parts of northern Massachusetts. They brought butter, cheese, lard, eggs, poultry,
potatoes, apples, cider, hams, pork, shoes, wooden ware, chairs,
and other articles of the field and shop, and returned with supplies needed at home. Teamers put up their teams at one of
the numerous taverns in the immediate neighborhood of Boston and, discharging their freight in the city early the next
morning, reloaded their wagons and returned to their putting
up place, starting for home the next day. The taverns, which
depended for support almost entirely on these teamsters, were
the Norfolk House in Roxbury, the Cattle Fair Hotel in
Brighton, the Punch-bowl in Brookline, Porter's Tavern in
North Cambridge, and others in Cambridgeport, Medford,
Watertown, Waltham, East Cambridge and Charlestown,
The best known of these were Porter's and the Cattle Fair,
and hardly a night did they fail to find numerous patrons who
sat around a huge wood fire playing checkers or loosening their
tongues with plentiful libations of mulled wine or flip. In the
vicinity of Porter's there was for some years a race course,
which afforded to the students of Harvard frequent opportunities to violate the rules of the college. Both at Port-

er's and the Cattle Fair house weekly cattle fairs were held, and cattle, horses and sheep and hogs, were sold to customers, who with fat wallets had come from many scores of towns to buy. These customers were market men and stable keepers from towns within a radius of at least fifty miles, and drove their purchases home over the roads and yarded them until ready for slaughter or sale. I have heard it said that no keener eye, or shrewder judgment of the value of a fat yoke of oxen than those of the late Amasa Holmes of Plymouth were to be found in the cattle yards of Cambridge and Brighton.

Having referred to the taverns in the vicinity of Boston, supported by the commerce on the road, and by the cattle fairs, I am led to speak of the hotel system in Boston, as I remember it seventy years ago, when the population was eighty thousand. At that time, omitting only very small taverns, I remember Doolittle's Tavern in Cambridge street, the Pemberton House in Howard street, the Pavilion, the Albion and the Tremont House in Tremont street, the New England House in Clinton street, two taverns near Haymarket Square, the American and Webster Houses in Hanover street, Wilde's Tavern in Elm street, the City Tavern in Brattle street, the Stackpole House on the corner of Milk and Devonshire streets, the Exchange Coffee House in Congress Square, the Pearl Street House on the upper corner of Milk and Pearl streets, the Commercial Coffee House on the lower corner of Milk and Battery March streets, the Bromfield House on the south side of Bromfield street, the Marlboro Hotel in Washington street, nearly opposite Franklin street, the Washington House on the east side of Washington street, a little south of Milk street, and the Lamb Tavern on or near the site of the present Boston Theatre. The United States Hotel which comes a little within the seventy years, was built by a company not far from 1840 on land bought of the South Cove Company. The South Cove Company owned flats bought of the city in 1833, extending from Essex street to the old Federal street bridge, measuring about seventy-three acres, and bounded on the west by Harrison avenue as far as Dover street bridge, including lands which for many years were the sites of the Boston and Albany and Old Colony Railroad stations. While workmen were excavating for the foundations of the United States Hotel, I remember seeing in the trench the timbers of an old wharf. Some of the houses I have mentioned have been historic. Paran Stevens, who kept the New England House, was engaged to keep the Revere House, when it was opened in 1844, and was the landlord later of the Tremont House, the Battle House in Mobile, and the Fifth Avenue Hotel in New York, in the last of which he made an ample fortune. The Tremont House was opened by Dwight Boyden in 1829, and with the exception of Mr. Stevens, he alone made the house profitable. The United States Hotel was opened and kept some years by Albert Clark and Ralph W. Holman. Mr. Clark went from the United States to the Brevoort House in New York, and retired a millionare. Up to the time during the Civil War, when the cost of living was advanced, the highest price per day for transients was two dollars, but on the claim that the cost of maintaining a boarder had doubled, the daily charge was doubled, and consequently the profits were also doubled. In 1845 I boarded at the United States Hotel, and paid for room and board five dollars a week, and during the winters of 1858 and 1859, while in the Senate, I boarded at the Tremont House and paid for board and room eight dollars per week. It is true that the comforts and conveniences in hotels have vastly improved. It is difficult to realize that at that time a visit to the lavatory involved in the winter an uncomfortable, if not dangerous exposure to the outer air. The sewage arrangements for hotels as for other houses, were entirely inadequate to the demands of the city, and the vaults were emptied by teams from Brighton, which were not permitted to enter the city until ten o'clock at night. In very many private yards there were pumps in close proximity to these vaults, and it is a wonder that the health of the city was not seriously impaired. The teams I have referred to were nightly strung along on Cambridge bridge, waiting for the hour, and were called by the college boys, "Brighton Artillery." The sewage question was an unsolved one in Boston for many years, and the necessity of ventilating sewers was little realized or understood. When water closets and set bowls were introduced, it was supposed that traps with standing water would prevent the passage of deleterious gas. It was, however, discovered

at last, that while odors might thus be excluded, the dangerous gases, which were inodorous, could not be kept back by
water. Thus two things became necessary, to wit, individual
ventilators connected with bathroom plumbing, and a proper
ventilation of public sewers. I remember that many years
ago the city Government in response to complaints of water
spouts which discharged their water on the sidewalks, passed
an ordinance requiring all spouts to enter the sewers. The
Board of Health at once protested against the adoption of such
an arrangement on the ground that spouts would discharge
sewer gases through the house gutters in the immediate vicinity of sleping room windows; but it was soon discovered that
such a general ventilation of the sewers prevented the formation of gases, and was a conservator of health.

CHAPTER XXXXIII.

I have suggested that some notice would be taken by me of the changes which have taken place in seventy years in the marine aspects of Boston. To a nautical eye these changes have been great. Seventy years ago the wharves from India wharf to what is now the Gas House wharf, were occupied by full rigged ships, square rigged brigs, topsail schooners and sloops, engaged in traffic with the northwest coast, Valparaiso, China, Calcutta, the Mediterranean, England, the Western Islands, Nova Scotia, the Penobscot and Kennebec rivers, Portland, New York, Philadelphia, Baltimore, the James river, Wilmington, Savannah, Charleston, New Orleans, and every New England port. There were the ships Akbah, Atlas, South America, St. Petersburg, Asia, Daniel Webster, and the brigs, Emerald, Ruby, Topaz and Amethyst in the European trade; the ships of Bryant and Sturgis in the northwest coast trade; of Elisha Atkins in the South American trade; John H. Pearson in the New Orleans trade; Daniel C. Bacon in the Calcutta trade, and shippers without number engaged in trade with many American ports. Besides these there were steamers running to Bangor, Bath and Portland, and during the summer to Plymouth, Barnstable, Hingham and Provincetown. The whole wharf front of Boston was not more than a mile long, but ship's royal masts and yards exhibited a tangle of spars in strong contrast with the scene to-day, South Boston at that time displayed an expanse of flats now covered with docks of the greatest capacity. East Boston was without wharves, and Charlestown outside of the Navy Yard, added little to the commercial aspect of the harbor. When the Cunard steamers began to arrive in 1840, there was not a towboat in the harbor, and when the steamer Brittannia of the Cunard line was getting ready on her return trip to Liverpool, set down for February 3, 1844, the harbor was closed solid with ice, which it was feared would prevent her departure. But the Boston merchants realizing the importance of holding Boston as the sailing port of the Cunard company, made a contract with Gage & Hittinger, a firm largely engaged in cutting

ice and shipping it to ports in warm latitudes, to cut a passage
to the sea one hundred feet wide, and seven miles long, through
ice nearly two feet thick. This was done, and the steamer
sailed on schedule time, much to the pleasure and profit of the
Cunard Company, and to the credit of the city. At about that
time the tug boat R. B. Forbes was built by the underwriters,
and was for some years in their service. One of her first opportunities to render aid was I think, in 1848, when the steamer Cambria, inward bound from Liverpool, went ashore back of
Truro. One Sunday morning, on my way to church, I met
Mr. George Baty Blake driving into town, who told me that
the Cambria, in which he was a passenger, was ashore, and
that he was on his way to Boston to obtain aid in hauling her
off. I went with him to see the station master, Henry Carter,
and Joseph Sampson, conductor, and in an hour he was on a
locomotive bound to Boston. So expeditiously was Mr.
Blake's service rendered, that before daylight the next morning the Cambria had been hauled off by the R. B. Forbes, and
was on her way to Boston. Mr. Blake had been a frequent
Cunard passenger, and told the captain that if he would put
him ashore he would send the R. B. Forbes down.

How things have changed. A ship is now rarely seen, brigs
have disappeared altogether, topsail schooners from Nova
Scotia occasionally visit Boston, and the old packet sloops have
lost the rosewood and bird's eye maple of their cabins, and
been degraded to uses of which they seem to be ashamed. Now
and then I read on the stern of a weather beaten coal barge
the name of a ship I knew in her prime, which seems to me like
a wing clipped eagle no longer able to soar, or a disembodied
spirit suffering for sins done in the body. In view of the
changes it is thoughlessly said that the commerce of Boston has
declined, but there can be no greater mistake. It must be remembered that the tonnage of vessels has largely increased.
The seven masted schooner Thomas W. Lawson alone, with a
carrying capacity of six thousand tons of coal, making ten
trips a year, represents the arrival of one hundred ships of the
carrying capacity of the largest tonnage seventy years ago,
while leaving out of the calculation tramp steamers, the regular liners with cargoes of two thousand tons each, represent
three hundred more. Coming down to actual statistics, the

customs receipts at Boston have increased from 1901 to 1905, inclusive, two millions of dollars, and the entering tonnage during the same time, has increased 456,392. The complaint of a sluggish condition of our commerce is based on the fact that our foreign trade is largely in the hands of aliens. Some seek a remedy in subsidy to American ships, but the question may be asked whether it will not be well, before taking a subsidy out of the treasury, a large portion of which will find its way into the pockets of the steel barons of Pennsylvania, to try the simpler remedy of taking the duty from coal and iron, and compelling manufacturers to sell at home structural steel used in building ships at prices as low as they sell to foreign ship builders.

Turning now to railroads, whose entire history is covered by the period of my life, I suppose I may say without the possibility of a denial, that no invention or discovery has within seventy years been more effective in developing the resources of our country, maintaining its integrity, and promoting its interests than the railroad system. The use of coal has been too great to be accurately measured, but without railroads that product of the mines would be still sleeping in its beds. The telegraph and telephone afford business facilities, which are thought indispensable, but they are only the inevitable followers of the railroad, and even depend on its lines for the stretching of their wires. Without gas or kerosene oil, and with wood for fuel, we could have still enjoyed life, though it be without present conveniences, comforts and luxury. Without railroads it is not too much to say that it would have been impossible to dispose of, and assimilate that vast immigration which during the last seventy years has sought a resting place in our land. It may also be said that the railroad system, which broke through the wall that separated the old Union from California, prevented the establishment of a new and distinct empire on the Pacific coast. Without attempting even a sketch of the history of the railroad system, it is sufficient to say that at its introduction the road bed, motive power and cars were rude and primitive. The locomotives weighed not far from eight tons; the cars running on a single truck were built after the fashion of stage coaches with doors on the sides, and the rails weighed fifty pounds per yard. When Gridley Bryant of Boston invented the double truck, I was told by his son, the late Gridley J. F. Bryant, that he was laughed out of the room of a committee of the Massachusetts Legislature when he suggested that long cars with two double trucks could safely run on a curved track. The committee had not learned the lesson, which the distinguished scientist, Professor Dionysius Lardner, learned at a later period, that it is never safe to deny the possibility of anything. In 1838 he declared that ocean steam navigation was impossible on account of the inability of any vessel to carry sufficient coal for a trans-Atlantic voyage, and yet before the year passed, in which the declaration was made, the steamship Sirius of seven hundred tons and two hundred and fifty horse power arrived in New York April 23d in nineteen days from Cork; and on the same day the steamship Great Western of thirteen hundred and forty tons and four hundred and fifty horse power, arrived in fifteen days from Bristol. I feel pretty sure when I deny that two and two make six, but if anyone should offer to bet with me that within five years it will be demonstrated that the earth stands still, I should be afraid to accept the offer. In June, 1827, when the construction of a road from Boston to Albany was first agitated, Jos. Tinker Buckingham, the learned editor of the Boston *Courier*, wrote an editorial for his columns, which contained the following paragraph:

"Alcibiades, or some other great man of antiquity, it is said, cut off his dog's tail, that *quid nuncs* might not become extinct for want of excitement. Some such motive, we doubt not, moved one or two of our natural and experimental philosophers to get up the project of a railroad from Boston to Albany; a project which every one knows, who knows the simplest rules in arithmetic to be impracticable but at an expense a little less than the market value of the whole territory of Massachusetts, and which if practicable, every person of common sense knows would be as useless as a railroad from Boston to the moon. Indeed a road of some kind from here to the heart of that beautiful satellite of our dusky planet would be of some practical utility, especially if a few of our national, public spirited men, our railway fanatics, could be persuaded to pay a visit to their proper country."

As is well known, the first railroad built in New England was a short road extending from the Quincy granite quarries to Neponset River, which was opened Oct. 7, 1826, to be used with horsepower for the transportation of granite to tide water.   In June, 1830, the Boston and Lowell railroad was incorporated, and in 1831 the Boston and Providence, and the Boston and Worcester.   I have heard it said that the curves on the easterly end of the Boston and Worcester were due to the expectation that horse power would be used, and to the consequent desirability of as level a track as possible.   Though when the construction of some of the Massachusetts roads was begun it was planned to run them by horse power, the plan was changed before the roads were completed.   On the Baltimore and Ohio road, which was begun in 1828, horses were used for some time, and the station between Baltimore and Washington, called the Relay House, took its name from the fact that relays of horses were taken there.   In 1830 there were only forty-eight miles of railroad in the United States.

The Boston and Worcester began to run trains as far as Newton, May 16, 1834, on a running time of eighteen miles an hour, and I remember well seeing one of the earliest trains start from the station which was then in Indiana Place, and I was as much astonished as I should be while writing these words to see an air car stop at my roof to receive passengers for Boston.

Some of the early railroads outside of New England were built with longitudinal sills of timber laid on ties, to which flat bars of iron from a half to three quarters of an inch thick were spiked, called strap rails.   In the summer of 1843 I went to Buffalo, passing over roads owned and controlled by I think, seven distinct corporations; the Boston and Worcester, the Western, as the road from Worcester to Albany was called, the Albany and Schenectady, the Schenectady and Utica, the Utica and Syracuse, the Syracuse and Rochester, and the Rochester and Buffalo.   At that time the cars, instead of being drawn by the locomotive around capitol hill as now, at Albany, were drawn to the summit of the hill by cables worked by stationary engines, and there attached to the locomotive.   The rail used at that time on all the above mentioned roads which were in New York, were strap rails.   It was soon found, however, that these rails became loosened at their butts, and being underrun by the wheels peeled up, often running through the car floors and in some cases fatally injuring passengers. These loose ends were called snake heads, and were as much to be feared as the snags on the Mississippi River sixty years ago.

On my return from Buffalo I took a passenger boat on the Erie Canal from Rochester to Syracuse, and had my first and only experience on the "raging canawl." The cabin of the boat was handsomely fitted up, and had sleeping berths so arranged as to be unfolded at night. The dinner furnished was good, and on the whole the novelty of the trip made it interesting. We were somewhat uncomfortable sitting on deck in the blazing sun, and when the cry of "low bridge" was called, obliging us to duck our heads as we passed under the various highways crossing the canal, I felt like one of the brakemen on the top of a freight car, liable to be swept off unless I was constantly on the alert. The rate of speed, not more than three or four miles an hour, was not especially exhilarating, but the operation of raising and lowering the locks relieved somewhat the monotony of the journey, and the opportunity afforded for an occasional run on the tow path, or a visit to the store of some shady hamlet for the purpose of purchasing such luxuries as the larder of the boat was unable to furnish, altogether made the trip one to be remembered.

It may surprise some of my readers to learn that, in the decade from 1835 to 1845, the United States was far in advance of both England and France in the construction of railroads. I speak from my own knowledge and experience when I say that after all the main railroad lines in the northern states had been completed some years, there was no railroad in England north of York on the east, or north of Manchester on the west. In the summer of 1846, in making the circuit from York through Newcastle, Edenboro, Perth, Dunkeld, the Trosacks, Glasgow, Carlisle and Lancaster to Manchester, I was obliged to go either by coach or post carriage all the way. So in France in the same summer, I found only one section of rail laid between Boulogne and Paris, and in December of that year not a finished mile between Paris and Marseilles. Gangs of men, who were called Navvies, were housed along the line between Lancaster and Carlisle grading a road bed, and in France I found on the route from Boulogne to Paris that a device had been adopted by which the railroad was utilized as fast and as far as its sections were finished.   On the 5th of July, 1846, I left Boulogne in a diligence for Paris.   The railroad from the latter city had been completed as far as Amiens about sixty miles. On reaching Amiens the diligence was driven under a crane with a chain sling attached, and after its body was loosened from the wheels it was swung round onto a platform car, to which it was securely attached, and the remainder of the journey was travelled by rail.

In 1843 a project was started to build a railroad from Boston to Plymouth, and on the 18th of March, 1844, the Old Colony railroad was incorporated.   A committee appointed by those interested in the enterprise, consisting of Col. John Sever of Kingston, Hon. Isaac L. Hedge and Jacob H. Loud of Plymouth, made a canvas of the towns on the route for the purpose of estimating the probable annual receipts of the road.   In their report they stated that the Plymouth receipts, including both to and from Boston, would probably be eighteen thousand dollars for passengers, but no estimate was made of the probable freight receipts.   They estimated the annual running expenses to be $46,250, and expressed the opinion that receipts of $100,000 would pay expenses, and a dividend of six per cent. on the cost of the road.   Their estimate of the cost of the road was as follows:

Gradients, masonry and bridges,	$176,595
Superstructure and turnouts,	290,650
Stations, buildings, furniture, etc.,	25,000
Fences,	23,500
Damages,	132,000
Engines and cars,	65,000
Contingent,	40,000
Total for 37 miles, a little over $20,000 per mile,	$752,745

When completed, the cost was found to have been $700,000. The weight of the first locomotives used was fourteen and a half tons, and the weight of the rails fifty pounds per yard, while the weight of those now in use is sixty tons for locomotives and ninety pounds per yard for rails.   On the Burlington route locomotives are now used weighing one hundred and eighty-seven tons, with tenders carrying twenty-six thousand pounds of coal, and six thousand gallons of water.   The first board of Directors chosen at a meeting held at the Exchange Coffee House in Boston, June 25, 1844, consisted of John Sever of Kingston, Addison Gilmore of Boston, Isaac L. Hedge of Plymouth, Nathan Carruth of Boston, Jacob H. Loud of Plymouth, William Thomas of Boston, and Uriel Crocker of Boston. Mr. Sever was chosen president; Mr. Gilmore, treasurer; and Mr. Loud, clerk. In December, 1844, the same officers were chosen, and December 31, 1845, the same officers were re-elected, except that Mr. Sever resigned as president, though remaining on the board, Mr. Carruth succeeding him as president, and Josiah Quincy, Jr., succeeding Mr. Gilmore, who resigned as director, but continued as treasurer. On the 8th of November, 1845, the road was opened and the Directors brought a party from Boston to dedicate it, among whom were Daniel Webster, John Quincy Adams, Judge John Davis, Josiah Quincy, Nathan Hale, E. Hasket Derby and P. P. F. Degrand. A collation had been prepared by the citizens in the lower Pilgrim Hall, at which Nathaniel Morton Davis presided, and speeches were made by the above gentlemen. The next day regular trains began to run twice a day at 7 a. m., and 3.30 p. m. from Plymouth, and 7.45 a. m. and 4.30 p. m. from Boston, with a running time of an hour and three quarters, while there are today eleven trains each way on week days, with various running times from 1.04 to 1.21, and five trains each way on Sundays. Until 1847 the road occupied the Boston and Worcester station in Lincoln street, and then removed to Kneeland street. The Directors believing that a hotel would be a profitable feeder to the business of the road, built the Samoset, which was dedicated and opened March 4, 1846. Joseph Stetson was employed to keep it, as the agent of the road, but in compliance with the recommendation of a committee chosen to investigate the affairs of the company, it was sold about 1850 to an association, as has been stated in a former chapter.

Some years after the incorporation of the Old Colony railroad, a branch from South Braintree to Fall River was incorporated as the Fall River railroad, which was consolidated with the Old Colony railroad, September 7, 1854, under the name of the Old Colony and Fall River railroad. After the extension of the road from Fall River to Newport, the name was changed to the Old Colony and Newport railroad. In 1872 the Cape

Cod railroad, extending from Middleboro to the Cape, was annexed, and the old name of Old Colony was resumed.   The South Shore railroad from Braintree to Cohasset was added October 1, 1876, the Duxbury and Cohasset from Cohasset to Kingston, October 1, 1878, and the Fall River, Warren and Providence, December 1, 1875.   The Bridgewater Branch was built at an early period, and the Middleboro and Taunton Branch was opened in 1856, the branch by way of Easton to Fall River in 1871, and the Raynham and Taunton Branch in 1882.   As this sketch brings the Old Colony railroad down to the memory of the present generation, it is unnecessary to pursue it further.

For twenty years the Old Colony railroad, like all other railroads in New England, used wood as fuel in their locomotives, and the lot of land on which the brick block stands, extending to the shore was constantly filled with piles of wood, which were kept supplied by Geo. Adams of Kingston, the purchasing agent.   The Providence road, more remote from wood lots, bought the standing wood on a large tract of land on the James River, and Franklin B. Cobb was sent one or more years to superintend its cutting and shipment.   Had not coal soon taken the place of wood it is probable that by this time the forests of the country would have been exhausted.   As it is, the enormous consumption of railroad ties presents a problem concerning a continual supply of these indispensable features of railroad construction which railroad men all over the country are beginning to seriously consider.   There are two hundred thousand miles of railroads in the United States, which, with twenty-five hundred ties to the mile, require for their construction 500,000,000 ties, or calling the life of a tie eight years, an annual supply of 62,000,000.   Counting sixteen feet to a tie the annual repair of two hundred thousand miles of road will require annually a supply of 992 million square feet.   With all the other uses to which lumber is put in houses, bridges, vessels, piling, box boards, barrels and wood pulp, to say nothing of the lumber destroyed by fires, it is easy to see that the end of our forests is not far off, unless some new material is discovered to meet the exigency.   The Pennsylvania railroad is experimenting with steel ties, weighing thirteen to a ton, and costing $2 each, but their inflexibility seriously increases the wear and tear of rails and cars, and it is feared that the experiment will prove a failure. When the Boston and Lowell railroad was built I feel quite sure that stone ties were used, and finally abandoned for the reason above suggested. Some railroad managers in the southwest are trying catalpa wood, which if its texture shall be found satisfactory, they think may be planted in large areas and furnish in twenty-five years a crop of trees, which set four feet apart will grow twenty-five hundred trees to the acre, or at the rate of two ties to a tree, five thousand ties. At this rate twelve thousand acres would supply a sufficient number of ties for a single year. But what shall be done while these trees are growing, and still another year's product of twelve thousand acres will be required, and after that another and another. All the while the cost of lumber is increasing. Within seventy years black walnut, before unknown as a furniture wood, has been so nearly exhausted as to bring in the Boston market one hundred dollars a thousand. Our legislators in Washington in their fear of the lumber barons of Michigan and Maine, who have even sent their invading axes into the mountains of New Hampshire and the forests of the Adirondacks, refuse to bring about even the slight amelioration of present conditions, which by the abolition of a duty on lumber, might be afforded by giving us access to the forests of the Dominion. Unlike France, where no man can cut down the forests on his own land without a government permit, we of the present generation in the United States are absolutely skinning the earth, as if future generations have no rights which we are bound to respect. If seventy years ago a law had been enacted requiring an acre of black walnut to be planted with so many trees to the acre, for every acre cut down, that wood would have continued in reasonably abundant supply. Unless some restraining laws be soon enacted to control the robbers of our forests, a lumber famine must sooner or later ensue.

The only effectual remedy for the existing evil, which I as a layman can see, is the discovery of a material to be made from some plant, weed or shrub raised in annual crops. For want of a better name let us call the material paper. What the plant or shrub will be, no man as yet knows. It may be now in our fields and yards growing under our very eyes, and

waiting to be called upon to do its share in the great work of
civilization.   It may be possible that with such an annual crop
the farmers of New England will see their hillsides and valleys
once more sources of wealth.   It may be possible to mould the
pulp made from this shrub into material of any form or shape
from house lumber and box boards to brush woods, and from
railroad ties to spools, as flexible as wood, as indistructible as
stone, and as incombustible as iron.   Fortune and fame await
the discoverer of this material. Young man, look for it, and
you will find it.   Who knows that it may not be the daisy—
not the common New England plant, but the daisy which has
been produced by Luther Burbank of Santa Rosa, California, a
combination of the New England, English and Japan daisies,
with stalks two feet long, which would probably yield four tons
to the acre.   Such a crop raised annually without constant
planting, and requiring little fertilization, would convert our
hillsides and valleys into mines of wealth, and what is now a
nuisance into an everlasting benefaction.

CHAPTER XXXXIV.

A few words may be interesting concerning the management of fires in my youth. Either there were very few fires in Plymouth during the colonial and provincial periods, or the record of them is very incomplete. It is known that on the 24th of January, 1620-21, the Common House on Leyden street caught fire from the lodgment of a spark on its thatched roof, and was burned to the ground. At a town meeting held on the fifth of February, 1664-5, it was voted, "to see what may be collected for the relief of Francis Billington, he having lately suffered great loss by the burning of his house." The house known as the "Crow House" at Seaside, was probably built in 1665, on the site of the "Billington House." The only other fire, of which there is any record before the Revolution, is referred to in a vote of the town passed March 21, 1757, "that Thomas Norrington, in consideration of his loss by fire, be abated his Province, County and Town rates for the last year." As there is no record of any house owned by Mr. Norrington, it is probable that he was a tenant of some house or store, and suffered the loss of furniture or goods. In Boston, either more complete records were kept, or there were many more fires during the periods above mentioned. In 1654 occurred what was known as the great fire. In 1676 a fire at the North end consumed forty-five dwelling houses, the North Church and several warehouses within a district enclosed by Richmond, Hanover and Clark streets. On the 8th of August, 1679, a fire occurred extending from what is now Blackstone street, westerly to Dock square, and southerly to the present Liberty square, which destroyed eighty dwelling houses, seventy warehouses, and many vessels with their cargoes, causing a loss of two hundred thousand pounds. The main reliance in extinguishing fires at that time was upon long handled hooks, with which every householder was required to be provided, and upon large swabs attached to poles twelve feet long, with which water was splashed on the walls and roofs. A few pumps and the dock were the only sources of water supply. All buildings in Boston at that

time were wooden, and at the next session of the General Court
a law was passed providing that no dwelling houses should be
erected in Boston except of stone or brick, and covered with
slate or tile, unless by permission of the magistrates, commissioners and selectmen.   October 1st, 1711, a fire beginning in
Williams Court, burned nearly one hundred buildings, including the First Church.

In 1778 a fire occurred at the South end, beginning at Beach
street, and extending southerly on both sides of Washington
street, as far as Common street, burning in its course the Hollis
street church; and in 1825 a fire in Kilby street destroyed fifty
stores.   The great fire in Boston, which burned from the evening of the 9th to the 11th of November, 1872, covered about
eighty acres, and extended from Bedford to State street, and
with the exception of a few buildings, from Washington street
to the harbor, causing a loss of about eighty millions of dollars.
Taking into consideration only the fires in Boston before the
Revolution, the number was entirely out of proportion to those
in Plymouth during the same period.

The first fire engine used in Boston with any effect, was
made in 1765 by David Wheeler, a blacksmith, who had his
house and shop on what is now Washington street, a little north
of Bedford street, and between the latter street and what is
now known as Avon place.   From the first settlement of Boston there was a pond belonging to the town abutting Wheeler's
land, which had been always used as a town watering place, and
which became a nuisance when dwellings were erected in its vicinity, and was finally sold to Mr. Wheeler in 1753.   The first
steam fire engine was introduced into Boston in 1854, and there
are now between thirty and forty in the city.

In 1792 the Massachusetts Charitable Fire Society was organized, and incorporated in 1794, to relieve sufferers by fire,
and to invent means by which fires might be extinguished.   For
many years its anniversary was celebrated by an oration and an
ode.   Several of the odes were written by Robert Treat Paine,
Jr., who changed his name from Thomas on account of his
aversion to Thomas Paine, the author of the "Age of Reason."
The celebrated song, "Adams and Liberty" was written by Mr.
Paine to be sung at one of the celebrations of the Society to the
tune, "To Anacreon in Heaven," which is now better known as

the tune of the "Star Spangled Banner." As most of my readers are probably unfamiliar with this song, I give below one of its stanzas:

"Ye sons of Columbia who bravely have fought,
   For those rights which unstained from your sires had descended,
May you long taste the blessings your valor has bought,
   And your sons reap the soil which their fathers defended;
      Mid the reign of mild peace,
      May your nation increase,
      With the glory of Rome and the wisdom of Greece,
And no son of Columbia shall e'er be a slave,
While the earth bears a plant, or the sea rolls a wave."

As far as I can learn there was no fire insurance on any building in Massachusetts until the very last years of the 18th century. There were no insurance companies in the state until then, but it is possible that there may have been individuals who took fire risks as Barnabas Hedge did at a later period in Plymouth. Until about 1798 or 1799, marine insurance was done entirely by underwriters, as they were called. A ship owner, for instance, about to send his vessel to sea, who wished insurance, would ask a few men of means how large risks each would take, and they would under write their names on printed blanks, stating the amounts they would insure. Of course the establishment of insurance companies put an end to this method of insurance except in outports like Plymouth, and the name underwriter was transferred to the companies. My great uncle Thomas Davis, was the first president of the first marine insurance company in Boston, from 1798 until his death in 1805, and I have hanging on the wall in my library, the barometer which hung in his office.

I have spoken of three fires which occurred in Plymouth during the colonial period. I am inclined to think that not more than forty fires have occurred since 1620, causing losses exceeding fire hundred dollars, and that the total loss by fire, exclusive of fires in the woods, has not exceeded three hundred thousand dollars. Of all the fires, which have occurred within my memory I can recall only one in which adjoining buildings were seriously damaged. While this bears testimony to the efficiency of the Plymouth fire department, I think that special mention should be made of the Unitarian Church fire, when only great skill and persistent effort saved the Bradford house, the Town house, and the Orthodox church.

For more than a hundred years Plymouth possessed no special means of extinguishing fires.   On the 27th of January, 1728, it was voted in town meeting "that every householder shall from time to time be provided with a sufficient ladder or ladders to reach from the ground to the ridge of such house at the charge of the owner therof; and in case the owner or owners of such house or houses be not an inhabitant of the town, then the occupiers thereof to provide the same and deduct the charge thereof out of his or their rent, on pain of the forfeiture of five shillings per month for every month's neglect after the tenth day of January next."   It was also voted that between the first day of March and the first of December every householder between Wood's Lane, now Samoset street, and Jabez Corner, should keep on his premises a hogshead or two barrels of water, or a cistern to the value of two hogsheads, exempting, however, any house standing twenty rods from the highway. So things went on with only the efforts of citizens to rely on, and the utmost care in the management of domestic fires, until the 16th of March, 1752, when it was voted to choose thereafter annually a board of five firewards; and on the 21st of March, 1757, it was voted to purchase what was called a 'garden engine' that would throw about fifty gallons of water a minute. On the 18th of February, 1765, it was voted that Gideon White, Wm. Rider, Samuel Cole, Wm. Rickard, Abiel Shurtleff, Zacheus Curtis, Lewis Bartlett, John May and Wm. Crombie, the managers of the engine, be exempted from the performance of all other town duties.   In 1770 two engines are referred to in the records, though there is no mention of the purchase of the second one, and both were kept in an addition at the easterly end of the present town house.   On the 2d of May, 1798, the town voted to buy a new engine, and on the 6th of April, 1801, another, these two taking the places of the two old ones. These two new engines called respectively Niagara No. 1 and Fountain No. 2, were bucket engines, and were kept under the Unitarian Meeting House until it was taken down in 1831, when the Fountain was removed to a house built on the southwest corner of Training Green, and the Niagara was removed to a house near the jail, and later to a house on Russell street.   An engine which was called No. 3, was presented to the town by Nathaniel Russell, William Davis and Barnabas Hedge, May 5,

1823, but was disposed of in 1836, when the Rapid was bought, and took its number. In 1829 the reservoirs in Town and Shirley squares were built, and in that year Torrent No. 4, a suction engine, was bought, and in the same year the Niagara was changed to a suction engine. In 1834 and later, reservoirs were built at Training Green, in High street and in Court street at the foot of Russell street and opposite Pilgrim Hall. The Torrent No. 4 was kept some years in the Northwesterly end of the Town House, and afterwards in Franklin street, while the Rapid was removed to Summer street. At the present time the Niagara built in 1798, the Fountain built in 1801, the Torrent built in 1828, and the Rapid built in 1836, are stored in the hospital of the Fire Department on Spring street, where I hope they will be permitted to long remain as veterans in the service, and relics of the past.

The earliest fire of which I have any recollection, was in 1828, when the anchor works, standing where the Plymouth Mills are now located, were burned. I was then attending Mrs. Maynard's school on the corner of Main street and Town Square, and saw one of the engines go round the corner. In the same year or the next, before the reservoirs were built, and before the first suction engine was bought, I remember seeing two lines of men and women carrying up one line buckets of water from the dock to a bucket engine at the head of North street, and carrying empty buckets down the other line back to the dock. In every house two leather fire buckets handsomely painted, and bearing the owner's name, hung in the front entry, and when the fire bells rang there was a general panic, and men half dressed and women bareheaded, and with disordered hair, seized their buckets and ran to the scene of the fire. In my boyhood the active men at fires were, Joseph Bradford, Samuel Doten, and Daniel and Isaac C. Jackson, each with his fire trumpet, calling as the occasion required, "Play away, No. 4," or "Play away, No. 1."

In 1835 an act was passed by the General Court, establishing the Plymouth Fire Department, under which the selectmen appoint annually a board of engineers, who now have full charge of the organization of the department and the management of fires. In May, 1870, in accordance with a vote of the town, steam fire engine No. 1 was bought, and in June, 1874, No. 2 was bought and named Jeremiah Farris. In 1893 No. 3 was bought, and named H. P. Bailey.   The question may well be asked why suction engines were not earlier invented.   For centuries water pumps were used, and the engine only needed an application of their well known principles to make them complete.   The saying that necessity is the mother of invention, is only another version of the statement that providence supplies what the actual wants of the people demand.   The carelessness of men, the cheap methods of building, and the introduction of new devices for heating houses, have alarmingly increased the liabilities to fires, and have led to a demand for better methods of extinguishing them, and lo, the engine appeared at call.   Nor does the steam fire engine mark more than another step towards more effective machines.   The time is undoubtedly near at hand when the auto engine will take the place of that drawn by horse power, and sooner or later will itself give way to some fire extinguisher, the nature of which time will disclose.

The Plymouth Fire Department, as now organized, is exceedingly creditable to the town.   It consists of a board of five engineers and 130 men, with the following apparatus and equipment:

In the two story brick central station in Main street, Steamer H. P. Bailey No. 3, hose wagon, ladder truck, chemical engine, hose reel, seven horses.

In the two story brick station on South street, Steamer No. 2, the Jeremiah Farris, hose wagon, ladder truck, and five horses.

At the Seaside station, Steamer No. 1, reel and hose.

At Hall Town, reel and hose.

At Whiting street, reel and hose.

At Baptist street, reel and hose.

At the Langford house, Chiltonville reel and hose.

Two hundred and twenty-eight hydrants: four hand engines, laid up; nine thousand feet of hose; twenty-five fire alarm signal boxes, and a battery room in the Central station.

It is only necessary to add that the appropriation for the maintenance of the department for the present year is eleven thousand dollars.

CHAPTER XXXXV.

Of funerals and their management, in early times, I have not much to say. Most of the funeral customs of ancient days had passed away before I was born. Funeral feasts and the gifts of gloves and scarfs and rings, a serious tax on the mourners, and a substantial profit to the officiating clergymen and pall bearers, who received them, were no longer in vogue. Until about the middle of the eighteenth century, prayers formed no part of a funeral ceremony, and it is said that the first prayer at a funeral in Boston was offered by Rev. Dr. Charles Chauncey at the interment of Rev. Dr. Jonathan Mayhew, pastor of the First Church, July 9, 1766. The sermon, which introduced the custom, which prevailed later of preaching funeral sermons, was preached by Dr. John Clarke in the Brattle street meeting house at the interment of Rev. Dr. Samuel Cooper, who died September 29, 1783. The rings given at funerals were of black enamel, edged with gold, inscribed with the name, age and date of the death of the deceased. The only one I ever saw was found a few years ago in the garden of the house which stood on the site of the Plymouth Savings Bank, and given to me. Recognizing the initials on the ring, and the date of death as those of one whose descendant at one time lived in the house referred to, I gave it to one of the family. It is said that Rev. Andrew Eliot, pastor of what was called the new North Church in Boston, received twenty-nine hundred and forty gloves at funerals, weddings and baptisms, a large number of which he sold, receiving therefor a very considerable addition to his salary. It was a custom which has not been abolished many years, on the Sunday after the death of a relative, to have a note read to the congregation asking prayers for the loss of a parent or wife or husband or friend. I have heard on some occasions as many as a dozen of these notes read before the announcement of the text of the sermon. An amusing story is told of a note, asking prayers for an inconsolable husband for the loss of a beloved wife, being found in a pulpit bible by a clergyman supplying the pulpit for the day only, who supposing it a new one, read it to the congregation, who

had listened to it a year before, much to the consternation of
the inconsolable husband, who was present in the church with a
new bride.   Though the custom of a funeral dinner, at which
the pall bearers were guests, which has been discribed as

> "Containing lots of fun,
> Like mourning coaches, when the funeral's done,"

had disappeared, I remember when it was the invariable custom
for the pall bearers to return with the mourners to the house
of the deceased and indulge in such wine or liquor as best
suited their tastes.   This custom continued until the temperance agitation about 1833, and has never been resumed.   Funeral customs were different in different places, some inherited
from the Dutch, and some from the English.   In New York
there were as in Massachusetts before the introduction of the
hearse, six bearers who relieved each other in carrying the coffin on a bier to the grave, and six others who walked beside the
bier, each holding a tassel of the pall or funeral cloth.   At
Mrs. Catalina de Peyster's funeral, six young ladies attended
as pall bearers dressed in white sarcinet jackets and petticoats
with their heads uncovered, and their hair powdered and done
up with white ribbon.   The first hearse was used in Boston in
1796, and the first in Plymouth was used at the funeral of
Thomas Pope, the father of the late Capt. Richard Pope, who
died July 6, 1820.   The first funeral which I remember, was
that of Henry Warren, which I saw forming in front of his
late residence on the corner of North street, but the first one I
attended, was that of my great uncle, Samuel Davis, at Mrs.
Nicolson's boarding house on Court Square, where he died July
10, 1829.   I can point out the very spot where, holding my
mother's hand, I listened to the passing bell, and waited im-
patiently for the procession to start.   I thought then that the
passing bell merely announced the march of the procession, and
did not realize that it was really the celebration of the passage
of a human soul through the gates of heaven.

The funeral hearse has a varied history, and in its present use
has been diverted from its original design and purpose.   At
various early times the hearse and the catafalque were the same,
and neither was ever used as a vehicle.   It was a temporary
structure set up in a chapel or house or place of burial, sometimes constructed at great cost, where the body lay for a time

in state. In Strype's Memorials the funeral ceremonies of the bishop of Winchester are described, after which, as he says, the body "was put into a wagon with four horses all covered with black." Strype also describes the funeral of Henry the Eighth at which "in the chapel was ordained a goodly formal hearse with four score square tapers; every light containing two foot in length poising in the whole eighteen hundred weight of wax garnished about with pensils and escutcheons banners and bannerols of descents, and at the four corners four banners of saints beaten in fine gold upon damask." He further says, that "on the 14th of February the chariot was brought to the Court hall door and the corpse with great reverence brought from the hearse to the same." These extracts show conclusively that the hearse was a temporary structure erected in a chapel, or elsewhere, and that since the abandonment of its use, its name has been transferred to the vehicle carrying the body to the grave.

In early chapters I have alluded to various habits and customs prevailing during my boyhood, but have left untouched many associated with every day life. A reference to these, like charity, must begin at home, and as I recall my boyhood days and everything associated with them, I realize,

"How cruelly sweet are the echoes that start,
When memory plays an old tune on the heart."

How well I remember the room, in which the family spent their evenings around the square centre table, lighted perhaps by two brass lamps, or by what was called an astral lamp, which was the first step in that series of illuminating contrivances, which included afterwards first the solar and then the carcel lamp, finally culminating in gas, which was introduced into Plymouth in 1855. For special occasions spermaceti candles were added, which were made at home in candle moulds with spermaceti bought at the Plymouth oil factory. Tallow candles and bayberry candles were used by many less well to do people, and to them kerosene oil, which came into use about the time of the introduction of gas at a price lower than whale oil, was a welcome boon. In the material world I know no greater civilizer than this oil has been among our people. The houses of those in the smaller towns, and in the suburbs of our own town, in which the sputtering oil lamp was extinguished at what was called early candle light, sending the occupants to bed, now display a cheerful sitting room, in which a centre table with books and magazines, and a parlor organ, or perhaps a piano, afford means of education and amusement, and promote a higher and a longer life.   Some years ago statistics showed that insanity was especially prevalent among farmers with their days of constant and anxious work, unrelieved by seasons of amusement and good cheer. But kerosene oil has changed all this, and has lifted the curtain which once shut out the light of a cheerful life, and has immeasurably broadened the horizon within which farmers live.

What evenings those were at our home, the mother with her children, unattracted by clubs and societies away from the grand functions of a mother's life; the children, out of the street, supplementing the instruction of school with that which only a parent could furnish.   I know no greater change within my lifetime than that exhibited by the lessening influence of home.   It has been brought about, partly by the disintegrating effect of civilized life, which with new means of heating and lighting, has scattered the members of a family, leaving no fireside to gather around, and has drawn them for intellectual and moral instructions beyond the limits of home; and partly, I am sorry to say, by the inculcation in some quarters of the idea that the management of a family and home is a drudgery, which should be avoided in the search for what is called a higher life. It seems useless to ask why the management of an institution incorporated by the acts of God, than which nothing can be nobler, is any more drudgery than the management of a railroad or steamboat or factory, incorporated by the legislature of the state.   I halt, however, on the threshold of a subject too broad for discussion here, and only alluded to because I believe it to be one touching the best and truest life of society.

Until about 1832 no attempt was made to heat our houses with any other fuel than wood.   In nearly every room there was a fireplace, that in the living room in some houses supplemented by a Franklin or Pierpont stove, which stood on the outer verge of the hearth, and with flaring sides, threw all the heat into the room without the loss of any by escape into the chimney.   When coal was introduced, perhaps a grate was set in the living room, and into some of the chambers a spitfire stove, and finally as the last step in methods of heating, came the furnace. Fires in chambers were in my day far from being universal. I do not think that at home I ever slept in a heated chamber, except when sick, until I was sixteen years of age. How well I remember lying in bed looking at the peacocks and other figures on the chintz curtain of my four post bedstead, dreading to get up and wash my face and hands with water frozen in the pitcher. Warming pans, now obsolete, were invaluable in those days. In making fires in the different fireplaces, instead of using shavings or newspapers and matches, a fire pan, a very important article in every house, was used to carry a brand, or a parcel of coals from the kitchen fire, which placed under the wood, with the aid of a bellows soon kindled into a cheerful blaze. The fire pan made of iron, had a wooden handle, a cover punched with holes, and its under side sloped up in front. The kitchen fire, like the chanukkah light of the Jews, which was intended to be perpetual, was supposed to never go out, and being covered up at night, was rekindled in the morning. If a neighbor lost his fire he would come to our house with a fire pan and borrow a brand. In connection with fires the foot stove must be mentioned, an article indispensable in those times when houses were insufficiently heated. It was also an indispensable article in the meeting house, where the heat from a box stove, with a long funnel running overhead the full length of the house, was supplemented by the foot stoves in the pews to a degree, which alone made the atmosphere tolerable. I recall the relief from the Sabbath imprisonment at home in those days, when it seemed to me,

"That congregations ne'er break up,
And Sabbaths never end."

when I was permitted to go to the meeting house with the foot stove and place it in the pew. The use of the foot stove in church was almost as ancient as the New England meeting house itself. On the fourth of March, 1744, it was voted by the town "that each person leaving his or her stove in any of the meeting houses in said town, after the people are all gone out (but the sexton) shall forfeit and pay the sum of five shillings to be improved as the law directs; and the stove so left to be forfeited to the sexton finding the same, and the sexton of each meeting house in the town is required carefully to inspect the pews and seats in each meeting house he or they have the care of, and to take into his possession all such stoves as may be so left in either or any of said meeting houses, and them keep in his possession until the owners thereof pay him the value of said stove or stoves so taken; and also each sexton is required and impowered to prosecute each person leaving his or her stove as aforesaid, and to recover the penalty set on such offender by this act."

The kitchen in our house was almost a baronial hall, nearly thirty feet long, with an open fireplace wide enough to take a four foot stick for a forestick, and deep enough to take an iron back log six inches square, bearing up a back stick with sticks between making a roaring fire capable of performing the multiplicity of duties assigned to it.   On the left side was a fire hole by which a wash boiler set in brick in the sink room was heated.   Over the fire was a long iron crane with its pot hooks and tramells from which a teakettle always hung, never permitting any usurpation of its place by pots and kettles of less royal station.   By its side hung the boiling kettle from whose recesses came at times those wonders of culinery art, the hard boiled puddings tied in a bag, of which the present generation knows nothing, and with which nothing has ever been seen since to furnish any comparison.   They were the hard boiled rice, plum rice, apple, Indian, Indian suet, batter, bread and huckleberry, sure proofs to all who remember them that the world has retrograded.   The hasty pudding was exempted from confinement in a bag, a pudding older than New England, and a favorite food of the Indians.   Joel Barlow described its preparation in the following lines:

"She learnt with stones to crack the well dried maize,
Thro' the rough sieve to shake the golden shower,
In boiling water stir the yellow flour;
The yellow flour bestrewed and stirred with haste,
Swells in the flood, and thickens to a paste,
Then puffs and wallops, rises to the brim,
Drinks the dry knobs that on the surface swim;
The knobs at last the busy ladle breaks,
And the whole mass its true consistence takes."

On the right hand side of the fireplace was a brick oven with an opening into the ash pit in front of the door to receive the coals and ashes when the oven was sufficiently heated.   This kind of oven is often called the "Dutch Oven," but it lacks that distinctive feature of the Dutch oven, a door on the outside of the house opening into a small lean-to under which the baking was done. In front of the fireplace was the tin kitchen, in which all the roasting was done, having a long spit running through it to hold the meat or turkey, the basting being done through a door on its back. The baking of bread, if not done in the oven when it happened to be heated, was done either in a creeper or in a tin Yankee baker before the fire. Inside the jams hung the indispensable bellows, and the waffle irons, which were often called into use. I supposed as others did, that when waffle irons were first used they were a new discovery in the culinary art. But bless you, my young admirers of waffles, they were older than the country, and were brought from Holland by the Dutch. The irons were called by the Dutch "Izers." In New York the waffles were called "Izer cookies," in New Jersey "split cakes," and in Philadelphia "squeeze cakes," and finally became known as waffles, a name which seems to have been an abbreviation of "wafers." As some of my readers may never have seen these irons, I will describe them as two iron handles, joined and worked like a pair of scissors, each having at its end a square or round plate five or six inches in diameter, fitting into each other and holding the dough, which is pressed, receiving the design cast in the inside of the plates. There is an old song remembered by Dutch descendants partly Dutch and partly English, which in its allusion to waffles shows the intiquity of the cakes, and which I submit to our high school scholars for translation:

"Ter roorches, ter roorches,
She mameche bucleche, borche
Ter roorches, ter roorches,
As me mither le waffles she boxes,
De butter la door de groches,
Ter roorches, ter rooches
She mameche backle che boo."

There are other articles of food which have come from the Dutch. The cooky from the Dutch word kockje, the cruller from the Dutch kruller, and noodles for soup from the Dutch noodlegees are well known. Our doughnut called in England in old times donnuts, are the same as the old Dutch oly-coecks, which originally had a raisin embedded in their centre.

In describing the old kitchen, I must not forget the coffee

grinder, which hung on the wall, in which our grandmothers knew enough not to grind more than sufficient for a day's use. Coffee was coffee in those days, and not the mixture of chicory and pease now imposed on those who buy what is called ground coffee. I say to my readers, pay no attention to the advertisers of postum and other substitutes for coffee, who magnify the ill effects of the genuine article. Always buy your coffee in the bean, roast and grind it yourself, and preserve its full flavor in an air tight box until used. I know that in Paris sixty years ago, coffee roasters were to be seen every morning along the sidewalks or in the court yards of the houses, showing the general importance attached to the morning beverage, and that everywhere in hotel and restaurant delicious coffee was always served. In 1895 no such scenes on the sidewalks came under my observation, and poor coffee had become the rule. No doubt the change is due to the use of ground coffee, which has either lost its flavour, or is an adulterated article.

In the autumn in my youth there was a solicitude concerning the articles to be laid in for the winter. First good potatoes must be found, twenty bushels of which with a barrel of sweet German turnips, and a bushel of carrots and onions must be put in brick bins in the cellar, where exposed to as little light as possible, they would in the days before furnaces keep well till spring. Then in a cool part of the cellar, places must be found for five barrels of apples, one each of Rhode Island Greenings, Baldwins, Russets, Holmes apples and sweet apples. Of course a firkin of good butter must be laid in, a jar of tamarinds, a jar of malaga grapes, and fifty pounds of well selected codfish, the last to be broad and thick, and not more than eighteen inches long including the tail. The fish must be kept in a close box, and placed in the garret. Never buy stripped codfish, for if you do you will probably get hake, polluck, skate and catfish, and other cheap denisons of the sea. In speaking of articles of food, in which there have been changes, there are other articles besides coffee and codfish not altogether creditable to those who provide them for public use. The sweet oil that you buy may be lard or cotton seed, the horseradish. which you wish for your veal in the spring, is largely flat turnip; some of the canned tomatoes are green and colored red, and much of your vinegar and whiskey is manufactured. The Philadelphia capons, Rhode Island turkeys and Vermont geese displayed on your hotel menus were raised in Plympton, Carver and Halifax. Our traders are honest, but they sell what they buy without analysis, leaving their protection to the law. Many of these misrepresentations are innocent enough, and cannot be classed with that which daily stares us in the face on the first page of a newspaper which is delivered at the hotels and newstands at half past twelve and dated 4.05. The worst feature of such misrepresentations as this is that it teaches the newsboys to make the false claim after 4.05, that the paper so dated is the last edition. One of the occasional domestic functions of our home was a quilting bee, in which friends and neighbors joined for the purpose of quilting a counterpane or bed quilt, made of patchwork. We had a set of quilting bars, four strips of wood about eight feet long, with holes a few inches apart, which when resting on the tops of chairs, could be put together by means of pegs at the corners, and enlarged as the quilt required more space between the side bars. As there were not many of these bars in town ours were constantly in demand, and loaned from one to another. I suppose these patchwork quilts are still in use, but the last one I ever saw was given to me by Mrs. Taylor, a daughter of Uncle Branch Pierce, in acknowledgment of service rendered her in securing the return of the body of her son, David A. Taylor, who was killed during the civil war. A part of my occupation at school in early boyhood was sewing patchwork squares together, to be used in quilts when needed.

Invariably on Saturday night my brother and I were given the weekly bath, which was not especially welcome in winter, but as cleanliness was next to Godliness, it was esteemed a proper preparation for Sunday. A countryman visiting New York for the first time must have been accustomed to the same habit, for he wrote home to his wife that "agin my room in the hotel is another room, with a bath tub and hot and cold water, and a lot of towels, and when I see them things I almost wished, begosh, that it was Saturday night." Notwithstanding the bath tub preparation for the Sabbath, I am sorry to say that the hours of that day were those of my youth which I recall with the least pleasure. A strict observance of the Sabbath was the custom of the time, and the day was devoted until late in the afternoon to Scripture reading and Sunday-school lessons in the morning, and attendance twice at church, with Sunday-school at noon. Parents in those days did not permit their children to loiter at home and on the street until the morning service was finished, and then send them to Sunday-school, for they believed that the religious and moral instruction received from the pulpit was as important as that received through catechisms from teachers in the pew.

After the second service my brother and I were sometimes permitted to take hold of hands and make a call at the house of my uncle Mr. Nathaniel Morton Davis, or at the house of my great aunt, Hannah White, then ninety years of age, a descendant of Peregrine White, who had talked with those who well knew the first born son of New England. Occasionally, also, I went with my mother to visit Miss Molly Jackson, an aunt of my grandmother Davis, who at the age of nearly one hundred occupied a second story room in the southwest corner of the house in Hobbs Hole, next south of that of Thos. E. Cornish. My visits to her connected me with an earlier date than any other incidents in my life, giving me an opportunity to see and talk with a person born one hundred and seventy-six years ago, or only twenty-five years after the death of Peregrine White. The lax observance of the Sabbath now prevailing in marked contrast with its observance in earlier times, believing as I do in the beneficent and conservative influence of stated days of rest for man and beast, aside from all religious considerations, should be considerately and wisely reformed.

CHAPTER XXXXVI.

Besides the quilting bee which has been mentioned, there were formerly many other kinds of bees, some within my own time, and others that I have heard about from my elders. There were the chopping and stone bees, by which a new comer in a settlement was assisted by all his neighbors in clearing the land for his house and farm; the apple gathering bee and the woodpile bee, in which under the full moon the fiddle and the dance played an important part. There was also the raising bee, when a house completely framed was ready to be set up, in which all the carpenters joined and found under the stimulating influence of Medford rum that in lifting plates and studs and rafters their yoke was easy, and their burden light. In raising the house on the upper westerly corner of High and Spring streets in 1799, the frame fell, precipitating from thirty to forty carpenters to the ground, twenty-one of whom were seriously, though none fatally injured. In that case the rum proved to be a little above proof, and the treenail fastenings a little below. The last house in Plymouth raised with the Medford accompaniment, was that now standing on the southerly corner of Howland street, built in 1834. The great bee, which was celebrated all over the corn growing parts of our country in olden times, was the husking bee, not the sham frolic of present days when, like the fox bought in a bag by Newport hunters, a load of corn on the stalk is bought for the occasion and piled on a floor glistening under electric lights, but the genuine husking frolic in a barn of ample proportions, where piles of pumpkins furnished the decorations, and cornstalk fiddles enlivened the scene. There the lads and lassies sat around the diminishing heap, and all knew the dangers and delights which attended the finding of a red or a smutty ear of corn.

> "In the barn the youths and maidens
> Strip the corn of husk and tassel,
> Warm the dullness of October
> With the life of spring and May;
> While through every chink the lanterns
> And sonorous gusts of laughter

> Make assault on night and silence
> With the counterfeit of day."

The literature of the husking bee is extensive, and there are mysterious legends of ancient date about the red ear of corn. As early as the year 1700, in the ceremony of marriage among the Caughnawaga Indians, the husband gave the wife a deer's leg, and the wife gave the husband a red ear, and in Hiawatha, Longfellow speaks of the husking as if it were a usage among the Indians.

> "When'er some lucky maiden
> Found a red ear in the husking,
> Found a red ear, red as blood is,
> Mushka; cried they altogether,
> Mushka; you shall have a sweetheart,
> You shall have a handsome husband."

John Barlow in his hasty pudding poem written in 1792 said:

> "The laws of husking every wight can tell—
> And sure no laws he ever keeps so well;
> For each red ear a general kiss he gains,
> With each smut ear he smuts the luckless swains;
> But when to some sweet maid a prize is cast,
> Red as her lips, and taper as her waist,
> She walks the round, and culls one favored beau,
> Who leaps the luscious tribute to bestow."

In "traits of American humor" a writer said, "there was a corn husking, and I went along with Sol. Stebbins. There was all the gals and boys setting around and I got sot down so near Sal Babit that I'll be darned if I didn't kiss her before I knowed what I was about." In the South the corn husk was called a shuck, and President Lincoln showed his familiarity with southern terms, when, after his conference at Fortress Monroe with Alexander H. Stephens, the vice president of the Confederacy, who was a very small man, weighing not more than ninety or a hundred pounds, and on that occasion wore an immense borrowed overcoat, which came down to his heels, he described Mr. Stevens as the smallest ear in the largest shuck he had ever seen.

Husking time among the negroes of North Carolina was always a season of relaxation and frolic. The following now no longer heard was among the husking songs they sang.

> "Oh boys! Come along and shuck the corn;
> Oh boys! Come along to the rattle of the horn!

We'll shuck and sing to the coming of the moon,
And den we'll ford the river.
 Oh Bob Ridley, O! O! O!
 How could you fool the possum so!"

There can be little doubt that at one time the harvest husking festival degenerated into noisy scenes, which called for earnest condemnation and earnest appeals for reform. Cotton Mather wrote in 1713 that "the riots that have too often accustomed our huskings, have carried in them fearful ingratitude and provocation unto the glorious God." But all through my boyhood pumpkin pie and sweet cider alone remained as relics of the ancient feast.

Christmas during my day came and went without observance or notice. It was not a holiday, presents were not exchanged, schools were kept, and the wish for a "Merry Christmas" was never heard. Puritan soil was not a favorable one for its observance. In 1659 any observance of Christmas "either by forbearing of labor, feasting, or any other way" was forbidden under a penalty of five shillings for each offence. Though this law was repealed in 1681 the leaders of the Massachusetts Colony, including Judge Samuel Sewall, still looked on Christmas revels as offensive to the Holy Son of God. During my boyhood the St. Andrews church in Scituate, which was later removed to Hanover, where it is now a flourishing church, was the only Episcopal church in Plymouth county. It is singular that in its early years it derived its membership and support from the Winslows and the Whites, descendants of Mayflower Pilgrims. As far as I can learn nearly all bearing those names in Marshfield and Scituate, among whom I include my own kinsmen, were Episcopalians, and some of those residing in Plymouth, were members of St. Andrew's church. The records of the Plymouth First Church contain a petition of my great aunt, Joanna Winslow, and her daughter, Mrs. Henry Warren, to be admitted to the Plymouth fold, on account of the distance of St. Andrew's from their homes in Plymouth. It is an anomaly difficult to understand that so many of Pilgrim blood should have returned to the faith from which their ancestors were glad to separate. With regard to Christmas I am inclined to think that its observance has found its way through its appeal to the æsthetic rather than the religious sense of the people.

Of the many cults and isms and doctrines, which have appeared within my recollection, I do not propose to speak. In the Bibliographia Antiquariana may be found, I think, nearly a hundred of their names terminating in "mancy," which at various times have found lodgment in the minds of men. Some of these still have their followers, and I am willing to accord to them as sound reasons for their faith as I claim for my own. The only limit to my tolerance is that set by the followers themselves in the contradictory acts of their every day life. Not long ago in a casual conversation with a devotee of an ism, the name of which I do not know, I incidentally said, "it is a stormy day, Madam," to which she answered, "It seems so, but it isn't." To my inquiry, "Why, then, do you carry an umbrella," she made no reply, and I bade her good morning.

In my early boyhood the primitive methods of kindling a fire were only a little in advance of the method of rubbing two sticks together, practised by the Indians. Until 1829, so far as my own observation went, the tinder box, with the flint and steel, was in use. Some used what was called the chemical match, a stick dipped first in sulphur, and then into a composition of chlorate of potash, and other ingredients, which dipped in a vial of sulphuric acid produced fire as the result of chemical action between the acid and potash. In 1829 it was found that sticks coated with chlorate of potash and phosphorus could be instantly ignited by rubbing them on sandpaper. This was the first step leading to the manufacture of the lucifer match, now in almost universal use. The lucifer match was at first called locofoco, a name derived from the Latin "loco foci," meaning "In the place of fire." The name loco foco applied to the democratic party had its origin in 1835 in the incident of relighting by means of matches the burners in a hall in New York, where a democratic meeting was held, and the light had been extinguished by party opponents. In recent years safety matches have been extensively used, the best of which are made in Sweden, which can be ignited only on the boxes in which they are sold. With the frequency of fires occasioned by the lucifer match, it is a wonder to me that either by law or by rules of insurance companies, some restriction is not put on its use. It is estimated that more than six million gross of lucifer matches, with 14,400 to a

gross, are annually consumed in the United States. A story
was told me by the late Rev. Dr. George E. Ellis, about John
Quincy Adams who died in 1848, nineteen years after the lucifer match came into use. Dr. Ellis attended with Mr. Adams
about 1840 an historical meeting in New York, and occupied
with him a double bedded room at the Astor House. In
those days only a few rooms in hotels were ever heated, and
those by means of a coal grate, which was kept full of kindlings
and coal ready to be lighted by matches, of which there was
always a supply on the mantel. When Mr. Adams got into
bed, though the fire had not been lighted, he opened a window
much to the discomfort of Mr. Ellis, who planned to close it
when his room-mate fell asleep. But Mr. Adams talked for an
hour, and then said, "I am going to repeat aloud the prayer
which I have said every night since I was nine years old, and
then turn over and go to sleep." He then said:

"Now I lay me down to sleep,
I pray the Lord my soul to keep;
If I should die before I wake.
I pray the Lord my soul to take.
            Amen."

After he was safely asleep, Dr. Ellis arose quietly and shut
the window. He was awakened in the morning by some noise,
and looking over his bedclothes, he saw Mr. Adams on his
knees by the side of his open valise, from which he had taken
his tinder box, and was getting a spark to touch off the kindlings in the grate. He scorned the use of the matches on the
mantel, preferring the friends of his youth and age, which
had been his faithful attendants through life.

There were few articles in domestic use in my youth more
popular than the apple, and few performing such a variety of
parts in the performances of the kitchen. A New England
supper would have been incomplete without an apple pie. The
English sneer at our corn, saying it is only fit for horses, while
they worship their oats, which are more fit for the horse trough
than the table. So, while they condemn our apple pie, made
with a crust thoroughly baked, they gorge themselves in July
and August and September with gooseberry and green gage
tarts, which no armored war ship could resist if fired from a
Whitworth gun at the distance of a mile. Behold the products of the apple, a roasted apple, a Marlboro pudding, look-

ing like an ordinary pie without crust, a pan-dowdy, or apple grunt baked with molasses in a deep pan, and the crust broken in, pork and apples cut up together and cooked, called by the Dutch "speck and apple jees," plain apple sauce, apple butter or Vermont apple sauce boiled with cider and put up for winter, apple brandy warranted to kill at thirty paces, called in New Jersey "Jersey lightning," and apple pudding. To the apple then, notwithstanding John Bull, let the toast go round.

Perhaps in the history of man no article in common use has undergone greater changes than that used in writing, and many of those changes have occurred within my memory. The stylus of the ancients used on waxen tablets, has become a factor in the advance of civilization, until it may now be said that:

> "Beneath the rule of men entirely great,
> The pen is mightier than the sword."

The stylus on waxen tablets gave way to reeds used with a fluid on papyrus, and reeds to quills of swans and geese and crows. For a long time geese were raised chiefly for their quills, and it is said that in one year twenty-seven millions of these quills were sent to England from St. Petersburg. Until the steel pen was introduced in my later youth, the goose quill held undivided sway in the United States, and for some years afterwards the price of the steel pen was not sufficiently reduced to admit of its popular use. In all the schools which I ever attended the teachers spent a large portion of their time in mending pens, an occupation so constant and universal as to introduce into our vocabulary the name "pen knife," which still holds its place, though the use for which it was designed has departed. As late as 1858 and 1859, when I was in the senate, among the articles of stationery distributed among the members, were a bunch of quills and a pen knife. As John Quincy Adams once wrote in a lady's album:

> "In days of yore the poet's pen
> From wing of bird was plundered,
> Perhaps of goose, but now and then
> From Jove's own eagle sundered."

Of the successive steps taken in the manufacture of pens until the steel pen, the gold pen with diamond point, and at last the fountain pen came into use, which was followed by the ·

typewriting machine I do not propose to speak.   In business
the machine seems to be coming rapidly into use, and is even
finding its way into social correspondence.   I have an old
man's notion, which if I live I may outgrow, that only with the
hand should a letter of friendship be written.   By the use
of the typewriter I fear that the accomplishment of letter writing has become a thing of the past.

CHAPTER XXXXVII.

The marriage laws of Massachusetts prevailing to-day are different from those in force all through my youth. As early as 1786 a law was passed by the General Court of Massachusetts establishing the methods to be pursued by those intending to enter into marriage, which provided that all persons intending to be joined in marriage, should "cause notice of their intention to be filed with the town clerk fourteen days before their marriage, which notice should be published by the clerk, either by posting up a written notice in some public place in the town of which he is clerk, fourteen days at least before the marriage or by making public proclamation thereof at three public religious meetings in the town on separate days, not less than three days distant from each other, exclusive of the days of publication." This law with slight amendments remained in force until 1850, when the present law was enacted requiring only a notice to the town clerk, by whom the necessary certificate would be issued. I remember well the little box with a glass front attached to the wall in the vestibule of the meeting house in which the marriage intention was posted, and I have often heard it read from the pulpit on the three Sundays required by law, much to the embarrassment of the loving pair sitting within the gaze of the congregation.

One of the most remarkable developments within my memory has been the number of articles claimed to be associated with the Mayflower and the Pilgrims. Not a month passes without the reception at Pilgrim Hall of a letter offering for sale a Mayflower relic. It may be a tea pot, though the Pilgrims had no tea; or a porcelain mug, though the inventories recorded in Plymouth contained no porcelain ware until 1660: or a fork, which the Pilgrims did not use, or a mahogany table, though no mahogany was known in England before 1700.

Three articles claimed to have been associated with the Pilgrims I have myself proved to bear fictitious labels. One of these exhibited a few years ago at a portrait exhibition in Copley Square as a miniature of Governor Edward Winslow, when he was six years of age, I have found to be a picture of a son of Capt. Thomas Dingley of Marshfield, painted about the time of the Revolution. Another article labelled the "Knocker" from the door of Governor Winslow's house, was taken from the door of a house built by Isaac Winslow, grandson of the governor, about 1720. Still another article presented to the Pilgrim Society as a part of the doorstep of a church in Delft-haven where the Pilgrims held service on the eve of their departure, owed the origin of its record to a miss-reported speech of one of the building committee of a church in Chicago, who had at its dedication stated that he had imbedded in its walls a piece of Plymouth Rock, a stone from Scrooby, and a piece of the pavement of a church in Delfthaven, which, perhaps, the Pilgrims may have visited. Of course the piece of doorstep has never found a lodgment in Pilgrim Hall. These fictitious historic relics are interesting as showing the veneration in which the Pilgrims are held, which is not shared by the Winthrop Colony, or by any other body of men since the days of Christ.

It will be remembered by my readers that at the dinner of the Old Colony Club on the 22d of December, 1769, the first course was "a large baked Indian Whortleberry pudding." I have often been asked how long the custom continued of serving the pudding before the meat, and whether I remembered such a custom, and my reply has been that the only relic of the custom existing within my day was a legend of the promise once made at dinner to children, that the more pudding they ate the more meat they might have. I always supposed that this promise was intended to restrict indulgence in meat, either from motives of economy, or to confine the youthful diet to a more wholesome food. I have recently read an extract from a book of travels written by Henry Bradshaw Fearon, an Englishman, who visited the United States in 1817. The book is in the Congressional Library in Washington, and probably never had a circulation on this side of the ocean. It contains much of interest to an American reader, including an approximately accurate answer to the question concerning the custom above mentioned. Mr. Fearon left New York on the 8th of September, 1817, on the steamboat Connecticut, bound for New Haven, and he described the boat as having an engine of forty horse power, and fitted up with one cabin for ladies, two for gentlemen, and an extensive kitchen.   Arriving at New Haven in twelve hours, he was transferred to the steamboat Fulton, bound to New London, from which place he took a stage via Providence for Boston.   The fare from New York to New Haven, including table board, was seven dollars. On a Sunday, while in Boston, he went to Quincy and dined with ex-president John Adams.   The dinner was served at one o'clock, and consisted of a first course of Indian meal pudding and molasses, and a second course of veal, bacon, neck of mutton, cabbage, carrots, and Indian beans, with Madeira wine.   He said that Boston was the headquarters of Federalism in politics and Unitarianism in religion, and that the Bostonians were the most intelligent and hospitable people he had met in America.   Thus it is certain that the pudding custom was in vogue in 1817, and was discontinued not long afterwards.

The allusion above made to the steamboats Connecticut and Fulton, leads me to again refer to the steamboat Eagle, which came to Plymouth in 1818 under the command of Capt. Lemuel Clark.   That boat was built in New York, but like other boats was enjoined under a New York law from operating in New York waters, on the ground of a monopoly in the use of the rivers and harbors of New York, which had been granted by the state.   Resistance to this monopoly led to the famous case of Gibbons against Ogden, in which, while the monopoly was held good by the state courts, it was decided by the Supreme Court of the United States to be unconstitutional. Pending the decision in that case, steamboats sought business in other waters, and the Eagle, before coming to Boston and Plymouth, cruised in Chesapeake bay, under the command of Capt. Moses Rogers, who was in 1819 commander of the steamship Savannah, which in that year was the first steamship to cross the Atlantic.   A picture of the Eagle is owned by the Pilgrim Society.   Capt. Rogers was the grandfather of our townsman, Dr. Charles Rufus Rogers, and it is the story of the Savannah, which leads me into a digression which may make necessary an additional chapter of memories which I had intended to close with the next chapter.   A memoir of Capt. Moses Rogers states that the Savannah was a full rigged ship of three hundred and fifty tons, built at Corlear's Hook, New York, by Francis Fickett, and launched August 22, 1818. She was bought by Scarborough and Isaacs of Savannah, and her machinery, with a ninety horse power engine, having forty-inch cylinders, and a five foot stroke, was put in under the supervision of Capt. Rogers. Besides the Eagle he had already commanded the steamboat Fulton on the Hudson river, and the Phenix on the Delaware river. A picture of the Savannah, a copy of which I have seen, represents her as a vessel of fine model, with round stern, a medium clipper bow, and a graceful, easy shear. Her wheels were made adjustable, and so affixed to the shaft as in stormy weather to be unshipped and removed to the deck in twenty minutes. Her wheels consisted of eight radial arms held in place by one flange, and arranged to close like a fan. With her allowance of seventy-five tons of coal and twenty-five cords of wood, she sailed from New York, March 28, 1819, and arrived at Savannah April 6, in two hundred and seven hours from Sandy Hook lightship, having steamed four days during the passage. On the 22d of May she began her voyage from Savannah to Liverpool, where she arrived on the 20th of June. Her log kept by Stevens Rogers, the sailing master, a brother-in-law of Capt. Moses Rogers, is in the possession of the descendants of Moses, and contains an interesting account of the voyage. On the 23d of July the Savannah set sail from Liverpool for Cronstadt, touching at Copenhagen and Stockholm on the way, reaching the first named port on the 9th of September. A few days later she arrived at St. Petersburg, where she remained until October 10, receiving while there visits from the Russian Lord High Admiral Marcus de Travys. On the 30th of November she again reached Savannah, and was run as a packet between that port and New York, until she was wrecked on Long Island.

Questions are often asked in newspapers and elsewhere concerning the circumstances attending the composition of popular hymns and songs, and I have already told my readers about the origin of "Sweet Home," and the "Star Spangled Banner." I have lately read in the Boston Sunday *Herald* an account of the composition of "My Country 'tis of Thee," by Samuel Francis Smith, which may be interesting to those of my readers who did not happen to see it. Mr. Smith was born in Sheafe street, Boston, October 21, 1808, and after attending the Eliot school and the Boston Latin school, graduated at Harvard in 1829. After graduating at the Andover Theological Seminary in 1832, he was settled as pastor of the Baptist church in Waterville, Me., and served as Professor of Modern languages in Colby University until he removed to Newton, Mass., where he resided until his death. At a meeting in the Old South Church in Boston, Mr. Smith said, in giving a history of the hymn, that many years before Mr. W. C. Woodbridge brought from Germany a number of books containing words and music used in the schools there, and gave them to Mr. Lowell Mason, who gave them to him, requesting him to either translate them or write words to such of the music as pleased him. In looking these books over, Mr. Smith found the notes of our National anthem attached to a patriotic hymn, and was inspired by it to write the hymn in question. To the tune of "God Save the King," Mr. Smith's hymn was sung for the first time at a Sunday-school celebration on the Fourth of July, 1832, and received at once such popular commendation as to re-christen the tune with the name of "America." We, of course, ought to accept Mr. Smith's word, but it seems almost incredible that he should have never heard of the tune until 1832, when it had been known in England as "God Save the King" at least two hundred years. It is also singular that the origin of many national airs should be involved in doubt. The Marseillaise, Yankee Doodle, and to a certain extent the "God Save the King" had an obscure, if not doubtful, authorship. The last, however, which has by some been attributed to Henry Carey, a musical composer who flourished in the time of James the First, seems to have been established by good evidence, to have been composed by John Bull, a contemporary with Carey, who died in 1622. As I have not been able to trace the name John Bull as applied to the English people, farther back than about the early part of the 17th century, I think it is a reasonable conjecture that Dr. Bull was not only the author of the National anthem, but also through his authorship of that popular air that he gave the name for all time to his fellow countrymen.

The compositon of the favorite Pilgrim hymn "Sons of Renowned Sires" by Judge John Davis of Boston in 1794, is interesting. Coming to Plymouth on the evening of the 21st of December to attend a celebration of the anniversary of the Landing on the next day, the regret was expressed to him that no original hymn had been prepared for the occasion, as had been intended. He expressed no intention to write one, but at an early hour retired to his chamber with his wife. Instead of going to bed he began to walk the room to the annoyance of his wife, and against her earnest remonstrances. Mrs. Davis fell asleep, waking occasionally, and finding him still walking, and the bed candle unsnuffed and smoking. Not having the remotest idea what he was doing, she became alarmed for his sanity, and again and again her sleep was broken by the noise of his footsteps. At last the candle was extinguished, and in the morning Mr. Davis surprised the committee with the hymn, which was sung that day to the tune of "God Save the King," thirty-eight years before Mr. Smith, the author of his anthem, had ever heard of it, and which has been sung probably at every Pilgrim celebration since.

The story of the inspiration of "The Breaking Waves Dashed High," written by Mrs. Hemans, is also an interesting one. In 1825 she was living with her brother at Rhyllon, a parish of St. Asaph at the mouth of the river Clwyd in North Wales. After shopping one day, one of her purchases was sent home in a bandbox covered with a newspaper, which she noticed was a Boston daily. Before throwing the paper away or burning it, she had the curiosity to look over its contents in which she found a long account of the Pilgrim celebration in Plymouth on December 22, 1824, and copious extracts from the oration delivered by Edward Everett. The Pilgrim story was a new one to her, and the account, which she read with great interest, was so circumstantial as to inspire her with the grandeur of the theme. She told Rev. Charles T. Brooks on a visit to her later home in Dublin, that she at once, after reading the account, turned to her desk and wrote the immortal lines. The original manuscript of the hymn she gave to James T. Fields of Boston, and it is now preserved in the cabinet of the Pilgrim Society, a gift from Mr. Fields.

It is singular how many of our best hymns have been the work of an hour. It has been said that the missionary hymn by Reginald Heber, was one of those sudden inspirations. It was written in 1819, while he was occupying a living in Hodnet in Shropshire, which had been given to him by his brother Richard, who was a member of parliament, and an owner of large estates in that shire. In 1823 he was consecrated Bishop of Calcutta, and died in India in 1826. Before going to India he devoted himself to literary pursuits, and wrote many hymns, which won a permanent place in hymnology, among which was that sweetly flowing hymn:

> "By cool Saloam's shady rill
> How sweet the lily grows."

I have heard it said that on one occasion Mr. Heber was invited by a brother clergyman in a neighboring parish to officiate at a missionary service to be held in his church. In the course of the evening, before the day of the service, his friend asked him if it would be possible for him to compose a hymn appropriate to the occasion. Mr. Heber said he would try, and retiring to another room, composed the hymn which for appropriateness and beauty, has rarely been equalled. His brother Richard was an author of note, and left at his death perhaps the largest private library ever collected in England. It contained 146,875 volumes, and after his death, the library was sold at an auction which continued through two hundred and sixteen days, and realized sixty thousand pounds.

Some years ago I heard the story of an incident which suggested "The Hanging of the Crane," one of the most charming poems of Longfellow. In the early married life of Aldrich, the poet, Longfellow dropped into his house one night and found him and his wife sitting alone at their evening meal. "Ah," said he, as he entered the supper room and took a seat at the table, "here Aldrich, is a whole poem, and I will give you the subject to work out." His friend, believing that the artist who paints a scene in his imagination, should put it on the canvas, said, "No, Longfellow, use it yourself." After some years of elaboration the poem appeared, depicting the changing scenes in married life, which the following selected extracts sufficiently describe. Happy are the father and mother who live to witness the scenes which time discloses as it unrolls the canvas:

"And now I sit and muse on what may be,
And in my vision, see or seem to see,
Through floating vapors interfused with light,
Shapes indeterminate, that gleam and fade,
As shadows passing into deeper shade,
Sink and elude the sight.
For two alone, there in the hall,
Is spread the table round and small.

* * * *

Seated I see the two again,
But not alone; they entertain
A little angel unaware.
With face as round as is the moon;
A royal guest with flaxen hair
Who throned upon his lofty chair
Drums on the table with his spoon.

* * * *

There are two guests at table now;
The King, deposed and older grown,
No longer occupies the throne—
The crown is on his sister's brow.

* * * *

I see the table wider grown,
I see it garlanded with guests,
As if fair Ariadne's crown
Out of the sky had fallen down.

* * * *

And now like the magician's scroll
That in the owner's keeping shrinks,
With every wish he speaks or thinks,
Till the last wish consumes the whole.
The table dwindles, and again
I see the two alone remain.
The crown of stars is broken in parts.
Its jewels brighter than the day
Have one by one been stolen away
To shine in other homes and hearts.

* * * *

What see I now? the night is fair;
The storm of grief, the clouds of care,
The wind, the rain have passed away;
The lamps are lit, the fires burn bright.
The house is full of life and light;
It is the Golden Wedding Day.
The guests come thronging in once more;
Quick footsteps sound along the floor;
The trooping children crowd the stair;

And in and out and everywhere
Flashes along the corridor
The sunshine of their golden hair.
On the round table, in the hall,
Another Ariadne's crown
Out of the sky hath fallen down;
More than one monarch of the moon
Is drumming with his silver spoon;
The light of love shines over all.
The ancient bridegroom and the bride
Smiling contented and serene
Upon the blithe, bewildering scene,
Behold well pleased on every side
Their forms and features multiplied."

The impromptu remark of Mr. Longfellow to Aldrich might have been like many other impromptus thought out before. If so, however, it was under authority of a poet's license. Perhaps it was like another of Mr. Longfellow's impromptus, of which I heard many years ago. While attending as a delegate the National Republican Convention in Cincinnati in 1876, a party composed of James Russell Lowell, Judge E. R. Hoar, Mr. Roosevelt, the father of the President, who were also delegates, and myself, took a carriage and drove out to the estate of Nicholas Longworth to call on him and see his wine vaults. Mr. Longworth told us that Mr. Longfellow had made a recent call on him, and when introduced had said: "Mr. Longworth, you have the advantage of me, for you know Pope says, "That worth makes the man, and the want of it the fellow.' " Some men would have thought of the *bon mot* the next day, and realized what the French call *l'esprit d'escallier*, a good thing thought of too late. But Mr. Longfellow was quick witted enough to think of the good thing "while going up stairs and not while going down." There have been severe critics of Longfellow who would not have hesitated to pronounce the above impromptu deliberately prepared. They have charged him with plagiarism, and have said that the "Psalm of Life" is composed of thoughts from Gœthe and Calderon and Schiller, and have declared that "there is not one striking image, and barely one striking phrase in the poem which originated absolutely with himself." They also claim that from Soame Jennyn's was taken the substance of those beautiful lines:

"Still like muffled drums are beating
Funeral marches to the grave."

But these critics cannot deny that the dress in which the above thoughts were clothed, and in which they captivate the reader, were his own.   Would any one on the following statement of facts claim that Webster was a plagiarist? Rev. Dr. John Pierpont wrote for the Plymouth celebration on the 22d of December, 1824, a hymn containing the following stanza:

> "The Pilgrim Fathers are at rest.
> When Summer's throned on high,
> And the world's warm breast is in verdure dressed
> Go stand on the hill where they lie.
> The earliest ray of the golden day
> On that hallowed spot is cast,
> And the evening sun as he leaves the world,
> Looks kindly on that spot last."

On the 17th of June, 1825, Mr. Webster delivered his memorable oration at the laying of the cornerstone of Bunker Hill monument, containing the well known passage, "Let it rise till it meet the sun in his coming; let the earliest light of the morning gild it, and parting day linger and play on its summit."

CHAPTER XXXXVIII.

During my boyhood there was an article which had been for many years in the cookery department of our house, but which had recently gone out of use.   It was called a roasting Jack, and preceded the tin kitchen in roasting meats and poultry.   I remember it well, but I have little doubt that like many another relic of the past, it found its way into the junk heap of William Nye on the approach of some muster or election day, when we boys wanted money for lobsters and lemonade and other promoters of a stomachache which, perhaps, in these days of fads would have been called appendicitis.   It was an iron cylinder about four inches in diameter and six inches long, attached at the top with an intermediate swivel to the chimney crane, and at the bottom to a hook or some other contrivance which held the meat.   Inside of the cylinder there was a clock work machinery, which when wound up would keep the hook constantly turning before the fire.   It probably went out of use between 1800 and 1820.

There was another kind of roasting Jack, consisting of a spit resting on hooks attached to the andirons to which a wheel was affixed, which was kept turning by a chain band running from a larger wheel moved by clock work attached to the under side of the mantel piece.   I have no doubt that many of my readers have seen the hooks on old andirons without knowing the purpose for which they were intended.   These hooks may be seen on a pair of andirons in the Pilgrim Hall Library.

There was another article closely associated with my childhood, which I have thus far omitted to mention.   How often have I sat in a high chair with a bib under my chin, and a pap spoon in hand, feeding myself out of a porringer.   I supposed that the porringer was the sole prerogative of children ; that it was designed expressly for their use, but I had not then learned the fictions of legendary lore, and that the world is all a fleeting show for a child's illusion given.   I learned the true origin and use of the porringer some years ago.   A lady wrote to me that an elderly lady in Roxbury in somewhat reduced circumstances owned a china soup tureen which was once used in the household of Queen Anne, and would be glad to sell it. I went to see it, and found a very handsome tureen, but I saw at once on its cover a knob representing a rabbit's ear, the exclusive mark of Wedgewood, who flourished during the time of Queen Charlotte, and made a very beautiful cream colored ware, of which this tureen was a specimen, and in honor of Queen Charlotte called it "queen's ware." The story accompanying the tureen was that an ancestor of its present owner was at one time attached to Queen Anne's Court, as one of the ladies in waiting, and afterwards becoming reduced, emigrated to New Brunswick, carrying with her the tureen, which she received as a present during her service in the household of the Queen. It is easy to account for the legend of its origin by the supposition of some later owner, knowing it was called queen's ware, that it was a part of the ware of the queen of whose household an ancestor was a member. Not being satisfied with the result of my examination I began a further investigation of the origin of soup tureens as articles of table ware, and found that in the reign of Queen Anne, they were neither used or known. The custom was to have soup brought to the table by the servants in porringers, one of which was placed before each guest. This was the design and purpose of the porringer, and this was its use until the appearance of the tureen about the middle of the eighteenth century, when it was relegated to the use of children. In my day the porringer was made of either silver or pewter, but as the fashion of its use has gradually gone out the silver porringer has found its way to the melting pot, and the pewter one to the bric-a-brac store.

There are doubtless many genuine relics of the Queen Anne period in existence. I have a hammered brass wine cooler of that period, which came down in my mother's family from John White, son of Peregrine White, born in Marshfield about 1660. It is about the size and shape of an ordinary soup tureen, with solid brass handles and slots around its edge, in which wine glasses were hung with their bowls in the water. It was called a "Monteth," and took its name from the inventor. The poet William King, who was born in 1663, and died in 1712, alluded to the article in the following lines:

"New names produce new words, and thus Monteth
Has by a vessel saved his name from death."

Among the books which I have examined with reference to the articles above mentioned, is a very interesting one entitled "Social life in the reign of Queen Anne," to which I refer the student of habits and customs in the early part of the 18th century.

In the flowers and fruits and trees of Plymouth the changes in my day have not been striking. The garden flora are the same as in my youth, except that new flowers have been introduced, and new and improved varieties of the old ones. Fashion has occasionally relegated some flowers to temporary obscurity, but in many instances has restored them to their old rank or to a higher one. In my youth the tulip filled every border in yard and garden, but in time fashion called it vulgar, and it retired from the floral social life. But it returned in due season, like a girl from a fashionable school with the flush of beauty and with cultivated taste, and became instead of the wall flower, one of the belles of the ball. The hollyhock once banished to the back yard, is now the guardian of our doorway, and nods a graceful welcome to every guest, while the sunflower, once the occupant of the poultry yard, now stands in splendid defiance under our windows, and hourly challenges the sun to do his best.

The most remarkable change in our gardens has been in connection with the tomato introduced from Mexico, and there called tomatl. In 1831 Dr. Jas. Thacher of Plymouth, who was fond of introducing new things, secured some seed and gave my mother some, which she planted. I remember the plant well, with its burdens of gorgeous fruit, which was looked upon rather as a garden ornament than food for the table. It was not long, however, before it came into general use as a summer vegetable, and finally as a preserve in cans for winter use, until it may now be said that in the extent of its use it stands next to the potato. Though long supposed to have been of Mexican origin, it has been recently found that nations in Africa had long used it, and esteemed it a valuable article of food. I have an impression that in the summer of 1831 it ripened much earlier than it does now. It is a serious objection that as a crop it ripens so late that practically the whole crop ripens at the same time, and as a perishable vegetable is rushed into the market at prices too low to make its cultivation profitable. The canning, however, of large quantities, has served in recent years to help prices by increasing the demand. A writer in Blackwood says, "the tomato is a noble fruit, as sweet in smell as the odors of Araby, and makes an illustrious salad. Its medicinal virtue is as great as its gastronomical goodness. It is the friend of the well to keep them well, and the friend of the sick to bring them back into the lost sheep-folds of Hygeia. The Englishman's travelling companion, the blue pill, would never be needed if he would pay proper court to the tomato."

Among the fruits brought into use in Plymouth from foreign fields, the banana has had the most striking history. I remember the first one I ever saw, and the first brought to Plymouth. It was about the year 1833 that Capt. Samuel Rogers in command of the schooner Capitol, belonging to Daniel and Abraham Jackson, brought to Plymouth several bunches of bananas, one of which he gave to Mr. Abraham Jackson, in whose yard I saw it hanging on a tree. The bunch was of the yellow variety, and Capt. Rogers called it plantain. As the demand for this fruit has increased, the banana fields of Porto Rico, Jamaica and Costa Rica have been immensely enlarged until regular lines of steamers from those places now bring into the United States twenty-five millions of bunches annually, or twenty-five hundred millions of bananas, enough to supply annually thirty bananas to every man, woman and child, including negroes. The fruit is now sold at so low a price, and is so universally used that I think it safe to say that no fruit, not excepting apples, has so large a consumption.

The most striking change in fruits during my time has been in the cultivation of cranberries. They have always been known as a native of New England, and John Smith found them in a visit here in 1614. They have always found their best natural growth in grassy meadows or swamps, where decay of vegetable matter has supplied the soil with organic acids. I know some patches of such meadows today where the cranberry has borne fruit hundreds of years. These natural berries are better than the cultivated ones, probably because the sand with which the made bog is covered has diminished the supply of organic acids. The general consumer has not yet discovered that the native berry weighs a number of pounds more to the bushel than the cultivated one, and has a richer flavor.   In 1855 the statistics of Plymouth showed an acre and a half of cranberry bog valued at $15—while at the present time there are 984 acres valued at $393,600.

Some fruits which were abundant in our gardens during my youth, have entirely disappeared.   I knew then scarcely a garden without its plums, gages and damsons, the latter of which were especially prized for preserving.   When it is asked what has become of these trees, it is often answered that they have run out.   But such an answer is absurd, because if they had run out in one place, they would have run out everywhere. But the plum and gage are raised in California and sold in Boston and Plymouth at a profit to the producer after a travel of three thousand miles across the continent.   The trouble is that the soil has run out after nearly three centuries of cultivation without renewal of those properties and ingredients which successive crops have exhausted.   If the virgin soils of California were analyzed, and their fertilizing constituents when discovered were applied to our worn out gardens, they would doubtless be rejuvenated.   Our people have not even been content with robbing the ground of its crops without adding to and restoring its vitality, but they have year after year raked out every stone, great and small, leaving the ground a mere black paste, instead of a vigorous loam.   They have yet to learn that the feldspar in granite contains potash enough if we knew how to extract it to fertilize the fields in which the farmer looks on stones as nuisances to be rid of.   I have seen some evidence in the rank growth of grass around stone heaps and under stone walls that nature may have found some method by chemical action of eliminating the feldspar potash which the rocks contain.   The condition of the trees on Boston Common, of which in late years we have heard much complaint illustrates in my opinion the necessity of restoring to the soil precisely those qualities which year after year the trees have been using up.   Mr. Doogue, the superintendent, last season, or the season before, ploughed the ground and planted grain as if the surface needed loosening and enriching to permit the access of rain to the roots of the trees, but I do not believe that he has reached or remedied the trouble.   If he would come to Plymouth I could show him by an object lesson what the trees need.

Let him make a visit to our woods, where with no more than two inches of soil on a substratum of sand and gravel, a thick growth of oaks and pines sends up every season a foot or more of upward growth, and preserves through the dryest summers a rich foliage. They simply live on the leaves which they shed in the autumn for their own use, and which they find in the spring that no robber has carried away. If Mr. Doogue, instead of raking the common and carting off the leaves will deposit them in trenches around the trees covered with a little earth, his trees will doubtless revive.

Among the trees which have practically disappeared in my day are the Buttonwood and Balm of Gilead. The Buttonwood or Sycamore or Plane tree, grew in various localities within the town, and until about the year 1845, a row of Buttonwoods stood on the front of the lot which now includes Cushman street and the lots on both sides. Jas. Russell Lowell was undoubtedly familiar with it when he wrote in his "Beaver Brook."

> "Beneath a bony buttonwood
> The mill's red door swings open wide;
> The whitened miller, dust imbued,
> Flits past the square of dark inside."

The Buttonwood bush is an entirely distinct plant deriving its name from the globules it bears resembling buttons in shape.

There was during my youth a row of Balm of Gileads or Balsam poplars five or six in number, standing below the stone wall opposite the North side of the Plymouth Rock House. The buds of the trees covered with a resinous matter, were much sought after as cures for cuts and wounds. Only a very few of these trees are now standing in Plymouth.

There is the hornbeam tree often spoken of in the division of lands in the early days of Plymouth Colony, of which very few specimens are now found in our woods. Wood in "New England's Prospect," under date of 1639 says, "the horn bound tree is a tough kind of wood that requires so much pains in riving as is almost incredible; being the best to make bowls and dishes, not being subject to crack or leak." He says:

> "The horn-bound tree that to be cloven scorns;
> Which from the tender vine oft takes his spouse
> Who twines embracing arms about his boughs."

The trees of New England seem to have been the same as

those which were natives of England. The English poet Spencer in the first book of the first canto of "The Færie Queen" enumerates the latter in the following lines:

"Much can they praise the trees so straight and hy,
The sayling Pine; the Cedar proud and tall;
The vine-propt Elme; the Popplar never dry;
The builder Oake, sole king of forrests all;
The Aspine, good for staves; the Cypresse funerall;
The Laurell, meed of mightie conquerors
And poets sage; the Firre that weepeth still;
The Willow, worne of forlorne paramours;
The Eugh, obedient to the bender's will;
The Birch for shaftes; the Sallow for the mill;
The Mirrhe, sweete-bleeding in the bitter wound;
The warlike Beech; the Ash for nothing ill;
The fruitful Olive, and the Platane round;
The corner Holme; the Maple seldom inward sound."

The sapling pine was the tree of which staffs were made; the builders' oak was the white oak; the sallow was a kind of willow; the platane was the plane, and the holm was the holly. The olive may have been some tree now known by another name.

The beech tree at one time within my recollection was almost extinct in Plymouth woods, and was rarely found except on islands in the woodland ponds. I have heard that the same was true of the beech in the Middlesex Fells, which suggests that woods fires which could not reach the islands may have thinned the beeches out. The fact that in recent years the beech is again making its appearance in the Plymouth Park and other protected localities, adds force to the suggestion.

Elm trees have always abounded in New England, doubtless including Plymouth, and are much handsomer than the English elms, though the latter retaining the custom of their habitat, leave out earlier in the spring than the American, and hold their leaves longer in the autumn. As far as I know there is no positive record of an elm tree from the natural forests in New England. The ages of the old elm on the Common in Boston, and of the Brookline and Pittsfield elms, is not known. There are contemporary records of an elm in New York city, standing on the corner of Wall and Broad streets as late as 1670, which measured more than thirty feet in circumference, and was called by the Dutch, "der Groot Tree." The trees now standing in Town Square, three of the five planted by my great-grandfather, Thomas Davis, in 1784, are young compared with the New York tree, and ought not to be in the languishing condition they now exhibit. With the ground in the square packed solid, it is impossible for rains to reach their roots. If a fence were built around each tree, and the ground within it dug up and kept loose, there can be no doubt that water would find its way to the roots and along them to the most distant rootlets. There is the same trouble with all the ornamental trees along our concreted sidewalks. We are spending hundreds of dollars each year in spraying their foliage to check the ravages of the beetle and miller, and at the same time by grass and concrete and macadamizing sentencing them to certain death. I commend the subject to the Plymouth Natural History Society, who on examination of the beautiful tree in the front of the new fire station, a central jewel in our coronet of trees, will find that we have been pursuing the policy of a physician who would treat a patient for loss of hair, who is dying of hunger and thirst.

Among other adopted trees are the European Linden, and the English Birch. Mr. George B. Emerson, the eminent naturalist, told me once he thought the latter the most beautiful tree in America. It undoubtedly has the merit of putting out its leaves earlier than our trees, and holding them longer, but I have never seen one standing erect if alone, or if more than forty years old retaining life and vigor in its upper branches. On the other hand I think the European Linden, of which we have noble specimens in Plymouth, is on the whole the most satisfactory ornamental tree for a bleak sea exposure like that of Plymouth. I have found in Holland, the country of Lindens, none to compare with the Lindens on North street, which grow straight and regular, under blasting winds, and I have seen them as late as the 6th of October without a yellow leaf.

Of the animals and birds and their changes within my day, I can say little. They are very much the same as in the days of the Pilgrims. The wild turkey disappeared before my time, and I think that they are only to be found in Massachusetts today in the Berkshire hills. All through my youth the wild pigeons were abundant in our grain fields and huckleberry woods, but they are now rare. Martins also were flying about our houses, and nearly every householder had a martin box under the eaves of his dwelling, or on a staff standing in his yard.   The English sparrow stole their nests, and they fled like the aborigines before the English immigrant.

The fish are the same as those described by Wood and Josselyn, writers in Pilgrim days, some, however having disappeared for a time and returned.   I remember being at Holmes Hole during the Civil War, and being told that the weak fish or squeteague had returned after an absence of twenty-five years.   In Josselyn's New England's rareties a fish called Gurnard is spoken of, and is also mentioned in a poem by Steendamn, a Dutchman, written, perhaps, about 1640 or 1650, in the following lines, descriptive of fish in New York waters:

"The bream and sturgeon, drum fish and gurnard
The sea-bass which a prince would not discard;
The cod and salmon cooked with due regard
Most palatable."

I am anxious to know what fish under its American name the gurnard is.   The Gurnet, at the entrance of Plymouth harbor, was named after a headland in the English Channel, which in shape resembled the Gurnet, a fish in English waters.   On the coast of Wales there is another headland named Gurnard, after the fish gurnard, the French name of the fish called in English, gurnet.   The gurnard has lost its French name with us, and I was not aware until I saw the name in Wood and Josselyn, that the gurnet fish was found in our waters under the name of gurnard.

There was a piece of household furniture in my youth which I believe has gone out of use.   The trundle bed was introduced by the Dutch, by whom it was called "een slaapbauck op rollen."   The bedsteads were universally four posted and high enough from the floor to permit the trundle bed to be kept under it, and to be rolled out at night when the younger children were sent to bed.   When the baby grew to be too large for the cradle, or was deposed by a new comer, it was promoted to the trundle bed, and when a newer comer appeared the trundle bed held two until the bedstead, with its chintz curtains, became the court of last resort.   In old Colonial days the bedsteads were made of sassafras wood, which was believed to be an effectual protection against vermin.   For hundreds of years the curative properties of sassafras were highly esteemed by the Indians, and when Champlain first sailed up the St. Lawrence he carried back to France large quantities of it to be used especially as a cure for venereal diseases. Within my day sassafras poles have been used as roosts in hen houses as a protection against hen lice.

The treatment of whiskers has changed almost as often as each generation came on the stage. The use of the razor is as old as the history of man. In the book of Isaiah it is written in the twentieth verse of the seventh chapter, "In the same day shall the Lord shave with a razor." Ezekiel, in the first verse of chapter five says, "Take thee a sharp knife, take thee a barber's razor and cause it to pass upon thy head and upon thy beard." Pliny states that barbers were common in his time, though only a short time before beards were allowed to grow. He also speaks of spider webs, applied with oil and vinegar to cuts received in barber shops, and also speaks of hones and whetstones for sharpening razors. In the time of Adrian beards were again allowed to grow, and so the changes and fashions went on. In the time of Queen Elizabeth the wearing of beards was controlled by law, and it was ordered that no fellow of Lincoln's Inn should wear a beard of more than two weeks' growth. The barber's brush was introduced in modern times. A writer named Stubb, in a work entitled "Anatomy of Abuses," published about 1550, in speaking of barbers, wrote, "When they came to washing, oh, how gingerly they behave themselves therein. For then shall your mouths be bossed with the lather or some that runneth off the balls, your eyes closed must be anointed therewith also." In the very beginning of the last century a poetical wag wrote the following lines showing that at that time the face was clean shaved by barbers.

"Strap that razor so keen! strap that razor again!
And Smallpiece will shave em, if he can come at em;
From his stool clad in aprons, he springs up amain
Like a barber refreshed by the smell of pomatum.
From the place where he lay,
He leaps in array
To lather and shave in the face of the day,
He has sworn from pollution our faces to clean
Our cheeks, necks and upper lips, whiskers and chin."

In 1829 a public meeting was held in New York against whiskers, and about the same time there was a movement in Plymouth against them.   Barbers and surgeons were incorporated as one company in the fifteenth century, and were called barber surgeons. Henry the Eighth dissolved the union and gave a new charter in 1540, in which it was provided "That no person using any shaving or barbery in London, shall occupy any surgery, letting of blood or other matter, excepting only the drawing of teeth."   Under the law barbers and surgeons were each to use a pole, that of the barber's, blue and white striped, and that of the surgeon's, the same, with the addition of a galipot and a red rag.   As near as I can learn the use of a pole began as early as the 13th century, when "a staff bound by a riband was held by persons being bled, and the pole was intended to denote the practice of blood letting."   The staff was about three feet long, with a ball on the top and a fillet or tape attached, which when not in use was wound around it.   So that the present barber's pole represents a part of the barber's business, that of blood letting, which long since passed to the prerogative of the surgeon.

During my youth beards were unknown among Americans, and until 1852 I do not think that a person of any nationality had in my time ever worn a moustache in Plymouth.   In the summer of 1854, while occupying for a time the house now occupied by Col. Wm. P. Stoddard, I was confined to the house by illness about three weeks, and during that time permitted my moustache to grow, intending to shave it off before going into the street.   When I had recovered sufficiently to go out I took an airing in the carriage of the late Ephraim Finney, having failed to carry out my intention, and my appendage was so roundly condemned by all my friends that I permitted it to grow, and I have never parted with it since.   During the next summer a meeting of the descendants of Elder Thomas Cushman, was held in Plymouth, and Rev. Dr. Robert W. Cushman, the orator of the occasion was a guest with his wife at my house.   I heard of his saying after he returned home, that he stayed with me while in Plymouth, and then adding—what a pity that a man like Mr. Davis should wear a moustache.   I doubt whether there are many older moustaches in Massachusetts than mine.

CHAPTER XXXXIX.

The habits of our people in the use of tobacco have been somewhat changeable. The use outside of medicine and surgery has been confined to smoking, chewing, snuffing and dipping. The last is practiced by applying moistened snuff with a brush to the gums, and has never been resorted to in New England to any considerable extent. I am inclined to think that it has been chiefly confined to the poor whites in the South. Snuff taking is a habit introduced into New England at a comparatively recent period, and of course was unknown to the aborigines. Its use had, however, a rapid growth, when once introduced, and in my youth was common among our people of both sexes, though I am inclined to think more so among women than men. In every grocery store there always stood on the counter two jars of snuff, and this fact alone shows its extensive use. I cannot recall more than thirty persons who were in the habit of carrying snuff boxes, and these did not belong to any special class or occupation. I remember that during the sessions of the Supreme and Common Pleas Courts an open box of snuff always lay on the clerk's desk, and was frequently visited by the members of the bar, as well as by the judges on the bench.

It is said that of all the tobacco habits that of snuff taking is the most difficult to abandon. The story is told of Charles Lamb and Thomas Hone, both inveterate snuffers, walking one day on Hamstead Heath, and coming to the resolution to give up the habit, threw their snuff boxes away. The next morning Lamb visited the Heath to recover his box, and there encountered Hone hunting in the shrubbery for his.

The practice of smoking is ancient. While the use of cigars in England and the United States cannot be traced to a period earlier than 1700, pipes were used by the aborigines, and have been found in the ancient mounds of the West. Whether tobacco was smoked before the days of the Pilgrims, so far as New England was concerned, is doubtful, while at an earlier period the natives of the South and West undoubtedly both used and cultivated it. It is certain that as late as King

Phillip's War in 1676, the New England Indian, while smoking tobacco when he could get it, used various substitutes. On this point we have the testimony of Mrs. Rowlandson, the wife of the minister of Lancaster, Mass., who was captured by the Indians and confined in the Camp of King Phillip. When a messenger was sent to King Phillip to negotiate for her release, she sent back word asking her husband to send her some tobacco for Phillip. She stated in a later narrative that when she saw Phillip, "he bade me come in and sit down, and asked me whether I would smoke it, but this no way suited me. For though I had formerly used tobacco, yet I had left it ever since I was first taken. It seems to be a bait the devil lays to make men loose their precious time. I remember with shame how formerly when I had taken two or three pipes I was presently ready for another, such a bewitching 'thing' it is, but I thank God he has now given me power over it; surely there are many who may be better employed than to lie sucking a stinking 'tobacco pipe.'" She further said that the Indians for want of tobacco smoked hemlock and ground ivy. From the above statement it will be seen that smoking was common to both sexes. The laws, however, from a very early period, were rigid in their provisions against smoking in public places. In 1638 the General Court ordered "that no man shall take any tobacco within twenty poles of any house, or so near as may endanger the same." One of the latest statutes on the subject was passed in 1798, which "forbade carrying fire through the streets, except in a covered vessel, as well as smoking or having in one's possession any lighted pipe or cigar in the streets or on the wharves." This law remained in force many years. In 1835 a by-law was adopted by the town of Plymouth, which I believe has never been repealed, forbidding smoking in any street, lane, public square or wharf within the town. I do not remember to have seen in all my boyhood any person smoking about the streets, or at his work. No ship carpenter in his yard, no rigger on the mast, no blacksmith at the forge, no digger in the garden or street, ever held a pipe in his mouth, wasting the time of his employer, in cutting tobacco, and filling his pipe. It was not because the practice was an expensive one, but because the fashion of the day was opposed to it. The mechanic and the farmer smoked in a leisure hour, or after his

meal, but no woman was seen at home or in the field, or anywhere else smoking at all.   Doctors and lawyers smoked occasionally in their offices, business men rarely behind their
counters, while a minister who used tobacco in any form was
unknown.   In later years, however, smoking has become a
frequent practice among the clergy, but so far as my observation has gone, chiefly among those of the Episcopalian and Unitarian denominations.   I once detected in the cheek of an
eminent divine a suspicious swelling, and when I spoke of it,
he said that it was his invariable habit to preach with a cud of
tobacco in his mouth.   Since the early days of which I speak,
pipe smoking has largely taken the place of cigar smoking,
and the use of both cigars and pipes has found its way into
times and places where forty years ago it would not have been
tolerated.   Several causes have contributed to this change.
In the first place cigars were much cheaper in 1840 and 1850,
and their higher cost has led to the more economical use of the
pipe.   When I began to smoke in 1838, Havana cigars sold at
retail at five dollars a quarter box of two hundred and fifty.
The same cigars today would cost twenty dollars.   In the second place the coming in of foreigners largely increased the use
of the pipe, and lastly the Civil War taught the use of the pipe
to soldiers in the camp, who under normal conditions would
not have taken it up.   Now we are seeing, to say nothing of
smelling, either the cigar or the pipe everywhere, in the street,
in the office, in court houses, in the state house, between the
lips of the mechanic at his work, the provision dealer on his
cart, and indeed almost in every place except the pulpit and
school, from which it is a matter of congratulation that they
are yet excluded.   Being a smoker myself, I cannot be charged with prejudice when I express the opinion that this excessive and ill-timed use of tobacco not only violates rules of good
taste and propriety, but is well nigh a nuisance.

The habit of using tooth picks is of recent origin.   In Boston on any day between twelve and two o'clock, nearly every
third woman met in the vicinity of Winter and West streets,
has a tooth pick between her lips.   This practice is made more
vulgar when at table the hand is held over the mouth, for
thus its vulgarity is acknowledged by those who persist in it.

The changing fashions in dress have been so constant that

it is futile to attempt to trace them.   The greatest change in
the United States occurred at the close of the revolution, when
what was called republican simplicity took the place of the
dress which characterized the first three-quarters of the 18th
century of which such fine illustrations may be found in the
works of Smybert, Blackburn and Copley.   There is something absurd about this so-called republican simplicity, which
compels a representative of our government to appear at foreign courts in the garb of an American citizen, while he has
his residence in one of the most lordly houses in London, and
makes it the vogue for a bridegroom to appear at his wedding
with nothing but the color of his skin to distinguish him from
the colored waiter, while he sets up a livery and hunts through
Herald's college for a coat of arms to have painted on the
door of his carriage.   I am inclined to think that a false pride
in the supposed possession of aristocratic blood has more to do
with the formation of so-called patriotic societies than a true
patriotic spirit.

In speaking of dress let me begin with the young.   In my
school days I wore a blue jacket with brass buttons and a stiff
linen collar buttoned to it on the inside, and turned over the
collar of the jacket.   I never wore an overcoat, or even owned
one, and when I entered college, the first thing I did was to
go to John Earle, the tailor, and get measured for a long tail
broadcloth coat, and buy a camlet cloak.   The frock coat was
unknown, and the cloak was indispensable in attending prayers
when hastily jumping out of bed I hurried to chapel often with
nothing under it but a night gown and trousers and boots.
During the summer months many boys went barefooted, not on
account of poverty, but simply for economy.   A writer in the
Old Colony Memorial in 1837 misrepresented this custom in
the statement that "old men had a great coat and a pair of
boots, the boots generally lasting for life.   Shoes and stockings were not worn by the young men, and by but few men in
farming business, and young women in their ordinary work
did not wear stockings and shoes."   I suppose that during the
school season there are fewer barefooted boys then formerly,
but at other times I do not think that there has been any change
as to footwear.   As to overcoats I have known many persons
who went without them from preference in the coldest weather.

Nathaniel Ingersoll Bowditch of Boston never wore one, and my old schoolmate, George Sampson, the late proprietor of the Boston directory, never did. I met the latter one afternoon in Boston when the thermometer was about zero, and I said, "George, I suspect that on such a day as this you wear a thicker undershirt?" To my surprise he said that he had never worn an undershirt in his life. I propose in speaking of dress to confine myself to those articles worn at various times which would strike the present generation as strange. About the year 1840, gentlemen's boots were two inches longer than the foot, and turned up like the dasher of a sleigh. At about the same time, or a little earlier, trousers skin tight, put on necessarily. with the boots already in them, were worn, and then immediately after loose trousers with plaits. For many years after the revolution, and continuing into my own days, the woolen cloths, of which dresses were made, were often spun and woven at home. During the 18th century in the small towns and country districts, nearly every family made a coarse cloth called lindsy-woolsy. with the warp of linen and the woof of wool. It is a mistake to suppose that in the earliest colonial times spinning wheels were much used until fulling mills were built in the last half of the 17th century, and it is not probable that Priscilla Alden ever used one until she was forty years of age. The small wheels known as flax wheels were first brought to Boston by the Scotch Irish in the first quarter of the 18th century. Of all articles of dress there is none in my opinion which so unerringly stamps the lady as a neat, tidy footgear. I say it with fear and trembling, but here goes, there must also be a white stocking. The contour of the foot is destroyed by a shoe, especially one without a heel, and the outlines of the ankle and limb are lost on any other color than white. The hat comes next, not set on the head like a liberty cap on a pole, but one whether large or small, as much belonging to the figure as the lily to its stem. Then comes the glove, never white in the street, a well fitting dress, not necessarily of expensive material, and withall as few ornaments as possible, and you have so far as flesh and blood are concerned, a faultless woman. A eulogist of the late Susan B. Anthony, herself a noble woman, said that she never was afraid to see her friend mount a table or platform to speak, because she knew that her boots and stockings were immaculate.

Ear-rings, concerning which I find many interesting items in the work of Alice Morse Earle on costumes, have come down to us from a period as early as the 16th century. They were, however, in their early days, worn by men more than by women, and in many cases only in one ear. Charles the First, on going to execution, wore a pearl pear shaped ear-ring, about five-eighths of an inch long, which is now owned by the Duke of Portland; and Shakespeare and Sir Walter Raleigh wore them. In my youth their use among women was almost universal, and I can recall many men who wore plain gold rings, and every young lady on leaving school had her ears bored as a matter of course.

Among the bonnets at various times in fashion I shall refer alone to the poke bonnet because its etymology is a little confused. This bonnet had plaits around its crown and sides. One of the many definitions of the word poke given in the Century dictionary, which no library is complete without, is, "to poke plaits in a ruff," and I have no doubt that "poke bonnet" meant merely a bonnet with plaits poked in the ruff. I must omit the scarlet cloak with its black silk quilted hood, worn by elderly women in my youth, the busks worn in the corsets, made of whalebone, steel or wood, the bustles below the waist behind, the quilted mandarins for cold weather, the India shawls now packed away in cedar closets awaiting their return in the revolving wheel of fashion, turbans, lace caps, night caps, hoops and other female paraphernalia, forming a sea without a shore, and speak lastly of pattens, which in my early boyhood were giving place to the overshoe and rubbers.

I remember a pair of pattens in an old closet where they had been consigned to an undeserved exile after many centuries of faithful service. The patten consisted of a wooden stock like the stock of a skate, with an oval iron ring attached to its under side, and with toe and heel pieces fastened by straps to the foot and ankle, its purpose being to protect the foot from mud and slush. It can be traced back to the 14th century, when it was called the galoe-shoe or galoshe. After its introduction into France, where it was called patin, the English galoshe became patten, but as if to revenge itself against the usurper, it has had a resurrection, and now lives in its legitimate successor, the galoshe of the present day.

I shall devote a portion of this chapter to a mention of those words and phrases which have made their appearance at various times, and have become incorporated for a longer or shorter time in the language of our people. Only a few of these are peculiar to Plymouth. Some have come down to us from our English ancestors, some owe their origin to the different languages of continental Europe, some are slang, which have found their way through unknown channels into the speech of men, and a few through ignorance of orthography have found a place in colloquial use. My reference to these must be restricted by necessarily limited space.

Some of my readers may be surprised at the number of words and names which have come to us from foreign tongues, and have made themselves as much at home as if they were to the manor born. We have the word wharf from the Swedish hworf, and the word dock from the Gothic dok, lane from the Dutch laan, alley from the French allee, derived from the verb aller, to go. The verb tedder meaning to ted or spread hay was introduced by the Irish when they began to work on our farms. Fishermen in Gloucester, Provincetown and Plymouth and other places, after drying codfish on flakes, yaffle them up and carry them into the fish house. The word yaffle is old English, and means an armful and the word stadle is the Scotch stathel, and means the stakes driven into a salt meadow, on which salt hay is to be piled. Scuttle comes from the French escoutelle, and the word kench, which means the bin in which salt codfish are piled, is old English. The word kid not only stands for an animal, but is also the name of the square bin on the deck of a fishing vessel by the side of each fisherman, in which he throws his fish. Sailors got into the way of calling any box without a cover a kid. I remember a story told by my mother when I was a boy of her going to church and finding a strange man in her pew, who jumped over the rail into the next pew, saying, I beg your pardon, Madam, I got into the wrong kid. The word coverlid, often called coverlet, is French derived from the French word couvrelit, cover bed. The word sass applied to vegetables, and also meaning impudence, is not as many suppose, a Yankee slang word, but has an English origin, and is still used in the county of Essex, in England. The word cabbage, as applied to the vegetable, came from Holland, and was introduced into England by Sir Anthony Ashley. He was accused of securing much loot, while holding a command in Spain, and he was so closely associated with the vegetable in the public mind, that on his monument at Wimbourne the head of a cabbage was sculptured, and in consequence of his looting the word became applied to looting in general, and finally to the odds and ends saved by tailors in their trade. The word arter, for after, came down to us from England, and if I remember right, was used by Governor Bradford in his history. The word fetch is an old Saxon word, used by Bacon, Shakespeare and many other old writers, and is worthy of respect, and continued use, though at present excluded from elegant speech. The word fetching expressing attractiveness in beauty or dress is a comparatively recent half slang innovation. The origin of the word contraptions, meaning new notions, I do not know, but I have heard it many times in my day. Arey or airey came from England, where it was sometimes called arrow or narrow. Hearth in two syllables, with emphasis on the e is a word I have never heard out of Plymouth. As long as I can remember it has been used by the deer hunters in Plymouth woods. Once Branch Pierce, the famous hunter, put Daniel Webster on a stand, and later in the day called out to him that the dogs had been out of hearth an hour, and that the hunt was up. The word dike as applied to a sloping grassy bank or terrace, is universal in Plymouth, and as far as I know, never used in that sense anywhere except in Plymouth, and its vicinity. Crojeck or crotchet, is a common corruption of crossjack in Plymouth and elsewhere as applied to the lower yard on the mizzen mast of a ship. Chimley for chimney, has been common in Scotland, and may be found in Scott's Rob Roy. In the United States it is usually spelled chimbley, but it is rarely heard in Plymouth.

James Russell Lowell has these lines:

> "Ag'in the chimbley crooknecks hung,
> An' in amongs 'em, rusted,
> The ole queen's arm that granther Young
> Fetched back from Concord, busted."

Sun-up for sunrise, I do not remember to have heard in

Plymouth more than once, but I have heard it often in other Plymouth county towns. As the opposite of sun-down, which is English, it seems as correct as sunset or sunrise, and may be properly used. Bile is often used for boil, and has been thought by some of the best writers to be more correct. It is, however, going out of use. Brewis is an English word meaning bread covered with broth, but when introduced into New England, it was applied to rye and Indian crusts boiled with milk and butter.

The word sleigh comes from the Dutch sluy; squash came down from the aborigines, by whom it was called estata, or vine apple; carrots came from Holland, and some growing wild bore a flower which the English called Queen Anne's lace. The cochroach was the Dutch kackenlack; potatoes, which have been said to have been introduced by the Irish, were raised by the Dutch in New York as early as 1654, and were called pataddes. It is not unlikely that as they were called Irish potatoes, the slang word paddies applied to the Irish, came from pataddes.

The word "certain" a few years ago came into use in answer to certain questions as for instance—are you going to Boston tomorrow? "Certain;" but it seems to have given place to the word "sure." For a time, "you bet," was used in the same way, as for instance to the statement, "that was a good dinner," the answer was, "you bet." Chores probably comes from the old English "char," as does also the word "charwomen." The word cow pronounced kyou, has been said to be peculiar to New England country towns, but there can be no greater mistake, for I have heard it so pronounced by natives of South Carolina, and it is so pronounced to-day in the shires of Essex and Sussex, in England. Fornent or fornenst was originally a Scotch word meaning opposite to, as for instance his house was fornent the church. It was carried to Ireland, and by the Irish introduced here. I heard it for the first time about 1854. "Gab," now common, was used by Chaucer as we use it. The English laugh at the word "guess," and call it a vulgar Americanism, but it was used by Locke, Milton and Chaucer.

> "Her yellow hair was braided in a tress,
> Behind her back a yard long I guess."

"Poke" in one of its many meanings is a pocket or bag, as in the words, to buy a pig in a poke, that is without seeing it.

"Streak it,"to run fast, was heard by me for the first time when hunting in the Plymouth woods. Branch Pierce, the hunter, after placing his party on their stands would take his son Tom and take short cuts through the woods to head off the deer. When a good chance occurred the old man could be heard calling out, Streak it, Tommy. There was another Thomas Pierce living in the neighborhood, so in order to distinguish them one was called Squire Tom, and the other Streak it Tommy. I have never heard the word "seen" in the sense of saw in Plymouth, but I have heard it frequently in Boston among Englishmen and immigrants from the Dominion. Muckrakes is a word recently rescued from oblivion, but with a wrong understanding of its meaning. According to Professor De-Vere, now or late Professor of modern languages in the University of Virginia, and author of "Studies in English" muckrakes are those who rake for the purpose of finding something valuable and worthy of preservation. Rag pickers are in one sense muckrakes. There are two offensive words which have recently found a lodgement in our vocabulary, chiefly, however, among inexperienced writers. One of these words, "one," taken out of its legitimate meaning, seems to be due either to a lack of taste or to a mistaken notion that it is elegant. The following sentence explains what I mean. "When one writes a letter one must be careful how one expresses oneself, lest one finds that one makes a mistake in using too many ones." The other is the word "gotten," which to me always suggests a writer who fancies himself an accurate scholar, and would call aisle of a church "oil," and one of its pillars, a "pillow." There are two other words not offensive, but objectionable, which I find constantly in new novels, "peering," for looking, and "perturbed" for disturbed, or agitated, or "annoyed." As for instance "in peering out of the window I was perturbed by an unusual sight."

The use of exaggerations and superlatives is every day becoming more common. Newspaper reporters and associated press men are responsible for many of these. With them it never rains, but it pours, every snow spit is a blizzard, every fresh breeze a gale, every gale a hurricane, every wave is mountain high, every collision is a crash, and every crowd a surging mob. New newspaper words are constantly creeping into our vocabulary. Among the most recent are "defi" for "defiance," and "confer" for "conference." There is another class of words and phrases having their origin in athletics and games of various kinds, which are constantly found in the newspapers, and even in congressional and other speeches. "Stand pat," "win out," "flush," and "full deck" are some of those which are unworthy of the press or the speech of a legislator. There is still another class quite frequently used which are really nothing but veiled oaths with the spirit if not the letter of profanity behind them. Among them are by-jingo, land-sakes, by-George, by-gum, by-thunder, good-gracious, dern it, thunder and Mars, heavens and earth, all fired for hell fired, gol darn it, darnation, Lord-a-mussy, mercy sakes alive, great Scott, by the eternal, and lastly, tarnation, as in the lines of John Noakes and May Styles:

> "Poor honest John 'tis plain he knows
> But little of life's range.
> Or he'd a know'd gals oft at fust
> Have ways tarnation strange."

In the above selections of words and phrases I have of course omitted a large number, the origin and etomology of which it would be interesting to trace. I must, however, in order to finish my memories in this chapter, proceed to the record of streets laid out since 1825, as proposed in the beginning of the chapter.

LeBaron alley, leading from Leyden street to Middle street, was laid out out as a townway Sept. 7 and 10, 1832.

The way around Cole's Hill from Leyden street was laid out Nov. 27, 1827, and May 14, 1829.

Pleasant street was laid out and altered at various times, June 5, 1820, May 12, 1825, Nov. 5, 1845, March 25, 1867, and January 4, 1887.

Russell street was laid out April 20, 1833.

Union street was laid out August 4, 1841, and Nov. 5, 1865.

Samoset street was laid out from Court street to the South Meadow Road, Dec. 8, 1854.

Cedarville Road was laid out Nov. 15, 1855.

The Manomet House Road was laid out September 23, 1851.

The way from Harvey Bartlett's to the Pine Hills was laid out July 13, 1848.

Warren Avenue was laid out Nov. 5, 1849, and August, 1850.

Robinson street was laid out April 6, 1859 and September 10, 1859.

Road from Chiltonville to the Manomet Road was laid out July 9, 1851, and April 9, 1866.

Cushman street was laid out Oct. 4, 1856.

Allerton street in part was laid out Oct. 4, 1856.

Allerton street in part was laid out March 26, 1877.

Chilton street was laid out April 3, 1882.

Cedar Village Road was laid out January 4, 1876.

Bradford street was laid out Sept. 10, 1859.

Cliff street was laid out March 20, 1876.

Oak street was laid out March 9, 1874, and March 1, 1875.

Davis street was laid out January 3, 1882.

Federal Road was laid out January 5, 1869.

Franklin street was laid out April 6, 1857, and July 6, 1865.

Fremont street was laid out Sept. 10, 1859.

Fremont street was extended June 22, 1895.

North Green street was laid out Oct. 4, 1856.

High street was widened June 24, 1870.

Corner of Court and North streets was laid out in 1892.

Main street was widened Aug. 3, 1886.

Jefferson street was laid out June 25, 1870.

Lothrop Place, laid out September 10, 1859, and Oct. 14, 1872.

Rocky Hill Road was laid out January 6, 1874.

Court Square, south side, laid out April 6, 1857.

South Russell street was laid out January 7, 1868.

Sagamore street was laid out June 25, 1870.

Street from Court street at Seaside to the railroad, was laid out January 6, 1874.

Sandy Gutter street laid out Oct. 21, 1871.

Stafford street laid out June 17, 1882.

Road from Manomet to Sandwich, January 2, 1872.

Road from Manomet to Fresh Pond, January 6, 1874.

Manomet Road, south of the bridge, February 7, 1857.

Manomet Road at the dam, January 1, 1884.

Market street, widened from the bake house, south, December 31, 1873.

Market street, widened at the corner of Leyden street, November 5, 1883.

Market street, widened at Spring Hill, January 1, 1890.

Massasoit street, laid out June 25, 1870.

Mayflower street, laid out April 6, 1857, and Sept. 10, 1859.

Mt. Pleasant street, laid out April 6, 1857.

Water street, extended April 4, 1881, Dec. 9, 1893, and June 22, 1895.

Thomas alley, discontinued March 28, 1885.

Waverly street, laid out October 4, 1856.

White Horse Road, laid out March 5, 1883.

Whiting street, laid out March 28, 1885.

Willard Place, laid out March 2, 1863.

Winslow street (Ocean Place), laid out April 3, 1882.

Spooner street at Seaside, laid out March 6, 1893.

Standish Avenue, laid out April 14, 1896, and March 6, 1899.

Vallerville road, laid out January 3, 1893, and March 19, 1901.

Washington street, laid out July 6, 1865.

Forest avenue, laid out February 20, 1904.

Billington street, laid out August 12, 1902.

Pump station Road, laid out August 12, 1902.

Road from Russell Mills to Long Pond Road, was laid out March 14, 1898.

Sever street was laid out January 26, 1901.

South Park Avenue, laid out January 26, 1901.

Clyfton street was laid out September 27, 1890.

Carver street was laid out March 28, 1854, February 12, 1884, and February 10, 1885.

Centre Hill Pond road was laid out August 6, 1895.

Cherry street was laid out March 6, 1899.

Alden street was laid out March 9, 1891, and April 6, 1891.

Atlantic street was laid out April 6, 1891.

Bartlett street was laid out March 13, 1886.

Brewster street was laid out December 1, 1884.

N. Wood & Co. Factory road at Chiltonville was laid out April 9, 1866.

Darby station entrance was laid out March 6, 1893.

Hall town road was laid out December 9, 1893.

Hamilton street was laid out June 5, 1897.

Highland Place was laid out April 2, 1888.

Howes Lane was laid out March 9, 1891, and March 7, 1892.

Leyden and Water street corner was widened March 9, 1891.

Lincoln street was laid out March 9, 1891.

Murray street was laid out March 5, 1883, and March 3, 1902.

Bay View avenue was laid out March 3, 1902.

Road from Manomet to Vallerville was laid out March 19, 1901.

Nelson street was laid out January 6, 1896.

Newfields street was laid out July 1, 1890, February 23, 1901.

Middle street was widened March 6, 1899.

Towns street was laid out February 10, 1906.

Main street was widened at the corner of Town Square, March 12, 1906.

Russell street was widened from Court street to the Registry, December 1, 1905.

Town Square was widened at corner of Main street, November 1, 1905.

Here, my readers, these memories must close. Any pleasure which you may have received in reading them has been more than equalled by my own in writing them. They present a meagre record of the memories of a long life whose beginning and end are mysteries.

> Helpless I lay upon the shore
> Of a world unknown to me;
> How, I wonder, came I o'er
> The dark mysterious sea.
>
> Tell me, oh tell me, whence I came;
> Is there another shore?
> This sun, these skies, are they the same
> That I have seen before?
>
> Now, life's journey nearly o'er,
> The land beyond the sea,
> As when I lay upon the shore,
> Is still unknown to me.
>
> Another shore before me lies,
> Bounding another sea;
> May I there find the sun and skies
> Before unknown to me.

Errata and Addenda

On page 26, 3rd line, "Contry" should be "country."
On page 28, 7th line, celebration of 1794 was private.
On page 41 "Hollinguer" should be "Hottinger."
On page 109, 11th line, "to" should be "so."
On page 233, 17th line, "Davee" should be "Davie."
On page 238, 17th line, "Longwood" should be "La Grange."
On page 319, 17th line, "Wooster" should be "Worcester."
On page 330, 25th line, "Nathan" should be "Nathaniel."
On page 399, 10th line from bottom, "Tuesday" should be "Monday."

To the blacksmiths on page 52, are to be added Nathan Delano and Moses Nichols. Mr. Delano lived on Middle street, and had his shop in the brick basement of the house, which once stood on Cole's Hill, with its rear on the way leading from Middle street to Water street.

Mr. Nichols came to Plymouth from Freetown, and building a shop in Chiltonville on the southwest corner of the Russell Mills road, worked on a vessel building on Eel River, a little below the Hayden factory. He later built a shop where the George Fuller shop now stands, and lived in the house in Wellingsley, lately occupied by John Bartlett. Still later he built a shop in what is now called Dublin, and built and occupied the house on the upper corner of Summer and Edes streets, where he died about 1809. After his death, his son Otis Nichols, born in the Bartlett house, occupied the Summer street house until he moved to Manomet, and established the farm now owned and occupied by his son Otis.

Among the whaling vessels mentioned on page 64, was the schooner Mercury. She sailed Nov. 12, 1842, and on the 2d of May, 1843, capsized in a gale, and Wm. H. Godfrey, Henry Missard, George L. Jones, Wm. Pierce and Wm. Hatch were lost. The remainder of the crew, consisting of John Winslow of Provincetown, Thomas D. Barnes, Lemuel Hall, Wm. H. Carver, Richard Pierce and Isaac Cole of Plymouth, and Robert Gardner and George Williams were taken off. When the vessel capsized Richard Pierce was in the cabin, and was taken out with a broken leg through a hole cut in the deck. I remember him well a cripple through life.

INDEX